新能源电力与低碳发展研究北京市重点实验室（华北电力大学）研究成果

新能源电力建设项目
选址、投资、风险决策研究

Research on Site Selection, Investment Decision and Risk Assessment of New Energy Power Construcion Project

乌云娜　许传博◎著

中国电力出版社
CHINA ELECTRIC POWER PRESS

内 容 提 要

本书通过论文集的形式展现，包含论文 15 篇（其中 SSCI/SCI 双检索论文 9 篇）：SCI 检索一区 11 篇，SCI 检索二区 4 篇（其中 ESI 高被引 2 篇）。论文集以新能源电力建设项目为研究主体，以前沿的决策理论与方法为手段进行了“选址决策研究—风险决策研究—投资决策研究”，补充和完善了新能源电力建设项目管理决策体系。

本书适合从事能源项目投资、决策方法理论等研究领域的专业人士、教师和学生阅读使用。

图书在版编目（CIP）数据

新能源电力建设项目选址、投资、风险决策研究 / 乌云娜，许传博著. —北京：中国电力出版社，2021.1

ISBN 978-7-5198-5338-9

Ⅰ. ①新… Ⅱ. ①乌… ②许… Ⅲ. ①新能源－电力工业－研究－中国 Ⅳ. ①F426.61

中国版本图书馆 CIP 数据核字(2021)第 022931 号

出版发行：中国电力出版社
地　　址：北京市东城区北京站西街19号（邮政编码100005）
网　　址：http://www.cepp.sgcc.com.cn
责任编辑：李　静（1103194425@qq.com）
责任校对：黄　蓓　常燕昆　马　宁　朱丽芳
装帧设计：九五互通　周　赢
责任印制：钱兴根

印　刷：三河市万龙印装有限公司
版　次：2021年1月第一版
印　次：2021年1月北京第一次印刷
开　本：787毫米×1092毫米　16开本
印　张：32.5
字　数：712千字
定　价：118.00元

前言

合理开发新能源电力建设项目是构建“清洁低碳、安全高效的现代能源体系”目标的有效途径。目前，在新能源电力建设项目的开发和建设中管理决策普遍缺乏理论和方法支撑，导致新能源电力建设项目显现厂址选择不科学、投资回报率不达预期及特殊风险事件缺乏识别和应对预案等现象。针对此类问题开展新能源电力建设项目管理决策研究对于推动我国能源低碳转型发展有着重要意义。

一、主要观点

1. 选址决策研究

第 1 章针对海上风电选址，应用 ELECTRE-Ⅲ在模糊和随机的环境下将值优先关系与基于似然的两两比较相结合，保留了信息的完整性，获得的排序关系更加合理。

第 2 章采用基于前景理论的 TODIM 方法对 GIS 技术预选的城市光伏充电站备选站点进行排序，针对不同的评价标准设置不同的遗憾系数，充分反映了决策者的主观偏好。

第 3 章在对秸秆生物质发电厂优化选址研究中创新性地运用三参数区间数和序关系来确定权重，并提出基于二维不确定语言变量和云模型的群决策排序方法，避免了信息丢失，解决了单个专家决策的片面性问题。

第 4 章针对垃圾发电厂选址，采用三角直觉模糊数来描述决策信息，运用拓展的 PROMETHEE-Ⅱ与 TODIM 方法对备选方案进行排序，更加符合实际需求。

第 5 章基于可持续发展的角度，将 TODIM 方法在三角直觉模糊数及其加权几何算子的应用下进行扩展，并结合 PROMETHEE-Ⅱ方法对聚光太阳能发电厂站址方案进行排序。

第 6 章考虑到指标间的相互影响，采用模糊 ANP 方法确定权重。此外，为了兼顾决策者的主观偏好，采用模糊 VIKOR 方法对商业屋顶光伏系统选址备选方案进行排序。

综上所述，新能源电力建设项目选址直接影响项目建设全过程并最终影响项目效益，甚至直接决定了项目的成败。本论文集针对海上风电、屋顶光伏、生物质发电及垃圾发电的选址问题，提出了信息融合的多属性决策选址方法，在指标体系构建、权重确定及站址排序方法上取得了创新性的成果，实现上述新能源电力建设项目的精准选址。

2. 投资决策研究

第 7 章首次提出将模糊集理论和累积前景理论结合应用于新能源项目投资决策，同时兼顾评估的不确定性和投资者的风险偏好，并通过案例分析论证了该方法的合理性和可行性。

第 8 章研究了企业在绿色发展战略、利益最大化战略、技术创新战略、稳定发展战略、和谐发展战略下如何进行分布式新能源项目投资组合选择的问题。

第 9 章首次将可持续性理念整合到新能源投资组合优化过程中，并提出将二型模糊数、WA 算子、AHP 方法与非支配排序遗传算法-Ⅱ结合用于新能源电力建设项目投资组合优化问题。

第 10 章综合考虑定量和定性指标，引入区间二型模糊 AHP-TOPSIS 技术用于风能耦合储氢项目评价。此外，启发式地提出了管理此类项目的改进思路。

第 11 章创新性地从垃圾分类的角度建立了焚烧发电厂性能评估指标体系。另外，基于组合权重法和模糊综合评价法建立了以绩效评价组合模型为基础的废弃物转化能源评估决策框架。

第 12 章利用 DEMATEL 方法和综合加权法确定指标权重。在考虑投资者风险规避心理的情况下，结合三角直觉模糊数和群决策理论，采用 TODIM 方法对可再生能源项目备选方案进行排序。

综上所述，论文集主要研究了包括垃圾发电项目、风能耦合储氢项目及高速公路服务区光伏发电项目在内的新能源电力建设项目的投资决策问题。新能源电力建设项目投资决策研究成果提高了模糊信息的保留、决策信息的可靠性及决策结果的合理性。

3. 风险决策研究

第 13 章针对光伏扶贫项目，从项目全生命周期的角度入手提取风险因素，避免了风险评估分析的局限性。此外，采用三角直觉模糊数来收集专家意见，减少了信息的损失。

第 14 章首次在海上光伏发电项目的评价指标中引入公众感受，增加了视觉影响风险这一指标，同时提出了一种基于犹豫模糊语言集和三角模糊数的海上光伏发电项目风险评估模型。

第 15 章构建了模糊环境下风险评估理论框架，弥补了 EPC 模式下城市屋顶分布式光伏风险评估的研究空白，同时运用直觉模糊理论改进了传统的 DEMATEL 法，增强了其实用性。

综上所述，论文集主要包括海上光伏发电项目、城市屋顶分布式光伏项目及光伏扶贫项目的风险决策问题。论文集中新能源电力建设项目风险评估研究实现了专家信息、公众意见保留的最大化，结合传统的风险评估理论，提高了风险决策方法的实践性。

二、学术贡献

本论文集充实了我国新能源电力建设项目管理决策研究，初步形成了新能源电力建设项目管理决策研究体系。主要学术贡献为：

1. 提出了信息融合的多属性决策选址方法

尽管 GIS 和 MCDM 已被应用于新能源电力建设项目区域优选中，现有研究仍停留在将 MCDM 应用于信息图层的权重确定，尚未解决站址的识别与排序问题。论文集在区域优选的基础上，首次使用了计算机视觉技术识别潜在的备选站址，并提出了 MCDM 与模糊集理论结合的方法（直觉模糊 DEMATEL、区间二型模糊 AHP-TOPSIS、直觉模糊 ELECTRE-Ⅲ）对备选站址进行了排序，实现了新能源电力建设项目的精准选址。

2. 提出项目群环境下“多属性+多目标”的投资决策方法

当前新能源电力项目投资决策多聚焦于单项目投资分析，忽视对项目组合效益的挖掘。此外，大部分研究定格于项目的经济效益，缺乏对综合效益、战略规划、决策偏好影响的考虑。计及新能源电力建设项目群协同与竞争关系，本论文集融合多属性决策与多目标优化理论，提出以“单项目投资分析—项目间协同刻画—多项目组合优化”为核心的多阶段多目标投资决策方法，为新能源电力项目在项目群环境下的投资组合提供决策范式。

3. 考虑了电力设备可循环再造的风险识别

风险决策管理贯穿于建设项目始终，从全生命周期角度来识别建设项目的各风险可保证风险管理决策体系的全面性。不同于传统建设项目风险决策的全生命周期划分方式，本论文集基于新能源电力设备材料的可循环再造特点，在新能源电力建设项目风险决策过程中首次考虑了电力设备回收问题，定义了规划设计阶段、建设施工阶段、运行维护阶段和设备回收阶段的新能源电力建设项目的全生命周期风险识别内涵。

三、理论创新和实践意义

1. 理论创新

（1）研究对象创新。本论文集有效把握新能源电力的发展趋势，针对沿海风电项目、高速公路服务区光伏项目、风电耦合储氢项目等新型项目展开研究，弥补了非典型新能源电力项目在管理决策方面的理论空白。

（2）研究视角创新。考虑到新能源电力建设项目之间的差异性，本论文集从可持续发展、企业战略、垃圾分类等新颖视角入手对特定约束下的新能源电力建设项目管理决策进行探究，提出了不同视角下的决策管理模型。

（3）研究方法创新。根据新能源电力建设项目决策信息的特点，论文集将模糊集理论引入决策框架并提出了以区间二型模糊 AHP、拓展犹豫模糊 DEMATEL 方法的指标权重模型和 TOMDIM-PROMETHEE 组合、改进偏好 PROMETHEE 方法的集成排序模型。

2. 实践意义

（1）对政府而言，论文集成果有助于政府相关部门对新能源电力建设项目进行统筹规划，为政府部门优化资源配置、制定新能源发展战略提供可靠的理论基础和智力支撑。

（2）对电力企业而言，论文集增强了企业进行项目投资、建设选址的科学性，提高了企业的风险管控中事前响应、主动监控的执行能力，有助于企业实现效益最大化。

（3）对研究人员而言，论文集中研究视角的创新及研究方法的改进，为学者和相关研究人员对新能源电力建设研究领域相关问题的理论和方法的研究，以及解决实践问题提供了借鉴和参考。

本书的撰写得到国家社科基金项目（19AGL027）、中央高校基金（No.2020MS066）及新能源电力与低碳发展研究北京市重点实验室等资助，在此表示衷心感谢。

鉴于作者水平有限，书中难免存在不足和错误之处，恳望读者批评指正。

目录

Contents

第一部分　选址决策研究

第 1 章针对海上风电选址，应用 ELECTRE-Ⅲ在模糊和随机的环境下将值优先关系与基于似然的两两比较相结合，保留了信息的完整性，获得的排序关系更加合理。

第 2 章采用基于前景理论的 TODIM 方法对 GIS 技术预选的城市光伏充电站备选站点进行排序，针对不同的评价标准设置不同的遗憾系数，充分反映了决策者的主观偏好。

第 3 章在对秸秆生物质发电厂优化选址研究中创新性地运用三参数区间数和序关系来确定权重，并提出基于二维不确定语言变量和云模型的群决策排序方法，避免了信息丢失，解决了单个专家决策的片面性问题。

第 4 章针对垃圾发电厂选址，采用三角直觉模糊数来描述决策信息，运用拓展的 PROMETHEE-Ⅱ与 TODIM 方法对备选方案进行排序，更加符合实际需求。

第 5 章基于可持续发展的角度，将 TODIM 方法在三角直觉模糊数及其加权几何算子的应用下进行扩展，并结合 PROMETHEE-Ⅱ方法对聚光太阳能发电厂站址方案进行排序。

第 6 章考虑到指标间的相互影响，采用模糊 ANP 方法确定权重。此外，为了兼顾决策者的主观偏好，采用模糊 VIKOR 方法对商业屋顶光伏系统选址备选方案进行排序。

综上所述，新能源电力建设项目选址直接影响项目建设全过程并最终影响项目效益，甚至直接决定了项目的成败。本论文集针对海上风电、屋顶光伏、生物质发电及垃圾发电的选址问题，提出了信息融合的多属性决策选址方法，在指标体系构建、权重确定及站址排序方法上取得了创新性的成果，实现上述新能源电力建设项目的精准选址。

Chapter 1

Study of decision framework of offshore wind power station site selection based on ELECTRE-III under intuitionistic fuzzy environment: a case of China

Yunna Wu [a], Jinying Zhang [b*], Jianping Yuan [c], Shuai Geng [d], Haobo Zhang [e]
North China Electric Power University, Beijing, China [a, b, c, e]
Ecological Research Institute of Shandong Academy of Sciences [d]
Email: zhangjinying8899@163.com
Phone: +86 15910896517

Abstract: Offshore wind power projects have been rapidly proposed in China due to policy promotion. Site selection immensely decides the success of any offshore wind power development and is a complex multi-criteria decision making (MCDM) problem. However, canonical MCDM methods tend to fail the site selection process due to the following three problems. Firstly, the compensation problem exists in information processing. Secondly, there exists the problem of incomplete utilization of decision information and information loss in the decision process. Thirdly, the interaction problem in the fuzzy environment is easy to be ignored. To deal with the above problems, this study builds a framework for offshore wind farm site selection decision utilizing Elimination et Choix Traduisant la REalité-III (ELECTRE-III) in the intuitionistic fuzzy environment. First of all, the comprehensive index system of OWPS site selection consisting of veto criteria and evaluation criteria is constructed. Then, the intuitionistic fuzzy set is used in the group decision for the decision makers to express the imperfect knowledge. Moreover, the generalized intuitionistic fuzzy ordered weighted geometric interaction averaging (GIFWGIA) operator is applied to deal with the interaction problem. Together with the likelihood-based valued comparisons, imprecise decision information is reasonably used and information loss problem is rationally avoided. Then a case of China is studied based on the proposed framework, demonstrating the site selection methodology valid and practical. This study implements evaluation method for offshore wind power site selection and also provides a theoretical basis for the development of offshore wind power decision-making in China.

Keywords: offshore wind power; site selection; multi-criteria decision making (MCDM); ELECTRE-III; intuitionistic fuzzy set

1. Introduction

In recent years, developing renewable energy in China has become an important step to achieve natural energy goals. In economically developed eastern coastal cities of China, demands for electricity grow rapidly. The desire of Chinese government for developing offshore wind farm resources is strong due to local offshore wind. The offshore wind power planning target till 2015 is 5 million kW, however, the target completion rate is less than 1/10 till 2013. Many projects are required to suspend or relocate because of wrong site selection problems.

The offshore wind power station (OWPS) site selection is a critical step toward a successful wind power project. It is a multi-criteria decision making (MCDM) problem, concerning conflicting criteria involving offshore wind resources, the environment, sea area planning, power grid access lines, economy, society, etc.. In last two years, imperfect consideration concerning these aspects have hold back the development of OWPS, as is shown in Fig. 1.1. At present, studies such as development of offshore wind turbines and wind power integration are widely performed in China, but studies on offshore wind farm site selection are scarce. China offshore wind farm site selection studies have been conducted outside by many researchers. Vafaeipour, Zolfani [1] presents a hybrid MCDM approach to identify suitable regions for implementation of future solar power plants. Uyan [2] proposes AHP model to select a suitable site for nuclear power plant. Shafiee [3] Studies on selecting appropriate risk mitigation strategy for offshore energy projects with ANP method. Choudhary and Shankar [4] propose TOPSIS method for evaluation and selection of optimal locations for thermal power plant. It can been seen that MCDM approaches provide effective framework for renewable energy plant selection with multiple conflicting criteria. However, there are still many problems in the existing decision process for OWPS site selection, which makes current decisions hardly conform to the real situations.

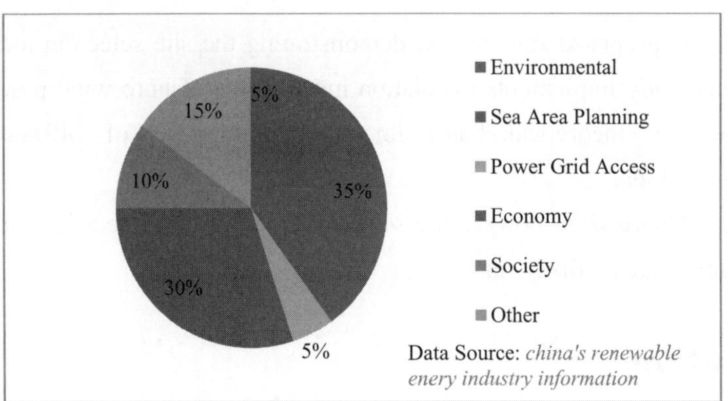

Fig. 1.1 Planning problems hold back OWPS construction in china.

(1) Firstly, vagueness generally exists in OWPS site selection decision problems. On one hand, site selection decision happens before the construction of OWPS, so the evaluation information is often hard to predict accurately or quantified precisely due to the complex situation with respect to OWPS and unforeseen factors. On the other hand, for decision makers (DMs), the practical judgments are often vague; neither the level of satisfaction nor the degree of dissatisfaction can be accurately estimated. That is to say, the site selection decision is under the imperfect and incomplete information environment. Therefore, determining how to express judgments integrally and sufficiently is a problem facing OWPS site selection.

(2) Secondly, the compensation problem exists in some canonical MCDM approaches, such as weighted synthesis method. As a result, for some alternatives, it may occur that the good performance in some criteria can make up for the poor performance in other criteria. That is to say, for instance, some site alternatives may have very poor scores in some criteria such as serious influence on the environment though, their superiority in other criteria like wind resources and construction conditions is magnificent. They still could rank at the top because of compensation problems; while some alternatives, which may work fine on every respect, are likely to be eliminated.

(3) Thirdly, incomplete utilization of decision information and information loss exist in the process of OWPS site selection decision, which could in turn give rise to decision failure. It mainly happens in the comparison stage in deciding the preferable plan of each pair of alternatives under multi-criteria, for there is a lack of feasible mechanism to distinguish different levels of preference. Although the existing outranking methods like ELECTRE-III has advantages in constructing preference degrees of real numbers by using valued outranking relations, it still needs to be extended in real-world applications to handle ambiguous information. Preference judgments need to be rationally processed to ensure the quality of decision-making under incomplete information environment.

This study aims at establishing a practical index system for OWPS site selection and developing an effective comprehensive evaluation framework to select the most satisfactory plan. We propose a new design of comprehensive MCDM framework based on the ELECTRE method to handle the OWPS site selection problems in the presence of multiple decision makers under incomplete information environment. To begin with, the comprehensive index system of OWPS site selection consisting of criteria and sub-criteria is constructed on the basis of experts consulting and literature analysis. In accordance with the evaluation criteria and veto factors, the potential competition sites can be identified. An integrated weight method is adopted for DMs to measure the relative importance of multiple criteria. The intuitionstic fuzzy numbers and linguistic variables are used for DMs to indicate the degree of satisfaction and dissatisfaction of the potential sites with respect to each criterion. Following this, the generalized intuitionistic fuzzy weighted geometric interaction averaging (GIFWGIA) operator is applied to integrate the DMs' evaluation on alternatives rating and criteria weights. Afterwards, the likelihood-based outranking relationship is proposed to define the indifferent, the strong preference and the weak preference relations by performing pairwise preference comparisons between the intuitionistic fuzzy numbers. A new concordance and discordance analytical measure is developed for providing partial and complete ranking orders. The MCDM framework of OWPS site selection in this study, provides insightful information for the managers to analyze and select the optimal site for OWPS decision-making. It is proposed for the following reasons.

- To handle the vague and imprecise information of the real world, the fuzzy set is normally utilized. Compared with Zadeh's traditional fuzzy set, Atanassov's intuitionistic fuzzy numbers convey more information for situation expression, including membership, non-membership and hesitation degree[5]. The intuitionistic fuzzy sets(IFSs) are proved to be more effective in dealing with inevitably imprecise or not totally reliable judgments, which is suitable for DMs to express their affirmation, negation and hesitation in decision-making applications [6-8]. Recently, the IFSs have aroused increasing concern and been widely performed in MCDM problems, revealing the capacity of handling the incomplete information [9-13].
- The compensatory problem is reasonably processed by the ELECTRE method. Different from fully compensatory methods such as TOPSIS, ELECTRE is partially compensatory, which means a severely dissatisfactory score with respect to a criterion would not be compensated by other content criterion rates, which conforms to the reality situations[14,15]. The ELECTRE method uses the outranking relation mechanism to handle decision information. The ranking order is determined by comparing the merits of every two attribute values, which counteract the effect of inaccurate attribute values on overall program to some extent, thus drawing a reasonable sorting results[16].
- The information loss is effectively avoided and important basic knowledge is reasonably

utilized by adopting the valued outranking relations and the likelihood-based pairwise comparisons. We uses ELECTRE-III rather than ELECTRE-I and ELECTRE-II because it constructs reasonable binary relations without sacrificing information. In addition, the likelihood-based comparison is used as it fully utilized the various aspects of fuzzy information. Therefore, the integration of the valued outranking relation and the likelihood-based pairwise comparisons has more advantages in obtaining reasonable outranking relations in the fuzzy and imprecise environment.

2. Literature review

Multi-criteria decision making (MCDM) methods, such as Analytic Hierarchy Process(AHP), Technique for Order Preferenceby Similarity to Ideal Solution(TOPSIS) and Elimination et Choix Traduisant la Realité(ELECTRE), are widely used by decision makers in the energy field. Lee et al. [17] use AHP to measure the relative efficiency of energy technologies. Kaya and Kahraman [18] study on a decision-making problem of energy planning using TOPSIS method. Grujić et al.[19] use ELECTRE method to choose the optimal heat demand solution. These researches promote the application of MCDM methods and verify the effectiveness of them in the decision support system for evaluation in energy field.

As there exists partial compensatory problems in real-world decision making [20], the ELECTRE method is applied by researchers to deal with this problems [21, 22]. ELECTRE, as an outranking method (OM), constructs a weaker binary relation (outranking relation) to decrease the compensation between indices and obtain reliable results within a large application scope[16]. ELECTRE-III method is based on the principle of fuzzy logic and uses the preference and indifference thresholds while determining the concordance and non-concordance indices[23]. As a valued outranking method, ELECTRE-III conveys more information than ELECTRE-I and ELECTRE-II [24]. The comparative analysis of multi-criteria decision making methodologies are shown in Table 1.1.

Table 1.1 Comparative analysis of multi-criteria decision making methodologies[69].

Characteristics	AHP	TOPSIS	ELECTRE-I	ELECTRE-II	ELECTRE-III
1. whether has the disadvantages of compensation	Yes	Yes	No	No	No
2. Number and type of outranking relations	$N(N-1)/2$	1	1	2	1
3. Consistency check	Provided	None	None	None	Provided
4. Suitable scope of criteria	Little	Large	Large	Large	Large

Recently, researchers started to apply Zadeh's fuzzy set theory to MCDM methods in order to make decisions more conform to the real-life situations. Perera, Attalage [25] proposed a decision support tool based on Fuzzy TOPSIS and level diagrams to support decision makers in the process of designing hybrid energy systems. Fuzzy Analytical Hierarchy Process (FAHP) and Technique for Order Preference by Similarity to Ideal Solution (TOPSIS) are integrated and proposed as Hybrid MCDM model to select appropriate source and blending of biodiesel[26]. Kaya, T.[18] put forward a modified fuzzy TOPSIS methodology for the selection of the best energy technology alternative. These researchers proved the effectiveness of fuzzy methods in solving MCDM problems.

Based on Zadeh's fuzzy set theory, it is admitted that the summation of the membership u and the non-membership v is 1. However, in real-life decisions, the summation of membership u and the non-membership v scored by the same person are often not equal to 1[20]. In order to solve the problem, Atanassov's intuitionistic fuzzy set is introduced as a generalization of Zadeh's fuzzy set. Both membership and the non-membership are fuzzy based on IFS theory, so it is well suited for DMs to express hesitation in decision-making problems and applications[27]. Therefore, the IFS has drawn increasing attention and been diffusely applied in decision-making problems in recent years [6, 20, 28-31].

As for basic operations, Xu [32] proposed the intuitionistic fuzzy weighted averaging (IFWA) operator to aggregate intuitionistic fuzzy numbers, which has been widely used to aggregate information in decision-making problems. Atanassov [33], Zhang [34] and He et al. [35] presented that there actually exists some interactions between the membership and non-membership functions, which have not been taken into consideration in some basic operations. In fact, the dealing with the interaction problem is convinced to be an effective way to improve the quality of evaluation in the intuitionistic fuzzy environment[35, 36]. As a solution, He et al. [35] proposed the GIFWGIA aggregation operator, which proved to be effective in handling the interactions.

In intuitionistic fuzzy ELECTRE(IF-ELECTRE), the construction of binary preference relations is also a critical issue directly and immensely affecting the evaluation quality. A few researchers have successfully processed the ELECTRE method in the intuitionistic fuzzy environment and constructed various kinds of binary preference relations[27, 30, 37-40]. For example, Wu and Chen [39] proposed three kinds of preference degree by comparing intuitionistic fuzzy parameters. Xu and Shen [40] processed the preference relations according to the score function $S(\tilde{A})$, $S(\tilde{B})$ and the accuracy function $H(\tilde{A})$, $H(\tilde{B})$. Chen [37] developed pairwise comparisons by likelihood-based preference functions. In conclusion, there are mainly three kinds of preference relations after reviewing the previous studies: ①Intuitionistic fuzzy parameters comparisons. It is commonly used and easy for DMs to conduct and calculate, but sometimes difficult to reveal all the conditions. ②Valued comparisons by intuitionistic fuzzy functions. This preference relation is useful for DMs to gain satisfaction degrees, but sometimes it is hard to reflect the preference of the DMs. ③Valued comparisons with DMs' preference parameters. Despite it is relatively complicated in calculation compared with the former ones, it considers the preference of the DMs, and effectively avoid information loss. The likelihood-based comparison, as a valued comparison method, is considered to be an effective way to construct the binary relations and a solid basis for the outranking method. However, it has not been used in the energy field yet.

In this study, the likelihood-based comparisons and the GIFWGIA operators are used together in the proposed ELECTRE-III method under the intuitionistic fuzzy environment for the following reasons. ①The working principles of the likelihood-based comparisons and the GIFWGIA operators are the same, both from the probability point of view. ②The data processing requirements of the likelihood-based comparisons can be met by the GIFWGIA operators. ③The compensation, interaction and information loss problems can be rationally processed. ④Using the likelihood-based comparisons and the GIFWGIA operators is more in line with the reality.

To conclude, on the basis of the aforementioned improvements, the comprehensive evaluation results of OWPS decision-making will be more reasonable than before.

3. Evaluation criteria system of OWPS site selection

The establishment of criteria system plays an important role in the OWPS site selection decision-making. Different from the on-shore wind farms, there are two sets of criteria in the OWPS decision-making: the veto criteria and the evaluation criteria. Due to the complex marine functional planning, there exist many sensitive sea areas where the OWPS cannot be built on. So the veto criteria are established to help recognize these sensitive areas and avoid any possible conflicts of marine functional planning. Marine sites concerning ecology, military, engineering uses and shipping lanes are significant marine uses according to Kapsimalis et al. [41]. Nobre et al. [42] defines non-implementing areas including military exercise areas, marine protected areas, cables locations, wave shadow areas, harbour entrances and navigation channels. After examining the Regulations on the Use of Sea Areas and Regulations on Marine Environmental Protection issued by the State Oceanic Administration (SOA) of China and related literatures, the experts identified four veto criteria as follows:

- Military activity area (V1): areas for military activities (e.g., maneuvers and exercises) and passage of submarines are excluded;
- Harbor and channel area (V2): the shipping lane and dock are excluded from the feasible area so that the navigation route and the potential OWPS sites do not interfere with each other;
- Natural reserve area (V3): areas for ecosystem protection (e.g., marine mammals and endangered species, ecosystems, natural monuments) are excluded;

- Engineering infrastructures (V4): areas near natural gas transmission pipeline, cable and other engineering facilities are excluded.

The other kind of criteria are called the evaluation criteria, whose value can be evaluated based on the investigation or analysis by the experts. Before the establishment of the evaluation criteria, the evaluation merits should be determined. Wind resources, economic factors, supporting conditions onshore are essential merits for OWPS site selection according to literatures [20, 43-45]. After the 18th CPC National Congress, the Chinese government pays more and more attention to the environmental and social influences caused by industrial process and the energy projects are no exception [46]. Hence, environment and society factors are considered as important merits for decision making in the current study. Last but not least, since the construction and maintenance conditions of OWPS are much more complicated and have more impacts on the plant benefits than onshore wind farm counterparts [47], they are also considered as the decisive factors for OWPS location selection. Based on the above analysis, the list of the OWPS evaluation criteria of the current study includes wind resources, construction and maintenance conditions, supporting conditions onshore, environmental impacts, economic and social benefits.

3.1 Wind resources (X1)

The wind energy resources assessment is key to OWPS site selection. It refers to the wind resources that enable high performance but do not damage wind turbines. The sub-criteria are mainly considered from two aspects: available wind resources and adverse influences of energy resources on plants operation and power generation [48-51].

(1) Wind speed and its distribution status (x11): refers to the speed of wind at the height of 30m, 50m and 100m which meet the most crew hub height requirements(m/s). This criterion is measured by the average speed during a full calendar year, and is amended according to the long-term representative wind speed series (five years) to decrease the influence of annual wind speed changes which represent long-term fluctuations.

(2) Wind power density (x12): measures kinetic power generated by the wind in the unit square meter and time (W/m^2). It indicates how much wind energy is available at the site for wind turbine generation. The average wind power density during a full calendar year is applied and amended according to the long-term representative wind speed series data from offshore wind towers.

(3) Effective wind hours (x13): refers to accumulative hours of effective wind per year(h).

(4) Wind shear (x14): evaluates the wind speed variation α with height in the atmosphere, according to the following equation: $\alpha = \ln(S_2 / S_1) / \ln(H_2 / H_1)$. S_1 and S_2 represent for the wind speeds at the height of H_1 and H_2, respectively. It influences the service life and operation

safety of blade and engine room.

(5) Turbulence (x15): measures ratio of standard deviation of the wind speed (m/s) to the average wind speed during a period of 10 min (m/s). It determines the fatigue load of wind turbine and largely affects the service life of the units. This criteria applies the integrated turbulence above 30 m, which is evaluated by the dominant wind turbulence intensity and partial sector turbulence intensity.

3.2 Construction and maintenance conditions (X2)

In consideration of the complex conditions on the sea, it is important to analyze whether the identified sites are suitable for OWPS construction and maintenance. Analysis of construction and maintenance conditions includes meteorological, marine, hydrological, and geological conditions [50, 52-55]. In addition, China's National Energy Administration (NEA) and the SOA have made special provisions on the sea water depth, distance from shore and beach width for OWPS.

(1) Meteorological conditions (x21): means complex natural threats (e.g., tropical cyclone in summer, extra tropical cyclone, cold anticyclone in winter, ice floes, salt fog).

(2) Marine conditions (x22): evaluates the threat of complex hydrological condition to project safety, including wave characteristics, tidal current, storm surge, sea ice, sea bed movement and erosion.

(3) Undersea geological condition (x23): evaluates the regional geological conditions and construction stability according to collected data and geological prospecting.

(4) Sea water depth, distance from shore and beach width (x24): refers to the suitability of plant construction including sea water depth, distance of offshore and beach width.

3.3 Supporting conditions onshore (X3)

Supporting conditions onshore refers to the favorable factors which facilitate construction and operation of the projects. Sub-criteria are considered from two aspects: Transportation and electrical conditions, after examination of relevant literatures [49, 56, 57].

(1) Traffic condition (x31): evaluates the convenience of large equipment transportation along the coast (e.g. highway, railway, bridge, airport, dock).

(2) Electrical transmission and distribution system (x32): evaluates whether the current power grid or its future planning meets the power supply requirements (e.g., substation, electrical grid).

(3) Distance to load center(x33): measures the electricity transmission distances(km).

3.4 Environmental impact (X4)

Sub-criteria in terms of environment are established to measure the OWPS's influence on the environment and the coordination with biology during the implementation of construction and operation [43, 58, 59].

(1) Marine environmental impact (x41): evaluates the plants' damage on the quality of marine ecosystem and biodiversity.

(2) Marine life coordination (x42): refers to the coordination degree with the sea area planning for marine life, which is measured by the distance between OWPS and migration for marine life.

(3) Birds coordination (x43): refers to the coordination degree with birds, which is measured by the distance between OWPS and the paths of migration for birds.

3.5 Economic (X5)

As for economic, sub-criteria are determined from two aspects: the internal economic assessment of the plants [49, 56, 60] and external subsidies from the local government (China has not introduced national offshore wind subsidy policies, but there are some provincial finance subsidies which can improve the enthusiasm of OWPS construction [46]).

(1) Total investment (x51): measures the total cost of offshore hybrid plant construction, operation and maintenance.

(2) Total project pay back period (x52): measures the length of total project pay pack period (The electric price of offshore wind power is 0.85RMB/kWh according to the officially launched offshore wind power benchmark price policy).

(3) Expected B/C (benefit to cost) ratio (x53): measures ratio of expected benefit to total cost.

(4) Operation and maintenance costs (x54): evaluates costs of the plant in the process of operation and maintenance.

(5) Local finance subsidies (x55): refers to the subsidies promoted by the local government finance.

3.6 Social benefits (X6)

Offshore wind power can affect the society in many aspects such as benefit to employment and living environment [61, 62]. Different locations of OWPS have different effects on the local society.

(1) Employment (x61): evaluates the motivation to employment in relevant industries including manufacturing industry transportation and iron industry, etc. on local location.

(2) Benefit to fog haze weather (x62): refers to the improvement to fog haze weather by reducing pollution emission through offshore wind power.

4. Decision framework of OWPS site selection

4.1 Basic theory of MCDM problem in the intuitionistic fuzzy environment

In order to express the DMs' imperfect knowledge in decision-making applications more effectively, the intuitionistic fuzzy set (IFS) is used in the MCDM method. This section describes a few definitions and operations of IFS related to the OWPS site selection MCDM problem.

Definition 1.[63] Let X be a non-empty finite set. An IFS A over X is defined as

$$A=\{(x,u_A(x),v_A(x))|x\in X\} \tag{1-1}$$

where $u_A(x):X\to[0,1]$, $v_A(x):X\to[0,1]$ represent for the membership degree and non-membership degree of x to the set A respectively, satisfying $0\leqslant u_A(x)+v_A(x)\leqslant 1$, $\forall x\in X$.

For the IFS A over X, the parameter $\pi_A(x)=1-u_A(x)-v_A(x)$ is defined as the intuitionistic index. It is the measurement of the hesitation degree of whether x belongs to A. $\pi_A(x)$ satisfies $0\leqslant\pi_A(x)\leqslant 1$, $\forall x\in X$.

Let an IFS $\tilde{A}_i$ denote the evaluation of the i th alternative. The characteristics of $\tilde{A}_i$ are represented by the IFS in the following manner:

$$\tilde{A}_i=\{\langle x_j,(u_{ij},v_{ij})\rangle|x\in X\} \tag{1-2}$$

where u_{ij} indicates the satisfactory degree of alternative A_i evaluated with respect to the criterion x_j, v_{ij} indicates the non-satisfactory degree of alternative A_i evaluated with respect to the criterion x_j, $i=1,2,\ldots,m$; $j=1,2,\ldots,n$.

To compute intuitionistic fuzzy numbers, Atanassov and De, Biswas [33, 64] introduced some basic operations as follows.

Definition 2.[33, 64] Let $A=\{(x,u_A(x),v_A(x))|x\in X\}$ and $B=\{(x,u_B(x),v_B(x))|x\in X\}$ be two intuitionistic fuzzy sets over the same finite set X. Then

$$A\otimes B=\{u_A\cdot u_B,u_A+u_B-u_A\cdot u_B\} \tag{1-3}$$

$$\lambda A=(1-(1-u_A)^{\lambda},u_A{}^{\lambda}),\lambda>0 \tag{1-4}$$

To deal with interactions, the operational laws on intuitionistic fuzzy numbers in definition 2 are redefined and listed as follows.

Definition 3.[65] Let $A=\{(x,u_A(x),v_A(x))|x\in X\}$ and $B=\{(x,u_B(x),v_B(x))|x\in X\}$ be two intuitionistic fuzzy sets over the same finite set X. Then

$$A\otimes B=\{(1-v_A)(1-v_B)-(1-(u_A+v_A))(1-(u_B+v_B)),1-(1-v_A)(1-v_B)\} \tag{1-5}$$

$$\lambda A = (1-(1-u_A)^{\lambda}, (1-u_A)^{\lambda} - (1-(u_A+v_A))), \lambda > 0 \quad (1\text{-}6)$$

In this study, a five-phase decision framework for OWPS site selection decision-making has been proposed, as shown in Fig. 1.2. The five phases of research methodology are described in the following subsections.

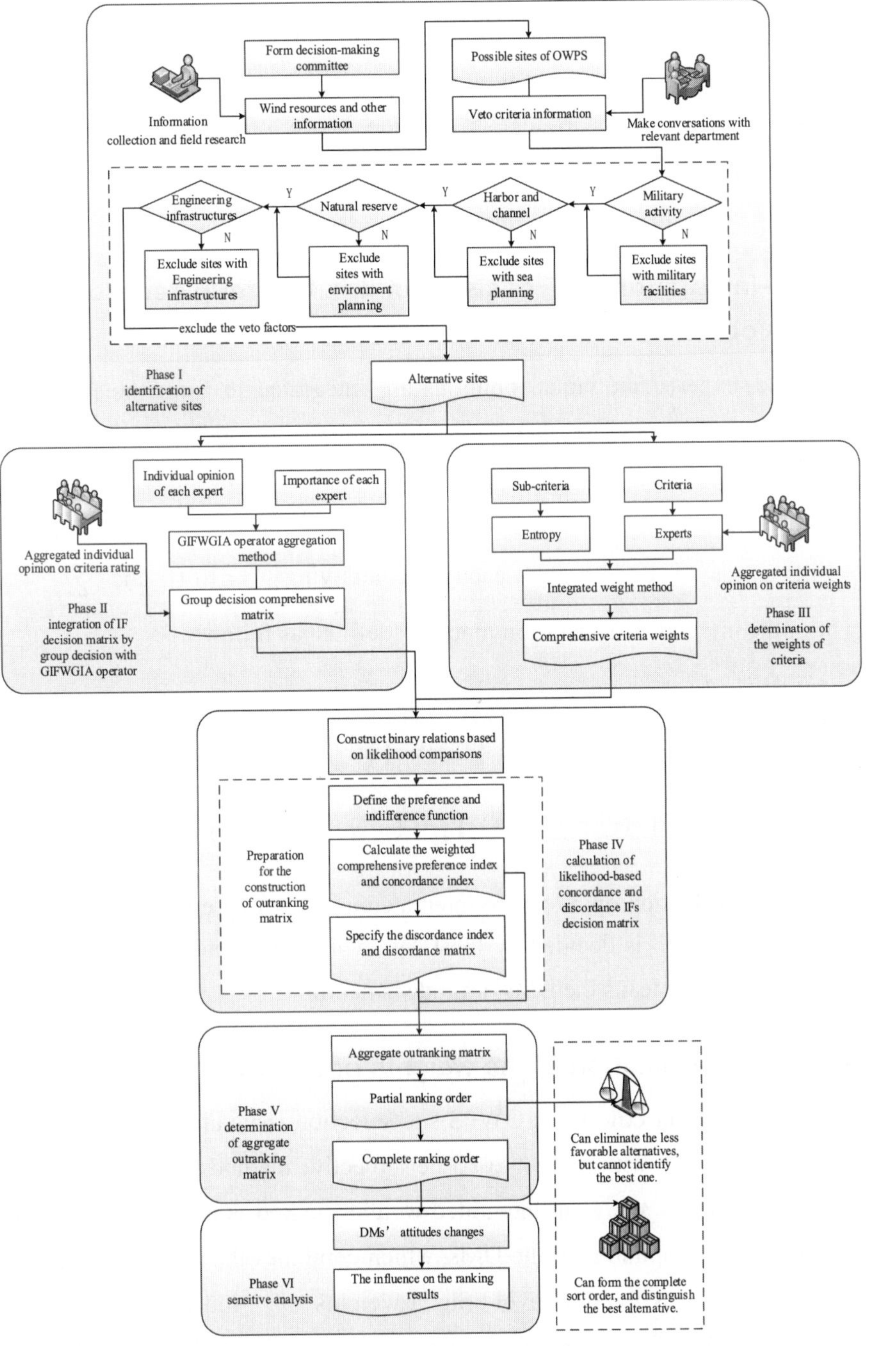

Fig. 1.2 Research methodology of OWPS site selection.

4.2 Phase I –identification of alternative sites

At this stage, experts are invited by OWPS investors to form the decision-making committee. Field research and information collection are conducted by the experts firstly. Then several possible sites of OWPS are identified in accordance with wind resources by satellite remote sensing data and wind resource maps and other information. After this, the experts make conversation with the related departments and collect materials including military activity area, harbor and channel area, natural reserve area, engineering infrastructures, and make full communication with relevant departments to exclude the veto factors [66], in order to avoid site election failure or project frozen caused by these factors. Finally, several alternative sites can be identified.

4.3 Phase II –integration of IF decision matrix by group decision with GIFWGIA operator

In this phase, experts' individual opinions are integrated to form the IF group decision comprehensive matrix. Considering there exist some interactions between IFS membership and non-membership[33, 34], the GIFWGIA operator[35] is used to form the aggregated decision matrix.

Definition 4.[35] Let $\tilde{A}_{ij}^{(l)}=[\tilde{a}_{ij}^{(l)}]_{m\times n}$ be the IF-decision matrix of k DMs, $l=1,2,\ldots,k$. $\lambda>0$, $w_l=(w_1,w_2,\ldots,w_k)$ is the weight of each DM, satisfying $w_l\in[0,1]$ and $\sum_{l=1}^{k}w_l=1$. Then each element of the integrated IF-decision matrix is defined as follows:

$$\begin{aligned}
a_{ij} &= GIFWGIA_w(a_{ij}^{(1)},a_{ij}^{(2)},\ldots,a_{ij}^{(l)})=\mathop{\oplus}_{k=1}^{l}(a_{ij}^{(l)})^{w_l}\\
&=\Bigg\{1-(1-\prod_{l=1}^{k}(1-(1-u_{ij}^{(l)})^{\lambda}+(1-(u_{ij}^{(l)}+v_{ij}^{(l)}))^{\lambda})^{w_l}+\prod_{l=1}^{k}(1-(u_{ij}^{(l)}+v_{ij}^{(l)}))^{\lambda w_l})^{1/\lambda},\\
&(1-\prod_{l=1}^{k}(1-(1-u_{ij}^{(l)})^{\lambda}+(1-(u_{ij}^{(l)}+v_{ij}^{(l)}))^{\lambda})^{w_l}+\prod_{l=1}^{k}(1-(u_{ij}^{(l)}+v_{ij}^{(l)}))^{\lambda w_l})^{1/\lambda}-\prod_{l=1}^{k}(1-(u_{ij}^{(l)}+v_{ij}^{(l)}))^{w_l}\Bigg\}
\end{aligned} \tag{1-7}$$

The individual evaluation opinions are integrated as the group evaluation opinion based on the GIFWGIA operator. λ is decided by the DMs, which represents the different attitude the DMs prefer. When $\lambda=1$, means the DMs' attitude is neutral[35].

4.4 Phase III –determination of the weights of criteria

The effects of different criteria on OWPS site selection issue are considered not equal. To decide the criteria weight W_j with respect to x_j, the subjective methods and the objective methods are commonly used. In this study, an integrated weight method is adopted to account for both objective information and opinions of the DMs, which combines the subjective method with the objective method. Firstly, as for first-level-criteria weights W_j^c, individual opinions of k DMs are aggregated using GIFWGIA operator; as for sub-criteria weights W_j^s, the entropy method is used through decision matrix. The IF entropy value with respect to sub-criterion x_j can be defined as follows.

Definition 5. Let $E(R_j)$ be the entropy values of R_j with respect to sub-criterion x_j, $R_{ij}=\left\{A_{1j},A_{2j},\ldots,A_{mj}\right\}$, IFS $A_{ij}=(u_{ij},v_{ij},\pi_{ij})$ .Then

$$E(R_j)=\frac{1}{m}\sum_{i=1}^{m}\frac{\min(u_{ij},v_{ij})+\pi_{ij}}{\max(u_{ij},v_{ij})+\pi_{ij}} \tag{1-8}$$

Then, the sub-criteria weights W_j^s is obtained by $E(R_j)$ after normalization. Following this, we integrate the first-level-criteria weights W_j^c and the sub-criteria weights W_j^c using Eq. (1-4) to get the final comprehensive criteria weights W_j. As a result, the obtained comprehensive criteria weights has both objective and subjective properties, which means either subjective information or the DMs' opinions have been taken into consideration.

4.5 Phase IV –calculation of likelihood-based concordance and discordance IFs decision matrix

In this phase, the binary relations of pairwise competing alternative sites are established, based on which the concordance and discordance IFs decision matrixes are constructed. The binary relation indicates the comparison relationship between two competing alternatives. Based on this concept, this paper introduces the likelihood-based comparisons into OWPS site selection decision to determine the binary relations between two alternatives by comparison possibilities under the incompletion information environment. Motivated by the likelihood concept, the comparison possibilities for each competing pair of alternatives are defined as follows.

Definition 6. Let $\tilde{A}_{ij}=(u_{ij},v_{ij},\pi_{ij})$ and $\tilde{A}_{i'j}=(u_{i'j},v_{i'j},\pi_{i'j})$ be two rating of alternatives with respect to criterion $x_j\in X$, $i,i'=1,2,\ldots,m$, $i\neq i'j=1,2\ldots,n;$ $\underline{C}_{ij}=u_{ij}$, $\overline{C}_{ij}=1-v_{ij}$, the comparison possibilities for each competing pair is defined by

$$L(\tilde{A}_{ij}\geqslant\tilde{A}_{i'j})=\max\left\{1-\max\left\{\frac{\overline{C}_{i'j}-\underline{C}_{ij}}{\pi_{ij}+\pi_{i'j}},0\right\},0\right\} \tag{1-9}$$

$L(\tilde{A}_{ij}\geqslant\tilde{A}_{i'j})$ represents for the likelihood degree that $\tilde{A}_{ij}$ is not smaller than $\tilde{A}_{i'j}$.

Step 1. Define the preference and indifference function.

Let $p(\tilde{A}_{ij},\tilde{A}_{i'j})$ be the preference function based on the likelihood comparison $L(\tilde{A}_{ij}\geqslant\tilde{A}_{i'j})$, indicating the degree of the preference of $\tilde{A}_{i'j}$ over $\tilde{A}_{ij}$ .The strict preference threshold p and the indifference threshold q are introduced, so that the DMs' preference opinions are reasonably considered in the decision process.

Definition 7.[37]

$$p(\tilde{A}_{ij},\tilde{A}_{i'j})=\begin{cases}1,\ \text{if}\, L(\tilde{A}_{ij}\geqslant\tilde{A}_{i'j})-0.5>p\\ \dfrac{\left|L(\tilde{A}_{ij}\geqslant\tilde{A}_{i'j})-0.5\right|-q}{p-q},\ \text{if}\ q<L(\tilde{A}_{ij}\geqslant\tilde{A}_{i'j})-0.5\leqslant p\\ 0,\ \text{otherwise}\end{cases}\tag{1-10}$$

$p(\tilde{A}_{ij},\tilde{A}_{i'j})$ represents for the preference function with the following substantial meanings: $p(\tilde{A}_{ij},\tilde{A}_{i'j})\sim 1$ indicates the preference of $\tilde{A}_{ij}$ over $\tilde{A}_{i'j}$ is strong; $p(\tilde{A}_{ij},\tilde{A}_{i'j})\sim 0.5$ indicates a weak preference; $p(\tilde{A}_{ij},\tilde{A}_{i'j})\sim 0$ indicates an indifference relationship between $\tilde{A}_{i'j}$ and $\tilde{A}_{ij}$. The strict preference threshold p and the indifference preference threshold q are decided by the DMs.

Step 2. Calculate the weighted comprehensive preference index $\tilde{p}_{ii'}$ and concordance index $I_{ii'}$.

The purpose of calculating the concordance decision index is to estimate the dominance of one alternative A_i over the other alternative $A_{i'}$ in each competing pair.

Firstly, the comprehensive preference index $\tilde{p}_{ii'}$ needs to be obtained, which can be calculated by the use of GIFWGIA operator in the following manner.

Definition 8. Let $W_j=\left\{\left\langle x_j,(w_u,w_v,w_\pi)\right\rangle \middle| x_j\in X\right\}$ be the comprehensive weights of the criteria. $p(\tilde{A}_{ij},\tilde{A}_{i'j})$ refers to the likelihood-based preference relationship. The comprehensive preference index $\tilde{p}_{ii'}$ is calculated by

$$\tilde{p}_{ii'}=GIFWGIA_{W_j}(p(\tilde{A}_{i1},\tilde{A}_{i'1}),p(\tilde{A}_{i2},\tilde{A}_{i'2}),\ldots,p(\tilde{A}_{in},\tilde{A}_{i'n}))=\overset{n}{\underset{j=1}{\oplus}}(p(\tilde{A}_{ij},\tilde{A}_{i'j}))\cdot W_j=(\rho_{ii'},\beta_{ii'},\tau_{ii'})\tag{1-11}$$

Then, the concordance index $I_{ii'}$ between A_i and $A_{i'}$ can be established based on the score function S [67, 68] as follows:

$$I_{ii'}=S(\tilde{p}_{ii'})=\rho_{ii'}-\tau_{ii'}\tag{1-12}$$

The concordance index $I_{ii'}$ reflects the relative preference degree that alternative A_i dominates $A_{i'}$. The higher the concordance index is, the more preferable the alternative A_i is over alternative $A_{i'}$. The threshold value $\overline{I}$ can help to judge the superior chance of A_i over $A_{i'}$. If the value of $I_{ii'}$ exceeds the threshold value $\overline{I}$, the chance increases[27]. The threshold value $\overline{I}$ can be calculated by

$$\overline{I}=\sum\nolimits_{i=1}^{m}\sum\nolimits_{i'=1}^{m}I_{ii'}/(m(m-1))\tag{1-13}$$

With threshold value $\overline{I}$ determined, the concordance relationship Boolean matrix H can be constructed and each element in the Boolean matrix is obtained as follows:

$$\begin{cases}h_{ii'}=1\ \text{ if } I_{ii'}\geqslant\overline{I}\\ h_{ii'}=0\ \text{ if } I_{ii'}<\overline{I}\end{cases}\tag{1-14}$$

Step 3. Specify the discordance index $DI_{ii'}$ and discordance matrix G.

The meaning of discordance index $DI_{ii'}$ is on the contrary to concordance index $I_{ii'}$, which indicates the degree that the alternative A_i is less favorable than the alternative $A_{i'}$. It can be obtained as follows:

$$DI_{ii'} = \frac{\sum_{j=1}^{n} p(\tilde{A}_{i'j}, \tilde{A}_{ij}) \cdot d_h(\tilde{A}_{ij}, \tilde{A}_{i'j})}{\sum_{j=1}^{n} d_h(\tilde{A}_{ij}, \tilde{A}_{i'j})} \tag{1-15}$$

$d_h(\tilde{A}_{ij}, \tilde{A}_{i'j})$ can be calculated by the following definition.

Definition 9.[27] The distance $d_h(\tilde{A}_{ij}, \tilde{A}_{i'j})$ between $\tilde{A}_{ij}$ and $\tilde{A}_{i'j}$ is defined by

$$d_h(\tilde{A}_{ij}, \tilde{A}_{i'j}) = \max\left\{\left|u_{ij} - u_{i'j}\right|, \left|v_{ij} - v_{i'j}\right|\right\} \tag{1-16}$$

The threshold value $\overline{DI}$ is calculated as follows:

$$\overline{DI} = \sum_{i=1}^{m} \sum_{i'=1}^{m} DI_{ii'} / (m(m-1)) \tag{1-17}$$

The higher the value of discordance index $DI_{ii'}$ is, the less satisfactory the alternative A_i is compared with alternative $A_{i'}$. Hence the discordance relationship can be evaluated as follows and the Boolean matrix G can be constructed as follows:

$$\begin{cases} g_{ii'} = 1 & \text{if } DI_{ii'} \leqslant \overline{DI} \\ g_{ii'} = 0 & \text{if } DI_{ii'} > \overline{DI} \end{cases} \tag{1-18}$$

4.6 Phase V –determination of aggregate outranking matrix

According to the concordance matrix H and discordance matrix G obtained before, the aggregate outranking matrix F can be established by

$$f_{ii'} = h_{ii'} \cdot g_{ii'} \tag{1-19}$$

$f_{ii'}$ refers to each element in the aggregate outranking matrix F with the following meaning: ① $f_{ii'} = 1$ indicates that the alternative A_i is superior to alternative $A_{i'}$ on the basis of both the concordance and discordance indices; ② $f_{ii'} = 0$ indicates that the alternative A_i is indifferent with or inferior to alternative $A_{i'}$. In this way, the initial ranking order can be obtained and the DMs can eliminate the less dissatisfactory alternatives.

However, the ranking results from the aggregate outranking matrix F is a partial-preference order, so that the DMs still cannot see clearly the complete rankings and decide which alternative is the best choice. In order to solve this problem, this paper puts forward a complete ordering method.

Let F' be the improved aggregate outranking matrix. Each element $f'_{ii'}$ in the outranking matrix F' is defined as follows:

$$f'_{ii'}=\begin{cases} SI_{ii'} & ,SDI_{ii'}\leqslant SI_{ii'} \\ SI_{ii'}\cdot\dfrac{1-SDI_{ii'}}{1-SI_{ii'}} & ,SDI_{ii'}>SI_{ii'} \end{cases} \tag{1-20}$$

where $SI_{ii'}$ and $SDI_{ii'}$ represent for the standard values of $I_{ii'}$ and $DI_{ii'}$, respectively, to make the concordance and discordance indices comparable, which are defined as below

$$SI_{ii'}=\frac{I_{ii'}-\min_{i'=1}^{m}\min_{i=1}^{m}I_{ii'}}{\max_{i'=1}^{m}\max_{i=1}^{m}I_{ii'}-\min_{i'=1}^{m}\min_{i=1}^{m}I_{ii'}} \tag{1-21}$$

$$SDI_{ii'}=\frac{DI_{ii'}-\min_{i'=1}^{m}\min_{i=1}^{m}DI_{ii'}}{\max_{i'=1}^{m}\max_{i=1}^{m}DI_{ii'}-\min_{i'=1}^{m}\min_{i=1}^{m}DI_{ii'}} \tag{1-22}$$

$f'_{ii'}$ denotes the outranking degree that the alternative A_i is preferable to alternative $A_{i'}$ in general. Let $\overline{F}$ be the threshold of the outranking matrix F', then the Boolean matrix F^B can be constructed and each element in the Boolean matrix is obtained as follows:

$$\begin{cases} f^b{}_{ii'}=1 \ \text{ if } f'_{ii'}\geqslant\overline{F} \\ f^b{}_{ii'}=0 \ \text{ if } f'_{ii'}<\overline{F} \end{cases} \tag{1-23}$$

Then a complete ranking orders can be obtained through coordinating the threshold values.

4.7 Phase VI-sensitive analysis

In order to learn how the ranking results will be influenced when decision information changes, we proposed a sensitive analysis, in that subjective judgment of decision makers may deviate from the objective facts. In the real-life decision-making practices, the DMs' attitudes do not always stay the same; they may vary with different conditions or factors. So the understanding of the DMs' attitudes changes and its influence on the ranking results is significant. Therefore, sensitive analysis will be made to reveal this influence and check the robustness of the decision results.

5. A real case study

To respond to the call of 2015 national energy plan of China, the Shandong Province would like to start a series of renewable energy plans, including building a 100MW OWPS. In order to choose a suitable location for OWPS, several experts and research analysts were invited by the Electric Power Research Institute of Shandong Province. These experts and research analysts formed an investigation and evaluation committee(hereinafter referred to as IEC). In IEC, there were two groups of experts: the professional group and the specialized group. The professional group was formed by experienced experts who had worked in the wind power industry for a long time and had comprehensive knowledge about wind power projects. The specialized group was formed by experts in different fields concerning the selection of the potential sites, including meteorology, hydrology, geology, electrical engineering, construction, technical economy, environment and sociology. The professional group was specialized in evaluating the influence degree of each site-selection factor on the full life circle of offshore wind power projects, while the specialized group was good at assessing the value of index in different fields. The two groups shared out the work and cooperated with one another in the decision process. This arrangement was to give full play of each expert's expertise and to avoid any deviation caused by specialty differences. The details are introduced in the following parts.

In phase I, the IEC identified feasible sites on the basis of field investigation and relevant documents. The conveyed investigation involved several potential coastal areas of Shandong, including Lubei, Laizhou Bay, Bozhong, Long Island, northern and southern peninsula. The IEC met the local power supply companies, the Development and Reform Commission and the Bureau of Commerce and collect information concerning wind resources, port planning and construction, offshore wind tower construction, offshore wind power planning, economic assessment and approved ocean area for construction. Seven potential sites were identified in the first place. After this, information conversations were conducted with the local power supply companies, the Development and Reform Commission, the Environmental Protection Agency, NEA, SOA, the local government and relative institutes, in order to exclude the areas concerning veto factors (V1~V4) for OWPS and get more information. Two identified sites were eliminated from the list because of the veto criteria V2 and V4. Then, the initial OWPS site selection scheme was formed by five potential alternatives, involving coasts of Bingzhou, Hekou, Laizhou Dongying, Laizhou Yantai, and Long Island, respectivelyA1, A2, A3, A4, A5. The evaluation criteria system for OWPS site selection is shown in Table 1.2.

Table 1.2 The criteria and sub-criteria of OWPS site selection.

Target	Criteria	Sub-criteria	Criteria type	Source
OWPS site selection	1.Wind resources	Wind speed and its distribution status x11	Quantitative (benefit)	Del Jesus et al.
		Wind power density x12	Quantitative (benefit)	Zhang et al. 2014
		Effective wind hours x13	Quantitative (benefit)	Yun-na et al. 2013
		Wind shear x14	Quantitative (cost)	Mycek et al. 2014
		Turbulence intensity x15	Quantitative (cost)	
	2.Construction and maintenance conditions	Meteorological conditions x21	Qualitative (benefit)	Ou et al. 2007, Hong and Möller 2012
		Marine conditions x22	Qualitative (benefit)	Mycek et al. 2014
		Undersea geological condition x23	Qualitative (benefit)	Fang et al. 2009

Continued

Target	Criteria	Sub-criteria	Criteria type	Source
OWPS site selection	2.Construction and maintenance conditions	Sea water depth, distance of Offshore and beach width x24	Qualitative (benefit)	China's National Energy Administration and the Oceanic Administration
	3. Supporting conditions onshore	Traffic condition x31	Qualitative (benefit)	Sánchez-Lozano et al., Yun-na et al. 2013
		Electrical transmission and distribution system x32	Qualitative (benefit)	Kim et al. 2013
		Distance to load center x33	Qualitative (benefit)	Yun-na et al. 2013
	4.Environme-ntal mpacts	Marine environmental impact x41	Qualitative (benefit)	Reubens et al. 2013, Thompson et al. 2013
		Marine life coordination x42	Qualitative (benefit)	According to the national conditions
		Birds coordination x43	Qualitative (benefit)	According to the national conditions
	5. Economic	Total investment x51	Quantitative (cost)	Yun-na et al. 2013
		Total project pay back period x52	Quantitative (benefit)	
		Expected B/C (benefit to cost) ratio x53	Quantitative (benefit)	Kim et al. 2013
		Operation and maintenance costs x54	Qualitative (cost)	Pérez et al. 2013
		Provincial finance subsidies x55	Qualitative (benefit)	Guo and Zheng 2011
	6. Society benefits	Employment x61	Qualitative (benefit)	According to Santora et al. 2004, Burkhard and Gee 2012 and the national conditions
		Benefit to fog haze weather x62	Qualitative (benefit)	

In phase II, criteria values were evaluated by the specialized group of IEC and individual opinions were aggregated based on the importance of each expert. Firstly, the specialized group was divided into different parts according to the corresponding criteria. In each part of the group, there were five related experts, whose professional title included two intermediate, two junior and one senior, numbered DM1, DM2, DM3, DM4, DM5, respectively. Then, based on the linguistic variables for the rating of alternatives shown in Table 1.3, the IFSs evaluation rating matrixes of the alternatives and criteria were established by each evaluation expert in the specialized group, as shown in Table 1.4 to Table1.9. Some data used in the evaluation is listed in Table 1.4. During this stage, the experts were required to score on their own instead of grading after discussion, in order to avoid interrupt and irrational interference, ensuring the independence of each DM. The importance of each DM was considered as not equal. The relative importance of DMs was decided by the professional title, which revealed individual's working experience and ability, given in Table 1.10. The attitude of the decision makers λ was decided by the experts as 1. With the weight of each expert determined, the aggregate evaluation ratings of the experts group were calculated using Eq. (1-7) as shown in Table 1.11.

Table1.3 linguistic variables for the rating of alternatives.

Linguistic variables	Intuitionistic fuzzy numbers
Extremely high(EH)	[1.00, 0.00]
Very very high(VVH)	[0.80, 0.10]
Very high(VH)	[0.80, 0.20]
High(H)	[0.60, 0.20]
Medium high(MH)	[0.60, 0.30]
Medium(M)	[0.40, 0.30]
Medium low(ML)	[0.40, 0.40]
Low(L)	[0.20, 0.40]
Very low(VL)	[0.20, 0.55]
Very very low(VVL)	[0.10, 0.80]

Table 1.4 Performance numerical values and the corresponding evaluation ratings.

Criteria	Sub-criteria		A1	A2	A3	A4	A5
X1	x11	30m (m/s)	5.33	4.91	5.51	5.23	4.50
		50m (m/s)	5.66	5.74	6.02	5.75	5.00
		100m (m/s)	7.54	7.68	7.96	7.23	6.90
		Evaluation ratings	MH MH VH ML ML	MH H M MH ML	EH H H VVH H	L L M M ML	VVL VVL VVL VVL VVL
	x12	30m (W/s^2)	292.6	233.4	330.0	320.7	284.0
		50m (W/s^2)	451.7	360.3	468.1	464.0	392.0
		100m(W/s^2)	544.7	434.5	640.0	492.8	421.8
		Evaluation ratings	L L MH L ML	VL VL ML VL VL	EH EH VH VVH VH	M M L ML VL	VVL VVL VVL VVL VVL
	x13	h	2334	2425	2462	2225	2198
		Evaluation ratings	M MH MH M MH	MH MH VVH MH MH	VVH VH H VH EH	MH M L ML ML	VL VVL VL VL VL
	x14	-	0.13	0.12	0.09	0.098	0.10
		Evaluation ratings	VVL VVL VL VVL VL	ML ML ML M ML	EH EH EH EH EH	VH VH MH MH VH	H H H H H
	x15	-	0.094	0.121	0.068	0.072	0.074
		Evaluation ratings	M M MH M L	ML VL VL VL ML	VVH EH VVH EH VVH	H H VVH H MH	H H H H H
X5	x51	¥	16400	17000	24400	18416	174550
		Evaluation ratings	MH ML M M L	M H H M M	VVL VVL VL VVL VVL	L L M L M	ML ML L L ML
	x52	Year	14	15	20	16	17
		Evaluation ratings	MH MH MH MH MH	MH MH ML MH MH	VL VVL VVL VVL VVL	M L M ML L	L L L L L

Continued

Criteria	Sub-criteria		A1	A2	A3	A4	A5
X5	x53	-	0.212	0.186	0.143	0.168	0.163
		Evaluation ratings	M M M M M	MH MH H MH H	M M ML ML L	M M ML M M	ML ML ML ML ML

Table 1.5 evaluation rating matrixes of alternative A_1 on the qualitative sub-criteria.

Xriteria	Sub-xriteria	DM1	DM2	DM3	DM4	DM5
X2	x21	M	M	ML	L	ML
	x22	L	VL	MH	M	L
	x23	ML	MH	VH	ML	ML
	x24	MH	MH	VH	ML	ML
X3	x31	M	L	H	ML	VL
	x32	M	M	H	ML	M
	x33	ML	MH	M	MH	ML
X4	x41	VVL	L	L	VVL	VVL
	x42	VL	VL	ML	VL	ML
	x43	ML	MH	ML	M	M
X5	x54	VL	VVL	VVL	VVL	VVL
	x55	MH	M	M	ML	M
X6	x61	M	H	MH	H	M
	x62	H	ML	M	MH	MH

Table 1.6 evaluation rating matrixes of alternative A_2 on the qualitative sub-criteria.

Criteria	Sub-criteria	DM1	DM2	DM3	DM4	DM5
X2	x21	MH	MH	VH	M	M
	x22	MH	M	MH	H	H
	x23	MH	M	ML	L	L
	x24	ML	MH	L	M	MH
X3	x31	MH	H	VH	H	MH
	x32	MH	M	MH	H	M
	x33	L	M	M	M	M
X4	x41	M	H	M	H	M
	x42	VH	MH	VH	H	MH
	x43	MH	MH	MH	VH	MH
X5	x54	MH	MH	MH	ML	MH
	x55	M	M	VH	MH	H
X6	x61	MH	VH	MH	VVH	M
	x62	VVH	VH	H	VH	MH

Table 1.7 evaluation rating matrixes of alternative A3 on the qualitative sub-criteria.

Criteria	Sub-criteria	DM1	DM2	DM3	DM4	DM5
X2	x21	L	VVL	VVL	L	L
	x22	ML	MH	MH	MH	MH
	x23	VH	H	EH	H	EH
	x24	VH	VH	VH	MH	MH
X3	x31	VH	H	M	MH	VH
	x32	VH	VH	VH	VH	H
	x33	VVL	VL	VL	VL	VVL
X4	x41	VL	VVL	VVL	VL	VL
	x42	L	L	L	ML	M
	x43	H	VVH	H	MH	H
X5	x54	EH	VVH	VVH	VVH	VVH
	x55	M	L	M	M	L
X6	x61	EH	VVH	H	EH	VH
	x62	VVH	H	H	H	VH

Table 1.8 evaluation rating matrixes of alternative A_4 on the qualitative sub-criteria.

Criteria	Sub-criteria	DM1	DM2	DM3	DM4	DM5
X2	x21	M	VL	M	M	L
	x22	VL	VL	VL	VL	VL
	x23	ML	L	ML	MH	ML
	x24	L	M	L	L	L
X3	x31	M	ML	L	ML	M
	x32	L	VL	L	VL	L
	x33	VL	VL	VL	ML	VL
X4	x41	ML	VL	ML	VL	ML
	x42	L	M	M	L	M
	x43	ML	MH	MH	ML	ML
X5	x54	MH	MH	VH	VH	VH
	x55	VL	VL	ML	VL	VL
X6	x61	M	M	H	VH	H
	x62	M	H	H	H	H

Table 1.9 evaluation rating matrixes of alternative A_5 on the qualitative sub-criteria.

Criteria	Sub-criteria	DM1	DM2	DM3	DM4	DM5
X2	x21	L	L	L	L	L
	x22	VL	VVL	VL	VVL	VVL
	x23	L	VL	L	VL	VL
	x24	VVL	VVL	VVL	VVL	VVL
X3	x31	VL	VVL	VL	VVL	VL
	x32	VL	VVL	VL	VVL	VL

Continued

Criteria	Sub-criteria	DM1	DM2	DM3	DM4	DM5
X3	x33	L	L	L	L	L
X4	x41	ML	L	L	L	ML
	x42	ML	ML	ML	ML	ML
	x43	ML	ML	ML	ML	ML
X5	x54	VH	VH	VH	VH	VH
	x55	VVL	VVL	VVL	VVL	VVL
X6	x61	ML	ML	ML	ML	ML
	x62	ML	ML	ML	ML	ML

Table1.10 relative importance of the DMs.

	DM1	DM2	DM3	DM4	DM5
Professional title	Intermediate	Intermediate	Junior	Junior	Senior
Linguistic terms	Important	Important	Medium	Medium	Very important
IF numbers	[0.7, 0.2]	[0.7, 0.2]	[0.5, 0.45]	[0.5, 0.45]	[0.9, 0.1]
Weights	0.2174	0.2174	0.1522	0.1522	0.2609

Table 1.11 aggregate evaluation ratings of the experts group.

Criteria	Sub-criteria	A1	A2	A3	A4	A5
X1	x11	[0.6703 0.3297]	[0.5276 0.3078]	[0.8816 0.1184]	[0.3230 0.3712]	[0.1000 0.8000]
	x12	[0.3439 0.3858]	[0.2285 0.5299]	[0.8974 0.1026]	[0.3142 0.4048]	[0.1000 0.8000]
	x13	[0.5499 0.3000]	[0.6273 0.2727]	[0.8699 0.1301]	[0.4328 0.3584]	[0.1724 0.6228]
	x14	[0.1336 0.7205]	[0.4015 0.3858]	[1.0000 0.0000]	[0.7681 0.2319]	[0.6000 0.2000]
	x15	[0.3988 0.3276]	[0.2917 0.4837]	[0.9357 0.0643]	[0.6364 0.2134]	[0.6000 0.2000]
X2	x21	[0.3765 0.3584]	[0.7143 0.2857]	[0.1601 0.6003]	[0.3000 0.3892]	[0.2000 0.4000]
	x22	[0.3108 0.4093]	[0.5706 0.2603]	[0.5607 0.3231]	[0.2000 0.5500]	[0.1296 0.7301]
	x23	[0.6482 0.3518]	[0.3914 0.3584]	[0.8772 0.1228]	[0.4050 0.3858]	[0.2031 0.4996]
	x24	[0.6703 0.3297]	[0.4915 0.3388]	[0.7570 0.2430]	[0.2447 0.3796]	[0.1000 0.8000]
X3	x31	[0.3322 0.3987]	[0.7505 0.2495]	[0.7681 0.2319]	[0.3761 0.3541]	[0.1553 0.6666]
	x32	[0.4326 0.3022]	[0.5264 0.2857]	[0.8000 0.2000]	[0.2033 0.4605]	[0.1553 0.6666]
	x33	[0.4856 0.3498]	[0.3576 0.3231]	[0.1440 0.6947]	[0.2285 0.5299]	[0.2000 0.4000]
X4	x41	[0.1332 0.6999]	[0.4772 0.2646]	[0.1553 0.6666]	[0.3223 0.4605]	[0.3129 0.4000]
	x42	[0.2788 0.4933]	[0.7505 0.2495]	[0.2907 0.3754]	[0.3276 0.3388]	[0.4000 0.4000]
	x43	[0.4579 0.3388]	[0.7143 0.2857]	[0.6494 0.1958]	[0.4804 0.3649]	[0.4000 0.4000]
X5	x51	[0.4171 0.3498]	[0.4772 0.2646]	[0.1113 0.7738]	[0.2843 0.3606]	[0.3530 0.4000]
	x52	[0.6000 0.3000]	[0.5726 0.3163]	[0.3165 0.5615]	[0.3115 0.3649]	[0.2000 0.4000]
	x53	[0.4000 0.3000]	[0.6065 0.2603]	[0.4030 0.3584]	[0.3704 0.3163]	[0.4000 0.4000]
	x54	[0.1165 0.7615]	[0.5726 0.3163]	[0.9208 0.0792]	[0.7549 0.2451]	[0.8000 0.2000]
	x55	[0.4616 0.3163]	[0.7397 0.2603]	[0.3060 0.3498]	[0.2285 0.5299]	[0.1000 0.8000]
X6	x61	[0.5169 0.2646]	[0.7487 0.2513]	[0.8913 0.1087]	[0.7549 0.2451]	[0.4000 0.4000]
	x62	[0.5371 0.3032]	[0.7926 0.2074]	[0.8207 0.1793]	[0.5587 0.2229]	[0.4000 0.4000]

In phase III, the criteria weights were decided by the professional group of IEC on the basis of the integrated weight method. The professional group was put on this job due to their thorough knowledge of wind power projects and understanding of how the projects were influenced by different site-selection factors. The professional group had the same personnel structure as each specialized group part. Based on the linguistic weighting terms and the corresponding intuitionistic fuzzy numbers (Table 1.12, the relative importance of the first-level-criteria were evaluated by the experts, as shown in Table 1.13. Then, the first-level-criteria weights evaluated by the experts were aggregated using Eq. (1-7), as shown in Table 1.14. Following this, the sub-criteria weights were obtained by using Eq. (1-8) after normalization, as shown in Table 1.15. Next, the first-level-criteria weights and the sub-criteria weights were integrated as the final comprehensive criteria weights by using Eq. (1-6) as shown in Table 1.16. From Table 1.16, we could find that the resources ([0.8183 0.1151]), economic ([0.7239 0.2043]), and the environment ([0.8570 0.0848]) were considered important to the overall goal for site selection. The environment was given a high weight in order to reduce the high risk of site selection failure, since the first franchise of OWPS projects in China were all required to be relocated due to the environmental problems.

Table1.12 linguistic variables for rating the importance of criteria and the DMs.

Linguistic varibles	Intuitionistic fuzzy numbers
Very important (VI)	[0.90, 0.10]
Important (I)	[0.70, 0.20]
Medium (M)	[0.50, 0.45]
Unimportant (UI)	[0.30, 0.60]
Very unimportant (VUI)	[0.10, 0.90]

Table 1.13 ratings of the first-level- criteria weights.

Decision makers	X1	X2	X3	X4	X5	X6
DM1	VI	I	M	VI	I	M
DM2	VI	M	UI	I	VI	UI
DM3	I	M	I	VI	M	I
DM4	VI	M	I	VI	M	I
DM5	I	M	UI	VI	VI	UI

Table 1.14 aggregated weights of the first-level-criteria.

	X1	X2	X3	X4	X5	X6
Weights	[0.8183, 0.1151]	[0.5387, 0.3613]	[0.4395, 0.4606]	[0.8570, 0.0848]	[0.7239, 0.2043]	[0.4395, 0.4606]

Table 1.15 sub-criteria weights.

	x11	x12	x13	x14	x15	x21	x22	x23	x24	x31	x32
Sub-criteria weight	0.1951	0.2181	0.2098	0.1665	0.2105	0.2825	0.2409	0.2628	0.2138	0.3165	0.3058
	x33	x41	x42	x43	x51	x52	x53	x54	x55	x61	x62
Sub-criteria weight	0.3777	0.2974	0.3715	0.3310	0.2372	0.2022	0.2731	0.1002	0.1873	0.4735	0.5265

Table 1.16 comprehensive criteria weights.

Criteria weight		Sub-criteria weight		Synthetic weight
X1	[0.8183 0.1151]	x11	0.1951	[0.2793, 0.6559]
		x12	0.2181	[0.3066, 0.6240]
		x13	0.2098	[0.2969, 0.6354]
		x14	0.1665	[0.2438, 0.6977]
		x15	0.2105	[0.2977, 0.6344]
X2	[0.5387 0.3613]	x21	0.2825	[0.1964, 0.7500]
		x22	0.2409	[0.1701, 0.7825]
		x23	0.2628	[0.1840, 0.7653]
		x24	0.2138	[0.1524, 0.8044]
X3	[0.4395 0.4606]	x31	0.3165	[0.1674, 0.7824]
		x32	0.3058	[0.1622, 0.7889]
		x33	0.3777	[0.1964, 0.7461]
X4	[0.8570 0.0848]	x41	0.2974	[0.3158, 0.6179]
		x42	0.3715	[0.3457, 0.5838]
		x43	0.3310	[0.3350, 0.5959]
X5	[0.7239 0.2043]	x51	0.2372	[0.2631, 0.6861]
		x52	0.2022	[0.2291, 0.7254]
		x53	0.2731	[0.2964, 0.6481]
		x54	0.1002	[0.1210, 0.8529]
		x55	0.1873	[0.2142, 0.7427]
X6	[0.4395 0.4606]	x61	0.4735	[0.1068, 0.8596]
		x62	0.5265	[0.1186, 0.8444]

In phase IV, the experts were informed of the essence meaning of the preference threshold p and indifference threshold q. The value of p and q was decided by the experts, respectively $p = 0.1$, $q = 0.5$. The comparison possibilities $L(\tilde{A}_{ij} \geqslant \tilde{A}_{i'j})$ and the preference function for each competing pair of alternative $\tilde{A}_{ij}$ and $\tilde{A}_{i'j}$ were calculated by Eq. (1-9) and Eq. (1-10), as shown in Table 1.17 and Table 1.18, respectively. Then the weighted comprehensive preference indices $\tilde{p}_{ii'}$ were obtained by Eq. (1-11)(Table 1.19), and the concordance indices $I_{ii'}$ were determined by Eq. (1-10)(Table 1.20). The threshold value $\overline{I} = 0.7647$, as calculated by Eq. (1-13). The concordance relationship Boolean matrix H could be constructed by Eq.

(1-16), as shown in Table 1.21. Then, the discordance indices $DI_{ii'}$ were obtained by Eq. (1-14) and Eq. (1-15), as shown in Table 1.22. The threshold value $\overline{DI} = 0.4838$, as calculated by Eq. (1-17) and discordance relationship Boolean matrix G were established using Eq. (1-18), as shown in Table 1.23. In the next phase, the partial-preference ranking orders were firstly sorted using the aggregate outranking matrix F established by Eq. (1-19), as shown in Table 1.24. From the above ranking orders, experts could only tell which alternative was less favorable; however, they still could not distinguish the dominant alternative, the dominant degree and the potential alternatives. Henceforth, the proposed ranking method was applied to obtain a complete preference sorting. Based on Eq. (1-20), the outranking degrees $f'_{ii'}$ were obtained and the improved aggregate outranking matrix F' is established accordingly, as shown in Table 1.25. The initial threshold decided by the experts is 0.6, according to which the outranking matrix F_1' was obtained. Based on F_1', we could find that the alternative sites A1 and A2 were indifferent. Then the experts adjust the threshold to 0.7, obtaining outranking matrix F_2', as shown in Table 1.26. As a result, the complete rankings were sorted, which is A3>A2>A4>A1>A5 . For the sake of the validity of the proposed ranking method, this study verified the ranking results by the complete-ranking method established by chen [37], which gained the same conclusion, proved the validity of the proposed complete-ranking method.

Table 1.17 the comparison possibilities for each competing pair of alternative.

$L(\tilde{A}_{ij} \geqslant \tilde{A}_{i'j})$	x11	x12	x13	x14	x15	x21	x22	x23	x24	x31	x32
$L(\tilde{A}_{1j} \geqslant \tilde{A}_{2j})$	0.87	0.75	0.29	0.00	0.76	0.00	0.04	1.00	1.00	0.00	0.38
$L(\tilde{A}_{1j} \geqslant \tilde{A}_{3j})$	1.00	0.00	0.00	0.00	0.00	0.95	0.08	1.00	0.00	0.00	0.00
$L(\tilde{A}_{1j} \geqslant \tilde{A}_{4j})$	1.00	0.54	0.74	0.00	0.08	0.59	0.74	1.00	1.00	0.42	0.82
$L(\tilde{A}_{1j} \geqslant \tilde{A}_{5j})$	1.00	1.00	1.00	0.00	0.15	0.66	1.00	1.00	1.00	1.00	1.00
$L(\tilde{A}_{2j} \geqslant \tilde{A}_{1j})$	0.13	0.25	0.71	1.00	0.24	1.00	0.96	0.00	0.00	1.00	0.62
$L(\tilde{A}_{2j} \geqslant \tilde{A}_{3j})$	0.00	0.00	0.00	0.00	0.00	1.00	0.63	0.00	0.00	0.00	0.00
$L(\tilde{A}_{2j} \geqslant \tilde{A}_{4j})$	0.78	0.30	0.95	0.00	0.00	1.00	1.00	0.52	0.76	1.00	0.98
$L(\tilde{A}_{2j} \geqslant \tilde{A}_{5j})$	1.00	1.00	1.00	0.03	0.00	1.00	1.00	0.80	1.00	1.00	1.00
$L(\tilde{A}_{3j} \geqslant \tilde{A}_{1j})$	1.00	1.00	1.00	1.00	1.00	0.05	0.92	0.00	1.00	1.00	1.00
$L(\tilde{A}_{3j} \geqslant \tilde{A}_{2j})$	1.00	1.00	1.00	1.00	1.00	0.00	0.37	1.00	1.00	1.00	1.00
$L(\tilde{A}_{3j} \geqslant \tilde{A}_{4j})$	1.00	1.00	1.00	1.00	1.00	0.18	1.00	1.00	1.00	1.00	1.00

Continued

$L(\tilde{A}_{ij} \geq \tilde{A}_{i'j})$	x11	x12	x13	x14	x15	x21	x22	x23	x24	x31	x32
$L(\tilde{A}_{3j} \geq \tilde{A}_{5j})$	1.00	1.00	1.00	1.00	1.00	0.31	1.00	1.00	1.00	1.00	1.00
$L(\tilde{A}_{4j} \geq \tilde{A}_{1j})$	0.00	0.46	0.26	1.00	0.92	0.41	0.26	0.00	0.00	0.58	0.18
$L(\tilde{A}_{4j} \geq \tilde{A}_{2j})$	0.22	0.70	0.05	1.00	1.00	0.00	0.00	0.48	0.24	0.00	0.02
$L(\tilde{A}_{4j} \geq \tilde{A}_{3j})$	0.00	0.00	0.00	0.00	0.00	0.82	0.00	0.00	0.00	0.00	0.00
$L(\tilde{A}_{4j} \geq \tilde{A}_{5j})$	1.00	1.00	1.00	0.84	0.53	0.58	0.82	0.81	1.00	1.00	0.75
$L(\tilde{A}_{5j} \geq \tilde{A}_{1j})$	0.00	0.00	0.00	1.00	0.85	0.34	0.00	0.00	0.00	0.00	0.00
$L(\tilde{A}_{5j} \geq \tilde{A}_{2j})$	0.00	0.00	0.00	0.97	1.00	0.00	0.00	0.20	0.00	0.00	0.00
$L(\tilde{A}_{5j} \geq \tilde{A}_{3j})$	0.00	0.00	0.00	0.00	0.00	0.69	0.00	0.00	0.00	0.00	0.00
$L(\tilde{A}_{5j} \geq \tilde{A}_{4j})$	0.00	0.00	0.00	0.16	0.47	0.42	0.18	0.19	0.00	0.00	0.25

$L(\tilde{A}_{ij} \geq \tilde{A}_{i'j})$	x33	x41	x42	x43	x51	x52	x53	x54	x55	x61	x62
$L(\tilde{A}_{1j} \geq \tilde{A}_{2j})$	0.60	0.00	0.00	0.00	0.35	0.60	0.22	0.00	0.00	0.00	0.00
$L(\tilde{A}_{1j} \geq \tilde{A}_{3j})$	1.00	0.42	0.38	0.03	1.00	1.00	0.55	0.00	0.67	0.00	0.00
$L(\tilde{A}_{1j} \geq \tilde{A}_{4j})$	1.00	0.00	0.32	0.50	0.62	0.92	0.54	0.00	0.98	0.00	0.37
$L(\tilde{A}_{1j} \geq \tilde{A}_{5j})$	0.80	0.00	0.25	0.65	0.62	1.00	0.60	0.00	1.00	0.80	0.83
$L(\tilde{A}_{2j} \geq \tilde{A}_{1j})$	0.40	1.00	1.00	1.00	0.65	0.40	0.78	1.00	1.00	1.00	1.00
$L(\tilde{A}_{2j} \geq \tilde{A}_{3j})$	1.00	1.00	1.00	0.42	1.00	1.00	0.91	0.00	1.00	0.00	0.00
$L(\tilde{A}_{2j} \geq \tilde{A}_{4j})$	0.80	0.87	1.00	1.00	0.74	0.86	0.83	0.00	1.00	0.00	1.00
$L(\tilde{A}_{2j} \geq \tilde{A}_{5j})$	0.66	0.77	1.00	1.00	0.76	0.95	1.00	0.00	1.00	1.00	1.00
$L(\tilde{A}_{3j} \geq \tilde{A}_{1j})$	0.00	0.58	0.62	0.97	0.00	0.00	0.45	1.00	0.33	1.00	1.00
$L(\tilde{A}_{3j} \geq \tilde{A}_{2j})$	0.00	0.00	0.00	0.58	0.00	0.00	0.09	1.00	0.00	1.00	1.00
$L(\tilde{A}_{3j} \geq \tilde{A}_{4j})$	0.19	0.03	0.44	1.00	0.00	0.00	0.49	0.00	0.72	1.00	1.00
$L(\tilde{A}_{3j} \geq \tilde{A}_{5j})$	0.19	0.04	0.42	1.00	0.00	0.07	0.55	1.00	1.00	1.00	1.00
$L(\tilde{A}_{4j} \geq \tilde{A}_{1j})$	0.00	1.00	0.68	0.50	0.38	0.08	0.46	1.00	0.02	1.00	0.63
$L(\tilde{A}_{4j} \geq \tilde{A}_{2j})$	0.20	0.13	0.00	0.00	0.26	0.14	0.17	1.00	0.00	1.00	0.00
$L(\tilde{A}_{4j} \geq \tilde{A}_{3j})$	0.81	0.97	0.56	0.00	1.00	1.00	0.51	1.00	0.28	0.00	0.00
$L(\tilde{A}_{4j} \geq \tilde{A}_{5j})$	0.42	0.45	0.49	0.66	0.48	0.60	0.55	0.00	1.00	1.00	0.90
$L(\tilde{A}_{5j} \geq \tilde{A}_{1j})$	0.20	1.00	0.75	0.35	0.38	0.00	0.40	1.00	0.00	0.20	0.17
$L(\tilde{A}_{5j} \geq \tilde{A}_{2j})$	0.34	0.23	0.00	0.00	0.24	0.05	0.00	1.00	0.00	0.00	0.00

Continued

$L(\tilde{A}_{ij} \geqslant \tilde{A}_{i'j})$	x33	x41	x42	x43	x51	x52	x53	x54	x55	x61	x62
$L(\tilde{A}_{5j} \geqslant \tilde{A}_{3j})$	0.81	0.96	0.58	0.00	1.00	0.93	0.45	1.00	0.00	0.00	0.00
$L(\tilde{A}_{5j} \geqslant \tilde{A}_{4j})$	0.58	0.55	0.51	0.34	0.52	0.40	0.45	0.00	0.00	0.00	0.10

Table 1.18 The preference function for each competing pair of alternatives.

$P(\tilde{A}_{ij} \geqslant \tilde{A}_{i'j})$	x11	x12	x13	x14	x15	x21	x22	x23	x24	x31	x32
$p(\tilde{A}_{1j} \geqslant \tilde{A}_{2j})$	0.91	0.61	0.00	0.00	0.64	0.00	0.00	1.00	1.00	0.00	0.00
$p(\tilde{A}_{1j} \geqslant \tilde{A}_{3j})$	1.00	0.00	0.00	0.00	0.00	1.00	0.00	1.00	0.00	0.00	0.00
$p(\tilde{A}_{1j} \geqslant \tilde{A}_{4j})$	1.00	0.06	0.59	0.00	0.00	0.19	0.57	1.00	1.00	0.00	0.80
$p(\tilde{A}_{1j} \geqslant \tilde{A}_{5j})$	1.00	1.00	1.00	0.00	0.00	0.38	1.00	1.00	1.00	1.00	1.00
$p(\tilde{A}_{2j} \geqslant \tilde{A}_{1j})$	0.00	0.00	0.50	1.00	0.00	1.00	1.00	0.00	0.00	1.00	0.27
$p(\tilde{A}_{2j} \geqslant \tilde{A}_{3j})$	0.00	0.00	0.00	0.00	0.00	1.00	0.28	0.00	0.00	0.00	0.00
$p(\tilde{A}_{2j} \geqslant \tilde{A}_{4j})$	0.70	0.00	1.00	0.00	0.00	1.00	1.00	0.00	0.64	1.00	1.00
$p(\tilde{A}_{2j} \geqslant \tilde{A}_{5j})$	1.00	1.00	1.00	0.00	0.00	1.00	1.00	0.74	1.00	1.00	1.00
$p(\tilde{A}_{3j} \geqslant \tilde{A}_{1j})$	1.00	1.00	1.00	1.00	1.00	0.00	1.00	0.00	1.00	1.00	1.00
$p(\tilde{A}_{3j} \geqslant \tilde{A}_{2j})$	1.00	1.00	1.00	1.00	1.00	0.00	0.00	1.00	1.00	1.00	1.00
$p(\tilde{A}_{3j} \geqslant \tilde{A}_{4j})$	1.00	1.00	1.00	1.00	1.00	0.00	1.00	1.00	1.00	1.00	1.00
$p(\tilde{A}_{3j} \geqslant \tilde{A}_{5j})$	1.00	1.00	1.00	1.00	1.00	0.00	1.00	1.00	1.00	1.00	1.00
$p(\tilde{A}_{4j} \geqslant \tilde{A}_{1j})$	0.00	0.00	0.00	1.00	1.00	0.00	0.00	0.00	0.00	0.16	0.00
$p(\tilde{A}_{4j} \geqslant \tilde{A}_{2j})$	0.00	0.48	0.00	1.00	1.00	0.00	0.00	0.00	0.00	0.00	0.00
$p(\tilde{A}_{4j} \geqslant \tilde{A}_{3j})$	0.00	0.00	0.00	0.00	0.00	0.79	0.00	0.00	0.00	0.00	0.00
$p(\tilde{A}_{4j} \geqslant \tilde{A}_{5j})$	1.00	1.00	1.00	0.84	0.03	0.15	0.79	0.77	1.00	1.00	0.60
$p(\tilde{A}_{5j} \geqslant \tilde{A}_{1j})$	0.00	0.00	0.00	1.00	0.86	0.00	0.00	0.00	0.00	0.00	0.00
$p(\tilde{A}_{5j} \geqslant \tilde{A}_{2j})$	0.00	0.00	0.00	1.00	1.00	0.00	0.00	0.00	0.00	0.00	0.00
$p(\tilde{A}_{5j} \geqslant \tilde{A}_{3j})$	0.00	0.00	0.00	0.00	0.00	0.44	0.00	0.00	0.00	0.00	0.00
$p(\tilde{A}_{5j} \geqslant \tilde{A}_{4j})$	0.00	0.00	0.00	0.00	0.00	0.00	0.00	0.00	0.00	0.00	0.00

$P(\tilde{A}_{ij} \geqslant \tilde{A}_{i'j})$	x33	x41	x42	x43	x51	x52	x53	x54	x55	x61	x62
$p(\tilde{A}_{1j} \geqslant \tilde{A}_{2j})$	0.22	0.00	0.00	0.00	0.00	0.22	0.00	0.00	0.00	0.00	0.00
$p(\tilde{A}_{1j} \geqslant \tilde{A}_{3j})$	1.00	0.00	0.00	0.00	1.00	1.00	0.08	0.00	0.39	0.00	0.00
$p(\tilde{A}_{1j} \geqslant \tilde{A}_{4j})$	1.00	0.00	0.00	0.00	0.27	1.00	0.05	0.00	1.00	0.00	0.00

Continued

$P(\tilde{A}_{ij} \geqslant \tilde{A}_{i'j})$	x33	x41	x42	x43	x51	x52	x53	x54	x55	x61	x62
$p(\tilde{A}_{1j} \geqslant \tilde{A}_{5j})$	0.73	0.00	0.00	0.34	0.26	1.00	0.21	0.00	1.00	0.74	0.80
$p(\tilde{A}_{2j} \geqslant \tilde{A}_{1j})$	0.00	1.00	1.00	1.00	0.34	0.00	0.70	1.00	1.00	1.00	1.00
$p(\tilde{A}_{2j} \geqslant \tilde{A}_{3j})$	1.00	1.00	1.00	0.00	1.00	1.00	1.00	0.00	1.00	0.00	0.00
$p(\tilde{A}_{2j} \geqslant \tilde{A}_{4j})$	0.74	0.92	1.00	1.00	0.57	0.88	0.81	0.00	1.00	0.00	1.00
$p(\tilde{A}_{2j} \geqslant \tilde{A}_{5j})$	0.38	0.67	1.00	1.00	0.62	1.00	1.00	0.00	1.00	1.00	1.00
$p(\tilde{A}_{3j} \geqslant \tilde{A}_{1j})$	0.00	0.16	0.25	1.00	0.00	0.00	0.00	1.00	0.00	1.00	1.00
$p(\tilde{A}_{3j} \geqslant \tilde{A}_{2j})$	0.00	0.00	0.00	0.16	0.00	0.00	0.00	1.00	0.00	1.00	1.00
$p(\tilde{A}_{3j} \geqslant \tilde{A}_{4j})$	0.00	0.00	0.00	1.00	0.00	0.00	0.00	0.00	0.53	1.00	1.00
$p(\tilde{A}_{3j} \geqslant \tilde{A}_{5j})$	0.00	0.00	0.00	1.00	0.00	0.00	0.08	1.00	1.00	1.00	1.00
$p(\tilde{A}_{4j} \geqslant \tilde{A}_{1j})$	0.00	1.00	0.42	0.00	0.00	0.00	0.00	1.00	0.00	1.00	0.30
$p(\tilde{A}_{4j} \geqslant \tilde{A}_{2j})$	0.00	0.00	0.00	0.00	0.00	0.00	0.00	1.00	0.00	1.00	0.00
$p(\tilde{A}_{4j} \geqslant \tilde{A}_{3j})$	0.76	1.00	0.09	0.00	1.00	1.00	0.00	1.00	0.00	0.00	0.00
$p(\tilde{A}_{4j} \geqslant \tilde{A}_{5j})$	0.00	0.00	0.00	0.38	0.00	0.21	0.09	0.00	1.00	1.00	1.00
$p(\tilde{A}_{5j} \geqslant \tilde{A}_{1j})$	0.00	1.00	0.61	0.00	0.00	0.00	0.00	1.00	0.00	0.00	0.00
$p(\tilde{A}_{5j} \geqslant \tilde{A}_{2j})$	0.00	0.00	0.00	0.00	0.00	0.00	0.00	1.00	0.00	0.00	0.00
$p(\tilde{A}_{5j} \geqslant \tilde{A}_{3j})$	0.77	1.00	0.16	0.00	1.00	1.00	0.00	1.00	0.00	0.00	0.00
$p(\tilde{A}_{5j} \geqslant \tilde{A}_{4j})$	0.16	0.08	0.00	0.00	0.01	0.00	0.00	0.00	0.00	0.00	0.00

Table 1.19 the weighted comprehensive preference indices.

	A1	A2	A3	A4	A5
A1	-	[0.71 0.20]	[0.81 0.12]	[0.87 0.07]	[0.96 0.02]
A2	[0.96 0.02]	-	[0.91 0.05]	[0.98 0.01]	[0.99 0.00]
A3	[0.96 0.01]	[0.94 0.02]	-	[0.97 0.01]	[0.97 0.01]
A4	[0.78 0.15]	[0.65 0.26]	[0.77 0.16]	-	[0.94 0.03]
A5	[0.74 0.18]	[0.53 0.38]	[0.75 0.17]	[0.07 0.92]	-

Table 1.20 concordance indices.

	A1	A2	A3	A4	A5
A1	-	0.62	0.74	0.81	0.93
A2	0.94	-	0.87	0.96	0.98
A3	0.94	0.91	-	0.94	0.96
A4	0.70	0.56	0.69	-	0.91
A5	0.66	0.44	0.68	0.05	-

Table 1.21 concordance relationship Boolean matrix.

	A1	A2	A3	A4	A5
A1	-	0	0	1	1
A2	1	-	1	1	1
A3	1	1	-	1	1
A4	0	0	0	-	1
A5	0	0	0	0	-

Table 1.22 discordance indices.

	A1	A2	A3	A4	A5
A1	-	0.44	1.00	0.64	0.33
A2	0.37	-	1.00	0.62	0.29
A3	0.08	0.00	-	0.00	0.00
A4	0.31	0.27	1.00	-	0.00
A5	0.65	0.71	1.00	0.95	-

Table 1.23 discordance relationship Boolean matrix.

	A1	A2	A3	A4	A5
A1	-	1	0	0	1
A2	1	-	0	0	1
A3	1	1	-	1	1
A4	1	1	0	-	1
A5	0	0	0	0	-

Table 1.24 the partial-preference ranking orders.

	A1	A2	A3	A4	A5
A1	-	0	0	0	1
A2	1	-	0	0	1
A3	1	1	-	1	1
A4	0	0	0	-	1
A5	0	0	0	0	-

Table 1.25 the improved aggregate outranking matrix.

	A1	A2	A3	A4	A5
A1	-	0.61	0.00	0.82	0.95
A2	0.95	-	0.00	0.98	1.00
A3	0.96	0.92	-	0.96	0.97
A4	0.70	0.55	0.00	-	0.92
A5	0.66	0.22	0.00	0.00	-

Table 1.26 the complete preference ranking orders.

	A1	A2	A3	A4	A5
A1	-	0	0	1	1
A2	1	-	0	1	1
A3	1	1	-	1	1
A4	0	0	0	-	1
A5	0	0	0	0	-

From the Table 1.11, the alternative site A3 is the most satisfactory selection. We can see that A3 performs better than the other alternatives in terms of the resources, supporting conditions onshore, and society. As the fact that the weight of these criteria accounts for the majority of the entire criteria weights, A3 obtains the most favorable results. However, A3 is inferior to the rest alternatives in terms of construction and maintenance conditions, economic and the environment. The alternative site A2 has advantages in economic, environment and society, but has disadvantage in the wind resources. The alternative site A4 has advantages in environment and society aspects, but has disadvantage in the construction and maintenance conditions. Yet, the alternative sites A2 and A4 are more satisfactory than A1 and A5, and can be the additional options for consideration.

In the decision analysis, as the fact that various attitudes of the decision makers can lead to different ranking orders, a sensitive analysis is processed on the parameter λ according to the decision makers' preference in order to examine to what extent the attitudes changes can affect the ranking orders and to know the robustness of the decision results. We let $\lambda = 10, 9, 8, 7, 6, 5, \ldots, 0.2$, respectively, which indicates the experts' different preference, and get the ranking orders of the alternatives correspondingly. The sensitive analysis results are shown in Table 1.27. From the analysis results, it can be seen that as the experts' attitudes changes, the rankings of the best and the worst sites have not altered, which testifies the robustness of the proposed method and suggests that the ranks are reliable and stable.

Table 1.27 sensitive analysis.

Sensitivity analysis run	Attitude change	Ranking of alternatives	Sensitivity analysis run	Attitude change	Ranking of alternatives
1	$\lambda=10$	A3> A2>A4>A1>A5	10	$\lambda=1$	A3> A2>A4>A1>A5
2	$\lambda=9$	A3> A2>A4>A1>A5	11	$\lambda=0.9$	A3> A2>A4>A1>A5
3	$\lambda=8$	A3> A2>A4>A1>A5	12	$\lambda=0.8$	A3> A2>A4>A1>A5
4	$\lambda=7$	A3> A2>A4>A1>A5	13	$\lambda=0.7$	A3> A2>A4>A1>A5
5	$\lambda=6$	A3> A2>A4>A1>A5	14	$\lambda=0.6$	A3> A2>A4>A1>A5
6	$\lambda=5$	A3> A2>A4>A1>A5	15	$\lambda=0.5$	A3> A4>A2>A1>A5
7	$\lambda=4$	A3> A2>A4>A1>A5	16	$\lambda=0.4$	A3> A4>A2>A1>A5
8	$\lambda=3$	A3> A2>A4>A1>A5	17	$\lambda=0.3$	A3> A4>A2>A1>A5
9	$\lambda=2$	A3> A2>A4>A1>A5	18	$\lambda=0.2$	A3> A4>A2>A1>A5

To take a closer look at the sensitivity analysis, we can find that the ranking of the alternatives stay the same when $\lambda = 10,9,8,\ldots,0.6$, respectively, but when $\lambda \leqslant 0.5$, although the best and the worst sites are stable, the less favorable alternatives starts to change slightly. We can see that the places of A2 and A4 exchange in the ranking of the alternatives, which reveals some influence of the decision makers' attitudes changes on the decision results. To study the reason of the changes, we examine the original data of the experts evaluation, and find that the evaluation values of alternative A4 with respect to the criteria are more fluctuant than that of alternative A2. However, the average value of the evaluation of alternative A4 is larger than that of alternative A2 with a slight advantage. That is to say, when the preference of the decision makers is becoming extremely optimistic or risky, alternative A4 ranks higher than alternative A2 considering the decision makers' attitudes. When the preference of the decision makers is pessimistic or conservative type /neutral type /relatively optimistic or risky type, the alternative A2 is superior to alternative A4 tably. In the real-life decision-making practice, different decision makers' attitudes can be considered by the proposed method.

Based on the aforementioned analysis, the experts choose the alternative A3 s the optimal site.

6. Conclusion

This study builds a comprehensive decision framework for OWPS site selection. Studies focused on this area are limited and there are still quite a few problems existing in the decision process for OWPS site selection. Firstly, the compensation problem lays in criteria information processing. Secondly, incomplete utilization of decision information and information loss exists in the decision process. Thirdly, the interaction problem in the fuzzy environment is easy to be ignored.

In this study, a new design of comprehensive MCDM framework based on the ELECTRE-III method in the presence of multiple decision makers under incomplete information environment is proposed to handle the OWPS site selection problems. Firstly, the comprehensive index system of OWPS site selection consisting of veto criteria and evaluation criteria is constructed to eliminate sensitive areas and identify potential alternatives. Then, the intuitionistic fuzzy set is used in group decision to express the imperfect knowledge of experts. Following this, an extended IF-ELECTRE-III method is proposed to solve compensation problem. Moreover, the GIFWGIA operator is applied to deal with interaction. Together with the likelihood-based valued comparisons, imprecise decision information is reasonably used and information loss is rationally avoided. Then a sensitive analysis is processed considering the attitude of the decision makers, testified the robustness of the proposed method. In conclusion, the aforementioned problems are effectively solved by the proposed intuitionistic fuzzy

ELECTRE-III method.

7. Acknowledgement

Project supported by the Fundamental Research Funds for the Central Universities (No.2015XS45), the National Nature Science Foundation of China (No.71271085) and National Philosophy and Social Science Foundation of Beijing (12JGB044), the Industry-University-Research Foundation of Beijing.

References

[1] Vafaeipour M, Zolfani S H, Varzandeh M H M, et al. Assessment of regions priority for implementation of solar projects in Iran: New application of a hybrid multi-criteria decision making approach[J]. Energ Convers Manage, 2014, 86: 653-663.

[2] Uyan M. GIS-based solar farms site selection using analytic hierarchy process (AHP) in Karapinar region, Konya/Turkey[J]. Renew Sust Energ Rev, 2013, 28 :11-17.

[3] Shafiee M.A fuzzy analytic network process model to mitigate the risks associated with offshore wind farms[J]. Expert Syst Appl, 2015, 42:2143-2152.

[4] Choudhary D, Shankar R. An STEEP-fuzzy AHP-TOPSIS framework for evaluation and selection of thermal power plant location: A case study from India[J]. Energy, 2012, 42:510-521.

[5] Qian G, Wang H, Feng X Q. Generalized hesitant fuzzy sets and their application in decision support system[J]. Knowl-Based Syst, 2013, 373:57-65.

[6] Behret H . Group decision making with intuitionistic fuzzy preference relations[J]. Knowl-Based Syst, 2014, 70:33-43.

[7] Lei Q, Xu Z S. Fundamental properties of intuitionistic fuzzy calculus[J]. Knowl-Based Syst, 2015, 76:1-16.

[8] Pekala B. Properties of Atanassov's intuitionistic fuzzy relations and Atanassov's operators[J]. Inform Sciences, 2012, 213:84-93.

[9] Ebrahimnejad S, Hashemi H, Mousavi S M, et al. A New Interval-Valued Intuitionistic Fuzzy Model to Group Decision Making for the Selection of Outsourcing Providers[J]. Econ Comput Econ Cyb, 2015, 49:269-290.

[10] Gao J W, Liu H H. Interval-valued intuitionistic fuzzy stochastic multi-criteria decision-making method based on Prospect theory[J]. Kybernetes, 2015, 44: 25-42.

[11] Ngan S C. Evidential Reasoning approach for multiple-criteria decision making: A simulation-based formulation[J]. Expert Syst Appl, 2015, 42 :4381-4396.

[12] Rostamzadeh R, Govindan K, Esmaeili A, et al. Application of fuzzy VIKOR for evaluation of green supply chain management practices[J]. Ecol Indic, 2015, 49: 188-203.

[13] Sevastjanov P, Dymova L. Generalised operations on hesitant fuzzy values in the framework of Dempster-Shafer theory[J]. Inform Sciences, 2015, 311:39-58.

[14] Cinelli M, Coles S R, Kirwan K. Analysis of the potentials of multi criteria decision analysis methods to conduct sustainability assessment[J]. Ecol Indic, 2014, 46:138-148.

[15] Ghoseiri K, Lessan J. Waste disposal site selection using an analytic hierarchal pairwise comparison and ELECTRE approaches under fuzzy environment[J]. J Intell Fuzzy Syst, 2014, 26:693-704.

[16] Vincke P. Analysis of multicriteria decision aid in Europe[J]. European Journal of Operational Research, 1986, 25: 160-168.

[17] Lee S K, Mogi G, Li Z, et al. Measuring the relative efficiency of hydrogen energy technologies for implementing the hydrogen economy: An integrated fuzzy AHP/DEA approach[J]. International Journal of Hydrogen Energy, 2011, 36:12655-12663.

[18] Kaya T, Kahraman C. Multicriteria decision making in energy planning using a modified fuzzy TOPSIS methodology[J]. Expert Syst Appl, 2011, 38: 6577-6585.

[19] Grujić M, Ivezić D, Živković M. Application of multi-criteria decision-making model for choice of the optimal solution for meeting heat demand in the centralized supply system in Belgrade[J]. Energy, 2014, 67:341-350.

[20] Wu Y N, Geng S, Xu H, et al. Study of decision framework of wind farm project plan selection under intuitionistic fuzzy set and fuzzy measure environment[J]. Energ Convers Manage, 2014, 87:274-284.

[21] López J, Chavira D, Ruiz M. An Application of a Multicriteria Approach to Compare Economic Sectors: The Case of Sinaloa, Mexico. in: R. Purshouse, P. Fleming, C. Fonseca, S. Greco, J. Shaw, (Eds.), Evolutionary Multi-Criterion Optimization[M]. Springer Berlin Heidelberg, 2013.

[22] Bouyssou D. Second EURO Summer InstituteSome remarks on the notion of compensation in MCDMSpringer Berlin Heidelberg[J]. Eur J Oper Res, 1986, 26:150-160.

[23] Roy B. The outranking approach and the foundations of ELECTRE methods[J]. Theory and Decision, 1991, 31:24.

[24] Mousseau V, Dias L. Valued outranking relations in ELECTRE providing manageable disaggregation procedures[J]. Eur J Oper Res, 2004, 156:467-482.

[25] Perera A T D, Attalage R A, Perera K K C K, et al. A hybrid tool to combine multi-objective optimization and multi-criterion decision making in designing standalone hybrid energy systems[J]. Appl Energ, 2013, 107 :412-425.

[26] Sakthivel G, Nagarajan G, Ilangkumaran M, et al. A hybrid multi-criteria decision support system for selection of optimum fuel blend[J]. Int J Exergy, 2013, 12:463-490.

[27] Vahdani B, Mousavi S M, Tavakkoli-Moghaddam R, et al. A new design of the elimination and choice translating reality method for multi-criteria group decision-making in an intuitionistic fuzzy environment[J]. Appl Math Model, 2013, 37: 1781-1799.

[28] Boran F E, Akay D. A biparametric similarity measure on intuitionistic fuzzy sets with applications to pattern recognition[J]. Inform Sciences, 2014, 255:45-57.

[29] Boran F E, Boran K, Menlik T. The Evaluation of Renewable Energy Technologies for Electricity Generation in Turkey Using Intuitionistic Fuzzy TOPSIS[J]. Energ Source Part B, 2012, 7:81-90.

[30] Devi K, Yadav S P. A multicriteria intuitionistic fuzzy group decision making for plant location selection with ELECTRE method[J]. Int J Adv Manuf Tech, 2013, 66: 1219-1229.

[31] Wu Y N, Geng S, Zhang H B, et al. Decision framework of solar thermal power plant site selection based on linguistic Choquet operator[J]. Appl Energ, 2014, 136:303-311.

[32] Xu Z S. Intuitionistic fuzzy aggregation operators[J]. Ieee T Fuzzy Syst, 2007, 15: 1179-1187.

[33] Atanassov K T. New Operations Defined over the Intuitionistic Fuzzy-Sets[J]. Fuzzy Set Syst, 1994, 61:137-142.

[34] Zhang Z M. Generalized Atanassov's intuitionistic fuzzy power geometric operators and their application to multiple attribute group decision making[J]. Inform Fusion, 2013, 14:460-486.

[35] He Y D, Chen H Y, Zhou L G, et al. Generalized intuitionistic fuzzy geometric interaction operators and their application to decision making[J]. Expert Syst Appl, 2014, 41:2484-2495.

[36] He Y D, Chen H Y, Zhou L G, et al. Intuitionistic fuzzy geometric interaction averaging operators and their application to multi-criteria decision making[J]. Inform Sciences, 2014, 259:142-159.

[37] Chen T Y. Multiple criteria decision analysis using a likelihood-based outranking method based on interval-valued intuitionistic fuzzy sets[J]. Inform Sciences, 2014, 286: 188-208.

[38] Wu M C, Chen T Y. The ELECTRE Multicriteria Analysis Approach Based on Intuitionistic Fuzzy Sets[J]. 2009 Ieee International Conference on Fuzzy Systems, Vols 1-3, 2009, 1383-1388.

[39] Wu M C, Chen T Y. The ELECTRE multicriteria analysis approach based on Atanassov's intuitionistic fuzzy sets[J]. Expert Syst Appl, 2011, 38:12318-12327.

[40] Xu J P, Shen F. A new outranking choice method for group decision making under Atanassov's interval-valued intuitionistic fuzzy environment[J]. Knowl-Based Syst, 2014, 70: 177-188.

[41] Kapsimalis V, Panagiotopoulos I, Hatzianestis I, et al. A screening procedure for selecting the most suitable dredged material placement site at the sea. The case of the South Euboean Gulf, Greece[J]. Environ Monit Assess, 2013, 185: 10049-10072.

[42] Nobre A, Pacheco M, Jorge R, et al. Geo-spatial multi-criteria analysis for wave energy conversion system deployment[J]. Renew Energ, 2009, 34:97-111.

[43] Fetanat A, Khorasaninejad E. A novel hybrid MCDM approach for offshore wind farm site selection: A case study of Iran[J]. Ocean Coast Manage, 2015, 109: 17-28.

[44] Kim J Y, Oh K Y, Kang K S, et al. Site selection of offshore wind farms around the Korean Peninsula through economic evaluation[J]. Renew Energ, 2013, 54:189-95.

[45] Wu Y N, Yang Y S, Feng T T, et al. Macro-site selection of wind/solar hybrid power station based on Ideal Matter-Element Model[J]. Int J Elec Power, 2013, 50: 76-84.

[46] http://www.carbontrust.com/media/510538/carbon-trust-offfshore -wind-policy-report.pdf.

[47] Scheu M, Matha D, Hofmann M, et al. Maintenance strategies for large offshore wind farms[J]. Selected Papers from Deep Sea Offshore Wind R&D Conference, 2012, 24:281-288.

[48] Zhang J, Chowdhury S, Messac A. A comprehensive measure of the energy resource: Wind power potential (WPP)[J]. Energy Conversion and Management, 2014, 86:388-398.

[49] Wu Y N, Yang Y S, Feng T T, et al. Macro-site selection of wind/solar hybrid power station based on Ideal Matter-Element Model[J]. International Journal of Electrical Power & Energy Systems, 2013, 50:76-84.

[50] Mycek P, Gaurier B, Germain G, et al. Experimental study of the turbulence intensity effects on marine current turbines behaviour. Part II: Two interacting turbines[J]. Renewable Energy, 2014, 68:876-892.

[51] Del Jesus F, Menendez M, Guanche R, et al. A wind chart to characterize potential offshore wind energy sites[J]. Comput Geosci-Uk, 2014, 71: 62-72.

[52] Ou J, Long X, Li Q S, et al. Vibration control of steel jacket offshore platform structures with damping isolation systems[J]. Engineering Structures, 2007, 29:1525-1538.

[53] Hong L, Möller B. An economic assessment of tropical cyclone risk on offshore wind farms[J]. Renewable Energy, 2012, 44 :180-192.

[54] Fang C L, Bao C, Qi W F. The Construction Goals and Spatial Layout Project of the Offshore Three Green Gorges in China[R]. 2009 World Non-Grid-Connected Wind Power and Energy Conference, 2009, 412-415.

[55] Le T M H, Eiksund G R, Strom P J, et al. Geological and geotechnical characterisation for offshore wind turbine foundations: A case study of the Sheringham Shoal wind farm[J]. Eng Geol, 2014, 177:40-53.

[56] Kim J-Y, Oh K-Y, Kang K-S, et al. Site selection of offshore wind farms around the Korean Peninsula through economic evaluation[J]. Renewable Energy, 2013, 54:189-195.

[57] Sanchez-Lozano J M, Garcia-Cascales M S, Lamata M T. Identification and selection of potential sites for onshore wind farms development in Region of Murcia, Spain[J]. Energy, 2014, 73:311-324.

[58] Reubens J T, Vandendriessche S, Zenner A N, et al. Offshore wind farms as productive sites or ecological traps for gadoid fishes? – Impact on growth, condition index and diet composition[J]. Marine Environmental Research, 2013, 90:66-74.

[59] Thompson P M, Hastie G D, Nedwell J, et al. Framework for assessing impacts of pile-driving noise from offshore wind farm construction on a harbour seal population[J]. Environ Impact Asses, 2013, 43: 73-85.

[60] Pérez B, Mínguez R, Guanche R. Offshore wind farm layout optimization using mathematical programming techniques[J]. Renewable Energy, 2013, 53:389-399.

[61] Santora C, Hade N, Odell J. Managing offshore wind developments in the United States: Legal, environmental and social considerations using a case study in Nantucket Sound[J]. Ocean & Coastal Management, 2004, 47: 141-164.

[62] Burkhard B, Gee K. Establishing the Resilience of a Coastal-marine Social-ecological System to the Installation of Offshore Wind Farms[J]. Ecol Soc, 2012, 17.

[63] Atanassov K T. Intuitionistic Fuzzy-Set[J]s. Fuzzy Set Syst, 1986, 20:87-96.

[64] De S K, Biswas R, Roy A R. Some operations on intuitionistic fuzzy sets[J]. Fuzzy Set Syst, 2000, 114:477-484.

[65] He Y D, Chen H Y, Zhou L G, et al. Generalized Interval-Valued Atanassov's Intuitionistic Fuzzy Power Operators and Their Application to Group Decision Making[J]. Int J Fuzzy Syst, 2013, 15: 401-411.

[66] Jin Y T, Hu L W, Zheng A L. Offshore wind farm site selection of topology optimization technology[J]. The people of the pearl river, 2012, 89-91.

[67] Chen N, Xu Z S, Xia M M. Interval-valued hesitant preference relations and their applications to group decision making[J]. Knowl-Based Syst, 2013, 37:528-540.

[68] Xu Z S. Approaches to multiple attribute group decision making based on intuitionistic fuzzy power aggregation operators[J]. Knowl-Based Syst, 2011, 24:749-760.

[69] Özcan T, Çelebi N, Esnaf Ş. Comparative analysis of multi-criteria decision making methodologies and implementation of a warehouse location selection problem[J]. Expert Systems with Applications, 2011, 38:9773-9779.

Chapter 2

A geographical information system based multi-criteria decision-making approach for location analysis and evaluation of urban photovoltaic charging station: a case study in Beijing

Jianli Zhou [a, b*], Yunna Wu [a, b], Chenghao Wu [a, b], Feiyang He [a, b], Buyuan Zhang [a, b], Fangtong Liu [a, b]

a. School of Economics and Management, North China Electric Power University, Beijing, 102206, China

b. Beijing Key Laboratory of New Energy and Low-Carbon Development (North China Electric Power University), Changping, Beijing, 102206, China

Abstract: The integration of photovoltaic (PV) power generation system and electric vehicle (EV) charging station can effectively promote the local consumption of renewable energy and reduce the indirect carbon emissions of EV. This paper aims to provide a practical model for location decision of PV charging station (PVCS) which combines geographic information system (GIS) with multi-criteria decision making (MCDM) methods. To verify the feasibility and practicality, an empirical study was conducted in Beijing. First, seven suitable areas were selected preliminarily by suitability analysis of GIS. This stage focused on traffic flow and road distribution. Second, MCDM methods were used to further evaluation. At this stage, a comprehensive evaluation index system of natural, economic, technical and social criteria was established. Interval number, triangular fuzzy number and hesitant fuzzy linguistic term set were utilized to collect and describe evaluation information. Then, the subjective and objective weights of the criteria were calculated by best-worst method and mixed information entropy method, respectively. Finally, the TODIM (an acronym in Portuguese of interactive and MCDM) method was used to rank the alternatives. The ranking results illustrated that alternative sites A3 and A7 are outstanding. Moreover, dual sensitivity analysis and comparative analysis proved the stability and reliability of the model. Scenario analysis expanded the application scope of TODIM method, which also showed that it is necessary to express decision preferences by setting different recession coefficients. This study can provide support for the layout of PVCS in urban, and enrich the application fields of GIS and MCDM methods.

Keywords: Electric vehicle (EV); Photovoltaic charging station (PVCS); Location decision; GIS application; Multi-criteria Decision making; TODIM

1. Introduction

The transportation sector is an important source of carbon dioxide production [1]. Under the dual pressures of energy and environment, electric vehicle (EV) came into being and received extremely close attention from the market and researchers. The "EV Charging Infrastructure Development Guide (2015-2020)" issued by the National Development and Reform Commission shows that the goal of China's charging infrastructure development is to build 12, 000 centralized charging stations and 4.8 million charging piles by 2020 to meet the needs of 5 million EVs in the country [2]. However, the sustainable development of EV still faces various obstacles and challenges [3]. First, EV has shorter driving mileage and lacks a complete charging infrastructure [4]. Driving mileage needs to be solved by further scientific technology.

Under the circumstance of limited mileage, more scientific and reasonable planning and construction of charging infrastructure to improve its utilization efficiency and convenience is the key to promote the development of EV [5]. Second, coal is still the main primary energy source in the power generation side of China's power system. EVs are directly connected to the grid through the charging infrastructure, and the actual indirect carbon emissions are not significantly superior to conventional fuel vehicles [6].

Faced with the above problems, it is an effective way to combine charging infrastructure with renewable energy power generation system to achieve true low carbon and sustainable development [3, 7]. The development of renewable energy utilization technology promotes the integration of photovoltaic (PV) power generation system and EV charging station (EVCS) [8]. The EVCS has stable power demand, and PV power generation equipment can provide power. These characteristics are the key to the combination and complementarity of them. In addition, the planning idea of PV power generation project is " nearby using the surplus to power grid". Correspondingly, PV charging stations (PVCSs) can promote the local consumption of PV power, reduce the dependence of charging stations on the grid, and directly reduce carbon emissions [3]. Therefore, the layout of PVCS would contribute to the sustainable development of EVs and society. PVCS has attracted the close attention of researchers. Tulpule et al. [9] analyzed the economic and environmental impact of PVCS by comparing the optimal charging scenario with uncontrolled charging scenario. Han et al. [10] presented an economic evaluation method for PVCS using retired EV batteries. Chaudhari et al. [11] proposed a hybrid optimization algorithm for energy storage of PVCS. Mouli and Bauer [12] designed a PVCS based on the idea of maximizing revenue. Farhadi [13] designed a novel grid-connected PVCS, which uses maximum power point tracking technology. Guo and Zhao [14] and Wu et al. [15] used multi-criteria decision-making methods to study the location of EVCS. But the research object is ordinary charging station. It can be seen these studies are mainly focusing on optimizing allocation and charging strategy and there are few studies on location decision of PVCS.

However, the location decision of PVCS is the prerequisite to solve the above problems. The specific reasons can be summarized as follows: Firstly, a scientific and reasonable site can reduce the cost of construction and operation, thereby improving the economic benefits of the investors. Secondly, only by choosing the suitable site can more users be served, thereby improving public recognition and satisfaction. Thirdly, the scientifically chosen location can provide an important guarantee for future expansion and sustainable development. Therefore, how to lay out scientifically and reasonably is a subject worthy of deep study. In the end, the aim of this paper is to provide investors and decision makers with a practical and reasonable approach for location decision of urban PVCS.

At present, commercial charging stations can be divided into ordinary charging stations and fast charging stations: ordinary charging stations are mainly distributed in residential areas, public parking lots and commercial buildings, which are closely integrated with parking spaces; fast charging stations are similar to gas stations, which are attached to main roads according to traffic flow layout. The PVCS studied in this paper belongs to the fast charging station, which mainly serves the pure EV. The layout of the PVCS should focus on the urban road layout and traffic flow. Therefore, this paper will use Geographic Information System (GIS) technology to analyze the urban road distribution and traffic flow, to provide a preliminary basis for site selection. Then, the MCDM methods are used to further optimize the sites.

The originality of this paper can be summarized as follows: ①Based on the latest geographic information data (road distribution, traffic flow, etc.), GIS technology is used to initially screen out the sites suitable for PVCS in Beijing. ②Through a deep study of related literature and industry reports, supplemented by expert consultation, the criteria system for further evaluation of the alternative sites is established. The criteria system covers four groups: natural, economic, technical and social factors. ③In order to make the evaluation results more accurate, this paper uses the corresponding information description tool to collect and express the index attribute values: the interval number is used to describe the quantitative economic indicators to reflect the influence of price and rate fluctuations; the hesitant fuzzy linguistic term set (HFLTS) is used to collect evaluation information of qualitative indicators. Then, the HFLTS can be converted into triangular fuzzy numbers for quantitative calculation and analysis. ④In this paper, TODIM method based on prospect theory is used to rank alternative sites selected by GIS technology. This method can represent the decision preference of decision makers for risk and loss avoidance. In addition, this paper extends the using environment of this method to the environment of mixed index attribute values, and sets different recession coefficients for different indicators to reflect different risk preferences of decision makers. The result of scenario analysis shows that this application change can extend the using scenario of TODIM method to a state closer to the actual decision-making. ⑤Based on the above methods and theories, this paper constructs a practical analysis and decision-making framework for the location decision of urban PVCS.

To this end, the rest of the paper is organized as follows: In view of the main points of this study, a literature review is carried out in Section 2. Section 3 introduces the geographic information data used in the stage of GIS suitability analysis and the criteria system for further evaluation of alternative sites. Section 4 introduces the main methods and related theories used in this paper. In Section 5, based on the proposed location decision framework, an empirical study is carried out to verify the overall model and framework of this paper. Further analysis and discussion are carried out in Section 6. Dual sensitivity analysis and comparative analysis are used to test the stability and applicability of the model. Through scenario analysis, this paper studies the changes of final results after different criteria adopting different recession coefficients. Conclusions are provided in Section 7.

2. Literature review

2.1 Location decision criteria for PVCS

Through the analysis of a large number of literatures, it can be found that the object of their topic is basically the conventional EVCS. Scholars have conducted extensive research on the location of EVCSs by considering various influencing factors and different decision-making perspectives. These research results provide important support for the location decision of PVCS studied in this paper.

Social, economic and environmental factors are the key considerations for scholars to plan the location of EVCS. On this basis, Lin et al. [16] established the weight coefficient of charging station. Guo and Zhao [14] evaluated the alternative charging station sites from three aspects of economy, society and environment based on the sustainable perspective. Wu et al. [15] optimized the appropriate site for EVCS from the perspectives of economy, society, environment and planning. Zhao and Li [17] screened out the optimal initial index of charging station location from the perspective of extended sustainability theory, and further determined the key index by Delphi method. Finally, they established an index system consisting of economic, social, environmental and technological aspects. Qing et al. [18] considered the constraints of land price, construction cost, operation and maintenance cost, traffic flow and service scope, and established a charging facility planning model. Sadeghi-Barzani et al. [19] proposed a hybrid integer non-linear optimization method for the optimal configuration of fast charging stations. The optimization method considers the development cost, energy consumption loss, power grid loss, the location of charging station and urban road. Besides, they pointed out that the reliability of power grid could affect the position of charging station. In addition to the above factors, Yan and Ma [20] also considered the market share of the EV industry, the safety of charging facilities and the technical maturity of the EV to provide a basis for the location of the EVCS. Davidov and Pantoš [21] believed that charging reliability and service quality are the key to the layout of charging facilities for EVs. YAĞCITEKİN et al. [22] focused on the convenience and scalability of the charging station.

Through the literature review and analysis above, it can be seen that the location decision of PVCS should consider the economic, social, technological, traffic flow, and geographical distribution factors. Therefore, the location decision of PV power plants should be a MCDM problem. In addition, due to the natural particularity of the PVCS, the solar energy resources and temperature of the alternative site should also be considered. The location decision factors and criteria considered in this study are summarized in Table 2.1. Besides, Section 3 will elaborate on the specific meaning of each factor and criterion.

Table 2.1 The location decision factors and criteria considered in this study.

Consideration mentioned in the literature	Factors and criteria constructed in this study	Analytical methods
Urban Road Distribution	Main Road distribution	GIS technology
Traffic flow	Interest points, Land use types	
Planning layout	Existing charging station layout	
Security	Waterway distribution, Gas station distribution	
Scalability	Possibility of capacity expansion in the future	Multi-criteria decision making
Economic performance	Construction cost, Payback period	
Technical factors	Impact on the power grid	
Social factors	Government support, Public recognition	
Natural environment	Direct normal irradiation, Annual average temperature	

2.2 Multi-criteria decision making methods for location decision

The main multi-criteria decision-making (MCDM) methods used in location decision can be divided into two categories: Weight determination methods and ranking methods. The former mainly include entropy method, AHP (Analytic hierarchy process), ANP (Analytic network process), DEMATEL (Decision Making Trial and Evaluation Laboratory), BWM (Best-worst method). The latter mainly include TOPSIS (Technique for Order Preference by Similarity to an Ideal Solution), VIKOR (VlseKriterijumska Optimizacija I Kompromisno Resenje), PROMETHEE (Preference Ranking Organization Method for Enrichment Evaluations), ELECTRE (Elimination et Choix Traduisant la Realite) and TODIM (an acronym in Portuguese of interactive and MCDM). The main characteristics of these methods are summarized in Appendix A.

In the determination of weights, both subjective and objective weights should be considered. Therefore, the combined weighting method is more suitable for determining the evaluation criteria of this location decision problem. BWM can greatly reduce the number of comparisons and the probability of comparison errors [23, 24]. It has been widely used in various research fields: determining the weight of green innovation obstacles [25], the weight of speaker prototype design selection criteria [26], the weight of biomass conversion technology selection criteria [27], olive harvester selection criteria [28], the weight of passenger experience criteria [29]. Besides, there is not obvious correlation among the evaluation criteria constructed in this paper, and the number of indicators is relatively moderate. Considering that the objective weight is easy to calculate, this study chooses BWM and entropy method to determine the subjective weight and objective weight respectively, and uses linear weighting method to fuse the calculation results.

In the actual location decision process, due to the influence of cognitive ability, emotional and psychological factors, decision-makers often have limited rational psychological characteristics, and there is a gap in their perception of the benefits and losses of each criterion. Therefore, compared with other ranking methods in Appendix A, the prospect theory represented by TODIM is more suitable for location decision. The validity of TODIM method lies in its solid mathematical foundation and simple application, which can obtain decision-making results in line with the preferences of decision makers. Therefore, TODIM method has been successfully applied to the field of location decision, such as airport site selection [30], landfill site selection [31], distributed PV project [32]. At the same time, it is necessary to extend the traditional TODIM method to the decision-making environment of mixed data type, so as to better solve the actual location decision problem of urban PVCS.

2.3 Combined application of GIS and multi-criteria decision making methods

As a mature platform of geospatial data processing and analysis, GIS has received attention in various fields. Location analysis is a specific application of GIS, which has been widely used in many researches. This paper will study the combination of GIS and MCDM.

Tahri et al. [33] and Uyan [34] used GIS technology and AHP method to evaluate the location of solar farms. The combination of TOPSIS, AHP and GIS has been applied to the location decision of solar farms [35] and wind farms [36]. Vasileiou et al. [37] also combined the AHP method with GIS to study the location of Greek hybrid offshore wind and wave energy systems. Hohn et al. [38] analyzed the potential biomasses and sites for biogas plants in southern Finland by using regional assessment method combined with GIS. Atici et al. [39] used GIS based MCDM method to study the location decision of wind farms. Gigović et al. [40] combined DEMATEL method with GIS to analyze Serbia's suitable location for tourism development. Giamalaki and Tsoutsos [41] used GIS and AHP methods to identify and determine the site suitable for installing solar power. The first step is to use GIS to identify suitable areas, and then use AHP to sort the alternative areas. Kamdar et al. [42] also used AHP method combined with GIS to study the suitable site of Municipal solid waste landfill. Ramya and Devadas [43] used MCDM methods and GIS to identify areas suitable for industrial development. The combinations are also used by Konstantinos et al. [44] to select suitable sites for wind farm layout. There are many cases and studies on the application of GIS and MCDM. Most of the above mentioned are related research in the energy field (solar and wind farms). Through the results of existing research, it can be concluded that their combined application is mature and effective.

GIS provides unique capabilities for automated geographic analysis and provides efficient data processing and description. MCDM is effective in dealing with the lack of valid data problems and merging subjective judgments into the decision-making process, and ultimately provides alternatives ranking result based on multi-criteria. Therefore, this paper will use the MCDM methods based on GIS to study the location decision of urban PVCS. Different from the above researches, this paper uses the TODIM method to perform the second stage of ranking. It is worth pointing out that in the multi-criteria evaluation stage, this paper sets up various scenarios to represent the different risk preferences of decision makers.

2.4 Findings of the literature review and contribution of this paper

Through the literature review above, it can be found that some issues have not been solved well by existing studies.

(1) There is currently no research on location decision for urban PVCS. The object of this research field is basically the general EVCS, without considering the combination with renewable energy power generation.

(2) In the existing decision researches of EVCS location, the alternative sites are often fictitious, lacking reliable sources and scientific access. This reduces the applicability and completeness of the whole study.

(3) The accuracy of the entire decision model needs to be improved by improving the evaluation information acquisition process.

(4) There is a need to improve the use environment of the MCDM method to match the actual decision scenario.

In order to solve the above issues, this paper makes the following improvements.

(1) The research object of this paper is PVCS. Different from the previous location decision of EVCS, the alternative sites of this study are obtained by using GIS through suitability analysis, which can fully consider the urban geographic information. Then, the MCDM methods are used to rank the alternative sites.

(2) This paper uses interval numbers to describe quantitative economic indicators to reflect the impact of price and rate fluctuations. The hesitant fuzzy linguistic terminology set is used to collect qualitative evaluation information.

(3) In view of the mixed type of evaluation information in this study, the entropy and TODIM method are extended to the mixed attribute value environment. In addition, the extended usage of TODIM method will be carried out through scenario analysis.

3. Location analysis and evaluation criteria for photovoltaic charging station

The determination of analysis and evaluation criteria is the basic work for selecting the suitable site of PVCS. One of the key contents of this paper is to construct two-stage criteria to prepare for the follow-up analysis work. Through consulting a large number of literature and industry reports (Table 2.1), and discussing with experts in energy development and EV related fields, these criteria were determined. In the first stage, based on a large number of detailed GIS data, this paper uses ArcGIS software to carry out suitability analysis, so as to preliminarily screen out the site with high suitability. In this stage, key geographic information such as roads, traffic, rivers, land use and interest points are mainly used. Based on the suitable areas analyzed in the first stage, this paper establishes four groups of evaluation criteria including natural factors G1, economic factors G2, technical factors G3 and social factors G4 in the second stage to further analyze the specific site suitable for the construction of PVCS. The specific GIS data and evaluation criteria used in the two stages are described below.

3.1 Data used for suitability analysis in GIS

Land use types [33-36, 39]. This kind of GIS data can reflect the land type of the area to be built. It can be divided into park, forest, farm, commercial land, industrial land, military zone, residential area, cemetery, orchard, shrub and other types. It is worth pointing out that alternative stations should be located in areas with human, building and traffic flows, so the barren and sparsely populated areas are excluded from this kind of data. The land use data used in this paper contains 18 classifications, which can serve the suitability analysis well. For the PVCS, the suitability of each type of land is different. 10-point scale is set in this paper. The closer the value is to 10, the better the suitability is. On the contrary, the closer the value is to 1, the worse the suitability of this kind of land is. For example, the suitability of military zones [39] and nature reserves is poor, and that of shrubs is better.

Road distribution [33, 34, 39]. The research object of this paper is PVCS, whose layout planning is similar to that of gas station to a certain extent, and is located near the main road according to traffic flow. Therefore, the suitability under this standard can be reflected by the distance between the selected area and the main road.

Waterway distribution [35, 36, 39]. This kind of data reflects in detail the distribution of rivers and waterways in the whole area to be selected. Considering the safety, the choice of charging station should be as far away from the water source as possible. Therefore, the suitability under this index can be reflected by the distance between the selected area and the waterway.

Gas station distribution. This kind of data reflects in detail the distribution of gas stations in the whole area to be selected. First of all, considering the safety, the charging station of EV should be as far away from the gas station as possible. In addition, in order to avoid traffic congestion and waste of road resources, EV supply points should be separated from fuel vehicle supply points. Therefore, the suitability under this index can be reflected by the distance between the selected area and the existing gas station.

Interest points [35, 36, 39, 40]. The point of interest is a landmark and attraction on the electronic map, which is used to indicate the government departments represented by the place, the commercial institutions of various industries, tourist attractions, historic sites, transportation facilities and other premises (such as park, playground, school, hotel). The more interest points in a region, the greater the traffic demand, the greater the charging demand of electric vehicles. Decision makers should give priority to the layout of PVCS in such regions.

Appendix B visually shows the geographic information map generated by the relevant GIS data used in this study. In the fifth chapter, based on GIS technology, suitability analysis will be used to preliminarily determine the suitable site for the construction of PVCS.

3.2 Further evaluation criteria for the location of PVCS

3.2.1 Natural factors G1

Direct normal irradiation [32, 45-48]. Solar energy resource is an important factor that affects the location of PVCS. The level of solar energy resource would directly affect the power generation of PVCS, and then influence the economic benefit of the project. The research area of this paper is the whole city of Beijing. Overall, the difference of solar energy resources in the whole city is not obvious. Therefore, this criterion was not used in the GIS stage. It is more intuitive to characterize the difference by collecting the specific values of the direct normal irradiation from the selected area.

Annual average temperature [32, 49-51]. Radiation and temperature are the main factors affecting the efficiency of PV power generation. When the temperature of solar cell module is high, the open circuit voltage decreases dramatically with the increase of temperature. In extreme cases, the charging point is seriously offset, which may cause the system to be undercharged and damaged. The output power of solar cells will also decrease dramatically with the increase of temperature, which makes the solar cell module unable to give full play to its maximum performance. In addition, the batteries used in the project would also be affected by temperature.

3.2.2 Economic factors G2

Construction cost [14, 15, 52, 53]. The PVCS can be divided into five sub-modules: PV power generation system, distribution system, charging system, battery dispatching system and charging station monitoring system. Correspondingly, the construction cost of PVCS is mainly composed of three parts: land acquisition fee, infrastructure cost, distribution facility cost. As a functional building with new concepts, the design and construction of PVCS need to consume a lot of funds. It is worth noting that the charging station will be built in the urban area with higher land prices, which is an important factor that investors have to consider. Therefore, the construction cost is a very important evaluation criterion.

Payback period [14, 15, 32, 54]. The payback period of PVCS investment refers to the time when the net income of the project offsets the total investment. The length of the payback period represents the risk in a certain degree. Therefore, it is an important index that needs the consideration of decision makers. And the calculation of investment payback period of PVCS project involves the construction cost, operation and maintenance cost, PV subsidy policy, charging standards, electricity need prediction for electric vehicles, etc. This paper would focus on the above aspects to study the payback period of PVCS.

3.2.3 Technical factors G3

Impact on the power grid [32, 55, 56]. When the PV power cannot meet the charging demand of EV, the distribution network will be used to charge EV together. In general, in order to prevent the power supply line from being overloaded, special high-voltage transmission network and step-down transformer are needed before the power grid is connected to the fast charging station of EV. High-voltage power is directly transmitted to the EVs through the transformer and the alternating current-direct current converter. Because there is no power buffer between them, the high-power and short-time charging characteristics of fast charging stations will affect the stability of power grid transmission, interfere with other users and even cause power accidents. Therefore, it is necessary to consider the impact of the charging station on the grid.

Possibility of capacity expansion in the future [15, 57, 58]. With the improvement of people's environmental awareness, EV has entered the public's vision more widely. It can be imagined that in the near future, more and more people will drive EV. Therefore, it is necessary to incorporate the possibility of capacity expansion into the criteria system of PVCS construction. The expansion of the capacity of charging stations needs to consider the number of charging users in the future, land resources nearby, government policies, and the upgrade of distribution network.

3.2.4 Social factors G4

Government support [32, 59, 60]. The PVCS project has a large initial investment cost and a long payback period, which is highly vulnerable to the influence of government policies. Specifically speaking, the approval of construction land, the upgrading and transformation of distribution network, the implementation of subsidy policy and the traffic planning near the charging station all need the support of the government. Therefore, government support is one of the indicators which is worthing considering in this study.

Public recognition [61, 62]. The PVCS would inevitably affect the local environment, transportation, power grid and so on in the early construction process, and also bring certain light pollution after the project is completed. But in the long run, the project will bring enormous economic and social benefits. It will not only benefit the environmental protection, but also promote the change of consumption concept of nearby residents. People may choose to purchase EV instead of traditional car because of the convenience of charging stations. The public could comprehensively analyze the pros and cons of the project and feedback their own attitudes toward the PVCS. Public awareness and support will affect the development of similar projects and the future development speed of EV.

According to the above specific analysis and elaboration, the further evaluation index system constructed in this paper are shown in Fig.2.1.

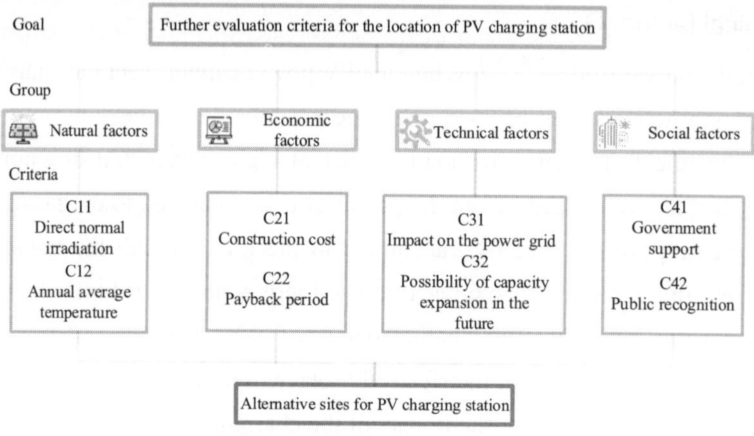

Fig. 2.1 Further evaluation criteria for the location of PV charging station.

4. Methodology

4.1 Geographic information system (GIS)

Geographic Information System, also referred to as GIS, is a comprehensive subject. Combining geography, cartography, remote sensing, surveying and mapping, and computer science, GIS is widely used in cartography, navigation, logistics, urban planning and other fields [63]. GIS is composed of spatial data, system hardware, system software and users. According to its functions, the software of GIS system can be divided into five parts: data input, data management, spatial analysis, data output and application module. ArcGIS is the world's leading GIS construction and application platform, but also the highest market share of the Global GIS software. This study uses the ArcGIS 10.2 Desktop software launched by ERSI in 2013 to achieve suitability analysis. Thematic layer is the basic framework of data analysis in GIS. GIS usually adopt the principle of classifying geographical objects by subject and layering them by category. The collection of the same elements is a thematic layer. Different themes are formed by overlapping different layers.

GIS technology has been applied in many fields, such as surveying and mapping science, resource investigation, environmental assessment, transportation, water conservancy and electricity, and plays an increasingly important role [35]. GIS can well match decision-making technology to provide decision-makers with more scientific and intuitive data analysis and data management functions. Geographic information data can be stored, managed, analyzed and visualized by GIS, so as to provide the initial suitable region or object for the evaluation of MCDM stage. GIS has been more and more used for spatial suitability analysis and modeling, which is an important means of location modeling using spatial data [64]. Therefore, this study uses GIS to make a preliminary suitability analysis of the area where the PVCS is laid out, so as to serve for further determining the optimal site.

This study mainly uses the following key steps to analyze the suitability of the location of PVCS. Firstly, distance analysis is carried out to calculate the Euclidean Distance of criteria elements corresponding to road layer, water layer and gas station layer based on the acquired geographic information data (Appendix B). The second step is to reclassify land use types, road distribution, waterway distribution and gas station distribution. In this part, the 10-point scoring method was used. For example, the closer the distance to the main road, the better the suitability, and the score given by the reclassification is closer to 10 points; the distribution of gas stations and waterways is reversed. The available land could be assigned different scores depending on whether it is suitable for building a PVCS. The third step is suitability analysis. After reclassification, each data set is unified into the same hierarchy, and the attributes considered appropriate in each data set are given higher values. Four factors are given different weights, and then data sets are merged to form intuitive maps for suitability analysis. The weighted formula for the final suitability data set is as follows:

$$\text{Suitability} = \alpha_1\text{Reclassroad} + \alpha_2\text{Reclassland} + \alpha_3\text{Reclasswater} + \alpha_4\text{Reclassgas} \quad (2\text{-}1)$$

where α_1, α_2, α_3 and α_4 represent the weight of these four factors and $\alpha_1 + \alpha_2 + \alpha_3 + \alpha_4 = 1$.

Then, regions with suitability greater than 6 are selected for further analysis. Besides, compare the number of interest points in these regions, and consider the distribution of existing charging stations. The area with a large number of interest points indicates that the charging demand of EVs is greater, and the layout of PVCS should be given priority. Finally, through the above operation and analysis, the alternative sites to be selected suitable for building the PVCS can be obtained.

4.2 Collection and description of evaluation information

4.2.1 Interval number

Definition 1. [65, 66] If $\tilde{x} = \left[x^l, x^u\right] = \left\{x \middle| x^l \leqslant x \leqslant x^u,\ x, x^l, x^u \in R\right\}$, then $\tilde{x}$ is called interval number (IN).

Where, x^u and x^l are the upper and lower limits supported by the interval number $\tilde{x}$. Besides, if $\tilde{x} = \left[x^l, x^u\right]$ also satisfies $0 < x^l \leqslant x^u < 1$, then $\tilde{x}$ is called a normative IN.

Distance calculation: If interval numbers $\tilde{a} = \left[a^l, a^u\right]$ and $\tilde{b} = \left[b^l, b^u\right]$ are known, the distance $D(\tilde{a}, \tilde{b})$ between them can be obtained by the following formula:

$$D(\tilde{a}, \tilde{b}) = \sqrt{\frac{(a^l - b^l)^2 + (a^u - b^u)^2}{2}} \quad (2\text{-}2)$$

Normalization of Interval Numbers: $D(\tilde{a}, \tilde{b})$ is known as the interval number in the decision matrix. Among them, i represents the ith decision attribute and j represents the jth alternative. The normalization method is as follows:

$$\text{Proift index}: \left[\frac{a_{ij}^{\ l}}{\max a_{ij}^{\ u}}, \frac{a_{ij}^{\ u}}{\max a_{ij}^{\ u}}\right] \quad (2\text{-}3)$$

$$\text{Cost index}: \left[\frac{\min a_{ij}^{\ l}}{a_{ij}^{\ u}}, \frac{\min a_{ij}^{\ l}}{a_{ij}^{\ l}}\right] \quad (2\text{-}4)$$

4.2.2 Triangular fuzzy number

Definition 2. [67] If $\tilde{\tilde{x}} = \left[x^l, x^m, x^u\right] = \left\{x \middle| 0 < x^l \leqslant x^m \leqslant x^u,\ x, x^l, x^m, x^u \in R\right\}$, then $\tilde{\tilde{x}}$ is called Triangular fuzzy number (TFN).

Where, x^u and x^l are the upper and lower limits supported by the triangular fuzzy number $\tilde{\tilde{x}}$. x^m is the median supported by the $\tilde{\tilde{x}}$. x^m is also called information preference value, usually the number with the largest discipline selected in the region. Besides, if $\tilde{\tilde{x}}$ also satisfies $0 < x^l \leqslant x^m \leqslant x^u < 1$, then $\tilde{\tilde{x}}$ is called a normative TFN.

If $x^l = x^m$ or $x^m = x^u$, then $\tilde{\tilde{x}} = [x^l, x^m, x^u]$ degenerates into an interval number $\tilde{\tilde{x}} = [x^m, x^u]$ or $\tilde{\tilde{x}} = [x^l, x^m]$.

Distance calculation: If two TFNs $\tilde{\tilde{a}} = (a^l, a^m, a^u)$ and $\tilde{\tilde{b}} = (b^l, b^m, b^u)$ are known, the distance $D(\tilde{\tilde{a}}, \tilde{\tilde{b}})$ between them can be obtained by the following formula:

$$D(\tilde{\tilde{a}}, \tilde{\tilde{b}}) = \sqrt{\frac{(a^l - b^l)^2 + (a^m - b^m)^2 + (a^u - b^u)^2}{3}} \tag{2-5}$$

4.2.3 Hesitant fuzzy linguistic term sets with credibility

In practical decision-making, due to the incompleteness and uncertainty of information, decision makers often hesitate among several possible linguistic terms when evaluating the attributes of the selected objects. To solve this problem, Rodriguez et al. proposed the concept of hesitant fuzzy linguistic term set (HFLTS). it increases the flexibility and application scope of evaluation linguistic term, and can collect and obtain evaluation information of qualitative attributes, especially risk indicators. The relevant definitions to be used are as follows:

Definition 3. Linguistic term set $S = \{s_i, s_{i+1}, s_{i+2}, \ldots, s_n\}$ is a finite ordered set, and the number of linguistic terms contained in S is odd [68]. The corresponding language terminology set S of HFLTS used in this paper is defined as follows:

$$S = \begin{Bmatrix} s_0: \text{Very Low (VL)},\ s_1: \text{Low (L)},\ s_2: \text{Relatively Low (RL)},\ s_3: \text{Medium(M)}, \\ s_4: \text{Relatively High (RH)},\ s_5: \text{High (H)},\ s_6: \text{Very High (VH)} \end{Bmatrix} \tag{2-6}$$

Definition 4. [69] Given the linguistic terminology set *S*, if H_S is a set of finite sequential linguistic terms in the linguistic terminology set *S*, then H_S is called a HFLTS on *S*. The mathematical form is:

$$H_S = \{\langle x, h(x)\rangle \mid x \in X\} \tag{2-7}$$

where function $h(x)$ denotes the possible membership of $x \in X$ mapped to set H_S, and $h(x)$ is a series of possible values in linguistic term set *S*.

Definition 5. [69] E_{G_H} represents a transformation relationship, which can convert the evaluation description (ED) given by experts according to the linguistic terminology set *S* into the corresponding HFLTS H_S. The logical relationship is as follows:

$$E_{G_H}: ED \rightarrow H_S$$

The specific rules are as follows:

$$E_{G_H}(s_i)=\{s_i|s_i \in S\}=\{s_i\} \tag{2-8}$$

$$E_{G_H}(\text{between } s_i \text{ and } s_j)=\{s_k|s_k \in S, s_i \leqslant s_k \leqslant s_j\}=\{s_i, s_{i+1},...,s_j\} \tag{2-9}$$

$$E_{G_H}(\text{below } s_i)=\{s_k|s_k \in S, s_k \leqslant s_i\}=\{s_0, s_1,...,s_i\} \tag{2-10}$$

$$E_{G_H}(\text{above } s_i)=\{s_k|s_k \in S, s_k \geqslant s_i\}=\{s_i, s_{i+1},...,s_g\} \tag{2-11}$$

When respondents evaluate the target criteria according to a given linguistic term set, they tend to prefer a linguistic term or some linguistic terms. Therefore, this paper uses the HFLTS with credibility [45, 70] to collect the evaluation information of qualitative criteria.

Example 1. Respondents consider that the public acceptance C42 of the alternative site A1 is between medium and high level. Use the transformation rules introduced in Definition 6. The HFLTS with credibility for this qualitative criterion can be obtained as follows:

$$H_S(C_{ij})=\left\{\frac{0.3}{M},\frac{0.6}{RH},\frac{0.1}{H}\right\}$$

The credibility of the linguistic value for evaluating the public acceptance C42 are 0.3, 0.6 and 0.1, which correspond to the medium, relatively high and high respectively.

After obtaining HFLTS with credibility, in order to facilitate further quantitative analysis and calculation, this paper further converts it into TFNs. The corresponding relationship between them is shown in Fig. 2.2 [45, 70].

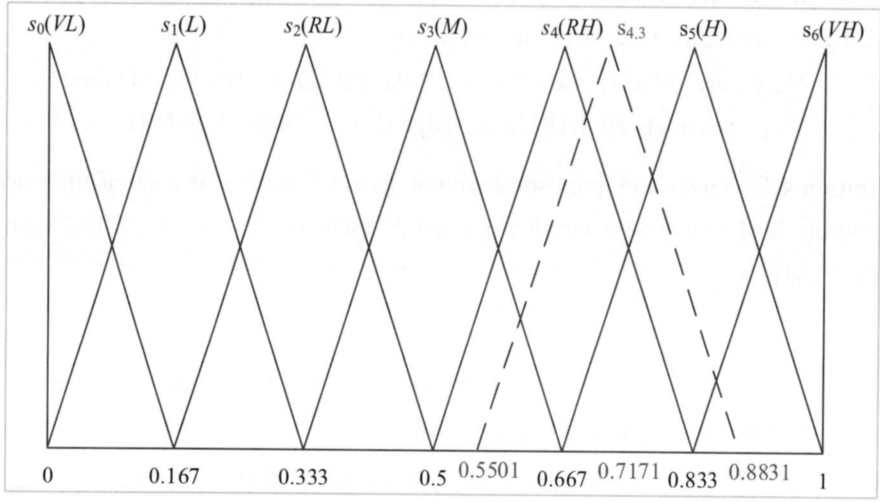

Fig. 2.2 The corresponding relationship between HFLTS and TFNs.

Example 2. Taking $s_{4.3}$ as an example:

$$S4.3:(0.5501,0.7171,0.8831)=(0.5+(1.3-1)\times 0.167,\ 0.667+(1.3-1)\times 0.167,\ 0.833+(1.3-1)\times 0.167)$$

According to the symmetric operation rules of subscripts, the correspondence between linguistic term set S and TFNs is obtained. The results are as follows:

$$S=\left\{\begin{array}{l} s_0:(0,0,0.167), s_1:(0,0.167,0.333), \\ s_2:(0.167,0.333,0.5), s_3:(0.333,0.5,0.667), \\ s_4:(0.5,0.667,0.833), s_5:(0.667,0.833,1), s_6:(0.833,1,1) \end{array}\right\}$$

Through the above theoretical analysis, HFLTS with credibility can be transformed into TFNs, and then can be calculated quantitatively according to the operation rules of TFNs [71]. The further processing of Example 1 is as follows:

$$\begin{aligned} H_S(C_{ij}) &= \left\{\frac{0.3}{M}, \frac{0.6}{RH}, \frac{0.1}{H}\right\} \\ &= (0.3s_3, 0.6s_4, 0.1s_5) \\ &= \left(0.3\times(0.333,0.5,0.667), 0.6\times(0.5,0.667,0.833), 0.1\times(0.667,0.833,1)\right) \\ &= (0.4666, 0.6335, 0.7999) \end{aligned}$$

4.3 Multi-criteria decision making methods

4.3.1 Best-worst method (BWM)

The BWM is a method of determining subjective weights. Generally, the MCDM problem needs to compare the indicators in pairs, and then obtain the evaluation matrix of the indicators. In the process of consistency test, if the consistency results of evaluation matrix cannot meet the requirements, it is necessary to revise the matrix. However, this amendment does not work very well [24]. The BWM method does not need to compare the indicators in pairs. It is only necessary to select the best and worst indicators, and compare the best and worst indicators with the rest [23, 24]. Fig. 2.3 illustrates the comparison principle of BWM method intuitively. The biggest advantage of BWM method is that it greatly reduces the number of comparisons. This method not only conforms to the evaluation habits of decision makers, but also greatly reduces the number of comparisons, and to a certain extent reduces the probability of comparative errors, making it more suitable for situations with relatively large standards. The specific steps of determining subjective weights with BWM can be summarized as follows:

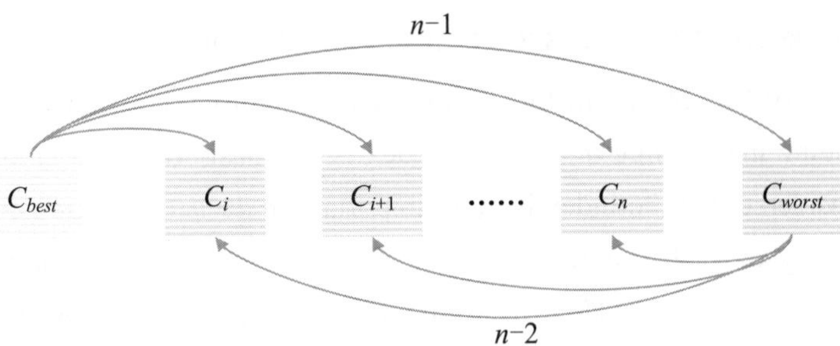

Fig. 2.3 The comparison principle of BWM method.

Step 1. Determine the best and worst criteria.

The best and worst are relative here. It aims to identify criteria that are more important and more valuable.

Step 2. Construct the judgment matrixs.

The scale of 1 to 9 is used to compare the relative importance of the best criterion C_{best} with other criteria and other criteria with the worst criterion C_{worst}. The judgment matrix $A_b = (a_{b1}, a_{b2}, \ldots, a_{b8})$ and $B_w = (a_{1w}, a_{2w}, \ldots, a_{8w})^T$ are obtained. It is obvious that $a_{bb} = 1$ and $a_{ww} = 1$.

Step 3. Calculate the optimal weight.

The optimal weight can be calculated by constructing a linear programming model. The objective function and constraints [23] are as follows:

$$
\begin{aligned}
&\min \xi \\
&\text{s.t.} \\
&\left| w_b - a_{bj} w_j \right| \leqslant \xi \text{, for all } j \\
&\left| w_j - a_{jw} w_w \right| \leqslant \xi \text{, for all } j \\
&\sum_j w_j = 1 \\
&w_j \geqslant 0
\end{aligned}
\tag{2-12}
$$

The optimal weight of each criterion and the value of ξ can be obtained by solving the above linear programming model. This paper would use LINGO software to solve this linear programming model.

Step 4. Conduct consistency test.

The final consistency test is carried out by calculating the consistency ratio of $\dfrac{\xi}{\max \xi}$ [23], where $\min \xi$ is obtained from Table 2.2.

Table 2.2 The consistency test index of BWM method [24].

a_{bw}	1	2	3	4	5	6	7	8	9
maxξ	0.00	0.44	1.00	1.63	2.30	3.00	3.73	4.47	5.23

4.3.2 Entropy weight method based on mixed information

The core idea of the entropy method is to analyze the difference between the index values. If the corresponding index value of a certain index is obviously different among the evaluation objects, it is considered that the index is more important in decision-making evaluation [72]. The information entropy of each criterion is calculated according to the quantitative information contained in the decision matrix. Then, according to the size of information entropy to reflect the size of the weight. The small information entropy indicates that the degree of information disorder is low, while the utility value of information is large, and the weight of corresponding indicator is large [32]. If the information entropy is large, the opposite is true. The final decision matrix in this paper contains real number, IN and TFN, so the entropy method would be developed under mixed information. The specific steps are described below.

Step 1. Calculate the average value of each evaluation criterion.

$$\tilde{f}_j = \left(f_{1j} \oplus \ldots \oplus f_{ij} \oplus \ldots \oplus f_{mj}\right)/m = \begin{cases} \frac{1}{m}\sum_{i=1}^{m} f_{ij}, f_{ij} \in I_1 \\ \left[\frac{1}{m}\sum_{i=1}^{m} f_{ij}^L, \frac{1}{m}\sum_{i=1}^{m} f_{ij}^U,\right], f_{ij} \in I_2 \\ \left(\frac{1}{m}\sum_{i=1}^{m} f_{ij}^L, \frac{1}{m}\sum_{i=1}^{m} f_{ij}^M, \frac{1}{m}\sum_{i=1}^{m} f_{ij}^U,\right), f_{ij} \in I_3 \end{cases} \tag{2-13}$$

where I_1 represents the attribute value of real number type, I_2 represents the attribute value of IN type, and I_3 represents the attribute value of TFN type.

Step 2. Calculate the information entropy of each criterion.

$$e_j = -\frac{1}{\ln(m)}\sum_{i=1}^{m}\left[\frac{d\left(f_{ij}, \tilde{f}_j\right)}{\sum_{i=1}^{m} d\left(f_{ij}, \tilde{f}_j\right)}\ln\left(\frac{d\left(f_{ij}, \tilde{f}_j\right)}{\sum_{i=1}^{m} d\left(f_{ij}, \tilde{f}_j\right)}\right)\right] \tag{2-14}$$

where $d\left(f_{ij}, \tilde{f}_j\right)$ represents the distance. For the specific calculation method, detail in Definition 1 and Definition 2.

Step 3. Calculate the objective weight of each criterion.

$$w_{oj} = \frac{1-e_j}{\sum_{j=1}^{n}\left(1-e_j\right)}, j = 1,2,\ldots,n \tag{2-15}$$

In this paper, a simple and effective linear weighting method is used to merge subjective and objective weights. The combined weights are calculated as follows:

$$w_j = \alpha w_{sj} + \beta w_{oj} \tag{2-16}$$

where α and β are two parameters, satisfying $\alpha + \beta = 1$ and $\alpha, \beta \geqslant 0$.

4.3.3 An extended TODIM method based on mixed information

PVCS have high one-time investment costs and long payback periods, so decision makers would avoid risks and losses when choosing the suitable site. TODIM method can solve the multi-criteria decision-making problem in this kind of situation very well. The core idea of TODIM method is to consider the dominance degree of alternatives under each index, then calculate the overall dominance degree, and finally rank alternatives according to the size of dominance degree [73]. Firstly, the classical TODIM method is extended to the mixed fuzzy information environment. Secondly, different recession coefficients are set for different criteria to reflect various scenarios in real decision-making. The above extension makes the application of the TODIM method closer to reality and the analysis angle is more flexible. The specific research process will be carried out in detail through scenario analysis.

Suppose that the number of alternate sites $A=(A_1,A_2,\ldots,A_m)$ is m and further evaluation criteria $C=(C_1,C_2,\ldots,C_n)$ is n. The decision matrix composed of the evaluation criteria values of each alternative is $R=\left[r_{ij}\right]_{m\times n}$, and r_{ij} represents the ith index evaluation value of the jth alternative. r_{ij} contains three data types: real number, IN, and TFN. The steps of the TODIM method [73] based on mixed information are as follows:

Step 1. Normalize the decision matrix and calculate the relative weights of the indicators.

The standardization of quantitative indicators has been explained above, and the data of qualitative indicators has met the requirements of standardization. The normalized matrix is $F=\left[f_{ij}\right]_{m\times n}$. Subsequently, the relative weight of indicator C_j is calculated:

$$w_{jr}=w_j/w_r \tag{2-17}$$

where $w_r=\max\left\{w_j\middle|j\in n\right\}$.

Step 2. Calculate the relative dominance under each criterion.

All kinds of data in decision matrix retain relatively complete evaluation information because they are not defuzzied. When calculating the gap of alternatives under a certain index, distance measure is used to reflect the difference. Therefore, the TODIM method can be well applied with using IN and TFN distance measurement methods correctly. The distance formulas of INs and TFNs have been explained above [Eq. (2-3) and Eq. (2-7)].

$$\Phi_j\left(A_i,A_k\right)=\begin{cases}\sqrt{\dfrac{w_{jr}}{\sum_{j=1}^{n}w_{jr}}}\tilde{d}\left(f_{ij},f_{kj}\right) & \text{if}\left(f_{ij}>f_{kj}\right)\\ 0 & \text{if}\left(f_{ij}=f_{kj}\right)\\ -\dfrac{1}{\tilde{\theta}}\sqrt{\dfrac{\sum_{j=1}^{n}w_{jr}}{w_{jr}}}\tilde{d}\left(f_{ij},f_{kj}\right) & \text{if}\left(f_{ij}<f_{kj}\right)\end{cases} \tag{2-18}$$

where $f_{ij}>f_{kj}$ indicates profit and $f_{ij}<f_{kj}$ indicates loss. $\tilde{d}\left(f_{ij},f_{kj}\right)$ represents the distance between two schemes and different types of values have corresponding calculation methods. $\tilde{\theta}$ is the recession coefficient. The smaller the $\tilde{\theta}$, the higher the psychological level of decision makers' loss avoidance. If $\tilde{\theta}<1$, the impact of the loss would be increased. On the contrary, when $\tilde{\theta}>1$, the impact of the loss would be reduced. The recession coefficient $\tilde{\theta}$ reflects the risk and loss avoidance psychology of decision makers.

Step 3. Calculate the global dominance of each alternate site.

According to the above calculation, the dominance matrix Φ_j under index C_j is constructed. The matrix form is as follows:

$$\Phi_j = \left[\Phi_{ik}^j\right] = \begin{matrix} & \begin{matrix} A_1 & A_2 & \cdots & A_m \end{matrix} \\ \begin{matrix} A_1 \\ A_2 \\ \vdots \\ A_m \end{matrix} & \begin{pmatrix} \Phi_{11}^j & \Phi_{12}^j & \cdots & \Phi_{1m}^j \\ \Phi_{21}^j & \Phi_{22}^j & \cdots & \Phi_{2m}^j \\ \vdots & \vdots & \ddots & \vdots \\ \Phi_{m1}^j & \Phi_{m2}^j & \cdots & \Phi_{mm}^j \end{pmatrix} \end{matrix}$$

where $\Phi_{ii}^j = 0$, $i,k = 1,2,...,m$ and $j = 1,2,...,n$.

Then the overall dominance $\delta(A_i, A_k)$ of alternative A_i over any other alternative A_k is calculated. The formula is as follows:

$$\delta(A_i, A_k) = \sum_{j=1}^{n} \Phi_j\left(A_i, A_k\right) \tag{2-19}$$

Step 4. Sort by the comprehensive ranking value.

By standardizing the overall dominance matrix, the comprehensive ranking values ξ_i of each alternative can be obtained. The calculation formula is as follows:

$$\xi_i = \frac{\sum_{k=1}^{m} \delta\left(A_i, A_k\right) - \min_i \sum_{k=1}^{m} \delta\left(A_i, A_k\right)}{\max_i \sum_{k=1}^{m} \delta\left(A_i, A_k\right) - \min_i \sum_{k=1}^{m} \delta\left(A_i, A_k\right)} \tag{2-20}$$

The alternatives are sorted and preferred based on ξ_i. The larger the value of ξ_i, the better the alternative.

4.4 A location analysis and evaluation framework for urban PV charging station

As more and more PVCSs will be laid out in cities in the future, decision makers will face the problem of selecting multiple alternative sites. Therefore, a reasonable and effective model framework can improve the efficiency of decision-making process. This section provides a location decision framework for PVCSs as shown in Fig.2.4. The decision framework consists of three main phases: Preliminary preparations, Implementation of suitability analysis and location evaluation, and Further discussion and analysis.

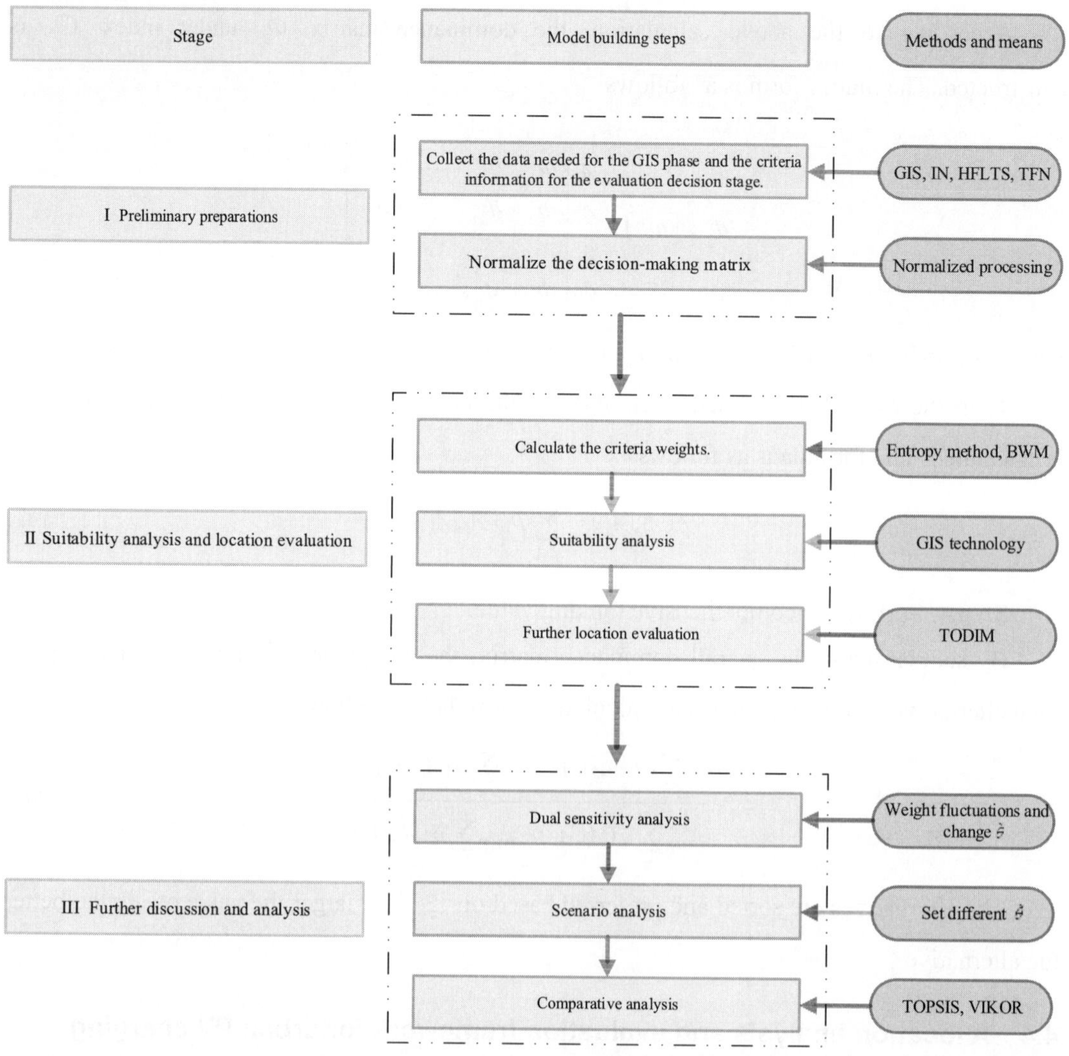

Fig. 2.4 The location analysis and evaluation framework for urban PV charging station.

5. Application of the proposed model

5.1 Problem statement

The scale of promotion and application of EVs in Beijing ranks in the forefront of China, and the level of construction of charging facilities is in the lead. In order to promote the development of EV industry and low carbon energy saving in cities, Beijing has implemented the 13th Five-Year Plan in an all-round way and vigorously promoted the construction of charging infrastructure. With the gradual enhancement of public awareness of environmental protection and the concept of green development, the PVCS will begin to be laid out in Beijing.

On the basis of market demand and policy support, an energy enterprise intends to invest in the construction of PVCS station in Beijing. In order to select a more suitable site, maximize the comprehensive utility of PVCS, the company decided to use the decision model built in this paper to optimize the site. The model integrates GIS technology, expert consultation and multi-criteria decision-making to solve this problem.

5.2 Data acquisition and processing

All kinds of data used for preliminary suitability analysis in the GIS part are shape format files. The data environment is unified into the same geographic coordinate system and then imported into ArcGIS software for operation and analysis. There are four quantitative criteria and four qualitative indicators in the multi-criteria evaluation part. Solar energy and temperature data on natural factors are obtained by reviewing the latest authoritative data. Economic indicators are obtained by calculation. Considering that these economic indicators would be affected by policy, price and rate fluctuations, this paper sets a 10% floating space to be described by IN. The criteria for judging the qualitative indicators are described in detail above, mainly through consultation with expert opinions and questionnaires. There are six experts consulted in this research, three of whom are professors from key universities in the field of energy and electricity, and the other three are professor-level senior engineers from the Research Institute of EV Development. For the collection of public acceptance evaluation information, this study obtains the evaluation information by issuing questionnaires to residents' committees in the areas where the alternative sites are located. During the one-month information collection period, the effective feedback rate of the questionnaires for each alternative site reached more than 45%. For the collection of qualitative index evaluation information, this study is based on HFLTS. The reliable sources of relevant data that need to be consulted are detailed below. The final decision matrix through information collection and processing is shown in Appendix C.

5.3 Weight calculation for each evaluation criterion

The weight calculation of eight evaluation indexes is divided into three parts. The first part is the calculation of subjective weight, which is obtained by BWM method introduced in Section 4.3.1. In this study, LINGO software was used to solve the issue. The linear programming model constructed based on Eq. (2-12) is detailed in Appendix D. The issue can be quickly solved by inputting the model into the LINGO software. The second part is the solution of objective weight. Based on the final decision matrix, the mixed information entropy method introduced in Section 4.3.2 is used to obtain the objective weight. Finally, this study sets the subjective and objective weights equally important (α=0.5). The combined weights of each evaluation index obtained by Eq. (1-16) are shown in Table 2.3.

Table 2.3 The combined weight of each evaluation criteria.

Criteria	Subjective weight	Objective weight	Combination weight	Order
C11	0.1139	0.1650	0.1395	4
C12	0.0407	0.0127	0.0267	8
C21	0.0854	0.1181	0.1018	5
C22	0.0684	0.1164	0.0924	6
C31	0.1139	0.0670	0.0904	7
C32	0.2929	0.1788	0.2358	1
C41	0.1139	0.1698	0.1419	3
C42	0.1709	0.1723	0.1716	2

It can be seen from Table 2.3 that the future scalability and social factors have greater weights, and the economic factors have lower weights. The results show that along with the green development and low-carbon travel concept, the layout of PVCS in Beijing is largely influenced by three factors: policy, public awareness and future development. Since the difference in solar energy resources and temperature across the whole municipality is not obvious, the importance of natural factors is average. However, as solar energy resources and temperature are two important factors affecting PV power generation, it is also necessary to consider them when further optimizing the site. The new energy EV has been showing a rapid growth and development trend. The economy of charging station is relatively considerable under a good operation mode, so the weight of economic factors is not high. It can be considered that investors need to focus on policies, public support and potential for further development in the layout of PVCS to select suitable sites.

5.4 Suitability analysis and further location evaluation

Geographic information data are processed based on the GIS functions described in Section 4.1. As shown in Fig. 2.5, the suitability of available land could be quantified by calculating Euclidean Distance (ED), reclassification and suitability analysis. It should be noted that after repeated consultations by the expert group, the weights of the four types of factors in Eq. (2-1) are determined as: $\alpha_1 = 0.4$, $\alpha_2 = 0.25$, $\alpha_3 = 0.1$, $\alpha_4 = 0.25$. Road layout is the most important, followed by land type and gas station distribution. Because the 10-point scoring method is used in the whole process of suitability analysis, after consulting experts, this stage screens out areas with suitability greater than 6 for further analysis: ①considering the number of points of interest in the suitable area; ②considering the road layout in the suitable area; ③considering the overall layout of charging stations in the surrounding area.

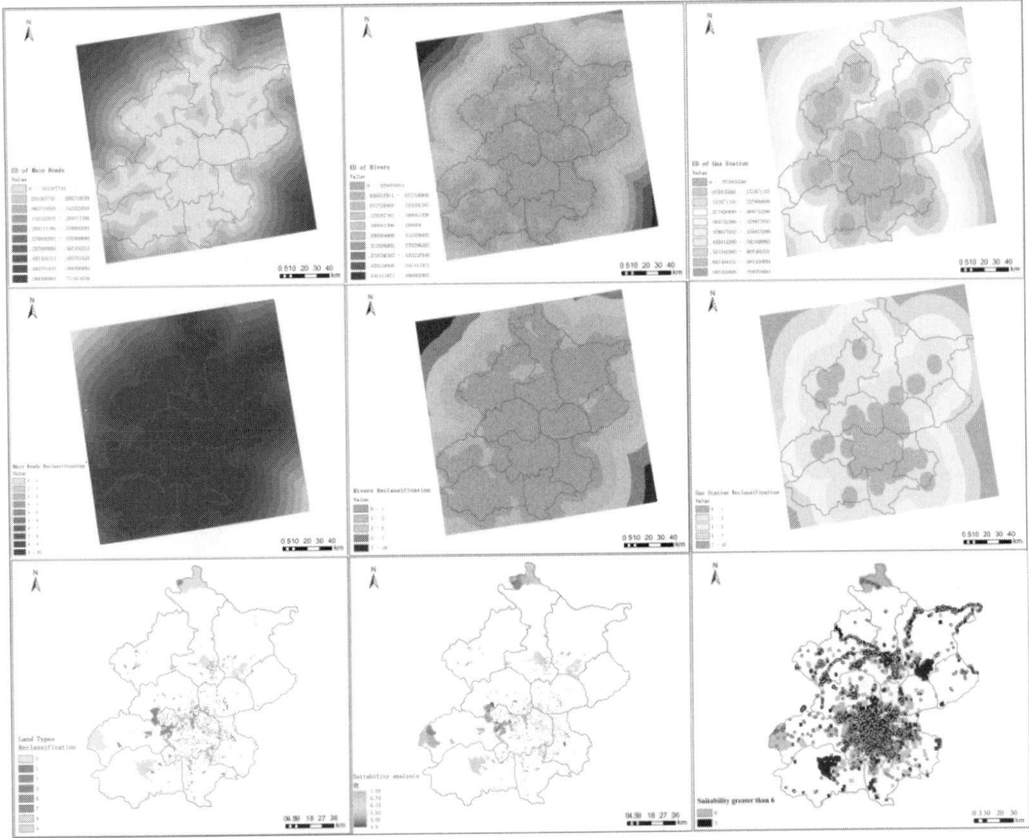

Fig. 2.5 Suitability analysis of the site of PV charging station in Beijing.

After the analysis of the above steps, the seven alternative sites selected in the GIS stage are shown in Fig. 2.6. A1 is located near Fanqi Road in Huairou District; A2 is located near Huilongguan East Avenue in Changping District; A3 is located near Shunping Road in Tongzhou District; A4 is located near Xitucheng in Haidian District; A5 is located near Shuguang West Road in Chaoyang District; A6 is located near Guangqumen Inner Avenue in Dongcheng District; A7 is located near Xinghua Street in Daxing District.

Then, the TODIM method is used to evaluate the seven alternative sites. The key step of TODIM method is to calculate the dominance of alternatives under each index. Dominance is reflected by distance measure. The distance measure methods of interval numbers and triangular fuzzy numbers are shown in Formula Eq. (2-2) and Eq. (2-5). Here, the index C11 is taken as an example to show the dominance matrix Φ_{11} as shown in Table 2.4. The dominance relationship between the two schemes under the criteria C_j is calculated according to Eq. (2-18), wherein the recession coefficient $\tilde{\theta}$ takes a value of 1[74-76].

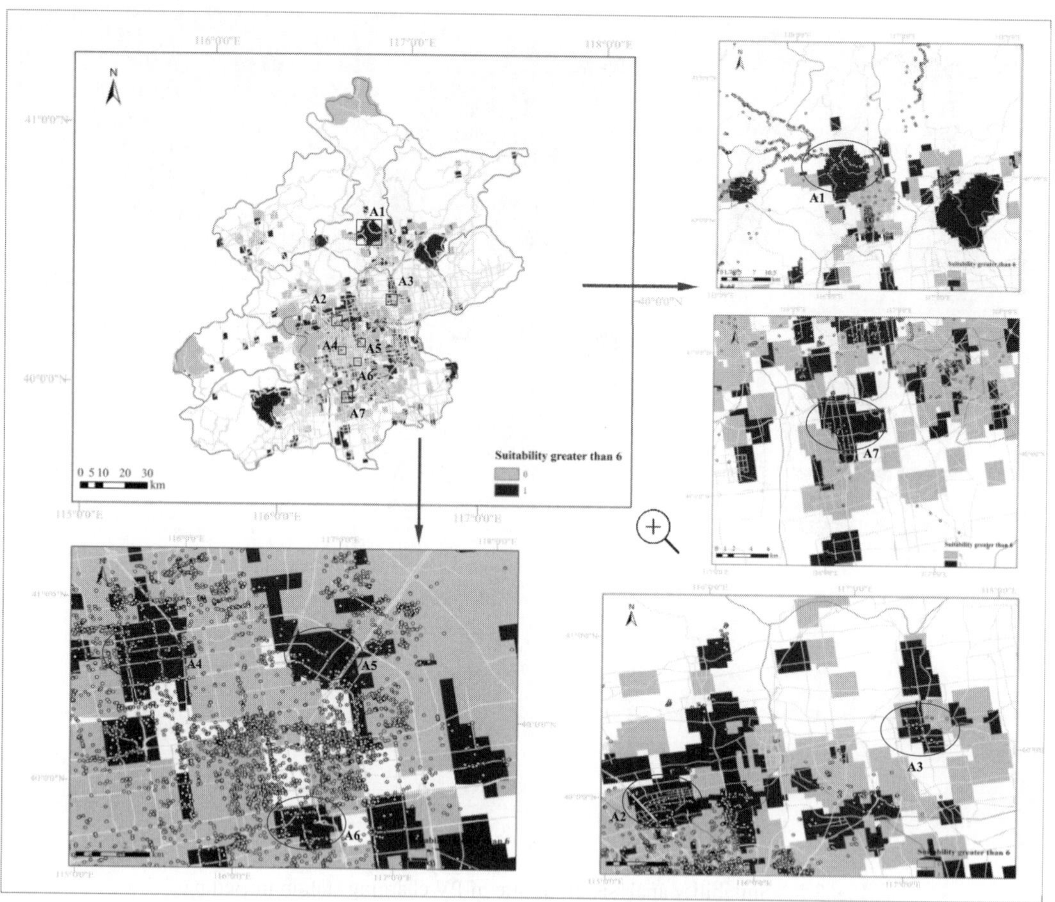

Fig. 2.6 Alternative sites of PVCS in Beijing.

Table 2.4 The dominance matrix under criteria C11.

C11	A1	A2	A3	A4	A5	A6	A7
	1.0000	0.9766	0.9948	0.9545	0.9557	0.9457	0.9448
A1	0.0000	0.0087	0.0019	0.0170	0.0165	0.0203	0.0206
A2	-0.0625	0.0000	-0.0487	0.0083	0.0078	0.0116	0.0119
A3	-0.0138	0.0068	0.0000	0.0151	0.0146	0.0184	0.0187
A4	-0.1218	-0.0593	-0.1080	0.0000	-0.0032	0.0033	0.0036
A5	-0.1186	-0.0560	-0.1048	0.0032	0.0000	0.0037	0.0041
A6	-0.1454	-0.0828	-0.1316	-0.0236	-0.0268	0.0000	0.0003
A7	-0.1478	-0.0853	-0.1340	-0.0260	-0.0292	-0.0024	0.0000

Repeat the above steps and get the dominance matrix of eight evaluation indicators. Then use Eq. (2-19) to summarize the dominance of the eight criteria to obtain the overall dominance matrix of each alternative site. According to Eq. (2-20), the ranking values of the alternative sites are calculated, and the results are shown in Table 2.5. Base on the calculation results, the order of the alternative sites can be determined as follows: A3>A7>A1>A2>A5>A4>A6. The comprehensive performance of top-ranking sites in natural, economic, technological and social aspects is excellent. Therefore, the energy planning department and investors can lay out the PVCS for Beijing based on the above analysis results. In the environment of limited resources, priority should be given to the layout of PVCS at site A3 and A7. The area covered by these sites has larger charging demand and good development conditions. Scientific and rational layout of PVCS in cities can effectively promote the use of renewable energy and reduce carbon emissions, which is consistent with the goal of energy conversion and energy management.

Table 2.5 The dominant matrix of all alternatives.

	A1	A2	A3	A4	A5	A6	A7	Summation	Standar-dization	Order
A1	0.0000	-0.2559	-0.9015	-0.9923	-0.9711	-0.9958	-1.0595	-5.1762	0.9195	3
A2	-1.9487	0.0000	-1.6304	-1.1787	-1.3193	-1.0121	-0.6389	-7.7282	0.6954	4
A3	-1.8640	-0.4445	0.0000	-0.4201	-0.4141	-0.1760	-0.9411	-4.2598	1.0000	1
A4	-3.4376	-1.6266	-2.4388	0.0000	-0.5281	-0.1342	-3.2109	-11.3762	0.3749	6
A5	-3.2842	-1.3341	-2.2563	-0.0763	0.0000	-0.1167	-2.2489	-9.3165	0.5559	5
A6	-4.2720	-2.6450	-3.5061	-0.9773	-1.0308	0.0000	-3.2139	-15.6450	0.0000	7
A7	-1.1434	-0.2294	-1.0293	-0.2615	-0.8651	-0.8753	0.0000	-4.4040	0.9873	2

The PVCS studied in this paper is suitable for the layout in such cities with good economic and social development, a certain scale market of EV and clean energy demand. The proposed model has a wide range of applications. It is not limited to the city of Beijing (China), other countries and regions can also be applied, because the location decision model constructed in this paper is universally applicable. For the Chapter 3: ①The land use type, road distribution, water distribution, gas station distribution, distribution of interest points and other indicators used in the GIS stage are all factors to be considered in the site selection of PVCS in every city. In addition, this study gives the source of geographic information data used in the GIS stage, which will be updated regularly and cover the world. ②The natural, economic, technological and social indicators constructed in the MCDM stage are also factors that need to be considered in the layout of PVCS in any region.

It is worth pointing out that the number of alternative sites is not constant. The threshold of suitability and interest points can be adjusted according to the preferences of decision makers to make the number of alternative sites more than or less than 7. The case study only takes Beijing as the research area (empirical case) to provide a complete model application process. Therefore, for the readers of this article, they can flexibly solve such problems in specific areas according to the model provided in this study.

6. Further analysis and discussion

6.1 Dual sensitivity analysis

The model built in this study mainly involves two kinds of parameters: one is the weight of evaluation index. The multi-criteria decision-making method used in the final scheme ranking is based on the criteria weights; the other is the core parameter of TODIM method, the recession coefficient $\tilde{\theta}$. Therefore, this section would carry out dual sensitivity analysis from these two perspectives to test the stability of the model.

Part 1. Change the weights of various evaluation criteria.

In this part, a total of 56 tests were conducted to analyze the impact of the change of index weight on the results. The weights of the eight evaluation criteria will fluctuate by 10% and 20% respectively to reflect the change of weights [77]. Through this operation, the influence caused by the weight change of each index can be visually expressed, and sensitivity analysis can be effectively carried out through unified mapping.

It can be seen intuitively from Fig. 2.7 that the final ranking results of seven alternative sites are very stable. Overall, the curve is relatively smooth, indicating that the results are stable. The sorting results have not changed and A3 and A7 are always in the first camp, which is the most suitable area for the layout of PVCS. Separately, the alternative site A6 shows a certain sensitivity to the index C11, and the ranking score decreases slightly with the increase of weight. The reason lies in the poor performance of solar energy resources in this area compared with other alternative sites. All the schemes show good stability when the weights of index C12, C22 and C41 fluctuate. Alternate site A6 is always the area with the lowest suitability. The fluctuation range is the most obvious in the whole test, but the range is always very small and does not exceed one unit. Therefore, it can be considered that the model built in this paper has good stability and applicability.

Part 2. Adjust the recession coefficient $\tilde{\theta}$ in TODIM method.

The recession coefficient $\tilde{\theta}$ is a direct parameter used in TODIM method to characterize decision makers to avoid risks and losses. The smaller the recession coefficient $\tilde{\theta}$ is, the larger the $1/\tilde{\theta}$ is; accordingly, the difference of the scheme under this index will be enlarged to show that decision makers pay more attention and sensitivity to the loss caused by this criterion. It is worth noting that such operations give all criteria the same recession coefficient. In the existing studies, $\tilde{\theta}=1$ and $\tilde{\theta}=2.25$ these two values are used at most [78]. In this part, the recession coefficient is set to 0.1, 0.3, 0.5, 0.7, 1, 1.3, 1.5, 1.7, 2 and 2.25[32] respectively, and then the overall dominance and ranking of schemes are calculated. The detailed data results of this sensitivity analysis are summarized in Table 2.6.

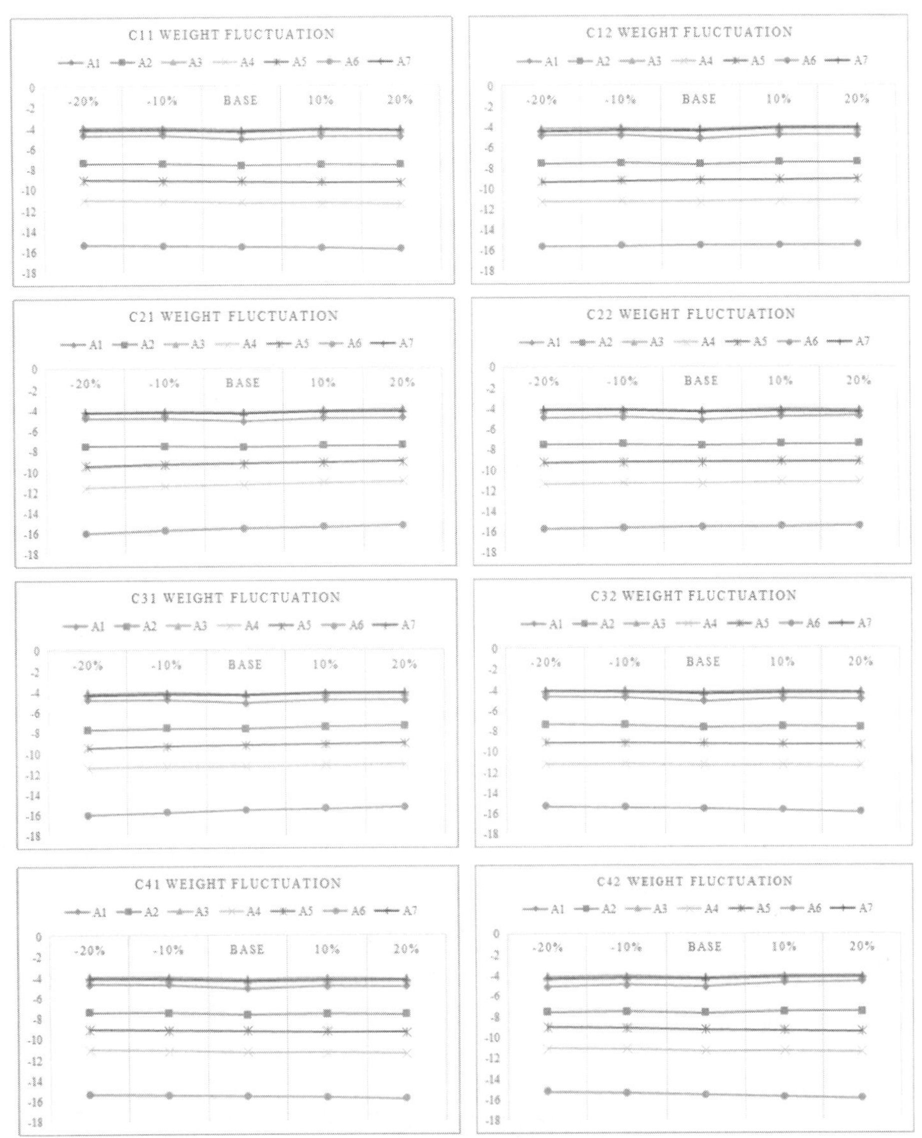

Fig. 2.7 Sensitivity analysis results of the Part 1.

Table 2.6 The schemes with different recession and order results.

	0.1		0.3		0.5		0.7		1.0	
	D	R	D	R	D	R	D	R	D	R
A1	-67.1716	3	-21.2490	3	-12.0645	3	-8.12832	3	-5.1762	3
A2	-85.7285	4	-27.9505	4	-16.3949	4	-11.4425	4	-7.7282	4
A3	-54.1758	1	-17.2010	1	-9.8060	1	-6.63674	1	-4.2598	1
A4	-120.5994	6	-39.6933	6	-23.5121	6	-16.5773	6	-11.3762	6
A5	-100.9547	5	-33.0745	5	-19.4985	5	-13.6802	5	-9.3165	5
A6	-163.5042	7	-53.9789	7	-32.0738	7	-22.6859	7	-15.6450	7
A7	-57.9389	2	-18.2834	2	-10.3523	2	-6.95326	2	-4.4040	2

Continued

	1.3		1.5		1.7		2.0		2.25	
	D	R	D	R	D	R	D	R	D	R
A1	-3.58653	3	-2.8800	3	-2.33977	3	-1.73197	3	-1.3493	3
A2	-5.72817	4	-4.8393	4	-4.15953	4	-3.39483	4	-2.9133	4
A3	-2.97989	1	-2.4110	1	-1.97605	2	-1.48667	2	-1.1785	2
A4	-8.57557	6	-7.3309	6	-6.37903	6	-5.30821	6	-4.6340	6
A5	-6.96678	5	-5.9225	5	-5.12388	5	-4.22546	5	-3.6598	5
A6	-11.8538	7	-10.1687	7	-8.88021	7	-7.43061	7	-6.5179	7
A7	-3.03128	2	-2.4212	2	-1.95466	1	-1.42981	1	-1.0993	1

Note: D and R represent dominance and ranking respectively.

From Table 2.6, it can be seen intuitively that during the process of increasing the recession coefficient $\tilde{\theta}$ from 0.1 to 1.5, there is no change in the ranking results. However, when the recession coefficient increased from 1.5 to 1.7, the position of the top two alternative sites A3 and A7 were exchanged. This change indicates that if the sensitivity of decision makers to the differences between alternatives is very low, the ranking results would be affected. Besides, it can be seen from Fig. 2.8 that the smaller the recession coefficient is, the more obvious the enlargement of the gap between schemes will be, which will lead to the increase of the difference of ranking values among schemes. Therefore, the above analysis shows that it is necessary to consider the decision makers' psychology of avoiding risks and losses. Generally speaking, the uniform change of the recession coefficient has no substantial impact on the final results. The model used in this paper has good stability and rationality. The scenario analysis in Section 6.2 will set different regression coefficients for different evaluation criteria to analyze the changes in the final results.

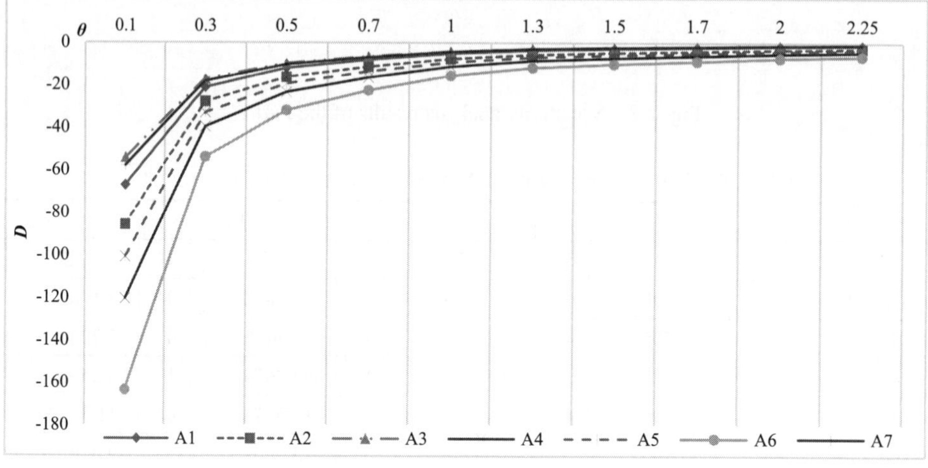

Fig. 2.8 Sensitivity analysis results of Part 2.

6.2 Scenario analysis

The traditional application of TODIM is to give all the evaluation criteria the same regression coefficient (Original Settings). That is to say, decision makers have the same sensitivity and risk aversion to all kinds of evaluation indicators. However, this setting does not correspond to the actual situation. Different decision-makers have different preferences, and the same decision-maker also shows local preferences under a set of evaluation criteria. Therefore, this paper will expand the application of TODIM method and set fourteen typical scenarios to explore the changes in the final results. The regression coefficient of sensitive indicator is set to 0.1[32]. The fourteen scenarios respectively show that the decision makers focus on the performance of one criteria group, two criteria groups, and three criteria groups. Details of the fourteen scenarios are shown in Fig. 2.9.

Criteria Group	G1	G2	G3	G4
Scenario 1	0.1	1	1	1
Scenario 2	1	0.1	1	1
Scenario 3	1	1	0.1	1
Scenario 4	1	1	1	0.1
Scenario 5	0.1	0.1	1	1
Scenario 6	0.1	1	0.1	1
Scenario 7	0.1	1	1	0.1

Criteria Group	G1	G2	G3	G4
Scenario 8	1	0.1	0.1	1
Scenario 9	1	0.1	1	0.1
Scenario 10	1	1	0.1	0.1
Scenario 11	1	0.1	0.1	0.1
Scenario 12	0.1	1	0.1	0.1
Scenario 13	0.1	0.1	1	0.1
Scenario 14	0.1	0.1	0.1	1

Fig. 2.9 The specific settings of scenario analysis.

Detailed ranking values and results for fourteen scenarios are summarized as shown in Appendix E.

It can be visually found from Fig. 2.10 that the ranking results in the fourteen scenarios have changed significantly compared to the original settings. In most scenarios, alternative site A6 ranks last. However, in scenarios 4 and 7, alternative site A6 ranks relatively high. This shows that the social performance (G4) of alternative site A6 is more prominent than other performance. The ranking results under fourteen scenarios show that alternative sites A1, A7, A3 and A5 may rank first. These four sites are outstanding in all kinds of scenarios as a whole. In most scenarios, A4 and A6 rank low, so decision makers can give priority to sites A1, A3, A5 and A7 when laying out PVCS. In addition, it can be found that the model constructed in this paper can not only provide a set of final results, but also provide corresponding decision results according to different actual scenarios (preferences of decision makers). This advantage is not available in most methods.

Scenarios	1st	2nd	3rd	4th	5th	6th	7th
1	A1	A3	A2	A7	A4	A5	A6
2	A7	A1	A2	A3	A5	A4	A6
3	A1	A7	A3	A2	A5	A4	A6
4	A5	A4	A6	A7	A3	A2	A1
5	A1	A7	A2	A3	A5	A4	A6
6	A1	A3	A7	A2	A5	A4	A6
7	A5	A3	A4	A6	A7	A2	A1
8	A7	A1	A3	A2	A5	A4	A6
9	A7	A3	A5	A2	A1	A4	A6
10	A3	A7	A5	A1	A4	A2	A6
11	A7	A3	A1	A2	A5	A4	A6
12	A3	A1	A7	A5	A4	A2	A6
13	A3	A7	A5	A2	A1	A4	A6
14	A1	A7	A3	A2	A5	A4	A6

Fig. 2.10 The ranking results under fourteen scenarios.

Therefore, the following conclusions can be drawn from the above analysis: The decision maker's psychology of avoiding risk and loss (gap sensitivity) should be considered when making decision; when using TODIM method to rank schemes, it is necessary to set different recession coefficients for different indicators to reflect the decision maker's risk preference.

6.3 Comparative analysis

The applicability and reliability of the methods used in this study need to be demonstrated by comparing with some mature and stable methods often used in existing studies. The TODIM method is the core part used in the multi-criteria evaluation model constructed in this paper. Fuzzy synthetic evaluation (FSE) is the most basic MCDM method. TOPSIS and VIKOR are mature methods often used in the field of location decision. In order to verify the reliability and applicability of this method, this section will use these three methods to calculate the problems again and compare the results.

It can be seen from Table 2.7 that the final results obtained by these four methods are generally consistent. A1, A7 and A3 are always the optimal alternative sites for the layout of PVCS. Alternative A6 is always the least suitable area for layout under the three methods. The alternate sites ranked fifth and sixth are also basically the same. However, it can be found that the alternative site A3 ranks first in the TODIM method, which is different from the results obtained by the other methods. The reason is that these four methods are based on different core ideas: FSE combines index value with index weight directly; TOPSIS and VIKOR focus on the distance between positive and negative ideal schemes; TODIM pays attention to the difference between schemes under each index. The difference under each criterion would lead to the decision-maker's psychology of avoiding risk and loss. This is the focus of practical decision-making. Overall, the comparative analysis results show that the model adopted in this study has good reliability.

Table 2.7 Ranking results by TOPSIS, VIKOR and TODIM.

	A1	A2	A3	A4	A5	A6	A7
Ranking value	0.7361	0.7000	0.7249	0.7091	0.7032	0.6760	0.7415
Ranking by FSE	2	6	3	4	5	7	1
D+	0.0230	0.0195	0.0254	0.0383	0.0409	0.0636	0.0177
D-	0.0539	0.0305	0.0248	0.0241	0.0178	0.0199	0.0488
Queuing value	0.7008	0.6103	0.4933	0.3860	0.3033	0.2381	0.7338
Ranking by TOPSIS	2	3	4	5	6	7	1
Si	0.3823	0.5335	0.4027	0.5708	0.5671	0.6665	0.4713
Ri	0.1419	0.1716	0.1374	0.2358	0.1920	0.2163	0.1395
Qi	0.0229	0.4398	0.0359	0.8316	0.6024	0.9006	0.1673
Ranking by VIKOR	1	4	2	6	5	7	3
Ranking by TODIM	3	4	1	6	5	7	2

Note: D+ and D- represent the distance between the scheme and the positive and negative ideal points in the TOPSIS method, respectively; Si and Ri represent group utility and individual regret for each scheme in the VIKOR method. The smaller the Qi, the better the corresponding scheme is.

7. Conclusions and outlooks

With the aggravation of environmental pollution and the depletion of fossil energy, EVs are increasingly favored by the market. However, the further development of EVs still faces challenges. Firstly, the lack of reasonable layout of EVCSs in cities leads to low utilization of charging infrastructure. Secondly, EVs are directly connected to the grid for charging, which indirectly generates carbon emissions. PVCS can promote local absorption of PV power generation, while reducing indirect emissions of carbon dioxide from EVs. Based on the above situation and problems, this paper carries out the location decision research of urban PVCS.

The location decision model proposed in this paper integrates GIS and MCDM methods. The empirical analysis is carried out in Beijing as the research area. In the first stage, geographic information data such as available land type, distribution of main roads, river distribution, distribution of gas stations and distribution of interest points are used to make suitability analysis using GIS platform. In this process, the suitable location of PVCS is selected preliminarily. The second stage is multi-criteria evaluation process. In this stage, four groups of evaluation indicators are established: natural factors, economic factors, technical factors and social factors. The weight results show that social factors and future expandable potential are more important. Then, the TODIM method is used to rank seven alternative sites. The results show that priority should be given to the layout of PVCS in A3 and A7. In the part of further analysis and discussion, this paper carries out dual sensitivity analysis by adjusting the weights of indicators and the recession coefficients of all indicators. The results show that the decision-making model constructed in this paper has good stability. In the comparative analysis part, this paper uses FSE, TOPSIS and VIKOR methods to reorder the alternative sites. The results show that TODIM method has good applicability and reliability when applied to this problem. When using the TODIM method for sorting, different regression coefficients are set for different evaluation criteria to reflect the risk preference of the decision maker. The results of scenario analysis show that considering the risk preferences in different scenarios could significantly change the final decision results. Therefore, the model provided in this paper can not only give a set of results, but also give corresponding results according to the risk preferences of decision makers. This improvement extends the usage of TODIM method.

This study provides a practical model combining decision-making methods with information technology for location decision of PVCS, and effectively improves decision-making level and work efficiency of decision-makers. Besides, it enriches the application fields of GIS and MCDM methods. Despite some contributions have been made, there are still some limitations in this paper. Based on this article, we will further deepen our research in our future work. In order to better promote the development and deployment of PVCS, we will study the capacity allocation of PV power generation and energy storage devices in PVCS, so that the entire charging station can produce optimal economic benefits. Besides, we will continue to study how to quantify the recession coefficient $\tilde{\theta}$ in TODIM, so as to clarify the exact relationship between the recession coefficient and the decision maker's psychology.

Acknowledgements

This research is supported by the National Social Science Fund of China (19AGL027), the Fundamental Research Funds for the Central Universities (No. 2018ZD14), the 2017 Special Project of Cultivation and Development of Innovation Base (No. Z171100002217024).

Appendix A

Table A.1 The main multi-criteria decision-making (MCDM) methods used in location decision.

Category	Method	Characteristics	Research object of location decision
Weight determination	AHP	This method does not consider the correlation between indicators and the number of comparisons is large, which is easy to cause consistency problems.	Carsharing station
	ANP	This method is suitable for situations where there are many indexes and there is obvious correlation between them. The index system with less correlation would get unsatisfactory results.	Wind farm
	Entropy method	This method is the most commonly used objective weight determination method, with good stability and reliability.	Distributed PV project
	λ-measure method	This method considers the correlation between indicators, but the measurement of correlation is too rigid, which may lead to the reduction of the rationality and effectiveness of the results.	Solar thermal power plant
	DEMATEL	This method is suitable for the case of causal relationship between indicators.	Wind/solar hybrid power station
	BWM	This method greatly reduces the number of comparisons, and to a certain extent reduces the probability of comparative errors.	Biomass cogeneration project
Ranking	TOPSIS	Although this kind of method can get the final ranking value of each scheme, it cannot show the reasons why a scheme satisfies or does not meet the conditions, which is not conducive to the improvement of the scheme after ranking.	Thermal Power Plant
	VIKOR		Waste Disposal Plant
	ELECTRE	Compared with method A, this method needs more parameters defined by decision makers, and the calculation process is more cumbersome.	Offshore wind farm
	PROMETHEE	This method does not need to standardize the indicators and avoids the loss of information to a certain extent, but does not consider the psychological behavior of decision makers.	Landfill site
	TODIM	This method is a typical behavioral MCDM method. It considers that the decision-maker is limited rationality, and focuses on the decision-maker's reference dependence and loss avoidance psychology.	Distributed PV project

Appendix B

The geographic information map generated by the relevant GIS data (©Geofabrik) used in this study.

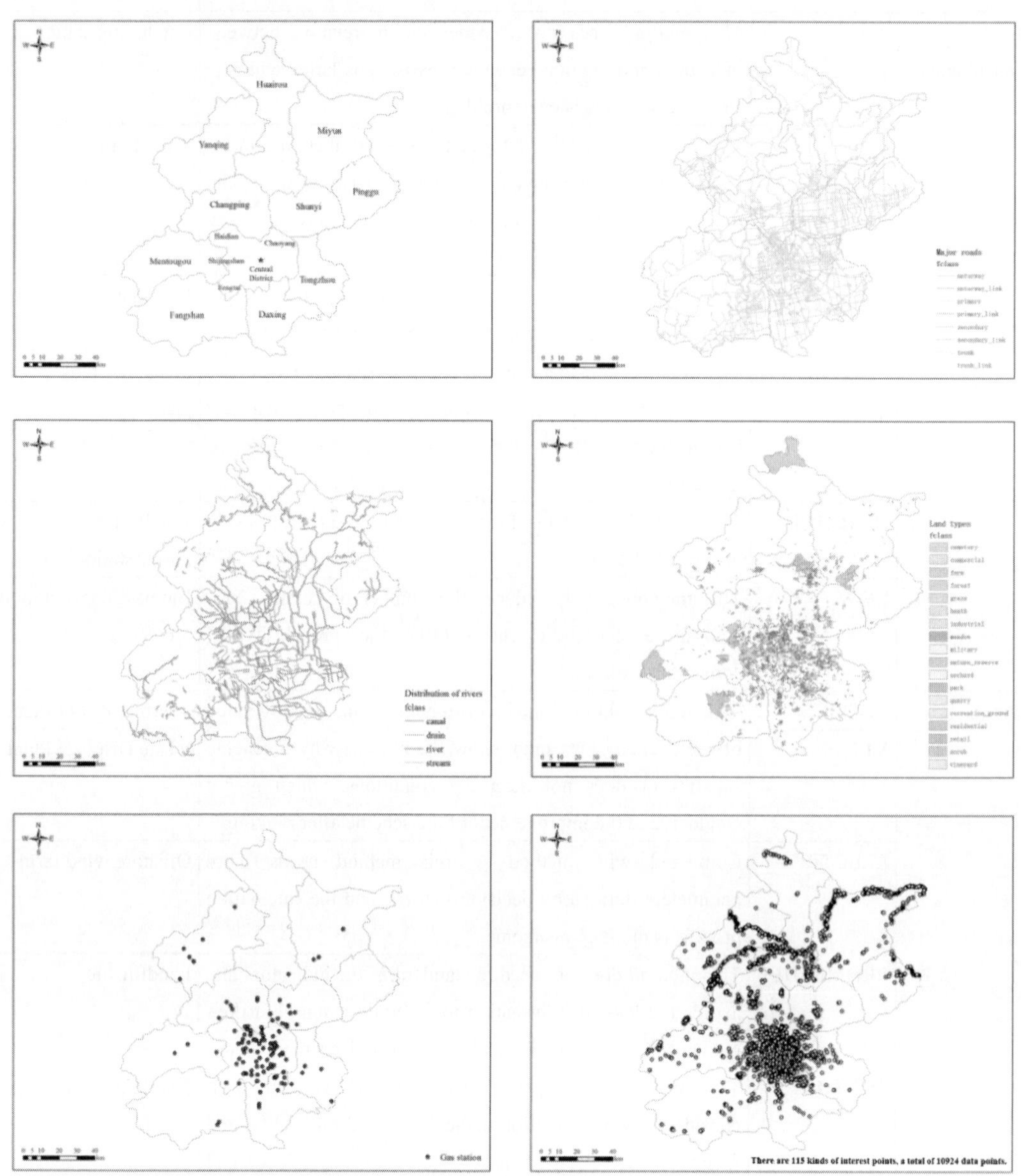

Fig. B.1 Geographic information map.

Appendix C

Table C.1 Performances of each alternative on each criterion (A standardized decision matrix).

	C11 kWh/m^2	C12 ℃	C21 Yuan	C22 Year	C31	C32	C41	C42
A1	3.3	8.9	[15058800, 18405200]	[10.08, 12.32]	[0.2220, 0.3666, 0.5336]	[0.5670, 0.7498, 0.9499]	[0.3333, 0.5003, 0.6943]	[0.4666, 0.6335, 0.7999]
A2	3.22	11.9	[18823500, 23006500]	[9.36, 11.44]	[0.3333, 0.5003, 0.6943]	[0.5536, 0.7220, 0.9332]	[0.4332, 0.6002, 0.7666]	[0.3780, 0.5555, 0.8109]
A3	3.28	11.8	[22588200, 27607800]	[8.64, 10.56]	[0.1943, 0.4165, 0.5835]	[0.4666, 0.6335, 0.7499]	[0.4833, 0.6502, 0.8165]	[0.6002, 0.7666, 0.9332]
A4	3.15	12.1	[30117600, 36810400]	[10.8, 13.2]	[0.378.0.5555, 0.8109]	[0.3112, 0.4722, 0.7387]	[0.6502, 0.8165, 0.9666]	[0.6943, 0.9165, 1]
A5	3.15	12.3	[26352900, 32209100]	[10.44, 12.76]	[0.4332, 0.6002, 0.7666]	[0.3832, 0.5501, 0.7167]	[0.5833, 0.8387, 0.9833]	[0.6666, 0.8998, 1]
A6	3.12	12.3	[33882300, 41411700]	[11.52, 14.08]	[0.5887, 0.9332, 1]	[0.3499, 0.5167, 0.6834]	[0.6666, 0.8998, 1]	[0.5887, 0.9332, 1]
A7	3.12	12.4	[18070560, 22086240]	[8.28, 10.12]	[0.2832, 0.4499, 0.6169]	[0.6502, 0.8165, 0.9666]	[0.378, 0.5555, 0.8109]	[0.4833, 0.6502, 0.8165]

Natural Factor Data Sources©: Solargis.
Land Cost Data Sources©: Beijing Municipal People's Government.

Appendix D

The specific model for calculating subjective weights.

$$\min = \xi$$
$$@abs(w_{C32} - 3w_{C11}) \leqslant \xi$$
$$@abs(w_{C32} - 6w_{C12}) \leqslant \xi$$
$$@abs(w_{C32} - 4w_{C21}) \leqslant \xi$$
$$@abs(w_{C32} - 5w_{C22}) \leqslant \xi$$
$$@abs(w_{C32} - 3w_{C31}) \leqslant \xi$$
$$@abs(w_{C32} - 3w_{C41}) \leqslant \xi$$
$$@abs(w_{C32} - 2w_{C42}) \leqslant \xi$$
$$@abs(w_{C11} - 2w_{C12}) \leqslant \xi$$
$$@abs(w_{C21} - 3w_{C12}) \leqslant \xi$$
$$@abs(w_{C22} - 2w_{C12}) \leqslant \xi$$
$$@abs(w_{C31} - 4w_{C12}) \leqslant \xi$$
$$@abs(w_{C41} - 4w_{C12}) \leqslant \xi$$
$$@abs(w_{C42} - 3w_{C12}) \leqslant \xi$$

$$w_{C11} + w_{C12} + w_{C21} + w_{C22} + w_{C31} + w_{C32} + w_{C41} + w_{C42} = 1$$
$$w_{C11}, w_{C12}, w_{C21}, w_{C22}, w_{C31}, w_{C32}, w_{C41}, w_{C42} \geqslant 0$$

Appendix E

Table E.1 Detailed ranking values and results for fourteen scenarios.

	Scenario 1		Scenario 2		Scenario 3		Scenario 4		Scenario 5		Scenario 6		Scenario 7	
	D	R	D	R	D	R	D	R	D	R	D	R	D	R
A1	-5.1762	1	-15.4200	2	-6.3311	1	-55.7728	7	-15.4200	1	-6.3311	1	-55.7728	7
A2	-13.7876	3	-18.8578	3	-28.9607	4	-47.3070	6	-24.9172	3	-35.0201	4	-53.3665	6
A3	-8.5867	2	-21.7126	4	-15.4203	3	-21.2356	5	-26.0395	4	-19.7472	2	-25.5625	2
A4	-21.5683	5	-63.6139	6	-51.2807	6	-18.2650	2	-73.8060	6	-61.4729	6	-28.4571	3
A5	-22.5908	6	-48.7745	5	-46.3728	5	-11.1660	1	-62.0488	5	-59.6471	5	-24.4403	1
A6	-30.1254	7	-84.2579	7	-75.7527	7	-20.3032	3	-98.7383	7	-90.2331	7	-34.7836	4
A7	-21.3786	4	-3.8706	1	-13.6457	2	-32.2559	4	-20.8453	2	-30.6203	3	-49.2306	5
	Scenario 8		Scenario 9		Scenario 10		Scenario 11		Scenario 12		Scenario 13		Scenario 14	
	D	R	D	R	D	R	D	R	D	R	D	R	D	R
A1	-16.5750	2	-66.0166	5	-56.9277	4	-67.1716	3	-56.9277	2	-66.0166	5	-16.5750	1
A2	-40.0903	4	-58.4366	4	-68.5395	6	-79.6691	4	-74.5989	6	-64.4960	4	-46.1497	4
A3	-32.8731	3	-38.6884	2	-32.3962	1	-49.8489	2	-36.7230	1	-43.0153	1	-37.2000	3
A4	-103.5184	6	-70.5027	6	-58.1695	5	-110.4072	6	-68.3617	5	-80.6948	6	-113.7105	6
A5	-85.8308	5	-50.6240	3	-48.2223	3	-87.6803	5	-61.4966	4	-63.8984	3	-99.1051	5
A6	-144.3656	7	-88.9161	7	-80.4109	7	-149.0238	7	-94.8913	7	-103.3965	7	-158.8459	7
A7	-13.1123	1	-31.7226	1	-41.4976	2	-40.9643	1	-58.4723	3	-48.6972	2	-30.0870	2

References

[1] Chukwu U C, Mahajan S M. V2G Parking Lot With PV Rooftop for Capacity Enhancement of a Distribution System[J]. IEEE Transactions on Sustainable Energy, 2013, 5:119-127.

[2] NDRC. Electric Vehicle Charging Infrastructure Development Guide (2015-2020). 2015; http://tzs.ndrc.gov.cn/zttp/cjmjtcwj/201606/t20160607 _806661.html.

[3] Brenna M, Dolara A, Foiadelli F. Urban Scale Photovoltaic Charging Stations for Electric Vehicles[J]. IEEE Transactions on Sustainable Energy, 2014, 5:1234-1241.

[4] Chung S H, Kwon C. Multi-period planning for electric car charging station locations: A case of Korean Expressways[J]. European Journal of Operational Research, 2015, 242:677-687.

[5] Veldman E, Verzijlbergh RA. Distribution Grid Impacts of Smart Electric Vehicle Charging From Different Perspectives[J]. IEEE Transactions on Smart Grid, 2015, 6:333-342.

[6] Jansen K H, Brown T, Samuelsen GS. Emissions impacts of plug-in hybrid electric vehicle deployment on the U.S. western grid[J]. Journal of Power Sources, 2010, 195:5409-516.

[7] Tan Z, Chen K, Liwei J U, et al. Issues and solutions of China's generation resource utilization based on sustainable development[J]. Modern power systems, 2016, 4:147-160.

[8] Fathabadi H. Utilizing solar and wind energy in plug-in hybrid electric vehicles[J]. Energy conversion and management, 2018, 156:317-328.

[9] Tulpule P J, Marano V, Yurkovich S, et al. Economic and environmental impacts of a P V powered workplace parking garage charging station[J]. Applied Energy, 2013, 108:323-332.

[10] Han X, Liang Y, Ai Y, et al. Economic evaluation of a PV combined energy storage charging station based on cost estimation of second-use batteries[J]. Energy, 2018, 165:326-339.

[11] Chaudhari K, Ukil A, Kumar K N, et al. Hybrid Optimization for Economic Deployment of ESS in PV-Integrated EV Charging Stations[J]. IEEE Transactions on Industrial Informatics, 2018, 14:106-116.

[12] Mouli G R C, Bauer P. Optimal System Design for a Solar Powered EV Charging Station[J]. IEEE Transportation Electrification Conference and Expo, 2018.

[13] Farhadi H. Novel solar powered electric vehicle charging station with the capability of vehicle-to-grid[J] . Solar Energy, 2017, 142:136-143.

[14] Guo S, Zhao H. Optimal site selection of electric vehicle charging station by using fuzzy TOPSIS based on sustainability perspective[J]. Applied Energy, 2015, 158:390-402.

[15] Wu Y, Xie C, Xu C, et al. A decision framework for electric vehicle charging station site selection for residential communities under an intuitionistic fuzzy environment: A case of beijing[J]. Energies, 2017, 10:1270.

[16] Lin X, Sun J, Ai S, et al. Distribution network planning integrating charging stations of electric vehicle with V2G[J]. International Journal of Electrical Power & Energy Systems, 2014, 63:507-512.

[17] Zhao H, Li N. Optimal siting of charging stations for electric vehicles based on fuzzy Delphi and hybrid multi-criteria decision making approaches from an extended sustainability perspective[J]. Energies, 2016, 9:270.

[18] Qing Y, Jinghua L, Qianfu Z, et al. Optimal planning of charging station for electric vehicle based on quantum ACQPSO algorithm[J]. Electrical Measurement & Instrumentation, 2017, 2017:20.

[19] Sadeghi-Barzani P, Rajabi-Ghahnavieh A, Kazemi-Karegar H. Optimal fast charging station placing and sizing[J]. Applied Energy, 2014, 125:289-299.

[20] Yan F, Ma X. Analysis on influencing factors of EV charging station planning based on AHP[J]. IOP Conference Series: Earth and Environmental Science, 2016:012054.

[21] Davidov S, Pantoš M. Planning of electric vehicle infrastructure based on charging reliability and quality of service[J]. Energy, 2017, 118:1156-1167.

[22] YAĞCITEKİN B, UZUNOĞLU M, KARAKAŞ A. A new deployment method for electric vehicle charging infrastructure[J]. Turkish Journal of Electrical Engineering & Computer Sciences, 2016,24:1292-1305.

[23] Rezaei J. Best-worst multi-criteria decision-making method: Some properties and a linear model[J]. Omega, 2016, 64:126-130.

[24] Rezaei J. Best-worst multi-criteria decision-making method[J]. Omega, 2015, 53:49-57.

[25] Gupta H, Barua M K. A framework to overcome barriers to green innovation in SMEs using BWM and Fuzzy TOPSIS[J]. Science of The Total Environment, 2018, 633:122-139.

[26] Maghsoodi A I, Mosavat M, Hafezalkotob A, et al. Hybrid hierarchical fuzzy group decision-making based on information axioms and BWM: Prototype design selection[J]. Computers & Industrial Engineering, 2019, 127:788-804.

[27] De Kaa GV, Kamp LM, Rezaei J. Selection of biomass thermochemical conversion technology in the Netherlands: A best worst method approach[J]. Journal of Cleaner Production, 2017, 166:32-39.

[28] Hafezalkotob A, Hamidindar A, Rabie N, et al. A decision support system for agricultural machines and equipment selection: A case study on olive harvester machines[J]. Computers and Electronics in Agriculture, 2018, 148:207-216.

[29] Groenendijk L, Rezaei J, Correia G. Incorporating the travellers' experience value in assessing the quality of transit nodes: A Rotterdam case study[J]. Case Studies on Transport Policy, 2018, 6:564-576.

[30] Li Y, Shan Y, Liu P. An Extended TODIM Method for Group Decision Making with the Interval Intuitionistic Fuzzy Sets[J]. Mathematical Problems in Engineering, 2015, 2015:1-9.

[31] Hanine M, Boutkhoum O, Tiknioune A, et al. Comparison of fuzzy AHP and fuzzy TODIM methods for landfill location selection[J]. SpringerPlus, 2016, 5:501.

[32] Wu Y, Zhou J, Hu Y, et al. A TODIM-based investment decision framework for commercial distributed PV projects under the energy performance contracting (EPC) business model: A case in East-Central China[J]. Energies, 2018, 11:1210.

[33] Tahri M, Hakdaoui M, Maanan M. The evaluation of solar farm locations applying Geographic Information System and Multi-Criteria Decision-Making methods: Case study in southern Morocco[J]. Renewable and Sustainable Energy Reviews, 2015, 51:1354-1362.

[34] Uyan M. GIS-based solar farms site selection using analytic hierarchy process (AHP) in Karapinar region, Konya/Turkey[J]. Renewable and Sustainable Energy Reviews, 2013, 28:11-17.

[35] Sánchez-Lozano J M, Teruel-Solano J, Soto-Elvira PL, et al. Geographical Information Systems (GIS) and Multi-Criteria Decision Making (MCDM) methods for the evaluation of solar farms locations: Case study in south-eastern Spain[J]. Renewable and Sustainable Energy Reviews, 2013, 24:544-556.

[36] Sánchez-Lozano J, García-Cascales M, et al. GIS-based onshore wind farm site selection using Fuzzy Multi-Criteria Decision Making methods. Evaluating the case of Southeastern Spain[J]. Applied Energy, 2016, 171:86-102.

[37] Vasileiou M, Loukogeorgaki E, Vagiona D G. GIS-based multi-criteria decision analysis for site selection of hybrid offshore wind and wave energy systems in Greece[J]. Renewable and sustainable energy reviews, 2017, 73:745-757.

[38] Hohn J G, Lehtonen E, Rasi S, et al. A Geographical Information System (GIS) based methodology for determination of potential biomasses and sites for biogas plants in southern Finland[J]. Applied Energy, 2014, 113:1-10.

[39] Atici K B, Simsek A B, Ulucan A, et al. A GIS-based Multiple Criteria Decision Analysis approach for wind power plant site selection[J]. Utilities Policy, 2015, 37:86-96.

[40] Gigović L, Pamučar D, Lukić D, et al. GIS-Fuzzy DEMATEL MCDA model for the evaluation of the sites for ecotourism development: A case study of "Dunavski ključ" region, Serbia[J]. Land Use Policy, 2016, 58:348-365.

[41] Giamalaki M, Tsoutsos T. Sustainable siting of solar power installations in Mediterranean using a GIS/AHP approach[J]. Renewable Energy, 2019, 141:64-75.

[42] Kamdar I, Ali S, Bennui A, et al. Municipal solid waste landfill siting using an integrated GIS-AHP approach: A case study from Songkhla, Thailand[J]. Resources, Conservation and Recycling, 2019, 149:220-235.

[43] Ramya S, Devadas V. Integration of GIS, AHP and TOPSIS in evaluating suitable locations for industrial development: A case of Tehri Garhwal district, Uttarakhand, India[J]. Journal of Cleaner Production, 2019, 238:117872.

[44] Konstantinos I, Georgios T, Garyfalos A. A Decision Support System methodology for selecting wind farm installation locations using AHP and TOPSIS: Case study in Eastern Macedonia and Thrace region, Greece[J]. Energy Policy, 2019, 132:232-246.

[45] Wu Y, Zhou J. Risk assessment of urban rooftop distributed PV in energy performance contracting (EPC) projects: An extended HFLTS-DEMATEL fuzzy synthetic evaluation analysis[J]. Sustainable Cities and Society, 2019, 47:101524.

[46] Sánchez-Lozano J, García-Cascales M, Lamata M. Comparative TOPSIS-ELECTRE TRI methods for optimal sites for photovoltaic solar farms[J]. Case study in Spain. Journal of Cleaner Production, 2016, 127:387-398.

[47] Liu J, Xu F, Lin S. Site selection of photovoltaic power plants in a value chain based on grey cumulative prospect theory for sustainability: A case study in Northwest China[J]. Journal of cleaner production, 2017, 148:386-397.

[48] Wu Y, Xu C, Ke Y, et al. An intuitionistic fuzzy multi-criteria framework for large-scale rooftop PV project portfolio selection: Case study in Zhejiang, China[J]. Energy, 2018, 143:295-309.

[49] Piano SL, Mayumi K. Toward an integrated assessment of the performance of photovoltaic power stations for electricity generation[J]. Applied energy, 2017, 186:167-174.

[50] Hong T, Koo C, Park J, et al. A GIS (geographic information system)-based optimization model for estimating the electricity generation of the rooftop PV (photovoltaic) system[J]. Energy, 2014, 65:190-199.

[51] Liu L, Sun Q, Li H, et al. Evaluating the benefits of Integrating Floating Photovoltaic and Pumped Storage Power System[J]. Energy Conversion and Management, 2019, 194:173-185.

[52] Seddig K, Jochem P, Fichtner W. Two-stage stochastic optimization for cost-minimal charging of electric vehicles at public charging stations with photovoltaics[J]. Applied energy, 2019, 242:769-781.

[53] Yang L, Ribberink H. Investigation of the potential to improve DC fast charging station economics by integrating photovoltaic power generation and/or local battery energy storage system[J]. Energy, 2019, 167:246-259.

[54] Jun D, Tian-tian F, Yi-sheng Y, et al. Macro-site selection of wind/solar hybrid power station based on ELECTRE-II[J]. Renewable and Sustainable Energy Reviews, 2014, 35:194-204.

[55] Wu Y, Geng S, Xu H, et al. Study of decision framework of wind farm project plan selection under intuitionistic fuzzy set and fuzzy measure environment[J]. Energy Conversion and Management, 2014, 87:274-284.

[56] Azoumah Y, Ramdé E, Tapsoba G, et al. Siting guidelines for concentrating solar power plants in the Sahel: Case study of Burkina Faso[J]. Solar Energy, 2010, 84:1545-1553.

[57] Yao W, Zhao J, Wen F, et al. A multi-objective collaborative planning strategy for integrated power distribution and electric vehicle charging systems[J]. IEEE Transactions on Power Systems, 2014, 29:1811-1821.

[58] Choudhary D, Shankar R. An STEEP-fuzzy AHP-TOPSIS framework for evaluation and selection of thermal power plant location: A case study from India[J]. Energy, 2012, 42:510-521.

[59] Branker K, Pearce J M. Financial return for government support of large-scale thin-film solar

photovoltaic manufacturing in Canada[J]. Energy Policy, 2010, 38:4291-4303.

[60] Hafeznia H, Aslani A, Anwar S, et al. Analysis of the effectiveness of national renewable energy policies: A case of photovoltaic policies[J]. Renewable and Sustainable Energy Reviews, 2017, 79:669-680.

[61] Mir-Artigues P, Cerdá E, del Río P. Analyzing the impact of cost-containment mechanisms on the profitability of solar PV plants in Spain[J]. Renewable and Sustainable Energy Reviews, 2015, 46:166-177.

[62] Carlisle J E, Solan D, Kane S L, et al. Utility-scale solar and public attitudes toward siting: A critical examination of proximity[J]. Land Use Policy, 2016, 58:491-501.

[63] Malczewski J. GIS and multicriteria decision analysis[M]. John Wiley & Sons, 1999.

[64] Lewis S M, Fitts G, Kelly M, et al. A fuzzy logic-based spatial suitability model for drought-tolerant switchgrass in the United States[J]. Computers and Electronics in Agriculture, 2014, 103:39-47.

[65] Sengupta A, Pal T K. On comparing interval numbers[J]. European Journal of Operational Research, 2000, 127:28-43.

[66] Moore R E, Lodwick W A. Interval analysis and fuzzy set theory[J]. Fuzzy Sets and Systems, 2003, 135:5-9.

[67] Van Laarhoven P J, Pedrycz W. A fuzzy extension of Saaty's priority theory[J]. Fuzzy sets and Systems, 1983, 11:229-241.

[68] Herrera F, Herrera-Viedma E, Verdegay J L. A sequential selection process in group decision making with a linguistic assessment approach[J]. Information Sciences, 1995, 85:223-239.

[69] Rodriguez R M, Martinez L, Herrera F. Hesitant fuzzy linguistic term sets for decision making[J] . IEEE Transactions on Fuzzy Systems, 2012, 20:109-119.

[70] Wu Y, Wang Y, Chen K, et al. Social sustainability assessment of small hydropower with hesitant PROMETHEE method[J]. Sustainable cities and society, 2017, 35:522-537.

[71] Wang X, Jia F, Wang Y. Evaluation of Clean Coal Technologies in China: Based on Rough Set Theory[J]. Energy & Environment, 2015, 26:985-995.

[72] Zeleny M. Multiple criteria decision making Kyoto 1975[M].Springer Science & Business Media, 2012.

[73] Gomes LFAM. An application of the TODIM method to the multicriteria rental evaluation of residential properties[J]. European Journal of Operational Research, 2009, 193:204-211.

[74] Xu C, Bai P, Xin T, et al. A novel solar energy integrated low-rank coal fired power generation using coal pre-drying and an absorption heat pump. [J].Applied energy, 2017, 200:170-179.

[75] Zhang X, Xu Z. The TODIM analysis approach based on novel measured functions under hesitant fuzzy environment[J]. Knowledge-Based Systems, 2014, 61:48-58.

[76] Zhang W, Ju Y, Gomes LFAM. The SMAA-TODIM approach: Modeling of preferences and a robustness analysis framework[J]. Computers & Industrial Engineering, 2017, 114.

[77] Wu Y, Wang J, Hu Y, et al. An extended TODIM-PROMETHEE method for waste-to-energy plant site selection based on sustainability perspective[J]. Energy, 2018, 156:1-16.

[78] Ren P, Xu Z, Gou X. Pythagorean fuzzy TODIM approach to multi-criteria decision making[J]. Applied Soft Computing, 2016, 42:246-259.

Chapter 3

Optimal site selection of straw biomass power plant under 2-dimension uncertain linguistic environment

Yunna Wu [a, b], Xiaokun Sun [a, b*], Zhiming Lu [c], Jianli Zhou [a, b], Chuanbo Xu [a, b]

a. School of Economics and Management, North China Electric Power University, Beijing, 102206, China

b. Beijing Key Laboratory of New Energy and Low-Carbon Development (North China Electric Power University), Changping, Beijing, 102206, China

c. China Gezhouba Group No.3 Engineering CO., LTD, Xi'an, 710077, China

Abstract: The optimal site selection is extremely important for straw biomass power plant. Uncertainty composed of fuzziness and randomness is an important issue in the site selection under increasingly complex environments. The 2-dimension linguistic information is a powerful tool to express the fuzziness of information, and meanwhile, the cloud model depicts the randomness of information with three numerical characteristics perfectly. Combining them together, this paper proposes the specialized decision framework of straw biomass power plant site selection. Firstly, a comprehensive set of index system is established to meet the need of scientific and reasonable evaluation. Secondly, the paper combines three-parameter interval number and order relation to determine the index weight, the importance of each factor is calculated. Thirdly, this paper uses the 2-dimension uncertain linguistic variable group decision-making model which solves the bias caused by individuals, fully expresses expert opinions and reflects the psychological states well, reduces the information missing. Finally, the paper proposes the specialized decision framework of straw biomass power plant site selection which clearly standardizes the decision-making process, provides the project managers with executable and real solutions. The results show that the model is very effective to study the straw biomass power plant site selection and is well worth popularizing in the future studies.

Keywords: clean energy; straw biomass power plant (SBPP); site selection; cloud model; 2-dimension uncertain linguistic variable

1. Introduction

Energy and economy have always been part of human life. China's economy has been developing rapidly and made great progress after the reform and opening up. However, the development of society and the advancement of technology for China are both chance and challenge. The deterioration of the environment and the excessive consumption of resources are becoming more and more serious. Traditional fossil fuel energy is no longer able to meet the needs of the current social development. Developing low-carbon economy which can effectively resolve above huge problems has become the main development model, new energies are confronted with the golden period of development.

Straw biomass which is one of them is favored by the government and relevant enterprises in the early stage of the twelfth five-year plan due to its remarkable environmental, economic and social benefits. For a time, SBPP and its relevant affiliates rose rapidly. At the moment, however, SBPP as the representative of biomass power generation companies has not achieved the original revenue plan and the development prospects are not optimistic. Many SBPPs operate at a loss and even some plants appear bankruptcy, which are far from the goals of the national twelfth five-year plan for a series of reasons. There are such drawbacks as the wasteful straw biomass, immature technique, imperfect laws and regulations, unreasonable optional location, difficulty of fuel procurement, insufficient local electricity demand, lack of experience, inconvenient traffic conditions, etc. Among them, unreasonable optional location, which cause that fuel supply can't satisfy the demand of power production and the unit cost of power generation is too high, is the fundamental and main reason. Some problems exist in present research on site selection of SBPP:

(1) Site selection is a complex problem, found to be influenced by many factors, and the influence factors analysis is not considerate. Biomass plants often fail due to the relatively high fuel cost. But the most present studies of biomass plant site selection are under the conditions of the transport distance, acquisition cost, environmental contamination and so on, this seemingly precise site selection model actually only considers a few factors, is unable to fully react to the difficulties that site selection are faced with.

(2) Most studies on biomass do not take the index weight into account. The importance of influenced factors is different, so the determination of weight is extremely important in the research domain of decision making. However, the weight is not fully considered in the current research.

(3) Most of the traditional researches are not suitable and innovative, exist very heavy

information missing which deserves special attentions. In practice, some of the indicators are in a state of dynamic change, are not constant. For example, purchase subsidy is decided by the specific development situation of biomass enterprise. Biomass purchase price, fuel supply, fuel storage fees, electricity demand and others also change overtime. Some traditional methods ignoring the risk of dynamic change of the factors uses the fixed value instead of the interval number, can't be comprehensive and dynamic response to the final results. Linear programming (Wan et al., 2015) which don't take the continuous dynamic changes of the factors into account is mostly used in the traditional studies of biomass plant. For linear programming, the number of constraint variables is very limited and the constraint variables are usually quantitative indexes, not qualitative indexes. It doesn't fully reflect the characteristics of biomass power plant and the opinions of the experts, may exclude the schemes in which the performances of some aspects are not eligible, but the overall performance is the best.

In addition, different experts have different opinions on the same question, the expert opinions and psychological states will change by the time. The subjective judgments of the experts can improve the scientific of decision making. However, in traditional researches, the subjective experience of the experts is not enough and the decision-making participation of project members is not high. Therefore, most traditional researches are unable to be fully reasonable, which produces information loss and has the potential to result in wrong decisions.

Other traditional several MCDM methods are also often used in the studies of the several key issues in many fields. Commonly used MCDM methods are VIKOR(Opricovic, 1998), ELECTRE III (Dias and Clímaco, 1999), ANP (Saaty, 2008), stochastic data envelopment analysis (Charnes et al., 1989), AHP (Saaty, 2001), TOPSIS (Hwang and Yoon, 1981), stochastic dominance, uncertain linguistic information and so on. Recently, other methods are well known and applied: BWM (Rezaei, 2015), SWARA (Keršuliene et al., 2010; Zolfani and Saparauskas, 2013), COPRAS (Mulliner et al., 2013), WASPAS (Zavadskas et al., 2014), MOORA (Brauers and Zavadskas, 2006), MULTIMOORA (Brauers and Zavadskas, 2010)... The MCDM methods are widely used in the fields of material selection, enterprise evaluation, system evaluation, investment strategy and so on (Wu et al., 2018a; Wu et al., 2018b). Moreover, applying sensitivity analysis can be better to deal with the risks. And yet, present studies are short of scheme sensitivity analysis. However, uncertain linguistic information gives performance evaluation of each alternative on each index but ignores the reliability of the evaluation result. Fortunately, the method is more than the problem. According to the characteristics of SBPP and the problems existing in the present studies, this paper makes some improvements as follows:

(1) Index system is the basis of evaluation research, this paper sets a relatively complete and uniquely index system for straw biomass study in site selection. The index system in this paper is much more perfect than some of the others, mainly includes four main aspects: economic factor, social factor, environmental factor, risk factor. Decision makers can obtain a

comprehensive and intuitive understanding of the straw biomass site selection, save a lot of wasted decision-making time.

(2) In this paper, weights are determined by innovatively combining three-parameter interval number and order relation. This method solves the problem that the amount of information contained in the two-parameter interval number is too small, makes up for the deficiency in determining the weights of evaluation factors only by the objective weight method. So, the result is more accurate than the result obtained only by traditional order relation method, project managers can be easy to understand what mainly plays a key role in the decision making.

(3) 2-dimension uncertain linguistic variable can provide continuous representation, avoid the information loss. Besides, group decision is used to rank the several same type alternatives. It not only makes the decision result limited to whether it is feasible, but also can consider a number of different views of experts, enhance the relevant staff participation, fully combine the subjective analysis with objective analysis.

(4) the decision framework for SBPP site selection is proposed. This decision framework mainly has the following two advantages: ①project managers of all levels can clearly grasp the decision-making process of optimal site selection of SBPP, so they can better perform their own tasks; ②it improves the process of traditional decision-making process, gives a concrete direction and a scientific decision way to the decision makers.

The rest of this paper is mainly composed of the following parts: Section 2 builds a comprehensive evaluation index system for the study of SBPP site selection and makes a detailed introduction of each index; Section 3 introduces the concepts and steps of the methods applied in this paper; Section 4 proposes the specialized decision framework for SBPP site selection; Section 5 performs an example analysis, chooses the best one from several alternatives.; Section 6 does the sensitivity analysis; Section 7 is the conclusion part.

2. Literature Review

In order to solve the development prospect of SBPP and bad real-world environment, domestic and foreign scholars have been carrying studies in many fields, which mainly involve the following areas: cost issue (Golecha, 2016; Yang, 2011), biomass supply chains, biomass utilization (ADIARSO et al., 2013; Pileidis and Titirici, 2016; Zhang et al., 2016), policy (Diban et al., 2016; Shan et al., 2016). At the same time, there are few researches on site selection.(Shi et al., 2008) study the site selection of biomass power plant (BPP) by using remote sensing and geographical information systems (GIS). (Cong et al., 2011) use the interval linear programming model to study the site selection of SBPP. (Perpiña et al., 2013) use the weighted linear summation (WLS) and ideal point method (IPM) to select the best site for biomass plants. (Chen et al., 2013) adopt the stochastic robust interval method to select the suitable site for BPP.

Unfortunately, there are some problems which lead to the unscientific and unbelievable results in the present studies of site selection. In a word, previous results are unbelievable and unsatisfactory.

Many traditional several MCDM methods are also often used in the studies of the several key issues in many fields. For example, an extended VIKOR-Based approach is employed for Pumped Hydro Energy Storage Plant Site Selection with Heterogeneous Information(Wu et al., 2017). ELECTRE III is frequently applied to study the problem of wind power plant site selection (Atici et al., 2015; Wu, Yunna et al., 2016). (Veza et al., 2015) apply the PROMETHEE (Mareschal et al., 1984) method to analysis industrial enterprises. (Azadeh et al., 2015)use the stochastic data envelopment analysis to study the electricity distribution units. (Al Garni and Awasthi, 2017) and (Aly et al., 2017) study the location of solar photovoltaic power stations, based on the extended-AHP method. (Şengül et al., 2015) use Fuzzy TOPSIS (Aouadni et al., 2017; Zavadskas et al., 2014; Zavadskas et al., 2016) method to compare the renewable energy supply systems and selected the best one. (Kuo et al., 2013) study optoelectronics industry site selection by using fuzzy integral method. There are also some methods that are widely used in engineering site selection, such as WASPAS (Zavadskas et al., 2014), SWARA (Zolfani and Saparauskas, 2013). Method (such as VIKOR, ELECTRE III, ANP, PROMETHEE, stochastic data envelopment analysis and AHP) not fully consider the fuzziness and randomness. So, the research results are not enough scientific and credible. The extended GRA method measures the correlations between factors, Fuzzy TOPSIS and fuzzy integral method considering the fuzziness of the factors introduce the fuzzy theory into decision making. These two methods take the reliability of the evaluation results into account, but the traditional stochastic dominance doesn't reflect the changes of the expert's opinions on interval.

Some method can give the performance evaluation of each alternative on each index and make the evaluation result reliable. Such as 2-tuples (Herrera and Martinez, 2001), the 2-dimension uncertain linguistic variable (Xu, 2006). Researches have done a few studies by using these kinds of methods. For example, (Wang et al., 2016) use 2-tuple linguistic aggregation operators in the decision-making study. (Xing and Xing, 2016)apply 2-tuple linguistic information to assess the virtual enterprise’s risk. (Liu and Yu, 2014) apply 2-dimension uncertain linguistic power generalized weighted aggregation operator in multiple attribute group decision making.

3. Evaluation index system for SBPP site selection

Siting plays a very important role in power development. It’s mainly divided into macro aspect and micro one. Macro site selection is the process of determining the location of the electric field in a larger area through the analysis and comparison of the resources, traffic, terrain and other construction conditions in a large area. The micro site selection is to study how to arrange the generator set in the small area selected by the macro location, so that the whole power plant will have better economic benefits. This paper studies the macro aspect. SBPP site selection is a complicated system task which can be decomposed into several sub-tasks. Many factors affect the results of SBPP site selection, identifying important influencing factors is a basic work of evaluating the alternatives, evaluation index system plays a very important role in SBPP site selection which is a heavy workload. Therefore, it is necessary to establish a set of comprehensive evaluation index system. (Liu, 2017) conduct research on the operation status of straw power generation project in China, involving power generation technology, policy environment, institutional factors and enterprise factors. (Chen et al., 2013) summarizes the factors that affect the location selection of biomass power plant as policy environment, economic environment, social environment and technical environment, and the selection of the scheme is made by using the center of gravity location model. Aiming at the site selection problem of waste-to-energy plant, (Wu, Y. et al., 2016) set up corresponding indicators and sub indicators from six aspects and apply cloud model to evaluate the plan. After the relevant literature review, field research, the questionnaire survey. This paper set up a set of relevant and perfect index system. Evaluation index system for SBPP site selection consists of the qualitative indexes and quantitative indexes, includes four main criteria: (a) economic factor, (b) social factor, (c) environmental factor, (d) risk factor. In addition, each first-class and second-class index are subdivided into several different sub-criteria. The evaluation index system for SBPP site selection is shown in Table 3.1.

Table 3.1 The evaluation index system for SBPP site selection.

Criteria	Sub-criteria
(a) economic factor	(a1) road traffic
	(a2) fuel reserve (t)
	(a3) biomass purchase price (CNY/t)
	(a4) grid connected distance(km)
	(a5) feed-in tariff (CNY/kWh)
	(a6) purchase subsidy (CNY/t)
	(a7) land cost (ten thousand)
(b) social factor	(b1) promote economic progress of surrounding region
	(b2) ease the demand for electricity
(c) environmental factor	(c1) environmental-impact assessment score
	(c2) carbon dioxide emission reduction (t)
	(c3) straw open burning reduction (t)
(d) risk factor	(d1) public acceptance
	(d2) policy support
	(d3) external competitiveness

On the one hand, sub-criteria in the Table 3.1 can be classified into seven qualitative indexes and eight quantitative indexes. Performance evaluation ways varies with types of sub-criteria, performances of eight quantitative indexes can be got though actual data, performances of seven qualitative indexes should be determined by experts in the specific fields. On the other hand, sub-criteria can be divided into two categories: cost indexes and benefit indexes. Among them, a1, a2, a5, a6, b1, b2, c1, c2, c3, d1 and d2 are benefit indexes; a3, a4, a7 and d3 are cost indexes. For the former, the smaller the better; For the latter, the larger the better.

3.1 Economic factor

For economic factor, it is one of the most important factors to be considered in the SBPP site selection, which can effectively measure the construction cost of SBPP, and provide valuable references for the investment decision-making activities. Economic factor is paid attention to in some other studies of site selection, such as wind farm site selection, site selection of electric vehicle charging stations, offshore wind power site selection and so on. The economic factor in SBPP site selection mainly includes seven sub-criteria, they are (a1) road traffic, (a2) fuel reserve (t), (a3) biomass purchase price (CNY/t), (a4) grid connected distance(km), (a5) feed-in tariff (CNY/kWh), (a6) purchase subsidy (CNY/t), (a7) land cost (ten thousand).

(a1) Road traffic: Has an important impact on the acquisition of biomass fuels. Good road traffic condition makes the transportation ways of fuel purchased become more flexible, decrease the distance from the site of fuel acquisition to transport destination, enhances the enthusiasm of the acquirers, promotes the sale of fuel in situ. At the same time, it is advantageous to the centralized acquisition, reduce the fuel transportation cost happening in the process of raw material acquisition.

(a2) Fuel reserve (t): SBPP should have sufficient fuel supply to maintain power generation. When local and surrounding fuel supply is not enough, SBPP requires long-distance fuel transportation to meet the demand, which increases the cost of SBPP. Therefore, fuel reserve is very important. The fuel reserve in this paper is considered within the scope of 50 km.

(a3) Biomass purchase price (CNY/t): Reasonable purchase price contributes to keep a good long-term cooperation relationship between growers and acquirers. For growers, it is a good return on the fruits of their labor, boosts the confidence of growers to continue growing in future. For acquirers, it will keep the cost of SBPP in an acceptable range. Biomass prices has significant impacts on bioenergy feedstock supply.

(a4) Grid connected distance(km)(Wu et al., 2014):Distance to transmission lines-(Atici et al., 2015; Fetanat and Khorasaninejad, 2015; Zoghi et al., 2017)has impact on site selection of new energy power plants. The distance between the SBPP and the local grid affects the complexity of the grid-connection involving the cost of wiring and line loss. The nearer the grid connected distance is, the better the coordination between SBPP and the local power grid is.

(a5) Feed-in tariff (CNY/kWh): Has a significant impact on the benefit of SBPP. The local government subsidies for on-grid price are helpful to reduce the cost of SBPP. The lower the unit cost is, the better the unit generation benefit is.

(a6) Purchase subsidy (CNY/t): The local government subsidies for biomass fuel purchase can change the feeble demand, promote the purchase of the biomass fuel, enhance the fuel supply security, lower the generation cost.

(a7) Land cost (ten thousand) (Choudhary and Shankar, 2012; Haaren and Fthenakis, 2011; Jelokhani-Niaraki and Malczewski, 2015): Is one of the SBPP cost. There are some differences in land cost in different places, the total land cost depends on the local unit land cost and the size of BPP. (Kontos et al., 2005) and (Pedrero et al., 2011) regard the land use as a significant evaluation index.

3.2 Social factor

The purpose of building the SBPP is to make important contributions to the economic development and people's livelihood of the society. Social factor has marked effect on our life. The impacts of the SBPP on the society specifically includes the two sub-criteria: (b1) promote economic progress of surrounding region, (b2) ease the demand for electricity.

(b1) Promote economic progress of surrounding region: SBPP can provide a lot of jobs to local people, drive the growth of other related industries (such as logistics), promote regional GDP growth, raise the level of the local per capita income, improve the quality of life.

(b2) Ease the demand for electricity: SBPP can effectively alleviate power demand of the local and surrounding areas. Construction scale of SBPP should be based on local and neighboring power demand.

3.3 Environmental factor

Environmental issues are related to people's health. In recent years, the environmental impacts of construction projects have been the focus of the society from all walks of life. Environmental issues are considered in offshore wind farm site selection. Straw biomass power plants' environmental impacts mainly appear in the construction stage and operation stage, environmental factor includes (c1) environmental-impact assessment score, (c2) carbon dioxide emission reduction and (c3) straw open burning reduction.

(c1) Environmental-impact assessment score: The construction process will cause damages to the local vegetation. Therefore, it is very meaningful to assess the assessment score.

(c2) Carbon dioxide emission reduction (t): Utilization of waste biomass fuel to produce electricity can effectively reduce the local carbon emission, contribute to cope with climate warming.

(c3) Straw open burning reduction (t): Biomass power generation using straw to generate electricity is a new energy, can reduce a lot of pollution produced by straw open burning.

3.4 Risk factor

Risk factor exists in the whole life cycle of SBPP, is related to the survival of SBPP and must be considered. Risk factor includes (dl) public acceptance, (d2) policy support, (d3) external competitiveness.

(dl) Public acceptance: Due to the noise influences produced by SBPP on local residents, public acceptance will affect the acquisition of biomass fuel in the field. They may interfere with the normal construction and operation of SBPP when they cannot accept the construction of SBPP. (Guikema, 2005) notes that public preference is very important for site selection. Socially acceptable affects the site selection (García et al., 2014)

(d2) Policy support (Ahi et al., 2009): Policies (such as clean energy projects subsidies, subsidies for carbon emissions) influence the prospect of SBPP. Investors should pay close attention to relevant policies.

(d3) External competitiveness: Other relevant industries (such as paper making) also have the big demand for biomass fuels. The quantity and scales of these enterprises that need biomass fuels have great influences on the fuel supply stability of SBPP. Strategies to overcome biomass supply problems are developed (Rauch, 2017).

In conclusion, it is reasonable to study SBPP site selection from four aspects: economy, society, environment and risk, establishment of evaluation index system lays a solid foundation for the later model research.

4. Preliminaries

4.1 Three-parameter interval number and order relation

Using the 2-dimension linguistic variable to reflect the experts' preferences is one way to depict the fuzziness and improve the evaluation quality. Another other way to improve the reasonability of risk assessment is to characterize the randomness of uncertainty. The optimal site selection of SBPP is conducted under the uncertain environment. The uncertainty is caused by the two following causes: ①Site Selection is carried out based on ex ante estimates about what the future value will be, so the resulting value is uncertain; ②the judgment of some decision information involved in site selection generally relies on experts' experiences, but experts cannot express their opinions as accurately as machines when describing a complex object, and vagueness always exists in the mode of thinking. Randomness is an important property of uncertainty due to the fact that conditions cannot determine outcomes sometimes.

Fortunately, the cloud model can characterize the randomness effectively, which makes decisions more realistic.

Definition 1. (Guangzhi and Zhang, 2001) Using three parameters to express the interval number is called three-parameter interval number. It is expressed as $u=[u^l,u^m,u^n]$, where $u^l \leqslant u^m \leqslant u^n$, u^l is the lower bound of the interval number; u^n is the upper bound of the interval number; u^m is the most possible acquired value within the interval, which is usually called the center of gravity and the ideal value of the interval number.

Assume there is n groups of three-parameter interval number $w=\{[r_1{}^a,r_1{}^b,r_1{}^c],[r_2{}^a,r_2{}^b,r_2{}^c],\ldots,[r_n{}^a,r_n{}^b,r_n{}^c]\}$, $i=1,2,\ldots,n$, so the normalized result is

$$w=\{[w_1{}^a,w_1{}^b,w_1{}^c],[w_2{}^a,w_2{}^b,w_2{}^c],\ldots,[w_n{}^a,w_n{}^b,w_n{}^c]\} \tag{3-1}$$

where, $w_i{}^a=r_i{}^a/\sum_{i=1}^{n}r_i{}^b$, $w_i{}^b=r_i{}^b/\sum_{i=1}^{n}r_i{}^b$, $w_i{}^c=r_i{}^c/\sum_{i=1}^{n}r_i{}^b$, $i=1,2,\ldots,n$.

Definition 2. (Yan et al., 2013) Assume there are three-parameter interval numbers $r=[r^l,r^m,r^n]$ and $s=[s^l,s^m,s^n]$, $d(r)=r^n-r^l$, $d(s)=s^n-s^l$, then

$$p_{r\geqslant s}=\min(1,\max(\frac{r^n+r^m-s^m-s^l}{d(r)+d(s)},0)) \tag{3-2}$$

where the result is true when it is greater than 0.5.

The importance ratio of the indicator $i-1$ to the indicator i is:

$$c_i=\frac{w_{i-1}{}'}{w_i{}'}, \quad i=1,2,\ldots,n \tag{3-3}$$

Then,

$$w_n=(1+\sum_{i=2}^{n}\prod_{j=i}^{n}c_j)^{-1}, \quad i=1,2,\ldots,n \tag{3-4}$$

$$w_{i-1}{}^*=c_i w_i{}^*, \quad i=n-1,n-2,\ldots,2 \tag{3-5}$$

The finally corresponding weight is $w^*=(w^*{}_1,w^*{}_2,\ldots,w^*{}_n)$.

4.2 2-dimension uncertain linguistic variable

Definition 3. (Xu, 2006) Let $\tilde{s}=[s_a,s_b]$, where $s_a,s_b\in\overline{S}$ and $a\leqslant b$, s_a and s_b are the lower and the upper limits, then $\tilde{s}$ is called an uncertain linguistic variable.

Definition4. (Yager, 2004) Let function $\rho:[0,1]\to[0,1]$ satisfy:

(1) $\rho(0)-0$;

(2) $\rho(1)=1$;

(3) If $x>y$, then $\rho(x)>\rho(y)$.

then ρ is called the basic unit-interval monotonic function (the BUM function).

Definition 5. (Zhang and Ze-Shui, 2005) If $[s_a, s_b]$ is the uncertain linguistic variable, and

$$f_\rho([s_a, s_b]) = s_{\int_0^1 \frac{d\rho(y)}{dy}(b-y(b-a))dy} \tag{3-6}$$

then f is called the uncertain linguistic variable OWA operator (the UL-OWA operator).

If $\rho(y) = y^\delta (\delta \geqslant 0)$, then

$$f_\rho([s_a, s_b]) = \frac{s_{b+\delta a}}{\delta + 1} \tag{3-7}$$

Definition 6. (Liu, 2012) Let $\hat{S} = ([\dot{s}_a, \dot{s}_b], [\ddot{s}_c, \ddot{s}_d])$, where $[\dot{s}_a, \dot{s}_b]$ is I class uncertain linguistic information, which represents decision maker's judgment to an evaluated object, and $\dot{s}_a, \dot{s}_b$ are the elements from the predefined linguistic assessment set $S_{\text{I}}=(\dot{s}_0, \dot{s}_1, .., \dot{s}_{t-1})$, while $[\ddot{s}_c, \ddot{s}_d]$ is II class uncertain linguistic information, which represents the subjective evaluation on the reliability of their given results, and $\ddot{s}_c, \ddot{s}_d$ are the elements from the predefined linguistic assessment set $S_{\text{II}}=(\ddot{s}_0, \ddot{s}_1, ..., \ddot{s}_{t-1})$, then $\hat{s}$ is called the 2-dimension uncertain linguistic variable.

In order to minimize the loss of linguistic information, the discrete linguistic assessment sets of 2-dimension uncertain linguistic information are extended to continuous linguistic assessment sets, such that $\dot{s}_a, \dot{s}_b \in \overline{S}_{\text{I}} = \{\dot{s}_\alpha \alpha \in [0, q]\}$ and $\ddot{s}_c, \ddot{s}_d \in \overline{S}_{\text{II}} = \{\ddot{s}_\alpha \mid \alpha \in [0, q']\}$. At the same time, for convenience, let $\hat{s}$ be the set of all 2-dimensionuncertain linguistic variables.

4.3 Cloud model

Definition 7. (Li et al., 2009) Let U be the universe of discourse and T be a qualitative concept in U, $x(x \in U)$ is a random instantiation of concept T, which satisfies $En' \sim N(En, He^2)$ and $x \sim N(Ex, En'^2)$, the certainty degree of x belonging to concept T satisfies $\mu = e^{\frac{(x-Ex)^2}{2(En')^2}}$.

Then the distribution of x in the universe U is called a normal cloud. The cloud model can effectively integrate the randomness and fuzziness of concepts, describe the overall quantitative property of a concept by the three numerical characteristics as follows:

Expectation Ex is the mathematical expectation of the cloud drops belonging to a concept in the universe and is the most representative and typical sample of the qualitative concept;

Entropy En represents the fuzziness measurement of a qualitative concept, which is determined by both the randomness and the fuzziness of the concept;

Hyper entropy He is the uncertain degree of entropy En, which reflects the dispersion of the cloud drops.

Assume that there are two clouds $A(Ex_1, En_1, He_1)$ and $B(Ex_2, En_2, He_2)$, operations between cloud A and cloud B are given by:

$(1)A+B=(Ex_1+Ex_2,\sqrt{En_1^2+En_2^2},\sqrt{He_1^2+He_2^2})$;

$(2)A-B=(Ex_1-Ex_2,\sqrt{En_1^2+En_2^2},\sqrt{He_1^2+He_2^2})$;

$(3)A\times B=(Ex_1\times Ex_2,\sqrt{(En_1Ex_2)^2+(En_2Ex_1)^2},\sqrt{(He_1Ex_2)^2+(He_2Ex_1)^2})$;

$(4)A^\lambda=(Ex_1{}^\lambda,\sqrt{\lambda}Ex_1{}^{\lambda-1}En_1,\sqrt{\lambda}Ex_1{}^{\lambda-1}He_1)$;

$(5)\lambda A=(\lambda Ex_1,\sqrt{\lambda}En_1,\sqrt{\lambda}He_1)$.

Definition 8. (Herrera et al., 2000) Let n be the number of the decision-makers' linguistic assessment scales (they can be selected randomly according to the real situation). The effective domain $[X_{\min},X_{\max}]$ is designated by experts, n clouds can be generated corresponding to the expression of linguistic values; denote the middle one as $Y_0(Ex_0,En_0,He_0)$, and if n is odd, then the left and right adjacent clouds are denoted as follows:

$Y_{-1}(Ex_{-1},En_{-1},He_{-1})$, $Y_{+1}(Ex_{+1},En_{+1},He_{+1})$

$Y_{-2}(Ex_{-2},En_{-2},He_{-2})$, $Y_{+2}(Ex_{+2},En_{+2},He_{+2})$

…

$Y_{-(n-1)/2}(Ex_{-(n-1)/2},En_{-(n-1)/2},He_{-(n-1)/2})$

$Y_{+(n-1)/2}(Ex_{+(n-1)/2},En_{+(n-1)/2},He_{+(n-1)/2})$

The Golden Section is used to generate seven clouds, where the corresponding numerical characters are shown as follows (Zhao et al., 2015):

$Ex_0=(X_{\min}+X_{\max})/2$, $Ex_{-3}=X_{\min}$, $Ex_{+3}=X_{\max}$

$Ex_{-2}=Ex_0-0.382(X_{\max}-X_{\min})/2$

$Ex_{+2}=Ex_0+0.382(X_{\max}-X_{\min})/2$

$Ex_{-1}=Ex_0-0.382(\frac{X_{\max}-X_{\min}}{2})/2$

$Ex_{+1}=Ex_0+0.382(\frac{X_{\max}-X_{\min}}{2})/2$

$En_{-1}=En_{+1}=0.382(X_{\max}-X_{\min})/6$

$En_0=0.618En_{+1}$, $En_{-2}=En_{+2}=En_{+1}/0.618$

$En_{-3}=En_{+3}=En_{+2}/0.618$

$He_{-1}=He_1=He_0/0.618$, $He_{-2}=He_2=He_1/0.618$

$He_{-3}=He_3=He_2/0.618$

It is noteworthy that He_0 is given beforehand.

Definition 9. (Wang et al., 2015) Let the interval linguistic value be $[s_i,s_j]$, convert s_i and s_j into two clouds $y_i=(Ex_i,En_i,He_i)$ and $y_i=(Ex_j,En_j,He_j)$. Then $\tilde{y}=([\underline{Ex},\overline{Ex}],En,He)$ can be called interval integrated cloud, where

$$\underline{Ex}=\min\{Ex_i,Ex_j\},\quad \overline{Ex}=\max\{Ex_i,Ex_j\} \tag{3-8}$$

$$En=\sqrt{En_i^2+En_j^2}\ ,\quad He=\sqrt{He_i^2+He_j^2} \tag{3-9}$$

The numerical characters of y are the expectation range $[\underline{Ex},\overline{Ex}]$, entropy En and hyper entropy He.

Definition 10. Let $A_i=([\underline{Ex_i},\overline{Ex_i}],En_i,He_i)$, $i=(1,2,...,n)$ be n adjacent interval integrated clouds in the domain U . $A=([\underline{Ex},\overline{Ex}],En,He)$ is called a floating interval integrated cloud, where the numerical characters $[\underline{Ex},\overline{Ex}]$, En , He are defined as follows:

$$[\underline{Ex},\overline{Ex}]=w_1[\underline{Ex_1},\overline{Ex_1}]+w_2[\underline{Ex_2},\overline{Ex_2}]+...+w_n[\underline{Ex_n},\overline{Ex_n}] \tag{3-10}$$

$$Ex_1=\frac{\underline{\underline{Ex_1}}+\overline{Ex_1}}{2},Ex_2=\frac{\underline{\underline{Ex_2}}+\overline{Ex_2}}{2},...,Ex_n=\frac{\underline{\underline{Ex_n}}+\overline{Ex_n}}{2} \tag{3-11}$$

$$En=\frac{w_1Ex_1En_1+w_2Ex_2En_2+...+w_nEx_nEn_n}{w_1Ex_1+w_2Ex_2+...+w_nEx_n} \tag{3-12}$$

$$He=\sqrt{He_1^2+He_2^2+...+He_n^2} \tag{3-13}$$

where $w_i(i=1,2,...,n)$ are the criteria weights satisfying $\sum_{i=1}^{n}w_i=1$.

Definition 11. Let $\tilde{y}_1=([\underline{Ex_1},\overline{Ex_1}],En_1,He_1)$ and $\tilde{y}_2=([\underline{Ex_2},\overline{Ex_2}],En_2,He_2)$ be two arbitrary interval integrated clouds. Then, $d(\tilde{y}_1,\tilde{y}_2)$ is defined as:

$$\begin{aligned}d(\tilde{y}_1,\tilde{y}_2)=\frac{1}{2}(|(1-\frac{En_1+He_1}{Ex_1})\underline{Ex_1}-(1-\frac{En_2+He_2}{Ex_2})\underline{Ex_2}|+\\|(1-\frac{En_1+He_1}{Ex_1})\overline{Ex_1}|-(1-\frac{En_2+He_2}{Ex_2})\overline{Ex_2})\end{aligned} \tag{3-14}$$

where $Ex_1=\frac{\underline{\underline{Ex_1}}+\overline{Ex_1}}{2}$, $Ex_2=\frac{\underline{\underline{Ex_2}}+\overline{Ex_2}}{2}$ .If En_1=He_1=En_2=He_2=0 , the interval integrated cloud is actually an interval number. In this case $\mathrm{d}(\tilde{y}_1,\tilde{y}_2)=\frac{1}{2}(|\underline{Ex_1}-\underline{Ex_2}|+|\overline{Ex_1}-\overline{Ex_2}|)$.

To illustrate the effectiveness of the proposed model concisely, the advantages and disadvantages of the existing models and the proposed model are summarized and shown in Table 3.2. As can be seen from the table, the proposed model overcomes some shortcomings of other models, such as not corresponding to the human cognitive habits, ignoring the reliability of the given evaluation result, and failing to handle the randomness. Therefore, based on the above improvements, the quality of Site selection can be improved largely. But the disadvantages of the proposed model are also obvious. That is, its calculation process is slightly complicated and the decision cost is high. However, compare with the loss of the decision-making mistake, the increasing decision cost and the complex calculation process may seem fairly trifling."

Table 3.2 The advantages and disadvantages of the existing models and the proposed model.

Description	Linguistic variable	2-Dimension linguistic variables	Cloud model	Model converting linguistic variable to cloud model	The proposed model
Advantages	It accords with the human cognitive habits, and can depict the fuzziness. The calculation process is simple	It accords with the human cognitive habits, and can depict the fuzziness and considers the reliability of the given evaluation result. The calculation process is simple	It can depict the fuzziness and randomness simultaneously. The calculation process is simple	It accords with the human cognitive habits, and can depict the fuzziness and randomness simultaneously	It accords with the human cognitive habits, at the same time considers the reliability of the given evaluation result. And it can depict the fuzziness and randomness simultaneously
Disadvantages	It ignores the reliability of the given evaluation result and fails to handle the randomness	It fails to handle the randomness	It is not in accordance with the human cognitive habits, and ignores the reliability of the given evaluation result	It ignores the reliability of the given evaluation result. And its calculation process is slightly complicated	Its calculation process is slightly complicated

5. Decision Framework for the optimal site selection of SBPP

In this paper, the decision framework for the optimal site selection of SBPP is divided into four stages, can be seen in Fig. 3.1 In order to avoid the bias of individual decision maker, a decision committee involving twenty-eight members is set up for the work of SBPP site selection. All those members including college professors, engineers, project managers, etc. They have rich theory and practice experience in different filed about SBPP, such as economic research, risk management, environment impact appraisal, power generation technology, operational management, construction management, etc. Each decision maker has their own tasks in the decision-making process of SBPP site selection.

According to the aforementioned definitions, specific and concrete work contents of four decision-making stages for SBPP based on 2-dimension uncertain linguistic variable are described as follows.

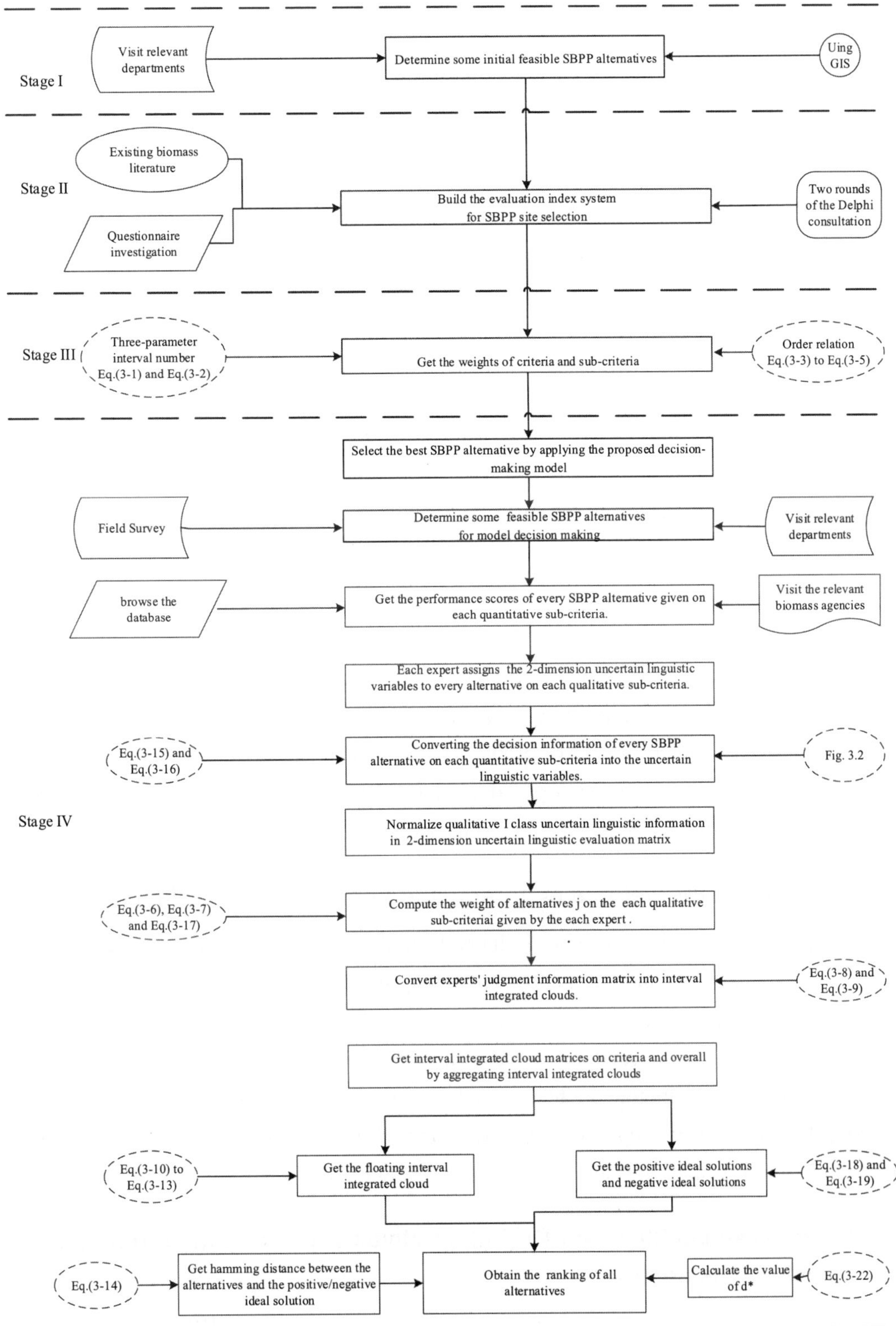

Fig.3.1 The four-stage decision framework for the optimal site selection of SBPP.

5.1 Stage I- determine some initial feasible SBPP alternatives

Rational application of information technology plays an important role in determine some initial feasible SBPP alternatives. In this stage, GIS is used as a tool of decision-making. The tasks made in stage I can simplify the process of SBPP optimal site selection, reduce the decision-making workload and improve decision efficiency. The stage I includes following two steps:

Step 1. Junior managers use the GIS to determine some preliminary alternatives, middle-level project managers do field investigation to form a list of alternatives according to the analysis of relevant data, such as local electric demand, straw-mulch amount, etc.

Step 2. Advanced project managers negotiate with local government departments to make further investigations on the sites listed in the table, adjust some alternatives so as to make the model evaluation.

5.2 Stage II- build the evaluation index system for SBPP site selection

The establishment of evaluation index for SBPP site selection should be based on the existing research and understanding of the current development situation of SBPP. Stage II includes following two steps:

Step 1. Doing the studies on the existing biomass literature and carry on questionnaire investigation to the experts, primary key factors associated with economy, social issue, environment and risk which have heavy impacts on SBPP site selection are obtained.

Step 2. Forming the evaluation index system though second rounds of the Delphi consultation. In this step, some factors are changed and canceled.

5.3 Stage III-get the weights of criteria and sub-criteria of evaluation indexes

This paper applies three-parameter interval number and order relation to determine the weights. Three-parameter interval number containing three possible values is the improvement to the traditional interval number which is composed of two parameters, scores given to each index can be more specific and more reasonable by using three-parameter interval number instead of employing the traditional interval number. Stage III include following two steps:

Step 1. Determine the importance of criteria and sub-criteria by Eq. (3-1) and Eq. (3-2).

Step 2. Index weights are calculated by Eq. (3-3) to Eq. (3-5).

5.4 Stage IV- select the best SBPP alternative by applying the proposed decision-making model

Stage IV mainly include eight steps designed for selecting the best SBPP alternative, details are as follows:

Step 1. Getting the decision information of every SBPP alternative on each quantitative sub-criteria.

In order to get the credible results, decision committee sends some engineers to conducted spot investigation of all SBPP alternatives. Moreover, some information managers visit the relevant biomass agencies and browse the database to collect the data on which the study is based. Finally, data processors are responsible to summarize and analyze the obtained data, satisfied performance scores are gotten.

This paper uses interval number $[u_{ij}, v_{ij}]$ to express the decision information of the alternative i on quantitative sub-criteria j.

Step 2. Each expert assigning the 2-dimension uncertain linguistic variables to every alternative on each qualitative sub-criteria.

First of all, committee members are divided into several specific groups according to knowledge, research direction and practice area. Then the members of those specific groups assess the specific groups of indicators. For example, risk factors are evaluated by the member groups of risk assessment.

In this paper, the 2-dimension uncertain linguistic variables are expressed as $E_{ij}^k = ([a_{ij}^k, b_{ij}^k], [c_{ij}^k, d_{ij}^k])$, $i = 1, 2, \ldots, m$, $j = 1, 2, \ldots, n$, $k = i, 2, \ldots, l$. Among them, $[a_{ij}^k, b_{ij}^k]$ represents that the judgment of the expert E_k to the SBPP alternatives i on qualitative sub-criteria j, $[c_{ij}^k, d_{ij}^k]$ represents the corresponding reliability.

In this paper, the linguistic judgment set is defined as $S =$ ($s_0 =$ extremely poor $s_1 =$ very poor , $s_2 =$ poor , $s_3 =$ fair , $s_4 =$ good , $s_6 =$ extremely good), the linguistic reliability set is defined as $H =$ ($h_0 =$ extremely poor , $h_1 =$ very unbelievable , $h_2 =$ unbelievable , $h_3 =$ fair , $h_4 =$ credible , $h_5 =$ very credible , h_6=extremely credible).

Step 3. Converting the decision information of every SBPP alternative on each quantitative sub-criteria into the uncertain linguistic variables.

Extremum processing is a very common and mature standardized processing method that is used in many studies to process data. The numerical values of performance of alternatives can be standardized through the following formulas:

$$y_{ji} = \frac{r_{ji} - \min_j r_{ji}}{\max_j r_{ji} - \min_j r_{ji}} \tag{3-15}$$

$$y_{ji} = \frac{\max_j r_{ji} - r_{ji}}{\max_j r_{ji} - \min_j r_{ji}} \tag{3-16}$$

where r_{ji} stands by the numerical value of the i_{th} alternative under the j_{th} index or sub-index. The concrete semantics of five linguistic assessment terms can be seen in Fig. 3.2 (Wu et al.,

2014).

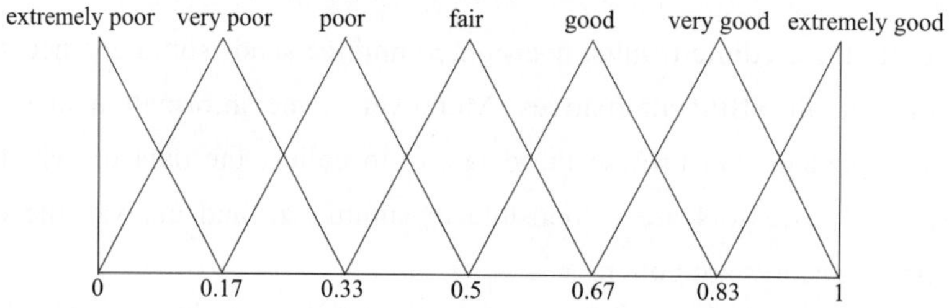

Fig. 3.2 The concrete semantics of seven linguistic assessment alternatives.

Therefore, the decision information $[u_{ij}, v_{ij}]$ can be converted into corresponding linguistic judgment value $[s_p, s_q]$ based on Fig. 3.2, can be normalized by Eq. (3-15) and Eq. (3-16), where $p = 1,2,...,5$, $q = 1,2,...,5$, $p \leqslant q$.

Step 4. Normalizing I class uncertain linguistic information in the 2-dimension uncertain linguistic evaluation matrix.

For the profit criteria, they require no change. For the cost benefit criteria, the normalized value is the opposite of the original value. For example, if linguistic judgment set is defined as $S = (s_0, s_1, ..., s_l)$, $[s_i, s_j]$ is I class uncertain linguistic information, $0 \leqslant i \leqslant j \leqslant l$, the normalized value is $[s_{l-j}, s_{l-i}]$.

Step 5. Computing the weight of alternatives i on the sub-criteria j given by the expert E_k.

The level of experts depends on their own knowledge and experience, so there are differences in the weight of alternatives i on the sub-criteria j given by the expert E_k. The weight p_{ij}^k in his paper is depended on the corresponding II class uncertain linguistic information, can be calculated by Eq. (3-7) and Eq. (3-17).

$$q_{ij}^k = \frac{p_{ij}^k}{\sum_{K=1}^{n} p_{ij}^k} \tag{3-17}$$

where $j = 1,2,...,n$, $i = 1,2,...,m$.

Step 6. Converting experts' judgment information matrix $E = [u_{ij}, v_{ij}]_{m\times n}$ into interval integrated clouds.

The matrix $E = [u_{ij}, v_{ij}]_{m\times n}$ can be converted into interval integrated clouds $\tilde{y}_{ij}^k = ([\underline{Ex_{ij}^k}, \overline{Ex_{ij}^k}], En_{ij}^k, He_{ij}^k)$, $i-1,2,...,m$, $j-1,2,...,n$, $k-i,2,...,l$ .by Eq. (3-8) and Eq. (3-9).

Step 7. Getting interval integrated cloud matrices on each criteria and overall by aggregating interval integrated clouds.

Using Eq. (3-10) to Eq. (3-13) to get the floating interval integrated cloud.

Step 8. Obtaining the sort order of all alternatives.

Getting the positive ideal solutions y_i^+ and negative ideal solutions y_i^- by Eq. (3-18)and Eq. (3-19).

$$y^+ = ([\max \underline{Ex_i}, \max \overline{Ex_i}], \min En_i, \min He_i) \tag{3-18}$$

$$y^- = ([\min \underline{Ex_i}, \min \overline{Ex_i}], \max En_i, \max He_i) \tag{3-19}$$

Hamming distance between the alternatives and the positive/negative ideal solution can be gotten by the Eq. (3-14). $d_i^+ = (y_i, y^+)$ is the Hamming distances between the alternatives and the positive ideal solution, $d_i^- = (y_i, y^-)$ is the Hamming distances between the alternatives and the negative ideal solution. Then, d_i^* can be obtained by Eq. (3-20).

$$d_i^* = \frac{d_i^-}{d_i^+ + d_i^-} \tag{3-20}$$

The larger d_i^* is, the better the performance is.

Then, managers get the orders of alternatives on each criteria and overall performance according to the corresponding ranking of the d_i^*, do the further analysis and select the best SBPP alternatives.

6. A case study

A foreign energy investment company M mainly involves in overseas investment business, regards the development of foreign investment as the company's long-term strategic objective to improve the company's comprehensive competitiveness and popularity in the international energy sector. Now company M has invested several SBPPs in many foreign countries, plans to enter the Chinese market to build a 25 MV SBPP. The company M adopts the following decision procedure to get the optimal SBPP site.

Stage I. Determining some initial feasible SBPP alternatives.

Due to the fact the company M is unfamiliar with Chinese biomass development situation, investment evaluation committee is made up of Chinese experts. The committee is composed of three main experts, all of whom are professors. Expert E1 is an outstanding scholar in the field of SBPP project management and has a solid foundation for theoretical research. The research direction of expert E2 is investment decision. He has been responsible for the investment decision analysis of power grid and government projects on many occasions. Expert E3 has many years of experience in power engineering construction. The three experts have certain understanding of the investment environment and policies for SBPP projects. At first, the company M understands the operation of the SBPP through company management information system, makes database analysis. Then, company M uses GIS to get some preliminary alternatives and conducts on-the-spot investigations and studies.

The investment evaluation committee chooses seven preliminary alternatives: A, B, C, D, E, F, G. However, E and F occupy the position of future highway traffic, the Local science and technology gardens will locate in G. That is to say, E, F and G clash with the local government development planning and must be excluded. So, A, B, C and D are finally four alternatives. A is located in Northwest of China, Gansu province. B is located at North China, Hebei Province. C is located at the Northeast of China, Jilin province. D is located at the coast of China, Jiangsu province.

Stage II. Building the evaluation index system for SBPP site selection.

Local thermal power plants can guarantee the normal supply heating in A, B and C The temperature is relatively high in D throughout the year. So, four places don't need heating in the winter, heating area is not included in the evaluation index system. Finally, the evaluation index system consists of 4 first class indicators and 15 second class indicators and all are shown in Table 3.1. Economic factor includes biomass purchase price and fuel reserve besides the feed-in tariff, land cost. Risk factor includes the policy support besides external competitiveness.

Stage III. Getting the weights of criteria and sub-criteria of evaluation indexes, the weight results can be seen in Table 3.3.

Table 3.3 The corresponding weights of the criteria and sub-criteria.

criteria	weights	sub-criteria	weights
a	0.4203	a1	0.0175
		a2	0.1223
		a3	0.3575
		a4	0.0506
		a5	0.2412
		a6	0.1912
		a7	0.0211
b	0.1327	b1	0.5372
		b2	0.4629
c	0.2108	c1	0.3823
		c2	0.4277
		c3	0.1903
d	0.2365	d1	0.2073
		d2	0.2529
		d3	0.5413

From the table 3.3, the weights of economic factor, social factor, environmental factor and risk factor are 0.4203, 0.1327, 0.2108, 0.2365. Economy is the most important factor, more important than the three others. The sub important one is the risk. Social factor is the least important one, has small impacts on the optimal site selection of SBPP.

The economic performances are mainly affected by the biomass purchase price (0.36), the feed-in tariff (0.24) and the purchase subsidy (0.19). Risk factor mainly comes from external competitiveness (0.54). So, the alternative which performances outstandingly good in economy and risk has the potential to be the best.

Stage IV. Selecting the best SBPP alternative by applying the proposed decision-making model.

Step 1. Getting the performance scores of every SBPP alternative on each quantitative sub-criterion, the corresponding performance scores are shown in Table 3.4.

Table 3.4 The decision information of alternatives on each qualitative indicator.

Sub-criteria	A	B	C	D
a2	[630, 810]	[840, 960]	[760, 840]	[820, 920]
a3	[230, 256]	[245, 285]	[230, 260]	[200, 235]
a4	[16.5, 19]	[16, 18]	[19, 21]	[17, 19]
a5	[0.2, 0.21]	[0.22, 0.24]	[0.23, 0.24]	[0.23, 0.25]
a6	[38, 48]	[42, 50]	[45, 58]	[46, 52]
a7	[6400, 6600]	[6300, 6500]	[6400, 6700]	[6600, 6800]
c2	[23, 26]	[25, 27]	[26, 28]	[25, 27]
c3	[17.5, 19]	[18, 19]	[19, 20]	[19, 20.5]

Step 2. Each expert assigns the 2-dimension uncertain linguistic variables to each qualitative sub-criteria of every alternative, so the performance of qualitative sub-criteria are measured by the corresponding scores of linguistic variables given by three experts E1, E2 and E3. the corresponding evaluation matrices made by E2 are shown in Table 3.5.

Table 3.5 Evaluation matrix of 2-dimension uncertain linguistic variables made by the expert E1.

Sub-criteria	A	B	C	D
a1	$[(s_0,s_2),(h_2,h_3)]$	$[(s_4,s_6),(h_1,h_2)]$	$[(s_4,s_6),(h_2,h_3)]$	$[(s_3,s_4),(h_3,h_4)]$
b1	$[(s_0,s_1),(h_4,h_5)]$	$[(s_2,s_3),(h_3,h_4)]$	$[(s_4,s_6),(h_2,h_3)]$	$[(s_2,s_3),(h_2,h_3)]$
b2	$[(s_2,s_4),(h_2,h_3)]$	$[(s_3,s_4),(h_2,h_3)]$	$[(s_2,s_4),(h_3,h_4)]$	$[(s_4,s_5),(h_3,h_5)]$
c1	$[(s_2,s_4),(h_2,h_3)]$	$[(s_3,s_4),(h_3,h_5)]$	$[(s_2,s_4),(h_2,h_4)]$	$[(s_4,s_5),(h_1,h_2)]$
d1	$[(s_1,s_2),(h_4,h_6)]$	$[(s_0,s_2),(h_3,h_5)]$	$[(s_2,s_4),(h_2,h_3)]$	$[(s_0,s_2),(h_1,h_3)]$
d2	$[(s_2,s_3),(h_3,h_5)]$	$[(s_1,s_3),(h_0,h_2)]$	$[(s_3,s_4),(h_1,h_2)]$	$[(s_2,s_3),(h_0,h_2)]$
d3	$[(s_2,s_4),(h_2,h_3)]$	$[(s_1,s_2),(h_3,h_5)]$	$[(s_0,s_3),(h_4,h_5)]$	$[(s_2,s_3),(h_3,h_5)]$

Step 3. Converting the decision information into the uncertain linguistic variables, the results can be seen in Table 3.6.

Table 3.6 The results of converting the qualitative decision information into the uncertain linguistic variables.

Sub-criteria	A	B	C	D
a2	$[s_0,s_3]$	$[s_4,s_6]$	$[s_2,s_4]$	$[s_3,s_5]$
a3	$[s_2,s_4]$	$[s_0,s_3]$	$[s_2,s_3]$	$[s_4,s_6]$
a4	$[s_2,s_5]$	$[s_4,s_6]$	$[s_0,s_2]$	$[s_2,s_5]$
a5	$[s_0,s_1]$	$[s_2,s_5]$	$[s_4,s_5]$	$[s_4,s_6]$
a6	$[s_0,s_3]$	$[s_1,s_4]$	$[s_2,s_6]$	$[s_3,s_4]$
a7	$[s_2,s_5]$	$[s_4,s_6]$	$[s_1,s_5]$	$[s_0,s_2]$
c2	$[s_0,s_4]$	$[s_2,s_5]$	$[s_4,s_6]$	$[s_2,s_5]$
c3	$[s_0,s_3]$	$[s_1,s_3]$	$[s_3,s_5]$	$[s_3,s_6]$

Step 4. Normalizing I class uncertain linguistic information; the normalized matrix is shown in Table 3.7.

Table 3.7 The standardized results of evaluation matrix of 2-dimension uncertain linguistic variables made by E1.

Sub-criteria	A	B	C	D
a1	$[(s_0,s_2),(h_2,h_3)]$	$[(s_4,s_6),(h_1,h_2)]$	$[(s_4,s_6),(h_2,h_3)]$	$[(s_3,s_4),(h_3,h_4)]$
b1	$[(s_0,s_1),(h_4,h_5)]$	$[(s_2,s_3),(h_3,h_4)]$	$[(s_4,s_6),(h_2,h_3)]$	$[(s_2,s_3),(h_2,h_3)]$
b2	$[(s_2,s_4),(h_2,h_3)]$	$[(s_3,s_4),(h_2,h_3)]$	$[(s_2,s_4),(h_3,h_4)]$	$[(s_4,s_5),(h_3,h_5)]$
c1	$[(s_2,s_4),(h_2,h_3)]$	$[(s_3,s_4),(h_3,h_5)]$	$[(s_2,s_4),(h_2,h_4)]$	$[(s_4,s_5),(h_1,h_2)]$
d1	$[(s_1,s_2),(h_4,h_6)]$	$[(s_0,s_2),(h_3,h_5)]$	$[(s_2,s_4),(h_2,h_3)]$	$[(s_0,s_2),(h_1,h_3)]$
d2	$[(s_2,s_3),(h_3,h_5)]$	$[(s_1,s_3),(h_0,h_2)]$	$[(s_3,s_4),(h_1,h_2)]$	$[(s_2,s_3),(h_0,h_2)]$
d3	$[(s_2,s_4),(h_2,h_3)]$	$[(s_4,s_5),(h_3,h_5)]$	$[(s_3,s_6),(h_4,h_5)]$	$[(s_3,s_4),(h_3,h_5)]$

Step 5. Computing the relative weight of alternatives i on the sub-criteria j given by the expert Ek, where the BUM function is $\rho(y)=y^4$, results is show in Table 3.8.

Table 3.8 Weight of alternatives *i* on the sub-criteria *j* given by the expert E1.

	A	B	C	D
a1	0.379	0.154	0.289	0.410
b1	0.700	0.471	0.244	0.314
b2	0.379	0.379	0.471	0.340
c1	0.250	0.472	0.300	0.214
d1	0.367	0.654	0.314	0.333
d2	0.370	0.065	0.240	0.095
d3	0.393	0.486	0.420	0.472

Step 6. Converting experts' judgment information matrix $E=[u_{ij},v_{ij}]_{m\times n}$ into interval integrated clouds.

Assume that the effective domain is $[0,14]$, therefore the numerical characteristics of seven clouds can be in Table 3.9. And the relevant cloud marix can be shown in Table 3.10 to Table 3.13.

Table 3.9 Numerical characteristics of seven clouds.

Linguistic term set	*Ex*	*En*	*He*
s6	14	2.334	0.212
s5	9.674	1.442	0.131
s4	8.337	0.891	0.081
s3	7	0.551	0.05
s2	5.663	0.891	0.081
s1	4.326	1.442	0.131
s0	0	2.334	0.212

Table 3.10 Interval integrated cloud matrix on quantitative sub-criteria.

Sub-criteria	A	B	C	D
a2	([0.00,7.00],2.40,0.22)	([8.34,14.00],2.50,0.23)	([5.66,8.34],1.26,0.11)	([7.00,9.67],1.54,0.14)
a3	([5.66,8.34],1.26,0.11)	([0.00,7.00],2.40,0.22)	([5.66,7.00],1.05,0.10)	([8.34,14.00],2.50,0.23)
a4	([5.66,9.67],1.70,0.15)	([8.34,14.00],2.50,0.23)	([0.00,5.66],2.50,0.23)	([5.66,9.67],1.70,0.15)
a5	([0.00,4.33],2.74,0.25)	([5.66,9.67],1.70,0.15)	([8.34,9.67],1.70,0.15)	([8.34,14.00],2.50,0.23)
a6	([0.00,7.00],2.40,0.22)	([4.33,8.34],1.70,0.15)	([5.66,14.00],2.50,0.23)	([7.00,8.34],1.05,0.10)
a7	([5.66,9.76],1.70,0.15)	([8.34,14.00],2.50,0.23)	([4.33,9.67],2.04,0.19)	([0.00,5.66],2.50,0.23)
c2	([0.00,8.34],2.50,0.23)	([5.66,9.67],1.70,0.15)	([8.34,14.00],2.50,0.23)	([5.66,9.67],1.70,0.15)
c3	([0.00,7.00],2.40,0.22)	([4.33,7.00],1.54,0.14)	([7.00,9.67],1.54,0.14)	([7.00,14.00],2.40,0.22)

Table 3.11 Interval integrated cloud matrix on qualitative sub-criteria by expert E1.

Sub-criteria	A	B	C	D
a1	([0.00,5.66],2.50,0.23)	([8.34,14.00],2.50,0.23)	([8.34,14.00],2.50,0.23)	([7.00,8.34],1.05,0.10)
b1	([0.00,4.33],2.74,0.25)	([5.66,7.00],1.05,0.10)	([8.34,14.00],2.50,0.23)	([5.66,7.00],1.05,0.10)
b2	([5.66,8.34],1.26,0.11)	([7.00,8.34],1.05,0.10)	([5.66,8.34],1.26,0.11)	([8.34,9.67],1.70,0.15)
c1	([5.66,8.34],1.26,0.11)	([7.00,8.34],1.05,0.10)	([5.66,8.34],1.26,0.11)	([8.34,9.67],1.70,0.15)
d1	([4.33,5.66],1.70,0.15)	([0.00,5.66],2.50,0.23)	([5.66,8.34],1.26,0.11)	([0.00,5.66],2.50,0.23)
d2	([5.66,7.00],1.05,0.10)	([8.34,9.67],1.70,0.15)	([7.00,8.34],1.05,0.10)	([5.66,7.00],1.05,0.10)
d3	([5.66,8.34],1.26,0.11)	([4.33,7.00],1.54,0.14)	([7.00,14.00],2.40,0.22)	([7.00,8.34],1.05,0.10)

Table 3.12 Interval integrated cloud matrix on qualitative indexes by experts' group.

Sub-criteria	A	B	C	D
a1	([3.47,7.28],1.52,0.29)	([6.49,8.90],1.54,0.28)	([7.77,10.93],1.92,0.31)	([8.20,11.68],2.13,0.35)
b1	([1.61,5.75],2.11,0.32)	([5.66,7.47],1.13,0.18)	([7.33,10.73],1.83,0.30)	([3.88,6.08],1.53,0.29)
b2	([5.66,8.34],1.26,0.20)	([5.34,7.18],1.34,0.23)	([4.19,6.69],1.51,0.31)	([7.88,10.60],1.82,0.29)
c1	([5.66,7.85],1.19,0.19)	([6.55,7.89],1.05,0.16)	([6.06,8.74],1.36,0.21)	([6.24,8.10],1.30,0.21)
d1	([4.68,6.02],1.49,0.24)	([1.70,5.87],1.99,0.29)	([2.65,6.50],1.73,0.30)	([3.78,6.68],1.34,0.27)
d2	([2.75,6.36],1.57,0.28)	([5.58,7.52],1.16,0.20)	([5.61,7.96],1.27,0.20)	([5.22,7.76],1.32,0.20)
d3	([5.95,8.62],1.33,0.21)	([7.23,9.25],1.55,0.24)	([5.77,9.94],1.93,0.28)	([7.00,8.78],1.22,0.19)

Step 7. Interval integrated cloud matrix on first-grade index and overall by aggregating interval integrated clouds.

Table 3.13 Interval integrated cloud matrix on first-grade index and overall.

	A	B	C	D
a	([2.50,7.03],1.74,0.30)	([3.89,9.26],2.09,0.33)	([6.04,9.20],1.64,0.28)	([7.62,11.98],2.15,0.33)
b	([3.47,6.94],1.58,0.14)	([5.51,7.34],1.22,0.08)	([5.88,8.87],1.72,0.19)	([5.72,8.16],1.71,0.17)
c	([2.15,7.90],1.82,0.13)	([5.75,8.49],1.42,0.07)	([7.22,11.18],1.98,0.12)	([6.13,9.90],1.74,0.12)
d	([4.88,7.51],1.40,0.18)	([5.66,8.11],1.51,0.18)	([5.07,8.72],1.74,0.21)	([5.88,8.09],1.26,0.15)
overall	([3.13,7.32],1.64,0.16)	([4.92,8.57],1.69,0.15)	([6.03,9.46],1.77,0.17)	([6.64,10.11],1.84,0.17)

Step 8. Obtaining the ranking order of all alternatives, the final decision information of alternatives under first-grade index and overall can be seen in Table 3.14 to Table 3.19.

(1) In terms of economic factor, $y_a^+ = ([7.62,11.98],1.68,0.28)$, $y_a^- = ([2.50,7.03],2.15,0.22)$.

Table 3.14 The final decision information of alternatives under the economic factor.

	A	B	C	D
d_{ai}^+	5.11	3.68	2.18	0.52
d_{ai}^-	0.44	1.87	3.37	5.03
d_{ai}^*	0.08	0.34	0.61	0.91
order	4	3	2	1

The ranking order of alternatives under economic factor is $D > C > B > A$.

(2) In terms of social factor, $y_b^+ = ([5.88,8.87],1.22,0.08)$, $y_b^- = ([3.47,6.94],1.72,0.19)$.

Table 3.15 The final decision information of alternatives under the social factor.

	A	B	C	D
d_{bi}^+	2.59	0.95	0.60	1.00
d_{bi}^-	0.18	1.82	2.17	1.77
d_{bi}^*	0.07	0.66	0.78	0.64
order	4	2	1	3

The ranking order of alternatives under social factor is $C > B > D > A$.

(3) In terms of environmental factor, $y_c^+ = ([7.22,11.18],1.42,0.07)$, $y_a^- = ([2.15,7.90],1.98,0.13)$.

Table 3.16 The final decision information of alternatives under the environmental factor.

	A	B	C	D
d_{ci}^+	4.63	2.08	0.61	1.54
d_{ci}^-	0.17	2.72	4.19	3.26
d_{ci}^*	0.04	0.57	0.87	0.68
order	4	3	1	2

The ranking order of alternatives under environmental factor is $C > D > B > A$.

(4) In terms of risk factor, $y_d^+ = ([5.88, 8.72], 1.26, 0.15)$, $y_d^- = ([4.88, 7.51], 1.74, 0.21)$.

Table 3.17 The final decision information of alternatives under the risk factor.

	A	B	C	D
d_{di}^+	1.27	0.69	0.93	0.32
d_{di}^-	0.36	0.94	0.70	1.31
d_{di}^*	0.22	0.58	0.43	0.80
order	4	2	3	1

The ranking order of alternatives under risk factor is $D > B > C > A$.

(5) In terms of the overall, $y_{overall}^+ = ([6.64, 10.11], 1.64, 0.15)$, $y_{overall}^- = ([3.13, 7.32], 1.84, 0.17)$.

Table 3.18 The final decision information of alternatives under the overall.

	A	B	C	D
$d_{overall\ i}^+$	3.16	1.68	0.78	0.22
$d_{overall\ i}^-$	0.21	1.69	2.60	3.15
$d_{overall\ i}^*$	0.06	0.50	0.77	0.93
order	4	3	2	1

The ranking order of alternatives under the overall is $D > C > B > A$.

Table 3.19 The rankings of alternatives under first-grade index and overall.

aspects of evaluation	A	B	C	D	rankings
(a) economic factor	0.08	0.34	0.61	0.91	$D > C > B > A$
(b) social factor	0.07	0.66	0.78	0.64	$C > B > D > A$
(c) environmental factor	0.04	0.57	0.87	0.68	$C > D > B > A$
(d) risk factor	0.22	0.58	0.43	0.80	$D > B > C > A$
overall	0.06	0.50	0.77	0.93	$D > C > B > A$

By comparing the performances of four alternatives under the economy, society, environment, risk and overall, the following conclusions can be drawn:

Among four alternatives, D performs best in economic factor and risk factor, has poor performance in social factor; C ranks first in social factor and environmental factor, performs worst in risk; A has worst performance in four criteria, the performance of B in four criteria is general or poor. On the overall, D is the best alternative, A is the worst alternative. For A and B, no further consideration is required. If C is chosen, risk factor should be improved substantially.

While the top managers regard the alternative D as the ideal project, the social factor should be paid more attention to. Moreover, the gap in d^* of the risk factor between C and D is wider than the gap in d^* of the social factor, the weight of social factor is bigger than the weight of risk factor. All in all, in general, D is better than C, can be considered as the best one of all alternatives.

The large gaps between the calculated results show that the method of 2-dimension uncertain linguistic variable and cloud model can synthetically aggregate the preference of experts in different indicators, more accurately reflect the expert's opinions, make a more intuitive and comprehensive comparison of the alternatives, well consider the reliability of the evaluation result. So, the decision makers can do a better decision-making according to the integrated information.

7. Discussion

In order to reflect the scientific nature and rationality of this decision-making method, in the process of sensitivity analysis, the paper changes the weight of one criteria while the weights of three other criteria are adjusted according to corresponding proportion of variations, the variations of one weight are graduated into five levels, which are −30%, −20%, −10%, 10%, 20% and 30%. The sensitivity analysis results can be seen in Fig. 3.3.

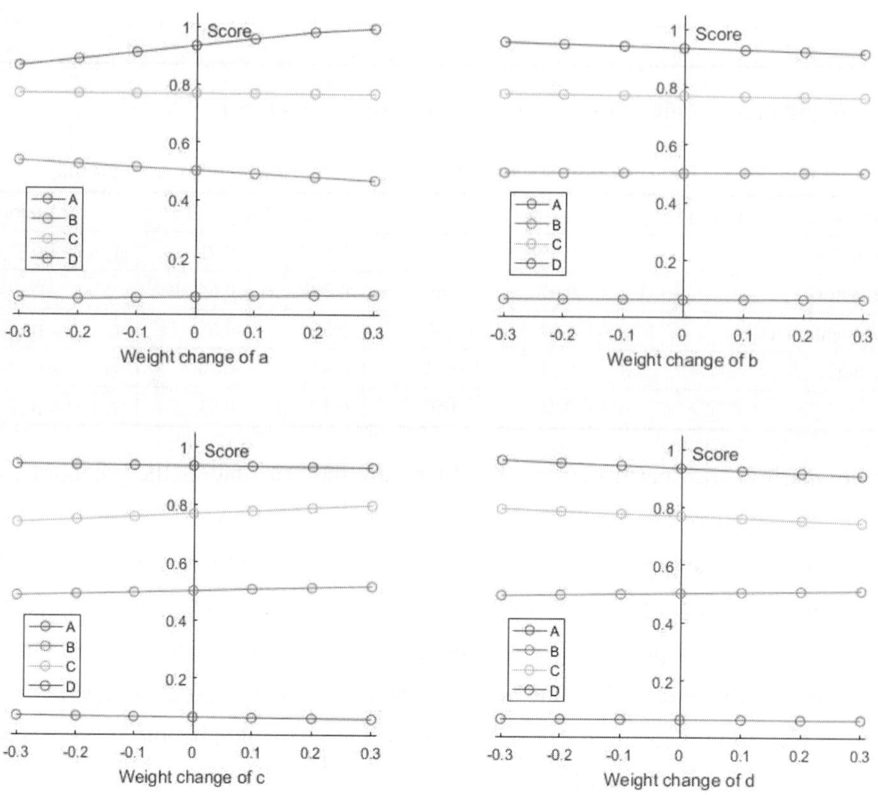

Fig. 3.3 The results of sensitivity analysis by changing the weights.

The overall consequences of the sensitivity analysis are that no matter how changes of criteria weights within plus or minus 30%, D is always the best alternative and its scores are much higher than other alternatives. At the same time, the ranking result of four alternatives is always D>C>B>A, which is extremely stable. Based on these robust results, it could be concluded that the method proposed in this study is effective and suitable for the optimal site selection of SBPP. In all the case of criteria weight fluctuation, the score of D remain relatively stable. In some extent, it means that D has less sensitive towards the changing of criteria weight. Nowadays, the government and general public are giving more and more attention to the ecological environment, and DMs consider more about ecological and environmental aspects when selecting a SBPP site. In terms of c (environment impacts), A, B, and D all have no chance to surpass C since the scores of four alternatives are all relatively stable. the evaluation results have strong robustness by using 2-dimension uncertain linguistic variable and cloud model to select the optimal site selection of SBPP.

8. Conclusion

The optimal site selection is extremely important for SBPP. Now there are some studies about SBPP, the pity is that some problems which reduce the quality of assessment are not resolved: Firstly, existing evaluation index system is not comprehensive and lacks pertinence and practicability for SBPP. Secondly, information loss and index weight are not given enough attention to. Thirdly, independence of experts is not well considered. All of the problems mentioned above are not conducive to make a reasonable optimal site selection for SBPP needed to be solved urgently.

Consequently, the research of this paper focuses on building an evaluation index system for optimal site selection of SBPP, calculating the important degree of evaluation indexes, proposing a novel and practical optimal site selection decision-making model and establishing the decision framework for SBPP site selection. Specifically, main works and results include: firstly, this paper establishes a relatively perfect evaluation index system for SBPP optimal site selection which includes 4 first class indexes (economy, society, environment, risk) and 15 second class indexes, lays a solid foundation for further research. In this process, this study refers to some site selection researches of other types of new energy power plants, considers the concrete characteristics of SBPP; secondly, determining the important degree of evaluation indexes by combining three-parameter interval number and order relation which enhances the accuracy of the weight calculation, lets project manager clearly understand the critical factors which largely influence the final decision result; Thirdly, a novel group decision model based on 2-dimension uncertain linguistic variable and cloud mode is proposed for SBPP optimal site selection. This model solves the heavy problems about information loss and independence of experts very well.

The improvements having been made can increase credibility of decision making result. Then, the specialized decision framework is designed for SBPP site selection. This framework can help decision makers save a lot time, raise their level of understanding of decision-making process. Furthermore, a case study is performed to rank and compare the four alternatives in China. The results show that the comprehensive performance of D is better than the three others. So, among the four alternatives, D is the best one. At the same time, the performances of the four alternatives in the first class, indicators are compared and analyzed in detail. Finally, the decision result is turned out to have good robustness by carrying out a sensitivity analysis.

Straw biomass power generation is a way of using clean energy. The model framework proposed in this paper not only provides reference for the site selection of straw biomass power plants, but also enriches the theoretical methods in the field of clean production. The significance of the research lies in that it both extends theoretical research, but also has guide meaning to practical engineering applications. Although this article has done a lot of work in the process of research, because of the limitations of various resources and time, the following aspects need to be further studied in the following aspects:

According to the needs of the construction of the evaluation index system, this paper can be divided into four categories and a total of fifteen sub categories. This paper holds that these four classifications cover the factors to be considered in the process of construction site selection, and can meet the requirements of the address. However, whether this classification method causes individual factors of SBPP projects to be omitted, this paper does not further prove it, which is needed to be supplemented in the future research. In addition, whether the classification method can be further applied to other similar fields and promote others. Monitoring and management of types of projects is also worth considering in further research.

In this paper, an example analysis is added to verify the flow of the model through the calculation of the whole process and the demonstration of the analysis process, and it is easy for readers to understand the research ideas in depth. However, due to time and resources constraints, this paper does not carry out empirical analysis on the research, and actually applies the research results to the construction projects. Therefore, a lot of empirical research is needed to confirm the effect of the research.

To sum up, this research topic still has the value of further research. In the future research, researchers can pay more attention to the empirical study of theory and method, and apply the research results to various types of construction projects as much as possible, and test the validity and applicability of the framework and model in the empirical process. In view of the deficiencies in the empirical process, the research results are continuously improved.

Conflict of interests

The authors declare that there is no conflict of interests regarding the publication of this paper.

Acknowledgement

This research is supported by the Fundamental Research Funds for the Central Universities (No. 2018ZD14), the 2017 Special Project of Cultivation and Development of Innovation Base (No. Z171100002217024) and Fundamental Research Funds for the Central Universities (No.2017XS098).

References

[1] Adiarso G, Murti, W, Priyanto U. utilization of Biomass for Energy: Prospect, Challenge and Industrialization Strategy in Indonesia[J]. Journal of the Japan Institute of Energy, 2013, 92(1): 89-98.

[2] Ahi L, Chen H H, Kang H Y. Multi-criteria decision making on strategic selection of wind farms[J]. Renewable Energy, 2009,34(1): 120-126.

[3] Al Garni H Z, Awasthi,A. Solar PV power plant site selection using a GIS-AHP based approach with application in Saudi Arabia. [J] Applied Energy, 2017, 206: 1225-1240.

[4] Aly A, Jensen S S, Pedersen A B. Solar power potential of Tanzania: Identifying CSP and PV hot spots through a GIS multicriteria decision making analysis[J]. Renewable Energy, 2017, 113: 159-175.

[5] Aouadni S, Rebai A, Turskis Z. The Meaningful Mixed Data TOPSIS (TOPSIS-MMD) Method and its Application in Supplier Selection[J]. Studies in Informatics and Control, 2017, 26(3): 353-363.

[6] Atici K B, Simsek A B, Ulucan A, et al. A GIS-based Multiple Criteria Decision Analysis approach for wind power plant site selection[J]. Utilities Policy, 2015, 37: 86-96.

[7] Azadeh A, Haghighi S M, Zarrin M, et al. Performance evaluation of Iranian electricity distribution units by using stochastic data envelopment analysis[J]. International Journal of Electrical Power & Energy Systems, 2015, 73: 919-931.

[8] Brauers W K M, Zavadskas E K. The MOORA method and its application to privatization in a transition economy[J]. Control & Cybernetics, 2006, 35(35): 445-469.

[9] Brauers W K M, Zavadskas E K. Project management by multimoora as an instrument for transition economies[J]. Technological and Economic Development of Economy, 2010, 16(1): 5-24.

[10] Charnes A, Cooper W W, Li S. Using data envelopment analysis to evaluate efficiency in the economic performance of Chinese cities [J]. Socio-Economic Planning Sciences, 1989, 23(6): 325-344.

[11] Chen C, Huang G H, Li Y P, et al. Model of risk analysis on site selection of biomass power plant based on stochastic robust interval method[J]. Transactions of the Chinese Society of Agricultural Engineering, 2013,29(20): 206-213.

[12] Choudhary D, Shankar R. An STEEP-fuzzy AHP-TOPSIS framework for evaluation and selection of

thermal power plant location: A case study from India[J]. Energy, 2012, 42(1): 510-521.

[13] Cong C, Wei L, Li Y F, et al. Biomass power plant site selection modeling and decision optimization[J]. Transactions of the Chinese Society of Agricultural Engineering, 2011, 27(1): 255-260(256).

[14] Dias L C, Clímaco J N. On computing ELECTRE's credibility indices under partial information[J]. Journal of Multi - Criteria Decision Analysis, 1999, 8(2): 74-92.

[15] Diban P, Mustafa Kamal A A, Foo D C Y, et al. Optimal biomass plantation replanting policy using dynamic programming[J]. Journal of Cleaner Production, 2016, 126: 409-418.

[16] Fetanat A, Khorasaninejad E. A novel hybrid MCDM approach for offshore wind farm site selection: A case study of Iran[J]. Ocean & Coastal Management, 2015, 109: 17-28.

[17] García J L, Alvarado A, Blanco J, et al. Multi-attribute evaluation and selection of sites for agricultural product warehouses based on an Analytic Hierarchy Process[J]. Computers & Electronics in Agriculture, 2014, 100(1): 60-69.

[18] Golecha R. Variations in biomass transport cost of cellulosic biorefineries[J]. International Journal of Innovation & Sustainable Development, 2016, 11(4): 309.

[19] Guangzhi B U, Zhang Y. Grey Fuzzy Comprehensive Evaluation Method Based on Interval Numbers of Three Parameters[J]. Systems Engineering & Electronics,2001,23(9):43-46.

[20] Guikema S D. An estimation of the social costs of landfill siting using a choice experiment[J]. Waste Management, 2005, 25(3): 331-333.

[21] Haaren R V, Fthenakis V. GIS-based wind farm site selection using spatial multi-criteria analysis (SMCA): Evaluating the case for New York State[J]. Renewable & Sustainable Energy Reviews, 2011, 15(7) 3332-3340.

[22] Herrera F, Herrera-Viedma E, Martínez L. A fusion approach for managing multi-granularity linguistic term sets in decision making[J]. Fuzzy sets and systems, 2000, 114(1): 43-58.

[23] Herrera F, Martinez L. A model based on linguistic 2-tuples for dealing with multigranular hierarchical linguistic contexts in multi-expert decision-making[J]. IEEE Transactions on Systems Man & Cybernetics Part B Cybernetics A Publication of the IEEE Systems Man & Cybernetics Society, 2001, 31(2): 227.

[24] Wang H C-L, Yoon K. Methods for multiple attribute decision making, Multiple attribute decision making[M]. Springer, 1981.

[25] Jelokhani-Niaraki M, Malczewski J. A group multicriteria spatial decision support system for parking site selection problem: A case study[J]. Land Use Policy, 2015, 42(42): 492-508.

[26] Keršuliene V, Zavadskas E K, Turskis Z. Selection of rational dispute resolution method by applying new step - wise weight assessment ratio analysis (SWARA) [J]. Journal of business economics and management, 2010, 11(2): 243-258.

[27] Kontos T D, Komilis D P, Halvadakis C P. Siting MSW landfills with a spatial multiple criteria analysis methodology[J]. Waste Management, 2005, 25(8): 818-832.

[28] Kuo Y C, Lu S T, Tzeng G H, et al. Using Fuzzy Integral Approach to Enhance Site Selection Assessment – A Case Study of the Optoelectronics Industry [J]. Procedia Computer Science, 2013, 17: 306-313.

[29] Li D, Liu C, Gan W. A new cognitive model: cloud model[J]. International Journal of Intelligent Systems, 2009, 24(3): 357-375.

[30] Liu P. The research note of 2-dimension uncertain linguistic variables[D]. Jinan:Shandong University of Finance and Economics, 2012.

[31] Liu P, Yu X. 2-Dimension uncertain linguistic power generalized weighted aggregation operator and its application in multiple attribute group decision making[J]. Knowledge-based systems, 2014, 57:69-80.

[32] Liu X. Operation Status and Development Suggestions of Straw Power Generation Project in China[J]. Agricultural Engineering, 2017, 7 (5):66-67, 101.

[33] Mareschal B, Brans J P, Vincke P. PROMETHEE: A new family of outranking methods in multicriteria analysis[D]. ULB—Universite Libre de Bruxelles, 1984.

[34] Mulliner E, Smallbone K, Maliene V. An assessment of sustainable housing affordability using a multiple criteria decision making method[J]. Omega, 2013, 41(2): 270-279.

[35] Opricovic S. Multicriteria optimization of civil engineering systems[J]. Faculty of Civil Engineering, Belgrade, 1998, 2(1): 5-21.

[36] Pedrero F, Albuquerque A, Monte H M D, et al. Application of GIS-based multi-criteria analysis for site selection of aquifer recharge with reclaimed water[J]. Resources Conservation & Recycling, 2011, 56(1): 105-116.

[37] Perpiña C, Martínez-Llario J C, Pérez-Navarro Á. Multicriteria assessment in GIS environments for siting biomass plants[J]. Land Use Policy, 2013, 31(2): 326-335.

[38] Pileidis F D, Titirici M M. Levulinic Acid Biorefineries: New Challenges for Efficient Utilization of Biomass. Chemsuschem, 2016, 47(21): 562-582.

[39] Rauch P. Developing and evaluating strategies to overcome biomass supply risks[J]. Renewable energy, 2017, 103: 561-569.

[40] Rezaei J. Best-worst multi-criteria decision-making method[J]. Omega, 2015, 53: 49-57.

[41] Saaty, T L. The Analytic Hierarchy Process[M]. New York: McGraw-Hill Company,1980.

[42] Saaty T L. Vargas L G. The analytlc net work process[M]. Boston:Springer,2013.

[43] Şengül Ü, Eren M, Shiraz S E, et al. Fuzzy TOPSIS method for ranking renewable energy supply systems in Turkey[J]. Renewable Energy ,2015,75(C): 617-625.

[44] Shan M, Li D, Jiang Y, et al. Re-thinking china's densified biomass fuel policies: Large or small scale? [J].Energy Policy, 2016, 93: 119-126.

[45] Shi X, Elmore A, Xia L, et al. Using spatial information technologies to select sites for biomass power plants: a case study in Guangdong Province, China[J]. Biomass & Bioenergy, 2008, 32(1):35-43.

[46] Veza I, Celar S, Peronja I. Competences-based Comparison and Ranking of Industrial Enterprises Using PROMETHEE Method [J]. Procedia Engineering, 2015, 100: 445-449.

[47] Wan S P, Wang F, Lin L L, et al. An intuitionistic fuzzy linear programming method for logistics outsourcing provider selection[J]. Knowledge-Based Systems, 2015, 82: 80-94.

[48] Wang J, Wang J-q, Zhang H-y, et al. Multi-criteria group decision-making approach based on 2-tuple linguistic aggregation operators with multi-hesitant fuzzy linguistic information[J]. International Journal of Fuzzy Systems 2016, 18(1): 81-97.

[49] Wang J Q, Peng J J, Zhang H Y, et al. An Uncertain Linguistic Multi-criteria Group Decision-Making Method Based on a Cloud Model[J]. Group Decision & Negotiation, 2015, 24(1): 171-192.

[50] Wu Y, Chen K, Zeng B, et al. Cloud-based decision framework for waste-to-energy plant site selection - A case study from China[J]. Waste Management, 2016, 48: 593-603.

[51] Wu Y, Geng S, Zhang H, et al. Decision framework of solar thermal power plant site selection based on linguistic Choquet operator[J]. Applied Energy, 2014, 136(C): 303-311.

[52] Wu Y, Liu L, Gao J, et al. An extended vikor-based approach for pumped hydro energy storage plant site selection with heterogeneous information[J]. Information, 2017, 8(3): 106.

[53] Wu Y, Xu C, Ke Y, et al. An intuitionistic fuzzy multi-criteria framework for large-scale rooftop PV project portfolio selection: Case study in Zhejiang, China[J]. Energy, 2018, 143: 295-309.

[54] Wu Y, Xu C, Zhang T. Evaluation of renewable power sources using a fuzzy MCDM based on cumulative prospect theory: A case in China[J]. Energy, 2018, 147:1227-1239.

[55] Wu Y, Zhang J, Yuan J, et al. Study of decision framework of offshore wind power station site selection based on ELECTRE-III under intuitionistic fuzzy environment: A case of China[J]. Energy Conversion & Management, 2016, 113: 66-81.

[56] Xing Y-J, Xing C. Model for evaluating the virtual enterprise's risk with 2-tuple linguistic information[J]. Journal of Intelligent & Fuzzy Systems, 2016, 31(1): 193-200.

[57] Xu Z. Induced uncertain linguistic OWA operators applied to group decision making[J]. Information fusion, 2006, 7(2): 231-238.

[58] Yager R R. OWA aggregation over a continuous interval argument with applications to decision making[J]. IEEE Transactions on Systems, Man, and Cybernetics, Part B (Cybernetics), 2004, 34(5): 1952-1963.

[59] Yan S L, Liu S F, Zhu J J, et al. TOPSIS Decision-Making Method with Three-Parameter Interval Number Based on Entropy Measure[J]. Chinese Journal of Management Science, 2013, 6:147-153

[60] Yang J. Review and Analysis of Research about Biomass Energy Cost Problem[J]. Anhui Agricultural Sciences, 2011, 16:9759-9760,9826.

[61] Zavadskas E K, Antucheviciene J, Hajiagha S H R, et al. Extension of weighted aggregated sum product assessment with interval-valued intuitionistic fuzzy numbers (WASPAS-IVIF) [J]. Applied Soft Computing, 2014, 24: 1013-1021.

[62] Zavadskas E K, Mardani A, Turskis, Z, et al. Development of TOPSIS method to solve complicated decision-making problems: An overview on developments from 2000 to 2015[J]. International Journal of Information Technology & Decision Making, 2016, 15(3): 645-682.

[63] Zhang D Z, Zhang X, Cai Z S. Research on Classification and Utilization Technology of Biomass Energy [J]Anhui Agricultural Sciences, 2016, 8:81-83.

[64] Zhang H M, Ze-Shui X U. Uncertain linguistic information based C-OWA and C-OWG operators and their applications[J]. Journal of Pla University of Science & Technology, 2016, 6(6): 604-608.

[65] Zhao K, Gao J, Qi Z, et al. Multi-criteria risky-decision-making approach based on prospect theory and cloud model[J]. Control and Decision, 2015, 30(3): 395-402.

[66] Zoghi M, Ehsani A H, Sadat M, et al. Optimization solar site selection by fuzzy logic model and weighted linear combination method in arid and semi-arid region: A case study Isfahan-IRAN[J]. Renewable & Sustainable Energy Reviews, 2017, 68: 986-996.

[67] Zolfani S H, Saparauskas J. New application of SWARA method in prioritizing sustainability assessment indicators of energy system[J]. Engineering Economics, 2013, 24(5): 408-414.

Chapter 4

An extended TODIM-PROMETHEE method for waste-to-energy plant site selection based on sustainability perspective

Yunna Wu [a, b], Jing Wang[a, b*], Yong Hu[a, b], Yiming Ke[a, b], Lingwenying Li [a, b]

a. School of Economics and Management, North China Electric Power University, Beijing, China

b. Beijing Key Laboratory of New Energy and Low-Carbon Development (North China Electric Power University), Changping Beijing, 102206

Abstract: The waste-to-energy (WtE) project has attracted much attention from the society mainly because of the characteristic of environmental friendliness. And plant site selection occupies a prominent position during the whole life cycle of waste-to-energy project. In consideration of the ambiguity of subjective judgments of decision makers (DMs) and the compensation problem existing in decision process, we build a framework for WtE plant site selection decision utilizing a novel method with triangular intuitionistic fuzzy numbers (TIFNs). First of all, the criteria for optimal WtE plant siting are determined based on extended sustainability theory including four perspectives of economic, environment, society, and technology to meet the demand of current social development. Then, the TIFNs and the triangular intuitionistic fuzzy weighted geometric (TIFWG) operator are applied to describing the indefinite information and completing the conversion, so that the uncertainty and hesitation of decision information can be well expressed. Furthermore, the extended TODIM (an acronym in Portuguese of interactive and multiple attribute decision making) method in conjunction with PROMETHEE-II (Preference Ranking Organization Method for Enrichment Evaluations) method is utilized to rank the alternatives, which makes this framework more practical and applicable. Finally, a case from China certifies the validity of the proposed framework.

Key words: WtE plant site selection; sustainability; triangular intuitionistic fuzzy numbers; TODIM- PROMETHEE method

1. Introduction

With the rapid expansion of civilization, the generated quantity of municipal solid waste (MSW) is appearing an increasing tendency, which brings forward a higher requirement for daily waste disposal. Currently, there are three common modes to deal with the waste internationally, mainly landfill, incinerate and compost, but many countries including China are still landfill based (see Fig.4.1 and Fig.4.2). Compared to other modes, the WtE technology has the advantages of shorter processing cycle, less space demand, more suitable use in urban areas and helping realize the comprehensive utilization on resources. It is verified that combustible content and calorific value of waste in China's large city has reached the level of direct combustion [1]. Moreover, the number of the WtE plants shows continued growth in China in recent years (see Fig. 4.3) [2]. It is obvious that due to the construction of the WtE plants satisfying basic conditions, it gradually arouses more attention from the government and whole society.

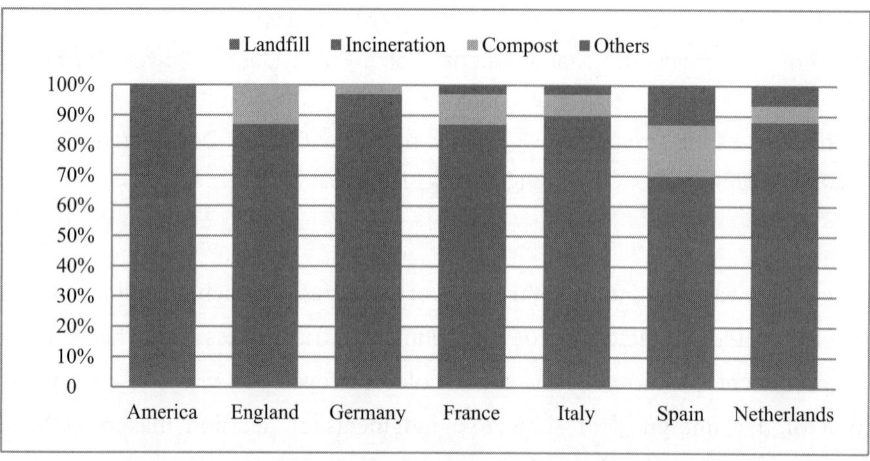

Fig. 4.1 The comparison of waste disposal methods among countries.

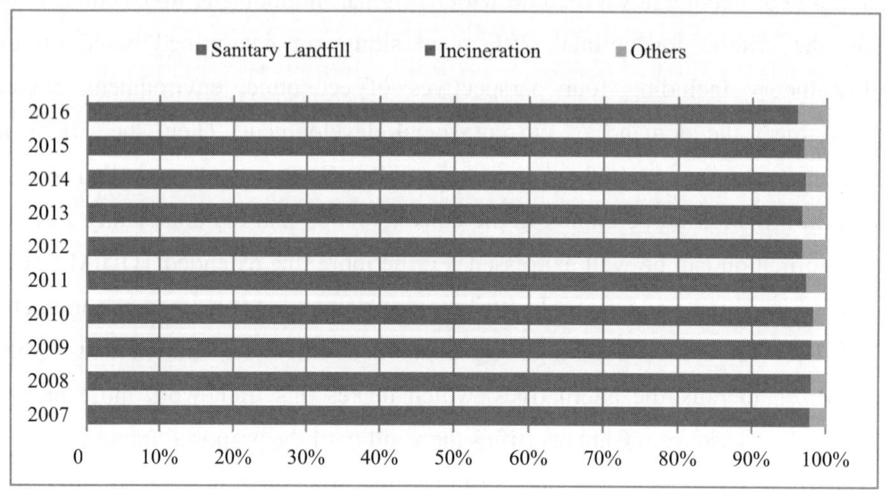

Fig. 4.2 The comparison of waste disposal methods in China.

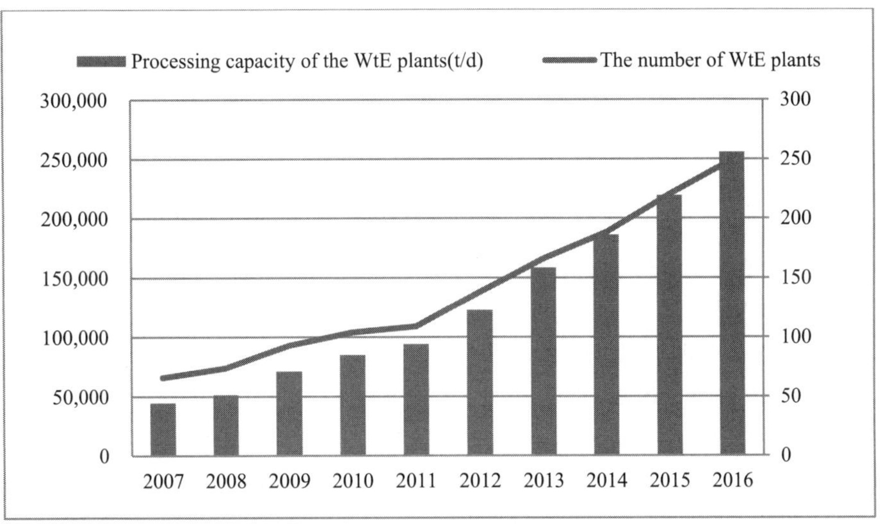

Fig. 4.3 The development of WtE plants in China.

The United Nations General Assembly (UNGA) first used the concept of "Sustainable development" in 1980. And in 1996, "Implement sustainable development" was definitely comprised in the strategic objectives in China. Many advantages as the WtE has, it is beneficial for us to select proper location to construct WtE plants. However, there existing numerous tangible and intangible factors influencing the site selection which need to be taken into consideration [2]. The WtE project is public welfare which has the characteristics of massive investment. Thus, it will exert a significant adverse impact on the residents living and sustainable development once the layout is unreasonable [3]. From this point of view, the WtE plant site selection will be performed based on the sustainability principles in this paper.

Generally speaking, "sustainability" stands for a long-term development which consists of three interlinked and inseparable dimensions: economic growth, social development and ecological protection [4, 5]. Squaring up the rapid development and diversity of technical conditions, it is conducive to append technology factors to expand the original concept to evaluate alternatives of the WtE plant site. The selection of the WtE plant site is a complex problem that relating to many aspects, for instance, it calls for favorable climate, geographical conditions, support of the residents and so forth. First, the natural terrain condition should get fully used in the site selection of the WtE plant project. Besides, the final layout is best to accord with local city planning. Second, the locations of WtE plants are far away from the city center in general. Thus, inappropriate siting will bring much inconvenience and increase unnecessary expenditure. Third, as for the support of residents, for one thing, waste incineration may produce harmful by-products, which may have a bad effect on health and normal life of local residents. For another, "Not In My Back Yard" (NIMBY) syndrome [6] widely occurring in residents will aggravate their resistance and dissatisfaction on the WtE project [7], and furthermore may become the biggest obstacle during the plant siting. As stated above, the WtE plant site selection means a MCDM problem actually. During the decision process, it is essential to incorporate the existing issues into consideration.

However, there are still many problems in the existing decision process for the WtE site selection, which makes current decision frameworks hardly fit in with the real situations. Thus this paper proposes a new tool for the WtE plant site selection based on a series of requirements for sustainable development.

(1) Due to the complexity and specificity of the environment in different regions, DMs usually have vague practical judgments. Besides, many factors influencing the WtE site selection are affected by DMs' preference, the level of both satisfaction and dissatisfaction cannot be accurately estimated [8]. For the sake of handling the vague and imprecise information in the real world, the fuzzy set is adopted to describe the vagueness. On the basis of Zadeh's traditional fuzzy set, we opt triangular intuitionistic fuzzy numbers (TIFNs) to describe the evaluation results. TIFNs take into consideration the maximum degree of membership, the minimum degree of non-membership and hesitation degree [9], so that it can convey more detailed information for situation description than triangular fuzzy numbers and help DMs express their opinions more easily and correctly during the WtE site selection.

(2) TODIM method is proposed to solve the MCDM problems according to DMs' behavior [10]. The classical TODIM method has two defects, on one hand, it is applicable for the problem in which attribute values are crisp numbers [11]; therefore, it is necessary to extend the TODIM method in order to adopt it to the circumstances that attributes values are in the form of fuzzy numbers in this paper. On the other hand, the compensation problem also exists in this method. As a result, the excellent performance in some criteria can make up for deficiencies in other criteria for some alternatives [12] and which may lead to inaccurate and dissatisfied results accordingly. In other words, some alternatives may have abysmal scores in some attributes while having significant advantages in else attributes, but it exerts little impact on ranking the forefront of all alternatives owing to the compensation problem. For these reasons, we combine PROMETHEE-II method with TODIM method to compensate for deficiencies to rank the alternatives. In real situations, this extended method is more practical and applicable which can help DMs choose the best WtE plant site.

The remainder of this paper is organized as follows: Section 2 reviews the literature which related to the WtE plant site selection and the current application of method used in this paper. Section 3 analyzes the factors affecting the site selection and builds an sustainable evaluation index system for WtE plant site selection. Section 4 elaborates the basic theories of fuzzy set, TIFNs and the extend TODIM method, illustrates the detailed framework for the WtE plant site selection as well. Section 5 demonstrates the whole process with a case in China. Section 6 proceeds a sensitivity analysis. Section 7 draws the conclusion.

2. Literature reviews

A scientific evaluation index system, an exact expression of indeterminate information and a convincing ranking method occupy a vital position in the decision making of WtE site selection.

2.1 WtE site selection criteria

In terms of the evaluation system, the characteristics of the WtE plant site selection are discussed from various angles in previous studies. Hu and Li [13] took into account environmental implication, public health and participation mainly and then established an evaluation system. Zhao et al. [14] comprehensively explored economic influence such as return on investment, net present value, internal rate of return, and so on. A set of sustainability assessment system was raised by Edmundas [2] which focused on 13 indicators in engineering, environmental, social and economic areas. Hadjibiros [15] devised solutions that the MSW should be in line with technical feasibility, public acceptance and environment sustainability. Mahnaz[16] divided the evaluation criteria into three categories from the standpoint of DMs: environmental, economical and socio-cultural. Savva [17] stood on environmental, economical and marketing aspects to illustrate the operation of WtE plants with a case. Huo and Cao [18] gave an in-depth assessment of the suitability of four alternative landfills in Guangzhou and chose natural, geographical factors, engineering geology factors as well as environmental factors for evaluation. Xiang et al. [19] further explored a more preferable site for the construction of WtE plants based on the scope of human health risk assessment. Even though previous studies have comprehensive coverage for indicators, rare papers discuss the WtE plant site selection out of consideration for sustainable points.

2.2 The fuzzy numbers

In the aspect of the description of information, more and more scholars started to generalize the use of Zadeh's fuzzy set theory to make decisions more applicable to the actual practice. The fuzzy numbers are usually employed by DMs to conduct their assessments, which are more available in disposing of uncertain, incomplete and ambiguous information compared with traditional quantitative representations [20]. In recent research of site selection, a triangular fuzzy number has become the most popular among fuzzy numbers. Li and Zhao [21] converted linguistic values to numerical values in determining the optimal siting of electric vehicle charging stations (EVCSs) within the context of triangular fuzzy numbers. Kengpol et al. [22] utilized the triangular fuzzy numbers to interpret the fuzzy event occurring in the decision-making of solar-thermal power plant locations. Besides, intuitionistic fuzzy sets (IFS) have also been widely applied in MCDM problems. Atanassov's intuitionistic fuzzy sets (A-IFSs) are used for performing transformations from linguistic terms to quantitative information [23]. Wu and Zhang [13] handled the incomplete information with the help of IFSs during the offshore wind power station site selection. However, IFSs are only applicable to discrete domains. Triangular intuitionistic fuzzy numbers (TIFNs) whose nonmembership and membership degrees are triangular fuzzy numbers instead of crisp values and intervals were put forward to applying to consecutive sets [24]. Hence, TIFNs may perform better in reflecting the indefinite and ill-known quantities of decision information than IFSs [25]. And that's why TIFNs are chosen to reveal the information of DMs in this paper.

2.3 Ranking methods

From the perspective of the selection of ranking methods, with a view to make it become more scientific and complete, many scholars have put their efforts in it. Pablo [26] applied the AHP and the ANP together to help the managing board of a Spanish investment company to determine whether to invest the solar power plant project. Liu and You [27] introduced attitudinal-based interval 2-tuple linguistic VIKOR method in the WtE plant site selection to select the best site. Sehnaz and Giovanni [28, 29] integrated AHP with a geographic information system (GIS) to screen the geographical information and get the most suitable site from alternatives. A modified fuzzy TOPSIS method was presented by Mehmet [30] to go about fuzzy multiple criteria analysis (MCA) during MSW management. In [3], an algorithm built on principal component analysis and back propagation (BP) neural network was proposed to help determine the WtE plant site selection, and through this method the training speed has got promoted. The Decision Making Trial and Evaluation Laboratory Model (DEMATEL) method combined with ANP were used for selecting the optimal renewable energy resources in Turkey on behalf of investors in [31]. Jia and Huang [32] assessed the WtE plant site selection by making use of a modified evaluation method with autonomous decision-making.

MCDM methods, such as Analytic Hierarchy Process (AHP), Analytic Network Process (ANP), Technique for Order Preference by Similarity to Ideal Solution (TOPSIS) and other hybrid methods are in widespread use in WtE plant site selection lately. In line with the review and analysis above, the extended TODIM- PROMETHEE method based on TIFNs is recommended to solve the above problems of processing qualitative information and ranking alternatives. Integrating fuzzy set theory and TODIM is a novel approach. The TODIM evaluation criteria have the characteristics of subjective and qualitative, and it articulates by linguistic information, which makes the fuzzy set gets more general use [33]. Tseng et al. [34] applied TODIM to examine and recommend options for green supply chain practices. Li [35] also extended TODIM technique built on the Hamming distance and Euclidean distance of the interval intuitionistic fuzzy sets and investigated the airport terminals siting. Qin and Liu [36] proposed the TODIM method to solve MCDM problems under the circumstance of interval type-2 fuzzy sets (IT2FSs) and applied it to green supplier selection. PROMETHEE-II is method used for ranking in MCA, but what should be noted is that it cannot distribute the weights of relative importance to the criteria in an organized way [37]. Therefore, the use of TODIM method is suggested to be conjunct with PROMETHEE-II in this paper. That is, TODIM is employed to work out overall appraisal values of alternatives, and then the PROMETHEE-II is used to get ranking results.

Unlike the previous studies, this paper shows the improvements below: first, this study targets the scope in WtE site selection and concentrates on four aspects of sustainability. Second, the vague and inexactitude content can be described simultaneously through TIFNs by means of comprehensive comparison to show DMs' performances precisely. Third, the extended TODIM-PROMETHEE integrated with TIFNs in this study will be used in the WtE site selection for the first time, which could provide a new idea for establishing an effective decision making framework to select the best WtE plant site. To conclude, on the basis of the improvements above, the comprehensive evaluation results of the WtE site selection decision-making will be more rational than before.

3. Evaluation index system for optimal siting of WtE plant

Although WtE is an efficient way to save energy, it has not been widespread in China yet. For the development of WtE, it is imperative for us to build a scientific and comprehensive evaluation index system to identify a satisfied site for WtE plants. The WtE plant site selection is dependent upon various factors. And since WtE is a sustainable way to contribute to energy conversion, sustainable decision factors are taken into consideration of necessity. Based on the relevant literature, feasibility reports and concerning the current situation, a sustainable evaluation index system has been established which covers economic factors, environmental factors, social factors and technical factors [21]. 17 sub-criteria are put forward to do the further explanation under this circumstance.

3.1 Economic factors

Economic factors exert significant impact on the initial WtE plant site planning, which mainly evaluate whether the alternative is worth investing or not. Waste supply plays a decisive role in inflammation efficiency and running cost [38]. Fuel acquisition costs, which include waste acquisition and transportation costs, determine the operation of the project directly. The land is the foundation of the plant construction, and the local land price is an important factor affecting investment funds. Besides, the average construction and maintenance cost [39] of local WtE plants is also needed to be investigated, for the reason that it can provide reference for prediction of the investment pay-back period preliminarily.

3.2 Environmental factors

Environmental factors characterize the position of the WtE plants concerning local ecological effects [2]. Compared with traditional waste disposal such as landfill, waste incineration can promote energy recycling and change the domestic status of coal power generation. Though waste incineration reduces greenhouse gases emission, it may still bring atmospheric particulate matter emission, such as severe toxic dioxin which not only causes severe air pollution but does great harm to human body and even causes cancer [17]. Furthermore, whether the WtE plant sits in the downwind of the dominant wind direction makes a difference to polluted range and level [39]. In addition, groundwater pollution and contaminants transportation in landfills are both of the leading environmental concerns relevant to long-term safety [40]. So it is a crucial indicator that whether the leachate and waste resulting from incineration are properly disposed of afterwards to reduce pressure on the environment [41]. Hydrogeological conditions deserve to be concerned for they are related to the speed of the infiltration of waste and decide directly the level of preventing the further pollution of local living water. Right hydrogeological conditions will help cut down the difficulty and the cost of construction to some extent.

3.3 Social factors

Social factors are criteria which cannot be omitted both in construction and in operation of the WtE plants. Public acceptability which consists of local and adjacent residents' opinion is crucial for future development. Negative public acceptability will bring the WtE to a standstill in the beginning, not to mention later operation. Therefore, the WtE project can hardly be completed without public support [7]. Service radius is used to measure the necessity of the project development for that a good site should benefit the residents as much as possible. Moreover, promotion of local economy development and urbanization should be taken into account to assess the social and economic benefits brought by the WtE plants [17]. Besides, sustainable development is people-oriented. From this perspective, improvement of living standards should be taken into consideration to help assure long-term operation.

3.4 Technical factors

Since WtE construction involves large numbers of technical conditions and the spending on technology make up the bulk of investments required for the plant construction[2], technical factors should be taken into consideration in the site selection process. First, transmission and distribution network convenience evaluates whether existing local power grid facilities such as grid voltage level and the length of transmission line support the project or not. It is crucial to make the plant connect into the grid without difficulty. Second, the distance between the WtE plant and power load center has an effect on practicality and future benefits. Third, adequate water supply will improve project efficiency and meet the demand for combined heat and power (CHP). Apart from these, according to the legislation, a WtE plant should be away from the residential district or public facilities for more than 300 meters owing to healthy concern [39]. Thus, it is apparently inappropriate to build a WtE plant in the city center. Under this circumstance, increasing traffic convenience is beneficial for materials transmission during both construction and operation stages.

In a word, in order to evaluate and select a more proper site for WtE plant seriously and responsibly from the perspective of sustainable development, it is essential to think over the economic, environmental, social as well as technical factors of alternatives. Based on these considerations, the evaluation index system is established and shown in Table 4.1.

Table 4.1 The evaluation index system for WtE plant site.

Target	Criteria	Sub-criteria
The WtE plant site selection	Economic factors	Fuel acquisition cost
		Local land price
		Average construction and maintenance cost of local WtE plants
	Environmental factors	Energy saving: standard coal
		Impact on air
		Dominant wind direction
		Waste discharge
		Hydrogeological conditions
	Social factors	Public acceptability
		Service radius
		Local economy development
		Urbanization
		Improvement of living standards
	Technical factors	Transmission and distribution network convenience
		Distance to power load center
		Distance to water supply network
		Traffic convenience

4. Methodology

4.1 Basic theory of MCDM problem in the intuitionistic fuzzy environment

There exists many problems in the actual situation, for instance, the information is not complete, and experts cannot give accurate values due to the impact of subjective or objective factors when evaluating. The introduction of fuzzy set theory will help express the uncertainty of DMs exquisitely in the process of decision-making in real decision environment.

Definition 1. [12] An intuitionistic fuzzy set (IFS) A over X is represented as:

$$A=\langle (x,\mu_A(x),\nu_A(x)) | x\in X\rangle \tag{4-1}$$

In this definition, $\mu_A(x)$ and $\nu_A(x)$ represents the membership and nonmembership degree of x in the IFS respectively. Let $\pi_A(x)=1-\mu_A(x)-\nu_A(x)$ be the intuitionistic index, standing for the hesitancy degree of A.

This expression should meet the following conditions:

(1) X is a nonempty set;

(2) $0\leqslant \mu_A(x)+\nu_A(x)\leqslant 1, 0\leqslant \pi_A(x)\leqslant 1, \forall x\in X$.

Definition 2. [42] Let $\tilde{a}$ be a triangular intuitionistic fuzzy number (TIFN), it is a special IFS on a crisp number set R, and it can be represented as (see Fig. 4.4):

$$\tilde{a}=\langle (\underline{a},a,\overline{a});\omega_{\tilde{a}},\mu_{\tilde{a}}\rangle \tag{4-2}$$

Its membership function and nonmembership function are defined as follows:

$$\omega_{\tilde{a}}(x)=\begin{cases} \dfrac{x-\underline{a}}{a-\underline{a}}\omega_{\tilde{a}}, & \text{if } \underline{a}\leqslant x<a \\ \omega_{\tilde{a}}, & \text{if } x=a \\ \dfrac{\overline{a}-x}{\overline{a}-a}\omega_{\tilde{a}}, & \text{if } a<x\leqslant \overline{a} \\ 0, & \text{if } x<\underline{a} \text{ or } x>\overline{a} \end{cases} \tag{4-3}$$

and

$$\mu_{\tilde{a}}(x)=\begin{cases} \dfrac{a-x+(x-\underline{a})\mu_{\tilde{a}}}{a-\underline{a}}, & \text{if } \underline{a}\leqslant x<a \\ \mu_{\tilde{a}}, & \text{if } x=a \\ \dfrac{x-a+(\overline{a}-x)\mu_{\tilde{a}}}{\overline{a}-a}, & \text{if } a<x\leqslant \overline{a} \\ 1, & \text{if } x<\underline{a} \text{ or } x>\overline{a} \end{cases} \tag{4-4}$$

In this definition, $\omega_{\tilde{a}}$ and $\mu_{\tilde{a}}$ represent the maximum degree of membership and the minimum degree of nonmembership, respectively, and satisfy the following descriptions: $0\leqslant \omega_{\tilde{a}}\leqslant 1$, $0\leqslant \mu_{\tilde{a}}\leqslant 1$ and $0\leqslant \omega_{\tilde{a}}+\mu_{\tilde{a}}\leqslant 1$, $\underline{a},a,\overline{a}\in R$. Let $\pi_{\tilde{a}}(x)=1-\omega_{\tilde{a}}(x)-\mu_{\tilde{a}}(x)$ be an intuitionistic fuzzy index of an element x in $\tilde{a}$ and represent the degree of indeterminacy membership of the element x to $\tilde{a}$. The smaller the value of $\pi_{\tilde{a}}(x)$ is, the clearer the fuzzy number is.

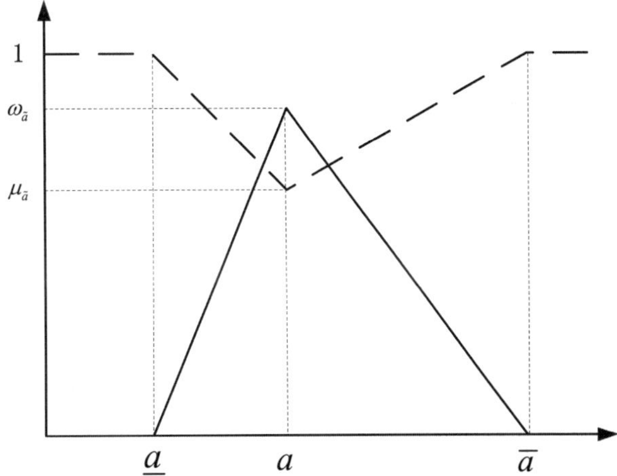

Fig. 4.4 A triangular intuitionistic fuzzy number $\tilde{a}=\langle(\underline{a},a,\overline{a});\omega_{\tilde{a}},\mu_{\tilde{a}}\rangle$.

Definition 3. [43] Let $\tilde{a}$, $\tilde{b}$ be two TIFNs: $\tilde{a}=\langle(\underline{a},a,\overline{a});\omega_{\tilde{a}},\mu_{\tilde{a}}\rangle$, $\tilde{b}=\langle(\underline{b},b,\overline{b});\omega_{\tilde{b}},\mu_{\tilde{b}}\rangle$ and $\lambda \geqslant 0$. Then we have these basic operations:

$$\tilde{a}+\tilde{b}=\langle(\underline{a}+\underline{b},a+b,\overline{a}+\overline{b});\omega_{\tilde{a}}\wedge\omega_{\tilde{b}},\mu_{\tilde{a}}\vee\mu_{\tilde{b}}\rangle \tag{4-5}$$

$$\tilde{a}\tilde{b}=\langle(\underline{ab},ab,\overline{ab});\omega_{\tilde{a}}\wedge\omega_{\tilde{b}},\mu_{\tilde{a}}\vee\mu_{\tilde{b}}\rangle \tag{4-6}$$

$$\lambda\tilde{a}=\langle(\lambda\underline{a},\lambda a,\lambda\overline{a});\omega_{\tilde{a}},\mu_{\tilde{a}}\rangle \tag{4-7}$$

$$\tilde{a}^{\lambda}=\langle(\underline{a}^{\lambda},a^{\lambda},\overline{a}^{\lambda});\omega_{\tilde{a}},\mu_{\tilde{a}}\rangle \tag{4-8}$$

In this definition, $\wedge$ and $\vee$ mean minimum and maximum operators, respectively.

Definition 4. [43] Let $\tilde{a}$, $\tilde{b}$ be two TIFNs: $\tilde{a}=\langle(\underline{a},a,\overline{a});\omega_{\tilde{a}},\mu_{\tilde{a}}\rangle,\tilde{b}=\langle(\underline{b},b,\overline{b});\omega_{\tilde{b}},\mu_{\tilde{b}}\rangle$. The distance between $\tilde{a}$ and $\tilde{b}$ is defined as follows:

$$d(\tilde{a},\tilde{b})=\frac{1}{6}\left\langle\begin{array}{l}|(1+\omega_{\tilde{a}}-\mu_{\tilde{a}})\underline{a}-(1+\omega_{\tilde{b}}-\mu_{\tilde{b}})\underline{b}| \\ +|(1+\omega_{\tilde{a}}-\mu_{\tilde{a}})a-(1+\omega_{\tilde{b}}-\mu_{\tilde{b}})b| \\ +|(1+\omega_{\tilde{a}}-\mu_{\tilde{a}})\overline{a}-(1+\omega_{\tilde{b}}-\mu_{\tilde{b}})\overline{b}|\end{array}\right\rangle \tag{4-9}$$

Definition 5. [44] The ranking index of the membership and nonmembership degree of the TIFN $\tilde{a}$ can be delimited as follows, respectively:

$$T_{\tilde{a};\omega_{\tilde{a}}}(\lambda)=\omega_{\tilde{a}}\langle\underline{a}(1-\lambda)+\overline{a}\lambda+a\rangle/2 \tag{4-10}$$

$$T_{\tilde{a};\mu_{\tilde{a}}}(\lambda)=(1-\mu_{\tilde{a}})\langle\overline{a}(1-\lambda)+\underline{a}\lambda+a\rangle/2 \tag{4-11}$$

where λ indicates the preference of DMs and varies from 0 to 1. If $\lambda=0$, the decision maker is risk-averse; if $\lambda=1$, the decision maker presents a propensity for risk; if $\lambda=0.5$, the decision maker is risk-neutral.

Definition 6. [44] In view of formula (4-10) through formula (4-11), a method for ranking TIFNs can be derived below:

$$R_{\tilde{a}}(\lambda)=(1-\lambda)T_{\tilde{a};\mu_{\tilde{a}}}(\lambda)+\lambda T_{\tilde{a};\omega_{\tilde{a}}}(\lambda) \tag{4-12}$$

Definition 7. [44] Let $\tilde{a}$ and $\tilde{b}$ are any two TIFNs, and then

(1) If $R_{\tilde{a}}(\lambda)<R_{\tilde{b}}(\lambda)$, then $\tilde{a}\succ\tilde{b}$;

(2) If $R_{\tilde{a}}(\lambda)=R_{\tilde{b}}(\lambda)$, then $\tilde{a}=\tilde{b}$.

4.2 Description of the decision making matrix with TIFNs information

The personal opinions of experts are integrated into a comprehensive decision matrix by using the triangular intuitionistic fuzzy weighted geometric (TIFWG) operator.

Definition 8. [45] Let $\tilde{a}_i\,(i=1,2,...,p)$ be a collection of TIFNs, and let $\text{TIFWG}:\Omega^p\to\Omega$ be TIFWG operator of n, satisfying:

$$\begin{aligned}\text{TIFWG}_w(\tilde{a}_1,\tilde{a}_2,...,\tilde{a}_p)&=\prod_{i=1}^{p}\tilde{a}_i^{\,w_i}\\&=\left\langle\left(\prod_{i=1}^{p}\underline{a}_i^{\,w_i},\prod_{i=1}^{p}a_i^{\,w_i},\prod_{i=1}^{p}\overline{a}_i^{\,w_i}\right);\prod_{i=1}^{p}\omega_{\tilde{a}_i}^{\,w_i},1-\prod_{i=1}^{p}(1-\mu_{\tilde{a}_i})^{w_i}\right\rangle\end{aligned} \tag{4-13}$$

In this definition, $w_i=(w_1,w_2,...,w_p)^T$ is the weight vector of, $\tilde{a}_i\,(i=1,2,...,p)$ $\sum_{i=1}^{p}w_i=1$, $w_i\in[0,1]$.

Since the criteria constructed in this paper include two types, cost criteria (the smaller, the better) and benefit criteria (the higher, the better), it is essential to standardize the appraisal to eliminate the interference from different physical dimensions on the decision-making results. Transform the resulting decision matrix $\tilde{A}=(\tilde{x}_{ij})_{m\times n}$ to standardized decision matrix $\tilde{R}=(\tilde{r}_{ij})_{m\times n}$, that is, normalize the element $\tilde{x}_{ij}=\langle(x_{ij\underline{a}},x_{ija},x_{ij\overline{a}});\omega_{x_{ij}},\mu_{x_{ij}}\rangle$ to $\tilde{r}_{ij}=\langle(r_{ij\underline{a}},r_{ija},r_{ij\overline{a}});\omega_{r_{ij}},\mu_{r_{ij}}\rangle$ as follows [25]:

For cost criteria:

$$\tilde{r}_{ij}=\left\langle\left(\frac{x_{ij\overline{a}}^{\;+}-x_{ij\overline{a}}}{x_{ij\overline{a}}^{\;+}-x_{ij\underline{a}}^{\;-}},\frac{x_{ij\overline{a}}^{\;+}-x_{ija}}{x_{ij\overline{a}}^{\;+}-x_{ij\underline{a}}^{\;-}},\frac{x_{ij\overline{a}}^{\;+}-x_{ij\underline{a}}}{x_{ij\overline{a}}^{\;+}-x_{ij\underline{a}}^{\;-}}\right);\omega_{x_{ij}},\mu_{x_{ij}}\right\rangle \tag{4-14}$$

For benefit criteria:

$$\tilde{r}_{ij}=\left\langle\left(\frac{x_{ij\underline{a}}-x_{ij\underline{a}}^{\;-}}{x_{ij\overline{a}}^{\;+}-x_{ij\underline{a}}^{\;-}},\frac{x_{ija}-x_{ij\underline{a}}^{\;-}}{x_{ij\overline{a}}^{\;+}-x_{ij\underline{a}}^{\;-}},\frac{x_{ij\overline{a}}-x_{ij\underline{a}}^{\;-}}{x_{ij\overline{a}}^{\;+}-x_{ij\underline{a}}^{\;-}}\right);\omega_{x_{ij}},\mu_{x_{ij}}\right\rangle \tag{4-15}$$

where $x_{ij\overline{a}}^{\;+}=\max_i(x_{ij\overline{a}})$ and $x_{ij\underline{a}}^{\;-}=\min_i(x_{ij\underline{a}})$.

4.3 Entropy weight method with TIFNS

The entropy weight method has been extensively used in decision-making situations since it derived from thermodynamics [35]. It has become a useful tool to measure the information providing by the data from an objected point of view. For this reason the entropy weight method is applied to gain the weight of attributes in this paper.

It is necessary to defuzzify fuzzy numbers before determining the weight. According to the method proposed by Wan [42], the TIFN $\tilde{x}_{ij}$ can be defuzzified to $\tilde{h}_{ij}$ as follows:

$$h(\tilde{a}) = \frac{1}{12}(\underline{a} + 4a + \overline{a})(1 - \mu_{\tilde{a}} + \omega_{\tilde{a}}) \tag{4-16}$$

Definition 9. [46] Let e_j be the entropy of attribute j:

$$e_j = -\frac{1}{\ln n}\sum_{i=1}^{m}\left\langle \frac{h_{ij}}{\sum_{i=1}^{m} h_{ij}} \times \ln\left(\frac{h_{ij}}{\sum_{i=1}^{m} h_{ij}}\right)\right\rangle \tag{4-17}$$

where $e_j \in [0,1]$.

Definition 10. [46] Let ω_j be the entropy weight of attribute j:

$$g_j = 1 - e_j \tag{4-18}$$

$$\omega_j = \frac{g_j}{\sum_{i=1}^{n} g_j} \tag{4-19}$$

In this definition, $\omega_j \in [0,1]$ and $\sum_{j=1}^{m}\omega_j = 1$. The value of ω_j reflects the difference between two attributes, that is the smaller the difference is, the smaller the weight is.

4.4 Description of TODIM method

TODIM is the extension of the prospect theory, which is a useful way to solve MCDM problems based on DMs' psychological behaviors. The TODIM algorithm uses paired comparisons between the criteria, where occasional inconsistencies resulting from these comparisons are eliminated and enables value judgment to perform on a verbal scale [33].

The TODIM method involves the following steps [47]:

Step 1. Calculate the relative attribute weight ϖ_{jr} for attribute b_j to reference attribute b_r as follows:

$$\varpi_{jr} = \frac{\varpi_r}{\varpi_j}\left(j = 1, 2, \ldots, m\right) \tag{4-20}$$

where $\varpi_j = \max\{\varpi_j | j = 1,2,...,m\}$.

Step 2. Calculate the dominance degree of the alternative T_p relative to the alternative T_q as below:

$$\phi_j(T_p,T_q)=\begin{cases}\sqrt{\dfrac{(r_{pj}-r_{qj})\varpi_{jr}}{\sum_{j=1}^{m}\varpi_{jr}}}, & \text{if } r_{pj}-r_{qj}>0\\ 0, & \text{if } r_{pj}-r_{qj}=0\\ -\dfrac{1}{\theta}\sqrt{\dfrac{(r_{qj}-r_{pj})\sum_{j=1}^{m}\varpi_{jr}}{\varpi_{jr}}}, & \text{if } r_{pj}-r_{qj}<0\end{cases} \tag{4-21}$$

In this definition, the parameter θ is the loss aversion coefficient.

Step 3. Calculate the overall dominance degree of each alternative T_p over each alternative T_q, and get

$$\delta(T_p,T_q)=\sum_{j=1}^{m}\phi_j(T_p,T_q) \tag{4-22}$$

Step 4. Calculate the global value of the alternative as follows:

$$\zeta_p=\frac{\sum_{q=1}^{n}\delta(T_p,T_q)-\min_p\left(\sum_{q=1}^{n}\delta(T_p,T_q)\right)}{\max_p\left(\sum_{q=1}^{n}\delta(T_p,T_q)\right)-\min_p\left(\sum_{q=1}^{n}\delta(T_p,T_q)\right)} \tag{4-23}$$

Step 5. Rank all the alternatives based on the global values of alternatives. The bigger ζ_p is, the better alternative T_p is.

4.5 Description of PROMETHEE-II method

PROMETHEE method is a multi-criteria decision-making method which judging the alternatives by using priority functions. PROMETHEE-I method and PROMETHEE-II method extend the PROMETHEE method and get extensive use.

The PROMETHEE-II method takes into consideration the preference function of each criterion determined by DMs, and each criterion is assessed on a different basis for the sake of making better decision [37]. The function takes values from 0 to 1, the smaller the function value is, the smaller the difference between the alternatives is. If the function value is 1, alternative a_i is strictly superior to alternative a_k.

Definition 11. Gaussian Criterion is chosen as the priority function $P(d)$.

$$P(d)=\begin{cases}0 & \text{if } d\leqslant 0\\ 1-\mathrm{e}^{\frac{-d^2}{2\sigma^2}} & \text{if } d>0\end{cases} \tag{4-24}$$

Definition 12. Based on the formula (20), $\Pi(a_i,a_k)$, the priority index between alternative a_i and a_k, can be calculated as:

$$\Pi(a_i,a_k)=\frac{\sum_{j=1}^{m} w_j p_j(a_i,a_k)}{\sum_{j=1}^{m} w_j} \tag{4-25}$$

In this definition, the value of w_j ($j=1,2,\ldots,m$) reflects the weight of each attribute in j alternatives. If the level of alternative a_i is higher than a_k, it meets $\Pi(a_i,a_k)=0$.

According to the priority index, outflow and inflow of each alternative can be derived as follows:

The outflow of alternative a_i:

$$\Phi^+(a_i)=\sum_{k=1}^{m}\Pi(a_i,a_k) \tag{4-26}$$

The inflow of alternative a_i:

$$\Phi^-(a_i)=\sum_{k=1}^{m}\Pi(a_k,a_i) \tag{4-27}$$

In this definition, i ($i=1,2,\ldots k,\ldots,m$) means the number of alternatives.

The net flow of alternative a_i:

$$\Phi(a_i)=\Phi^+(a_i)-\Phi^-(a_i) \tag{4-28}$$

On the basis of the net flow, the level relationship can be determined. If $\Phi(a_i)>\Phi(a_k)$, that is to say that the level of alternative a_i is higher than alternative a_k. If $\Phi(a_i)=\Phi(a_k)$, it represents that the level of two alternatives has no difference yet.

5. Decision framework of the WtE plant site selection

Generally speaking, classical TODIM method can only solve MCDM problems whose appraisal values are crisp numbers, so it is necessary to make it fit in the fuzzy numbers with some modification. The procedure of how to use the TODIM-PROMETHEE method can be summarized in the following steps:

Step 1. Determine the alternatives and evaluation criteria. There are K experts to evaluate attributes of n alternatives using the TIFNS to show the evaluation values. Then, an assessment matrix belonged to each expert can be derived.

Step 2. Based on step 1, utilize the TIFWG operator to aggregate the values of criteria. After that, all of the assessment values can be aggregated into an integrated matrix and standardize according to formula (4-14) through (4-15).

Step 3. According to the certain expert weights, the attribute weights can be calculated on the basis of formula (4-16) through (4-19).

Step 4. Compare the two fuzzy numbers $\tilde{r}_{pj}=\left\langle\left(\tilde{r}_{pj\underline{a}},\tilde{r}_{pja},\tilde{r}_{pj\bar{a}}\right);\omega_{\tilde{r}_{pj}},\mu_{\tilde{r}_{pj}}\right\rangle$ and $\tilde{r}_{qj}=\left\langle\left(\tilde{r}_{qj\underline{a}},\tilde{r}_{qja},\tilde{r}_{qj\bar{a}}\right);\omega_{\tilde{r}_{qj}},\mu_{\tilde{r}_{qj}}\right\rangle$ on the ground of definition 5 to definition 7.

Step 5. [48] Calculate the dominance degree of the alternative T_p relative to the alternative T_q as below according to the extended TODIM method:

$$\delta\left(T_p,T_q\right)=\sum_{j=1}^{m}\phi_j\left(T_p,T_q\right)$$

where

$$\phi_j\left(T_p,T_q\right)=\begin{cases}\sqrt{\dfrac{\varpi_{jr}}{\sum_{j=1}^{m}\varpi_{jr}}}d\left(\tilde{r}_{pj},\tilde{r}_{qj}\right), & \text{if } \tilde{r}_{pj}-\tilde{r}_{qj}>0\\ 0, & \text{if } \tilde{r}_{pj}-\tilde{r}_{qj}=0\\ -\dfrac{1}{\theta}\sqrt{\dfrac{\sum_{j=1}^{m}\varpi_{jr}}{\varpi_{jr}}}d\left(\tilde{r}_{qj},\tilde{r}_{pj}\right), & \text{if } \tilde{r}_{pj}-\tilde{r}_{qj}<0\end{cases} \tag{4-29}$$

In this definition, $d\left(\tilde{r}_{pj},\tilde{r}_{qj}\right)$ represents the distance between $\tilde{r}_{pj}$ and $\tilde{r}_{qj}$ which can be calculated by formula (4-9).

Step 6. Calculate the overall appraisal value by normalizing the final dominance matrix. To eliminate compensation problem between attributes in classical TODIM method for fear of affecting the decision results, PROMETHEE-II method is used to solve this problem as formula (4-25) through (4-28) and get the value of $\Phi\left(a_i\right)$ finally.

Step 7. Rank according to the judgment rules, and then choose the optimal alternative in the light of ranking results.

The algorithm implementation for the WtE site selection decision-making has been proposed, as shown in Fig. 4.5.

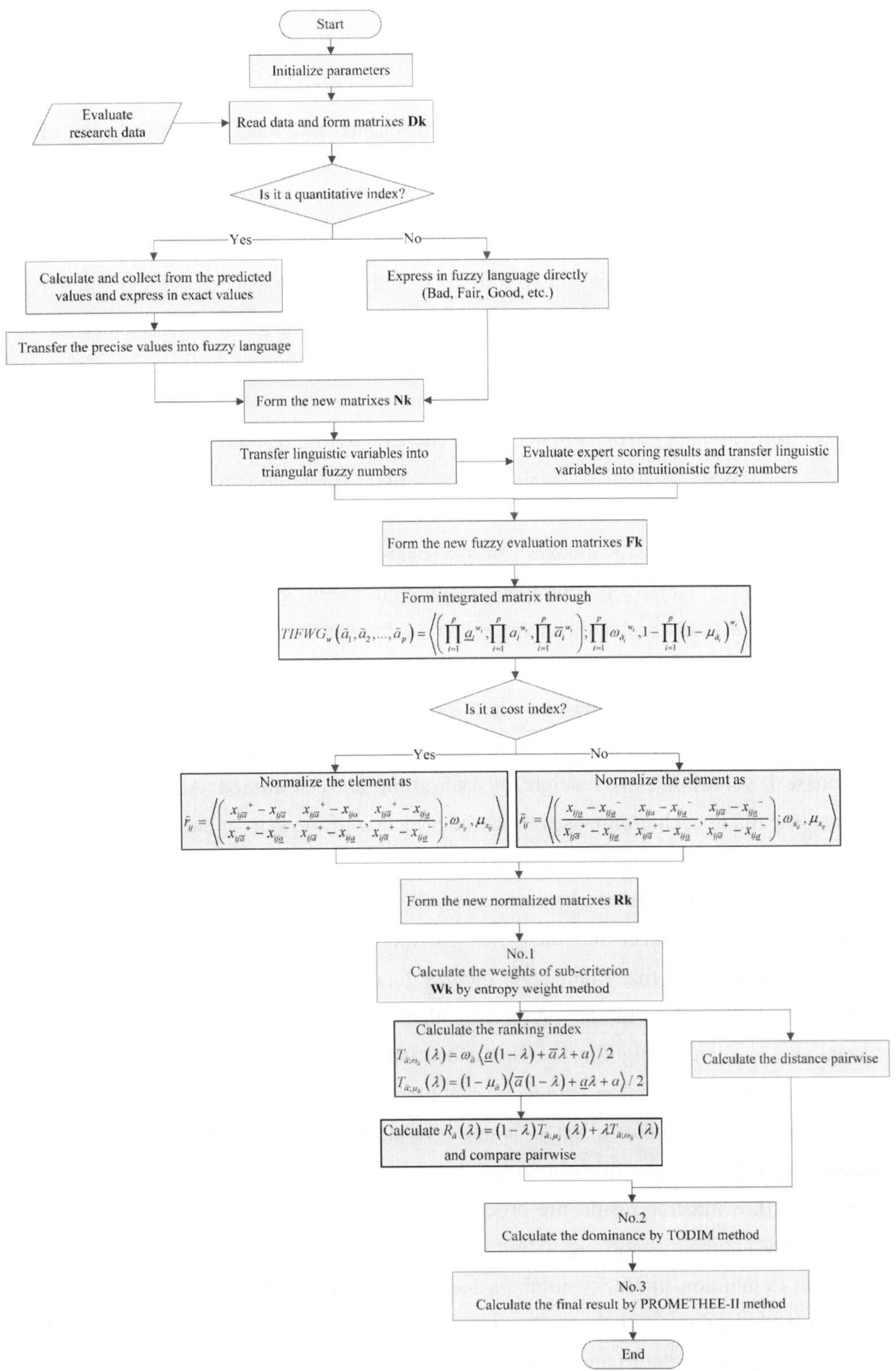

Fig. 4.5 The flowchart of algorithm implementation about proposed framework.

6. A case study

In order to make full use of a large number of MSW to achieve the goal of energy recycling, the government of Yulin City, located in Shaanxi province, China, is ready to build a new WtE plant to respond to national development policies and crack the garbage siege dilemma.

Considering the amount of the waste and the distance from the residential areas to Yulin City center, four sites located respectively in Jia County, Hengshan District, Shenmu City, and Yuyang District, are determined as the alternatives by the top managers. The alternatives denoted as A1, A2, A3 and A4, meet the basic standards of construction.

For the purpose of making a more comprehensive and convincing assessment of the four alternatives, four groups of experts in economy, energy, environmental protection, transportation and other related fields are invited to establish an expert evaluation committee to help make the decision on the WtE plant site selection. Based on the principles of sustainable development, experts formulate a series of indexes on the basis of professional knowledge and work experience. A set of relatively complete evaluation index system is established through continuous modifications and adjustments. The evaluation criteria system for the WtE site selection based on sustainable perspective is shown in Table 4.1.

After determining the criteria and alternatives in the early planning stage, it should be started to collect and process the project data. The details are as follows.

In phase I, values of expert weight of each group are determined. According to personal capacity of experts in each group, as well as the principle of the sum of expert weight is 1, four groups of expert weight can be determined as 0.20, 0.30, 0.25, 0.25, respectively.

In phase II, primary data of alternatives is collected. Experts score the attribute values on the basis of their experience, and then evaluate the degree of the membership. Qualitative attributes are expressed in fuzzy language, such as good, fair or bad. Quantitative attributes are calculated and collected from the predicted values and further expressed in exact values. However, as the direct weighting of the exact values may exaggerate the gaps between alternatives, and these prediction values are ambiguous to some extent, experts choose to use fuzzy language to evaluate the collected quantitative attributes and convert the precise values of the quantitative indicators into fuzzy language.

In phase III, evaluation results are processed preliminarily. Convert the attribute values to triangular fuzzy numbers according to Fig. 4.6, and then evaluate expert scoring results and convert them to intuitionistic fuzzy numbers according to Table 4.2. The attribute values are all represented in the form of TIFNs by this transformation. On account of the large number of attributes, we only show the triangular intuitionistic fuzzy decision matrix of expert group 1 as Table 4.3.

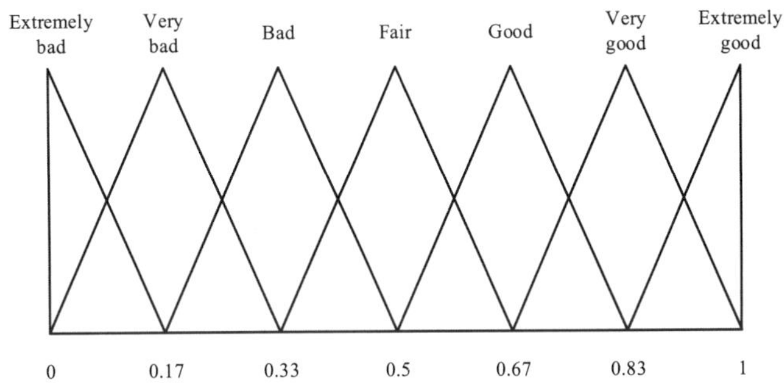

Fig. 4.6 Seven semantic terms and their intervals[49].

Table 4.2 The relationship between linguistic variables and intuitionistic fuzzy values[25].

Linguistic variables	Intuitionistic fuzzy values
Very high	(0.9, 0.1)
High	(0.8, 0.1)
Medium	(0.6, 0.3)
Poor	(0.3, 0.6)
Very poor	(0.1, 0.9)

Table 4.3 Attribute scoring and decision matrix of A1 given by expert group 1.

Index	Assessment language	TIFNs
C11	Very good; Medium	<(0.67, 0.83, 1); 0.6, 0.3>
C12	Bad; High	<(0.17, 0.33, 0.5); 0.8, 0.1>
C13	Bad; High	<(0.17, 0.33, 0.5); 0.8, 0.1>
C21	Good; Medium	<(0.5, 0.67, 0.83); 0.6, 0.3>
C22	Bad; High	<(0.17, 0.33, 0.5); 0.8, 0.1>
C23	Very good; Medium	<(0.67, 0.83, 1); 0.6, 0.3>
C24	Bad; Poor	<(0.17, 0.33, 0.5); 0.3, 0.6>
C25	Fair; Poor	<(0.33, 0.5, 0.67); 0.3, 0.6>
C31	Very good; High	<(0.67, 0.83, 1); 0.8, 0.1>
C32	Very good; High	<(0.67, 0.83, 1); 0.8, 0.1>
C33	Fair; High	<(0.33, 0.5, 0.67); 0.8, 0.1>
C34	Fair; Medium	<(0.33, 0.5, 0.67); 0.6, 0.3>
C35	Very good; High	<(0.67, 0.83, 1); 0.8, 0.1>
C41	Good; Very high	<(0.5, 0.67, 0.83); 0.9, 0.1>
C42	Very good; High	<(0.67, 0.83, 1); 0.8, 0.1>
C43	Fair; Medium	<(0.33, 0.5, 0.67); 0.6, 0.3>
C44	Very good; Medium	<(0.67, 0.83, 1); 0.6, 0.3>

In phase IV, aggregate the decision matrices to an integrated matrix. The expert weight matrix is $E=(0.20,0.30,0.25,0.25)^T$. Get integrated matrix of A1 through A4 by using TIFWG operator and normalize. The standardized decision matrix is shown in Table 4.4.

Table 4.4 Integrated decision matrix after being standardized.

Index	A1	A2	A3	A4
C11	<(0.05, 0.28, 0.49); 0.76, 0.14>	<(0.02, 0.2, 0.4); 0.85, 0.1>	<(0.29, 0.48, 0.68); 0.82, 0.1>	<(0.23, 0.47, 0.7); 0.68, 0.22>
C12	<(0.58, 0.8, 0.97); 0.57, 0.32>	<(0.39, 0.58, 0.77); 0.44, 0.45>	<(0.17, 0.34, 0.54); 0.62, 0.29>	<(0.18, 0.41, 0.64); 0.76, 0.14>
C13	<(0.57, 0.8, 1); 0.64, 0.36>	<(0.19, 0.58, 0.77); 0.8, 0.1>	<(0.40, 0.59, 0.78); 0.76, 0.14>	<(0.41, 0.64, 0.88); 0.52, 0.38>
C21	<(0.30, 0.52, 0.73); 0.54, 0.35>	<(0.45, 0.65, 0.84); 0.5, 0.39>	<(0.41, 0.61, 0.79); 0.6, 0.29>	<(0.19, 0.42, 0.66); 0.54, 0.35>
C22	<(0.47, 0.68, 0.9); 0.73, 0.17>	<(0.31, 0.5, 0.69); 0.48, 0.41>	<(0.17, 0.34, 0.54); 0.59, 0.32>	<(0.3, 0.53, 0.77); 0.51, 0.49>
C23	<(0.41, 0.62, 0.82); 0.7, 0.2>	<(0.51, 0.7, 0.9); 0.73, 0.17>	<(0.41, 0.6, 0.79); 0.76, 0.14>	<(0.42, 0.66, 0.88); 0.64, 0.26>
C24	<(0.49, 0.71, 0.94); 0.44, 0.33>	<(0.49, 0.68, 1); 0.59, 0.3>	<(0.41, 0.61, 1); 0.74, 0.15>	<(0.53, 0.77, 1); 0.38, 0.51>
C25	<(0.25, 0.48, 0.68); 0.46, 0.44>	<(0.48, 0.68, 0.88); 0.74, 0.15>	<(0.46, 0.64, 0.83); 0.75, 0.17>	<(0.41, 0.64, 0.88); 0.68, 0.22>
C31	<(0.22, 0.43, 0.66); 0.58, 0.31>	<(0.24, 0.42, 0.63); 0.77, 0.15>	<(0.22, 0.41, 0.6); 0.7, 0.22>	<(0.18, 0.42, 0.66); 0.64, 0.25>
C32	<(0.33, 0.54, 0.76); 0.68, 0.22>	<(0.6, 0.8, 0.98); 0.7, 0.2>	<(0.5, 0.69, 0.88); 0.53, 0.38>	<(0.3, 0.53, 0.77); 0.55, 0.34>
C33	<(0.25, 0.48, 0.68); 0.6, 0.29>	<(0.51, 0.7, 0.9); 0.87, 0.1>	<(0.56, 0.74, 0.92); 0.79, 0.15>	<(0.34, 0.58, 0.81); 0.7, 0.2>
C34	<(0.25, 0.48, 0.68); 0.69, 0.33>	<(0.5, 0.7, 0.9); 0.72, 0.2>	<(0.63, 0.82, 1); 0.8, 0.1>	<(0.55, 0.77, 1); 0.51, 0.4>
C35	<(0.47, 0.68, 0.89); 0.83, 0.1>	<(0.63, 0.81, 1); 0.65, 0.25>	<(0.37, 0.56, 0.74); 0.7, 0.2>	<(0.27, 0.52, 0.75); 0.65, 0.27>
C41	<(0.42, 0.63, 0.84); 0.64, 0.27>	<(0.57, 0.76, 0.94); 0.69, 0.25>	<(0.3, 0.5, 0.69); 0.47, 0.42>	<(0.14, 0.37, 0.6); 0.7, 0.2>
C42	<(0.18, 0.38, 0.59); 0.83, 0.1>	<(0.01, 0.19, 0.39); 0.83, 0.1>	<(0.13, 0.32, 0.51); 0.69, 0.21>	<(0.12, 0.34, 0.58); 0.64, 0.25>
C43	<(0.42, 0.63, 0.85); 0.56, 0.33>	<(0.13, 0.32, 0.51); 0.64, 0.26>	<(0.03, 0.21, 0.4); 0.76, 0.15>	<(0.18, 0.41, 0.64); 0.82, 0.1>
C44	<(0.58, 0.78, 1); 0.66, 0.25>	<(0.51, 0.7, 0.9); 0.68, 0.23>	<(0.17, 0.56, 0.74); 0.64, 0.21>	<(0.30, 0.53, 0.77); 0.69, 0.21>

In phase V, work out the values of the attribute weights through formula (4-16) through (4-19). The results are as shown in Table 4.5.

Table 4.5. The weights of indexes.

Index	e_j	g_j	ω_j
C11	0.961	0.039	0.109
C12	0.970	0.030	0.084
C13	0.995	0.005	0.015
C21	0.990	0.010	0.029
C22	0.953	0.047	0.133
C23	0.998	0.002	0.006
C24	0.971	0.029	0.080
C25	0.997	0.003	0.007
C31	0.997	0.003	0.007
C32	0.980	0.020	0.055
C33	0.974	0.026	0.072
C34	0.973	0.027	0.077
C35	0.985	0.015	0.042
C41	0.966	0.034	0.095
C42	0.980	0.020	0.057
C43	0.962	0.038	0.106
C44	0.990	0.010	0.027

In phase VI, calculate the values of $T_{\tilde{a};\mu_{\tilde{a}}}(\lambda)$, $T_{\tilde{a};\omega_{\tilde{a}}}(\lambda)$ and $R_{\tilde{a}}(\lambda)$, and then compare pairwise according to rules. The value of parameter λ is given as 0.5 here, for assuming that DMs are risk-neutral. After that, calculate the distance between the TIFNs based on the formula (4-9) and the results are shown in Table 4.6.

Table 4.6 The distance between the alternatives.

Index	d(A1,A2)	d(A1,A3)	d(A1,A4)	d(A2,A3)	d(A2,A4)	d(A3,A4)
C11	0.041	0.194	0.119	0.236	0.161	0.075
C12	0.202	0.257	0.157	0.054	0.077	0.099
C13	0.079	0.027	0.139	0.066	0.118	0.112
C21	0.051	0.088	0.056	0.036	0.107	0.143
C22	0.266	0.311	0.261	0.045	0.013	0.050
C23	0.086	0.024	0.012	0.063	0.098	0.035
C24	0.071	0.139	0.062	0.069	0.133	0.202
C25	0.301	0.269	0.230	0.032	0.071	0.039
C31	0.071	0.026	0.024	0.045	0.056	0.021
C32	0.198	0.033	0.074	0.198	0.272	0.074
C33	0.315	0.299	0.125	0.021	0.190	0.174
C34	0.212	0.373	0.110	0.161	0.103	0.264

Continued

Index	d(A1,A2)	d(A1,A3)	d(A1,A4)	d(A2,A3)	d(A2,A4)	d(A3,A4)
C35	0.042	0.171	0.234	0.152	0.215	0.063
C41	0.113	0.171	0.154	0.284	0.267	0.052
C42	0.161	0.095	0.091	0.067	0.071	0.013
C43	0.169	0.218	0.055	0.049	0.132	0.181
C44	0.045	0.204	0.160	0.160	0.115	0.050

Next, the dominance of alternative Ai overreach alternative Aj under 17 criteria can be work out by formula (4-29). To be in line with the real situations, we suppose the parameter θ is 0.5. We only show the dominance matrix under C11 here similarly in Table 4.7.

Table 4.7 The dominance matrix under C11.

Alternative	A1	A2	A3	A4
A1	0	-0.250	0.064	0.039
A2	0.014	0	0.078	0.053
A3	-1.177	-1.427	0	-0.454
A4	-0.723	-0.973	0.025	0

In the next phase, priority index of alternative Ai overreach alternative Aj under each criterion are got through formula (4-25) firstly. The priority indexes under C11 is listed in Table 4.8 and the global priority index of alternative Ai overreach alternative Aj is shown in Table 4.9.

Table 4.8 The priority index under C11.

Alternative	A1	A2	A3	A4
A1	0	-0.027	0.007	0.004
A2	0.001	0	0.008	0.006
A3	-0.128	-0.156	0	-0.050
A4	-0.079	-0.106	0.003	0

Table 4.9 The global priority index of alternative Ai overreach alternative Aj.

Alternative	A1	A2	A3	A4
A1	0	-0.557	-0.786	-0.720
A2	-0.554	0	-0.499	-0.741
A3	-0.635	-0.325	0	-0.543
A4	-0.219	-0.256	-0.247	0

According to formula (4-26) through (4-28), we can get the net flow and rank all the alternatives $A_i(i=1,2,3,4)$ in accordance with the value $\Phi(a_i)$ in Table 4.10.

Table 4.10 Ranking of alternatives.

Alternative	A1	A2	A3	A4
$\Phi(a_i)$	-0.654	-0.655	0.029	1.281
Ranking	3	4	2	1

According to the above calculation process, the final result is $A4 > A3 > A1 > A2$. Therefore, A4, namely the WtE plant site at Yuyang District should be selected as the optimal site.

7. Sensitivity analysis

Based on previous analysis, it can be concluded that the ranking of all the WtE plant selections in descending order are A4, A3, A1, A2. In order to test the robustness of evaluation model, the sensitivity analysis on the impacts of sub-criteria weights on the WtE plant site selection and θ value are performed in this section.

First, a sensitivity analysis of sub-criteria weights is presented. It aims to see whether the results would qualitatively change if the index weights fluctuate. Seventeen sub-criteria are classified as four analysis groups, namely economic group, environmental group, social group and technical group. All sub-criteria have 10%, 20% and 30% less weight than the base weight and 10%, 20% and 30% more weight than the base weight [21], then we can observe the changes in net flow from line charts intuitively.

Fig. 4.7 shows the cases where the sub-criteria in economic group has 10%, 20% and 30% less weight and 10%, 20% and 30% more weight than the base weight. As we can see from the figure, the net flow of A3, A4 decreases while the net flow of A1, A2 increases with the increasing of the proportion of $C11$ weight. Thus, $C11$ is the sensitive factor in this case. As $C12$, $C13$ is given more importance, the net flow of all alternatives remains steady. It can be concluded that A4 is still the optimal site to select even if economic factors weights change.

Cases where the sub-criteria in environmental group has 10%, 20% and 30% less weight and 10%, 20% and 30% more weight than the base weight are shown in Fig.4.8. It reveals that the net flow variations brought by $C23$ and $C25$ are tiny and the results have little difference from the initial data. As $C21$ and $C24$ is given more importance, respectively, the net flow of A2 and A3 shows a small decreasing tendency. It is worth mentioning that the net flow of A2 and A3 increases clearly with the importance of $C22$ growing and A2 even surpasses A1. Therefore, $C22$ is the sensitive sub-criterion in this group. However, no matter how the weight changes in the environmental group, the net flow of A4 always has the highest value, indicating the best alternative.

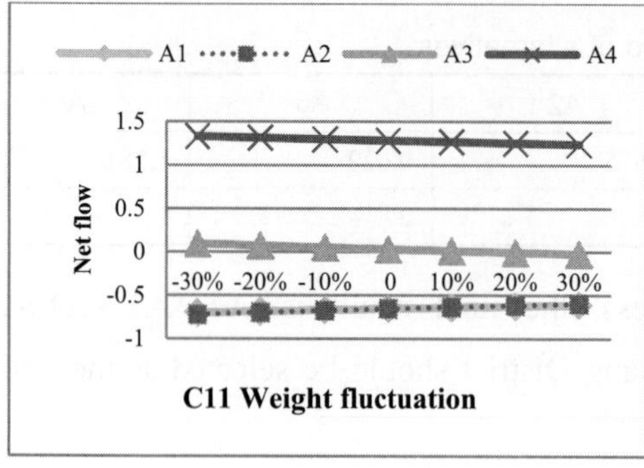

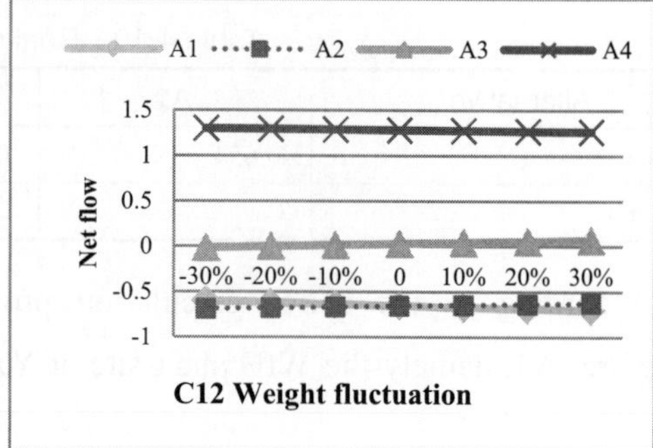

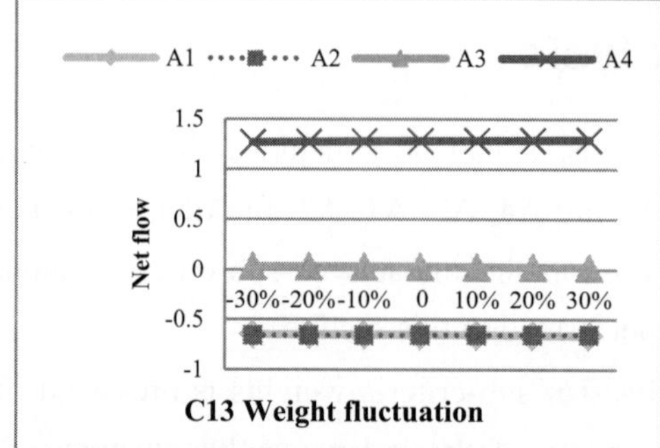

Fig. 4.7 Sensitivity analysis results of the sub-criteria in the economic group.

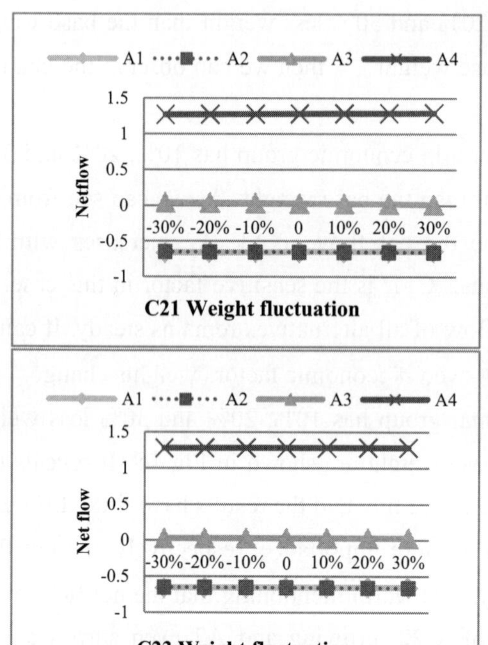

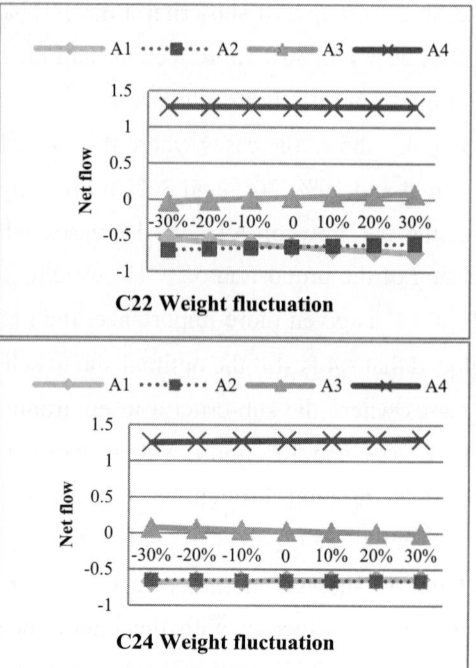

Fig. 4.8 Sensitivity analysis results of the sub-criteria in the environmental group.

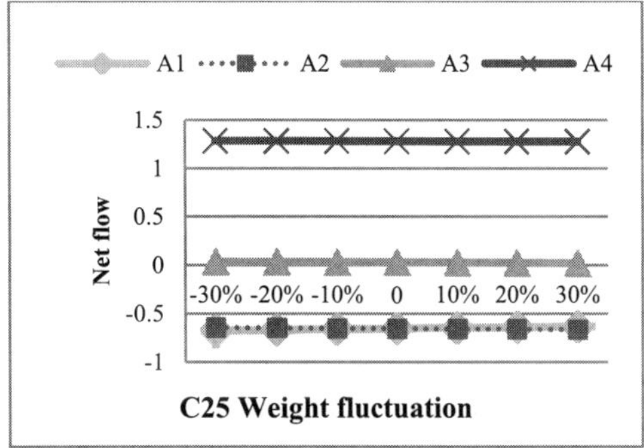

Fig. 4.8 Sensitivity analysis results of the sub-criteria in the environmental group (coutinued).

For the sub-criteria in the social group (see Fig.4.9), the net flow of four alternatives remains stable when C31 becomes more critical. However, as the sub-criteria C32 and C35 are given more importance, the net flow of A3, A4 increases slightly while the net flow of A2 keeps the weakened trend slightly compared to the initial data and then affects the ranking of Al and A2. Notably, with the weight changes of C33 and C34, the net flow of A3 show an decreasing tendency along with increase of weights, the net flow of A4 remains stable with the weight variation, while A2 ranks forth, surpassed by Al. Therefore, the WtE site alternative A4 is finally chosen as the optimal WtE site in overall ranking.

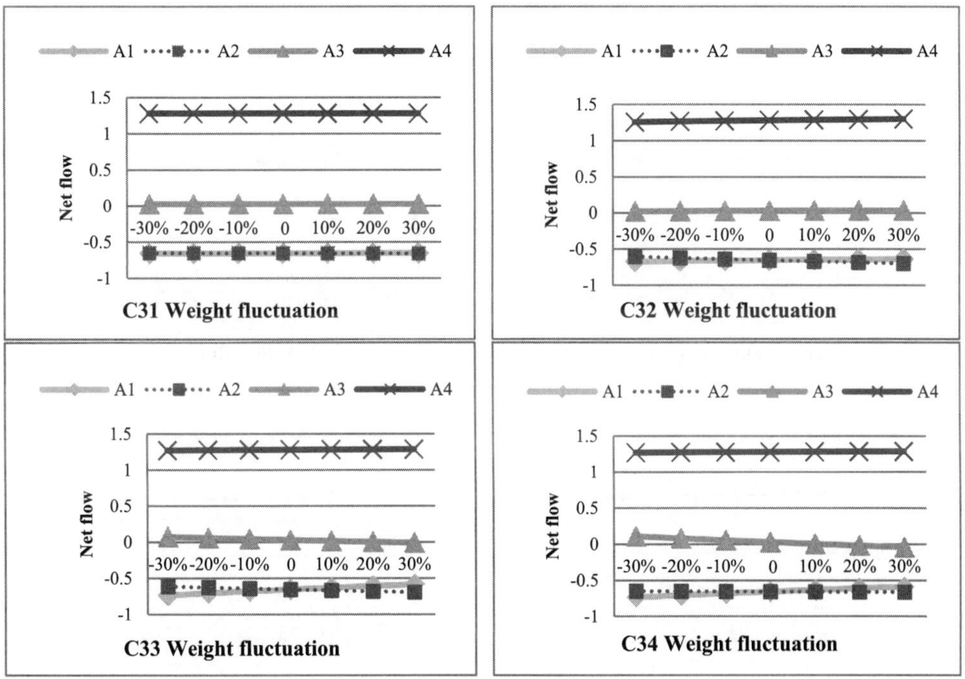

Fig. 4.9 Sensitivity analysis results of the sub-criteria in the social group.

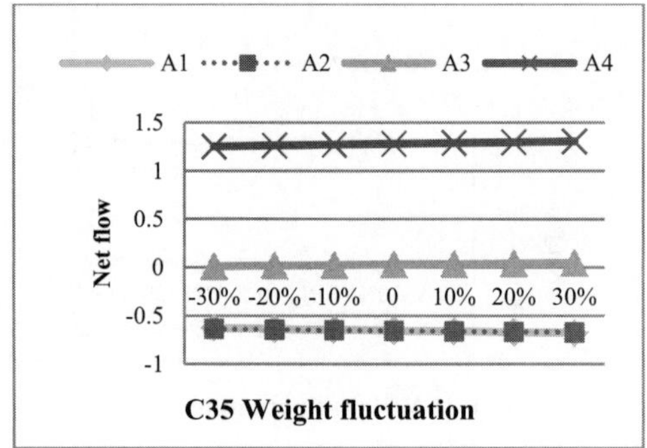

Fig. 4.9 Sensitivity analysis results of the sub-criteria in the social group (continued).

Fig. 4.10 shows those cases where the sub-criteria in technical group has 10%, 20% and 30% less weight and 10%, 20% and 30% more weight than the base weight. In this group, it can be seen that the net flow of four alternatives has similar variation trend in the case of C42 weight fluctuation and C44 weight fluctuation. In these two cases, the net flow of A2 and A3 shows a rising trend slightly while A2 and A4 are on the opposite position. In the case of C41, the net flow of A1 and A4 stay relatively stable, meanwhile A2 and A3 present opposite trend instead. In the case of C43, A4 shows a decline trend. Meanwhile, the net flow of A2 increases and surpasses A1. Therefore, A4 secures its top ranking no matter how changes of sub-criteria weight in technical group just as the other three groups mentioned above.

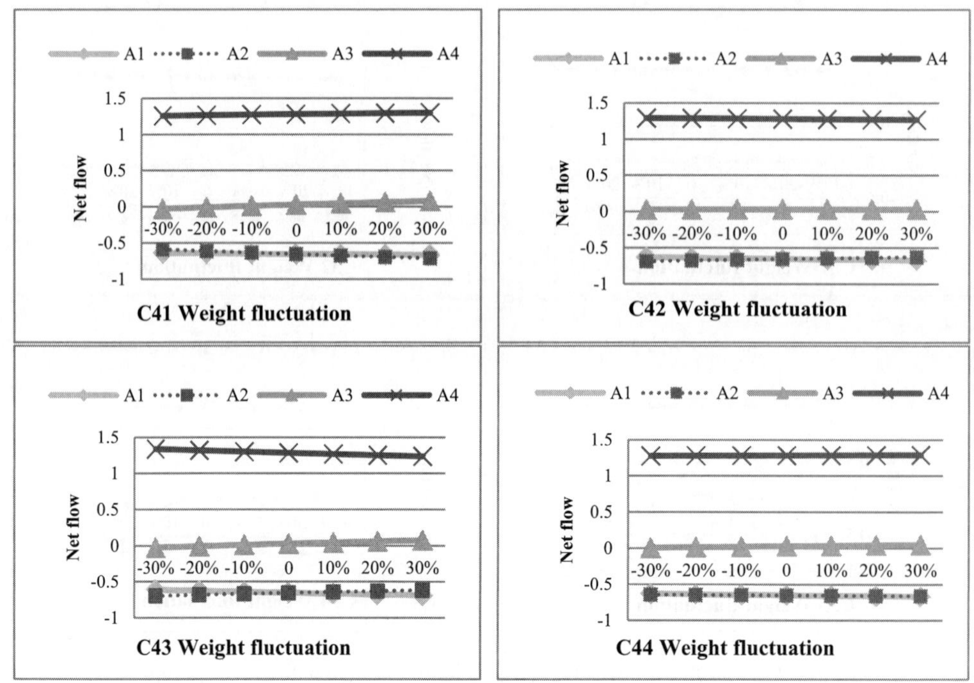

Fig. 4.10 Sensitivity analysis results of the sub-criteria in the technical group.

Based on the analysis above, it can be summarized that no matter how the sub-criteria weights change, A4 always secures its ranking as No. 1 in the WtE plant site selection and the robustness of this method is verified.

Next, as the fact that different attitudes of DMs may lead to different ranking orders, we use various values of parameter θ according to the attitudes of DMs to examine how these changes affect the ranking orders and assess the robustness of the obtained ranking.

We let $\theta = 6,5,4,3,2,1,0.9,0.8,0.7,0.6,0.5,0.4,0.3,0.2$, respectively, which indicates the experts' different attitudes to losses and get the ranking orders of the alternatives correspondingly. The results are shown in Table 4.11. From the results, we can see that A4 is always the best alternative, followed by A3. The correctness and robustness of the proposed method in the paper can be testified. However, the worst alternative is changed to A2 instead of A1 with the decrease of θ. The reason can be explained that under the condition that the evaluation results of the alternatives are similar, the psychological behavior characteristics of DMs play a significant role. In fact, the TODIM model considers DMs' performances and DMs are more inclined to reduce the risk of loss, so the final result gained by using the proposed framework, $A4 > A3 > A1 > A2$, is more precise and credible in the real word.

To visualize the influence, a radar diagram based on Table 11 is drawn to present the result of the sensitivity analysis, which is shown in Fig. 4.11. It's evident that the gap of the net flow is getting more prominent between A4 and other alternatives with the decrease of the value of θ. In other words, in spite of whether DMs tend to avoid risk and pursue profit or not, A4 is the optimal and the most reliable site to choose.

Above all, DMs can draw the conclusion that A4 is the optimal site of all alternatives in this case and the method using extended TODIM-PROMETHEE to determine the best location from multiple alternatives is robust and stable.

Table 4.11 Ranking orders of alternatives with different θ.

Sensitivity analysis run	Different values of θ	A1	A2	A3	A4	Ranking of alternatives
1	θ=6	-0.093	-0.059	0.012	0.140	A4 > A3 > A2 > A1
2	θ=5	-0.104	-0.069	0.012	0.161	A4 > A3 > A2 > A1
3	θ=4	-0.119	-0.086	0.013	0.192	A4 > A3 > A2 > A1
4	θ=3	-0.144	-0.113	0.014	0.244	A4 > A3 > A2 > A1
5	θ=2	-0.195	-0.167	0.015	0.347	A4 > A3 > A2 > A1
6	θ=1	-0.348	-0.330	0.020	0.659	A4 > A3 > A2 > A1
7	θ=0.9	-0.382	-0.366	0.021	0.728	A4 > A3 > A2 > A1
8	θ=0.8	-0.425	-0.399	0.010	0.814	A4 > A3 > A2 > A1
9	θ=0.7	-0.480	-0.469	0.023	0.925	A4 > A3 > A2 > A1
10	θ=0.6	-0.552	-0.547	0.026	1.074	A4 > A3 > A2 > A1
11	θ=0.5	-0.654	-0.655	0.029	1.281	A4 > A3 > A1 > A2

Continued

Sensitivity analysis run	Different values of θ	A1	A2	A3	A4	Ranking of alternatives
12	θ=0.4	-0.807	-0.818	0.033	1.592	A4 > A3 > A1 > A2
13	θ=0.3	-1.063	-1.089	0.040	2.111	A4 > A3 > A1 > A2
14	θ=0.2	-1.573	-1.631	0.055	3.149	A4 > A3 > A1 > A2

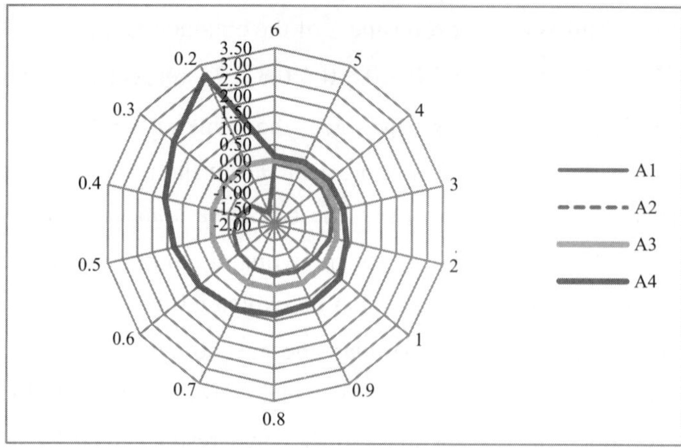

Fig. 4.11 The radar plot showing the result of the sensitivity analysis.

8. Conclusions

This study builds a comprehensive decision framework for the WtE site selection from the sustainability perspective. Previous studies focused on this field are limited, and there are still quite a few problems existing in the decision process for the WtE site selection. Firstly, the frameworks proposed are short of a systematic mode fitting in with social development. Secondly, the indeterminacy of decision information doesn't get thorough expression. Thirdly, the compensation problem occurring in criteria information processing remains unheeded.

Therefore, this paper proposes a new design of comprehensive MCDM framework to handle the aforementioned problems. We extend TODIM method under the circumstance of TIFNs and TIFWG operator to deal with the WtE plant site selection considering the concept of extended sustainability. Firstly, a sustainable evaluation index system for WtE site selection is framed, which consists of four aspects of sustainability, namely economic factors, environmental factors, social factors and technical factors. Following this, the indeterminacy of information gets complete description by converting from the linguistic variables to TIFNs. Finally, an extended TODIM algorithm combined with PROMETHEE-II method is utilized to rank the alternatives and solve compensation problem. After that, when applied to a case from China, it turns out that the decision framework performs excellent suitability. The DMs can well understand the decision-making process and results through the linguistic data. In short, from our theoretical modeling and empirical research, the proposed decision framework can effectively overcome the deficiencies and help DMs choose a more reasonable WtE plant site efficiently.

Due to the practical experience of writers, there are some limitations in this paper. Firstly, although there is certain theoretical basis on applying the evaluation model proposed in this paper to WtE plant site researches, further researches and practice are needed for the practical construction projects. Secondly, on the account of more complicated characters of practical construction projects, the index system should be slightly modified when used for the decision making of practical WtE projects in order to meet the requirement of the practical situation. Only in this way can we obtain the decision result that is more consistent with the practical result.

Acknowledgements

Project supported by the 2017 Special Project of Cultivation and Development of Innovation Base (No. Z171100002217024) and the Fundamental Research Funds for the Central Universities (No. 2018ZD14).

References

[1] Xu S, Yu Y. Optimized research of municipal solid waste incineration plant location [D]. Chongqing University, Chongqing, 2007.

[2] Kazimieras Zavadskas E, Baušys R, Lazauskas M. Sustainable Assessment of Alternative Sites for the Construction of a Waste Incineration Plant by Applying WASPAS Method with Single-Valued Neutrosophic Set[J]. Sustainability, 2015, 7 (12): 15923-15936.

[3] Zheng Y, Zhao B. Optimizing BP Neural Network Used in Refuse Incineration Power Plant Addressing[J]. Electric Power Construction, 2011, 32 (6):67-69.

[4] Subhadra B G. Sustainability of algal biofuel production using integrated renewable energy park (IREP) and algal biorefinery approach[J]. Energy Policy, 2010, 38 (10): 5892-5901.

[5] Guo S, Zhao H. Optimal site selection of electric vehicle charging station by using fuzzy TOPSIS based on sustainability perspective[J]. Applied Energy, 2015, 158:390-402.

[6] Ch Achillasa, Ch Vlachokostasa, N Moussiopoulosa, et al. Social acceptance for the development of a waste-to-energy plant in an urban[J]. Resources, Conservation and Recycling, 2011, 55: 857-863.

[7] Lv H. Research on the Location Problem of Straw-based Power Generation Plant: Considering the Influence of Carbon Emission[D]. Nanjing University of Aeronautics and Astronautics Nanjing, 2014.

[8] Wang Q. Triangular Intuitionsic Fuzzy Multiple Attribute Group Decision Making Method and Its Application in Supplier Selection[D]. Jiangxi Unversity of Finance & Economics, Nanchang, 2014.

[9] Wu Y, Xie C, Xu C, et al. A Decision Framework for Electric Vehicle Charging Station Site Selection for Residential Communities under an Intuitionistic Fuzzy Environment: A Case of Beijing[J]. Energies, 2017, 10 (9): 1270.

[10] Fan Z-P, Zhang X, Chen F-D, et al. Extended TODIM method for hybrid multiple attribute decision making problems[J]. Knowledge-Based Systems, 2013, 42: 40-48.

[11] Krohling R A, Pacheco A G C, Siviero A L T, et al. IF-TODIM: An intuitionistic fuzzy TODIM to multi-criteria decision making[J]. Knowledge-Based Systems, 2013, 53: 142-146.

[12] Wu Y, Zhang J, Yuan J, et al . Study of decision framework of offshore wind power station site selection based on ELECTRE-III under intuitionistic fuzzy environment: A case of China[J]. Energy Conversion and Management, 2016, 113: 66-81.

[13] Hu H, Li X, Nguyen A D, et al. A Critical Evaluation of Waste Incineration Plants in Wuhan (China) Based on Site Selection, Environmental Influence, Public Health and Public Participation[J]. International journal of environmental research and public health, 2015, 12(7): 7593-7614.

[14] Zhao X G, Jiang G W, Li A, et al. Economic analysis of waste-to-energy industry in China[J]. Waste management, 2016, 48: 604-618.

[15] Hadjibiros K, Dermatas D, Laspidou C S. Municipal Solid Waste Management and Landfill Site Selection in Greece: Irrationality Versus Efficiency[J]. Global NEST, 2011, 13 (2): 150-161.

[16] Eskandari M, Homaee M, Mahmodi S. An integrated multi criteria approach for landfill siting in a conflicting environmental, economical and socio-cultural area[J]. Waste management, 2012, 32 (8):1528-38.

[17] Savva P G, Costa C N, Charalambides A G. Environmental, Economical and Marketing Aspects of the Operation of a Waste-to-Energy Plant in the Kotsiatis Landfill in Cyprus[J]. Waste and Biomass Valorization, 2012, 4, (2): 259-269.

[18] Huo P, Cao L, Tian Y. Application and Comparison of AHP and Fuzzy Evaluation Method in Landfill Sting[J]. Environmental Engineering, 2015, (3):131-135.

[19] Xiang M, Yang L, Yu Y, et al. The study on location selection of municipal solid waste incineration power plant based on health risk assessment[J]. China Environmental Science, 2013, 33 (1): 165-171.

[20] Fetanat A, Khorasaninejad E. A novel hybrid MCDM approach for offshore wind farm site selection: A case study of Iran[J]. Ocean & Coastal Management, 2015, 109: 17-28.

[21] Zhao H, Li N. Optimal Siting of Charging Stations for Electric Vehicles Based on Fuzzy Delphi and Hybrid Multi-Criteria Decision Making Approaches from an Extended Sustainability Perspective[J]. Energies, 2016, 9 (4): 270.

[22] Kengpol A, Rontlaong P, Tuominen M. A Decision Support System for Selection of Solar Power Plant Locations by Applying Fuzzy AHP and TOPSIS: An Empirical Study[J]. Journal of Software Engineering and Applications, 2013, 6 (9): 470-481.

[23] Hao Z, Xu Z, Zhao H, et al. Novel Intuitionistic Fuzzy Decision Making Models in the Framework of Decision Field Theory[J]. Information Fusion, 2017, 33: 57-70.

[24] Xu J, Sun S, Ionita S, et al. A risk attitudinal ranking approach of triangular intuitionistic fuzzy numbers and their application to MADM problems[J]. Journal of Intelligent & Fuzzy Systems, 2016, 31 (6): 2919-2925.

[25] Dong J, Wan S. A new method for multi-attribute group decision making with triangular intuitionistic fuzzy numbers[J]. Kybernetes, 2016, 45 (1): 158-180.

[26] Aragonés-Beltrán P, Chaparro-González F, Pastor-Ferrando J-P, et al. An AHP (Analytic Hierarchy Process)/ANP (Analytic Network Process)-based multi-criteria decision approach for the selection of solar-thermal power plant investment projects[J]. Energy, 2014, 66: 222-238.

[27] Liu H, You J, Fan X, et al. Site selection in waste management by the VIKOR method using linguistic assessment[J]. Applied Soft Computing, 2014, 21: 453-461.

[28] Sener S, Sener E, Nas B, et al. Combining AHP with GIS for landfill site selection: a case study in the Lake Beysehir catchment area (Konya, Turkey) [J]. Waste management, 2010, 30 (11): 2037-2046.

[29] De Feo G, De Gisi S. Using MCDA and GIS for hazardous waste landfill siting considering land scarcity for waste disposal[J]. Waste management, 2014, 34 (11): 2225-2238.

[30] Ekmekcioglu M, Kaya T, Kahraman C. Fuzzy multicriteria disposal method and site selection for municipal solid waste[J]. Waste management, 2010, 30 (8-9): 1729-1736.

[31] Büyüközkan G, Güleryüz S. An integrated DEMATEL-ANP approach for renewable energy resources selection in Turkey[J]. International Journal of Production Economics, 2016, 182: 435-448.

[32] Jia C, Huang Y. Study on Garbage Power Plant Location Selection Based on Comprehensive Evaluation Method with Autonomous Decision-making[J]. Shaanxi Electric Power, 2014, 42 (8): 11-16.

[33] Chen R-H, Lin Y, Tseng M-L. Multicriteria analysis of sustainable development indicators in the construction minerals industry in China[J]. Resources Policy, 2015, 46: 123-133.

[34] Tseng M-L, Lin Y-H, Tan K, et al. Using TODIM to Evaluate Green Supply Chain Practices under Uncertainty[J]. Applied Mathematical Modelling, 2014, 38 (11-12): 2983-2995.

[35] Li Y, Shan Y, Liu P. An Extended TODIM Method for Group Decision Making with the Interval Intuitionistic Fuzzy Sets[J]. Mathematical Problems in Engineering, 2015: 1-9.

[36] Qin J, Liu X, Pedrycz W. An extended TODIM multi-criteria group decision making method for green supplier selection in interval type-2 fuzzy environment[J]. European Journal of Operational Research, 2017, 258 (2): 626-638.

[37] Kessili A, Benmamar S. Prioritizing sewer rehabilitation projects using AHP-PROMETHEE II ranking method[J]. Water science and technology: a journal of the International Association on Water Pollution Research, 2016, 73 (2): 283-291.

[38] Song J, Song D, Zhang X, et al. Risk identification for PPP waste-to-energy incineration projects in China[J]. Energy Policy, 2013, 61: 953-962.

[39] Wu Y, Chen K, Zeng B, et al. Cloud-based decision framework for waste-to-energy plant site selection - A case study from China[J]. Waste management, 2016, 48: 593-603.

[40] Gorsevski P V, Donevska K R, Mitrovski C D, et al. Integrating multi-criteria evaluation techniques with geographic information systems for landfill site selection: a case study using ordered weighted average[J]. Waste management, 2012, 32 (2): 287-296.

[41] Wu Y, Yang M, Zhang H, et al. Optimal Site Selection of Electric Vehicle Charging Stations Based on a Cloud Model and the PROMETHEE Method[J]. Energies, 2016, 9 (3): 157.

[42] Wan S, Wang Q, Dong J. The extended VIKOR method for multi-attribute group decision making with triangular intuitionistic fuzzy numbers[J]. Knowledge-Based Systems, 2013, 52: 65-77.

[43] Wan S, Wang F, Lin L, et al.Some new generalized aggregation operators for triangular intuitionistic fuzzy numbers and application to multi-attribute group decision making[J]. Computers & Industrial Engineering, 2016, 93: 286-301.

[44] Sun H, Li Y. VIKOR Method with Triangular Intuitionistic Fuzzy Numbers[J]. Operations Research and Management Science, 2015, 24 (4): 288-294.

[45] Liang C, Zhao S, Zhang J. Aggregation Operators on Triangular Intuitionistic Fuzzy Numbers and its Application to Multi-Criteria Decision Making Problems[J]. Foundations of Computing and Decision Sciences, 2014, 39 (3).

[46] Tang Y. Scientific Project Performance Evaluation of Zhejiang Colleges' Based on AHP&Entropy[D]. Zhejiang University of Technology, Hangzhou, 2011.

[47] Liu P, Teng F. An extended TODIM method for multiple attribute group decision-making based on 2-dimension uncertain linguistic Variable[J]. Complexity, 2016, 21 (5): 20-30.

[48] Wang X, Dang Y-g. Multiple attribute decision-making model with interval grey number based on improved TODIM method[J]. Control and Decision, 2016, 31: 261-266.

[49] Wu Y, Geng S, Zhang H, et al. Decision framework of solar thermal power plant site selection based on linguistic Choquet operator[J]. Applied Energy, 2014, 136: 303-311.

Chapter 5

An intuitionistic fuzzy multi-criteria framework for parabolic trough concentrating solar power plant site selection: a case in China

Yunna Wu [a, b], Buyuan Zhang [a, b*]

a. School of Economics and Management, North China Electric Power University, Beijing, China

b. Beijing Key Laboratory of New Energy and Low-Carbon Development (North China Electric Power University), Changping Beijing 102206, China

Abstract: The Parabolic Trough Concentrating Solar Power Plant (PT-CSPP) is one of the most promising technologies for electricity generation to tackle the rapid increase in energy demand and the limited resources of fossil fuel in the near future. Site selection immensely determines the whole life cycle of PT-CSPP projects in need of considering the impact on environment and society. In consideration of the information inadequacies, the interaction problem and the ambiguity of subjective preferences of decision makers (DMs) existing in decision process, this study establishes a decision framework for PT-CSPP site selection utilizing Fuzzy Vlsekriterijumska Optimizacija IKompromisno Resenje (Fuzzy VIKOR) method combined with a triangular intuitionistic fuzzy generalized ordered weighted averaging (TIFGOWA) operator. First, the triangular intuitionistic fuzzy numbers (TIFNs) are introduced to describe indefinite information. Second, the TIFGOWA operator is adopted to solve the interaction problem involved in different DMs' evaluation on alternative ratings and criteria weights. Third, fuzzy VIKOR is presented to rank the options on the basis of DMs' subjective judgments. Finally, to certificate the feasibility of the proposed framework, a case study of China with sensitive analysis and comparative analysis is conducted. The result illustrates the PT-CSPP site located in Qinghai Golmud would be the optimal site.

Keywords: parabolic trough concentrating solar power plant; site selection; triangular intuitionistic fuzzy number; TIFGOWA; VIKOR

1. Introduction

Energy demand is increasing owing to the rapid growth in global energy consumption, and the limited resources of fossil fuel is depleting with alarming rate. It is estimated that electric energy consumption will double within the next 15-20 years due to an increase in population, industrialization, and urbanization [1]. The total primary 80% energy consumed worldwide is supplied by the fossil fuels, and their maximum uses will be serious issue in near future [2]. Moreover, fossil-fuel energy sources are responsible for an increasing pace of climate change, thus developing countries are imperatively forced to seek alternative energy sources for their respective power sectors to ease carbon emissions. Renewable energy sources provide a viable option to address the key energy demand issues in providing energy services in a sustainable manner and, in particular, in mitigating climate change [3]. Based on the features of green, low-cost and renewable, solar energy is universally recognized as one of the most competitive and effective alternatives among all the renewables [4]. However, solar photovoltaic power generation has certain severe and striking demerits like low efficiency, large surface etc. Fortunately, these two primary problems are being incorporated in the concentrating solar power (CSP) [5]. CSP is one of the most attractive technologies to generate electricity due to the durability and dispatchability especially in countries which are abundant in solar energy resources [1]. In current times, the most advanced technology for solar thermal power production is represented by CSP [6]. The key distinction of CSP comparing with other renewables is the heat storage system to product electricity even with cloudy skies or after the sunset. Thus, the rising economic competitiveness of CSP with fossil fuels will perform a determinant role in the near future [7]. The CSP technology can be classified into parabolic trough, solar tower, linear Fresnel and parabolic dish, based on the way they focus the sun's ray and whether the receiver is fixed or mobile [8]. The parabolic trough concentrating solar power plant (PT-CSPP) is the lowest cost large-scale and most versatile solar power alternative available today and is also one of the primary renewable energy alternatives for electricity production [6]. The PT-CSPP represents the most mature, prominent and developed CSP technology for electricity generation. A schematic diagram of a PT-CSPP is illustrated in Fig.5.1. Chinese government has put forward ambitious development goals for CSP, especially setting up PT-CSPPs. According to the 13th Five-Year electric power plan and Renewable Energy Development Roadmap of China 2050, the expected total installed capacity in 2020, 2030 and 2050 may reach 5 GW, 30GW and 180GW, respectively [9]. In order to implement planning goals, the Chinese government and public are strongly motivated to accelerate the utilization of PT-CSPP to offer potential and sustainable energy supply for the development of cities and society in the future.

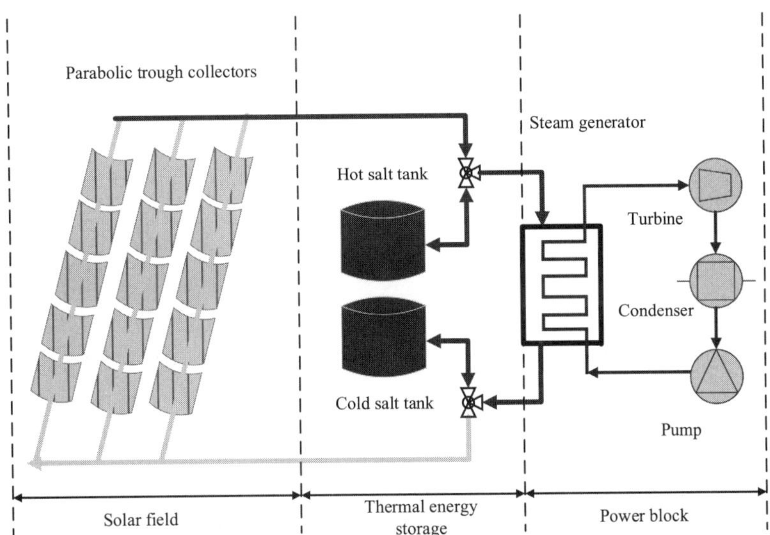

Fig. 5.1 The schematic diagram of a PT-CSPP.

In the entire life cycle of PT-CSPP, the optimal location is extremely critical from the perspective of sustainable development. Firstly, the optimal location would have a necessary impact on the cost, which might determine the funded feasibility of the project. Secondly, a wrongly chosen site could have a hostile influence on the public living life, which would destruct the sustainable development of society. Finally, the alternative site which fails to fit environmental demands would not play a role to protect the environment but to destroy it instead. However, the adequate exiting researches on the PT-CSPP mainly focus on the following aspects: performance optimization [10-14], potential analysis [1,15-17] and techno-economic evaluation [18-23]. Distinct from the aforementioned fields, the issue of PT-CSPP project site selection from the perspective of sustainable development has not acquired plentiful scholarly attention. Beltrán et al. [24] proposed an ordinary method for a solar power investment company in Spanish to determine whether to invest in a CSP project. Aly et al. [25] investigated the spatial suitability for CSP installations using Geographic Information System (GIS) analysis complimented by Multi-criteria Decision Making (MCDM) technique. However, their researches have not taken into consideration the environmental and social influences and benefits for sustainable cities and society. Moreover, shortcomings and inadequacies existing in the decision process decrease the evaluation quality of PT-CSPP site selection. Firstly, the vague and imprecise information generally exist in the process of site selection due to the complex situation as follows: ①the chosen location of a project is in the early period that depends on ex ante predicts what the values may be; ②the energy investment market is always dynamic and unpredictable based on the undulation of market price and energy policy; ③the judgment and determination of some factors relies on DMs' experience, which could not reflect DMs' opinions as exactly as precise machines do when depicting an intricate object. Secondly, the interaction problem exists in different DMs' evaluation on alternative ratings and criteria weights, which are not taken seriously. Thirdly, the ranking order techniques utilized in previous studies could not describe the DMs' subjective preferences for evaluating the PT-CSPP site selection problem accurately. Fortunately, the value of this study would make up for the shortcomings and inadequacies in current researches, which is vitally significant for the development prospect of PT-CSPP.

The site selection decision making for PT-CSPP based on sustainable cites and society is a complex MCDM problem due to its uncertainties and specificity. This study aims at building up a practical comprehensive index system based on sustainability perspective for PT-CSPP site selection and establishing an effective realistic decision framework to choose the most satisfactory scheme. A novel design of fuzzy MCDM framework based on the fuzzy VIKOR method is proposed to handle the PT-CSPP site selection problem combined with a TIFGOWA operator under incomplete information environment. The originality and intention of this study derives from the following details. Firstly, based on the sustainable development of cites and society, the comprehensive index system for PT-CSPP site selection is set up practically. Secondly, in order to describe the vague and inaccurate judgment and determination of information in the site selection for PT-CSPP, the TIFNs are normally utilized in the group decision for the DMs. Thirdly, the TIFGOWA operator is introduced to integrate the DMs' evaluation opinions on alternative ratings and criteria weights. Moreover, the fuzzy VIKOR method is employed to rank the options on the basis of the distinct views of different DMs. This proposed fuzzy MCDM framework provides the ranking of alternative PT-CSPP sites under the goal of sustainable society and practicable evaluation criteria to insure the effectiveness of decision making. Finally, the reasonability and practicality of this research are illustrated through an example of China.

2. Literature review

MCDM ranking order methods, such as Analytic Hierarchy Process (AHP), Analytic Network Process (ANP), Perference Ranking Organization Methods for Enrichment Evaluations (PROMETHEE), Elimination et Choix Traduisant la Realité (ELECTRE), Technique for Order Preference by Similarity to Ideal Solution (TOPSIS) and VIKOR are applied diffusely in the site selection field. Baseer et al. [26] employed AHP technique to assign appropriate weights of criteria in the site suitability analysis for wind farm. The ANP method was used to determine the weight of coefficients of criteria when selecting the wind farm location [27]. Inamdar et al. [28] proposed PROMETHEE II method to rank potential stormwater harvesting sites. Wu et al. [29] built a decision framework for offshore wind farm site selection based on ELECTRE-III technique. Fang et al. [30] presented a novel integrated method based on TOPSIS to select sustainable sites for PV power plant. Liu et al. [31] introduced a decision making model via a hybrid modified VIKOR method to improve and select the location for the food waste composting facilities. These aforementioned studies clarify the utilization of MCDM techniques and certificate the practicality and feasibility of them in the site selection field of the decision support system for evaluation.

Fuzzy set theory [32] has emerged as a vigorous way to describe uncertain phenomena for solving site selection problem. The presentation of fuzzy set theory promoted fuzzy numbers to be widely applied in the field of site selection to express uncertainties. For instance, Zhang et al. [33] employed the picture fuzzy set to describe large amounts of uncertain information in the location selection of offshore wind power station. Rikalovic et al. [34] proposed a fuzzy approach in the intelligent decision support system for industrial site classification. However, to some extent, the DMs exhibit some hesitation degrees for the estimation since they depends on intuition and experience to assess the complex attributes of available sites in the decision-making problems [35]. Intuitionistic fuzzy set (IFS) [36] is more feasible and practical than traditional fuzzy set in dealing with uncertainties since IFSs include membership, non-membership and hesitation degrees simultaneously. TIFN, as an advanced version of IFN, has acquired considerable preferences since it expresses DMs' opinions more accurately by employing a triangular fuzzy number (TFN) to replace a linguistic variable [37]. Constantly, sufficient researchers have begun to adopt TIFNs to solve MCDM problems for the goal of making decision results be in line with real-life situations. Qin et al. [38] applied TIFNs combined with an extended TODIM method to deal with the multi-criteria group decision making problems. Chen and Huang [39] explored the applications of TIFNs in three methods of MCDM problems. Wu et al. [40] utilized a novel method with TIFNs to build a framework for waste-to-energy plant site selection decision. Wu et al. [41] used TIFNs to establish a practical electric vehicle charging station site selection decision framework. The TIFNs are certified to be more predominant in settling incompletely reliable or inevitably imprecise judgments and decisions in MCDM problems, which is appropriate and acceptable for DMs to represent their affirmation, negation and hesitation in decision-making applications [35, 38]. Since the pre-project evaluation site selection problem is filled with diverse uncertain information, applying the TIFNs to express the uncertainties of PT-CSPP site selection would have significant practical value.

Based on current researches, the aggregating techniques, such as weighted arithmetic aggregation operators or geometric aggregation operators, are widely used to solve MCDM problems with intuitionistic fuzzy numbers (IFNs) and TIFNs. Yin and Li [42] transformed numerous aspirations into integrated aspirations using intuitionistic fuzzy geometric weighted Heronian mean (IFGWHM) operator. Wu et al. [29] applied the generalized intuitionistic fuzzy ordered weighted geometric interaction averaging (GIFWGIA) operator to deal with the interaction problem. Compared with the aggregating techniques diffusely applied in IFNs, the integrated operators of TIFNs only attract a minority of researchers. The weighted arithmetic interaction averaging operator of TIFN (TIFN-WAIA) was defined to aggregate the weight vector [38]. Wu et al. [40] integrated the opinions of experts into a comprehensive decision matrix by the triangular intuitionistic fuzzy weighted geometric (TIFWG) operator. The TIFGOWA operator unifies most of aggregation operators of TIFNs, for example, the TIFWG is a special case of the TIFGOWA operator [35]. Since the TIFGOWA operator has distinct forms through choosing different function g, the DMs could receive different decision results by applying the TIFGOWA operator, which exceedingly enhances the flexibility and effectiveness of decision-making technique. Thus, this study employs the TIFGOWA operator to integrate the DMs' different evaluation results, which solves the interaction problem validly and accurately.

The ranking technique VIKOR is one of the most widely applied MCDM methods, which has been extended to multiple kinds of fuzzy situations. Sakthivel et al. [43] proposed a fuzzy VIKOR method to select the optimum fuel biodiesel blend for the IC engine. Xu et al. [44] assessed alternatives using the fuzzy VIKOR approach in the service performance evaluation of electric vehicle sharing programs. Gul and Ak [45] provided a fuzzy AHP-VIKOR integrated method in quantifying risk ratings. Majumder and Maity [46] combined VIKOR with the fuzzy logic system to predict and optimize wire electrical discharge machining responses for nickel-titanium shape memory alloy. Chen [47] presented novel VIKOR-based methods to deal with multiple criteria decision analysis involving Pythagorean fuzzy information. Wang et al. [48] constructed an integrated picture fuzzy normalized projection VIKOR-based method for the risk evaluation. Awasthi et al. [49] employed an integrated fuzzy AHP-VIKOR approach-based framework for sustainable global supplier selection. Yang et al. [50] obtained the optimal solution closest to ideal solution via VIKOR method in the fuzzy environment. Ren et al. [51] put forward a dual hesitant fuzzy VIKOR method for solving the multi-criteria group decision making problems. Zhao et al. [52] used fuzzy VIKOR for ranking alternatives to evaluate the comprehensive benefit of eco-industrial parks. Obviously, the fuzzy VIKOR technique was utilized diffusely in the realistic MCDM problems, which demonstrated the feasibility and rationality of the proposed model to select the optional location.

According to the literature review above, we could definitely prove the applicability and superiority of our research. The fuzzy VIKOR-based framework combined with TIFGOWA operator under the TIFN environment is established for PT-CSPP project site selection because: ①various kinds of uncertainties and fuzziness are existed in the PT-CSPP project for its complicated and inconstant environment and technical conditions, and the TIFN is a powerful and useful tool for representing such uncertainties; ②the interaction problem is involved in different DMs' evaluation on alternative ratings and criteria weights, and the TIFGOWA operator is introduced to integrate the DMs' evaluation opinions; ③the DM's subjective preferences may not be taken into account, and fuzzy VIKOR is proposed to rank the options on the basis of DMs' opinions. Thus, based on the aforementioned improvements, the decision results of PT-CSPP project site selection will be more scientific and reasonable than before.

3. Evaluation criteria system of PT-CSPP site selection

Although building PT-CSPP is a valid way to save energy, it has not been widespread in China yet. In the entire life cycle of PT-CSPP, it is imperative for us to establish a scientific and comprehensive evaluation index system to identify a satisfied site for PT-CSPPs. The PT-CSPP site selection is dependent upon various factors. And since building PT-CSPP is a sustainable way to contribute to energy conversion, it is necessary to take sustainable decision factors into consideration. According to the relevant literature, feasibility reports and concerning the current situation, a scientific and sustainable evaluation index system has been established which covers resource factor (C1), economy factor (C2), infrastructure and construction factor (C3), environmental factor (C4), and social factor (C5).

3.1 Resource factor

The resource factor includes annual sunshine hours (C11), annual solar radiation (C12) and average temperature (C13) which are the essential sub-criteria to assess the solar energy and available resources. The amount of solar energy, such as annual sunshine hours and annual sunshine radiation received at the alternative sites will impact on the quality of project operation [53]. The annual solar radiation was taken as a climatological factor applied to determine the intensity of sunshine for a candidate site [54]. Distinct from solar photovoltaic, CSP applies only the direct normal irradiation (DNI) and can supply carbon-free heat and power only in regions with high DNI [7]. The working temperature of solar radiation concentrating collectors influence the performance and high temperature driven losses [55]. The performance of PT-CSPP extremely depends on the meteorological conditions at the specific location of the plant. Thus, resource assessment is the primary and essential exercise for the decision-making in PT-CSPP site selection.

3.2 Economy factor

The economy factor adopts the levelized cost of energy (LCOE) evolution (C21) which is one of the most common methodologies to evaluate the economic situation of an electric energy generation project [56]. LCOE weights the overall unit energy costs of building and operating a power system throughout its entire life [57]. All the expenses and revenues, which occur during the lifetime of CSP systems, shall be accounted for the present value of money when we calculate LCOE [9]. Unfortunately, the previous studies on LCOE of CSP systems ignore partial taxes or costs and cannot accurately reflect the cost-benefit of CSP systems. The objective of the economic assessment is to investigate the profitability of PT-CSPP projects regardless of their financing system, which gives the DMs an overall idea about the funding limitations and economic risks of these projects to enable them to plan for their PT-CSPP projects in a more feasible and precise way.

3.3 Infrastructure and construction factor

The infrastructure and construction factor has the components of grid connection convenience (C31), water supply convenience (C32), transportation convenience (C33), soil structure and the geology (C34) and land tenure (C35). Power grid is another essential factor for the site selection of CSP systems in China, since the electricity generated by CSP systems is not only needed to satisfy the demand of local economics, but also to transmit the surplus electricity to the load center (eastern China) that is facing the power shortage through the grid [58]. In contrast to other renewable technologies such as solar PV or wind farm, CSP systems require a considerable amount of water, mainly for cooling and spinning steam turbines [3, 59]. The transportation convenience is to evaluate the transportation comfort level at the construction period, which is interrelated to the costs and risk of projects [60]. The nature of the soil has impact on the type of civil work to be conducted on the location especially the foundation and the earthwork. Land cover should not conflict with other land usage such as housing, farming, protected natural reserves and industrial zones [58, 59]. Ideal locations of PT-CSPP are near cities with appropriate grid connection distance, sufficient water resource, good transportation, favorable geology and approved land tenure.

3.4 Environmental factor

The environmental factor consists of impact on the surrounding environment (C41) and pollutant emission reduction benefits (C42). The CSP projects will disturb the surrounding environment and living people, such as noise pollution, light pollution, soil quality degradation, acidification potential and waste disposal [61]. The pollutant emission reduction benefit indicates that the amount of CO_2, SO_2, NO_2 and dust will be decreased by using a PT-CSPP to replace a thermal power station at the same electricity production amount [62]. The main objective of PT-CSPP projects is developing emission reduction electric energy generation projects. Thus, in order to evaluate the sustainability of a chosen project, determination of environmental factor is a critical step.

3.5 Social factor

The social factor contains impact on the local economy (C51) and public support (C52). People might attach importance to that CSP deployment has the potential for substantial local value addition through localization of production of components, services and operation and maintenance, thus driving local economic development and creating job opportunities [63]. For countries that are net fossil fuel energy importers, CSP deployment may be an appealing alternative to lessen this dependence. The social acceptability of a technology can be critical for its deployment [63].

In conclusion, in order to evaluate and select the best site for PT-CSPP scientifically and responsibly from the perspective of sustainable development, it is essential to take into account resource factor, economy factor, environmental factor, social factor as well as infrastructure and construction factor. The evaluation criteria system for PT-CSPP site selection including five specific criteria and thirteen sub-criteria is set up, shown in Table 5.1.

Table 5.1 The criteria and sub-criteria of the PT-CSPP site selection.

Criteria	Sub-criteria	Remark
(C1) Resource factor	(C11) Annual sunshine hours	It determines local solar energy level
	(C12) Annual solar radiation	It directly influences the generating capacity and decides whether the PT-CSPP will be implemented
	(C13) Average temperature	The working temperature will affect the performance of the PT-CSPP
(C2) Economy factor	(C21) Levelized cost of energy evolution	It reflects the lifecycle cost of the PT-CSPP
(C3) Infrastructure and construction factor	(C31) Grid connection convenience	It will influence the power losses and the transmission cost
	(C32) Water supply convenience	The PT-CSPP requires a water source for their operation
	(C33) Transportation convenience	It reflects the transportation comfort level at the construction period
	(C34) Soil structure and the geology	It determines the type of civil work
	(C35) Land tenure	It determines the ownership to build the PT-CSPP
(C4) Environmental factor	(C41) Impact on the surrounding environment	It will influence the surrounding ecological environment
	(C42) Pollutant emission reduction benefits	Energy generated by the PT-CSPP is non-polluting
(C5) Social factor	(C51) Impact on the local economy	The utilization of the PT-CSPP will affect local economy
	(C52) Public support	It affects the popularity of the PT-CSPP

4. Decision framework of PT-CSPP site selection

4.1 Basic theory of MCDM problem in the triangular intuitionistic fuzzy environment

In order to express the DMs' incomplete and imperfect knowledge in decision-making utilization more effectively, the triangular intuitionistic fuzzy number (TIFN) is introduced in the MCDM method. This section describes a few definitions and operations of TIFN related to the PT-CSPP site selection MCDM problem.

Definition 1. [64] A TIFN $\tilde{a}$ is defined as $\tilde{a}=((\underline{a},a,\overline{a});w_{\tilde{a}},u_{\tilde{a}})$ on the real number set R, whose membership function and non-membership function are defined as:

$$\mu_{\tilde{a}}(x)=\begin{cases}(x-\underline{a})w_{\tilde{a}}/(a-\underline{a}) & \text{if } \underline{a}\leqslant x<a,\\ w_{\tilde{a}} & \text{if } x=a,\\ (\overline{a}-x)w_{\tilde{a}}/(\overline{a}-a) & \text{if } a<x\leqslant\overline{a},\\ 0 & \text{if } x<\underline{a} \text{ or } x>\overline{a}\end{cases}$$

and

$$\nu_{\tilde{a}}(x)=\begin{cases}[a-x+u_{\tilde{a}}(x-\underline{a})]/(a-\underline{a}) & \text{if } a\leqslant x<a,\\ u_{\tilde{a}} & \text{if } x=a,\\ [x-a+u_{\tilde{a}}(\overline{a}-x)]/(\overline{a}-a) & \text{if } a<x\leqslant\overline{a},\\ 1 & \text{if } x<\underline{a} \text{ or } x>\overline{a}\end{cases}$$

respectively, where the values $w_{\tilde{a}}$ and $u_{\tilde{a}}$ mean the maximum membership degree and the minimum non-membership degree which meet the conditions: $0\leqslant w_{\tilde{a}}\leqslant 1$, $0\leqslant u_{\tilde{a}}\leqslant 1$ and $w_{\tilde{a}}+u_{\tilde{a}}\leqslant 1$. Let $\pi_{\tilde{a}}(x)=1-w_{\tilde{a}}(x)-u_{\tilde{a}}(x)$ represent an intuitionistic fuzzy index of the TIFN $\tilde{a}$, which implies hesitancy degree of the element x to $\tilde{a}$, the definition is visualized in Fig. 5.2.

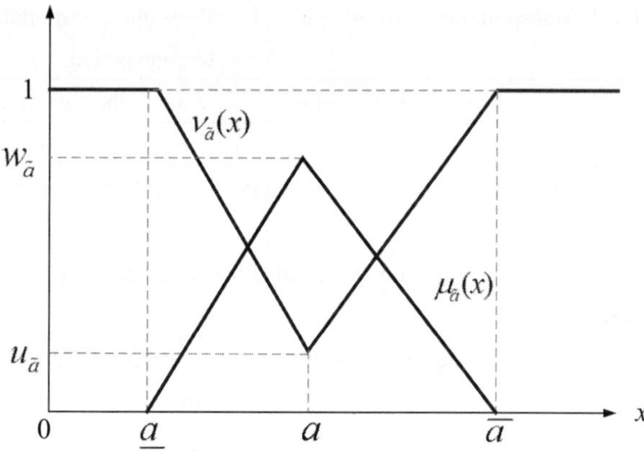

Fig. 5.2 A TFIN $\tilde{a}=((\underline{a},a,\overline{a});w_{\tilde{a}},u_{\tilde{a}})$.

A TIFN $\tilde{a}=((\underline{a},a,\overline{a});w_{\tilde{a}},u_{\tilde{a}})$ represents an ill-known quantity "approximate a", whose meaning is approximately equal to a. That is to say, the ill-known quantity "approximate a" is represented by any value between $\underline{a}$ and $\overline{a}$ with distinct degrees of membership and degrees of non-membership. Namely, the most probable value is a with the degree $w_{\tilde{a}}$ of membership and the degree $u_{\tilde{a}}$ of non-membership; the pessimistic value is $\underline{a}$ while the optimistic value is $\overline{a}$ with the degree 0 of membership and the degree 1 of non-membership. Moreover, other values are equal to any $x\in(\underline{a},\overline{a})$ with the degree $\mu_{\tilde{a}}(x)$ of membership and the degree $\nu_{\tilde{a}}(x)$ of non-membership.

Definition 2.[40] Let $\tilde{a}_1=((\underline{a}_1,a_1,\overline{a}_1);w_{a_1},u_{a_1})$ and $\tilde{a}_2=((\underline{a}_2,a_2,\overline{a}_2);w_{a_2},u_{a_2})$ represent two TIFNs and λ be a real number. Then the arithmetical operations for TIFNs are defined as:

$$\tilde{a}_1+\tilde{a}_2=((\underline{a}_1+\underline{a}_2,a_1+a_2,\overline{a}_1+\overline{a}_2);w_{\tilde{a}_1}\wedge w_{\tilde{a}_2},u_{\tilde{a}_1}\vee u_{\tilde{a}_2}) \tag{5-1}$$

$$\tilde{a}_1\tilde{a}_2=\begin{cases}((\underline{a}_1\underline{a}_2,a_1a_2,\overline{a}_1\overline{a}_2);w_{\tilde{a}_1}\wedge w_{\tilde{a}_2},u_{\tilde{a}_1}\vee u_{\tilde{a}_2}), \text{ if } \tilde{a}_1>0 \text{ and } \tilde{a}_2>0\\((\underline{a}_1\overline{a}_2,a_1a_2,\overline{a}_1\underline{a}_2);w_{\tilde{a}_1}\wedge w_{\tilde{a}_2},u_{\tilde{a}_1}\vee u_{\tilde{a}_2}), \text{ if } \tilde{a}_1<0 \text{ and } \tilde{a}_2>0\\((\overline{a}_1\overline{a}_2,a_1a_2,\underline{a}_1\underline{a}_2);w_{\tilde{a}_1}\wedge w_{\tilde{a}_2},u_{\tilde{a}_1}\vee u_{\tilde{a}_2}), \text{ if } \tilde{a}_1<0 \text{ and } \tilde{a}_2<0\end{cases} \tag{5-2}$$

$$\lambda\tilde{a}_1=\begin{cases}((\lambda\underline{a}_1,\lambda a_1,\lambda\overline{a}_1);w_{\tilde{a}_1},u_{\tilde{a}_1}), \text{ if } \lambda>0\\((\lambda\overline{a}_1,\lambda a_1,\lambda\underline{a}_1);w_{\tilde{a}_1},u_{\tilde{a}_1}), \text{ if } \lambda<0\end{cases} \tag{5-3}$$

$$\tilde{a}_1^{\lambda}=((\underline{a}_1^{\lambda},a_1^{\lambda},\overline{a}_1^{\lambda});w_{\tilde{a}_1},u_{\tilde{a}_1}) \tag{5-4}$$

where the notations "$\wedge$" and "$\vee$" imply min and max operators, respectively.

Definition 3. [64] Let $\tilde{a}_i=((\underline{a}_i,a_i,\overline{a}_i);w_{a_i},u_{a_i})$ represent a set of TIFNs. A ratio ranking procedure can be presented for ranking the TIFNs $a_i(i=1,2,\ldots,n)$, which is summarized as follows:

$$R(\tilde{a}_i,\lambda)=\frac{(\underline{a}_i+4a_i+\overline{a}_i)+(\lambda w_{\tilde{a}_i}^2+(1-\lambda)(1-u_{\tilde{a}_i})^2)}{6+(\overline{a}_i-\underline{a}_i)(\lambda w_{\tilde{a}_i}^2+(1-\lambda)(1-u_{\tilde{a}_i})^2)} \tag{5-5}$$

where $\lambda\in[0,1]$ is a weight which reflects the DM's opinion toward the degree of uncertainty; $\lambda\in[0,1/2)$ indicates that the DM prefers uncertainty or negative feeling; $\lambda\in(1/2,1]$ means that the DM prefers certainty or positive feeling; $\lambda=1/2$ implies that the DM is unconcerned between positive feeling and negative feeling. Thus, the ambiguity parameter λ expresses the DM's subjectivity opinion to the TIFN.

Definition 4. [40] Let $\tilde{a}_1=((\underline{a}_1,a_1,\overline{a}_1);w_{a_1},u_{a_1})$ and $\tilde{a}_2=((\underline{a}_2,a_2,\overline{a}_2);w_{a_2},u_{a_2})$ represent two TIFNs. The distance between them is defined as follows:

$$d(\tilde{a}_1,\tilde{a}_2)=\frac{1}{6}\left\langle\begin{array}{l}|(1+w_{a_1}-u_{a_1})\underline{a}_1-(1+w_{a_2}-u_{a_2})\underline{a}_2|\\+|(1+w_{a_1}-u_{a_1})a_1-(1+w_{a_2}-u_{a_2})a_2|\\+|(1+w_{a_1}-u_{a_1})\overline{a}_1-(1+w_{a_2}-u_{a_2})\overline{a}_2|\end{array}\right\rangle \tag{5-6}$$

The personal opinions of experts are integrated into a comprehensive decision matrix by using the triangular intuitionistic fuzzy generalized ordered weighted averaging (TIFGOWA) operator.

Definition 5. [35] Let $\tilde{a}_i=((\underline{a}_i,a_i,\overline{a}_i);w_{a_i},u_{a_i})$ be a set of TIFNs, and let TIFGOWA: $\Omega^k\rightarrow\Omega$, satisfying

$$
\begin{aligned}
TIFGOWA_{\omega}(\tilde{a}_1,\tilde{a}_2,\ldots,\tilde{a}_n)&=g^{-1}\left(\sum_{i=1}^{k}\omega_i g(\tilde{a}_{(i)})\right)\\
&=\left(\left(g^{-1}\left(\sum_{i=1}^{k}\omega_i g(\underline{a}_{(i)})\right),g^{-1}\left(\sum_{i=1}^{k}\omega_i g(a_{(i)})\right),g^{-1}\left(\sum_{i=1}^{k}\omega_i g(\overline{a}_{(i)})\right)\right);\wedge_{i=1}^{k}w_{\overline{a}_{(i)}},\vee_{i=1}^{k}u_{\overline{a}_{(i)}}\right)
\end{aligned}
\tag{5-7}
$$

where g is a continuous strictly monotone increasing function, $\omega=(\omega_1,\omega_2,\ldots,\omega_n)^T$ is the weight vector of $a_i(i=1,2,\ldots,k)$, satisfying $0\leqslant\omega_i\leqslant1$ and $\sum_{i=1}^{k}\omega_i=1$.

4.2 Description of the decision making matrix with TIFNs information

The criteria can be assorted into three types: ①quantitative criteria that can be measured accurately; ②quantitative criteria that cannot be measured accurately; and ③qualitative criteria. For the first type of criteria, though their values are equal to real numbers, which will be converted into TIFNs to keep the consistency; for the second type of criteria, their imprecise values are computed firstly, and then experts appraise them by applying TIFNs to express the uncertainties; for the last type of criteria, their qualitative values are directly evaluated by experts using linguistic scales in Table 5.2.

Table 5.2 The fuzzy linguistic scale for the alternatives.

Linguistic Variable	Abbreviation	TIFNs
Very poor	VP	((0, 0, 1);0.7,0.2)
Poor	P	((0, 1, 3);0.8,0.1)
Medium poor	MP	((1, 3, 5);0.9,0)
Fair	F	((3, 5, 7);1,0)
Medium good	MG	((5, 7, 9);0.9,0)
Good	G	((7, 9, 10);0.8,0.1)
Very good	VG	((9, 10, 10);0.7,0.2)

Hypothesis that this MCDM problem has $k(k=1,2,\ldots,K)$ experts, m alternatives $A_i(i=1,2,\ldots,m)$, and n sub-criteria $C_j(j=1,2,\ldots,n)$. Let $\tilde{x}_{ijk}=((\underline{x}_{ijk},x_{ijk},\overline{x}_{ijk}),w_{x_{ijk}},u_{x_{ijk}})$ represent the fuzzy rating of the i th alternative on the j th sub-criterion provided by the k_{th} experts by TIFNs, and $\omega_k(k=1,2,\ldots,K)$ represent the relative importance weights of the K experts, satisfying $\sum_1^K\omega_k=1$ and $\omega_k>0$ for $k=1,2,\ldots,K$.

The aggregated fuzzy ratings $\tilde{x}_{ij}=((\underline{x}_{ij},x_{ij},\overline{x}_{ij});w_{x_{ij}},u_{x_{ij}})$ of alternatives with respect to each criterion could be calculated utilizing the TIFGOWA operator according to Eq. (5-7), then the aggregated decision matrix $[\tilde{x}_{ij}]_{m\times n}$ is constructed. In order to evaluate the influence of distinct physical dimensions and measurements on the final decision, the decision matrix $[\tilde{x}_{ij}]_{m\times n}$ need be normalized as $[\tilde{r}_{ij}]_{m\times n}$ where $\tilde{r}_{ij}=(\underline{r}_{ij},r_{ij},\overline{r}_{ij},w_{r_{ij}},u_{r_{ij}})$ with $w_{r_{ij}}=w_{x_{ij}}$, $u_{r_{ij}}=u_{x_{ij}}$ and

$$(\underline{r}_{ij},r_{ij},\overline{r}_{ij})=\begin{cases}(\frac{\underline{x}_{ij}}{\overline{x}_{\max j}},\frac{x_{ij}}{\overline{x}_{\max j}},\frac{\overline{x}_{ij}}{\overline{x}_{\max j}}) & \text{if } x_j\in F^B\\ (\frac{\underline{x}_{\min j}}{\overline{x}_{ij}},\frac{\underline{x}_{\min j}}{x_{ij}},\frac{\underline{x}_{\min j}}{\underline{x}_{ij}}) & \text{if } x_j\in F^C\end{cases}\tag{5-8}$$

where $\overline{x}_{\max j}=\max\{\overline{x}_{ij}\mid i=1,2,\ldots,m\}$, $\underline{x}_{\min j}=\min\{\underline{x}_{ij}\mid i=1,2,\ldots,m\}$. F^B and F^C are the subsets of benefit criteria and cost criteria, respectively.

4.3 Entropy-weighting approach with TIFNs

The entropy-weighting approach has been extensively applied in decision-making situations since it derived from thermodynamics. It has become a useful tool to measure the information providing by the data from an objected point of view. In this paper, the entropy-weighting approach is utilized to obtain the weight of criteria.

The step to defuzzify fuzzy numbers must be conducted before determining the weight using Eq. (5-5). The TIFN $\tilde{x}_{ij}=((\underline{x}_{ij},x_{ij},\overline{x}_{ij});w_{x_{ij}},u_{x_{ij}})$ can be defuzzified as follows (here $\lambda=0.5$):

$$x_{ij}=\frac{(\underline{x}_i+4x_i+\overline{x}_i)+(0.5w_{\tilde{x}_i}^2+0.5(1-u_{\tilde{x}_i})^2)}{6+(\overline{x}_i-\underline{x}_i)(0.5w_{\tilde{x}_i}^2+0.5(1-u_{\tilde{x}_i})^2)},i<j\tag{5-9}$$

Definition 6. [65] Let e_j represent the entropy of sub-criterion j, satisfying:

$$e_j=-\frac{1}{\ln m}\sum_{i=1}^{m}\left[\frac{x_{ij}}{\sum_{i=1}^{m}x_{ij}}\times\ln\left(\frac{x_{ij}}{\sum_{i=1}^{m}x_{ij}}\right)\right]\tag{5-10}$$

where $e_j\in[0,1]$.

Definition 7. [65] Let ω_j^c represent the entropy of sub-criterion j, satisfying:

$$h_j=1-e_j\tag{5-11}$$

$$\omega_j^c=\frac{h_j}{\sum_{j=1}^{n}h_j}\tag{5-12}$$

where $\sum_{j=1}^{n}\omega_j^c=1$.

4.4 Description of fuzzy VIKOR method

The fuzzy VIKOR method involves the following steps [64].

Step 1. Calculate the fuzzy best $\tilde{f}_j^*$ and the fuzzy worst $\tilde{f}_j^-$ values of all criteria ratings according to the normalized decision matrix $[\tilde{r}_{ij}]_{m\times n}$, $i=1,2,\ldots,m$, $j=1,2,\ldots,n$.

$$\tilde{f}_j^*=\left\{\begin{array}{ll}\max\limits_i \tilde{r}_{ij}=((\max\limits_i \underline{r}_{ij},\max\limits_i r_{ij},\max\limits_i \overline{r}_{ij});1,0), & \text{for benefit criteria}\\ \min\limits_i \tilde{r}_{ij}=((\min\limits_i \underline{r}_{ij},\min\limits_i r_{ij},\min\limits_i \overline{r}_{ij});0,1), & \text{for cost criteria}\end{array}\right\} \tag{5-13}$$

$$\tilde{f}_j^-=\left\{\begin{array}{ll}\min\limits_i \tilde{r}_{ij}=((\min\limits_i \underline{r}_{ij},\min\limits_i r_{ij},\min\limits_i \overline{r}_{ij});0,1), & \text{for benefit criteria}\\ \max\limits_i \tilde{r}_{ij}=((\max\limits_i \underline{r}_{ij},\max\limits_i r_{ij},\max\limits_i \overline{r}_{ij});1,0), & \text{for cost criteria}\end{array}\right\} \tag{5-14}$$

Step 2. Determine the normalized fuzzy distance $d_{ij}, i=1,2,\ldots,m$, $j=1,2,\ldots,n$ based on Eq. (5-6).

$$d_{ij}=\frac{d(\tilde{f}_j^*,\tilde{r}_{ij})}{d(\tilde{f}_j^*,\tilde{f}_j^-)} \tag{5-15}$$

Step 3. Determine group utility S_i and individual regret R_i for each alternative i.

$$S_i=\sum_{j=1}^{n}\omega_j^c d_{ij}, i=1,2,\ldots,m \tag{5-16}$$

$$R_i=\max_j(\omega_j^c d_{ij}), i=1,2,\ldots,m \tag{5-17}$$

where ω_j^c means the relative weights of sub-criteria acquired from the above subsection.

Step 4. Determine aggregating index Q_i for each alternative i.

$$Q_i=v\frac{S_i-S^*}{S^- -S^*}+(1-v)\frac{R_i-R^*}{R^- -R^*}, i=1,2,\ldots,m \tag{5-18}$$

where $S^*=\min\limits_i S_i$, $S^-=\max\limits_i S_i$, $R^*=\min\limits_i R_i$, $R^-=\max\limits_i R_i$, and v represents the weight of the strategy of the majority of sub-criteria. The value of v is set to 0.5 in this study.

Step 5. Rank the alternatives, sorting by the values S, R and Q in the increasing order.

Step 6. Determine a compromise solution, the alternative ($A^{(1)}$), which is the best ranked by the measure Q (minimum) if the following two conditions are satisfied:

Condition 1. Acceptable advantage: $Q(A^{(2)})-Q(A^{(1)})\geqslant 1/(m-1)$ where $A^{(2)}$ represents the alternative with second position in the ranking list by Q.

Condition 2. Acceptable stability in decision making: The best alternative $A^{(1)}$ must also be the best alternative in terms of both S_i and R_i. This compromise solution is stable within a decision-making process, which could be: "voting by majority rule" (when $v > 0.5$ is needed), or "by consensus" ($v \approx 0.5$), or "with veto" ($v < 0.5$).

If one of the conditions is not conformed, then a set of compromise solutions is presented, which includes:

Alternatives $A^{(1)}$ and $A^{(2)}$ if only condition 2 is not accorded.

Alternatives $A^{(1)}, A^{(2)}$,…, $A^{(M)}$ if condition 1 is not accorded. Alternative $A^{(M)}$ is determined by $Q(A^{(M)}) - Q(A^{(1)}) < 1/(m-1)$.

4.5 Decision framework of the PT-CSPP site selection

The intuitionistic fuzzy multi-criteria decision framework proposed in this work combining TIFN, TIFGOWA operator, the entropy-weighting approach and fuzzy VIKOR together in a very structure and systematic framework. The proposed framework composes of five main steps, which can be seen in Fig. 5.3. A detailed description of each step composing the suggested site selection framework is presented as follows.

Step 1. Determine the alternative PT-CSPP sites. A number of experts are invited by the project DMs to establish the decision-making committee. Firstly the decision-making committee applies the satellite remote sensing data, traffic maps, grid maps and other information to select feasible alternative PT-CSPP sites. Then the decision-making committee visits and inspects these alternative PT-CSPP sites to collect socio-political and other relevant information of each site from revenue records and local administration, for the purpose of avoiding any possible delay in getting final approval of chosen optimal sites for establishing the new PT-CSPP from various State and Central Government Departments. Finally, the decision-making committee will determine the alternative PT-CSPP sites and obtain some relevant data of the quantitative criteria.

Step 2. Determine the decision making matrix with TIFNs. For the first two types of criteria, their values are converted into TIFNs. For the last type of criteria, their qualitative values are directly evaluated by the decision-making committee using linguistic scales based on Table 2 firstly, and then the linguistic values are transformed into TIFNs which represents the opinions of them. Then, the decision making matrix $\tilde{x}_{ijk} = ((\underline{x}_{ijk}, x_{ijk}, \overline{x}_{ijk}), w_{x_{ijk}}, u_{x_{ijk}})$ belonged to each expert can be derived.

Step 3. Construct the aggregated decision matrix utilizing the TIFGOWA operator. Based on Eq. (5-7), the aggregated decision matrix $[\tilde{x}_{ij}]_{m\times n}$ is constructed. Then, the normalized decision matrix $[\tilde{r}_{ij}]_{m\times n}$ is calculated to keep the consistency, as shown in Eq. (5-8).

Step 4. Determine the weight of criteria using the entropy-weighting approach. The aggregated decision matrix $[\tilde{x}_{ij}]_{m\times n}$ can be defuzzified using Eq. (5-9), and then the weight of criteria can be calculated on the basis of Eq. (5-10) to Eq. (5-12).

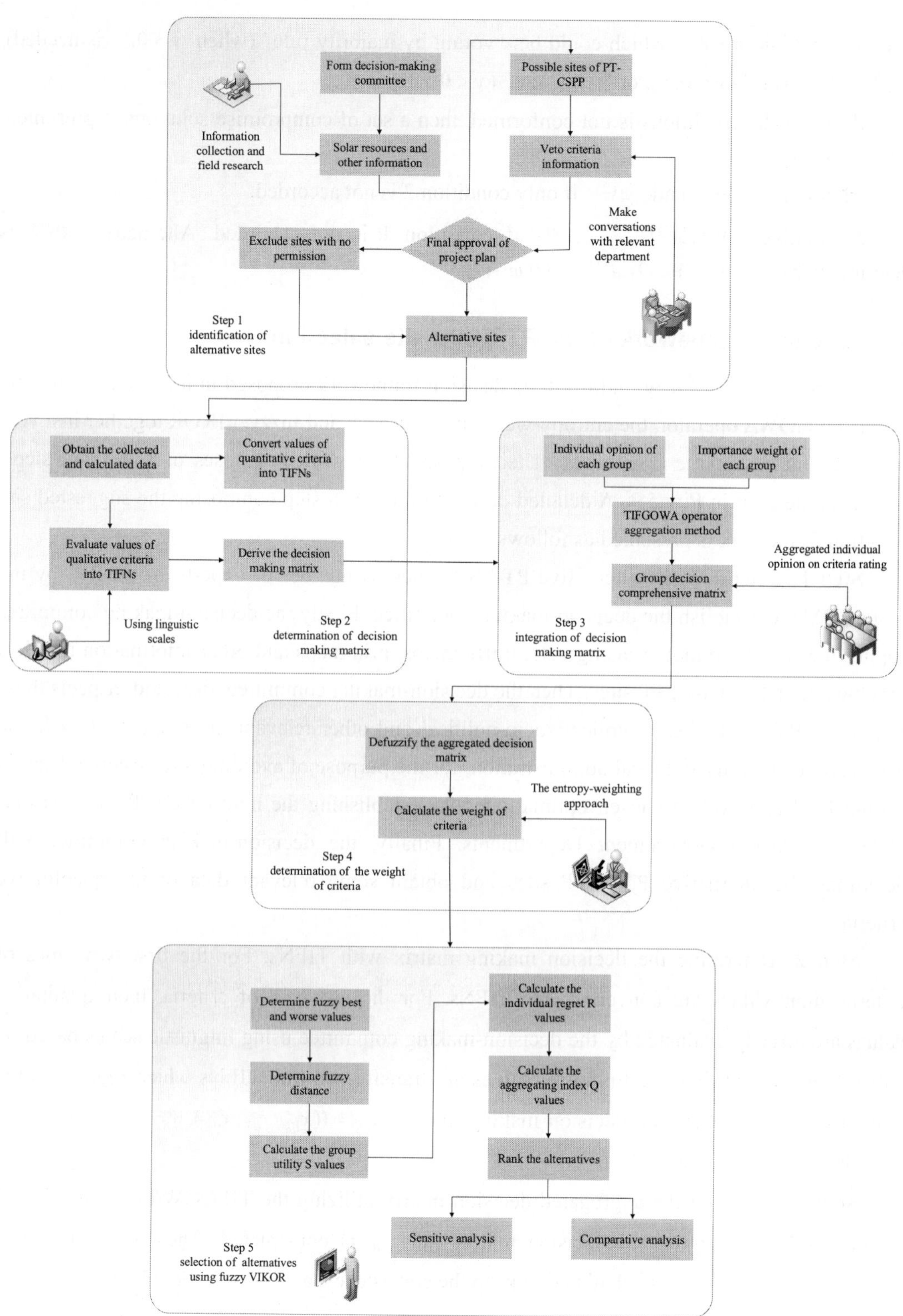

Fig. 5.3 The decision framework for PT-CSPP site selection.

Step 5. Select the optimal site by fuzzy VIKOR method. Calculate the scores for each alternative based on Eq. (5-13) to Eq. (5-18). Rank the alternatives according to the judgment rules, and then choose the optimal alternative in the light of ranking results.

Then, the sensitive analysis will be proposed to check the robustness of the evaluation results. Moreover, the comparative analysis based on the same illustrative case with the results of other previous methods will be carried out to examine the feasibility and effectiveness of the decision framework proposed.

5. A case study

5.1 Problem statement and identification of alternatives

Large amounts of renewable energy is demanded in China's western regions while the conventional fossil fuels are scarce, which brings an essential impact on the socio-economic development of the areas. Plentiful energy generated by the PT-CSPP provides a good choice for these areas. A Chinese renewable energy company located in Shanghai intends to invest a 50 MW PT-CSPP project in China's western regions. These areas are the economically backward, minority areas and the energy plans differ with various areas. Consequently, besides the traditional factors of PT-CSPP site selection, social factors are needed to be considered carefully, such as the acceptance degree of the local residents and the support degree of the local government. Thus the company's DMs make up their mind to invite an expert decision-making committee to help them to select the best site for the PT-CSPP.

The expert decision-making committee composes of four expert groups. In each group, members' academic research backgrounds are energy, economical, engineering, social and environmental field respectively. Each group is in charge of the whole evaluation and data collection of the PT-CSPP sites. Each group must be responsible to evaluate the performance linguistic variables of the alternatives relative to the sub-criteria, which will be converted into TIFNs in the following decision-making. Based on personal capacity of experts in each group, as well as the principle of the sum of expert weight is 1, four groups of expert weight can be determined as 0.20, 0.30, 0.25, and 0.25, respectively.

Firstly, the committee uses satellite remote sensing data, traffic maps and grid maps to identify the potential PT-CSPP sites. Seven feasible PT-CSPP sites are obtained on the list. Then, the committee visits these places to gather more information of the PT-CSPP sites in order to avoid any possible delay in getting final approval of chosen optimal project plan for a new PT-CSPP project from various State and Central Government Departments and to find out whether any other problems exist. After investigation, two alternatives are wiped off from the list, due to the fact that they are located at the ecological preservation and the military reservation area, respectively. The other five potential alternatives on the list, involving Xinjiang Hami, Tibet Shigatse, Qinghai Golmud, Gansu Jiuquan, Inner Mongolia Bayannur, are labeled as A1, A2, A3, A4 and A5. Due to convenient solar irradiation, Gansu, Tibet, Qinghai, Xinjiang and Inner Mongolia would be appropriate areas for the deployment of large scale CSP projects [7]. After that, the evaluation index system is established by the committee as shown in Table 5.1.

5.2 Attribute data collection

Based on Table 5.1, thirteen attributes are identified and classified into five categories i.e. resource, economy, infrastructure and construction, environment and society. As mentioned in Section 4.2, these attributes can be classified into three types.

The first type consists of C11 (annual sunshine hours), C12 (annual solar radiation) and C13 (average temperature) since their values can be measured precisely. Based on the locations of PT-CSPP projects identified by the expert decision-making committee, data of C11, C12 and C13 are acquired by inputting geodetic coordinates system on National Aeronautics and Space Administration (NASA) website.

The second type includes C21 (levelized cost of energy evolution) and C42 (pollutant emission reduction benefits) since their values can be measured roughly.

The value of C21 can be calculated as [9]:

$$LCOE_t=\frac{(L+C_t)\left[1-\frac{t_{In}}{DP}\sum_{i=1}^{DP}\frac{1}{(1+d)^i}+(1-t_{In})lr\sum_{i=1}^{RP}(1-\frac{i=1}{RP})\right]+(1-t_{In})\sum_{i=1}^{T}\frac{[(OPEX+x)\times C_t]}{(1+d)^i}+(\beta-\beta t_{In}-t_{Ad})\times t_{VAT}\sum_{i=3}^{T}\frac{\alpha\times OPEX\times C_t}{(1+d)^i}}{(1-t_{In})\sum_{i=1}^{T}\frac{DNI\times TF\times\eta(1-DR)^i}{(1+d)^i}+(\beta-\beta t_{In}-t_{Ad})\times t_{VAT}\sum_{i=3}^{T}\frac{DNI\times TF\times\eta(1-DR)^i}{(1+d)^i}} \tag{5-19}$$

where $LCOE_t$ represents the levelized cost of energy associated with PT- CSPP systems. The value of L can be calculated based on some related data of the first PT-CSPP pilot plants in China (See Table 5.3). We discover that the average area of land demanded for PT- CSPP is about 2.51 km^2 per 50MW. In addition, based on the compensation standards of land expropriation of China, the compensation for wastelands is \$4.52/m^2. Therefore, we obtain that the average land cost for PT-CSPP is approximately \$0.227/W. In addition, the other nomenclatures and values of parameters are listed in Table 5.4.

Table 5.3 Information on the first PT-CSPP demonstration projects of China.

No.	Projects	DNI (kWh/m^2/year)	Initial cost ($/W)	Electricity production (GWh/year)	Area (km^2/MW)	TES capacity(h)
PT_1	Yumen East Town 50MW thermal oil PT-CSPP	1800	4.11	169.3	2.477	9
PT_2	Gansu Akesai 50MW molten-salt PT-CSPP	2056.5	6.07	256	-	15
PT_3	Yumen East Town 50MW thermal oil PT-CSPP	1800	-	-	2.9	9
PT_4	Urat Middle Banner 100MW thermal oil PT-CSPP	2025	4.28	350	4.67	10
PT_5	Delingha 50MW thermal oil PT-CSPP	1976	5.93	225	2.6	9
PT_6	Gansu Gulang 100MW thermal oil PT-CSP	1913	-	-	-	7
PT_7	Zhangjiakou 64MW molten salt PT-CSP	1700	4.30	300	2.867	16

Note: Information on the first PT-CSPP demonstration projects of China is mainly from CSPPLAZA website, which is the only professional website in CSP industry of China; the datasources of Table 5.3 are shown in Appendix.

Table 5.4 Parameters means and values of the LCOE mode associated with PT-CSPP systems [9].

Symbols	Means	Values
L	Average land cost of the PT-CSPP	$0.227/W
C_t	Costs of PT-CSPP system installations	$4.303/W
t_{In}	Income tax rate	15%
DP	Depreciation period	15 years
d	Discount rate	10%
l	Loan ratio in the total investment	0.8
r	Long-term loans interest rate	4.9%
RP	Repayment period	15 years
T	Life-cycle	25 years
$OPEX$	Operation and maintenance(O&M) costs ratio	1.5%
I	Insurance costs ratio	0.5%
β	Ratio of value added tax refunds	50%
t_{Ad}	Additional taxes rate	8%
t_{VAT}	Value added tax rate	17%
α	Ratio with involving input tax in the O&M costs	57%
DNI	Direct normal irradiation	Equal to C12
TF	Tracking factor of PT-CSPP systems	97.11%
η	Performance factor of PT-CSPP systems	2.171m^2/kW
DR	Degradation factor	0.2%

The value of C42 can be calculated by the amount of carbon emission reduction as:

$$S_{CO_2} = E_T \times C_c \times C_d \tag{5-20}$$

where S_{CO_2} is the amount of carbon dioxide, E_T is the total electricity generated by the PT-CSPP in the life cycle which is equal to the denominator of $LCOE$, C_c is the average coal consumption for power supply which is measured by g/kWh, and C_d is the amount of carbon dioxide produced by burning a ton of standard coal which is measured by t. Based on the present stage of China, the appropriate value of C_c and C_d is about 335g/kWh and 2.62t [37].

The last type consists of C31 (grid connection convenience), C32 (water supply convenience), C33 (transportation convenience), C34 (soil structure and the geology), C35 (land tenure), C41 (impact on the surrounding environment), C51 (impact on the local economy) and C52 (public support) since they cannot be quantified. Their qualitative values are directly evaluated by the decision-making committee using linguistic scales in Table 2 firstly, and then the linguistic values are transformed into TIFNs.

5.3 Decision-making process

In this section, the proposed intuitionistic fuzzy multi-criteria decision framework is applied for the renewable energy company to select a suitable location for establishing a PT-CSPP in China's western regions.

In step 1, the decision-making committee is established, and the alternative PT-CSPP sites are determined, as mentioned in Section 5.1. The initial PT-CSPP site selection scheme is formed within five potential alternatives, containing Xinjiang Hami, Tibet Shigatse, Qinghai Golmud, Gansu Jiuquan, Inner Mongolia Bayannur, respectively A1, A2, A3, A4, and A5. The evaluation criteria system for PT-CSPP site selection is shown in Table 1.

In step 2, based on criteria data collection and calculation mentioned in Section 5.2, construct two decision matrices for the first and second categories of sub-criteria using Eq. (5-19) and Eq. (5-20), as shown in Table 5.5 and Table 5.6. For the last type of criteria, their qualitative values are evaluated by four expert groups (G1-G4) using linguistic scales, and the evaluation results are presented in Table 5.7, and then the linguistic values are transformed into TIFNs, as shown in Table 5.8.

Table 5.5 Performance numerical values in TIFNs of the first category of sub-criteria.

	A1	A2	A3	A4	A5
C11(h)	((3115,3121.7,3125); 0.8,0.1)	((3175,3182.7,3185); 0.8,0.1)	((3050,3056.4, 3060); 0.7,0.2)	((3210,3214.7,3220); 0.6,0.3)	((2970,2978.2, 2980);0.6,0.3)
C13(℃)	((3.7,7.3,11.6); 0.8,0.1)	((3.4,6.3,10.5); 0.7,0.2)	((5.4,8.0,10.4); 0.8,0.1)	((1.2,4.3,6.8); 0.8,0.1)	((5.4,8.7,12.4); 0.7,0.2)

Table 5.6 Performance numerical values in TIFNs of the second category of sub-criteria.

		A1	A2	A3	A4	A5
C12(10^3MJ/m^2)	Value	≈6.42	≈7.62	≈6.13	≈6.86	≈6.21
	TINF	((6.41,6.42,6.43); 0.7,0.2)	((7.61,7.62,7.63); 0.7,0.2)	((6.12,6.13,6.14); 0.6,0.3)	((6.85,6.86,6.87); 0.7,0.2)	((6.20,6.21,6.22); 0.7,0.2)
C21(10^2\$/MWh)	Value	≈2.53	≈1.96	≈3.02	≈2.14	≈2.85
	TINF	((2.52,2.53,2.54); 0.7,0.1)	((1.95,1.96,1.97); 0.6,0.2)	((3.01,3.02,3.03); 0.7,0.1)	((2.13,2.14,2.15); 0.7,0.1)	((2.84,2.85,2.86); 0.7,0.1)
C42(10^3t)	Value	≈3.36	≈3.87	≈3.12	≈3.48	≈3.23
	TINF	((3.35,3.36,3.37); 0.6,0.2)	((3.86,3.87,3.88); 0.5,0.3)	((3.11,3.12,3.13); 0.6,0.2)	((3.47,3.48,3.49); 0.5,0.2)	((3.22,3.23,3.24); 0.5,0.3)

Table 5.7 Evaluation results of alternative A1-A5 on the qualitative sub-criteria.

		A1	A2	A3	A4	A5
C31	G1	MP	P	G	VG	VP
	G2	P	VP	MG	MG	P
	G3	F	P	MG	G	P
	G4	F	MP	G	G	P
C32	G1	MG	F	G	MG	MG
	G2	G	MP	MG	F	F
	G3	MG	MP	F	MG	G
	G4	MG	P	MG	G	MG
C33	G1	G	MG	F	F	F
	G2	MG	F	MP	MG	MG
	G3	G	G	P	F	MP
	G4	MG	MG	MP	MP	MG
C34	G1	G	P	MG	F	G
	G2	G	VP	F	P	VG
	G3	MG	P	G	MP	G
	G4	MG	P	MG	MP	MG
C35	G1	F	VP	MG	F	MP
	G2	MG	P	F	MG	MG
	G3	F	VP	MG	F	F
	G4	F	P	MG	MG	F
C41	G1	VP	MP	P	P	VP
	G2	P	MP	P	MP	P
	G3	P	F	VP	MP	P
	G4	VP	F	MP	P	MP
C51	G1	VG	G	F	F	MG
	G2	G	VG	G	MG	F
	G3	G	G	F	MG	F
	G4	MG	G	MG	MP	MG

Continued

		A1	A2	A3	A4	A5
C52	G1	F	G	MP	MG	F
	G2	MP	G	F	MG	MP
	G3	MP	MG	F	F	MP
	G4	F	MG	MP	MG	F

Table 5.8 The linguistic values are transformed into TIFNs.

		A1	A2	A3	A4	A5
C31	G1	((2,3,4);0.7,0.1)	((0,1,2);0.6,0.2)	((8,9,10);0.7,0.1)	((9,10,10);0.6,0.2)	((0,0,1);0.7,0.2)
	G2	((0,1,2);0.6,0.2)	((0,0,1);0.6,0.3)	((6,7,8);0.6,0.3)	((6,7,8);0.7,0.1)	((0,1,3);0.6,0.3)
	G3	((3,4,6);0.6,0.3)	((0,1,2);0.7,0.2)	((6,7,9);0.7,0.2)	((7,9,10);0.6,0.2)	((0,1,2);0.6,0.3)
	G4	((4,5,7);0.7,0.2)	((2,3,4);0.7,0.1)	((7,8,9);0.6,0.2)	((7,8,9);0.7,0.1)	((0,1,3);0.7,0.2)
C32	G1	((6,7,8);0.6,0.2)	((4,5,7);0.6,0.2)	((8,9,10);0.6,0.3)	((6,7,8);0.7,0.2)	((5,6,7);0.6,0.2)
	G2	((7,8,9);0.6,0.1)	((2,3,4);0.7,0.1)	((6,7,9);0.5,0.3)	((4,5,7);0.6,0.3)	((4,5,7);0.7,0.1)
	G3	((5,7,8);0.5,0.3)	((1,3,4);0.6,0.3)	((4,5,7);0.6,0.2)	((6,7,8);0.7,0.1)	((8,9,10);0.6,0.2)
	G4	((6,7,9);0.5,0.3)	((0,1,3);0.7,0.1)	((6,7,9);0.5,0.4)	((8,9,10);0.6,0.1)	((6,7,8);0.6,0.3)
C33	G1	((7,9,10);0.6,0.2)	((6,7,9);0.8,0.1)	((4,5,6);0.6,0.3)	((4,5,7);0.7,0.1)	((4,5,6);0.6,0.3)
	G2	((5,7,9);0.7,0.1)	((3,5,6);0.6,0.3)	((2,3,4);0.6,0.2)	((6,7,9);0.6,0.3)	((5,7,9);0.5,0.3)
	G3	((7,8,9);0.6,0.2)	((7,8,9);0.7,0.1)	((0,1,2);0.6,0.2)	((3,5,7);0.6,0.2)	((2,3,4);0.6,0.2)
	G4	((5,7,8);0.7,0.1)	((6,7,8);0.6,0.3)	((1,3,5);0.7,0.2)	((2,3,5);0.6,0.2)	((5,7,8);0.5,0.3)
C34	G1	((7,8,9);0.6,0.2)	((0,1,3);0.7,0.1)	((5,7,9);0.6,0.3)	((3,5,6);0.7,0.1)	((7,9,10);0.5,0.4)
	G2	((8,9,10);0.7,0.1)	((0,0,1);0.6,0.2)	((4,5,6);0.7,0.2)	((0,1,3);0.6,0.3)	((9,10,10);0.6,0.3)
	G3	((6,7,8);0.5,0.3)	((0,1,2);0.6,0.3)	((7,8,9);0.8,0.1)	((2,3,5);0.7,0.1)	((7,8,9);0.7,0.1)
	G4	((5,7,8);0.6,0.2)	((0,1,3);0.7,0.2)	((6,7,8);0.7,0.1)	((1,3,5);0.6,0.2)	((5,7,8);0.6,0.3)
C35	G1	((4,5,6);0.6,0.3)	((0,0,1);0.6,0.3)	((5,7,9);0.6,0.2)	((4,5,7);0.7,0.1)	((2,3,4);0.6,0.2)
	G2	((6,7,9);0.7,0.1)	((0,1,3);0.7,0.1)	((3,5,7);0.6,0.3)	((6,7,9);0.6,0.3)	((6,7,8);0.5,0.3)
	G3	((3,5,7);0.7,0.1)	((0,0,1);0.6,0.2)	((6,7,8);0.7,0.2)	((3,5,6);0.7,0.2)	((4,5,6);0.6,0.2)
	G4	((4,5,7);0.6,0.2)	((0,1,3);0.7,0.1)	((5,7,8);0.6,0.2)	((5,7,8);0.6,0.2)	((3,5,6);0.7,0.2)
C41	G1	((0,0,1);0.7,0.1)	((2,3,4);0.7,0.1)	((0,1,3);0.7,0.1)	((0,1,3);0.7,0.2)	((0,0,1);0.7,0.1)
	G2	((1,1,2);0.6,0.3)	((2,3,5);0.6,0.3)	((0,1,2);0.6,0.2)	((2,3,4);0.6,0.3)	((0,1,3);0.6,0.2)
	G3	((0,1,3);0.5,0.3)	((4,5,6);0.6,0.2)	((0,0,1);0.7,0.1)	((1,3,5);0.7,0.1)	((0,1,2);0.6,0.3)
	G4	((0,0,1);0.6,0.2)	((4,5,7);0.7,0.2)	((2,3,4);0.6,0.1)	((0,1,3);0.6,0.3)	((1,3,5);0.6,0.2)
C51	G1	((9,10,10);0.7,0.2)	((8,9,10);0.6,0.2)	((3,5,6);0.6,0.2)	((4,5,6);0.6,0.2)	((6,7,8);0.5,0.3)
	G2	((7,8,9);0.6,0.3)	((9,10,10);0.7,0.2)	((7,9,10);0.5,0.3)	((5,7,8);0.7,0.2)	((4,5,6);0.6,0.2)
	G3	((8,9,10);0.7,0.1)	((7,9,10);0.6,0.3)	((3,5,6);0.7,0.1)	((6,7,9);0.6,0.3)	((4,5,7);0.7,0.1)
	G4	((6,7,9);0.6,0.2)	((7,8,9);0.7,0.1)	((6,7,8);0.6,0.2)	((1,3,4);0.6,0.2)	((5,7,9);0.6,0.2)
C52	G1	((4,5,6);0.6,0.3)	((7,9,9);0.6,0.2)	((1,3,4);0.6,0.2)	((5,7,8);0.7,0.1)	((3,5,7);0.6,0.2)
	G2	((2,3,5);0.6,0.2)	((8,9,10);0.7,0.1)	((4,5,7);0.8,0.1)	((6,7,8);0.6,0.3)	((1,3,5);0.7,0.1)
	G3	((1,3,4);0.7,0.1)	((6,7,8);0.6,0.1)	((3,5,6);0.7,0.1)	((4,5,6);0.6,0.2)	((1,3,5);0.6,0.1)
	G4	((4,5,7);0.8,0.1)	((5,7,9);0.6,0.3)	((2,3,5);0.6,0.3)	((6,7,9);0.6,0.3)	((3,5,7);0.5,0.4)

In step 3, aggregate the decision matrices to an integrated matrix. The expert weight matrix is $\omega=(0.2,0.3,0.25,0.25)^T$. Get integrated matrix of A1 through A5 by using TIFGOWA operator (here $g=x^2, x$ is the independent variable of g), which is shown in Table 5.9, and then the standardized decision matrix is obtained easily.

In step 4, the values of the attribute weights are calculated using Eq. (5-9)to Eq.(5-12), and the results are presented in Table 5.10.

Table 5.9 The integrated matrix on the qualitative sub-criteria.

	A1	A2	A3	A4	A5
C31	((2.66,3.51,5.06); 0.6,0.3)	((1.00,1.64,2.47); 0.6,0.3)	((6.70,7.69,8.93); 0.6,0.3)	((7.17,8.42,9.19); 0.6,0.2)	((0.00,0.89,2.48); 0.6,0.3)
C32	((6.10,7.31,8.56); 0.5,0.3)	((2.16,3.19,4.57); 0.6,0.3)	((6.05,7.03,8.76); 0.5,0.4)	((6.08,7.06,8.28); 0.6,0.3)	((5.90,6.87,8.09); 0.6,0.3)
C33	((5.98,7.69,8.97); 0.6,0.2)	((5.58,6.75,7.95); 0.6,0.3)	((2.16,3.19,4.39); 0.6,0.3)	((4.15,5.31,7.25); 0.6,0.3)	((4.24,5.85,7.18); 0.5,0.3)
C34	((6.65,7.85,8.84); 0.5,0.3)	((0.00,0.83,2.31); 0.6,0.3)	((5.57,6.75,7.95); 0.6,0.3)	((1.75,3.13,4.73); 0.6,0.3)	((7.25,8.63,9.29); 0.5,0.4)
C35	((4.50,5.67,7.48); 0.6,0.3)	((0.00,0.74,2.32); 0.6,0.3)	((4.79,6.47,7.93); 0.6,0.3)	((4.74,6.18,7.69); 0.6,0.3)	((4.22,5.39,6.36); 0.5,0.3)
C41	((0.55,0.74,1.97); 0.5,0.3)	((3.16,4.12,5.65); 0.6,0.3)	((1.00,1.66,2.69); 0.6,0.2)	((1.20,2.32,3.89); 0.6,0.3)	((0.50,1.67,3.19); 0.6,0.3)
C51	((7.48,8.47,9.46); 0.6,0.3)	((7.85,9.08,9.76); 0.6,0.3)	((5.27,6.91,7.89); 0.5,0.3)	((4.47,5.85,7.12); 0.6,0.3)	((4.72,5.98,7.49); 0.5,0.3)
C52	((2.94,4.02,5.56); 0.6,0.3)	((6.65,8.06,9.08); 0.6,0.3)	((2.87,4.22,5.76); 0.6,0.3)	((5.37,6.56,7.83); 0.6,0.3)	((2.14,4.02,5.98); 0.5,0.4)

Table 5.10 The weights of sub-criteria.

	C11	C12	C13	C21	C31	C32	C33	C34	C35	C41	C42	C51	C52
Weight	0.0846	0.0893	0.0594	0.1132	0.1096	0.0592	0.0181	0.0432	0.0813	0.0524	0.0954	0.0927	0.1016

In step 5, the fuzzy best $\tilde{f}_j^*$ and the fuzzy worst $\tilde{f}_j^-$ values of all criteria ratings are calculated by Eq. (5-13) and Eq. (5-14). The normalized fuzzy distance can be obtained using Eq. (5-15). The values of S_i, R_i and Q_i are calculated for each alternative i according to Eq. (5-16) to Eq. (5-18), as shown in Table 5.11.

According to Table 5.11, the priority orders of five alternatives by Q_i in increasing order is A3>A1>A4>A2>A5. For alternative A3, the Condition 1 and 2 are both satisfied clearly. Thus, based on the comprehensive evaluation results obtained by the proposed decision framework, A3 is the best alternative for the renewable energy company to set up a PT-CSPP.

Table 5.11 The values S_i, R_i and Q_i of five alternatives.

	A1	A2	A3	A4	A5
S_i	0.4665	0.5075	0.4495	0.4602	0.5356
R_i	0.0773	0.0949	0.0659	0.0829	0.0999
Q_i	0.2665	0.7633	0	0.3123	1

5.4 Sensitivity analysis

Since the objective facts may deviate from the DMs' subjective judgment, a sensitivity analysis is carried out to inspect whether the results of a sequence will be qualitatively influenced when the decision-making information changes. In the presented fuzzy VIKOR model, the parameter v has been employed as weight of the strategy of the group utility. Thus, in the process of selecting optional alternatives for setting up PT-CSPPs, the parameter v plays an indispensable role. In general, the value of v is set to 0.5. However, v can take any value from 0 to 1, which indicates the DMs' different preferences. In the decision analysis, as the fact that different various attitudes of the DMs may result in various ranking orders. Consequently, it is necessary to perform a sensitivity analysis on the parameter v based on the DMs' preference to examine the validity and robustness of the obtained evaluation results. According to the different values of v from 0 to 1, the values of Q_i are calculated using Eq. (5-18) in Table 5.12, and the changes of collective comprehensive values are vividly demonstrated in Fig. 5.4.

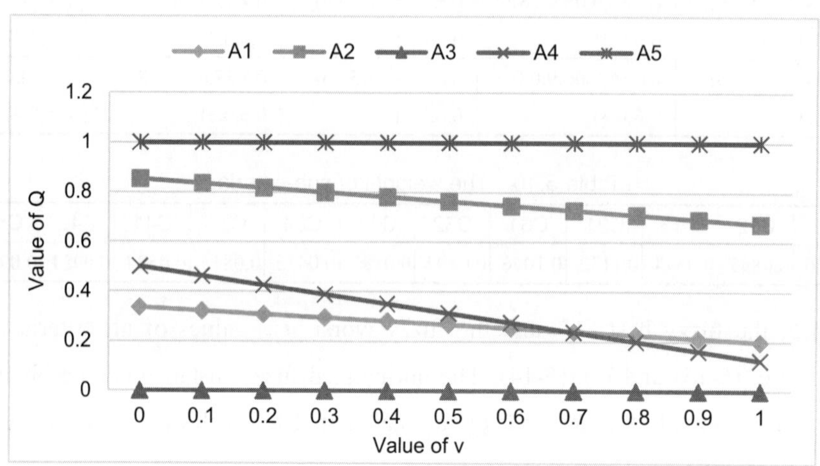

Fig. 5.4 The collective comprehensive values of the alternatives.

Table 5.12 The values of Q_i based on v from 0 to 1.

	A1	A2	A3	A4	A5
$v = 0$	0.5625	0.9554	0	1	0.8394
$v = 0.1$	0.5318	0.9027	0	1	0.7727
$v = 0.2$	0.5012	0.8500	0	1	0.7060

Continued

	A1	A2	A3	A4	A5
$v = 0.3$	0.4705	0.7974	0	1	0.6392
$v = 0.4$	0.4399	0.7447	0	1	0.5725
$v = 0.5$	0.4093	0.6920	0	1	0.5057
$v = 0.6$	0.3786	0.6393	0	1	0.4390
$v = 0.7$	0.3480	0.5867	0	1	0.3722
$v = 0.8$	0.3173	0.5340	0	1	0.3055
$v = 0.9$	0.2867	0.4813	0	1	0.2387
$v = 1$	0.2560	0.4286	0	1	0.1720

From Fig. 5.4, the ranking order sequences of three alternatives containing A2, A3 and A5 are stable relatively no matter what the v value is. Especially, the ranking order sequence of A3 demonstrates that it is constantly the best site to establish a PT-CSPP, which certificates that the acquired evaluation results from the proposed fuzzy VIKOR model are robust and reliable.

In addition, to take a closer look at the Fig. 5.4, the ranking order of the five alternatives stays the same when v takes values from 0 to 0.6, yet when v takes values from 0.7 to 1, though the best and the worst alternatives do not change, the less favorable alternative have changed obviously. Alternatives A1 and A4 exchange their order in the ranking results, which reveals some impact of the DMs' attitudes changes on the decision results. The changes manifest that alternative A1 ranks higher than alternative A4 when the preference of the DMs is extremely irrelevant to the group utility. Nevertheless, when the DMs show more preferences to the group utility, alternative A1 is superior to alternative A4 stably. Therefore, variation in the v values provides flexibility for the DMs to make their subjective preferences available. In the realistic decision-making practice, each DMs' opinion can be considered by the proposed method.

5.5 Comparative analysis

In order to certificate the decision framework proposed above for the PT-CSPP site selection applying the fuzzy VIKOR method is effective and feasible, a comparison according to the same illustrative case with the ranking results acquired by fuzzy TOPSIS, PROMETHEE-II and ELECTRE-III is analyzed.

The ranking order sequences of the fuzzy TOPSIS method are obtained by the relative closeness $RC(A_i)$. Distinguishing from VIKOR and TOPSIS methods based on the relative closeness to the ideal solution, PROMETHEE-II and ELECTRE-III methods are conducted to rank the alternatives based on the net flow $\varphi(A_i)$. The calculation results and ranking orders are listed in Table 5.13.

Table 5.13 The calculation results of VIKOR, TOPSIS, PROMETHEE-II and ELECTRE-III.

	Calculation Results					Ranking Orders
VIKOR	$Q(A_1)$	$Q(A_2)$	$Q(A_3)$	$Q(A_4)$	$Q(A_5)$	A3>A1>A4>A2>A5
	0.2665	0.7633	0	0.3123	1	
TOPSIS	$RC(A_1)$	$RC(A_2)$	$RC(A_3)$	$RC(A_4)$	$RC(A_5)$	A3>A4>A1>A2>A5
	0.6314	0.6231	0.6745	0.6342	0.6018	
PROMETHEE-II	$\varphi(A_1)$	$\varphi(A_2)$	$\varphi(A_3)$	$\varphi(A_4)$	$\varphi(A_5)$	A3>A4>A1>A2>A5
	0.1782	0.0136	0.2148	0.1843	-0.0014	
ELECTRE-III	$\varphi(A_1)$	$\varphi(A_2)$	$\varphi(A_3)$	$\varphi(A_4)$	$\varphi(A_5)$	A3>A1=A4>A2>A5
	1	0	2	1	-1	

According to Table 5.13, alternative A3 is invariably the best site with the greatest relative closeness to the ideal solution and the maximum of net flow, which stays the same as the results acquired by proposed fuzzy VIKOR method. In addition, the worst site is always alternative A4. The primary difference in the ranking orders exists between alternative A1 and A5. The reasons for difference could be interpreted as follows.

The fuzzy TOPSIS method identifies a solution with the shortest distance from the ideal solution, however, it does not take the relative importance of the ideal solution and the negative-ideal solution into account. Moreover, the ranking order based on fuzzy VIKOR method in the decision framework when v takes 0.7 to 1, is the same as the result obtained by fuzzy TOPSIS method. That indicates the evaluation results from fuzzy TOPSIS method are as part of the results list of the fuzzy VIKOR method which considers different preferences of the DMs.

Instead ofconsidering the individual regret, the fuzzy PROMETHEE-II method only takes maximum of group utility into account. Based on the calculation results, the main difference is the ranking order between A1 and A4. According to the preferences of decision-making group, the score of A1 is superior to A4, but the ranking result obtained by fuzzy PROMETHEE-II method is opposite. That is not consistent with the opinions of the decision-making group.

Without taking the group utility into consideration, the fuzzy ELECTRE-III method determines a solution pursuing the minimum of individual regret applying thresholds of indifference and preference. Based on the calculation results, the ranking order between A1 and A4 cannot be decided by the fuzzy ELECTRE-III method clearly, so the distinct evaluation results cannot be acquired.

After the comparative analysis conducted, the final ranking order derived from the fuzzy VIKOR method A3>A1>A4>A2>A5 is more accurate and credible than those acquired by other mentioned methods. Therefore, the proposed fuzzy VIKOR method determines not only the solution closer to the ideal one, but also a balance between the maximum group utility of the "majority" and the minimum individual regret for the "opponent". Moreover, the fuzzy VIKOR method takes the preferences of DMs into consideration. Consequently, the fuzzy VIKOR method is more suitable and feasible than other mentioned methods for PT-CSPP site selection.

6. Conclusions

This study sets up a comprehensive decision framework for PT-CSPP site selection on the basis of the sustainable perspective. Current researches focused on this field are extremely finite and quite a quantity of problems and flaws still exist in the decision process for PT-CSPP site selection. Firstly, uncertainties and randomness generally are involved in the site selection for PT-CSPP. Secondly, the interaction problem exists in distinct DMs' evaluation opinions on alternative ratings and criteria weights. Thirdly, the ranking techniques used in previous studies could not reflect the DMs' subjective preferences for evaluating the PT-CSPP site selection problem. The justifiability of the decision-making results would decline and the probability of decision-making mistakes would increase unless the aforementioned problems are not ignored.

In this research, a novel design of comprehensive MCDM framework on the basis of the fuzzy VIKOR method combined with a TIFGOWA operator under imprecise information environment is proposed to deal with the PT-CSPP site selection problem. Firstly, the comprehensive index system towards sustainability for PT-CSPP site selection is constructed to recognize and eliminate potential alternatives. Secondly, the TIFNs are introduced to reflect the imperfect knowledge of experts and express the uncertainties of information. Thirdly, the TIFGOWA operator is applied to handle the interaction problem derived from different DMs' evaluation opinions. Moreover, the fuzzy VIKOR is employed to rank the optimal alternatives on the basis of the integrated DMs' scores. Finally, a case of northwestern part of China with the sensitive analysis and comparative analysis is preformed to demonstrate the feasibility and robustness of the proposed decision framework.

In the presented comprehensive index system, the economic, environmental and social criteria attract more attention than other criteria in the decision-making for PT-CSPP site selection on the basis of sustainable cities and society. By applying the proposed decision framework, alternative A3 is chosen as the most optimal site to establish a PT-CSPP project, and alternative A1 is considered as the sub-optimal site. According to the sensitivity analysis and comparative analysis, the obtained ranking order would not change in general, which indicates the acquired results have rationality and practicality.

Consequently, based on presented theoretical modeling and empirical research, the proposed MCDM decision framework on the basis of sustainability perspective could solve such a complex problem validly and bring about a remarkable result.

Acknowledgments

This paper is supported by the 2017 Special Project of Cultivation and Development of Innovation Base (No. Z171100002217024) and the Fundamental Research Funds for the Central Universities (No. 2018ZD14).

Appendix A

Table A.1 The datasources of Table 5.3.

No.	Datasources
PT_1	http://www.docin.com/p-1871037172.html
PT_2	http://www.cspplaza.com/article-8085-2.html
PT_3	http://www.cspplaza.com/article-8085-2.html
PT_4	http://www.cspplaza.com/article-8085-2.html
PT_5	http://www.cspplaza.com/article-8085-2.html
PT_6	http://www.cspplaza.com/article-8085-2.html
PT_7	http://www.cspplaza.com/article-3735-1.html

References

[1] Belgasim B, Aldali Y, Abdunnabi M J R, et al. The potential of concentrating solar power (CSP) for electricity generation in Libya[J]. Renewable & Sustainable Energy Reviews, 2018, 90:1-15.

[2] Islam M T, Huda N, Abdullah A B, et al. A comprehensive review of state-of-the-art concentrating solar power (CSP) technologies: Current status and research trends[J]. Renewable and Sustainable Energy Reviews, 2018, 91:987-1018.

[3] Purohit I, Purohit P. Technical and economic potential of concentrating solar thermal power generation in India[J]. Renewable & Sustainable Energy Reviews, 2017, 78:648-667.

[4] Sun J, Liu Q, Hong H. Numerical study of parabolic-trough direct steam generation loop in recirculation mode: Characteristics, performance and general operation strategy[J]. Energy Conversion & Management, 2015, 96:287-302.

[5] Kumar A, Prakash O, Dube A. A review on progress of concentrated solar power in India[J]. Renewable & Sustainable Energy Reviews, 2017, 79:304-307.

[6] Bouhal T, Agrouaz Y, Kousksou T, et al. Technical feasibility of a sustainable Concentrated Solar Power in Morocco through an energy analysis[J]. Renewable & Sustainable Energy Reviews, 2018, 81:1087-1095.

[7] Vieira de Souza L E, Gilmanova Cavalcante A M. Concentrated Solar Power deployment in emerging economies: The cases of China and Brazil[J]. Renewable and Sustainable Energy Reviews, 2017, 72:1094-1103.

[8] Yushchenko A, Bono A D, Chatenoux B, et al. GIS-based assessment of photovoltaic (PV) and concentrated solar power (CSP) generation potential in West Africa[J]. Renewable & Sustainable Energy Reviews, 2017, 81:2088-2103.

[9] Ren L Z, Zhao X G, Yu X X, et al. Cost-benefit evolution for Concentrated Solar Power in China[J]. Journal of Cleaner Production, 2018, 190:471-482.

[10] Wang R, Qu W, Hong H, et al. Experimental performance of 300 kWth prototype of parabolic trough collector with rotatable axis and irreversibility analysis[J]. Energy, 2018, 161:595-609.

[11] Javanshir A, Sarunac N, Razzaghpanah Z. Thermodynamic analysis and optimization of single and combined power cycles for concentrated solar power applications[J]. Energy, 2018, 157:65-75.

[12] Yu Q, Jia L M, Qi W W, et al. An experimental study on the heat transfer performance of a prototype molten-salt rod baffle heat exchanger for concentrated solar power[J]. Energy, 2018, 156:63-72.

[13] Mihoub S, Chermiti A, Beltagy H. Methodology of determining the optimum performances of future concentrating solar thermal power plants in Algeria[J]. Energy, 2017, 122:801-810.

[14] Almonacid F, Fernández E F, Almonacid-Cruz B, et al. Spectral-matching-ratio modelling based on ANNs and atmospheric parameters for the electrical characterization of multi-junction concentrator PV systems[J]. Energy, 2018, 156:409-417.

[15] Fichter T, Soria R, Szklo A, et al. Assessing the potential role of concentrated solar power (CSP) for the northeast power system of Brazil using a detailed power system model[J]. Energy, 2017, 121:695-715.

[16] Balghouthi M, Trabelsi S E, Amara M B, et al. Potential of concentrating solar power (CSP) technology in Tunisia and the possibility of interconnection with Europe[J]. Renewable & Sustainable Energy Reviews, 2016, 56:1227-1248.

[17] Seyf H R, Henry A. Thermophotovoltaics: a potential pathway to high efficiency concentrated solar power[J]. ENERGY & ENVIRONMENTAL SCIENCE, 2016, 9(8):2654-2665.

[18] Haneklaus N, Schroders S, Yanhua Z, et al. Economic evaluation of flameless phosphate rock calcination with concentrated solar power and high temperature reactors[J]. Energy, 2017, 140:1148-1157.

[19] Jin H L, Dally B B, Chinnici A, et al. Techno-economic evaluation of modular hybrid concentrating solar power systems[J]. Energy, 2017, 129:158-170.

[20] Bendato I, Cassettari L, Mosca M, et al. Stochastic techno-economic assessment based on Monte Carlo simulation and the Response Surface Methodology: The case of an innovative linear Fresnel CSP (concentrated solar power) system[J]. Energy, 2016, 101:309-324.

[21] Rea J E, Oshman C J, Olsen M L, et al. Performance modeling and techno-economic analysis of a modular concentrated solar power tower with latent heat storage[J]. Applied Energy, 2018, 217:143-152.

[22] Du E, Zhang N, Hodge B-M, et al. Economic justification of concentrating solar power in high renewable energy penetrated power systems[J]. Applied Energy, 2018, 222:649-661.

[23] Miguel G S, Corona B. Economic viability of concentrated solar power under different regulatory frameworks in Spain[J]. Renewable and Sustainable Energy Reviews, 2018, 91:205-218.

[24] Aragonés-Beltrán P, Chaparro-González F, Pastor-Ferrando J P, et al. An AHP (Analytic Hierarchy Process)/ANP (Analytic Network Process)-based multi-criteria decision approach for the selection of solar-thermal power plant investment projects[J]. Energy., 2014, 66(2):222-238.

[25] Aly A, Jensen S S, Pedersen A B. Solar power potential of Tanzania: Identifying CSP and PV hot spots through a GIS multicriteria decision making analysis[J]. Renewable Energy, 2017, 113:159-175.

[26] Baseer M A, Rehman J P, Meyer J P, et al. GIS-based site suitability analysis for wind farm development

in Saudi Arabia[J]. Energy, 2017, 141:1166-1176.

[27] Gigović L, Pamučar D, Božanić D, et al. Application of the GIS-DANP-MABAC multi-criteria model for selecting the location of wind farms: A case study of Vojvodina, Serbia[J]. Renewable Energy, 2017, 103:501-521.

[28] Inamdar P M, Sharma A K, Cook S, et al. Evaluation of stormwater harvesting sites using multi criteria decision methodology[J]. Journal of Hydrology, 2018, 562:181-192.

[29] Wu Y, Zhang J, Yuan J, et al. Study of decision framework of offshore wind power station site selection based on ELECTRE-III under intuitionistic fuzzy environment: A case of China[J]. Energy Conversion & Management, 2016, 113:66-81.

[30] Fang H, Li J, Song W. Sustainable site selection for photovoltaic power plant: An integrated approach based on prospect theory[J]. Energy Conversion and Management, 2018, 174:755-768.

[31] Liu K-M, Lin S-H, Hsieh J-C, et al. Improving the food waste composting facilities site selection for sustainable development using a hybrid modified MADM model[J]. Waste Management, 2018, 75:44-59.

[32] Zadeh LA. Fuzzy sets[J]. Information & Control, 1965, 8(3):338-353.

[33] Zhang X-y, Wang X -k, Yu S-m, et al. Location selection of offshore wind power station by consensus decision framework using picture fuzzy modelling[J]. JOURNAL OF CLEANER PRODUCTION, 2018, 202:980-992.

[34] Rikalovic A M, Cosic I, Labati R D, et al. Intelligent Decision Support System for Industrial Site Classification: A GIS-Based Hierarchical Neuro-Fuzzy Approach[J]. IEEE Systems Journal, 2017, PP(99):1-12.

[35] Wan S P, Wang F, Lin L L, et al. Some new generalized aggregation operators for triangular intuitionistic fuzzy numbers and application to multi-attribute group decision making[J]. Computers & Industrial Engineering, 2016, 93(C):286-301.

[36] Atanassov K T. Intuitionistic fuzzy sets[J]. Fuzzy Sets & Systems, 2012, 20(1):87-96.

[37] Wu Y, Xua C, Ke Y, et al. An intuitionistic fuzzy multi-criteria framework for large-scale rooftop PV project portfolio selection: case study in Zhejiang, China[J]. ENERGY, 2017, 143:295-309.

[38] Qin Q, Liang F, Li L, et al. A TODIM-based multi-criteria group decision making with triangular intuitionistic fuzzy numbers[J]. APPLIED SOFT COMPUTING, 2017, 55:93-107.

[39] Chen J, Huang X. Hesitant triangular intuitionistic fuzzy information and its application to multi-attribute decision making problem[J]. JOURNAL OF NONLINEAR SCIENCES AND APPLICATIONS, 2017, 10(3):1012-1029.

[40] Wu Y, Wang J, Hu Y, et al. An Extended TODIM-PROMETHEE Method for Waste-to-energy Plant Site Selection Based on Sustainability Perspective[J]. Energy, 2018, 156:1-16.

[41] Wu Y, Xie C, Xu C, et al. A Decision Framework for Electric Vehicle Charging Station Site Selection for Residential Communities under an Intuitionistic Fuzzy Environment: A Case of Beijing[J]. ENERGIES, 2017, 10(9):1270.

[42] Yin S, Li B. Matching management of supply and demand of green building technologies based on a novel matching method with intuitionistic fuzzy sets[J]. JOURNAL OF CLEANER PRODUCTION, 2018, 201:748-763.

[43] Sakthivel, Sivakumar, Saravanan, et al. A decision support system to evaluate the optimum fuel blend in an IC engine to enhance the energy efficiency and energy management[J]. Energy, 2017,

140:566-583.

[44] Xu F, Liu J, Lin S, et al. A VIKOR-based approach for assessing the service performance of electric vehicle sharing programs: A case study in Beijing[J]. Journal of Cleaner Production, 2017, 148:254-267.

[45] Gul M, Ak M F. A comparative outline for quantifying risk ratings in occupational health and safety risk assessment[J]. Journal of Cleaner Production, 2018, 196:653-664.

[46] Majumder H, Maity K. Application of GRNN and multivariate hybrid approach to predict and optimize WEDM responses for Ni-Ti shape memory alloy[J]. Applied Soft Computing, 2018, 70:665-679.

[47] Chen T Y. Remoteness Index-Based Pythagorean Fuzzy VIKOR Methods with a Generalized Distance Measure for Multiple Criteria Decision Analysis[J]. Information Fusion, 2017, 41:129-150.

[48] Wang L, Zhang H Y, Wang J Q, et al. Picture fuzzy normalized projection-based VIKOR method for the risk evaluation of construction project[J]. Applied Soft Computing, 2018, 64:216-226.

[49] Awasthi A, Govindan K, Gold S. Multi-tier sustainable global supplier selection using a fuzzy AHP-VIKOR based approach[J]. International Journal of Production Economics, 2018, 195:106-117.

[50] Yang Z, Li J, Huang L, et al. Developing dynamic intuitionistic normal fuzzy aggregation operators for multi-attribute decision-making with time sequence preference[J]. Expert Systems with Applications An International Journal, 2017, 82(C):344-356.

[51] Ren Z, Xu Z, Wang H. Dual hesitant fuzzy VIKOR method for multi-criteria group decision making based on fuzzy measure and new comparison method[J].INFORMATION SCIENCES , 2017.

[52] Zhao H, Zhao H, Guo S. Evaluating the comprehensive benefit of eco-industrial parks by employing multi-criteria decision making approach for circular economy[J]. Journal of Cleaner Production, 2017, 142:2262-2276.

[53] Wu Y, Geng S. Multi-criteria decision making on selection of solar–wind hybrid power station location: A case of China[J]. Energy Conversion & Management, 2014, 81(81):527-533.

[54] Liu J, Xu F, Lin S. Site selection of photovoltaic power plants in a value chain based on grey cumulative prospect theory for sustainability: A case study in Northwest China[J]. Journal of Cleaner Production, 2017, 148:386-397.

[55] Andika R, Kim Y, Yoon S H, et al. Techno-economic assessment of technological improvements in thermal energy storage of concentrated solar power[J]. Solar Energy, 2017, 157:552-558.

[56] Dowling A W, Zheng T, Zavala V M. Economic assessment of concentrated solar power technologies: A review[J]. Renewable & Sustainable Energy Reviews, 2017, 72:1019-1032.

[57] Gu Y, Zhang X, Myhren J A, et al. Techno-economic analysis of a solar photovoltaic/thermal (PV/T) concentrator for building application in Sweden using Monte Carlo method[J]. Energy Conversion & Management, 2018, 165:8-24.

[58] Li Y, Liao S, Rao Z, et al. A dynamic assessment based feasibility study of concentrating solar power in China[J]. Renewable Energy, 2014, 69(3):34-42.

[59] Ogunmodimu O, Okoroigwe E C. Concentrating solar power technologies for solar thermal grid electricity in Nigeria: A review[J]. Renewable and Sustainable Energy Reviews, 2018, 90:104-119.

[60] Wu Y, Geng S, Zhang H, et al. Decision framework of solar thermal power plant site selection based on linguistic Choquet operator[J]. Applied Energy, 2014, 136(C):303-311.

[61] Simsek Y, Watts D, Escobar R. Sustainability evaluation of Concentrated Solar Power (CSP) projects

under Clean Development Mechanism (CDM) by using Multi Criteria Decision Method (MCDM)[J]. Renewable & Sustainable Energy Reviews, 2018, 93:421-438.

[62] Corona B, Cerrajero E, López D, et al. Full environmental life cycle cost analysis of concentrating solar power technology: Contribution of externalities to overall energy costs[J]. Solar Energy, 2016, 135:758-768.

[63] Río P d, Peñasco C, Mir-Artigues P. An overview of drivers and barriers to concentrated solar power in the European Union[J]. Renewable and Sustainable Energy Reviews, 2018, 81:1019-1029.

[64] Wu Y, Zhang B, Xu C, et al. Site selection decision framework using fuzzy ANP-VIKOR for large commercial rooftop PV system based on sustainability perspective[J]. Sustainable Cities & Society, 2018, 40:454-470.

[65] Jing R, Wang M, Brandon N, et al. Multi-criteria evaluation of solid oxide fuel cell based combined cooling heating and power (SOFC-CCHP) applications for public buildings in China[J]. Energy, 2017, 141:273-289.

Chapter 6

Site selection decision framework using fuzzy ANP-VIKOR for large commercial rooftop PV system based on sustainability perspective

Yunna Wu [a, b], Buyuan Zhang [a, b*], Chuanbo Xu [a, b], Lingwenying Li [a, b]

a. School of Economics and Management, North China Electric Power University, Beijing, China

b. Beijing Key Laboratory of New Energy and Low-Carbon Development (North China Electric Power University), Changping Beijing 102206, China

Abstract: The Large Commercial Rooftop Photovoltaic System (LCRPS) projects have been rapidly proposed in China due to policy promotion towards sustainability. Site selection immensely determines the life cycle of LCRPS projects based on sustainability perspective, in need of considering the impact on environment and society. However, inadequacies still exist in the decision for LCRPS site selection. Firstly, uncertainties of information cannot be described integrally. Secondly, consideration of the correlation among criteria from sustainability perspective is lacking. Thirdly, the ranking methods in previous studies cannot reflect decision makers' subjective preferences. Therefore, this study establishes a decision framework for LCRPS site selection utilizing Fuzzy Analytic Network Process (Fuzzy ANP) method and Fuzzy Vlsekriterijumska Optimizacija IKompromisno Resenje (Fuzzy VIKOR) method. First, the triangular intuitionistic fuzzy numbers (TIFNs) are adopted to describe indeterminate information. Second, fuzzy ANP is introduced to reflect the correlation among criteria based on sustainability perspective. Third, fuzzy VIKOR is employed to rank the options on the basis of decision makers' subjective preferences. Finally, to validate the effectiveness of the proposed framework, a case study of Guangdong province with sensitive analysis and comparative analysis is conducted. The result shows the LCRPS site located in Dongguan should be selected as the optimal site.

Keywords: large commercial rooftop photovoltaic system; site selection; triangular intuitionistic fuzzy number; ANP; VIKOR

1. Introduction

With the rapid development of Chinese economy, traditional fossil fuels cannot provide sustainable energy supply to meet China's demand Therefore, China is faced with an urgent situation of severe energy shortages nowadays. Solar PV power is currently, following wind and hydro power, the third most significant renewable energy source in terms of globally installed capacity (S. Zhang, 2016). However, the overcapacity is caused by local limited energy consumption level, the lagging construction of cross-regional transmission channel and the complexity existed in connected power grid, which leads to a phenomenon of light abandoning extremely severe in the three northern regions of China. Fortunately, the application of distributed PV (DPV) is a valid way to conquer this problem towards the current sustainable cites and society since the DPV system is located close to demand centers and generates energy where needed (F. Zhang, Deng, Margolis, & Su, 2015). The DPV system is largely installed on household and commercial rooftops since the rooftop PV calls for little building architecture pre-design and is compatible to refurbish (W. Zhang, Hao, Li, Liu, & Yao, 2015). In addition, commercial rooftops draw more attention than household rooftops because they are capable to install more PV panels and always possessed by a single stakeholder (Wu, Xu, Ke, Chen, & Sun, 2017). The LCRPS refers to the DPV system installed on large commercial rooftops. Simultaneously, the "13th Five-Year Plan for Electric Power Development" points out that it is essential to promote the DPV system development vigorously, indicating DPV has become the policy priority of sustainable and renewable energy development in China. With the vigorous rise of LCRPS market, available LCRPS project alternatives will far exceed the quantity of projects that can be executed with a PV enterprise' limited resources at any time. Thus, the Chinese government and public are strongly motivated to accelerate the utilization of LCRPS that is expected to provide potential and sustainable energy supply for cities and society in the future. An example of LCRPS is shown in Fig. 6.1.

Fig. 6.1 An example of LCRPS.

In the entire life cycle of LCRPS, the optimal location is necessary from the perspective of sustainable development. Firstly, the optimal location would have a significant impact on the cost, which could determine the success or failure of the project. Secondly, a wrongly chosen site might have an adverse influence on cites and society, which would affect the sustainable development of LCRPS. Finally, the alternative failing to satisfy environmental demands would not kick in to protect the environment but to destroy it instead. However, the current abundant valuable researches on the LCRPS predominantly focus on the following fields: installation performance (Sueyoshi & Wang, 2017; Sweet, Khatib, Bristow, Drysdale, & Jenkins, 2016; Wang & Sueyoshi, 2017), economic feasibility (Ghosh, Nair, & Krishnan, 2015; Lang, Ammann, & Girod, 2016; Peerapong & Limmeechokchai, 2015), technical potential (Byrne, Taminiau, Kurdgelashvili, & Kim, 2015; Hong, Lee, Koo, Jeong, & Kim, 2016; Singh & Banerjee, 2015) and so on. Compared with the aforementioned aspects, the issue of LCRPS project site selection from the perspective of sustainable development has not received sufficient scholarly attention. Koo, Hong, Lee, and Kim (2016) proposed an integrated multi-objective model to select the optimal location in implementing rooftop PV system, which was in absence of the sustainable aspect for cites and society yet. Haghdadi, Copper, Bruce, and Macgill (2017) presented a method to estimate the location and orientation of small-scale DPV systems. Compared to Haghdadi's study on small-scale DPV systems, the application of LCRPS can install more PV panels to produce more power, so this paper on LCRPS will receive more attention from decision makers (DMs) and senior managers in PV enterprises. Up till now, flaws and inadequacies still exist in the decision process for LCRPS site selection. Firstly, information uncertainties generally exist in the site selection for LCRPS as follows: ①the site selection of a project is in the early stage which relies on ex ante estimates about what the values will be; ②the PV market is always dynamic and changeable due to the fluctuation of price and policy; ③the judgment and decision of some data relies on DMs' experience, which cannot reflect DMs' opinions as accurately as machines do when describing a intricate object. Secondly, the relationships between the criteria based on sustainable cites and society are not taken seriously. Thirdly, the ranking methods applied in previous studies cannot reflect the DMs' subjective preferences for evaluating the LCRPS site selection problem. Therefore, the study of this paper makes up for the flaws and inadequacies in current researches, which is of vital significance for the prospect of LCRPS.

The site selection for LCRPS based on sustainability perspective is a complex multi-criteria decision-making (MCDM) problem. This study aims at establishing a practical index system based on sustainable cites and society for LCRPS site selection and developing an effective comprehensive evaluation framework to select the most satisfactory plan. A new design of fuzzy MCDM framework based on the ANP and VIKOR method is proposed to handle the LCRPS site selection problem in the presence of multiple DMs under incomplete information environment. The originality of this paper comes from the following folds. First, based on the sustainable cites and society prospective, the comprehensive index system for LCRPS site selection is established. Second, to dispose the vague and imprecise information in the site selection for LCRPS, the TIFNs are normally utilized. Third, Fuzzy ANP is introduced to measure the correlation of the criteria and create appropriate weights. Additionally, the Fuzzy VIKOR method is described and employed to rank the options on the basis of the opinions of different DMs. This fuzzy MCDM framework not only provides the ranking of alternative LCRPS sites under the goal of sustainable cites and society, but also offers the rankings under the sub-goals and the evaluation criteria for the sake of insuring the reasonability of decision-making. Finally, the effectiveness and practicality of this research are demonstrated through an example of China.

2. Literature review

MCDM methods, such as Analytic Hierarchy Process (AHP), ANP, Technique for Order Preference by Similarity to Ideal Solution (TOPSIS), VIKOR, Perference Ranking Organization Methods for Enrichment Evaluations (PROMETHEE) and Elimination et Choix Traduisant la Realité (ELECTRE) are applied widely in the site selection field. Vasileiou, Loukogeorgaki, and Vagiona (2017) used the AHP method to evaluate criteria in the site selection of hybrid offshore wind and wave energy systems. Wu, Yang, Zhang, Chen, and Wang (2016) applied the ANP method to measure the correlation of the indicators in electric vehicle charging station site selection. Rezaei, Mostafaeipour, Qolipour, and Tavakkoli-Moghaddam (2018) proposed TOPSIS for evaluation and selection of optimal locations for wind-solar hybrid plants. The VIKOR method was adopted to determine the optimal site of electric vehicle charging stations (Zhao & Li, 2016). The PROMETHEE method was developed in social sustainability assessment of small hydropower stations (Wu, Wang, Chen, Xu, & Li, 2017). Wu, Zhang, Yuan, Geng, and Zhang (2016) built a framework for offshore wind farm site selection decision utilizing the ELECTRE method. These researches promote the application of MCDM methods and verify the effectiveness and practicality of them in the decision support system for evaluation in the site selection field. The advantages and disadvantages of these methods are shown in Table 6.1.

Table 6.1 The advantages and disadvantages of MCDM methods

(Choudhary & Shankar, 2012; Kumar et al., 2017; Pätäri, Karell, Luukka, & Yeomans, 2017).

	Advantages	Disadvantages
AHP	It is suitable for quantitative and qualitative criteria. It uses hierarchical structures to evaluate	With the increasing number of criteria and alternatives, the massive pairs of comparisons are required

Continued

	Advantages	Disadvantages
AHP	The consistency of the evaluation process can be measured effectively	More DMs involved could make the problem more complex while assigning weights. Data in need are collected based on experience
ANP	It is capable of handling feedbacks and interdependencies. It depicts the dependence and influences of the criteria involved in the goal or higher-level performance objective. Specific software can be applied to solve it conveniently	More pairwise comparison matrices in ANP than AHP are required. It cannot be evaluated for one element in isolation
TOPSIS	It is easy to utilize and well understandable. It works with fundamental ranking. It can easily be revised to eliminate all the subjectivity in the decision process	It does not consider any difference between negative and positive values. It cannot check the consistency. It does not consider the relative importance of these distances
VIKOR	It reflects DMs' subjective preferences. It calculates ration of positive and negative ideal solution to remove the impact. It presents a compromise solution with an advantage rate	Difficult when conflicting situation arises. Needs modification while handling some terse data as it is difficult to build a real time model
PROMETHE	It involves group level decision. It incorporates imprecise and fuzzy information	Does not structure the objective properly. Depends on DMs to assign weight
ELECTRE	Decision making by utilizing thresholds of indifference and preference, and outranking method. It is suitable even when incomparable alternatives exist	It is comparatively difficult because of complex computational procedure. It may not figure out the preferred alternatives

The intuitionistic fuzzy number (IFN), first introduced by Atanassov in 1986, is a generalization of fuzzy number (Atanassov, 1986). Compared with Zadeh's traditional fuzzy number, Atanassov's intuitionistic fuzzy numbers convey more information for situation expression, including membership, non-membership and hesitation degree (Qian, Wang, & Feng, 2013). TIFN, as a special kind of IFN, has drawn considerable attention since it reflects DMs' opinions more accurately by applying a triangular fuzzy number to replace a linguistic variable. Recently, some researchers start to apply TIFNs to MCDM problems in order to make decisions more conform to real-life situations. Wu, Xie, Xu, and Li (2017) used TIFNs to build a comprehensive electric vehicle charging station site selection decision framework. The TIFNs are proved to be more effective in dealing with inevitably imprecise or incompletely reliable judgments in MCDM problems, which is suitable for DMs to express their affirmation, negation and hesitation in decision-making applications (Qin, Liang, Li, Chen, & Yu, 2017; Wan, Wang, Lin, & Dong, 2016). The site selection, a pre-project evaluation problem, is filled with multiple imprecise information and uncertain phenomena. Consequently, introducing the TIFNs to model the uncertainties of LCRPS project site selection would have important theoretical value and practical significance.

The ANP, first proposed by Saaty in 1996, is derived from the AHP (Saaty, 1996). ANP is a comprehensive decision-making technique that captures the outcome of dependency between criteria (Saaty, 1996). It handles interdependence between criteria very well by obtaining the composite weights through the development of supermatrix (Arsić, Nikolić, Mihajlović, Fedajev, & Živković, 2017). Arsić, Nikolić, and Živković (2017) applied a fuzzy MCDM model containing fuzzy ANP to prioritization strategies of sustainable development of ecotourism. Fetanat and Khorasaninejad (2015) employed fuzzy ANP to achieve the principal eigenvector of criteria and sub-criteria in offshore wind farm site selection. Govindan, Shankar, and Kannan (2016) established a framework to evaluate the remanufacturing drivers utilizing fuzzy ANP. Tosarkani, Amin, Tosarkani, and Amin (2017) proposed fuzzy ANP to transform the qualitative measurements to the measurable parameters. Ghadikolaei and Parkouhi (2017) applied fuzzy ANP to determine the importance level of the criteria effectively in resilient supplier selection. ANP, which captures the interdependence, appears to be one of the most feasible and accurate solutions for generating the weights of the selection criteria (Chang, Liao, Tseng, & Liao, 2015). The fuzzy ANP handles ambiguity and uncertainty evidence of human judgment and enhances the capability of ANP to acquire more precise and authentic results (Khoshnava, Rostami, Valipour, Ismail, & Rahmat, 2016). The great correlation between the evaluation indicators of LCRPS optional locations cannot be neglected, and thus the usage of the fuzzy ANP is meaningful and beneficial work for the LCRPS project site selection in this study.

VIKOR is one of the classical MCDM methods, which has been extended to diverse kinds of fuzzy and imprecise situations. The MCDM methods VIKOR and TOPSIS are both based on an aggregating function representing "closeness to the ideal". However, VIKOR is an updated version of TOPSIS, which can fully reflect DM's subjective preferences. Wu, Xie, et al. (2017) utilized fuzzy VIKOR method to rank the alternative electric vehicle charging station sites. Awasthi, Govindan, and Gold (2017) employed fuzzy VIKOR method for multi-tier sustainable global supplier selection. Chen (2017) proposed fuzzy VIKOR method for diverse criteria decision analysis. Sakthivel, Sivakumar, Saravanan, Ikua, and Bernard (2017) presented a novel hybrid MCDM technique concluding fuzzy VIKOR method to evaluate and select the optimum fuel biodiesel blend. Liao, Xu, and Zeng (2015) put forward a fuzzy VIKOR method to solve the MCDM problem in which the criteria conflict with each other. Wan, Yuan, and Dong (2017) applied fuzzy VIKOR method for multiple criteria decision-making with linguistic hesitant fuzzy information. These researchers prove the effectiveness and universality of fuzzy VIKOR method in solving MCDM problems. Hence, this study employs fuzzy VIKOR method to solve the site selection decision-making of LCRPS, which has not been explored by researchers.

Based on the review above, we can explicitly state the applicability and superiority of our study. The framework including fuzzy ANP and fuzzy VIKOR considering correlations between the evaluation indicators under the TIFNs environment is established for LCRPS project site selection because: ①various kinds of uncertainties are involved in the LCRPS project for its complicated and changeable environment and technical conditions, and the TIFN is a powerful tool for describing such uncertainties; ②criteria associated with LCRPS project evaluation have correlations which could not be ignored, and the fuzzy ANP method takes this point into account; ③the DM's subjective preferences need be taken into consideration, and fuzzy VIKOR is employed to rank the options on the basis of the opinions of DMs. In conclusion, on the basis of the aforementioned improvements, the decision results of LCRPS project site selection will be more reasonable and suitable than before.

3. Evaluation criteria system of LCRPS site selection

The establishment of criteria system plays an important role in the LCRPS site selection decision-making based on sustainability perspective. In order to achieve the entire life cycle project management of LCRPS, derived from an extensive literature review on site selection decision-making, we summarize the evaluation attributes of the LCRPS site selection from the sustainability perspective, including resource factor (C1), economy factor (C2), risk factor (C3), environmental factor (C4), and social factor (C5).

The resource factor consists of annual sunshine hours (C11), annual total solar radiation (C12), average temperature (C13) and rooftop available area (C14) since these factors are the indispensable sub-criteria to assess the solar energy and available resources. Wu and Geng (2014) selected solar–wind hybrid power station by calculating annual sunshine hours. The annual total solar radiation was considered as a climatological factor which was applied to measure the intensity of sunshine for a candidate site (J. Liu, Xu, & Lin, 2017), and the total amount of solar radiation on a tilted surface has the components of direct, diffused and ground-reflected radiation. Hong, Koo, Park, and Park (2014) demonstrated the working temperature of solar cells and batteries is one of the most important factors influencing the performance of rooftop PV system. The quantity of solar panels relies on the rooftop available area, which was considered as an important sub-criteria affecting the daily generating capacity and thus the output value of power generation as a result (Dong, Xu, & Lin, 2017).

For the economic factor, the corresponding important financial criteria are initial investment cost (C21), annual capital income (C22), payback period (C23), operation and maintenance cost (C24), local government subsidies (C25). J. Liu et al. (2017) utilized initial investment cost to cover the facility location cost and the procurement cost in the site selection of PV power plants. Wu, Xu, et al. (2017) indicated the annual capital income intuitively reflects the profitability of large-scale rooftop PV projects and is concerned by PV enterprises most. Payback period, the most widely applied metric for PV investments, was chosen as the key financial indicator for the probabilistic model of the present study (Shakouri, Lee, & Kim, 2017). Dong et al. (2017) calculated operation and maintenance cost to cover daily maintenance and cleaning, configuration of basic tools and salary. Local government subsidy is a key to promote the development of distributed PV as well as a source of considerable revenue (Dong et al., 2017).

The risk factor includes extreme weather damage risk (C31) and policy risk (C32). Extreme weather such as storm and persistent rain will reduce generating capacity, or even damage equipment (Guerin, 2017). The policy risk mainly comes from the national energy policy, since every province has its own energy plan (Frisari & Stadelmann, 2015). Thus, the alternative project plans of LCRPS will meet different government support degrees.

For the environmental factor, the main criteria are light pollution (C41), pollutant emission reduction benefits (C42) and energy-saving benefit (C43). Wu and Geng (2014) took light pollution into account in the selection of solar–wind hybrid power station location. The pollutant emission reduction benefit refers to the number of CO_2, SO_2 and dust decreased by using the LCRPS to replace a thermal power station at the same electricity production amount (Wu, Geng, Zhang, & Gao, 2014). The energy-saving benefit indicates that the alternative project will save the amount of the stand coal compared to a thermal power station at the same annual electricity production (Wu et al., 2014).

For the social factor, the impact on the local economy (C51) and public support (C52) must be considered when selecting the optimal LCRPS location, which will decide whether the project construction and operation can run smoothly. The sub-criteria impact on the local economy was considered by numerous scholars to select the optimal sites (Wu & Geng, 2014; Wu et al., 2014). In addition, public support must also be considered in the site selection (Wu et al., 2014), which determines whether the LCRPS will be put into use widely.

In conclusion, the alternative LCRPS site should be evaluated from resource, economy, risk, environmental and social factors based on the sustainability perspective. The evaluation criteria system for LCRPS site selection including five specific criteria and sixteen sub-criteria is set up, shown in Table 6.2.

Table 6.2 The criteria and sub-criteria of LCRPS site selection.

Criteria	Sub-criteria	Remark
(C1) Resource factor	(C11) Annual sunshine hours	It determines local solar energy level.
	(C12) Annual total solar radiation	It directly influences the generating capacity and decides whether LCRPS project will be implemented.
	(C13) Average temperature	The working temperature will affect the performance of LCRPS.
	(C14) Rooftop available area	It determines how many solar panels can be installed on the rooftop.
(C2) Economy factor	(C21) Initial investment cost	It must be considered due to the limited capital resources.
	(C22) Annual capital income	It reflects the profitability of projects.
	(C23) Payback period	It reflects how long the capital return is.
	(C24) Annual operation and maintenance cost	It calculates the cost produced in the operation and maintenance of LCRPS.
	(C25) Local government subsidies	Local government subsidies influence the profitability of projects.
(C3) Risk factor	(C31) Extreme weather damage risk	It will reduce generating capacity and make equipment damaged.
	(C32) Policy risk	Policy will affect the development of LCRPS industry.
(C4) Environmental factor	(C41) Light pollution	It will influence public normal life.
	(C42) Pollutant emission reduction benefits	Energy generated by LCRPS is non-polluting.
	(C43) Energy-saving benefit: standard coal	The application of LCRPS will save a great deal of energy.
(C5) Social factor	(C51) Impact on the local economy	It reflects the utilization of LCRPS will affect local economy.
	(C52) Public support	It affects the popularity of LCRPS.

4. Decision framework of LCRPS site selection

4.1 Basic theory of MCDM problem in the triangular intuitionistic fuzzy environment

For the sake of expressing the DMs' imperfect knowledge in decision-making utilization more effectively, the triangular intuitionistic fuzzy number (TIFN) is applied in the MCDM method. This section describes a few definitions and operations of TIFN related to the LCRPS site selection MCDM problem.

Definition 1. (Li, 2010) A TIFN $\tilde{a}$ on the real number set R is defined as

$\tilde{a}=((\underline{a},a,\overline{a});w_{\tilde{a}},u_{\tilde{a}})$, whose membership function and non-membership function are defined as follows:

$$\mu_{\tilde{a}}(x)=\begin{cases}(x-\underline{a})w_{\tilde{a}}/(a-\underline{a}) & \text{if } \underline{a}\leqslant x<a,\\ w_{\tilde{a}} & \text{if } x=a,\\ (\overline{a}-x)w_{\tilde{a}}/(\overline{a}-a) & \text{if } a\leqslant x<\overline{a},\\ 0 & \text{if } x<\underline{a} \text{ or } x>\overline{a},\end{cases}$$

and

$$\nu_{\tilde{a}}(x)=\begin{cases}[a-x+u_{\tilde{a}}(x-\underline{a})]/(a-\underline{a}) & \text{if } \underline{a}\leqslant x<a,\\ u_{\tilde{a}} & \text{if } x=a,\\ [x-a+u_{\tilde{a}}(\overline{a}-x)]/(\overline{a}-a) & \text{if } a\leqslant x<\overline{a},\\ 0 & \text{if } x<\underline{a} \text{ or } x>\overline{a},\end{cases}$$

respectively, where the values $w_{\tilde{a}}$ and $u_{\tilde{a}}$ represent the maximum membership degree and the minimum non-membership degree such that they satisfy the conditions: $0\leqslant w_{\tilde{a}}\leqslant 1$, $0\leqslant u_{\tilde{a}}\leqslant 1$ and $w_{\tilde{a}}+u_{\tilde{a}}\leqslant 1$. Let $\pi_{\tilde{a}}(x)=1-w_{\tilde{a}}(x)-u_{\tilde{a}}(x)$ be called an intuitionistic fuzzy index of the TIFN $\tilde{a}$, which reflects hesitancy degree of the element x to $\tilde{a}$.

A TIFN $\tilde{a}=((\underline{a},a,\overline{a});w_{\tilde{a}},u_{\tilde{a}})$ expresses an ill-known quantity "approximate *a*", which is approximately equal to *a*. Namely, the ill-known quantity "approximate *a*" is expressed using any value between $\underline{a}$ and $\overline{a}$ with different degrees of membership and degrees of non-membership. In other words, the most possible value is *a* with the degree $w_{\tilde{a}}$ of membership and the degree $u_{\tilde{a}}$ of non-membership; the pessimistic value is $\underline{a}$ while the optimistic value is $\overline{a}$ with the degree 0 of membership and the degree 1 of non-membership. Other values are any $x\in(\underline{a},\overline{a})$ with the degree $\mu_{\tilde{a}}(x)$ of membership and the degree $\nu_{\tilde{a}}(x)$ of non-membership.

Definition 2. (Li, 2010) Let $\tilde{a}_1=((\underline{a}_1,a_1,\overline{a}_1);w_{a_1},u_{a_1})$ and $\tilde{a}_2=((\underline{a}_2,a_2,\overline{a}_2);w_{a_2},u_{a_2})$ be two TIFNs and λ be a real number. Then the arithmetical operations for TIFNs are defined as follows:

(1) $\tilde{a}_1+\tilde{a}_2=((\underline{a}_1+\underline{a}_2,a_1+a_2,\overline{a}_1+\overline{a}_2);w_{\tilde{a}_1}\wedge w_{\tilde{a}_2},u_{\tilde{a}_1}\vee u_{\tilde{a}_2})$

(2) $$\tilde{a}_1\tilde{a}_2=\begin{cases}((\underline{a}_1\underline{a}_2,a_1a_2,\overline{a}_1\overline{a}_2);w_{\tilde{a}_1}\wedge w_{\tilde{a}_2},u_{\tilde{a}_1}\vee u_{\tilde{a}_2}), \text{ if } \tilde{a}_1>0 \text{ and } \tilde{a}_2>0\\ ((\underline{a}_1\overline{a}_2,a_1a_2,\overline{a}_1\underline{a}_2);w_{\tilde{a}_1}\wedge w_{\tilde{a}_2},u_{\tilde{a}_1}\vee u_{\tilde{a}_2}), \text{ if } \tilde{a}_1<0 \text{ and } \tilde{a}_2>0\\ ((\overline{a}_1\overline{a}_2,a_1a_2,\underline{a}_1\underline{a}_2);w_{\tilde{a}_1}\wedge w_{\tilde{a}_2},u_{\tilde{a}_1}\vee u_{\tilde{a}_2}), \text{ if } \tilde{a}_1<0 \text{ and } \tilde{a}_2<0\end{cases}$$

(3) $$\lambda\tilde{a}_1=\begin{cases}((\lambda\underline{a}_1,\lambda a_1,\lambda\overline{a}_1);w_{\tilde{a}_1},u_{\tilde{a}_1}), \text{ if } \lambda>0\\ ((\lambda\overline{a}_1,\lambda a_1,\lambda\underline{a}_1);w_{\tilde{a}_1},u_{\tilde{a}_1}), \text{ if } \lambda<0\end{cases}$$

where the symbols "$\wedge$" and "$\vee$" mean min and max operators, respectively.

Definition 3. (Li, 2010) Let $\tilde{a}_i=((\underline{a}_i,a_i,\overline{a}_i);w_{a_i},u_{a_i})$ be TIFNs. A ratio ranking procedure can be developed for ranking the TIFNs $a_i(i=1,2,\ldots,n)$, which is summarized as follows:

$$R(\tilde{a}_i,\lambda)=\frac{(\underline{a}_i+4a_i+\overline{a}_i)+(\lambda w_{\tilde{a}_i}^2+(1-\lambda)(1-u_{\tilde{a}_i})^2)}{6+(\overline{a}_i-\underline{a}_i)(\lambda w_{\tilde{a}_i}^2+(1-\lambda)(1-u_{\tilde{a}_i})^2)} \tag{6-1}$$

where $\lambda \in [0,1]$ is a weight which represents the DM's attitude toward the degree of uncertain; $\lambda \in [0,1/2)$ shows that the DM prefers uncertainty or negative feeling; $\lambda \in (1/2,1]$ shows that the DM prefers certainty or positive feeling; $\lambda = 1/2$ shows that the DM is indifferent between positive feeling and negative feeling. Therefore, the ambiguity parameter λ reflects the DM's subjectivity attitude to the TIFN.

Definition 4. (Wan, Wang, & Dong, 2013) Let $\tilde{a}_1=((\underline{a}_1,a_1,\overline{a}_1);w_{a_1},u_{a_1})$ and $\tilde{a}_2=((\underline{a}_2,a_2,\overline{a}_2);w_{a_2},u_{a_2})$ be two TIFNs. The Hamming distance between them are respectively defined as follows:

$$d(\tilde{a}_1,\tilde{a}_2)=\frac{1}{3}(|\underline{a}_1-\underline{a}_2|+|a_1-a_2|+|\overline{a}_1-\overline{a}_2|)+\max(|w_{a_1}-w_{a_2}|,|u_{a_1}-u_{a_2}|) \tag{6-2}$$

In this study, a four-phase decision framework for LCRPS site selection decision-making is proposed, as shown in Fig. 6.2. The four phases of research methodology are described in the following subsections.

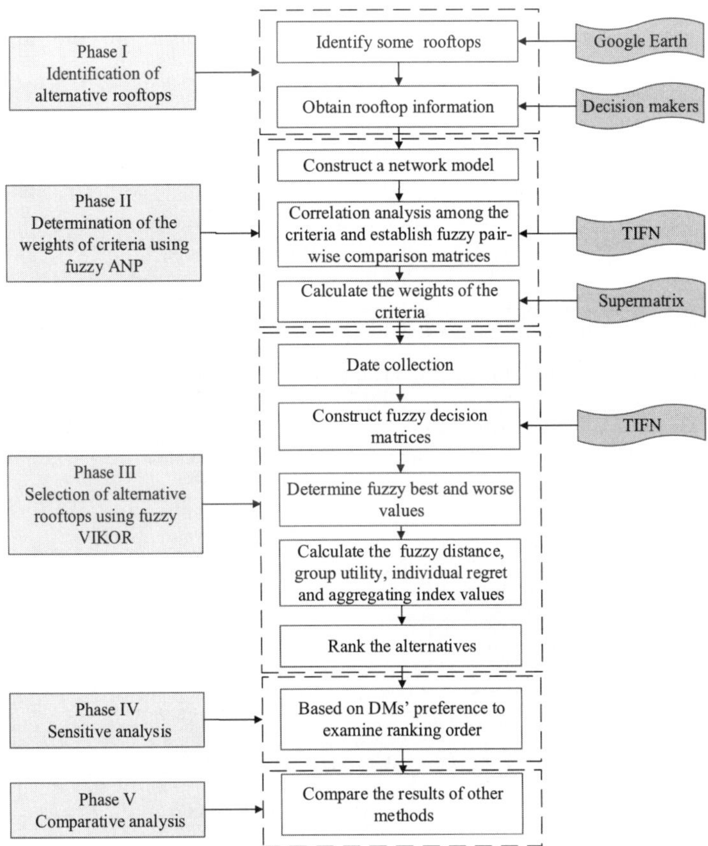

Fig. 6.2 The decision framework of LCRPS site selection.

4.2 Phase I – identification of alternative rooftops

Step 1. The software of Google Earth is applied to identify some alternative rooftops with large enough area.

Step 2. The DMs inspect these rooftops to obtain some relevant information such as radiation intensity, building height, roof area, roof slope, roof type, etc.

4.3 Phase II – determination of the weights of criteria

The steps of fuzzy ANP are presented as follows (Lee, Kang, & Liou, 2017; Wu, Yang, et al., 2016):

Step 1. Construct a network model and determine the interrelationships among the criteria. A network model is established using criteria, sub-criteria and alternatives for the site selection of LCRPS, as shown in Fig. 6.3. Brainstorming is held with experts invited from relative fields to determine the interrelationships among the sub-criteria. First, the opinion of every expert ought to be collected separately. Next, several collective discussions concentrating on the divergence should be held until consensus has been reached. The final mutual influence concern of the sub-criteria is shown in Table 6.3 based on the agreement. The symbol "√" means that the sub-criterion in the row would have an effect on the sub-criterion in the column.

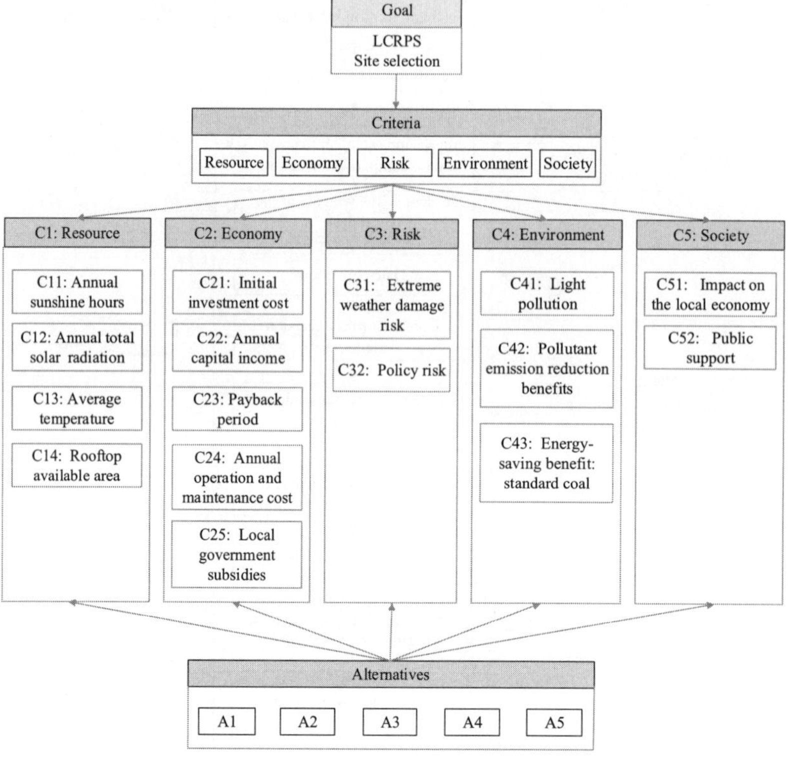

Fig. 6.3 A network model for the site selection of LCRPS.

Table 6.3 Mutual influence concerns of the factors.

	Resource factors				Economy factors					Risk factors		Environmental factors			Social factors	
	C11	C12	C13	C14	C21	C22	C23	C24	C25	C31	C32	C41	C42	C43	C51	C52
C11		√	√	√	√	√	√	√	√		√	√	√	√	√	√
C12	√		√	√	√	√	√	√	√		√	√	√	√	√	√
C13	√	√		√	√	√	√	√	√	√	√				√	√
C14					√	√	√	√	√	√	√	√	√	√	√	√
C21			√	√		√	√	√	√	√	√	√	√	√	√	√
C22	√	√	√	√	√		√	√	√	√	√	√	√	√	√	√
C23	√	√	√	√	√	√		√	√	√	√	√	√	√	√	√
C24			√	√	√	√	√		√	√	√	√	√	√	√	√
C25	√	√	√	√	√	√	√	√		√	√	√	√	√	√	√
C31	√	√	√	√	√	√	√	√	√		√	√	√	√	√	√
C32	√	√	√	√	√	√	√	√	√	√		√	√	√	√	√
C41	√	√	√	√	√	√	√	√	√	√	√		√	√	√	√
C42	√	√	√	√	√	√	√	√	√	√	√	√		√	√	√
C43	√	√	√	√	√	√	√	√	√	√	√	√	√		√	√
C51	√	√	√	√	√	√	√	√	√	√	√	√	√	√		√
C52	√	√	√	√	√	√	√	√	√	√	√	√	√	√	√	

Step 2. Determine fuzzy aggregated pairwise comparison matrices. Based on linguistic variables in Table 6.4, experts determine the degree of importance of each sub-criterion using pair-wise comparisons. The consequences from every expert are transformed into TIFNs based on Table 6.4. The fuzzy pairwise comparison matrix of criteria for expert k is as follows:

Table 6.4 The fuzzy linguistic scale for the weights.

Linguistic Variable	Abbreviation	TIFNs
Very low	VL	((1/5, 1/4, 1/3); 0.7, 0.2)
Low	L	((1/4, 1/3, 1/2); 0.8, 0.1)
Medium low	ML	((1/3, 1/2, 1); 0.9, 0)
Equal	E	((1, 1, 1); 1, 0)
Medium high	MH	((1, 2, 3); 0.9, 0)
High	H	((2, 3, 4); 0.8, 0.1)
Very high	VH	((3, 4, 5); 0.7, 0.2)

$$\tilde{W}_{CK} = \begin{bmatrix} & C_1 & C_2 & \cdots & C_N \\ C_1 & 1 & \tilde{a}_{12k} & \cdots & \tilde{a}_{1Nk} \\ C_2 & \tilde{a}_{21k} & 1 & \cdots & \tilde{a}_{2Nk} \\ \vdots & \vdots & \vdots & \tilde{a}_{ijk} & \vdots \\ C_N & \tilde{a}_{N1k} & \tilde{a}_{N2k} & \cdots & 1 \end{bmatrix}, i = 1, 2, \ldots, N; j = 1, 2, \ldots, N \tag{6-3}$$

where $\tilde{a}_{ijk}$ is the pairwise comparison value between criterion i and j determined by expert k. Experts' opinions are integrated using an arithmetic average approach. With K experts, the arithmetic average for the pairwise comparison value between criteria i and j is:

$$\tilde{f}_{ij} = \sum_{k=1}^{K} \mu_k \tilde{a}_{ijk} = ((\underline{f}_i, f_i, \overline{f}_i); w_{f_i}, u_{f_i}), i = 1,2,\ldots,N; j = 1,2,\ldots,N \tag{6-4}$$

where μ_k is the importance weights of the K experts, satisfying $\sum_1^K \mu_k = 1$ and $\mu_k > 0$ for $k = 1,2,\ldots,K$.

The fuzzy aggregated pairwise comparison matrix for the criteria is:

$$\tilde{W}_C = \begin{bmatrix} & C_1 & C_2 & \cdots & C_N \\ C_1 & 1 & \tilde{f}_{12} & \cdots & \tilde{f}_{1N} \\ C_2 & \tilde{f}_{21} & 1 & \cdots & \tilde{f}_{2N} \\ \vdots & \vdots & \vdots & \tilde{f}_{ij} & \vdots \\ C_N & \tilde{f}_{N1} & \tilde{f}_{N2} & \cdots & 1 \end{bmatrix}, i = 1,2,\ldots,N; j = 1,2,\ldots,N \tag{6-5}$$

Step 3. Calculate defuzzified aggregated pairwise comparison matrices. If $i < j$, the fuzzy aggregated pairwise comparison values are transformed into defuzzified aggregated pairwise comparison values based on Eq. (6-1) (here $\lambda = 0.5$), as shown in Eq. (6-6). If $i = j$, the defuzzified aggregated pairwise comparison values are equal to 1. The rest values can be obtained by the reciprocal, as shown in Eq. (6-7).

$$f_{ij} = \frac{(\underline{f}_i + 4f_i + \overline{f}_i) + (0.5w_{\overline{f}_i}^2 + 0.5(1 - u_{\overline{f}_i})^2)}{6 + (\overline{f}_i - \underline{f}_i)(0.5w_{\overline{f}_i}^2 + 0.5(1 - u_{\overline{f}_i})^2)}, i < j \tag{6-6}$$

$$W_C = \begin{bmatrix} & C_1 & C_2 & \cdots & C_N \\ C_1 & 1 & f_{12} & \cdots & f_{1N} \\ C_2 & 1/f_{12} & 1 & \cdots & f_{2N} \\ \vdots & \vdots & \vdots & f_{ij} & \vdots \\ C_N & 1/f_{1N} & 1/f_{2N} & \cdots & 1 \end{bmatrix}, i = 1,2,\ldots,N; j = 1,2,\ldots,N \tag{6-7}$$

Step 4. Calculate the importance vector of the criteria. For example, the importance vector for the defuzzified aggregated pairwise comparison for the criteria is as follows:

$$W_C \times w_C = \lambda_{\max} \times w_C \tag{6-8}$$

where W_C is the defuzzified aggregated comparison matrix for the criteria, w_C is the eigenvector, and $\lambda_{\max}$ is the largest eigenvalue of W_C.

Step 5. Examine the consistency of each defuzzified aggregated pairwise comparison matrix. The consistency index (CI) and consistency ratio (CR) for the defuzzified aggregated comparison matrix for the criteria are calculated as follows:

$$CI_C = \frac{\lambda_{\max} - N}{N - 1} \tag{6-9}$$

$$CR_C = \frac{CI_C}{RI} \tag{6-10}$$

where RI is the random index. If the consistency ratio exceeds 0.1, an inconsistency is emerging, then the experts will be invited to revise the pairwise comparison values. The calculations will be carried out again.

Step 6. Calculate the weight of the criteria. First, utilize the importance vector of the criteria to form an unweighted supermatrix. Then, transform the unweighted supermatrix into a weighted supermatrix to ensure column stochastic. By taking powers, the weighted supermatrix can converge into a stable supermatrix, called the limit supermatrix. The final weights of the sub-criteria w_j^C are found in the limit supermatrix.

4.4 Phase III – selection of alternative rooftops

The steps of fuzzy VIKOR are proposed as follows (Liu, You, You, & Shan, 2015; Wu, Xu, et al., 2017):

Step 1. Constructing the decision matrix. The criteria can be classified into three types: ①quantitative criteria that can be measured precisely; ②quantitative criteria that cannot be measured precisely; and ③qualitative criteria. For the first category of criteria, their values are equal to real numbers, which will be converted into TIFNs to keep the consistency; for the second category of criteria, their imprecise values are calculated firstly, and then DMs assess them by applying TIFNs to reflect the uncertainties; for the last category of criteria, their values are directly evaluated by DMs using linguistic scales in Table 6.5. Suppose that this MCDM problem has $DM_k(k=1,2,\ldots,K)$, m alternatives $A_i(i=1,2,\ldots,m)$, and n sub-criteria $C_j(j=1,2,\ldots,n)$. Let $\tilde{x}_{ijk}=((\underline{x}_{ijk},x_{ijk},\overline{x}_{ijk}),w_{x_{ijk}},u_{x_{ijk}})$ be the fuzzy rating of the i th alternative on the j th sub-criterion provided by the k th DM using TIFNs, and $\lambda_k(k=1,2,\ldots,K)$ be the relative importance weights of the K DMs, satisfying $\sum_1^K \lambda_k = 1$ and $\lambda_k > 0$ for $k=1,2,\ldots,K$.

The aggregated fuzzy ratings ($\tilde{x}_{ij}$) of alternatives with respect to each criterion can be calculated using an arithmetic average approach as:

$$\tilde{x}_{ij} = \sum_{k=1}^{K} \lambda_k \tilde{x}_{ijk} = ((\underline{x}_{ij}, x_{ij}, \overline{x}_{ij}); w_{x_{ij}}, u_{x_{ij}}), i=1,2,\ldots,m; j=1,2,\ldots,n \tag{6-11}$$

then the aggregated decision matrix $[\tilde{x}_{ij}]_{m\times n}$ is constructed. To evaluate the impact of various physical dimensions and measurements on the final decision, the decision matrix $[\tilde{x}_{ij}]_{m\times n}$ needs be normalized as $[\tilde{r}_{ij}]_{m\times n}$ where $\tilde{r}_{ij}=(\underline{r}_{ij},r_{ij},\overline{r}_{ij},w_{r_{ij}},u_{r_{ij}})$ with $w_{r_{ij}}=w_{x_{ij}}$, $u_{r_{ij}}=u_{x_{ij}}$ and

$$(\underline{r}_{ij}, r_{ij}, \overline{r}_{ij}) = \begin{cases} (\dfrac{\underline{x}_{ij}}{\overline{x}_{\max j}}, \dfrac{x_{ij}}{\overline{x}_{\max j}}, \dfrac{\overline{x}_{ij}}{\overline{x}_{\max j}}) & \text{if } x_j \in F^B \\ (\dfrac{\underline{x}_{\min j}}{\overline{x}_{ij}}, \dfrac{\underline{x}_{\min j}}{x_{ij}}, \dfrac{\underline{x}_{\min j}}{\underline{x}_{ij}}) & \text{if } x_j \in F^C \end{cases} \tag{6-12}$$

where $\overline{x}_{\max j} = \max\{\overline{x}_{ij} \mid i = 1,2,\ldots,m\}$, $\underline{x}_{\min j} = \min\{\underline{x}_{ij} \mid i = 1,2,\ldots,m\}$. F^B and F^C are the subsets of benefit criteria and cost criteria, respectively.

Table 6.5 The fuzzy linguistic scale for the alternatives.

Linguistic Variable	Abbreviation	TIFNs
Very poor	VP	((0, 0, 1); 0.7, 0.2)
Poor	P	((0, 1, 3); 0.8, 0.1)
Medium poor	MP	((1, 3, 5); 0.9, 0)
Fair	F	((3, 5, 7); 1, 0)
Medium good	MG	((5, 7, 9); 0.9, 0)
Good	G	((7, 9, 10); 0.8, 0.1)
Very good	VG	((9, 10, 10); 0.7, 0.2)

Step 2. Determine the fuzzy best $\tilde{f}_j^*$ and the fuzzy worst $\tilde{f}_j^-$ values of all criteria ratings, $i = 1,2,\ldots,m$, $j = 1,2,\ldots,n$.

$$\tilde{f}_j^* = \begin{cases} \max_i \tilde{r}_{ij} = ((\max_i \underline{r}_{ij}, \max_i r_{ij}, \max_i \overline{r}_{ij}); 1, 0), & \text{for benefit criteria} \\ \min_i \tilde{r}_{ij} = ((\min_i \underline{r}_{ij}, \min_i r_{ij}, \min_i \overline{r}_{ij}); 0, 1), & \text{for cost criteria} \end{cases} \tag{6-13}$$

$$\tilde{f}_j^- = \begin{cases} \min_i \tilde{r}_{ij} = ((\min_i \underline{r}_{ij}, \min_i r_{ij}, \min_i \overline{r}_{ij}); 0, 1), & \text{for benefit criteria} \\ \max_i \tilde{r}_{ij} = ((\max_i \underline{r}_{ij}, \max_i r_{ij}, \max_i \overline{r}_{ij}); 1, 0), & \text{for cost criteria} \end{cases} \tag{6-14}$$

Step 3. Calculate the normalized fuzzy distance $d_{ij}, i = 1,2,\ldots,m$, $j = 1,2,\ldots,n$ based on Eq. (6-2).

$$d_{ij} = \frac{d(\tilde{f}_j^*, \tilde{r}_{ij})}{d(\tilde{f}_j^*, \tilde{f}_j^-)} \tag{6-15}$$

Step 4. Calculate group utility S_i and individual regret R_i for each alternative i.

$$S_i = \sum_{j=1}^{n} w_j^C d_{ij}, i = 1,2,\ldots,m \tag{6-16}$$

$$R_i = \max_j (w_j^C d_{ij}), i = 1,2,\ldots,m \tag{6-17}$$

where w_j^C is the relative weights of sub-criteria acquired from Phase II.

Step 5. Calculate aggregating index Q_i for each alternative i.

$$Q_i = v\frac{S_i - S^*}{S^- - S^*} + (1-v)\frac{R_i - R^*}{R^- - R^*}, i = 1,2,\ldots,m \tag{6-18}$$

where $S^* = \min_i S_i$, $S^- = \max_i S_i$, $R^* = \min_i R_i$, $R^- = \max_i R_i$, and v is the weight of the strategy of the majority of sub-criteria. The value of v is set to 0.5 in this study.

Step 6. Rank the alternatives, sorting by the values S, R and Q in increasing order. The results are three ranking lists.

Step 7. Propose a compromise solution, the alternative ($A^{(1)}$), which is the best ranked by the measure Q (minimum) if the following two conditions are satisfied:

Condition 1. Acceptable advantage: $Q(A^{(2)}) - Q(A^{(1)}) \geqslant 1/(m-1)$ where $A^{(2)}$ is the alternative with second position in the ranking list by Q.

Condition 2. Acceptable stability in decision making: The best alternative $A^{(1)}$ must also be the best alternative in terms of both S_i and R_i. This compromise solution is stable within a decision-making process, which could be: "voting by majority rule" (when $v > 0.5$ is needed), or "by consensus" ($v \approx 0.5$), or "with veto" ($v < 0.5$).

If one of the conditions is not satisfied, then a set of compromise solutions is proposed, which consists of:

Alternatives $A^{(1)}$ and $A^{(2)}$ if only condition 2 is not met.

Alternatives $A^{(1)}$, $A^{(2)}$,..., $A^{(M)}$ if condition 1 is not met. Alternative $A^{(M)}$ is determined by $Q(A^{(M)}) - Q(A^{(1)}) < 1/(m-1)$.

4.5 Phase IV – sensitive analysis

For the sake of discovering how the ranking results will be impacted when decision information changes, a sensitive analysis is required because subjective judgment of DMs may deviate from objective facts. In the process of realistic decision-making, the DMs' opinions do not always keep consistent; they may vary due to various conditions or factors. So the understanding of the change of DMs' opinions and its impact on the ranking results is necessary. As a consequence, sensitive analysis will be proposed to reveal this impact and check the robustness of the evaluation results.

4.6 Phase V –comparative analysis

In order to examine the feasibility and effectiveness of the decision framework proposed for the LCRPS site selection, a comparative analysis based on the same illustrative case with the results of other previous methods will be carried out. The comparative analysis will be performed by obtained calculation results from other previous methods, so the comparison of differences between the ranking orders obtained by other methods may certificate the suitability and feasibility of the proposed method.

5. A case study

5.1 Problem statement

Large amounts of energy is demanded in China's coastal regions while the conventional fossil fuels are scarce, which brings an essential impact on the socio-economic development of the areas. Plentiful energy generated by LCRPS provides a good choice for these areas. Based on market requirements, A PV enterprise located in Shanghai intends to invest a LCRPS project in Guangdong province. After investigation and information collection, a total of five LCRPS projects located in various cities are identified, as shown in Fig. 6.4. All these alternatives have an adequate area larger than 10 thousand square meters. Due to the insufficient funds, the PV enterprise has to select an optimal alternative.

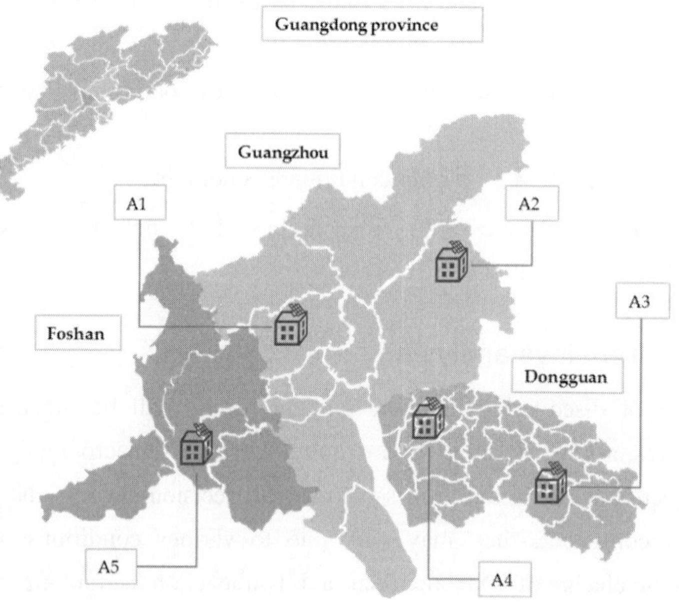

Fig.6.4 The geographical positions of five alternatives.

5.2 Attribute data collection

Based on Table 6.2, sixteen attributes are identified and classified into five categories i.e. resource, economy, risk, environment and society. As mentioned in Section 4.4, these attributes can be classified into three types.

The first type includes C11 (annual sunshine hours), C13 (average temperature), C14 (rooftop available area) since their values can be measured precisely. Based on the locations of LCRPS projects, data of C11 and C13 are acquired through input geodetic coordinates system on

National Aeronautics and Space Administration (NASA) website. Data of C14 are measured from urban maps obtained from Google Earth.

The second type consists of C12 (annual total solar radiation), C21 (initial investment cost), C22 (annual capital income), C23 (payback period), C24 (annual operation and maintenance cost), C25 (local government subsidies), C42 (pollutant emission reduction benefits), C43 (energy-saving benefit: standard coal) since their values cannot be measured precisely.

The value of C12 can be calculated as (Dan, Mohajeri, & Scartezzini, 2017):

$$G_t = G_{Bt} + G_{Dt} + G_{Rt} = G_B R_b + G_D R_d + G_h R_r \tag{6-19}$$

where G_t is the total solar radiation on a tilted surface measured by MJ/m2, G_B, G_D and G_h are the direct, diffused and ground-reflected irradiation respectively, which are acquired on NASA website. The tilted coefficients R_b, R_d and R_r represent the main variables: R_b represents the direct radiation factor, R_d represents the diffuse radiation factor, and R_r represents the reflected radiation factor. The calculation of R_b, R_d and R_r are shown in Appendix A.

The value of C21 can be calculated as (Wu, Xua, Ke, Chen, & Sun, 2017):

$$C_{ic} = \sum_{t=1}^{n}\left(C_{ar} \bullet A_r \bullet (1+I_c)^{-t}\right) + C_p \tag{6-20}$$

where C_{ic} is the initial investment cost, n is the lifetime of the LCRPS project, C_{ar} is the annual rooftop rent cost measured by CNY/m^2, A_r is the effective PV module area of the rooftop measured by m^2 and I_c is the discount rate. C_p is the procurement cost that refers to the cost of raw materials from suppliers consisting of PV modules, support structure forms, batteries and inverters (Cucchiella, D'Adamo, & Koh, 2015). In this study, the values of n and I_c are assumed to be 25 years and 10%, respectively.

The value of C22 can be calculated as (Wu, Xua, et al., 2017; Xu, 2016):

$$B_t = (P_s \bullet (G_t \bullet T \bullet A_r \bullet \theta \bullet \eta) \times \kappa_i + P_o \bullet (G_t \bullet T \bullet A_r \bullet \theta \bullet \eta) \times (1-\kappa_i) + SU)_t \tag{6-21}$$

where B_t is the annual capital income measured by CNY, T is the annually average effective solar radiation hour measured by h, θ is the PV conversion efficiency and η is the corrected coefficient taking some reduction factors into consideration such as inverter power loss and operating temperature loss. Therefore, $(G_t \bullet T \bullet A_r \bullet \theta \bullet \eta)$ refers to the total power generation produced by the LCRPS project. κ_i is the proportion of the self-consumed power in the total power generation, so $(1-\kappa_i)$ is the proportion of the power amount which is connected into the grid in the total power generation. P_s is the price of the old-way supplied energy that is supplanted by the LCRPS project. Thus, $P_s \bullet (G_t \bullet T \bullet A_r \bullet \theta \bullet \eta) \times \kappa_i$ refers to a cost-saving, treated as a part of income. The value of P_s is 0.9 CNY/kWh. P_o is PV station feed-in tariff whose value is regulated to be 0.85 CNY/kWh for Guangdong province belonging to Region III.

SU is the subsidies of local municipal government, the value of C25, which is various between cities, as shown in Table 6.6. The value of C25 can be calculated as:

$$SU = SU_i + SU_p \tag{6-22}$$

where SU_i is the subsidies based on installed capacity, SU_p is the subsidies based on power generation. In this study, the value of θ is 17.5% while the value of η is 75%.

The value of C23 can be calculated as:

$$PP = C_{ic} / B_t \tag{6-23}$$

where PP is the payback period measured by year.

The value of C24 can be calculated as (Wu, Xua, et al., 2017):

$$C_m = C_{ic} \cdot R_i \tag{6-24}$$

where C_m is annual operation and maintenance cost, and R_i is the maintenance rate of various regions.

The value of C42 can be calculated by the amount of carbon emission reduction as (Wu, Xua, et al., 2017):

$$S_{CO_2} = (G_t \cdot T \cdot A_r \cdot \theta \cdot \eta) \cdot g \cdot m \tag{6-25}$$

where S_{CO_2} is the amount of carbon dioxide, g is the average coal consumption for power supply which is measured by g/kWh, and m is the amount of carbon dioxide produced by burning a ton of standard coal which is measured by t so the value of C43 is equal to $(G_t \cdot T \cdot A_r \cdot \theta \cdot \eta) \cdot g$. Based on the present stage of China, the appropriate value of g and m is about 335g/kWh and 2.62t.

Table 6.6 Various municipal subsidies in Guangdong province.

City	Subsidy
Guangzhou	0.2(CNY/W) based on installed capacity and 0.1(CNY/kWh) based on power generation for 10 years.
Dongguan	0.25(CNY/W) based on installed capacity and 0.1(CNY/kWh) based on power generation for 5 years.
Foshan	0.4(CNY/W) based on installed capacity and 0.15(CNY/kWh) based on power generation for 3 years.

The last type contains C31 (extreme weather damage risk), C32 (policy risk), C41 (light pollution), C51 (impact on the local economy) and C52 (public support) since they are not easy to be quantified. Thus, TIFNs are employed by DMs to evaluate them based on linguistic variables in Table 6.4.

5.3 Decision-making process

In this section, the proposed four-phase decision framework is applied for the PV enterprise to select a suitable location for establishing a LCRPS in Guangdong province.

In phase I, the initial LCRPS site selection scheme is formed within five potential alternatives, involving cities of Guangzhou, Dongguan and Foshan, respectively A1, A2, A3, A4, A5. The evaluation criteria system for LCRPS site selection is shown in Table 6.2.

In phase II, the network model and the mutual influence concern of criteria are shown in Fig. 6.2 and Table 6.3, respectively. Based on the linguistic weighting terms and the corresponding TIFNs in Table 6.4, the relative importance of the first-level-criteria are evaluated by three experts, and the linguistic variables are transformed into TIFNs, as shown in Appendix A. Then, suppose the experts have the same weights, so the fuzzy aggregated pairwise comparison matrix for the first-level-criteria using Eq. (6-4) and Eq. (6-5) is shown in Appendix A. Following this, the fuzzy aggregated pairwise comparison matrices for the sub-criteria are shown in Appendix A. Then, calculate defuzzified aggregated pairwise comparison matrices for the first-level-criteria and sub-criteria using Eq. (6-6) and Eq. (6-7), as shown in Appendix A. Subsequently, the importance vector of the criteria are calculated by Eq. (6-8) and the consistency test is performed by Eq. (6-9) and Eq. (6-10). Then, an unweighted supermatrix is formed using the importance vector of the criteria, as shown in Table A1. The weighted supermatrix and the limit supermatrix are also calculated, as shown in Table A2 and A3, respectively. The final importance weights of the sub-criteria are shown in Table 6.7.

Table 6.7 Sub-criteria weights.

	C11	C12	C13	C14	C21	C22	C23	C24	C25	C31	C32	C41	C42	C43	C51	C52
Weight	0.0649	0.0767	0.0497	0.0733	0.0468	0.0443	0.0403	0.0358	0.0397	0.0900	0.0740	0.0715	0.0909	0.0837	0.0680	0.0504

In phase III, based on criteria date collection and calculation mentioned above, construct two decision matrices for the first and second categories of sub-criteria, as shown in Table 6.8 and Table 6.9. Then, construct the third aggregated decision matrix using Eq. (6-11) after three DMs with the same weight evaluate the last category of sub-criteria using linguistic variables in Table 6.5, as shown in Appendix B. The aggregated decision matrices need to be normalized using Eq. (6-12), as shown in Appendix B. Then, the fuzzy best $\tilde{f}_j^*$ and the fuzzy worst $\tilde{f}_j^-$ values of all criteria ratings are determined by Eq. (6-13) and Eq. (6-14). The normalized fuzzy distance can be calculated using Eq. (6-15). The values of S, R_i and Q_i are calculated for each alternative i using Eq. (16-16) to Eq. (16-18), as shown in Table 6.10.

Table 6.8 Performance numerical values in TIFNs of the first category of sub-criteria.

	A1	A2	A3	A4	A5
C11(h)	((4410, 4412.2, 4415); 0.8, 0.1)	((4420, 4424, 4425); 0.8, 0.1)	((4420, 4423.8, 4425); 0.7, 0.2)	((4418, 4420.4, 4423); 0.6, 0.3)	((4417, 4419.3, 4422); 0.6, 0.3)
C13(℃)	((17, 20.4, 24.1); 0.8, 0.1)	((17.2, 20.6, 24.6); 0.7, 0.2)	((19.4, 22.1, 25); 0.8, 0.1)	((18.5, 21.7, 25.4); 0.8, 0.1)	((18, 21.3, 25); 0.7, 0.2)
C14(m^2)	((15237, 15237.4, 15239); 0.8, 0.1)	((14345, 14345.2, 14347); 0.8, 0.1)	((17085, 17085.6, 17087); 0.7, 0.2)	((13640, 13640.1, 13642); 0.7, 0.2)	((16420, 16420.7, 16423); 0.8, 0.1)

Table 6.9 Performance numerical values in TIFNs of the second category of sub-criteria.

		A1	A2	A3	A4	A5
C12	Value	≈4.93	≈5.08	≈5.36	≈5.24	≈5.13
(103MJ/m²)	TINF	((4.90, 4.93, 5.00); 0.7, 0.2)	((5.00, 5.08, 5.10); 0.7, 0.2)	((5.30, 5.36, 5.40); 0.6, 0.3)	((5.20, 5.24, 5.30); 0.7, 0.2)	((5.10, 5.13, 5.20); 0.7, 0.2)
C21	Value	≈1.52	≈1.36	≈1.74	≈1.28	≈1.64
(107CNY)	TINF	((1.45, 1.52, 1.55); 0.6, 0.2)	((1.30, 1.36, 1.40); 0.7, 0.1)	((1.70, 1.74, 1.80); 0.6, 0.2)	((1.25, 1.28, 1.35); 0.7, 0.1)	((1.60, 1.64, 1.70); 0.6, 0.1)
C22	Value	≈4.40	≈4.32	≈4.67	≈3.64	≈4.19
(106CNY)	TINF	((4.35, 4.40, 4.45); 0.7, 0.1)	((4.25, 4.32, 4.35); 0.6, 0.2)	((4.60, 4.67, 4.70); 0.8, 0)	((3.60, 3.64, 3.70); 0.7, 0.1)	((4.15, 4.19, 4.25); 0.7, 0.1)
C23	Value	≈3.45	≈3.15	≈3.73	≈3.52	≈3.91
(Year)	TINF	((3.40, 3.45, 3.50); 0.6, 0.2)	((3.10, 3.15, 3.20); 0.5, 0.3)	((3.70, 3.73, 3.80); 0.6, 0.2)	((3.45, 3.52, 3.55); 0.5, 0.2)	((3.85, 3.91, 3.95); 0.5, 0.3)
C24	Value	≈3.04	≈2.72	≈3.48	≈2.56	≈3.28
(105CNY)	TINF	((3.00, 3.04, 3.10); 0.6, 0.3)	((2.65, 2.72, 2.75); 0.5, 0.3)	((3.45, 3.48, 3.55); 0.6, 0.3)	((2.50, 2.56, 2.60); 0.6, 0.2)	((3.25, 3.28, 3.35); 0.6, 0.3)
C25	Value	≈2.00	≈2.00	≈1.75	≈1.36	≈1.50
(106CNY)	TINF	((1.99, 2.00, 2.01); 0.9, 0)	((1.99, 2.00, 2.01); 0.9, 0)	((1.70, 1.75, 1.80); 0.7, 0.1)	((1.30, 1.36, 1.40); 0.6, 0.2)	((1.40, 1.50, 1.60); 0.7, 0.1)
C42	Value	≈2.40	≈2.33	≈2.61	≈2.29	≈2.51
(103t)	TINF	((2.35, 2.40, 2.45); 0.6, 0.3)	((2.30, 2.33, 2.40); 0.5, 0.3)	((2.55, 2.61, 2.65); 0.6, 0.3)	((2.25, 2.29, 2.35); 0.6, 0.2)	((2.45, 2.51, 2.55); 0.6, 0.3)
C43	Value	≈9.17	≈8.90	≈9.95	≈8.73	≈9.58
(102t)	TINF	((9.15, 9.17, 9.25); 0.6, 0.3)	((8.85, 8.90, 8.95); 0.6, 0.2)	((9.90, 9.95, 10.00); 0.5, 0.3)	((8.70, 8.73, 8.80); 0.6, 0.3)	((9.55, 9.58, 9.65); 0.6, 0.3)

Table 6.10 The values S_i, R_i and Q_i of five alternatives.

	A1	A2	A3	A4	A5
S_i	0.5390	0.5582	0.5105	0.6218	0.5296
R_i	0.0643	0.0680	0.0590	0.0685	0.0669
Q_i	0.4093	0.6920	0	1	0.5057

From Table 10, the priority orders of five alternatives by Q_i in increasing order is A3>A5>A1>A2>A4. For alternative A3, the Condition 1 and 2 are both met obviously. Consequently, based on the comprehensive evaluation results, A3 is the best alternative for the PV enterprise to set up a LCRPS.

5.4 Sensitivity analysis

In the proposed fuzzy VIKOR model, the parameter v has been applied as weight of the strategy of the group utility. In the process of ranking optional alternatives for establishing

LCRPSs, the parameter v plays an indispensable role. Generally, the value of v is set to 0.5. Nevertheless, v can take any value from 0 to 1. In the decision analysis, as the fact that various opinions of the DMs can give rise to different ranking orders. Consequently, it is essential to conduct a sensitivity analysis on the parameter v according to the DMs' preference to examine or prove the validity and robustness of the presented evaluation results. Based on the various values of v from 0 to 1, the values of Q_i are calculated using Eq. (6-18) in Table 6.11, and the ranking order trend is vividly demonstrated in Fig. 6.5.

Table 6.11 The values of Q_i based on v from 0 to 1.

	A1	A2	A3	A4	A5
$v = 0$	0.5625	0.9554	0	1	0.8394
$v = 0.1$	0.5318	0.9027	0	1	0.7727
$v = 0.2$	0.5012	0.8500	0	1	0.7060
$v = 0.3$	0.4705	0.7974	0	1	0.6392
$v = 0.4$	0.4399	0.7447	0	1	0.5725
$v = 0.5$	0.4093	0.6920	0	1	0.5057
$v = 0.6$	0.3786	0.6393	0	1	0.4390
$v = 0.7$	0.3480	0.5867	0	1	0.3722
$v = 0.8$	0.3173	0.5340	0	1	0.3055
$v = 0.9$	0.2867	0.4813	0	1	0.2387
$v = 1$	0.2560	0.4286	0	1	0.1720

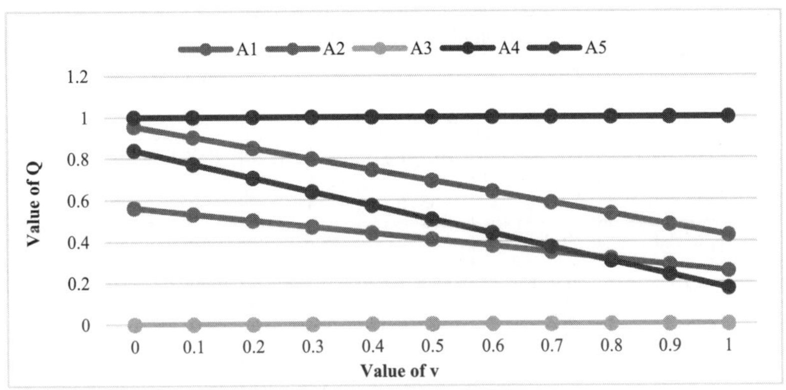

Fig. 6.5 The ranking order trend.

As can be seen in Fig. 6.5, the ranking order trend of three alternatives are not at all influenced by the v value. Especially, the ranking order trend of A3 illustrates that it is constantly the best a lternative, which is not impacted by the v value. This result certificates that the acquired evaluation results of the proposed fuzzy VIKOR model are robust and reliable.

To take a closer look at the sensitivity analysis, it can be seen that the ranking of the alternatives stays the same when v takes values from 0 to 0.7, respectively, yet when v takes values from 0.8 to 1, though the best and the worst alternatives have not altered, the less favorable alternative have changed slightly. We can find that A1 and A5 exchange in the ranking of the alternatives, which reveals some influence of the DMs' opinion changes on the decision results. The changes manifest that alternative A1 ranks higher than alternative A5 when the preference of the DMs is extremely irrelevant to the group utility. However, when the DMs take the group utility into consideration, alternative A1 is superior to alternative A5 stably. In the realistic decision-making practice, various DMs' attitudes can be considered by the proposed method.

5.5 Comparative analysis

For the sake of proving that the decision framework proposed above for the LCRPS site selection utilizing the fuzzy VIKOR method is feasible and valid, a comparative analysis based on the same illustrative case with the results obtained by fuzzy TOPSIS, PROMETHEE-II and ELECTRE-III is carried out.

The ranking order results of the fuzzy TOPSIS method relies on the relative closeness $RC(A_i)$ by applying Eq. (6-2). Varying from the VIKOR and TOPSIS methods, PROMETHEE-II and ELECTRE-III based on the net flow $\varphi(A_i)$ are conducted to rank the alternatives, respectively. The calculation results and ranking orders are listed in Table 6.12.

Table 6.12 The calculation results and ranking orders.

	Calculation Results					Ranking Orders
VIKOR	$Q(A_1)$	$Q(A_2)$	$Q(A_3)$	$Q(A_4)$	$Q(A_5)$	A3>A1>A5>A2>A4
	0.4093	0.6920	0	1	0.5057	
TOPSIS	$RC(A_1)$	$RC(A_2)$	$RC(A_3)$	$RC(A_4)$	$RC(A_5)$	A3>A5>A1>A2>A4
	0.5890	0.5642	0.6876	0.5413	0.6054	
PROMETHEE-II	$\varphi(A_1)$	$\varphi(A_2)$	$\varphi(A_3)$	$\varphi(A_4)$	$\varphi(A_5)$	A3>A5>A1>A2>A4
	0.1026	-0.011	0.2361	–0.134	0.2073	
ELECTRE-III	$\varphi(A_1)$	$\varphi(A_2)$	$\varphi(A_3)$	$\varphi(A_4)$	$\varphi(A_5)$	A3>A5=A1>A2>A4
	1	0	2	–1	1	

According to Table 6.12, the best alternative is invariably A3 with the greatest relative closeness to the ideal solution and the maximum of net flow, which is the same as the sequence through the proposed fuzzy VIKOR method. Moreover, the worst alternative is always A4. The main difference exists in the ranking orders between A1 and A5, for which the reasons could be explained as follows.

The fuzzy TOPSIS method determines a solution with the shortest distance from the ideal solution, but it does not consider the relative importance of the ideal solution and the negative-ideal solution. In addition, in the decision framework based on fuzzy VIKOR method

$v \geqslant 0.8$, the ranking order is the same as the result of the fuzzy TOPSIS method. That illustrates the calculation results of fuzzy TOPSIS method are as part of the results list of the fuzzy VIKOR method with different preferences of the DMs.

In the process of ranking alternatives, the fuzzy PROMETHEE-II method only considers maximum of group utility, without taking the individual regret into consideration. According to the calculation results, the primary difference is the ranking order of A1 and A5. Based on the DMs' opinions, the score of A1 is superior to A5, but the ranking result of fuzzy PROMETHEE-II method is opposite. That is not consistent with the preferences of the DMs.

The fuzzy ELECTRE-III method determines a solution for the purpose of the minimum of individual regret utilizing thresholds of indifference and preference without taking the group utility into account. According to the calculation results, the fuzzy ELECTRE-III method cannot decide the ranking order of A1 and A5 clearly, so the distinct decision results cannot be acquired.

After the comparative analysis above, the final ranking order derived from the fuzzy VIKOR method A3>A1>A5>A2>A4 is more precise and credible than the results acquired by other mentioned methods. Consequently, the fuzzy VIKOR method provides not only the solution closer to the ideal one, but also a balance between the maximum group utility of the "majority" and the minimum individual regret for the "opponent". In addition, the fuzzy VIKOR method takes the preferences of DMs into consideration. In summary, the fuzzy VIKOR method is more feasible and valid than other methods for LCRPS site selection.

6. Conclusions

This study builds a comprehensive decision framework for LCRPS site selection based on sustainability perspective. Studies focused on this area are limited exceedingly and quite a few problems still exists in the decision process for LCRPS site selection. Firstly, uncertainties generally exist in the site selection for LCRPS. Secondly, the relationships between criteria based on sustainability perspective are not taken seriously. Thirdly, the ranking methods applied in previous studies cannot reflect the DMs' subjective preferences for evaluating the LCRPS site selection problem. The rationality of the decision-making results will decline and the probability of decision-making mistake will increase if the above problems are ignored.

In this study, a new design of comprehensive MCDM framework based on the fuzzy ANP and VIKOR method under incomplete information environment is proposed to handle the LCRPS site selection problems. Firstly, the comprehensive index system of LCRPS site selection towards sustainability is constructed to eliminate and identify potential alternatives. Secondly, the TIFNs are applied to express the imperfect knowledge of experts and describe the uncertainties of information. Thirdly, the fuzzy ANP is introduced to create appropriate weights, which takes the relationships between the criteria into consideration. Moreover, the fuzzy

VIKOR is introduced to rank the optimal alternatives on the basis of the opinions of different DMs. Finally, a case of Guangdong province with the sensitive analysis and comparative analysis is conducted to testify the rationality and robustness of the proposed decision framework.

In the proposed comprehensive index system, the environmental and social criteria play a more significant role than the economic criteria in the LCRPS site selection decision-making based on sustainable cities and society. By applying the presented decision framework, alternative A3 is selected as the most optimal location to establish a LCRPS project, and alternative A1 is accounted as the sub-optimal site. Based on the sensitivity analysis and comparative analysis, the ranking order does not vary in general, which manifests the obtained conclusions have effectiveness and practicality.

Consequently, from our theoretical modeling and empirical research, the MCDM decision framework based on sustainability perspective can effectively handle such a complex problem and bring about an outstanding result.

Acknowledgments

This paper is supported by the 2017 Special Project of Cultivation and Development of Innovation Base (No. Z171100002217024) and the Fundamental Research Funds for the Central Universities (No. 2018ZD14).

Appendix A

Table A.1 The unweighted supermatrix.

	C11	C12	C13	C14	C21	C22	C23	C24	C25	C31	C32	C41	C42	C43	C51	C52
C11	0.0000	0.7154	0.4357	0.3456	0.2162	0.1541	0.2324	0.2223	0.1418	0.0000	0.3026	0.4026	0.2142	0.2040	0.2548	0.2346
C12	0.6623	0.0000	0.5643	0.3612	0.2164	0.3752	0.3124	0.2254	0.3678	0.0000	0.2874	0.4153	0.3846	0.3976	0.2678	0.2478
C13	0.3377	0.2846	0.0000	0.2932	0.2043	0.1020	0.1526	0.2045	0.1356	0.3546	0.2022	0.0000	0.0000	0.0000	0.1759	0.1864
C14	0.0000	0.0000	0.0000	0.0000	0.3631	0.3687	0.3026	0.3478	0.3548	0.6454	0.2078	0.1821	0.4012	0.3984	0.3015	0.3312
C21	0.0000	0.0000	0.2846	0.3012	0.0000	0.2385	0.3016	0.2287	0.3415	0.3214	0.2431	0.3651	0.2145	0.2018	0.2248	0.2345
C22	0.4658	0.4326	0.2034	0.2846	0.1846	0.0000	0.3045	0.3456	0.0959	0.1104	0.1234	0.1042	0.2345	0.2320	0.2456	0.2478
C23	0.1729	0.2326	0.1846	0.2014	0.3245	0.2245	0.0000	0.1245	0.3013	0.2345	0.1347	0.2243	0.1978	0.1846	0.1678	0.2016
C24	0.0000	0.0000	0.2013	0.1546	0.4013	0.2344	0.2078	0.0000	0.2613	0.2441	0.1652	0.2106	0.1516	0.1706	0.1846	0.1215
C25	0.3613	0.3348	0.1261	0.0582	0.0896	0.3026	0.1861	0.3012	0.0000	0.0896	0.3336	0.0958	0.2016	0.2110	0.1772	0.1946
C31	0.8645	0.8056	0.7645	0.4516	0.3478	0.6248	0.4659	0.3746	0.5478	0.0000	1.0000	0.6513	0.5648	0.5548	0.4458	0.4352
C32	0.1355	0.1944	0.2355	0.5484	0.6522	0.3752	0.5341	0.6254	0.4522	1.0000	0.0000	0.3487	0.4352	0.4452	0.5542	0.5648
C41	0.3618	0.3517	0.4013	0.3416	0.4415	0.2767	0.3346	0.4016	0.2546	0.5412	0.3014	0.0000	0.1630	0.1034	0.1023	0.3786
C42	0.3416	0.3346	0.3026	0.3354	0.2940	0.3687	0.3578	0.3021	0.4139	0.2315	0.3516	0.5514	0.0000	0.8966	0.5046	0.3346
C43	0.2966	0.3137	0.2961	0.3230	0.2645	0.3546	0.3076	0.2963	0.3315	0.2273	0.3470	0.4486	0.8370	0.0000	0.3931	0.2868

Continued

	C11	C12	C13	C14	C21	C22	C23	C24	C25	C31	C32	C41	C42	C43	C51	C52
C51	0.7648	0.8046	0.6134	0.4216	0.5648	0.5548	0.5134	0.5531	0.5013	0.5416	0.6210	0.6014	0.5641	0.5323	0.0000	1.0000
C52	0.2352	0.1954	0.3866	0.5784	0.4352	0.4452	0.4866	0.4469	0.4987	0.4584	0.3790	0.3986	0.4359	0.4677	1.0000	0.0000

Table A.2 The weighted supermatrix.

	C11	C12	C13	C14	C21	C22	C23	C24	C25	C31	C32	C41	C42	C43	C51	C52
C11	0.0000	0.1834	0.1117	0.0886	0.0732	0.0522	0.0787	0.0753	0.0480	0.0000	0.1127	0.0676	0.0359	0.0342	0.0525	0.0483
C12	0.1698	0.0000	0.1447	0.0926	0.0733	0.1271	0.1058	0.0764	0.1246	0.0000	0.1071	0.0697	0.0645	0.0667	0.0552	0.0511
C13	0.0866	0.0730	0.0000	0.0752	0.0692	0.0346	0.0517	0.0693	0.0459	0.1321	0.0753	0.0000	0.0000	0.0000	0.0362	0.0384
C14	0.0000	0.0000	0.0000	0.0000	0.1230	0.1249	0.1025	0.1178	0.1202	0.2404	0.0774	0.0306	0.0673	0.0669	0.0621	0.0683
C21	0.0000	0.0000	0.0438	0.0463	0.0000	0.0487	0.0616	0.0467	0.0697	0.0939	0.0710	0.0613	0.0360	0.0339	0.0658	0.0687
C22	0.0717	0.0666	0.0313	0.0438	0.0377	0.0000	0.0621	0.0705	0.0196	0.0323	0.0361	0.0175	0.0394	0.0389	0.0719	0.0726
C23	0.0266	0.0358	0.0284	0.0310	0.0662	0.0458	0.0000	0.0254	0.0615	0.0685	0.0394	0.0376	0.0332	0.0310	0.0491	0.0590
C24	0.0000	0.0000	0.0310	0.0238	0.0819	0.0478	0.0424	0.0000	0.0533	0.0713	0.0483	0.0353	0.0254	0.0286	0.0540	0.0356
C25	0.0556	0.0515	0.0194	0.0090	0.0183	0.0618	0.0380	0.0615	0.0000	0.0262	0.0975	0.0161	0.0338	0.0354	0.0519	0.0570
C31	0.0842	0.0785	0.0745	0.0440	0.0348	0.0625	0.0466	0.0375	0.0548	0.0000	0.1433	0.1767	0.1532	0.1505	0.1024	0.1000
C32	0.0132	0.0189	0.0229	0.0534	0.0652	0.0375	0.0534	0.0625	0.0452	0.1433	0.0000	0.0946	0.1181	0.1208	0.1273	0.1298
C41	0.1271	0.1235	0.1410	0.1200	0.1234	0.0774	0.0936	0.1123	0.0712	0.0659	0.0367	0.0000	0.0375	0.0238	0.0162	0.0601
C42	0.1200	0.1175	0.1063	0.1178	0.0822	0.1031	0.1000	0.0845	0.1157	0.0282	0.0428	0.1268	0.0000	0.2061	0.0801	0.0531
C43	0.1042	0.1102	0.1040	0.1135	0.0740	0.0991	0.0860	0.0828	0.0927	0.0277	0.0423	0.1031	0.1924	0.0000	0.0624	0.0455
C51	0.1079	0.1135	0.0865	0.0595	0.0438	0.0430	0.0398	0.0429	0.0389	0.0380	0.0436	0.0982	0.0921	0.0869	0.0000	0.1126
C52	0.0332	0.0276	0.0545	0.0816	0.0338	0.0345	0.0377	0.0347	0.0387	0.0322	0.0266	0.0651	0.0711	0.0763	0.1126	0.0000

Table A.3 The limit supermatrix.

	C11	C12	C13	C14	C21	C22	C23	C24	C25	C31	C32	C41	C42	C43	C51	C52
C11	0.0649	0.0649	0.0649	0.0649	0.0649	0.0649	0.0649	0.0649	0.0649	0.0649	0.0649	0.0649	0.0649	0.0649	0.0649	0.0649
C12	0.0767	0.0767	0.0767	0.0767	0.0767	0.0767	0.0767	0.0767	0.0767	0.0767	0.0767	0.0767	0.0767	0.0767	0.0767	0.0767
C13	0.0497	0.0497	0.0497	0.0497	0.0497	0.0497	0.0497	0.0497	0.0497	0.0497	0.0497	0.0497	0.0497	0.0497	0.0497	0.0497
C14	0.0733	0.0733	0.0733	0.0733	0.0733	0.0733	0.0733	0.0733	0.0733	0.0733	0.0733	0.0733	0.0733	0.0733	0.0733	0.0733
C21	0.0468	0.0468	0.0468	0.0468	0.0468	0.0468	0.0468	0.0468	0.0468	0.0468	0.0468	0.0468	0.0468	0.0468	0.0468	0.0468
C22	0.0443	0.0443	0.0443	0.0443	0.0443	0.0443	0.0443	0.0443	0.0443	0.0443	0.0443	0.0443	0.0443	0.0443	0.0443	0.0443
C23	0.0403	0.0403	0.0403	0.0403	0.0403	0.0403	0.0403	0.0403	0.0403	0.0403	0.0403	0.0403	0.0403	0.0403	0.0403	0.0403
C24	0.0358	0.0358	0.0358	0.0358	0.0358	0.0358	0.0358	0.0358	0.0358	0.0358	0.0358	0.0358	0.0358	0.0358	0.0358	0.0358
C25	0.0397	0.0397	0.0397	0.0397	0.0397	0.0397	0.0397	0.0397	0.0397	0.0397	0.0397	0.0397	0.0397	0.0397	0.0397	0.0397
C31	0.0900	0.0900	0.0900	0.0900	0.0900	0.0900	0.0900	0.0900	0.0900	0.0900	0.0900	0.0900	0.0900	0.0900	0.0900	0.0900
C32	0.0740	0.0740	0.0740	0.0740	0.0740	0.0740	0.0740	0.0740	0.0740	0.0740	0.0740	0.0740	0.0740	0.0740	0.0740	0.0740
C41	0.0715	0.0715	0.0715	0.0715	0.0715	0.0715	0.0715	0.0715	0.0715	0.0715	0.0715	0.0715	0.0715	0.0715	0.0715	0.0715
C42	0.0909	0.0909	0.0909	0.0909	0.0909	0.0909	0.0909	0.0909	0.0909	0.0909	0.0909	0.0909	0.0909	0.0909	0.0909	0.0909
C43	0.0837	0.0837	0.0837	0.0837	0.0837	0.0837	0.0837	0.0837	0.0837	0.0837	0.0837	0.0837	0.0837	0.0837	0.0837	0.0837
C51	0.0680	0.0680	0.0680	0.0680	0.0680	0.0680	0.0680	0.0680	0.0680	0.0680	0.0680	0.0680	0.0680	0.0680	0.0680	0.0680
C52	0.0504	0.0504	0.0504	0.0504	0.0504	0.0504	0.0504	0.0504	0.0504	0.0504	0.0504	0.0504	0.0504	0.0504	0.0504	0.0504

The calculation of R_b, R_d and R_r in Eq. (6-19) are as follows (Dan et al., 2017):

$$R_b = \frac{\int_{\omega_{sr}}^{\omega_{ss}} \cos\theta_T(\omega)d\omega}{\int_{\omega_r}^{\omega_s} \cos\theta_Z(\omega)d\omega} = \frac{R_{b1}}{R_{b2}}$$

$$R_{b1} = [\cos(\beta)\sin(\delta)\sin(\phi)]\frac{\pi}{180}[\omega_{ss} - \omega_{sr}] - [\sin(\delta)\cos(\phi)\sin(\beta)\cos(\gamma)] \times \frac{\pi}{180}[\omega_{ss} - \omega_{sr}] + [\cos(\phi)\cos(\delta)\cos(\beta)][\sin\omega_{ss} - \sin\omega_{sr}] + [\cos(\delta)\cos(\gamma) \times \sin(\phi)\sin(\beta)][\sin\omega_{ss} - \sin\omega_{sr}] + [\cos(\delta)\sin(\beta)\sin(\gamma)][\cos\omega_{ss} - \cos\omega_{sr}]$$

$$R_{b2} = 2[\cos(\phi)\cos(\delta)\sin(\omega_s) + \left(\frac{\pi}{180}\right)\omega_s \sin(\phi)\sin(\delta)]$$

where θ_T and θ_Z are the angle of incidence on the tilted surface and the sun zenith angle, respectively. ω_{sr} and ω_{ss} are the sunrise and sunset hour angles on the tilted surface. ω_r and ω_s are the sunrise and sunset hour angles over horizon. β, ϕ and γ are the roof tilt angle, latitude, and roof azimuth angle, respectively.

$$\omega_{sr} = \begin{cases} -\min\left[\omega_s, \arccos\left(\dfrac{AB + \sqrt{A^2 - B^2 + 1}}{A^2 + 1}\right)\right], & \text{if } \gamma < 0 \\ -\min\left[\omega_s, \arccos\left(\dfrac{AB - \sqrt{A^2 - B^2 + 1}}{A^2 + 1}\right)\right], & \text{if } \gamma > 0 \end{cases}$$

$$\omega_{ss} = \begin{cases} -\min\left[\omega_s, \arccos\left(\dfrac{AB - \sqrt{A^2 - B^2 + 1}}{A^2 + 1}\right)\right], & \text{if } \gamma < 0 \\ -\min\left[\omega_s, \arccos\left(\dfrac{AB + \sqrt{A^2 - B^2 + 1}}{A^2 + 1}\right)\right], & \text{if } \gamma > 0 \end{cases}$$

where A and B are given by:

$$A = \frac{\cos(\phi)}{\sin(\gamma)\tan(\beta)} + \frac{\sin(\phi)}{\tan(\gamma)}$$

$$B = \tan(\delta)\left[\frac{\cos(\phi)}{\tan(\gamma)} - \frac{\sin(\phi)}{\sin(\gamma)\tan(\beta)}\right]$$

and δ is the monthly declination angle and can be computed as:

$$\delta = 23.45^\circ \sin\left(\frac{360 \times (284 + m)}{365}\right)$$

where m is the representative day of the year given for each month.

$$R_d = CR_b + (1-C)\left[\frac{1+\cos\beta}{2}\right]\left[1+\sqrt{\frac{G_B}{G_h}}\sin^3(\frac{\beta}{2})\right]$$

where C is given by:

$$C = \frac{G_B}{G_{oh}}$$

and G_{oh} is the extra-terrestrial horizontal radiation.

$$R_r = \rho\left(\frac{1-\cos\beta}{2}\right)$$

where ρ is the surface reflectance or albedo (typical albedo of 0.2 for urban settings is used in this study).

The first-level-criteria are evaluated by three experts using linguistic variables as follows:

$$\begin{pmatrix} D^1 & C1 & C2 & C3 & C4 & C5 \\ C1 & E & ML & MH & L & E \\ C2 & MH & E & MH & ML & H \\ C3 & ML & ML & E & MH & H \\ C4 & H & MH & ML & E & ML \\ C5 & E & L & L & MH & E \end{pmatrix} \begin{pmatrix} D^2 & C1 & C2 & C3 & C4 & C5 \\ C1 & E & MH & H & ML & MH \\ C2 & ML & E & MH & L & MH \\ C3 & L & ML & E & E & MH \\ C4 & MH & H & E & E & MH \\ C5 & ML & ML & ML & ML & E \end{pmatrix}$$

$$\begin{pmatrix} D^3 & C1 & C2 & C3 & C4 & C5 \\ C1 & E & H & VH & E & H \\ C2 & L & E & H & E & VH \\ C3 & VL & L & E & ML & MH \\ C4 & E & E & MH & E & MH \\ C5 & L & VL & ML & ML & E \end{pmatrix}$$

The linguistic variables are transformed into TIFNs as follows:

$$\begin{pmatrix} D^1 & C1 & C2 & C3 & C4 & C5 \\ C1 & ((1,1,1);1,0) & ((\frac{1}{3},\frac{1}{2},1);0.9,0) & ((1,2,3);0.7,0.2) & ((\frac{1}{4},\frac{1}{3},\frac{1}{2});0.8,0.1) & ((1,1,1);0.8,0.1) \\ C2 & ((1,2,3);0.9,0) & ((1,1,1);1,0) & ((1,2,3);0.8,0.1) & ((\frac{1}{3},\frac{1}{2},1);0.8,0.1) & ((2,3,4);0.7,0.2) \\ C3 & ((\frac{1}{3},\frac{1}{2},1);0.7,0.2) & ((\frac{1}{3},\frac{1}{2},1);0.8,0.1) & ((1,1,1);1,0) & ((1,2,3);0.8,0.1) & ((2,3,4);0.8,0.1) \\ C4 & ((2,3,4);0.8,0.1) & ((1,2,3);0.8,0.1) & ((\frac{1}{3},\frac{1}{2},1);0.8,0.1) & ((1,1,1);1,0) & ((\frac{1}{3},\frac{1}{2},1);0.7,0.2) \\ C5 & ((1,1,1);0.8,0.1) & ((\frac{1}{4},\frac{1}{3},\frac{1}{2});0.7,0.2) & ((\frac{1}{4},\frac{1}{3},\frac{1}{2});0.8,0.1) & ((1,2,3);0.7,0.2) & ((1,1,1);1,0) \end{pmatrix}$$

$$\begin{pmatrix} D^2 & C1 & C2 & C3 & C4 & C5 \\ C1 & ((1,1,1);1,0) & ((1,2,3);0.8,0.1) & ((2,3,4);0.7,0.2) & ((\frac{1}{3},\frac{1}{2},1);0.8,0.1) & ((1,2,3);0.8,0.1) \\ C2 & ((\frac{1}{3},\frac{1}{2},1);0.8,0.1) & ((1,1,1);1,0) & ((1,2,3);0.8,0.1) & ((\frac{1}{4},\frac{1}{3},\frac{1}{2});0.8,0.1) & ((1,2,3);0.7,0.2) \\ C3 & ((\frac{1}{4},\frac{1}{3},\frac{1}{2});0.7,0.2) & ((\frac{1}{3},\frac{1}{2},1);0.8,0.1) & ((1,1,1);1,0) & ((1,1,1);0.8,0.1) & ((1,2,3);0.7,0.2) \\ C4 & ((1,2,3);0.8,0.1) & ((2,3,4);0.8,0.1) & ((1,1,1);0.8,0.1) & ((1,1,1);1,0) & ((1,2,3);0.8,0.1) \\ C5 & ((\frac{1}{3},\frac{1}{2},1);0.8,0.1) & ((\frac{1}{3},\frac{1}{2},1);0.7,0.2) & ((\frac{1}{3},\frac{1}{2},1);0.7,0.2) & ((\frac{1}{3},\frac{1}{2},1);0.8,0.1) & ((1,1,1);1,0) \end{pmatrix}$$

$$\begin{pmatrix} D^3 & C1 & C2 & C3 & C4 & C5 \\ C1 & ((1,1,1);1,0) & ((2,3,4);0.8,0.1) & ((3,4,5);0.7,0.2) & ((1,1,1);0.8,0.1) & ((2,3,4);0.8,0.1) \\ C2 & ((\frac{1}{4},\frac{1}{3},\frac{1}{2});0.8,0.1) & ((1,1,1);1,0) & ((2,3,4);0.7,0.2) & ((1,1,1);0.8,0.1) & ((3,4,5);0.7,0.2) \\ C3 & ((\frac{1}{5},\frac{1}{4},\frac{1}{3});0.7,0.2) & ((\frac{1}{4},\frac{1}{3},\frac{1}{2});0.7,0.2) & ((1,1,1);1,0) & ((\frac{1}{3},\frac{1}{2},1);0.7,0.2) & ((1,2,3);0.8,0.1) \\ C4 & ((1,1,1);0.8,0.1) & ((1,1,1);0.8,0.1) & ((1,2,3);0.7,0.2) & ((1,1,1);1,0) & ((1,2,3);0.7,0.2) \\ C5 & ((\frac{1}{4},\frac{1}{3},\frac{1}{2});0.8,0.1) & ((\frac{1}{5},\frac{1}{4},\frac{1}{3});0.7,0.2) & ((\frac{1}{3},\frac{1}{2},1);0.8,0.1) & ((\frac{1}{3},\frac{1}{2},1);0.7,0.2) & ((1,1,1);1,0) \end{pmatrix}$$

The fuzzy aggregated pairwise comparison matrix for the first-level-criteria is shown as:

$$\begin{pmatrix} & C1 & C2 & C3 & C4 & C5 \\ C1 & ((1,1,1);1,0) & ((1.11,1.83,2.67);0.8,0.1) & ((2.00,3.00,4.00);0.7,0.2) & ((0.53,0.61,0.83);0.8,0.1) & ((1.33,2.00,2.67);0.8,0.1) \\ C2 & ((0.53,0.94,1.50);0.8,0.1) & ((1,1,1);1,0) & ((1.33,2.33,3.33);0.7,0.2) & ((0.53,0.61,0.83);0.8,0.1) & ((2.00,3.00,4.00);0.7,0.2) \\ C3 & ((0.26,0.36,0.61);0.7,0.2) & ((0.31,0.44,0.83);0.7,0.2) & ((1,1,1);1,0) & ((0.78,1.17,1.67);0.7,0.2) & ((1.33,2.33,3.33);0.7,0.2) \\ C4 & ((1.33,2.00,2.67);0.8,0.1) & ((1.33,2.00,2.67);0.8,0.1) & ((0.78,1.17,1.67);0.7,0.2) & ((1,1,1);1,0) & ((0.78,1.50,2.33);0.7,0.2) \\ C5 & ((0.53,0.61,0.83);0.8,0.1) & ((0.26,0.36,0.61);0.7,0.2) & ((0.31,0.44,0.83);0.7,0.2) & ((0.56,1.00,1.67);0.7,0.2) & ((1,1,1);1,0) \end{pmatrix}$$

The fuzzy aggregated pairwise comparison matrices for the sub-criteria are shown as:

$$\begin{pmatrix} & C11 & C12 & C13 & C14 \\ C11 & ((1,1,1);1,0) & ((0.56,1.00,1.67);0.7,0.2) & ((1.33,2.00,2.67);0.8,0.1) & ((0.31,0.44,0.83);0.7,0.2) \\ C12 & ((0.78,1.50,2.33);0.7,0.2) & ((1,1,1);1,0) & ((1.33,2.00,2.67);0.8,0.1) & ((0.26,0.36,0.61);0.7,0.2) \\ C13 & ((0.53,0.61,0.83);0.8,0.1) & ((0.53,0.61,0.83);0.8,0.1) & ((1,1,1);1,0) & ((0.56,1.00,1.67);0.7,0.2) \\ C14 & ((1.33,2.33,3.33);0.7,0.2) & ((2.00,3.00,4.00);0.7,0.2) & ((0.78,1.50,2.33);0.7,0.2) & ((1,1,1);1,0) \end{pmatrix}$$

$$\begin{pmatrix} & C21 & C22 & C23 & C24 & C25 \\ C21 & ((1,1,1);1,0) & ((0.53,0.94,1.50);0.8,0.1) & ((0.56,1.00,1.67);0.7,0.2) & ((1.33,2.33,3.33);0.7,0.2) & ((0.56,1.00,1.67);0.7,0.2) \\ C22 & ((1.11,1.83,2.67);0.8,0.1) & ((1,1,1);1,0) & ((0.53,0.94,1.50);0.8,0.1) & ((1.33,2.00,2.67);0.8,0.1) & ((2.00,3.00,4.00);0.7,0.2) \\ C23 & ((0.78,1.50,2.33);0.7,0.2) & ((1.11,1.83,2.67);0.8,0.1) & ((1,1,1);1,0) & ((1.11,1.83,2.67);0.8,0.1) & ((1.33,2.33,3.33);0.7,0.2) \\ C24 & ((0.31,0.44,0.83);0.7,0.2) & ((0.53,0.61,0.83);0.8,0.1) & ((0.53,0.94,1.50);0.8,0.1) & ((1,1,1);1,0) & ((0.53,0.94,1.50);0.8,0.1) \\ C25 & ((0.78,1.50,2.33);0.7,0.2) & ((0.26,0.36,0.61);0.7,0.2) & ((0.31,0.44,0.83);0.7,0.2) & ((1.11,1.83,2.67);0.8,0.1) & ((1,1,1);1,0) \end{pmatrix}$$

$$\begin{pmatrix} & C31 & C32 \\ C31 & ((1,1,1);1,0) & ((1.11,1.83,2.67);0.8,0.1) \\ C32 & ((0.53,0.94,1.50);0.8,0.1) & ((1,1,1);1,0) \end{pmatrix}$$

$$\begin{pmatrix} & C41 & C42 & C43 \\ C41 & ((1,1,1);1,0) & ((0.31,0.44,0.83);0.7,0.2) & ((0.53,0.61,0.83);0.8,0.1) \\ C42 & ((1.33,2.33,3.33);0.7,0.2) & ((1,1,1);1,0) & ((0.78,1.50,2.33);0.7,0.2) \\ C43 & ((1.33,2.00,2.67);0.8,0.1) & ((0.56,1.00,1.67);0.7,0.2) & ((1,1,1);1,0) \end{pmatrix}$$

$$\begin{pmatrix} & C51 & C52 \\ C51 & ((1,1,1);1,0) & ((1.11,1.83,2.67);0.8,0.1) \\ C52 & ((0.53,0.94,1.50);0.8,0.1) & ((1,1,1);1,0) \end{pmatrix}$$

The defuzzified aggregated pairwise comparison matrices for the first-level-criteria and sub-criteria are shown as:

$$\begin{pmatrix} & C1 & C2 & C3 & C4 & C5 \\ C1 & 1 & 1.66 & 2.60 & 0.73 & 1.83 \\ C2 & 0.6 & 1 & 2.04 & 0.73 & 2.60 \\ C3 & 0.38 & 0.49 & 1 & 1.18 & 2.04 \\ C4 & 1.37 & 1.37 & 0.85 & 1 & 1.41 \\ C5 & 0.55 & 0.38 & 0.49 & 0.71 & 1 \end{pmatrix} \begin{pmatrix} & C11 & C12 & C13 & C14 \\ C11 & 1 & 1.03 & 1.83 & 0.55 \\ C12 & 0.98 & 1 & 1.83 & 0.46 \\ C13 & 0.55 & 0.55 & 1 & 1.03 \\ C14 & 1.82 & 2.16 & 0.98 & 1 \end{pmatrix}$$

$$\begin{pmatrix} & C21 & C22 & C23 & C24 & C25 \\ C21 & 1 & 0.97 & 1.03 & 2.04 & 1.03 \\ C22 & 1.03 & 1 & 0.97 & 1.83 & 2.60 \\ C23 & 0.98 & 1.03 & 1 & 1.66 & 2.04 \\ C24 & 0.49 & 0.55 & 0.60 & 1 & 0.97 \\ C25 & 0.98 & 0.38 & 0.49 & 1.03 & 1 \end{pmatrix} \begin{pmatrix} & C31 & C32 \\ C31 & 1 & 1.6 \\ C32 & 0.625 & 1 \end{pmatrix} \begin{pmatrix} & C41 & C42 & C43 \\ C41 & 1 & 0.55 & 0.73 \\ C42 & 1.82 & 1 & 1.41 \\ C43 & 1.37 & 0.71 & 1 \end{pmatrix}$$

$$\begin{pmatrix} & C51 & C52 \\ C51 & 1 & 1.6 \\ C52 & 0.625 & 1 \end{pmatrix}$$

Appendix B

Three DMs evaluate the last category of sub-criteria using linguistic variables as follows:

$$\begin{pmatrix} D^1 & A1 & A2 & A3 & A4 & A5 \\ C31 & MG & G & MG & MG & F \\ C32 & MP & MP & P & P & MP \\ C41 & MG & G & F & MG & F \\ C51 & P & MP & F & F & MG \\ C52 & F & MG & MG & G & MG \end{pmatrix} \begin{pmatrix} D^2 & A1 & A2 & A3 & A4 & A5 \\ C31 & MG & MG & VG & G & G \\ C32 & F & MP & MP & P & P \\ C41 & G & MG & MG & F & MG \\ C51 & MP & P & G & MG & MG \\ C52 & G & MG & MG & G & MG \end{pmatrix}$$

$$
\begin{pmatrix}
D^3 & A1 & A2 & A3 & A4 & A5 \\
C31 & G & MG & VG & G & G \\
C32 & P & F & MG & MP & F \\
C41 & MG & VG & MP & MG & P \\
C51 & MP & MG & F & MP & MG \\
C52 & G & MG & MP & P & MG
\end{pmatrix}
$$

Three decision matrices are transformed into TIFNs as follows:

$$
\begin{pmatrix}
D^1 & A1 & A2 & A3 & A4 & A5 \\
C31 & ((5,7,9);0.7,0.1) & ((7,9,10);0.7,0.1) & ((6,7,8);0.7,0.2) & ((5,7,8);0.6,0.2) & ((3,5,7);0.7,0.1) \\
C32 & ((1,3,5);0.6,0.2) & ((2,3,4);0.7,0.2) & ((0,1,2);0.7,0.1) & ((0,1,3);0.7,0.1) & ((1,3,5);0.6,0.2) \\
C41 & ((6,7,9);0.6,0.1) & ((8,9,10);0.8,0.1) & ((3,5,7);0.7,0.1) & ((5,7,9);0.7,0.1) & ((4,5,7);0.7,0.1) \\
C51 & ((0,1,3);0.7,0.1) & ((1,3,4);0.6,0.2) & ((3,5,6);0.6,0.2) & ((4,5,6);0.7,0.2) & ((6,7,9);0.6,0.1) \\
C52 & ((3,5,7);0.7,0.1) & ((6,7,8);0.7,0.1) & ((5,7,9);0.7,0.1) & ((7,9,10);0.7,0.1) & ((5,7,8);0.7,0.1)
\end{pmatrix}
$$

$$
\begin{pmatrix}
D^2 & A1 & A2 & A3 & A4 & A5 \\
C31 & ((5,7,9);0.6,0.3) & ((5,7,9);0.7,0.2) & ((9,10,10);0.6,0.2) & ((8,9,10);0.6,0.3) & ((7,9,10);0.6,0.2) \\
C32 & ((3,5,7);0.5,0.2) & ((1,3,5);0.6,0.2) & ((2,3,5);0.6,0.2) & ((0,1,2);0.5,0.1) & ((0,1,3);0.6,0.2) \\
C41 & ((8,9,10);0.6,0.3) & ((5,7,8);0.6,0.2) & ((5,7,9);0.7,0.1) & ((3,5,7);0.6,0.2) & ((6,7,9);0.5,0.1) \\
C51 & ((1,3,5);0.5,0.2) & ((0,1,3);0.7,0.1) & ((7,9,10);0.6,0.2) & ((6,7,8);0.6,0.2) & ((5,7,8);0.6,0.3) \\
C52 & ((7,9,10);0.5,0.2) & ((6,7,8);0.6,0.2) & ((6,7,9);0.6,0.2) & ((7,9,10);0.6,0.2) & ((6,7,9);0.6,0.2)
\end{pmatrix}
$$

$$
\begin{pmatrix}
D^3 & A1 & A2 & A3 & A4 & A5 \\
C31 & ((8,9,10);0.6,0.2) & ((5,7,9);0.6,0.2) & ((9,10,10);0.5,0.4) & ((8,9,10);0.6,0.3) & ((7,9,10);0.5,0.4) \\
C32 & ((0,1,3);0.5,0.2) & ((3,5,7);0.5,0.2) & ((5,7,8);0.6,0.2) & ((1,3,5);0.5,0.1) & ((4,5,7);0.6,0.3) \\
C41 & ((6,7,9);0.6,0.2) & ((9,10,10);0.5,0.2) & ((1,3,4);0.5,0.2) & ((6,7,8);0.6,0.2) & ((0,1,3);0.5,0.1) \\
C51 & ((1,3,5);0.5,0.2) & ((6,7,8);0.5,0.2) & ((4,5,7);0.5,0.2) & ((2,3,5);0.5,0.2) & ((6,7,9);0.6,0.2) \\
C52 & ((7,9,10);0.5,0.2) & ((5,7,9);0.6,0.3) & ((2,3,5);0.5,0.3) & ((0,1,2);0.6,0.2) & ((5,7,9);0.5,0.2)
\end{pmatrix}
$$

The third fuzzy aggregated decision matrix is shown as follows:

$$
\begin{pmatrix}
 & A1 & A2 & A3 & A4 & A5 \\
C31 & ((6.00,7.67,9.33);0.6,0.3) & ((5.67,7.67,9.33);0.6,0.2) & ((8.00,9.00,9.33);0.5,0.4) & ((7.00,8.33,9.33);0.6,0.3) & ((5.67,7.67,9.00);0.5,0.4) \\
C32 & ((1.33,3.00,5.00);0.5,0.2) & ((2.00,3.67,5.33);0.5,0.2) & ((2.33,3.67,5.00);0.6,0.2) & ((0.33,1.67,3.33);0.5,0.1) & ((1.67,3.00,5.00);0.6,0.3) \\
C41 & ((6.67,7.67,9.33);0.5,0.2) & ((7.33,8.67,9.33);0.5,0.2) & ((3.00,5.00,6.67);0.5,0.2) & ((4.67,6.33,8.00);0.6,0.2) & ((3.33,4.33,6.33);0.5,0.1) \\
C51 & ((0.67,2.33,4.33);0.5,0.2) & ((2.33,3.67,5.00);0.5,0.2) & ((4.67,6.33,7.67);0.5,0.2) & ((4.00,5.00,6.33);0.5,0.2) & ((5.67,7.00,8.67);0.6,0.3) \\
C52 & ((5.67,7.67,9.00);0.5,0.2) & ((5.67,7.00,8.33);0.6,0.3) & ((4.33,5.67,7.67);0.5,0.3) & ((4.67,6.33,7.33);0.6,0.2) & ((5.33,7.00,8.67);0.5,0.2)
\end{pmatrix}
$$

References

[1] Arsić S, Nikolić D, Mihajlović I, et al. A New Approach Within ANP-SWOT Framework for Prioritization of Ecosystem Management and Case Study of National Park Djerdap, Serbia[J]. Ecological Economics, 2017, 146:85–95.

[2] Arsić S, Nikolić D, Živković Ž. Hybrid SWOT - ANP - FANP model for prioritization strategies of sustainable development of ecotourism in National Park Djerdap, Serbia[J]. Forest Policy & Economics, 2017, 80:11-26.

[3] Atanassov K T. Intuitionistic fuzzy sets[J]. Fuzzy Sets & Systems, 1986, 20(1), 87-96.

[4] Awasthi A, Govindan K, Gold S. Multi-tier sustainable global supplier selection using a fuzzy AHP-VIKOR based approach[J]. International Journal of Production Economics, 2017, 195:106-117.

[5] Byrne J, Taminiau J, Kurdgelashvili L, et al. A review of the solar city concept and methods to assess rooftop solar electric potential, with an illustrative application to the city of Seoul[J]. Renewable & Sustainable Energy Reviews, 2015, 41: 830-844.

[6] Chang K L, Liao S K, Tseng T W, et al. An ANP based TOPSIS approach for Taiwanese service apartment location selection[J]. Asia Pacific Management Review, 2015, 20(2):49-55.

[7] Chen T Y. Remoteness Index-Based Pythagorean Fuzzy VIKOR Methods with a Generalized Distance Measure for Multiple Criteria Decision Analysis[J]. Information Fusion, 2017, 41:129-150.

[8] Choudhary D, Shankar R. An STEEP-fuzzy AHP-TOPSIS framework for evaluation and selection of thermal power plant location: A case study from India[J]. Energy, 2012, 42(1):510-521.

[9] Cucchiella F, D'Adamo I, Koh S C L. Environmental and economic analysis of building integrated photovoltaic systems in Italian regions[J]. Journal of Cleaner Production, 2015, 98:241-252.

[10] DanA, Mohajeri N, Scartezzini J L. Quantifying rooftop photovoltaic solar energy potential: A machine learning approach[J]. Solar Energy, 2017, 141:278-296.

[11] Dong R, Xu J, Lin B. ROI-based study on impact factors of distributed PV projects by LSSVM-PSO[J]. Energy, 2017, 124:336-349.

[12] Fetanat A, Khorasaninejad E. A novel hybrid MCDM approach for offshore wind farm site selection: A case study of Iran[J]. Ocean & Coastal Management, 2015, 109:17-28.

[13] Frisari G, Stadelmann M. De-risking concentrated solar power in emerging markets: The role of policies and international finance institutions[J]. Energy Policy, 2015, 82:12-22.

[14] Ghadikolaei A S, Parkouhi S V. A resilience approach for supplier selection: Using Fuzzy Analytic Network Process and grey VIKOR techniques[J]. Journal of Cleaner Production, 2017, 161:431-451.

[15] Ghosh S, Nair A, Krishnan S S. Techno-economic review of rooftop photovoltaic systems: Case studies of industrial, residential and off-grid rooftops in Bangalore, Karnataka[J]. Renewable & Sustainable Energy Reviews, 2015, 42:1132-1142.

[16] Govindan K, Shankar K M, Kannan D. Application of fuzzy analytic network process for barrier evaluation in automotive parts remanufacturing towards cleaner production – a study in an Indian scenario[J]. Journal of Cleaner Production, 2016, 114: 199-213.

[17] Guerin T F. Evaluating expected and comparing with observed risks on a large-scale solar photovoltaic construction project: A case for reducing the regulatory burden[J]. Renewable & Sustainable Energy Reviews, 2017, 74:333-348.

[18] Haghdadi N, Copper J, Bruce A, et al. A method to estimate the location and orientation of distributed photovoltaic systems from their generation output data[J]. Renewable Energy, 2017, 108:390-400.

[19] Hong T, Koo C, Park J, et al. A GIS (geographic information system)-based optimization model for estimating the electricity generation of the rooftop PV (photovoltaic) system[J]. Energy, 2014, 65(2):190-199.

[20] Hong T, Lee M, Koo C, et al. Development of a method for estimating the rooftop solar photovoltaic (PV) potential by analyzing the available rooftop area using Hillshade analysis[J]. Applied Energy, 2016, 194:320-332.

[21] Khoshnava S M, Rostami R, Valipour A, et al. Rank of green building material criteria based on the three pillars of sustainability using the hybrid multi criteria decision making method[J]. Journal of

Cleaner Production, 2016, 173:82-99.

[22] Koo C, Hong T, Lee M., et al. An integrated multi-objective optimization model for determining the optimal solution in implementing the rooftop photovoltaic system[J]. Renewable & Sustainable Energy Reviews, 2016, 57:822-837.

[23] Kumar A, Sah B, Singh A R, et al. A review of multi criteria decision making (MCDM) towards sustainable renewable energy development[J]. Renewable & Sustainable Energy Reviews, 2017, 69:596-609.

[24] Lang T, Ammann D, Girod B.Profitability in absence of subsidies: A techno-economic analysis of rooftop photovoltaic self-consumption in residential and commercial buildings[J]. Renewable Energy, 2016, 87:77-87.

[25] Lee A, Kang H Y, Liou Y J. A Hybrid Multiple-Criteria Decision-Making Approach for Photovoltaic Solar Plant Location Selection[J]. Sustainability, 2017, 9(2):184.

[26] Li D F. A ratio ranking method of triangular intuitionistic fuzzy numbers and its application to MADM problems[J]. Computers & Mathematics with Applications, 2010, 60(6):1557-1570.

[27] Liao H, Xu Z, Zeng X J. Hesitant Fuzzy Linguistic VIKOR Method and Its Application in Qualitative Multiple Criteria Decision Making[J]. IEEE Transactions on Fuzzy Systems, 2015, 23(5):1343-1355.

[28] Liu You J X, You X Y, Shan M M. A novel approach for failure mode and effects analysis using combination weighting and fuzzy VIKOR method[J]. Applied Soft Computing, 2015, 28:579-588.

[29] Liu J, Xu F, Lin S. Site selection of photovoltaic power plants in a value chain based on grey cumulative prospect theory for sustainability: A case study in Northwest China[J]. Journal of Cleaner Production, 2017, 148:386-397.

[30] Pätäri E, Karell V, Luukka P, et al. Comparison of the multicriteria decision-making methods for equity portfolio selection: The U.S. evidence[J]. European Journal of Operational Research, 2017, 265:655-672.

[31] Peerapong P, Limmeechokchai B. Optimal Photovoltaic Resources Harvesting in Grid-connected Residential Rooftop and in Commercial Buildings: Cases of Thailand [J]. Energy Procedia, 2015, 79(2175):39-46.

[32] Qian G, Wang H, Feng X. Generalized hesitant fuzzy sets and their application in decision support system[J]. Knowledge-Based Systems, 2013, 37(4):357-365.

[33] Qin Q, Liang F, Li L, et al. A TODIM-based multi-criteria group decision making with triangular intuitionistic fuzzy numbers[J]. Applied Soft Computing, 2017, 55:93-107.

[34] Rezaei M, Mostafaeipour A, Qolipour M, et al. Investigation of the optimal location design of a hybrid wind-solar plant: A case study[J]. International Journal of Hydrogen Energy, 2018, 43(1):100-114.

[35] Saaty T L. Decision Making with Dependence and Feedback: The Analytic Network Process[J]. International, 1996, 95(2):129-157.

[36] Sakthivel, Sivakumar, Saravanan, et al. A decision support system to evaluate the optimum fuel blend in an IC engine to enhance the energy efficiency and energy management[J]. Energy, 2017, 140:566-583.

[37] Shakouri M, Lee H W, Kim Y W. A probabilistic portfolio-based model for financial valuation of community solar[J]. Applied Energy, 2017, 191:709-726.

[38] Singh R, Banerjee R. Estimation of rooftop solar photovoltaic potential of a city[J]. Solar Energy,

2015, 115:589-602.

[39] Sueyoshi T, Wang D. Measuring Scale Efficiency and Returns to Scale on Large Commercial Rooftop Photovoltaic Systems in California[J]. Energy Economics, 2017, 65:389-398.

[40] Sweet T K N, Khatib K E, Bristow N, et al. Commercial photovoltaic system design for Cardiff City Hall[J]. Energy, 2016, 169(1): 18-29.

[41] Tosarkani B M, Amin S H, Tosarkani B M, et al. A possibilistic solution to configure a battery closed-loop supply chain: multi-objective approach[J]. Expert Systems with Applications, 2017, 92: 12-26.

[42] Vasileiou M, Loukogeorgaki E, Vagiona D G. GIS-based multi-criteria decision analysis for site selection of hybrid offshore wind and wave energy systems in Greece[J]. Renewable & Sustainable Energy Reviews, 2017, 73: 745-757.

[43] Wan S P, Wang F, Lin L L, et al. Some new generalized aggregation operators for triangular intuitionistic fuzzy numbers and application to multi-attribute group decision making[J]. Computers & Industrial Engineering, 2016, 93(C): 286-301.

[44] Wan S P, Wang Q Y, Dong J Y. The extended VIKOR method for multi-attribute group decision making with triangular intuitionistic fuzzy numbers[J]. Knowledge-Based Systems, 2013, 52(6): 65-77.

[45] Wan S P, Yuan F F, Dong J Y. Extended VIKOR method for multiple criteria decision-making with linguistic hesitant fuzzy information[J]. Computers & Industrial Engineering, 2017, 112:305-319.

[46] Wang D D, Sueyoshi T. Assessment of large commercial rooftop photovoltaic system installations: Evidence from California[J]. Applied Energy, 2017, 188: 45-55.

[47] Wu Y, Geng S. Multi-criteria decision making on selection of solar–wind hybrid power station location: A case of China[J]. Energy Conversion & Management, 2014, 81(81):527-533.

[48] Wu Y, Geng S, Zhang H, et al. Decision framework of solar thermal power plant site selection based on linguistic Choquet operator[J]. Applied Energy, 2014, 136: 303-311.

[49] Wu Y, Wang Y, Chen K, et al. Social sustainability assessment of small hydropower with hesitant PROMETHEE method[J]. Sustainable Cities & Society, 2017, 35: 522-537.

[50] Wu Y, Xie C, Xu C, et al. A Decision Framework for Electric Vehicle Charging Station Site Selection for Residential Communities under an Intuitionistic Fuzzy Environment: A Case of Beijing[J]. Energies, 2017, 10(9):1270.

[51] Wu Y, Xu C, Ke Y, et al. An intuitionistic fuzzy multi-criteria framework for large-scale rooftop PV project portfolio selection: case study in Zhejiang, China[J]. Energy, 2017, 143:295-309.

[52] Wu Y, Xua C, Ke Y, et al. An intuitionistic fuzzy multi-criteria framework for large-scale rooftop PV project portfolio selection: case study in Zhejiang, China[J]. Energy, 2017, 143:295-309.

[53] Wu Y, Yang M, Zhang H, et al. Optimal Site Selection of Electric Vehicle Charging Stations Based on a Cloud Model and the PROMETHEE Method[J]. Energies, 2016, 9(3):157.

[54] Wu Y, Zhang J, Yuan J, et al. Study of decision framework of offshore wind power station site selection based on ELECTRE-III under intuitionistic fuzzy environment: A case of China[J]. Energy Conversion & Management, 2016, 113: 66-81.

[55] Xu R. The restriction research for urban area building integrated grid-connected PV power generation potential[J]. Energy, 2016, 113:124-143.

[56] Zhang F, Deng H, Margolis R, et al. Analysis of distributed-generation photovoltaic deployment,

installation time and cost, market barriers, and policies in China[J]. Energy Policy, 2015, 81: 43-55.
[57] Zhang S. Analysis of DSPV (distributed solar PV) power policy in China[J]. Energy, 2016, 98(4):92-100.
[58] Zhang W, Hao B, Li N, et al. Investigation on Photovoltaic Application in Buildings in China [J]. Energy Procedia, 2015, 70:673-682.
[59] Zhao H, Li N. Optimal Siting of Charging Stations for Electric Vehicles Based on Fuzzy Delphi and Hybrid Multi-Criteria Decision Making Approaches from an Extended Sustainability Perspective[J]. Energies, 2016, 9(4):270.

第二部分　投资决策研究

第 7 章首次提出将模糊集理论和累积前景理论结合应用于新能源项目投资决策，同时兼顾评估的不确定性和投资者的风险偏好，并通过案例分析论证了该方法的合理性和可行性。

第 8 章研究了企业在绿色发展战略、利益最大化战略、技术创新战略、稳定发展战略、和谐发展战略下如何进行分布式新能源项目投资组合选择的问题。

第 9 章首次将可持续性理念整合到新能源投资组合优化过程中，并提出将二型模糊数、WA 算子、AHP 方法与非支配排序遗传算法-II 结合用于新能源电力建设项目投资组合优化问题。

第 10 章综合考虑定量和定性指标，引入区间二型模糊 AHP-TOPSIS 技术用于风能耦合储氢项目评价。此外，启发式地提出了管理此类项目的改进思路。

第 11 章创新性地从垃圾分类的角度建立了焚烧发电厂性能评估指标体系。其次，基于组合权重法和模糊综合评价法建立了以绩效评价组合模型为基础的废弃物转化能源评估决策框架。

第 12 章利用 DEMATEL 方法和综合加权法确定指标权重。在考虑投资者风险规避心理的情况下，结合三角直觉模糊数和群决策理论，采用 TODIM 方法对可再生能源项目备选方案进行排序。

综上所述，本部分主要研究了包括垃圾发电项目、风能耦合储氢项目及高速公路服务区光伏发电项目在内的新能源电力建设项目的投资决策问题。新能源电力建设项目投资决策研究成果提高了模糊信息的保留、决策信息的可靠性及决策结果的合理性。

Chapter 7

Portfolio selection of distributed energy generation projects considering uncertainty and project interaction under different enterprise strategic scenarios

Yunna Wu [a, b], Chuanbo Xu [a, b*], Yiming Ke [a, b], Xinying Li [a, b], Lingwenying Li [a, b]
a. School of Economics and Management, North China Electric Power University, PCR, Beijing, China
b. Beijing Key Laboratory of New Energy and Low-Carbon Development (North China Electric Power University), Changping, Beijing, 102206, China

Abstract: Selecting a rational distributed energy generation (DEG) project portfolio is the key to achieving the strategic objectives of energy enterprises. The complexity associated with the selection of DEG project portfolio comes from uncertainties in decision-making environment, interactions between projects, and necessary alignment with the strategic objectives of enterprises. However, previous researches did not address the three issues simultaneously. To fill such gap, this study establishes a multi-criteria decision-making framework to select the optimal DEG project portfolio(s) under different strategic scenarios, where uncertainty and project interaction are considered. The framework consists of two stages. In the first phase, the weights of criteria are determined by the interval type-2 fuzzy analytic hierarchy process technique, and the strategic alignment indexes of each candidate distributed energy generation project are obtained using the interval type-2 fuzzy weighted averaging operator. In the second stage, considering the strategic interactions, a nonlinear 0-1 programming is formulated while satisfying the budget constraints, and the non-dominated sorting genetic algorithm-II is utilized to obtain the optimal portfolio of DEG projects under different strategic scenarios. The proposed framework is applied in a case study to illustrate its suitability and effectiveness. The results show that the selected portfolios vary with the strategic objectives of enterprises. This research has practical applied value for project managers in project portfolio management.

Keywords: distributed energy source; project portfolio; multi-criteria decision-making; interval type-2 fuzzy analytic hierarchy process; interval type-2 fuzzy weighted averaging; non-dominated sorting genetic algorithm-II.

1. Introduction

China's large-scale power generation bases of renewable energy are mainly located in the western and northwestern regions currently due to the sufficient resources and cheap land prices. There are usually two schemes for dealing with generated renewable energy power. The first scheme is the local consumption and the second is the cross-regional long-distance transmission [1]. However, the local electricity consumption in the western and northwestern regions is limited [2]. Although using ultra-high voltage transmission system to deliver electricity to economically developed areas could be another scheme, related construction costs are too high [3]. For these reasons, the phenomena of wind and solar photovoltaic (PV) energy curtailment in the western and northwestern regions was severe, reaching 12% and 6% respectively in 2017 according to the data released by National Energy Administration (NEA). Fortunately, the utilization of distributed energy sources in the areas with large electricity demand could solve the problem of energy curtailment because the distributed energy systems are geographically close to demand centers [4]. Moreover, high energy efficiency is another prominent feature of the distributed energy system. Under such circumstances, many policies have been formulated to support the development of distributed energy generation (DEG) projects, as shown in Table 7.1.

Table 7.1 Policies supporting for DEG project development.

No.	Document	Issuing time	Issuing agency	Core content
1	12th Five-Year plan for renewable energy development	Aug. 2012	National Development and Reform Commission (NDRC)	Combination development of centralized and decentralized renewable energy
2	Strategic action plan for energy development (2014-2020)	Jun. 2014	State Council	South and the Middle East are the key regions for the development of decentralized energy resources
3	13th Five-Year plan for renewable energy	Dec. 2016	NDRC	Comprehensively promoting the development and utilization of wind energy resources in the South and the Middle East regions
4	Guidance on energy work in 2018	Mar. 2018	NEA	Giving priority to the development of decentralized wind power and distributed photovoltaic power generation

Distributed energy sources mainly consist of natural gas, solar PV power, wind power and some other forms of energy. Among all distributed energy sources, natural gas distributed energy was the first one to be developed in China. By 2015, the amount of China's natural gas distributed energy projects had increased to 288, and the total installed capacity had reached 11.12 GW, about 4 times what it was in 2014 [5]. In 2016, the cumulative installed capacity of the national natural gas distributed generation was 12 GW. However, this data is far to reach the goal of 50 GW in the Guidelines for Developing Natural Gas Distributed Energy Sources [6].

China's distributed solar PV grows explosively in recent years. By the end of 2016, the cumulative installed capacity of China's distributed solar PV power projects had increased to 10.32 GW. By the end of September 2017, the cumulative installed capacity of solar PV power generation had reached 120 GW nationwide, including 25.62 GW of distributed solar PV projects. The 13th Five-Year Plan for Energy Development [7] issued by NDRC and NEA set an ambitious goal that the cumulative installed capacity of distributed solar PV should reach 60 GW by 2020.

In contrast, the scale of decentralized wind power in China is still relatively small due to its late start. To speed up its development, the Interim Measures for the Development and Construction of Decentralized Wind Power Projects [8] issued by the NEA clarified the standard, the price and the subsidy policy for the grid-connection of decentralized wind power in the first quarter of 2018,, which means that the decentralized wind power will enter a new stage with rapid development.

To summarize, the industry of DEG has enormous investment potential. For energy enterprises, the investment of DEG projects has become an inherent realistic demand for their own survival and improvement. Therefore, many of them take advantage of such an excellent opportunity. For example, State Power Investment Group has proposed to promote natural gas distributed energy and distributed solar PV power generation actively, and Huadian Group has proposed to control conventional coal-fired power generation and vigorously boost the development of distributed energy strictly. With the outbreak of the distributed energy market, the number of potential DEG projects will inevitably exceed the number of executable projects under the limited resource constraints of energy enterprises. As a result, project managers in energy enterprises would be strongly advised to pay more attention to the problem of DEG project portfolio selection. Project portfolio selection, as a critical link of project management, refers to the process of selecting multiple projects to meet the strategic objectives of an enterprise under the constraints of resources and some other conditions [9]. A proper DEG project portfolio is essential for energy enterprise to create competitive advantages in today's highly competitive distributed energy market. On the contrary, an improper selection of DEG project portfolio may lead to the waste of resources and the deviation from the strategic direction of the enterprise. Regarding the DEG project portfolio selection problem, there are three critical issues that need to be valued and addressed.

Firstly, the chosen project portfolio should be in line with the enterprise's strategic objectives. Investors make investment decisions in order to achieve specific strategic objectives, perhaps for the largest gains, perhaps for sustainable development, or perhaps for market occupation. Project portfolios are vehicles for strategy implementation [10]. With the deepening of the new round of China's power system reformation, the competition of energy enterprises becomes increasingly fierce [11]. To survive sustainably and develop in such a new competitive situation, energy enterprises should ensure that the selected project portfolio is highly consistent with their strategic objectives.

Secondly, uncertainties in portfolio selection should be fully described. The uncertainties mainly stem from the following two aspects. On the one hand, given that project portfolio selection is a forward-looking activity, it is hard to predict the future performances of the criteria accurately due to the dynamics and complexity of electricity market [12]. On the other hand, some evaluation contents in DEG project portfolio selection are qualitative, which mainly depend on the knowledge of experts. Because of the vagueness of human thinking as well as the limitation of cognitive, it is relatively difficult for experts to make accurate judgements on the criteria. Thus, mistakes may occur while ignoring those uncertainties.

Thirdly, interactions between projects should not be overlooked. Interactions between projects can be divided into the complementary effect and the substitute effect [13]. The complement effect between DEG projects occurs because facilities such as electricity transmission line are shared between close-range projects. Besides, the strong complementary effect is also observed in different types of DEG projects. For instance, distributed solar PV and distributed wind energy have complementary characteristics in both resource condition and technical application [14]. The substitute effect between DEG projects exists because projects are competing as resource conditions constrain the whole decision process.

Current researches have made significant contributions to one or two of the above issues. As illustrated in Table 7.2, the three problems are dealt with separately in most cases, and in the other cases, two of the three problems are solved. However, to the best of our knowledge, there is no research covering all these three issues simultaneously, which motivates our research.

Table 7.2 Literature review on project portfolio selection.

Literature	Strategy	Uncertainty	Interaction
Smith-Perera, García-Melón [15]	×		
Garcíamelón, Povedabautista [16]	×		
Jeng, Huang [17]	×		
Mohagheghi, Mousavi [18]		×	

Continued

Literature	Strategy	Uncertainty	Interaction
Tavana, Keramatpour [19]		×	
Khalili-Damghani, Sadi-Nezhad [20]		×	
Mohagheghi, Mousavi [21]		×	
Pendharkar, Rodger [22]			×
Killen [23]			×
Lopes, Almeida [24]			×
Eilat, Golany [25]			×
Jiang, Zhang [26]			×
Pendharkar [27]			×
Neumeier, Radszuwill [28]			×
Lin, Hsieh [29]	×	×	
Relich, Pawlewski [30]	×	×	
Ghapanchi, Tavana [31]		×	×
Bhattacharyya, Kumar [32]		×	×
Alvarez-García, Fernández-Castro [33]		×	×
Liu, Liu [34]		×	×
Wu, Xu [4]		×	×
Jafarzadeh, Akbari [35]		×	×

Due to the lack of theoretical models, the selection of the DEG project portfolio in reality relies on empirical rules and experience heavily, which hinder the progress of the project portfolio management. Therefore, under the premise of combining theory with practice, this paper tries to provide some useful methods and ideas for project managers in energy enterprise to carry out DEG project portfolio selection. The purpose of this paper is to select the optimal portfolio of DEG projects under different strategic scenarios, in which uncertainty and project interactions are considered. To achieve this goal, this paper firstly identifies the strategic objective of realistic energy enterprises and constructs an evaluation criteria system for portfolio selection on DEG projects through a questionnaire survey. Secondly, to describe uncertainty inherent in DEG project portfolio selection, internal type-2 fuzzy numbers (IT2FNs) are adopted to represent the performance of projects, the weight of criteria and the interactions between projects. Compared with other fuzzy numbers such as triangular fuzzy numbers and trapezoidal fuzzy numbers, the fuzzification degree of IT2FNs is higher and thus is more suitable for complex decision making like DEG project portfolio selection. Thirdly, the weights of the criteria determined by interval type-2 fuzzy analytic hierarchy process (IT2FAHP) technique are integrated into the interval type-2 fuzzy weighted averaging (IT2FWA) operator to obtain the strategic alignment index for each DEG project. Finally, a nonlinear integer programming is formulated, and the non-dominated sorting genetic algorithm-II (NSGA-II) is used to obtain an optimal-Pareto set under different strategic scenarios. The reason for using the NSGA-II is that it has the advantages of less complexity algorithm, fast running speed, and good convergence of the solution set. The originality of the paper is solving the issues of uncertainty, project interaction, and strategic alignment simultaneously for the project portfolio selection problem.

The rest of this paper is structured as follows: after the Introduction, we conduct a literature review in Section 2; in Section 3, some related materials and methods are introduced; we further provide an example in Zhejiang province, China in section 4. Section 5 is the discussion and the last section concludes the paper.

2. Literature review

2.1 Project portfolio selection

The project portfolio selection can be defined as a problem of selecting a subset from a group of projects, and the selected subset is considered as a portfolio. Project portfolio selection is a popular research topic in the field of project management [36]. Nowadays, the researches in this topic are quite abundant, mainly focused on new product development (NDP) projects [37], research and development (R&D) projects [38] and information technology (IT) projects [31]. Besides, some valuable researches on energy project portfolio selection have also been conducted. For example, Wu, Li [39] proposed an energy project portfolio management system using energy portfolio management technology, including the introduction of energy projects, the selection and evaluation of energy projects, and the evaluation of project portfolios. To assist the U.S. Department of Energy, Golabi, Kirkwood [40] selected a portfolio of solar energy projects using the multiattribute preference theory. Similarly, Wu, Xu [4] selected a rational large-scale rooftop PV project portfolio based on an intuitionistic fuzzy multi-criteria framework.

Various methods have been applied to select the optimal portfolio of projects. Among them, multi-criteria decision-making (MCDM) techniques are the most commonly used methods currently because the project portfolio selection usually involves numerous conflicting objectives or criteria. Generally, MCDM is classified into multi-attribute decision making (MADM) and multi-objective decision making (MODM) depending on whether the decision alternative is limited or infinite [41]. In project portfolio selection, MADM can be used to evaluate individual project while MODM is used to optimize project portfolio [4]. Nowadays, many scholars have successfully applied the MCDM technique to the project portfolio issues. For instance, Khalili-Damghani, Sadi-Nezhad [20] established a hybrid MCDM framework integrates Data Envelope Analysis (DEA) model and an Evolutionary Algorithm (EA) for the problem of sustainable project portfolio selection. Lopes and Almeida [24] selected an Exploration and

Production projects portfolio in the petroleum industry based on a multi-attribute utility theory (MAUT). Moreover, some researches also use MADM techniques to evaluate distributed energy systems or projects. Ren, Gao [42] selected the optimal of distributed residential energy systems based on a multi-criteria evaluation. Jing, Zhu [43] proposed an framework consists of multi-criteria evaluation and multi-objective optimization for distributed energy system planning. Väisänen, Mikkilä [44] used a hybrid multi-criteria approach for decision-making about a sustainable local distributed energy system. In addition to the aspect of project portfolio, MCDM techniques have also been used to other fields such as power demand response planning [45], solar PV power plant site selection [46], wind speed forecasting [47] and so on. Therefore, inspired by them, the MCDM technique is utilized to select the optimal DEG project portfolio in this study.

2.2 Strategic alignment in project portfolio selection

Enterprise strategy determines the rise and fall of enterprise development. For project-oriented enterprises such as power generation enterprises, decision-makers (DMs) must select the optimal portfolio that is aligned with the strategic objectives for each project. Some literatures made an emphasis on the importance of consistency between projects and enterprise strategies. Voss and Kock [48] stated clearly that today's enterprises should carry out portfolio management to cope with the growing number of projects and apply it to guarantee strategic alignment. Kaiser, Arbi [49] hold that the project portfolio management is a common technology to make the project portfolio consistent with the enterprise strategic goals. Hernandez-Perdomo, Mun [50] indicated that ranking and selecting multiple projects in portfolio management will affect multiple strategic goals. Although the acceptance of strategic alignment is one of the major objectives of portfolio selection, the literature on it is relatively limited [51].

Turner's model [52] is one of the well-known models that connect a portfolio of projects to enterprise strategic objectives. Smith-Perera, García-Melón [15] prioritized a project portfolio by using a novel approach based on the strategic goals of an energy enterprise. In their study, firstly, three strategic goals including human resources, technique and quality as well as a total of ten critical criteria were identified. Then, the analytic network process (ANP) was used to obtain the project strategic index (PSI) of each project. Garcíamelón, Povedabautista [16] used the strategic relative alignment index in the selection of portfolio projects. Nine strategic objectives and associated critical criteria were identified in this study, and the ANP was also used to calculate the relative alignment index (RAI) of each project. Jeng and Huang [17] conducted a strategic project portfolio selection by using a systematic hybrid technique. A four-dimension framework including need, solution, differentiation, and benefit was constructed which consisted of 16 critical criteria. Then, a systematic technique consisting of a modified Delphi, a decision-making trial and evaluation laboratory (DEMATEL) and an ANP was employed. Considering that DMs always make decision-makings under uncertain circumstances, Lin and Hsieh [53] proposed an decision support system based framework that incorporates fuzzy theory into strategic portfolio selection, which could provide DMs with a flexible, expandable and interactive tool to select projects for strategic portfolio management.

2.3 Uncertainty description in project portfolio selection

As uncertainties such as technical innovation or policy changes increase, decision-makers must make decisions about DEG project portfolio under nondeterministic conditions. Thus, determining the exact values of the identified criteria is often difficult or even impossible when uncertainty is taken into account [54]. Fuzzy set theory, introduced by Zadeh [55], has emerged as an effective tool to depict such uncertainties.

Fuzzy sets have been widely used in the selection of project portfolios. For example, Huang, Chu [56] used a trapezoidal fuzzy number based analytic hierarchy process (AHP) for R&D portfolio selection. Similarly, Chen and Cheng [57] employed a fuzzy MCDM method under the trapezoidal fuzzy environment and ranked portfolios of information system projects. More recently, the Data Envelopment Analysis (DEA) was used by Ghapanchi, Tavana [31] to select the best portfolio of information system/IT projects under the triangular fuzzy environment. Mohagheghi, Mousavi [18] proposed a new optimizing model for project evaluation and project portfolio selection under interval-valued fuzzy (IVF) environment. To deal with the uncertainties of the levelized cost of electricity and risk levels of failure modes in the problem of energy generation portfolio, Zeng, Nasri [58] introduced the triangular fuzzy numbers. Tavana, Keramatpour [19] developed a triangular fuzzy numbers hybrid project portfolio selection method using DEA, TOPSIS and integer programming. Mohagheghi, Mousavi [21] proposed a new model of R&D project portfolio selection under uncertainty. The uncertain environment of projects is well handled by using interval type-2 fuzzy sets.

2.4 Interactions modeling in project portfolio selection

The interaction effect between projects was first proposed by Baker and Freeland [59], and they held the view that the current models for portfolio selection had considerable limitations of ignoring the interaction between projects. This issue was also recognized by Mcfarlan [60] and Keil and Marchewka [61], and they suggested that calculating the risk and value of an IT project portfolio was a non-addition problem since some interactions exist between projects in a portfolio. At present, it is generally recognized that an enterprise must be capable of understanding the interactions between projects in a portfolio for selecting the best portfolio [23].

Pendharkar and Rodger [22] indicated that selecting an IT project portfolio may have some organizational tax incentives that could provide synergies and increase the value of an IT project portfolio. Killen [23] argued that interactions between projects increase information overload and time pressure, so they used decision scenario experiments to evaluate the visualizations of project interactions. Lopes and Almeida [24] assessed interactions between projects in the context of selecting an exploration and production project portfolio based on a multi-attribute utility function. Three widely present synergies were considered consisting of project scope synergy, fiscal synergy and information synergy. Eilat, Golany [25] considered the interactions between R&D projects, which can be classified into resource interactions, benefit interactions, and outcome interactions. Jiang, Zhang [26] took into consideration the interactions among the different types of technologies for each remanufacturing technology portfolio. Alvarez-García and Fernández-Castro [62] presented a fuzzy interactive multi-objective model aiming to address the scarcity of interaction models, which elicited the evaluation of interactions from a group of experts in a natural way.

2.5 Findings of the literature review

Through the literature review, the findings can be summarized as follows:

- The current researches solve one or two issue above, but none of them solve the above three issues at the same time. However, the three issues are significant and cannot be ignored in the selection of DEG project portfolio.
- The literature on strategic alignment of project portfolio selection is in a limitation, and the current strategic types are not related to energy enterprises.
- The uncertainty has not been fully described in project portfolio selection. Most of the previous researches were carried out in a deterministic environment or type-1 fuzzy environment.
- Various kinds of project interactions have been proposed, such as benefit, outcome, resource, and technical interactions. However, the interactions at the strategic level have not been proposed.

Based on these findings, the main contributions of this study are as follows. Firstly, the strategic objectives of energy enterprises have been reviewed from official websites, and critical criteria associated with these strategies have been identified. The criteria system decomposes the strategic objectives into an operational level. Secondly, the interval type-2 fuzzy set (IT2FS) is used to represent the uncertainties in the process of DEG project portfolio selection. It is worth mentioning that the combination of IT2FS and NSGA-II is first introduced in fields of both energy and project portfolio management. Thirdly, the concept of strategic interaction coefficient (SIC) is proposed for the first time. The SIC describes the degree of interaction between two

DEG projects in a specific strategy. Based on the above improvements, in summary, the decision-making results of DEG project portfolio selection would be better, which is mainly reflected in the following two aspects: ①the results are credible because the proposed framework is more closely related to the actual situation of the project portfolio; ②the results are more reasonable due to the applicability of the adopted methods.

3. Materials and methods

3.1 Strategic objective and critical criteria for DEG project portfolio selection

The strategic objectives of the state large power generation enterprises, such as China Huaneng Group Corporation Limited and State Power Investment Corporation Limited, are reviewed from China Energy Network, shown as follows:

- Green development strategy
- Benefit maximization strategy
- Technological innovation strategy
- Stable development strategy
- Harmonious development strategy

Criteria that are associated with the above five strategies are identified by the following steps: firstly, the academic literature related to the DEG project evaluation are collected and studied, and the initial evaluation criteria system is built which consists a total of 48 initial criteria, as shown in Appendix A. Secondly, an online questionnaire survey method, which has been used frequently in the critical success factors identification [63], is sent to the experts in the fields of energy project management and energy strategy management. The main context of the questionnaire survey is to require respondents to evaluate the importance of each criterion for each strategy. In details, for example, to investigate the critical criteria associated with the technological innovation strategy, the questionnaire is designed as: What do you think is the importance of this factor in achieving the technological innovation strategy? What additional factors do you think are included in the technology innovation strategy?

A five-point scale is defined for this evaluation (1-5). A total of 30 questionnaires are sent out to experts whose backgrounds are related to energy project management, and feedbacks from 8 of them are received, with a response rate of 26.67%. Experts' opinions are aggregated by the mean score. The risk factors with a mean value greater than 3 are deemed as critical criteria. Finally, the critical criteria associated with each strategic objective are identified, as shown in Fig. 7.1.

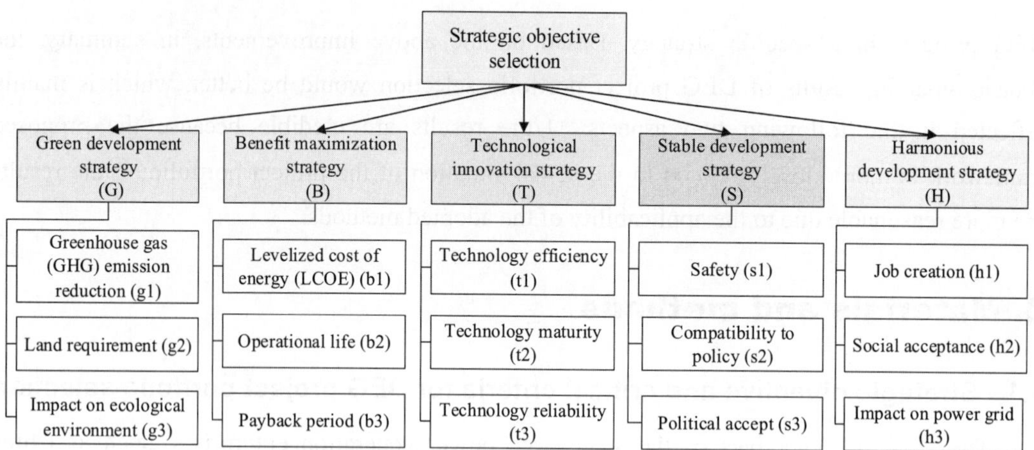

Fig. 7.1 Critical criteria associated with each strategic objective.

3.2 Basic conception of IT2FSs

Definition 1. [64] Let $\tilde{A}_i$ be a trapezoidal IT2FS. $\tilde{\tilde{A}}_i=[\tilde{A}_i^U,\tilde{A}_i^L]=\left[\left(a_{i1}^U,a_{i2}^U,a_{i3}^U,a_{i4}^U;H_1(\tilde{A}_i^U),H_2(\tilde{A}_i^U)\right),\left(a_{i1}^L,a_{i2}^L,a_{i3}^L,a_{i4}^L;H_1(\tilde{A}_i^L),H_2(\tilde{A}_i^L)\right)\right]$, where $\tilde{A}_i^U$ and $\tilde{A}_i^L$ are type-1 fuzzy sets, $a_{i1}^U,a_{i2}^U,a_{i3}^U,a_{i4}^U,a_{i1}^U,a_{i2}^U,a_{i3}^U,a_{i4}^U$ are the reference points of $\tilde{\tilde{A}}_i$. $H_j(\tilde{A}_i^U)$ denotes the membership value of the element $a^U{}_{i(j+1)}$ in the upper trapezoidal membership function $\tilde{A}_i^U$, $1\leqslant j\leqslant 2$, $H_j(\tilde{A}_i^L)$ denotes the membership value of the element $a^L{}_{i(j+1)}$ in the lower trapezoidal membership function. A classical trapezoidal IT2FS is depicted in Fig. 7.2.

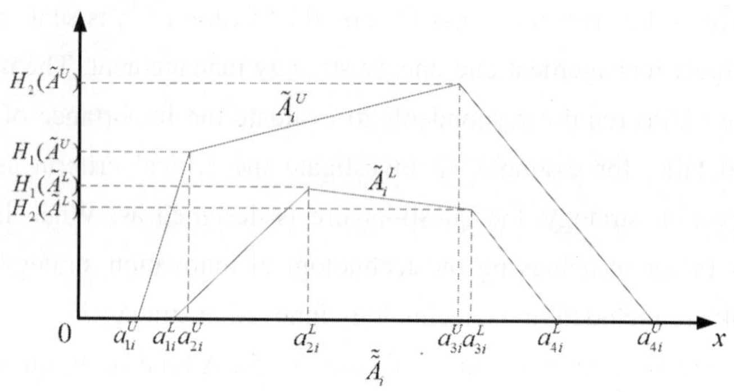

Fig. 7.2 The upper trapezoidal membership function $\tilde{A}_i^U$ and the lower trapezoidal membership function $\tilde{A}_i^L$ of the interval type-2 fuzzy set $\tilde{\tilde{A}}_i$.

3.3 IT2FWA operator

Definition 2. Let $\tilde{\tilde{A}}_i=\left[\left(a_{i1}^U,a_{i2}^U,a_{i3}^U,a_{i4}^U;H_1(\tilde{A}_i^U),H_2(\tilde{A}_i^U)\right),\left(a_{i1}^L,a_{i2}^L,a_{i3}^L,a_{i4}^L;H_1(\tilde{A}_i^L),H_2(\tilde{A}_i^L)\right)\right]$ $(i=1,2,\ldots,n)$ be a collection of trapezoidal IT2FS. The IT2FWA operator of the elements

$\tilde{\tilde{A}}_1, \tilde{\tilde{A}}_2, \ldots, \tilde{\tilde{A}}_m$ is shown as follows:

$$TI2FWA(\tilde{\tilde{A}}_1, \tilde{\tilde{A}}_2, \ldots, \tilde{\tilde{A}}_m) = \mathop{\oplus}_{j=1}^{m} \varpi_j \otimes \tilde{\tilde{A}}_j \tag{7-1}$$

The basic operation of interval type-2 fuzzy numbers is as follows:

(1)

$$\tilde{\tilde{A}}_1 \oplus \tilde{\tilde{A}}_2 = (\tilde{A}_1^U, \tilde{A}_1^L) \oplus (\tilde{A}_2^U, \tilde{A}_2^L) =$$
$$\begin{pmatrix} a_{11}^U + a_{21}^U, a_{12}^U + a_{22}^U, a_{13}^U + a_{23}^U, a_{14}^U + a_{24}^U; \min\left(H_1(\tilde{A}_1^U), H_1(\tilde{A}_2^U)\right), \min\left(H_2(\tilde{A}_1^U), H_2(\tilde{A}_2^U)\right), \\ a_{11}^L + a_{21}^L, a_{12}^L + a_{22}^L, a_{13}^L + a_{23}^L, a_{14}^L + a_{24}^L; \min\left(H_1(\tilde{A}_1^L), H_1(\tilde{A}_2^L)\right), \min\left(H_2(\tilde{A}_1^L), H_2(\tilde{A}_2^L)\right) \end{pmatrix}$$

(2)

$$\tilde{\tilde{A}}_1 \otimes \tilde{\tilde{A}}_2 = (\tilde{A}_1^U, \tilde{A}_1^L) \otimes (\tilde{A}_2^U, \tilde{A}_2^L) =$$
$$\begin{pmatrix} a_{11}^U \times a_{21}^U, a_{12}^U \times a_{22}^U, a_{13}^U \times a_{23}^U, a_{14}^U \times a_{24}^U; \min\left(H_1(\tilde{A}_1^U), H_1(\tilde{A}_2^U)\right), \min\left(H_2(\tilde{A}_1^U), H_2(\tilde{A}_2^U)\right), \\ a_{11}^L \times a_{21}^L, a_{12}^L \times a_{22}^L, a_{13}^L \times a_{23}^L, a_{14}^L \times a_{24}^L; \min\left(H_1(\tilde{A}_1^L), H_1(\tilde{A}_2^L)\right), \min\left(H_2(\tilde{A}_1^L), H_2(\tilde{A}_2^L)\right) \end{pmatrix}$$

(3) $$k \otimes \tilde{\tilde{A}}_1 = \begin{pmatrix} \left(ka_{11}^U, ka_{12}^U, ka_{13}^U, ka_{14}^U; H_1(\tilde{A}_1^U), H_2(\tilde{A}_1^U)\right), \\ \left(ka_{11}^L, ka_{12}^L, ka_{13}^L, ka_{14}^L; H_1(\tilde{A}_1^L), H_2(\tilde{A}_1^L)\right) \end{pmatrix}$$

3.4 IT2FAHP technique

AHP, proposed by Saaty [65], is a popular MCDM method for its rational hierarchy structure and clear logic relations. Subsequently, Buckley [66] extended Saaty's AHP into fuzzy AHP by combining fuzzy sets. In this paper, AHP method under interval type-2 fuzzy set environment is used to obtain the fuzzy weights of criteria.

The steps of IT2FAHP technique are presented as follows:

Step 1. The pairwise comparison matrix under IT2FSs is established. The linguistic terms and their corresponding IT2FNs are shown in Table 7.3.

Table 7.3 Linguistic terms for importance weights of factors [67].

Linguistic variables	IT2FN	Reciprocal IT2FN
Absolutely Strong (AS)	((7, 8, 9, 9; 1, 1), (7.2, 8.2, 8.8, 9; 0.8, 0.8))	((0.11, 0.11, 0.12, 0.14; 1, 1), (0.11, 0.11, 0.12, 0.14; 0.8, 0.8))
Very Strong (VS)	((5, 6, 8, 9; 1, 1), (5.2, 6.2, 7.8, 8.8; 0.8, 0.8))	((0.11, 0.12, 0.17, 0.2; 1, 1), (0.11, 0.13, 0.16, 0.19; 0.8, 0.8))
Fairly Strong (FS)	((3, 4, 6, 7; 1, 1), (3.2, 4.2, 5.8, 6.8; 0.8, 0.8))	((0.14, 0.17, 0.25, 0.33; 1, 1), (0.15, 0.17, 0.24, 0.31; 0.8, 0.8))
Slightly Strong (SS)	((1, 2, 4, 5; 1, 1), (1.2, 2.2, 3.8, 4.8; 0.8, 0.8))	((0.2, 0.25, 0.5, 1; 1, 1), 0.21, 0.26, 0.45, 0.83; 0.8, 0.8))
Exactly Equal (E)	((1, 1, 1, 1; 1, 1), (1, 1, 1, 1; 1, 1))	((1, 1, 1, 1; 1, 1), (1, 1, 1, 1; 1, 1))

Step 2. Test the consistency of the IT2FSs pair wise comparison. The IT2FSs matrices are defuzzified as Eq. (7-4) [68] and checked for consistency.

$$Defuzzified(\tilde{\tilde{a}}_i)=\frac{\dfrac{(a_{i4}^U-a_{i1}^U)+\left(H_1(\tilde{A}_i^U)\times a_{i2}^U-a_{i1}^U\right)+\left(H_2(\tilde{A}_i^U)\times a_{i3}^U-a_{i1}^U\right)}{4}+a_{i1}^U+\dfrac{(a_{i4}^L-a_{i1}^L)+\left(H_1(\tilde{A}_i^L)\times a_{i2}^L-a_{i1}^L\right)+\left(H_2(\tilde{A}_i^L)\times a_{i3}^L-a_{i1}^L\right)}{4}+a_{i1}^L}{2} \tag{7-2}$$

In order to identify the consistency ratio (CR) of a matrix, the matrix consistency index CI is found as follows:

$$CI=(\lambda_{\max}-m)/(m-1) \tag{7-3}$$

where $Aw=\lambda_{\max}w$, $\lambda_{\max}$ is the largest or principal eigen value of the A decision matrix of pairwise comparison; m is the matrix order.

It turns out that A is consistent if the value of CR less than 0.1 is considered acceptable. The matrix consistency ratio CR is calculated as:

$$CR=CI/RI \tag{7-4}$$

Step 3. Aggregate the evaluations of DMs by using geometric means.

$$\tilde{\tilde{A}}_{ij}=\left[\tilde{\tilde{A}}^1\otimes\cdots\otimes\tilde{\tilde{A}}^n\right]^{1/n} \tag{7-5}$$

where $\sqrt[n]{\tilde{\tilde{A}}_{ij}}=\begin{pmatrix}\sqrt[n]{\tilde{\tilde{A}}_{ij1}{}^U},\sqrt[n]{\tilde{\tilde{A}}_{ij2}{}^U},\sqrt[n]{\tilde{\tilde{A}}_{ij3}{}^U},\sqrt[n]{\tilde{\tilde{A}}_{ij4}{}^U};H_1(a_{ij}{}^U),H_2(a_{ij}{}^U),\\ \sqrt[n]{\tilde{\tilde{A}}_{ij1}{}^L},\sqrt[n]{\tilde{\tilde{A}}_{ij2}{}^L},\sqrt[n]{\tilde{\tilde{A}}_{ij3}{}^L},\sqrt[n]{\tilde{\tilde{A}}_{ij4}{}^L};H_1(a_{ij}{}^L),H_2(a_{ij}{}^L)\end{pmatrix}$

Step 4. Calculate the fuzzy weights of each criterion as follows.

$$\tilde{\tilde{w}}_i=\tilde{\tilde{r}}_i\times(\tilde{\tilde{r}}_1+\tilde{\tilde{r}}_2+\ldots+\tilde{\tilde{r}}_m)^{-1} \tag{7-6}$$

where $\tilde{\tilde{r}}_i$ represents the geometric mean of each row of matrix.

3.5 NSGA-II algorithm

Portfolio selection of a DEG project based on strategy alignment is a MODM problem since an enterprise generally implements multiple strategies at the same time. For such multi-objective optimization problems, the most widely and popularly used multi-objective evolutionary algorithms include NSGA-II, improved strength Pareto evolutionary algorithm (SPEA2) and Pareto envelope-based selection algorithm II (PESA-II) and so on. Gong, Jiao [69] have made comparisons among these algorithms. They supported that in solving most problems, the Pareto-optimal set obtained by NSGA-II algorithm has a more diversified set of optimal solutions than PAES-II and SPEA2 algorithms, and its convergence is closer to the actual Pareto-optimal level. In this point of view, the NSGA-II algorithm is utilized in this work.

NSGA-II algorithm was proposed by Deb, Pratap [70] in 2000 on the basis of NSGA. Its advantages over the NSGA algorithm lie in the following three aspects: ①a fast non-dominated sorting algorithm is proposed. The complexity of the calculation is reduced from O(MN3) to O(MN2); ②the elitist strategy is introduced to ensure that some excellent individuals are not discarded during the evolution process, thereby improving the accuracy of optimization results; ③the comparison operator is adopted. It not only overcomes the defect that the NSGA needs to specify the shared parameters in the population, but also makes it a comparison standard among individuals in the population. Therefore, the individual in the quasi Pareto domain can be extended to the whole Pareto domain evenly, and the diversity of the population is guaranteed.

3.6 Decision framework of DEG project portfolio selection

The MCDM framework integrates the IT2FAHP technique, the IT2FWA operator, and the NSGA-II algorithm together. The IT2FAHP technique and the IT2FWA operator are used to determine the weights of criteria and aggregate the criteria respectively while the role of the NSGA-II algorithm is to obtain optimal project portfolios. The proposed framework consists of three main phases, including the preparatory phase, the individual project evaluation phase, and the portfolio optimization phase (as shown in Fig. 7.3).

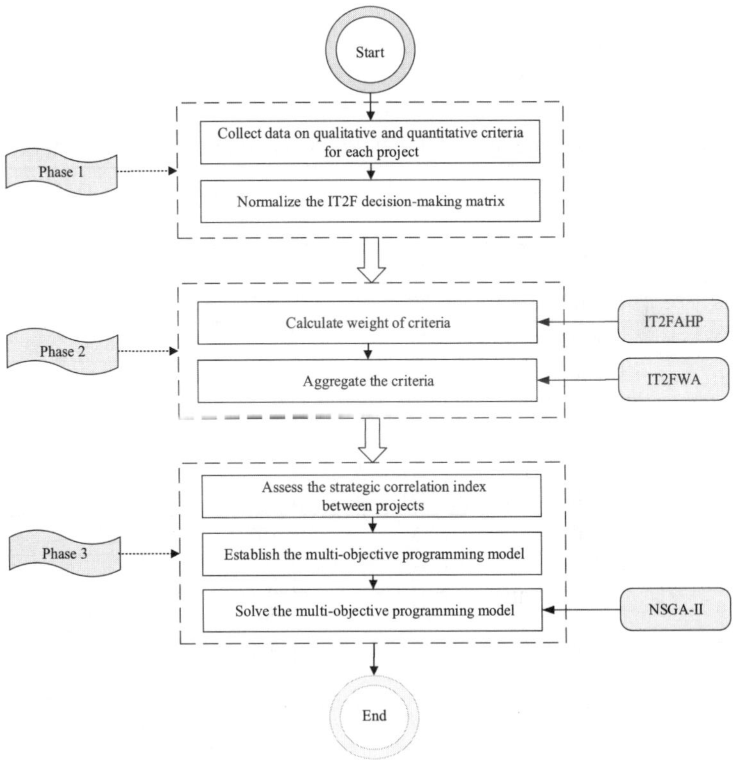

Fig. 7.3 Decision framework of DEG project portfolio selection.

4. A case study

4.1 Problem statement

A large energy investment enterprise plans to invest in DEG projects. Zhejiang Province is selected as the targeted investment area because of its abundant natural resources such as wind, sunshine and natural gas as well as the huge demand for electricity there. Through an early-stage investigation of resources, market, and site, a total of 15 feasible DEG projects near the load center are identified, including six distributed solar PV projects, five distributed wind energy projects and four distributed natural gas projects.

Due to limited funds of the investment enterprise, only a part of DEG projects that meet the enterprise's strategic objectives can be selected to invest. For this purpose, an investment decision-making committee, consisting of an internal senior project manager and three external authoritative experts whose backgrounds are project management of energy engineering, is established. The responsibilities of the senior project manager are to provide project information and organize expert meetings while the tasks of these experts are to evaluate the performances of the qualitative criteria, evaluate the weights of the criteria and evaluate the SICs of the projects.

4.2 Data collection

The quantitative criterion information of the 15 projects are collected from the feasibility study report, as shown in Table 7.4.

Table 7.4 Performances of the alternatives on the qualitative criteria.

Project	g2 (m^2)	b1 (yuan/kWh)	b2 (year)	b3 (year)	t1 (%)	h1 (jobs)
P1	3748	0.439	15	10.3	25%	86
P2	1294	0.506	25	7.8	24%	67
P3	2108	0.613	20	8.2	26%	68
P4	2972	0.503	22	9.5	28%	50
P5	3000	0.782	15	8.7	25%	90
P6	3367	0.497	20	9.8	25%	110
P7	4019	0.507	17	12	19%	70
P8	3118	1.080	25	9.5	30%	61
P9	3448	0.608	18	10	22%	44
P10	3278	0.632	22	7	25%	57
P11	4359	0.958	25	8.2	31%	63
P12	1635	0.591	20	9.5	23%	74
P13	3278	0.578	25	9	26%	54
P14	2539	0.520	18	8	25%	34
P15	2700	0.515	20	8.7	26%	57

Then, the performances of these alternatives on the qualitative criteria are evaluated by the three experts, as shown in Table 7.5.

Table 7.5 Performances of the alternatives on the qualitative criteria.

Project	g1	g3	t2	t3	s1	s2	s3	h2	h3
P1	VL, VL, VL	VL, L, L	MH, M, M	MH, MH, M	ML, M, M	L, ML, M	ML, M, M	ML, M, M	M, M, ML
P2	VL, VL, VL	ML, L, ML	MH, MH, H	MH, M, H	M, M, MH	ML, M, M	H, H, VH	M, M, MH	M, H, MH
P3	VL, VL, L	L, L, L	MH, MH, MH	M, M, MH	M, M, M	ML, M, M	H, MH, H	M, M, M	MH, H, MH
P4	L, L, VL	L, VL, ML	M, MH, MH	M, M, MH	MH, M, MH	M, MH, M	H, MH, M	ML, M, ML	M, M, MH
P5	L, L, VL	L, VL, ML	M, MH, MH	M, MH, MH	M, M, MH	M, MH, M	M, M, MH	M, M, MH	M, MH, M
P6	VL, VL, L	ML, L, ML	MH, H, MH	M, H, MH	MH, H, M	MH, M, MH	M, MH, MH	M, M, MH	M, M, MH
P7	VL, L, VL	M, ML, L	ML, L, L	ML, ML, L	M, M, M	M, MH, H	ML, M, M	ML, ML, M	MH, MH, M
P8	VL, VL, VL	L, VL, ML	VL, L, VL	VL, L, ML	ML, M, MH	H, H, MH	M, M, MH	L, L, ML	M, M, MH
P9	L, VL, VL	ML, M, ML	L, L, L	L, VL, L	ML, ML, M	M, M, MH	MH, M, H	ML, ML, M	M, M, M
P10	VL, L, VL	M, M, L	ML, L, ML	ML, ML, ML	MH, M, MH	MH, M, MH	M, M, MH	ML, M, ML	ML, M, M
P11	VL, VL, VL	L, ML, L	L, L, VL	L, VL, VL	M, ML, MH	M, M, MH	ML, M, M	M, M, ML	M, M, ML
P12	ML, L, ML	M, MH, M	M, M, MH	M, MH, MH	MH, H, M	M, MH, MH	MH, M, M	MH, MH, M	L, L, ML
P13	L, VL, ML	ML, M, M	ML, M, ML	ML, MH, ML	ML, L, L	MH, H, M	M, ML, M	MH, M, M	ML, ML, L
P14	ML, VL, VL	M, M, M	ML, M, MH	ML, MH, MH	ML, ML, ML	MH, MH, H	M, M, M	M, M, M	ML, M, M
P15	L, L, ML	ML, ML, M	M, M, MH	M, M, MH	L, ML, M	M, M, H	M, M, ML	MH, M, MH	M, M, ML

The linguistic variables are transformed into IT2FSs using the following mapping relations, as shown in Table 7.6.

Table 7.6 Linguistic variables and their corresponding IT2FSs [71].

Linguistic variables	Trapezoidal IT2FSs
Very Low (VL)	(0, 0, 0, 0.1; 1, 1), (0, 0, 0, 0.05; 0.9, 0.9)
Low (L)	(0, 0.1, 0.1, 0.3; 1, 1), (0.05, 0.1, 0.1, 0.2; 0.9, 0.9)
Medium Low (ML)	(0.1, 0.3, 0.3, 0.5; 1, 1), (0.2, 0.3, 0.3, 0.4; 0.9, 0.9)
Medium (M)	(0.3, 0.5, 0.5, 0.7; 1, 1), (0.4, 0.5, 0.5, 0.6; 0.9, 0.9)
Medium high (MH)	(0.5, 0.7, 0.7, 0.9; 1, 1), (0.6, 0.7, 0.7, 0.8; 0.9, 0.9)
High (H)	(0.7, 0.9, 0.9, 1; 1, 1), (0.8, 0.9, 0.9, 0.95; 0.9, 0.9)
Very High (VL)	(0.9, 1, 1, 1; 1, 1), (0.95, 1, 1, 1; 0.9, 0.9)

Then, the IT2FWA is adopted based on Eq. (7-4) to aggregate the different opinions of experts. The normalized decision matrix can be obtained, as shown in Appendix B.

Subsequently, experts individually make the importance comparison of the criteria, as shown in Table 7.7 to Table 7.11. Consistency check is carried out using Eq. (7-2) to Eq. (7-4), and results show that all the comparison matrixes pass the consistency test.

Table 7.7 Importance comparison of the criteria within green development strategy.

Criteria	g1	g2	g3
g1	E, E, E	VS, VS, FS	FS, SS, FS
g2	1/VS, 1/VS, 1/FS	E, E, E	1/FS, 1/FS, 1/SS
g3	1/FS, 1/SS, 1/FS	FS, FS, SS	E, E, E

Table 7.8 Importance comparison of the criteria within benefit maximization strategy.

Criteria	b1	b2	b3
b1	E, E, E	FS, SS, FS	SS, FS, SS
b2	1/FS, 1/SS, 1/FS	E, E, E	E, 1/SS, SS
b3	1/SS, 1/FS, 1/SS	E, SS, 1/SS	E, E, E

Table 7.9 Importance comparison of the criteria within technological innovation strategy.

Criteria	t1	t2	t3
t1	E, E, E	FS, FS, SS	SS, SS, SS
t2	1/FS, 1/FS, 1/SS	E, E, E	E, E, E
t3	1/SS, 1/SS, 1/SS	E, E, E	E, E, E

Table 7.10 Importance comparison of the criteria within stable development strategy.

Criteria	s1	s2	s3
s1	E, E, E	SS, SS, E	E, E, SS
s2	1/SS, 1/SS, E	E, E, E	E, E, E
s3	E, E, 1/SS	E, E, E	E, E, E

Table 7.11 Importance comparison of the criteria within harmonious development strategy.

Criteria	h1	h2	h3
h1	E, E, E	FS, FS, VS	E, SS, E
h2	1/FS, 1/FS, 1/VS	E, E, E	1/FS, 1/FS, 1/SS
h3	E, 1/SS, E	FS, FS, SS	E, E, E

Following this, the fuzzy weights of these criteria are calculated using Eq. (7-5) to Eq. (7-6)and are given in Table 7.12.

Table 7.12 Fuzzy weights of the criteria.

Criteria	Fuzzy weight
g1	((0.37, 0.52, 0.91, 1.24; 1, 1), (0.40, 0.55, 0.86, 1.15; 0.8, 0.8))
g2	((0.05, 0.06, 0.11, 0.16; 1, 1), (0.05, 0.06, 0.10, 0.14; 0.8, 0.8))
g3	((0.12, 0.17, 0.32, 0.48; 1, 1), (0.13, 0.18, 0.30, 0.43; 0.8, 0.8))
b1	((0.27, 0.45, 0.93, 1.38; 1, 1), (0.31, 0.49, 0.87, 1.26; 0.8, 0.8))
b2	((0.09, 0.12, 0.24, 0.40; 1, 1), (0.09, 0.13, 0.22, 0.35; 0.8, 0.8))
b3	((0.09, 0.13, 0.26, 0.45; 1, 1), (0.10, 0.13, 0.24, 0.39; 0.8, 0.8))
t1	((0.26, 0.44, 0.90, 1.31; 1, 1), (0.29, 0.48, 0.84, 1.21; 0.8, 0.8))

Continued

Criteria	Fuzzy weight
t2	((0.11, 0.14, 0.22, 0.33; 1, 1), (0.12, 0.14, 0.21, 0.30; 0.8, 0.8))
t3	((0.12, 0.15, 0.26, 0.42; 1, 1), (0.12, 0.16, 0.24, 0.37; 0.8, 0.8))
s1	((0.27, 0.37, 0.56, 0.67; 1, 1), (0.29, 0.39, 0.54, 0.65; 0.8, 0.8))
s2	((0.19, 0.22, 0.30, 0.39; 1, 1), (0.20, 0.22, 0.29, 0.37; 0.8, 0.8))
s3	((0.23, 0.25, 0.32, 0.39; 1, 1), (0.23, 0.26, 0.32, 0.38; 0.8, 0.8))
h1	((0.32, 0.43, 0.65, 0.82; 1, 1), (0.35, 0.45, 0.63, 0.78; 0.8, 0.8))
h2	((0.06, 0.07, 0.12, 0.18; 1, 1), (0.06, 0.08, 0.11, 0.16; 0.8, 0.8))
h3	((0.23, 0.30, 0.48, 0.64; 1, 1), (0.24, 0.31, 0.46, 0.60; 0.8, 0.8))

Based on the performances of the projects on criteria and the weights of criteria, the performances of the alternative on the five strategic objectives are aggregated using the IT2FWA operator and are shown in Table 7.13.

Table 7.13 Performances of the alternatives on the five strategic objectives.

	Green development strategy (G)	Benefit maximization strategy (B)	Technological innovation strategy (T)	Stable development strategy (S)	Harmonious development strategy (H)
P1	((0.102, 0.171, 0.320, 0.636; 1, 1), (0.12, 0.18, 0.3, 0.501; 0.8, 0.8))	((0.301, 0.494, 1.018, 1.533; 1, 1), (0.344, 0.534, 0.952, 1.393; 0.8, 0.8))	((0.222, 0.394, 0.739, 1.258; 1, 1), (0.265, 0.421, 0.691, 1.076; 0.8, 0.8))	((0.142, 0.334, 0.471, 0.866; 1, 1), (0.217, 0.347, 0.459, 0.697; 0.8, 0.8))	((0.317, 0.495, 0.769, 1.166; 1, 1), (0.371, 0.518, 0.739, 1.019; 0.8, 0.8))
P2	((0.118, 0.190, 0.355, 0.732; 1, 1), (0.137, 0.198, 0.33, 0.563; 0.8, 0.8))	((0.407, 0.632, 1.291, 2.013; 1, 1), (0.451, 0.678, 1.2, 1.805; 0.8, 0.8))	((0.209, 0.44, 0.826, 1.383; 1, 1), (0.297, 0.469, 0.773, 1.192; 0.8, 0.8))	((0.32, 0.538, 0.746, 1.151; 1, 1), (0.398, 0.559, 0.73, 0.998; 0.8, 0.8))	((0.191, 0.316, 0.494, 0.814; 1, 1), (0.232, 0.334, 0.474, 0.685; 0.8, 0.8))
P3	((0.121, 0.214, 0.399, 0.805; 1, 1), (0.148, 0.224, 0.372, 0.626; 0.8, 0.8))	((0.337, 0.523, 1.068, 1.668; 1, 1), (0.374, 0.560, 0.993, 1.495; 0.8, 0.8))	((0.251, 0.44, 0.826, 1.383; 1, 1), (0.297, 0.469, 0.773, 1.192; 0.8, 0.8))	((0.271, 0.489, 0.676, 1.093; 1, 1), (0.351, 0.507, 0.662, 0.929; 0.8, 0.8))	((0.199, 0.337, 0.527, 0.855; 1, 1), (0.245, 0.355, 0.505, 0.725; 0.8, 0.8))
P4	((0.107, 0.209, 0.388, 0.826; 1, 1), (0.138, 0.22, 0.363, 0.63; 0.8, 0.8))	((0.367, 0.576, 1.178, 1.819; 1, 1), (0.408, 0.62, 1.097, 1.637; 0.8, 0.8))	((0.287, 0.504, 0.962, 1.58; 1, 1), (0.338, 0.539, 0.899, 1.374; 0.8, 0.8))	((0.286, 0.517, 0.727, 1.182; 1, 1), (0.371, 0.536, 0.709, 1.04; 0.8, 0.8))	((0.131, 0.246, 0.389, 0.68; 1, 1), (0.17, 0.259, 0.372, 0.559; 0.8, 0.8))
P5	((0.106, 0.209, 0.387, 0.824; 1, 1), (0.137, 0.219, 0.362, 0.629; 0.8, 0.8))	((0.239, 0.367, 0.748, 1.179; 1, 1), (0.264, 0.392, 0.695, 1.053; 0.8, 0.8))	((0.23, 0.404, 0.754, 1.28; 1, 1), (0.273, 0.43, 0.705, 1.096; 0.8, 0.8))	((0.253, 0.476, 0.669, 1.112; 1, 1), (0.336, 0.493, 0.652, 0.972; 0.8, 0.8))	((0.311, 0.487, 0.755, 1.148; 1, 1), (0.366, 0.511, 0.726, 1.001; 0.8, 0.8))
P6	((0.084, 0.167, 0.311, 0.707; 1, 1), (0.11, 0.176, 0.291, 0.526; 0.8, 0.8))	((0.357, 0.563, 1.153, 1.774; 1, 1), (0.398, 0.607, 1.073, 1.598; 0.8, 0.8))	((0.23, 0.404, 0.757, 1.272; 1, 1), (0.273, 0.431, 0.707, 1.095; 0.8, 0.8))	((0.317, 0.557, 0.784, 1.231; 1, 1), (0.403, 0.577, 0.764, 1.097; 0.8, 0.8))	((0.396, 0.6, 0.926, 1.363; 1, 1), (0.458, 0.63, 0.892, 1.207; 0.8, 0.8))

Continued

	Green development strategy (G)	Benefit maximization strategy (B)	Technological innovation strategy (T)	Stable development strategy (S)	Harmonious development strategy (H)
P7	((0.066, 0.143, 0.266, 0.641; 1, 1), (0.09, 0.151, 0.249, 0.467; 0.8, 0.8))	((0.303, 0.484, 0.995, 1.506; 1, 1), (0.338, 0.526, 0.927, 1.364; 0.8, 0.8))	((0.012, 0.058, 0.097, 0.303; 1, 1), (0.03, 0.061, 0.091, 0.203; 0.8, 0.8))	((0.23, 0.447, 0.629, 1.054; 1, 1), (0.313, 0.462, 0.612, 0.882; 0.8, 0.8))	((0.2, 0.34, 0.528, 0.854; 1, 1), (0.246, 0.356, 0.508, 0.725; 0.8, 0.8))
P8	((0.104, 0.172, 0.322, 0.653; 1, 1), (0.122, 0.18, 0.301, 0.509; 0.8, 0.8))	((0.135, 0.185, 0.37, 0.625; 1, 1), (0.14, 0.195, 0.34, 0.545; 0.8, 0.8))	((0.242, 0.428, 0.867, 1.382; 1, 1), (0.278, 0.466, 0.809, 1.22; 0.8, 0.8))	((0.286, 0.51, 0.711, 1.145; 1, 1), (0.37, 0.526, 0.693, 1.014; 0.8, 0.8))	((0.169, 0.294, 0.459, 0.762; 1, 1), (0.21, 0.307, 0.441, 0.639; 0.8, 0.8))
P9	((0.067, 0.143, 0.265, 0.654; 1, 1), (0.091, 0.15, 0.248, 0.472; 0.8, 0.8))	((0.3, 0.47, 0.961, 1.484; 1, 1), (0.333, 0.506, 0.895, 1.335; 0.8, 0.8))	((0.065, 0.134, 0.264, 0.524; 1, 1), (0.082, 0.145, 0.247, 0.418; 0.8, 0.8))	((0.214, 0.419, 0.578, 1.004; 1, 1) (0.293, 0.432, 0.565, 0.867; 0.8, 0.8))	((0.121, 0.232, 0.37, 0.658; 1, 1), (0.158, 0.244, 0.354, 0.538; 0.8, 0.8))
P10	((0.07, 0.146, 0.271, 0.648; 1, 1), (0.094, 0.153, 0.254, 0.473; 0.8, 0.8))	((0.358, 0.55, 1.121, 1.767; 1, 1), (0.396, 0.587, 1.042, 1.579; 0.8, 0.8))	((0.149, 0.298, 0.579, 1.008; 1, 1), (0.187, 0.321, 0.541, 0.853; 0.8, 0.8))	((0.284, 0.515, 0.726, 1.182; 1, 1) (0.369, 0.534, 0.707, 1.039; 0.8, 0.8))	((0.191, 0.326, 0.513, 0.841; 1, 1), (0.234, 0.341, 0.492, 0.711; 0.8, 0.8))
P11	((0.076, 0.142, 0.267, 0.588; 1, 1), (0.095, 0.15, 0.25, 0.445; 0.8, 0.8))	((0.21, 0.304, 0.614, 1.004; 1, 1), (0.225, 0.322, 0.568, 0.886; 0.8, 0.8))	((0.26, 0.454, 0.923, 1.457; 1, 1), (0.296, 0.495, 0.862, 1.317; 0.8, 0.8))	((0.204, 0.418, 0.589, 1.015; 1, 1), (0.286, 0.432, 0.573, 0.839; 0.8, 0.8))	((0.221, 0.365, 0.572, 0.918; 1, 1), (0.266, 0.382, 0.549, 0.783; 0.8, 0.8))
P12	((0.097, 0.248, 0.448, 0.983; 1, 1), (0.148, 0.259, 0.419, 0.622; 0.8, 0.8))	((0.323, 0.504, 1.032, 1.598; 1, 1), (0.359, 0.543, 0.96, 1.436; 0.8, 0.8))	((0.179, 0.321, 0.589, 1.039; 1, 1), (0.217, 0.341, 0.551, 0.874; 0.8, 0.8))	((0.317, 0.557, 0.784, 1.231; 1, 1), (0.403, 0.577, 0.764, 1.097; 0.8, 0.8))	((0.336, 0.516, 0.81, 1.145; 1, 1), (0.388, 0.54, 0.777, 1.057; 0.8, 0.8))
P13	((0.074, 0.187, 0.341, 0.797; 1, 1), (0.112, 0.196, 0.32, 0.586; 0.8, 0.8))	((0.355, 0.55, 1.124, 1.751; 1, 1), (0.393, 0.592, 1.045, 1.571; 0.8, 0.8))	((0.198, 0.373, 0.718, 1.217; 1, 1), (0.241, 0.401, 0.671, 1.043; 0.8, 0.8))	((0.145, 0.309, 0.422, 0.818; 1, 1), (0.212, 0.317, 0.412, 0.647; 0.8, 0.8))	((0.252, 0.403, 0.639, 0.93; 1, 1), (0.296, 0.422, 0.611, 0.852; 0.8, 0.8)
P14	((0.078, 0.173, 0.316, 0.72; 1, 1), (0.109, 0.181, 0.295, 0.533; 0.8, 0.8))	((0.389, 0.605, 1.237, 1.926; 1, 1), (0.432, 0.649, 1.15, 1.728; 0.8, 0.8))	((0.207, 0.375, 0.707, 1.208; 1, 1), (0.249, 0.401, 0.661, 1.032; 0.8, 0.8))	((0.166, 0.361, 0.498, 0.907; 1, 1), (0.243, 0.372, 0.486, 0.735; 0.8, 0.8))	((0.102, 0.205, 0.332, 0.617; 1, 1), (0.136, 0.216, 0.316, 0.496; 0.8, 0.8))
P15	((0.091, 0.227, 0.414, 0.941; 1, 1), (0.136, 0.238, 0.388, 0.698; 0.8, 0.8))	((0.382, 0.594, 1.215, 1.886; 1, 1), (0.423, 0.64, 1.13, 1.694; 0.8, 0.8))	((0.236, 0.421, 0.797, 1.339; 1, 1), (0.281, 0.45, 0.745, 1.152; 0.8, 0.8))	((0.172, 0.359, 0.496, 0.907; 1, 1), (0.246, 0.369, 0.484, 0.734; 0.8, 0.8))	((0.123, 0.175, 0.273, 0.398; 1, 1), (0.138, 0.187, 0.261, 0.354; 0.8, 0.8))

As for the determination of SICs, the linguistic variable is also adopted since it is much closer to the decision-maker's thinking mode and at the same time can alleviates decision-maker's working pressure. The SICs between two DEG projects on each strategic objective are identified, as shown in Fig. 7.4.

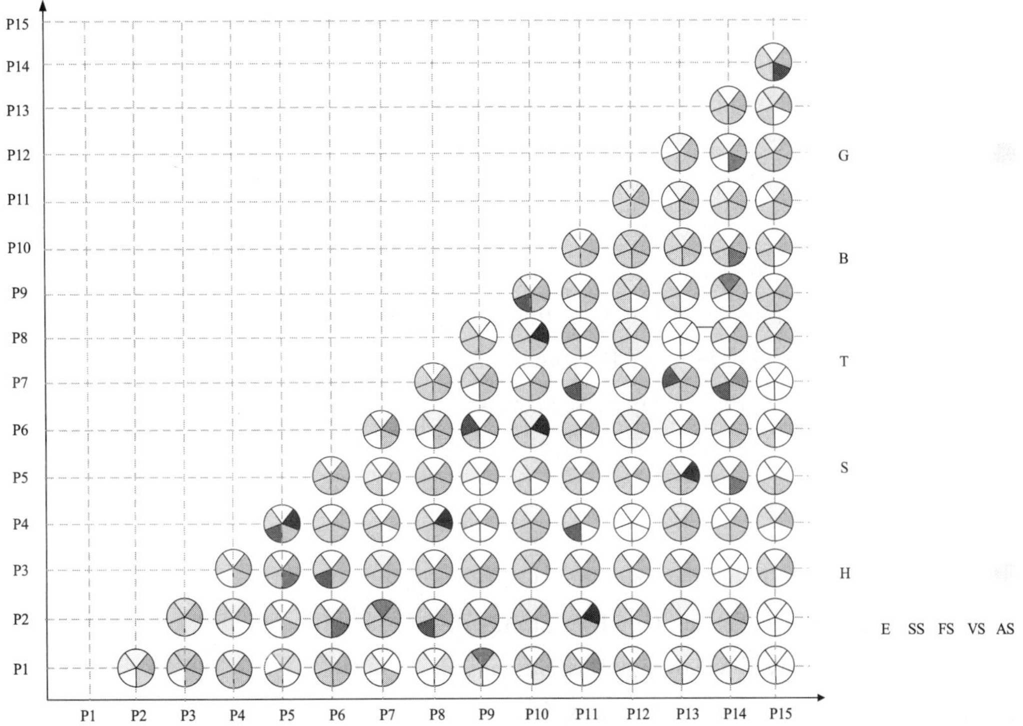

Fig. 7.4 SIC between two DEG projects on each strategic objective.

Considering the strategic interactions, a nonlinear 0-1 programming is established, in which various strategic objectives is optimized, subject to total cost constraints. It is formulated as follows:

$$\max\left\{\left(\sum_{i=1}^{n}\tilde{\tilde{V}}_i^k x_i+\sum_{i=1}^{n}\sum_{j=1,j>i}^{n}s_{ij}{}^k(\tilde{\tilde{V}}_i^k+\tilde{\tilde{V}}_j^k)x_i x_j\right)\right\}$$

$$\text{s.t.}\begin{cases}\sum_{i=1}^{n}\tilde{\tilde{C}}_i x_i\leqslant C\\ x_i=\begin{cases}1,\ \text{selected}\\0,\ \text{not selected}\end{cases}\end{cases}\tag{7-7}$$

where the objective is to maximize the strategic objectives of a portfolio, and $\tilde{\tilde{V}}^k$ is the fuzzy value of project i in term of objective k, $(k=1,2,3,4,5)$. $s_{ij}{}^k$ is the SIC between two DEG projects on each strategic objective, which represents an additive benefit of joint implementation projects i and i. This issue is constrained by total cost C constraint, and $\tilde{\tilde{C}}_i$ represents the fuzzy investment cost of project i.

However, it is complex to solve a multi-objective model when it comes to fuzzy variables [58]. An effective solution is to apply a defuzzification technique to transform the current fuzzy variable into a determined variable. Thus, Eq. (7-2) is applied to remove the fuzziness.

4.3 Result

4.3.1 Strategic scenario analysis

In this section, the scenario series of implementing two or three strategic objectives are analyzed since these two kinds of scenarios are the most common among energy enterprises. Considering that there are five strategies, a total of 20 scenarios can be obtained as follows.

- Scenario series of implementing two strategic objectives:

Scenario 1: Strategy G & Strategy B; Scenario 2: Strategy G & Strategy T;

Scenario 3: Strategy G & Strategy S; Scenario 4: Strategy G & Strategy H;

Scenario 5: Strategy B & Strategy T; Scenario 6: Strategy B & Strategy S;

Scenario 7: Strategy B & Strategy H; Scenario 8: Strategy T & Strategy S;

Scenario 9: Strategy T & Strategy H; Scenario 10: Strategy S & Strategy H.

- Scenario series of implementing three strategic objectives:

Scenario 11: Strategy G & Strategy B & Strategy T;

Scenario 12: Strategy G & Strategy B & Strategy S;

Scenario 13: Strategy G & Strategy B & Strategy H;

Scenario 14: Strategy G & Strategy T & Strategy S;

Scenario 15: Strategy G & Strategy T & Strategy H;

Scenario 16: Strategy G & Strategy S & Strategy H;

Scenario 17: Strategy B & Strategy T & Strategy S;

Scenario 18: Strategy B & Strategy T & Strategy H;

Scenario 19: Strategy B & Strategy S & Strategy H;

Scenario 20: Strategy T & Strategy S & Strategy H.

Then, the data are inputted into the NSGA-II and the programming model is performed in environment of MATLAB 7.1. The results are shown in Fig. 7.5 and Fig.7.6.

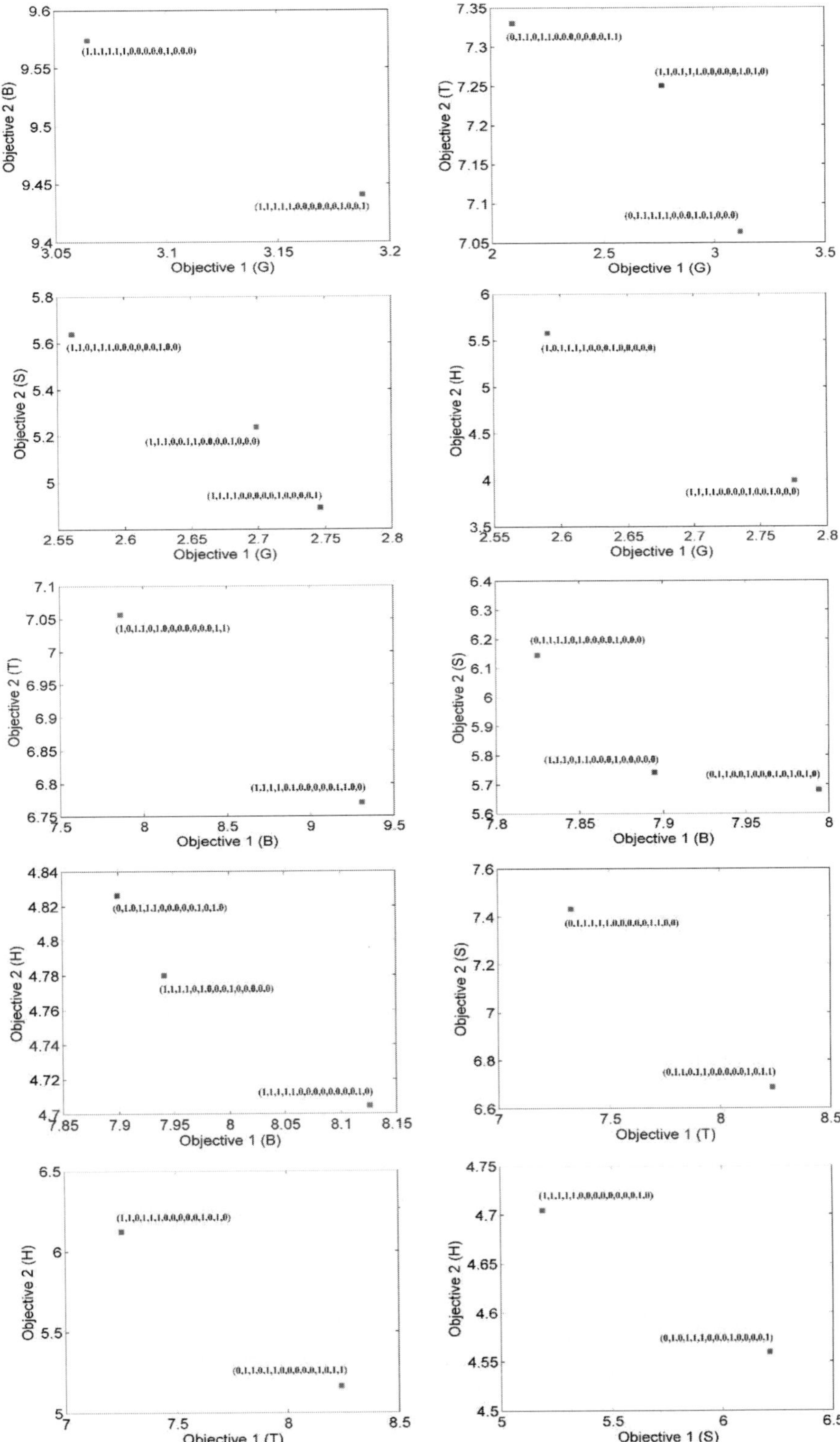

Fig.7.5 Pareto sets in the scenario series of implementing two strategic objectives (scenario 1-10).

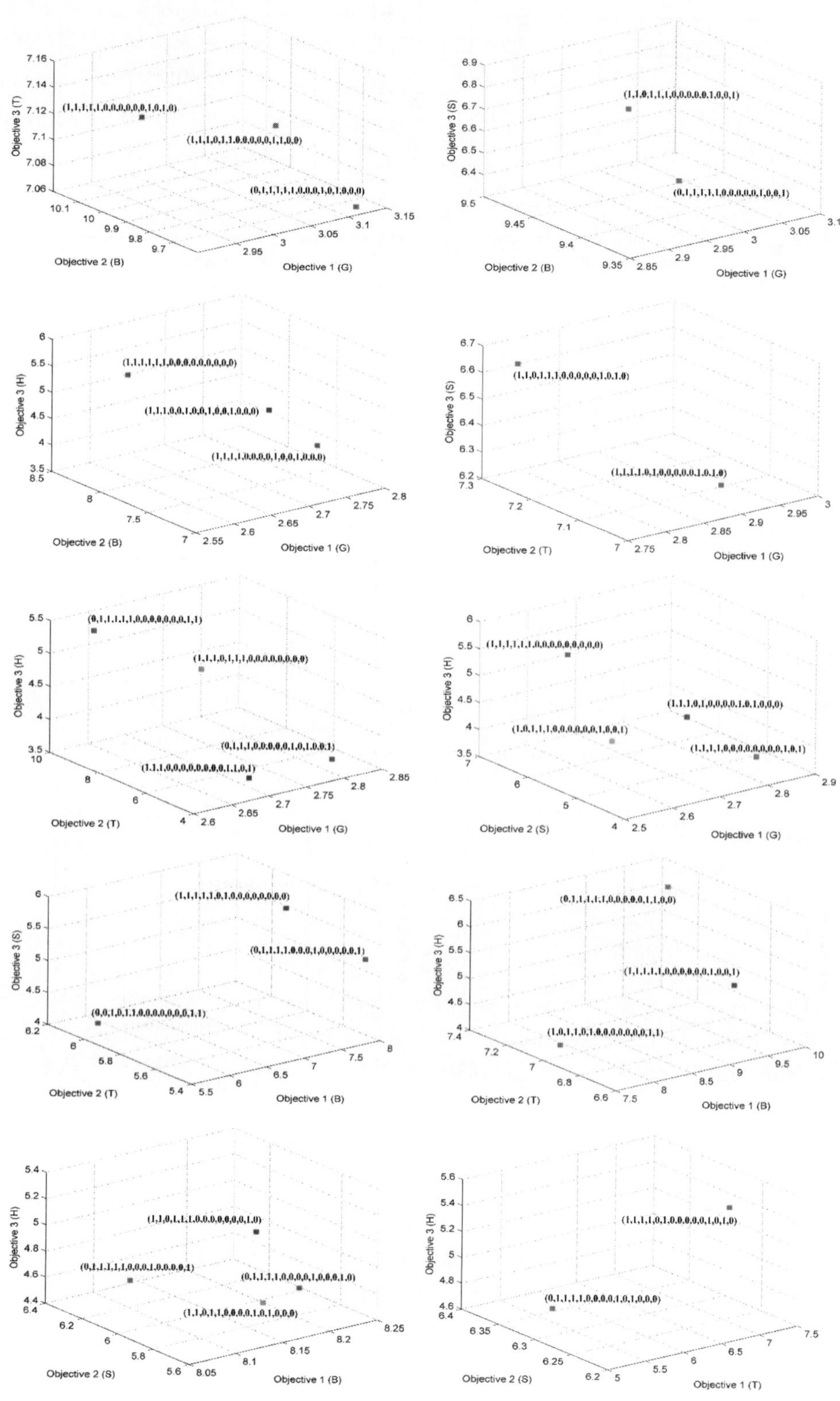

Fig. 7.6 Pareto sets in the scenario series of implementing two strategic objectives (scenario 11-20).

4.3.2 Comparative analysis

The main advantage of the proposed methods is that they can take into account the uncertainty, the project interaction, and the strategic alignment in the process of project portfolio selection. In order to highlight this advantage, a comparative analysis is carried out in this section. Different scenarios considering only one issue, two issues, and three issues are analyzed, as shown in Table 7.14. Given that there are many strategic combinations, this research takes the Strategy G & Strategy B (Scenario 1 in section 4.3) as an example.

Table 7.14 Scenario series of considering different issue combinations.

Scenario series	Uncertainty	Project interaction	Strategic alignment
Scenario I	√		
Scenario II		√	
Scenario III			√
Scenario IV	√	√	
Scenario V	√		√
Scenario VI		√	√
Scenario VII	√	√	√

In various scenarios, the programming models are different, which may lead to diverse results. The programming models in each scenario are presented as follows:

- Scenario I: Considering the uncertainty while ignoring the project interaction and strategic alignment.

Corresponding model: single-objective nondeterministic linear programming model [Eq. (7-8)].

$$\max\left\{\sum_{i=1}^{n}\tilde{\tilde{V}}_i\ x_i\right\}$$

$$\text{s.t.}\begin{cases}\sum_{i=1}^{n}\tilde{\tilde{C}}_i x_i \leqslant C \\ x_i=\begin{cases}1,\ \text{selected}\\0,\ \text{not selected}\end{cases}\end{cases} \tag{7-8}$$

- Scenario II: considering the project interaction while ignoring the uncertainty and strategic alignment.

Corresponding model: single-objective deterministic nonlinear programming model [Eq. (7-9)].

$$\max\left\{\left(\sum_{i=1}^{n} V_i x_i + \sum_{i=1}^{n}\sum_{j=1,j>i}^{n} s_{ij}(V_i + V_j)x_i x_j\right)\right\}$$
$$\text{s.t.}\begin{cases}\sum_{i=1}^{n} C_i x_i \leqslant C \\ x_i = \begin{cases}1, \text{ selected} \\ 0, \text{ not selected}\end{cases}\end{cases} \tag{7-9}$$

- Scenario III: considering the strategic alignment while ignoring the uncertainty and project interaction.

Corresponding model: mulit-objective deterministic linear 0-1 programming model [Eq. (7-10)].

$$\max\left\{\sum_{i=1}^{n} V_i^k x_i\right\}$$
$$\text{s.t.}\begin{cases}\sum_{i=1}^{n} C_i x_i \leqslant C \\ x_i = \begin{cases}1, \text{ selected} \\ 0, \text{ not selected}\end{cases}\end{cases} \tag{7-10}$$

- Scenario IV: considering the uncertainty and project interaction while ignoring the strategic alignment.

Corresponding model: single-objective nondeterministic nonlinear programming model [Eq. (7-11)].

$$\max\left\{\left(\sum_{i=1}^{n} \tilde{\tilde{V}}_i x_i + \sum_{i=1}^{n}\sum_{j=1,j>i}^{n} s_{ij}(\tilde{\tilde{V}}_i + \tilde{\tilde{V}}_j)x_i x_j\right)\right\}$$
$$\text{s.t.}\begin{cases}\sum_{i=1}^{n} \tilde{\tilde{C}}_i x_i \leqslant C \\ x_i = \begin{cases}1, \text{ selected} \\ 0, \text{ not selected}\end{cases}\end{cases} \tag{7-11}$$

- Scenario V: considering the uncertainty and strategic alignment while ignoring the project interaction.

Corresponding model: multi-objective nondeterministic linear programming model [Eq. (7-12)].

$$\max\left\{\sum_{i=1}^{n}\tilde{\tilde{V}}_i^k x_i\right\}$$

$$\text{s.t.}\begin{cases}\sum_{i=1}^{n}\tilde{\tilde{C}}_i x_i \leqslant C \\ x_i=\begin{cases}1, \text{ selected}\\ 0, \text{ not selected}\end{cases}\end{cases} \tag{7-12}$$

- Scenario VI: considering the project interaction and strategic alignment while ignoring the uncertainty.

Corresponding model: multi-objective deterministic nonlinear programming model [Eq. (7-13)].

$$\max\left\{\left(\sum_{i=1}^{n}V_i^k x_i+\sum_{i=1}^{n}\sum_{j=1,j>i}^{n}s_{ij}^k(V_i^k+V_j^k)x_i x_j\right)\right\}$$

$$\text{s.t.}\begin{cases}\sum_{i=1}^{n}C_i x_i \leqslant C \\ x_i=\begin{cases}1, \text{ selected}\\ 0, \text{ not selected}\end{cases}\end{cases} \tag{7-13}$$

- Scenario VII: considering the uncertainty, project interaction and strategic alignment.

Corresponding model: multi-objective nondeterministic nonlinear programming model [Eq. (7-7)].

The way to deal with the deterministic programming model is to use the crisp number instead of IT2FNs. Without loss of generality, the linguistic variables used to represent the project performance (VL, L, ML, M, MH, H, VL) are transformed into the crisp number from 0 to 1 with uniform spacing. The performances of the alternatives on the qualitative criteria in the form of crisp number are shown in Table 7.15. Moreover, the linguistic variables used to represent the criteria importance (E, SS, FS, VS, AS) are transformed into the crisp number from 1 to 5 with one interval. The weight vector of the selected criteria is calculated as $(0.295, 0.066, 0.140, 0.272, 0.112, 0.117)^{\mathrm{T}}$. The method of processing the single-objective programming model is to aggregate the criteria g1, g2, g3, b1, b2, b3 together rather than sub-objective aggregation.

Table 7.15 Performances of the alternatives on the qualitative criteria in the form of crisp number.

Project	g1	g3	t2	t3	s1	s2	s3	h2
P1	0	0.111	0.556	0.611	0.444	0.333	0.444	0.444
P2	0	0.278	0.723	0.667	0.556	0.444	0.889	0.556
P3	0.056	0.167	0.667	0.556	0.5	0.444	0.778	0.5
P4	0.111	0.167	0.611	0.556	0.611	0.556	0.667	0.389
P5	0.111	0.167	0.611	0.611	0.556	0.556	0.556	0.556

Continued

Project	g1	g3	t2	t3	s1	s2	s3	h2
P6	0.056	0.278	0.723	0.667	0.667	0.611	0.611	0.556
P7	0.056	0.333	0.222	0.278	0.5	0.667	0.444	0.389
P8	0	0.167	0.056	0.167	0.5	0.778	0.556	0.222
P9	0.056	0.389	0.167	0.111	0.389	0.556	0.667	0.389
P10	0.056	0.389	0.278	0.333	0.611	0.611	0.556	0.389
P11	0	0.222	0.111	0.056	0.5	0.556	0.444	0.444
P12	0.278	0.556	0.556	0.611	0.667	0.611	0.556	0.611
P13	0.167	0.444	0.389	0.444	0.222	0.667	0.444	0.556
P14	0.111	0.5	0.5	0.556	0.333	0.723	0.5	0.5
P15	0.222	0.389	0.556	0.556	0.333	0.611	0.444	0.611

The NSGA-II with the same parameters is performed in environment of MATLAB 7.1 to deal with the above programming models. The produced portfolio(s) and their objective function values of the seven scenarios are described in Fig.7.7.

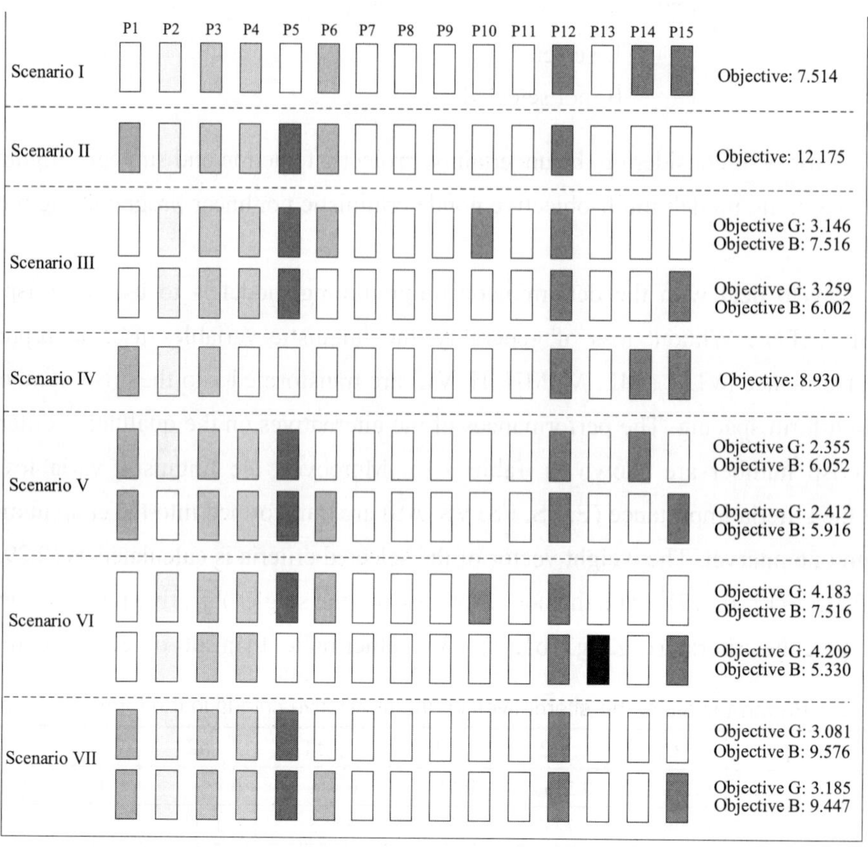

Fig. 7.7 Portfolios and their objective values of various scenarios.

From this figure, we compare the objective values between the scenario I, II and VI. It can be found in the comparison of the scenario I and VI that the project interactions produce synergistic benefits to increase the objective values. Therefore, ignoring the project interaction will underestimate the overall effectiveness of a portfolio. For this reason, the portfolio selected in the scenario I and VI are different from each other, which indicates that an abnormal result will take place because of neglecting the project interaction. An interesting phenomenon is that the uncertainty sometimes reduces the objective value when the objective values between scenario II and VI are compared. Similar phenomena can be observed from the scenario III and V. This is because various elements are still in the state of ambiguity in the early stage of project decision-making, which increases the risk of early decision-making. So, the uncertainty that provides enough flexibility for project portfolio selection cannot be ignored. Moreover, it can be also observed that one selected portfolio (1, 1, 1, 1, 1, 1, 0, 0, 0, 0, 0, 1, 0, 0, 1) in the scenario VII contains many portfolios in other scenarios, such as the portfolio (1, 1, 1, 1, 1, 1, 0, 0, 0, 0, 0, 0, 0, 0, 1) in scenario II.

Some more information can be excavated according to the frequency of the project occurrence. On the one hand, the project P2 and P4 occur in most scenarios with the frequency of 11, which means that these projects are up-and-coming. However, the two projects are not included in the scenario VI and V. On the other hand, the project P10 and P13 are rarely selected in most scenarios. However, the scenario III and the scenario VI include one or both of them. In both the cases, the selected portfolios obtained by these scenarios are unreasonable. The main reason for the situation is that the scenario III, V and VI fail to consider the uncertainty or the project interaction. The scenario VI does not take into account the strategic alignment. In effect, energy enterprise project portfolio selection is guided by its strategic objectives. Thus, ignoring the strategic alignment will lead to mistakes in decision-making.

It can be concluded that the results obtained from the scenario I-VI are undesired. By comparison, the scenario VII has achieved satisfactory results. These conclusions highlight the importance of considering uncertainty, project interaction and strategic alignment in the process of project portfolio selection. At the same time, the advantages of the proposed methods including the IT2FNs, SIC, and criteria system can be justified.

The above results can provide some ideas for real applications in project portfolio management. Firstly, various uncertain factor such as technical innovation or policy change cannot be predicted accurately due to the complexity of the environment. In general, the knowledge and experience of experts are used to assess these uncertain factors in this situation. The IT2FNs employed in this research can be used by experts to reflect the essence of the uncertainty entirely, and thus help project managers to understand these uncertain factors better. Secondly, the interaction between DEG projects such as wind-solar complementary is significant, which will significantly affect the results of portfolio selection. It is necessary for project managers to evaluate the project interaction reasonably. The proposed SIC is an effective tool to describe the degree of interaction between two DEG projects in a specific strategy. Thirdly, on the principle that the enterprise strategy determines investment directions, DMs of energy enterprise should establish an operable evaluation criteria system for their own strategic objectives. The established evaluation criteria system consisting of five strategies and fifteen criteria can serve as a valuable reference to for taking such measures.

5. Discussions

In order to reflect the criteria weights more intuitively, the fuzzy weights are defuzzified based on Eq. (7-2), the results are shown in Fig. 7.8. Among all the criteria, the weight of GHG emission reduction is the largest and has the most significant influence on the results of the project portfolio selection. The reason is that environmental problems are attracting increasing attention nowadays. This phenomenon also demonstrates that an energy enterprise should focus on GHG emission issues. Besides this criterion, some other important factors should also be considered in project investment such as LCOE and technology efficiency. LCOE is an essential index for the international energy industry to evaluate the economic benefits of power generation projects from the perspective of the life cycle. For the latter, the current distributed generation technology is not yet perfect, and the efficiency of power generation is the critical factor affecting the economic benefits of projects. Under this circumstance, LCOE and technology efficiency should be attached importance to as well.

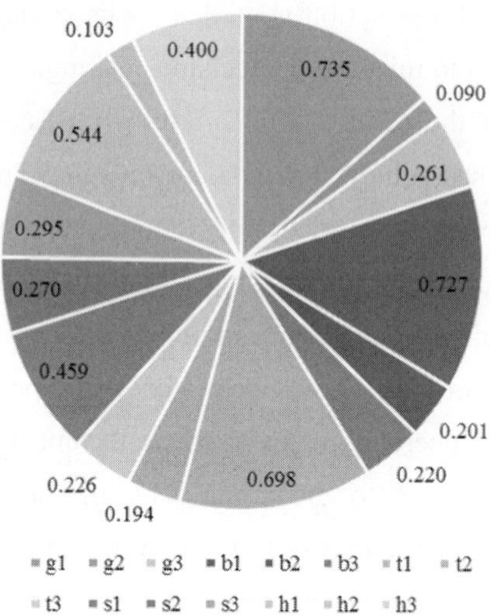

Fig. 7.8 Defuzzified weights of criteria.

Besides, the defuzzified values of DEG projects on each strategic objective can be obtained, as described vividly in Fig. 7.9. As can be seen, none of DEG performs equally well on all five strategic objectives. The project P12 ranks first within the context of green development strategy and stable development strategy while the project P6 holds absolute advantages regarding the stable development strategy and harmonious development strategy. Whereas, the project P2 is inclined towards the benefit maximization strategy. However, although these projects are promising, they may not be selected. For example, two of the three solutions in scenario 3, (1, 1, 1, 0, 0, 1, 1, 0, 0, 0, 0, 1, 0, 0, 0) and (1, 1, 0, 1, 1, 1, 0, 0, 0, 0, 0, 0, 1, 0, 0), do not include P12, although it performs well in green development strategy and stable development strategy. The reason is that the project portfolio selection requires more considerations of the project interaction and resource allocation than individual project selection, which is a main difference between the two.

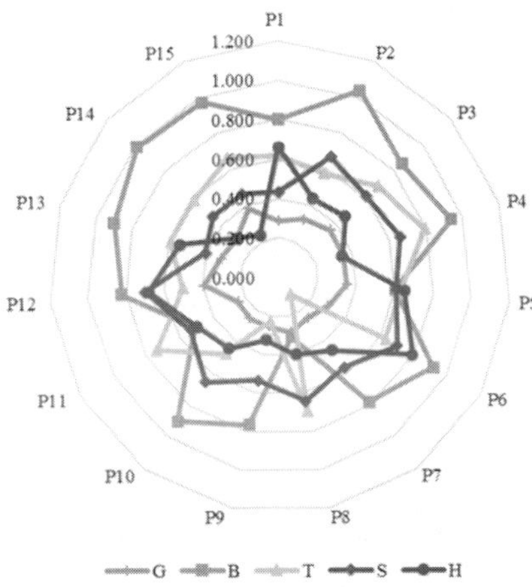

Fig. 7.9 Defuzzified values of DEG projects on each strategic objective.

From the results of scenario analysis, it can be seen that the Pareto sets are different under 20 scenario experiences. The importance of considering strategic objective is highlighted in the process of DEG project portfolio selection. Furthermore, it is not difficult to find that every portfolio is superior to some strategic objectives but is disadvantaged on other strategic objectives. Take scenario 1 as an example. The portfolio (1, 1, 1, 1, 1, 1, 0, 0, 0, 0, 0, 1, 0, 0, 0) is superior to another portfolio (1, 1, 1, 1, 1, 0, 0, 0, 0, 0, 0, 1, 0, 0, 1) under the objective of benefit maximization strategy, while the situation is opposite under the green development strategy. In this case, it is difficult to compare the two portfolios since the two strategic objectives are incomparable. In order to make further decisions, it is necessary to consider the preferences of the decision-makers on these two objectives.

6. Conclusions and managerial implications

With the outbreak of the distributed energy industry, the portfolio selection becomes essential for distributed energy generation projects in the case of limited resources. This paper aims to construct a hybrid multi-criteria decision-making method to select the optimal distributed energy generation project portfolio. First, five types of strategic objectives are identified including technological innovation strategy, green development strategy, harmonious development strategy, benefit maximization strategy and stable development strategy. Then, associated 15 crucial criteria are also identified. Subsequently, internal type-2 fuzzy numbers are adopted to represent the performance of each project on these criteria to describe the inherent uncertainties. After that, the criteria weights determined by internal type-2 fuzzy analytic hierarchy process method are incorporated into the interval type-2 fuzzy weighted averaging operator to obtain the strategic alignment index of each project. Last but not least, by considering the strategic interactions, a nonlinear integer programming is established, and the non-dominated sorting genetic algorithm-II is used to obtain the optimal distributed energy generation project portfolio under different strategic scenarios. To validate the practicability and effectiveness of the proposed framework, a case study is provided. The results show that the selected portfolios vary according to the enterprise strategic objectives. The research provides theoretical guidance for project manager in the practice of project portfolio management as well as offering a new idea for relative scholars to make more research on project portfolio management.

According to the evaluation results, some broader managerial implications can be deduced:

(1) For each strategic objective, various criteria should be considered. The realization of strategic goals is always complicated, which cannot be fully represented by a single criterion. In order to achieve comprehensiveness, various kinds of criteria must be taken into account simultaneously to decompose a strategic objective.

(2) Project portfolio selection is more difficult than single project selection. The former should consider the project interactions and resource allocation while the latter only needs to consider the project itself.

(3) To achieve enterprise strategic objectives, decision-makers and project managers should make the project portfolio coincident with enterprise strategic objectives in the process of project portfolio selection, especially in project-oriented enterprises.

(4) Project interactions at the strategic level have a significant impact on the project portfolio. If this issue is ignored, the reality of the results would reduce, and the probability of raising errors would also increase.

Acknowledgment: This project is supported by the 2017 Special Project of Cultivation and Development of Innovation Base (No. Z171100002217024), the Fundamental Research Funds for the Central Universities (No. 2017XS099) and (No. 2018ZD14), and the NCEPU "Double First-Class" Graduate Talent Cultivation Program. The authors would also like to thank Ph.D. Student Siyuan Huang from UCLA for his instructive advices on the writing of this manuscript.

Appendix A

Table A.1 The initial evaluation criteria system.

Factors	References								
	Kahraman, Kaya [72]	Büyüközkan and Güleryüz [73]	Haddad, Liazid [74]	Wu, Xu [75]	Amer and Daim [76]	Kaya and Kahraman [77]	Streimikiene, Balezentis [78]	Şengül, Eren [79]	Tasri and Susilawati [80]
Technology maturity	×	×	×	×	×	×	×		×
Technology efficiency	×	×		×	×	×	×		×
Capital cost	×		×	×		×	×	×	×
O &M cost	×		×	×		×	×	×	×
Job creation	×	×		×	×	×	×	×	×
GHG emission reduction	×	×	×	×	×	×		×	×
Social acceptance	×		×	×	×	×	×		×
Land requirement	×	×		×	×	×	×		×
Technology reliability		×	×	×		×	×		×
Operational life		×	×	×	×		×		
Impact on environment	×	×	×	×	×				
Social benefit			×			×	×		×
Levelized energy cost		×		×		×	×		
National energy security				×		×		×	×
Payback period		×	×				×		
Resource availability	×					×			×
Safety			×	×			×		
Net present value							×		×
Availability of funds	×	×		×					
Energy production capacity		×	×						
Compatibility to policy		×		×					×
Political accept		×	×	×					
Stress on ecosystem				×		×			×
Cost of grid connection				×				×	
Installed capacity		×							x
Lead time	×				×				
deployment time				×		×			
Expert human resource				×		×			
R & D cost				×		×			
Technology cost					×				×
Contribution to economy		×		×					
Primary energy ratio							×		
Grid connectivity	×					×			

Continued

Factors	References								
	Kahraman, Kaya [72]	Büyüközkan and Güleryüz [73]	Haddad, Liazid [74]	Wu, Xu [75]	Amer and Daim [76]	Kaya and Kahraman [77]	Streimikiene, Balezentis [78]	Şengül, Eren [79]	Tasri and Susilawati [80]
Impact on human health				×				×	
Need of waste disposal		×		×					
Electricity supply availability				×					
Ease of decentralization				×					
Network stability				×					
Reserves /production ratio									
Peak load response								×	
Feed-in tariff rate					×				
Financial structure									×
Affordability		×							
Market maturity				×					
Site advantage				×					
Severe accidents								×	
Noise							×		
Benefit to national economy						×			

Appendix B

Table B.1 The normalized decision matrix (1).

	g1	g2	g3
P1	((0, 0, 0, 0.1; 1, 1), (0, 0, 0, 0.05; 0.9, 0.9))	((0.199, 0.199, 0.199, 0.199; 1, 1), (0.199, 0.199, 0.199, 0.199; 1, 1))	((0.767, 0.933, 0.933, 1; 1, 1) (0.85, 0.933, 0.933, 0.967; 0.9, 0.9))
P2	((0, 0, 0, 0.1; 1, 1), (0, 0, 0, 0.05; 0.9, 0.9))	((1, 1, 1, 1; 1, 1), (1, 1, 1, 1; 1, 1))	((0.567, 0.767, 0.767, 0.933; 1, 1), (0.667, 0.767, 0.767, 0.85; 0.9, 0.9))
P3	((0, 0.033, 0.033, 0.167; 1, 1), (0.017, 0.033, 0.033, 0.1; 0.9, 0.9))	((0.734, 0.734, 0.734, 0.734; 1, 1), (0.734, 0.734, 0.734, 0.734; 1, 1))	((0.7, 0.9, 0.9, 1; 1, 1), (0.8, 0.9, 0.9, 0.95; 0.9, 0.9))
P4	((0, 0.067, 0.067, 0.233; 1, 1), (0.033, 0.067, 0.067, 0.15; 0.9, 0.9))	((0.453, 0.453, 0.453, 0.453; 1, 1), (0.453, 0.453, 0.453, 0.453; 1, 1))	((0.7, 0.867, 0.867, 0.967; 1, 1), (0.783, 0.867, 0.867, 0.917; 0.9, 0.9))
P5	((0, 0.067, 0.067, 0.233; 1, 1), (0.033, 0.067, 0.067, 0.15; 0.9, 0.9))	((0.443, 0.443, 0.443, 0.443; 1, 1), (0.443, 0.443, 0.443, 0.443; 1, 1))	(0.7, 0.867, 0.867, 0.967; 1, 1), (0.783, 0.867, 0.867, 0.917; 0.9, 0.9)
P6	((0, 0.033, 0.033, 0.167; 1, 1), (0.017, 0.033, 0.033 0.1; 0.9, 0.9))	((0.324, 0.324, 0.324, 0.324; 1, 1), (0.324, 0.324, 0.324, 0.324; 1, 1))	((0.567, 0.767, 0.767, 0.933; 1, 1), (0.667, 0.767, 0.767, 0.85; 0.9, 0.9))
P7	((0, 0.033, 0.033, 0.167; 1, 1), (0.017, 0.033, 0.033 0.1; 0.9, 0.9))	((0.111, 0.111, 0.111, 0.111; 1, 1), (0.111, 0.111, 0.111, 0.111; 1, 1))	((0.5, 0.7, 0.7, 0.867; 1, 1) (0.6, 0.7, 0.7 0.783; 0.9, 0.9))

Continued

	g1	g2	g3
P8	((0, 0, 0, 0.1; 1, 1), (0, 0, 0, 0.05; 0.9, 0.9))	((0.405, 0.405, 0.405, 0.405; 1, 1), (0.405, 0.405, 0.405, 0.405; 1, 1))	((0.7, 0.867, 0.867, 0.967; 1, 1), (0.783, 0.867, 0.867, 0.917; 0.9, 0.9))
P9	((0, 0.033, 0.033, 0.167; 1, 1), (0.017, 0.033, 0.033 0.1; 0.9, 0.9))	((0.297, 0.297, 0.297, 0.297; 1, 1), (0.297, 0.297, 0.297, 0.297; 1, 1))	((0.433, 0.633, 0.633 0.833; 1, 1), (0.533, 0.633, 0.633, 0.733; 0.9, 0.9))
P10	((0, 0.033, 0.033, 0.167; 1, 1), (0.017, 0.033, 0.033 0.1; 0.9, 0.9))	((0.353, 0.353, 0.353, 0.353; 1, 1), (0.353, 0.353, 0.353, 0.353; 1, 1))	((0.433, 0.633, 0.633, 0.8; 1, 1) (0.533, 0.633, 0.633, 0.717; 0.9, 0.9))
P11	((0, 0, 0, 0.1; 1, 1), (0, 0, 0, 0.05; 0.9, 0.9))	((0, 0, 0, 0; 1, 1), (0, 0, 0, 0; 1, 1))	((0.633, 0.833, 0.833, 0.967; 1, 1), (0.733, 0.833, 0.833, 0.9; 0.9, 0.9))
P12	((0.067, 0.233, 0.233, 0.433; 1, 1), (0.15, 0.233, 0.233 0.233; 0.9, 0.9))	((0.889, 0.889, 0.889, 0.889; 1, 1), (0.889, 0.889, 0.889, 0.889; 1, 1))	((0.233, 0.433, 0.433, 0.633; 1, 1), (0.333, 0.433, 0.433, 0.533; 0.9, 0.9))
P13	((0.033, 0.133, 0.133, 0.3; 1, 1), (0.083, 0.133, 0.133 0.217; 0.9, 0.9))	((0.353, 0.353, 0.353, 0.353; 1, 1), (0.353, 0.353, 0.353, 0.353; 1, 1))	((0.367, 0.567, 0.567, 0.767; 1, 1) (0.467, 0.567, 0.567, 0.667; 0.9, 0.9))
P14	((0.033, 0.1, 0.1, 0.233; 1, 1), (0.067, 0.1, 0.1, 0.167; 0.9, 0.9))	((0.594, 0.594, 0.594, 0.594; 1, 1), (0.594, 0.594, 0.594, 0.594; 1, 1))	((0.3, 0.5, 0.5, 0.7; 1, 1) (0.4, 0.5, 0.5, 0.6; 0.9, 0.9))
P15	((0.033, 0.167, 0.167, 0.367; 1, 1), ((0.1, 0.167, 0.167, 0.267; 0.9, 0.9)	((0.541, 0.541, 0.541, 0.541; 1, 1), (0.541, 0.541, 0.541, 0.541; 1, 1))	((0.433, 0.633, 0.633 0.833; 1, 1), (0.533, 0.633, 0.633, 0.733; 0.9, 0.9))

Table B.2 The normalized decision matrix (2).

	b1	b2	b3
P1	((1, 1, 1, 1; 1, 1), (1, 1, 1, 1; 1, 1))	((0, 0, 0, 0; 1, 1), (0, 0, 0, 0; 1, 1))	((0.34, 0.34, 0.34, 0.34; 1, 1), (0.34, 0.34, 0.34, 0.34; 1, 1))
P2	((0.895, 0.895, 0.895, 0.895; 1, 1), (0.895, 0.895, 0.895, 0.895; 1, 1))	((1, 1, 1, 1; 1, 1), (1, 1, 1, 1; 1, 1))	((0.84, 0.84, 0.84, 0.84; 1, 1), (0.84, 0.84, 0.84, 0.84; 1, 1))
P3	((0.729, 0.729, 0.729, 0.729; 1, 1), (0.729, 0.729, 0.729, 0.729; 1, 1))	((0.8, 0.8, 0.8, 0.8; 1, 1), (0.8, 0.8, 0.8, 0.8; 1, 1))	((0.76, 0.76, 0.76, 0.76; 1, 1), (0.76, 0.76, 0.76, 0.76; 1, 1))
P4	((0.9, 0.9, 0.9, 0.9; 1, 1), (0.9, 0.9, 0.9, 0.9; 1, 1))	((0.88, 0.88, 0.88, 0.88; 1, 1), (0.88, 0.88, 0.88, 0.88; 1, 1))	((0.5, 0.5, 0.5, 0.5; 1, 1), (0.5, 0.5, 0.5, 0.5; 1, 1))
P5	((0.465, 0.465, 0.465, 0.465; 1, 1), (0.465, 0.465, 0.465, 0.465; 1, 1))	((0.6, 0.6, 0.6, 0.6; 1, 1), (0.6, 0.6, 0.6, 0.6; 1, 1))	((0.66, 0.66, 0.66, 0.66; 1, 1), (0.66, 0.66, 0.66, 0.66; 1, 1))
P6	((0.910, 0.910, 0.910, 0.910; 1, 1), (0.910, 0.910, 0.910, 0.910; 1, 1))	((0.8, 0.8, 0.8, 0.8; 1, 1), (0.8, 0.8, 0.8, 0.8; 1, 1))	((0.44, 0.44, 0.44, 0.44; 1, 1), (0.44, 0.44, 0.44, 0.44; 1, 1))
P7	((0.894, 0.894, 0.894, 0.894; 1, 1), (0.894, 0.894, 0.894, 0.894; 1, 1))	((0.68, 0.68, 0.68, 0.68; 1, 1), (0.68, 0.68, 0.68, 0.68; 1, 1))	((0, 0, 0, 0; 1, 1), (0, 0, 0, 0; 1, 1))
P8	((0, 0, 0, 0; 1, 1), (0, 0, 0, 0; 1, 1))	((1, 1, 1, 1; 1, 1), (1, 1, 1, 1; 1, 1))	((0.5, 0.5, 0.5, 0.5; 1, 1), (0.5, 0.5, 0.5, 0.5; 1, 1))
P9	((0.736, 0.736, 0.736, 0.736; 1, 1), (0.736, 0.736, 0.736, 0.736; 1, 1))	((0.72, 0.72, 0.72, 0.72; 1, 1), (0.72, 0.72, 0.72, 0.72; 1, 1))	((0.4, 0.4, 0.4, 0.4; 1, 1), (0.4, 0.4, 0.4, 0.4; 1, 1))
P10	((0.699, 0.699, 0.699, 0.699; 1, 1), (0.699, 0.699, 0.699, 0.699; 1, 1))	((0.88, 0.88, 0.88, 0.88; 1, 1), (0.88, 0.88, 0.88, 0.88; 1, 1))	((1, 1, 1, 1; 1, 1), (1, 1, 1, 1; 1, 1))

Continued

	b1	b2	b3
P11	((0.190, 0.190, 0.190, 0.190; 1, 1), (0.190, 0.190, 0.190, 0.190; 1, 1))	((1, 1, 1, 1; 1, 1), (1, 1, 1, 1; 1, 1))	((0.76, 0.76, 0.76, 0.76; 1, 1), (0.76, 0.76, 0.76, 0.76; 1, 1))
P12	((0.763, 0.763, 0.763, 0.763; 1, 1), (0.763, 0.763, 0.763, 0.763; 1, 1))	((0.8, 0.8, 0.8, 0.8; 1, 1), (0.8, 0.8, 0.8, 0.8; 1, 1))	((0.5, 0.5, 0.5, 0.5; 1, 1), (0.5, 0.5, 0.5, 0.5; 1, 1))
P13	((0.783, 0.783, 0.783, 0.783; 1, 1), (0.783, 0.783, 0.783, 0.783; 1, 1))	((1, 1, 1, 1; 1, 1), (1, 1, 1, 1; 1, 1))	((0.6, 0.6, 0.6, 0.6; 1, 1), (0.6, 0.6, 0.6, 0.6; 1, 1))
P14	((0.874, 0.874, 0.874, 0.874; 1, 1), (0.874, 0.874, 0.874, 0.874; 1, 1))	((0.9, 0.9, 0.9, 0.9; 1, 1), (0.9, 0.9, 0.9, 0.9; 1, 1))	((0.8, 0.8, 0.8, 0.8; 1, 1), (0.8, 0.8, 0.8, 0.8; 1, 1))
P15	((0.881, 0.881, 0.881, 0.881; 1, 1), (0.881, 0.881, 0.881, 0.881; 1, 1))	((1, 1, 1, 1; 1, 1), (1, 1, 1, 1; 1, 1))	((0.6, 0.6, 0.6, 0.6; 1, 1), (0.6, 0.6, 0.6, 0.6; 1, 1))

Table B.3 The normalized decisions matrix (3).

	t1	t2	t3
P1	((0.5, 0.5, 0.5, 0.5; 1, 1), (0.5, 0.5, 0.5, 0.5; 1, 1))	((0.367, 0.567, 0.567, 0.767; 1, 1), (0.467, 0.567, 0.567, 0.667; 0.9, 0.9))	((0.433, 0.633, 0.633, 0.833; 1, 1), (0.533, 0.633, 0.633, 0.733; 0.9, 0.9))
P2	((0.417, 0.417, 0.417, 0.417; 1, 1), (0.417, 0.417, 0.417, 0.417; 1, 1))	((0.367, 0.567, 0.567, 0.767; 1, 1), (0.467, 0.567, 0.567, 0.667; 0.9, 0.9))	((0.5, 0.7, 0.7, 0.867; 1, 1), (0.6, 0.7, 0.7, 0.783; 0.9, 0.9))
P3	((0.583, 0.583, 0.583, 0.583; 1, 1), (0.583, 0.583, 0.583, 0.583; 1, 1))	((0.5, 0.7, 0.7, 0.9; 1, 1), (0.6, 0.7, 0.7, 0.8; 0.9, 0.9))	((0.367, 0.567, 0.567, 0.767; 1, 1), (0.467, 0.567, 0.567, 0.667; 0.9, 0.9))
P4	((0.75, 0.75, 0.75, 0.75; 1, 1), (0.75, 0.75, 0.75, 0.75; 1, 1))	((0.433, 0.633, 0.633, 0.833; 1, 1), (0.533, 0.633, 0.633, 0.733; 0.9, 0.9))	((0.367, 0.567, 0.567, 0.767; 1, 1), (0.467, 0.567, 0.567, 0.667; 0.9, 0.9))
P5	((0.5, 0.5, 0.5, 0.5; 1, 1), (0.5, 0.5, 0.5, 0.5; 1, 1))	((0.433, 0.633, 0.633, 0.833; 1, 1), (0.533, 0.633, 0.633, 0.733; 0.9, 0.9))	((0.433, 0.633, 0.633, 0.833; 1, 1), (0.533, 0.633, 0.633, 0.733; 0.9, 0.9))
P6	((0.5, 0.5, 0.5, 0.5; 1, 1), (0.5, 0.5, 0.5, 0.5; 1, 1))	((0.367, 0.567, 0.567, 0.767; 1, 1), (0.467, 0.567, 0.567, 0.667; 0.9, 0.9))	((0.5, 0.7, 0.7, 0.867; 1, 1), (0.6, 0.7, 0.7, 0.783; 0.9, 0.9))
P7	((0, 0, 0, 0; 1, 1), (0, 0, 0, 0; 1, 1))	((0.033, 0.167, 0.167, 0.367; 1, 1), (0.1, 0.167, 0.167, 0.267; 0.9, 0.9))	((0.067, 0.233, 0.233, 0.433; 1, 1), (0.15, 0.233, 0.233, 0.333; 0.9, 0.9))
P8	((0.917, 0.917, 0.917, 0.917; 1, 1), (0.917, 0.917, 0.917, 0.917; 1, 1))	((0, 0.033, 0.033, 0.167; 1, 1), (0.017, 0.033, 0.033, 0.1; 0.9, 0.9))	((0.033, 0.133, 0.133, 0.3; 1, 1), (0.083, 0.133, 0.133, 0.217; 0.9, 0.9))
P9	((0.25, 0.25, 0.25, 0.25; 1, 1), (0.25, 0.25, 0.25, 0.25; 1, 1))	((0, 0.1, 0.1, 0.3; 1, 1), (0.05, 0.1, 0.1, 0.2; 0.9, 0.9))	((0, 0.067, 0.067, 0.233; 1, 1), (0.033, 0.067, 0.067, 0.15; 0.9, 0.9))
P10	((0.5, 0.5, 0.5, 0.5; 1, 1), (0.5, 0.5, 0.5, 0.5; 1, 1))	(0.067, 0.233, 0.233, 0.433; 1, 1), (0.15, 0.233, 0.233, 0.333; 0.9, 0.9))	((0.1, 0.3, 0.3, 0.5; 1, 1), (0.2, 0.3, 0.3, 0.4; 0.9, 0.9))
P11	((1, 1, 1, 1; 1, 1), (1, 1, 1, 1; 1, 1))	((0, 0.067, 0.067, 0.233; 1, 1), (0.033, 0.067, 0.067, 0.15; 0.9, 0.9))	((0, 0.033, 0.033, 0.167; 1, 1), (0.017, 0.033, 0.033, 0.1; 0.9, 0.9))
P12	((0.333, 0.333, 0.333, 0.333; 1, 1), (0.333, 0.333, 0.333, 0.333; 1, 1))	((0.367, 0.567, 0.567, 0.767; 1, 1), (0.467, 0.567, 0.567, 0.667; 0.9, 0.9))	((0.433, 0.633, 0.633, 0.833; 1, 1), (0.533, 0.633, 0.633, 0.733; 0.9, 0.9))
P13	((0.583, 0.583, 0.583, 0.583; 1, 1), (0.583, 0.583, 0.583, 0.583; 1, 1))	((0.167, 0.367, 0.367, 0.567; 1, 1), (0.267, 0.367, 0.367, 0.467; 0.9, 0.9))	((0.233, 0.433, 0.433, 0.633; 1, 1), (0.333, 0.433, 0.433, 0.533; 0.9, 0.9))

Continued

	t1	t2	t3
P14	((0.5, 0.5, 0.5, 0.5; 1, 1), (0.5, 0.5, 0.5, 0.5; 1, 1))	((0.3, 0.5, 0.5, 0.7; 1, 1), (0.4, 0.5, 0.5, 0.6; 0.9, 0.9)	((0.367, 0.567, 0.567, 0.767; 1, 1), (0.467, 0.567, 0.567, 0.667; 0.9, 0.9))
P15	((0.583, 0.583, 0.583, 0.583; 1, 1), (0.583, 0.583, 0.583, 0.583; 1, 1))	((0.367, 0.567, 0.567, 0.767; 1, 1), (0.467, 0.567, 0.567, 0.667; 0.9, 0.9))	((0.367, 0.567, 0.567, 0.767; 1, 1), (0.467, 0.567, 0.567, 0.667; 0.9, 0.9))

Table B.4 The normalized decision matrix (4).

	s1	s2	s3
P1	((0.233, 0.433, 0.433, 0.633; 1, 1) (0.333, 0.433, 0.433, 0.533; 0.9, 0.9))	((0.133, 0.3, 0.3 0.5; 1, 1), (0.217, 0.3, 0.3, 0.4; 0.9, 0.9))	((0.233, 0.433, 0.433, 0.633; 1, 1), (0.333, 0.433, 0.433, 0.533; 0.9, 0.9))
P2	((0.367, 0.567, 0.567, 0.767; 1, 1), (0.467, 0.567, 0.567, 0.667; 0.9, 0.9))	((0.233, 0.433, 0.433, 0.633; 1, 1), (0.333, 0.433, 0.433, 0.533; 0.9, 0.9))	((0.767, 0.933, 0.933, 1; 1, 1), (0.85, 0.933, 0.933, 0.967; 0.9, 0.9))
P3	((0.3, 0.5, 0.5, 0.7; 1, 1) (0.4, 0.5, 0.5, 0.6; 0.9, 0.9))	((0.233, 0.433, 0.433, 0.633; 1, 1), (0.333, 0.433, 0.433, 0.533; 0.9, 0.9))	((0.633, 0.833, 0.833, 0.967; 1, 1), (0.733, 0.833, 0.833, 0.9; 0.9, 0.9))
P4	((0.433, 0.633, 0.633, 0.833; 1, 1), (0.533, 0.633, 0.633, 0.733; 0.9, 0.9))	((0.367, 0.567, 0.567, 0.767; 1, 1), (0.467, 0.567, 0.567, 0.667; 0.9, 0.9))	((0.433, 0.633, 0.633, 0.833; 1, 1), (0.533, 0.633, 0.633, 0.733; 0.9, 0.9))
P5	((0.367, 0.567, 0.567, 0.767; 1, 1), (0.467, 0.567, 0.567, 0.667; 0.9, 0.9))	((0.367, 0.567, 0.567, 0.767; 1, 1), (0.467, 0.567, 0.567, 0.667; 0.9, 0.9))	((0.367, 0.567, 0.567, 0.767; 1, 1), (0.467, 0.567, 0.567, 0.667; 0.9, 0.9))
P6	((0.5, 0.7, 0.7, 0.867; 1, 1), (0.6, 0.7, 0.7, 0.783; 0.9, 0.9))	((0.433, 0.633, 0.633, 0.833; 1, 1), (0.533, 0.633, 0.633, 0.733; 0.9, 0.9))	((0.433, 0.633, 0.633, 0.833; 1, 1), (0.533, 0.633, 0.633, 0.733; 0.9, 0.9))
P7	((0.3, 0.5, 0.5, 0.7; 1, 1) (0.4, 0.5, 0.5, 0.6; 0.9, 0.9))	((0.5, 0.7, 0.7, 0.867; 1, 1), (0.6, 0.7, 0.7, 0.783; 0.9, 0.9))	((0.233, 0.433, 0.433, 0.633; 1, 1), (0.333, 0.433, 0.433, 0.533; 0.9, 0.9))
P8	((0.3, 0.5, 0.5, 0.7; 1, 1), (0.4, 0.5, 0.5, 0.6; 0.9, 0.9)	((0.633, 0.833, 0.833, 0.967; 1, 1), (0.733, 0.833, 0.833, 0.9; 0.9, 0.9))	((0.367, 0.567, 0.567, 0.767; 1, 1), (0.467, 0.567, 0.567, 0.667; 0.9, 0.9))
P9	((0.167, 0.367, 0.367, 0.567; 1, 1), (0.267, 0.367, 0.367, 0.467; 0.9, 0.9))	((0.367, 0.567, 0.567, 0.767; 1, 1), (0.467, 0.567, 0.567, 0.667; 0.9, 0.9))	((0.433, 0.633, 0.633, 0.833; 1, 1), (0.533, 0.633, 0.633, 0.733; 0.9, 0.9))
P10	((0.433, 0.633, 0.633, 0.833; 1, 1), (0.533, 0.633, 0.633, 0.733; 0.9, 0.9))	((0.433, 0.633, 0.633, 0.833; 1, 1), (0.533, 0.633, 0.633, 0.733; 0.9, 0.9))	((0.367, 0.567, 0.567, 0.767; 1, 1), (0.467, 0.567, 0.567, 0.667; 0.9, 0.9))
P11	((0.3, 0.5, 0.5, 0.7; 1, 1), (0.4, 0.5, 0.5, 0.6; 0.9, 0.9))	((0.367, 0.567, 0.567, 0.767; 1, 1), (0.467, 0.567, 0.567, 0.667; 0.9, 0.9))	((0.233, 0.433, 0.433, 0.633; 1, 1), (0.333, 0.433, 0.433, 0.533; 0.9, 0.9))
P12	((0.5, 0.7, 0.7, 0.867; 1, 1), (0.6, 0.7, 0.7, 0.783; 0.9, 0.9))	((0.433, 0.633, 0.633, 0.833; 1, 1), (0.533, 0.633, 0.633, 0.733; 0.9, 0.9))	((0.433, 0.633, 0.633, 0.833; 1, 1), (0.533, 0.633, 0.633, 0.733; 0.9, 0.9))
P13	((0.033, 0.167, 0.167, 0.367; 1, 1), (0.1, 0.167, 0.167, 0.267; 0.9, 0.9))	((0.433, 0.633, 0.633, 0.833; 1, 1), (0.533, 0.633, 0.633, 0.733; 0.9, 0.9))	((0.233, 0.433, 0.433, 0.633; 1, 1), (0.333, 0.433, 0.433, 0.533; 0.9, 0.9))
P14	((0.1, 0.3, 0.3, 0.5; 1, 1), (0.2, 0.3, 0.3, 0.4; 0.9, 0.9))	((0.367, 0.567, 0.567, 0.767; 1, 1), (0.467, 0.567, 0.567, 0.667; 0.9, 0.9))	((0.3, 0.5, 0.5, 0.7; 1, 1) (0.4, 0.5, 0.5, 0.6; 0.9, 0.9))
P15	((0.133, 0.3, 0.3 0.5; 1, 1), (0.217, 0.3, 0.3, 0.4; 0.9, 0.9))	((0.433, 0.633, 0.633, 0.8; 1, 1), (0.533, 0.633, 0.633, 0.717; 0.9, 0.9))	((0.233, 0.433, 0.433, 0.633; 1, 1) (0.333, 0.433, 0.433, 0.533; 0.9, 0.9))

Table B.5 The normalized decision matrix (5).

	h1	h2	h3
P1	((0.684, 0.684, 0.684, 0.684; 1, 1), (0.684, 0.684, 0.684, 0.684; 1, 1))	((0.233, 0.433, 0.433, 0.633; 1, 1), (0.333, 0.433, 0.433, 0.533; 0.9, 0.9))	((0.367, 0.567, 0.567, 0.767; 1, 1), (0.467, 0.567, 0.567, 0.667; 0.9, 0.9))
P2	((0.434, 0.434, 0.434, 0.434; 1, 1), (0.434, 0.434, 0.434, 0.434; 1, 1))	((0.367, 0.567, 0.567, 0.767; 1, 1), (0.467, 0.567, 0.567, 0.667; 0.9, 0.9))	((0.133, 0.3, 0.3 0.5; 1, 1), (0.217, 0.3, 0.3, 0.4; 0.9, 0.9))
P3	((0.447, 0.447, 0.447, 0.447; 1, 1), (0.447, 0.447, 0.447, 0.447; 1, 1))	((0.3, 0.5, 0.5, 0.7; 1, 1) (0.4, 0.5, 0.5, 0.6; 0.9, 0.9))	((0.167, 0.367, 0.367, 0.567; 1, 1), (0.267, 0.367, 0.367, 0.467; 0.9, 0.9))
P4	((0.211, 0.211, 0.211, 0.211; 1, 1), (0.211, 0.211, 0.211, 0.211; 1, 1))	((0.167, 0.367, 0.367, 0.567; 1, 1), (0.267, 0.367, 0.367, 0.467; 0.9, 0.9))	((0.233, 0.433, 0.433, 0.633; 1, 1), (0.333, 0.433, 0.433, 0.533; 0.9, 0.9))
P5	((0.737, 0.737, 0.737, 0.737; 1, 1), (0.737, 0.737, 0.737, 0.737; 1, 1))	((0.367, 0.567, 0.567, 0.767; 1, 1), (0.467, 0.567, 0.567, 0.667; 0.9, 0.9))	((0.233, 0.433, 0.433, 0.633; 1, 1), (0.333, 0.433, 0.433, 0.533; 0.9, 0.9))
P6	((1, 1, 1, 1; 1, 1), (1, 1, 1, 1; 1, 1))	((0.367, 0.567, 0.567, 0.767; 1, 1), (0.467, 0.567, 0.567, 0.667; 0.9, 0.9))	((0.233, 0.433, 0.433, 0.633; 1, 1), (0.333, 0.433, 0.433, 0.533; 0.9, 0.9))
P7	((0.474, 0.474, 0.474, 0.474; 1, 1), (0.474, 0.474, 0.474, 0.474; 1, 1))	((0.167, 0.367, 0.367, 0.567; 1, 1), (0.267, 0.367, 0.367, 0.467; 0.9, 0.9))	((0.167, 0.367, 0.367, 0.567; 1, 1), (0.267, 0.367, 0.367, 0.467; 0.9, 0.9))
P8	((0.355, 0.355, 0.355, 0.355; 1, 1), (0.355, 0.355, 0.355, 0.355; 1, 1))	((0.033, 0.167, 0.167, 0.367; 1, 1), (0.1, 0.167, 0.167, 0.267; 0.9, 0.9))	((0.233, 0.433, 0.433, 0.633; 1, 1), (0.333, 0.433, 0.433, 0.533; 0.9, 0.9))
P9	((0.132, 0.132, 0.132, 0.132; 1, 1), (0.132, 0.132, 0.132, 0.132; 1, 1))	((0.167, 0.367, 0.367, 0.567; 1, 1), (0.267, 0.367, 0.367, 0.467; 0.9, 0.9))	((0.3, 0.5, 0.5, 0.7; 1, 1) (0.4, 0.5, 0.5, 0.6; 0.9, 0.9))
P10	((0.303, 0.303, 0.303, 0.303; 1, 1), (0.303, 0.303, 0.303, 0.303; 1, 1))	((0.167, 0.367, 0.367, 0.567; 1, 1), (0.267, 0.367, 0.367, 0.467; 0.9, 0.9))	((0.367, 0.567, 0.567, 0.767; 1, 1), (0.467, 0.567, 0.567, 0.667; 0.9, 0.9))
P11	((0.382, 0.382, 0.382, 0.382; 1, 1), (0.382, 0.382, 0.382, 0.382; 1, 1))	((0.233, 0.433, 0.433, 0.633; 1, 1), (0.333, 0.433, 0.433, 0.533; 0.9, 0.9))	((0.367, 0.567, 0.567, 0.767; 1, 1), (0.467, 0.567, 0.567, 0.667; 0.9, 0.9))
P12	((0.526, 0.526, 0.526, 0.526; 1, 1), (0.526, 0.526, 0.526, 0.526; 1, 1))	((0.367, 0.567, 0.567, 0.767; 1, 1), (0.467, 0.567, 0.567, 0.667; 0.9, 0.9))	((0.633, 0.833, 0.833, 0.967; 1, 1), (0.733, 0.833, 0.833, 0.9; 0.9, 0.9))
P13	((0.263, 0.263, 0.263, 0.263; 1, 1), (0.263, 0.263, 0.263, 0.263; 1, 1))	((0.367, 0.567, 0.567, 0.767; 1, 1), (0.467, 0.567, 0.567, 0.667; 0.9, 0.9))	((0.633, 0.833, 0.833, 0.967; 1, 1), (0.733, 0.833, 0.833, 0.9; 0.9, 0.9))
P14	((0, 0, 0, 0; 1, 1), (0, 0, 0, 0; 1, 1))	((0.3, 0.5, 0.5, 0.7; 1, 1) (0.4, 0.5, 0.5, 0.6; 0.9, 0.9))	((0.367, 0.567, 0.567, 0.767; 1, 1), (0.467, 0.567, 0.567, 0.667; 0.9, 0.9))
P15	((0.303, 0.303, 0.303, 0.303; 1, 1), (0.303, 0.303, 0.303, 0.303; 1, 1))	((0.433, 0.633, 0.633, 0.833; 1, 1), (0.533, 0.633, 0.633, 0.733; 0.9, 0.9))	((0.367, 0.567, 0.567, 0.767; 1, 1), (0.467, 0.567, 0.567, 0.667; 0.9, 0.9))

References

[1] Sun B, Yu Y, Qin C. Should China focus on the distributed development of wind and solar photovoltaic power generation? A comparative study[J]. Applied Energy, 2017, 185:421-439.

[2] Lu Z, Li H, Qiao Y. Probabilistic Flexibility Evaluation for Power System Planning Considering its Association with Renewable Power Curtailment[J]. IEEE Transactions on Power Systems, 2018, 33:3285-3295.

[3] Fan X C, Wang W Q, Shi R J, et al. Analysis and countermeasures of wind power curtailment in China[J]. Renewable & Sustainable Energy Reviews, 2015, 52:1429-1436.

[4] Wu Y, Xu C, Ke Y, et al. An intuitionistic fuzzy multi-criteria framework for large-scale rooftop PV project portfolio selection: case study in Zhejiang, China[J]. Energy, 2018, 143:295-309.

[5] Wang Z, Luo D, Liu L. Natural gas utilization in China: Development trends and prospects[J]. Energy Reports, 2018, 4:351-356.

[6] NDRC. Guidelines for Developing Natural Gas Distributed Energy Sources. http://www.ndrc.gov.cn/zcfb/zcfbtz/201110/t20111013_438374.html. 2011.

[7] NDRC, NEA. 13th Five-Year Plan for Energy Development. http://www.ndrc.gov.cn/zcfb/zcfbtz/201701/t20170117_835278.html. 2016.

[8] NEA. Interim Measures for the Development and Construction of Decentralized Wind Power Projects. http://zfxxgk.nea.gov.cn/auto87/201804/t20180416_3150.htm. 2018.

[9] Sefair J A, Méndez C Y, Babat O, et al. Linear solution schemes for mean-semivariance project portfolio selection problems: An application in the oil and gas industry[J]. Omega, 2016, 68:39-48.

[10] Unger B N, Kock A, Gemünden HG, et al. Enforcing strategic fit of project portfolios by project termination: An empirical study on senior management involvement[J]. International Journal of Project Management, 2012, 30:675-685.

[11] Liu P, Tan Z. How to develop distributed generation in China: In the context of the reformation of electric power system[J]. Renewable & Sustainable Energy Reviews, 2016, 66:10-26.

[12] Anadón L D, Baker E, Bosetti V. Integrating uncertainty into public energy research and development decisions. Nature Energy, 2017, 2:17071.

[13] Debnath D, Whistance J, Thompson W, et al. Complement or substitute: Ethanol's uncertain relationship with gasoline under alternative petroleum price and policy scenarios[J]. Applied Energy, 2017, 191:385-397.

[14] Wu Y, Geng S. Multi-criteria decision making on selection of solar–wind hybrid power station location: A case of China[J]. Energy Conversion & Management, 2014, 81:527-533.

[15] Smith-Perera A, García-Melón M, Poveda-Bautista R, et al. A Project Strategic Index proposal for portfolio selection in electrical company based on the Analytic Network Process[J]. Renewable & Sustainable Energy Reviews, 2010, 14:1569-1579.

[16] Garcíamelón M, Povedabautista R, Del VM, José L. Using the strategic relative alignment index for the selection of portfolio projects application to a public Venezuelan Power Corporation[J]. International Journal of Production Economics, 2015, 170:54-66.

[17] Jeng J F, Huang K H. Strategic project portfolio selection for national research institutes[J]. Journal of Business Research, 2015, 68:2305-2311.

[18] Mohagheghi V, Mousavi S M, Vahdani B. A New Optimization Model for Project Portfolio Selection Under Interval-Valued Fuzzy Environment[J]. Arabian Journal for Science & Engineering, 2015, 40:3351-3361.

[19] Tavana M, Keramatpour M, Santos-Arteaga F J, et al. A fuzzy hybrid project portfolio selection method using Data Envelopment Analysis, TOPSIS and Integer Programming[J]. Expert Systems with Applications, 2015, 42:8432-8444.

[20] Khalili-Damghani K, Sadi-Nezhad S, Lotfi F H, et al. A hybrid fuzzy rule-based multi-criteria framework for sustainable project portfolio selection[J]. Information Sciences, 2013, 220:442-462.

[21] Mohagheghi V, Mousavi S M, Vahdani B, et al. R&D project evaluation and project portfolio selection by a new interval type-2 fuzzy optimization approach[J]. Neural Computing & Applications,

2017, 28:3869-3888.

[22] Pendharkar P C, Rodger J A. Information technology capital budgeting using a knapsack problem[J]. International Transactions in Operational Research, 2010, 13:333-351.

[23] Killen C P. Evaluation of project interdependency visualizations through decision scenario experimentation [J]. International Journal of Project Management, 2013, 31:804-816.

[24] Lopes Y G, Almeida A T D. Assessment of synergies for selecting a project portfolio in the petroleum industry based on a multi-attribute utility function[J]. Journal of Petroleum Science & Engineering, 2015, 126:131-140.

[25] Eilat H, Golany B, Shtub A. Constructing and evaluating balanced portfolios of R&D projects with interactions: A DEA based methodology[J]. European Journal of Operational Research, 2006, 172:1018-1039.

[26] Jiang Z, Zhang H, Sutherland J W. Development of multi-criteria decision making model for remanufacturing technology portfolio selection[J]. Journal of Cleaner Production, 2011, 19:1939-1945.

[27] Pendharkar P C. A decision-making framework for justifying a portfolio of IT projects[J]. International Journal of Project Management, 2014, 32:625-639.

[28] Neumeier A, Radszuwill S, Garizy T Z. Modeling project criticality in IT project portfolios[J]. International Journal of Project Management, 2018, 36:833-844.

[29] Lin C, Hsieh P J. A fuzzy decision support system for strategic portfolio management[J]. Decision Support Systems, 2005, 38:383-398.

[30] Relich M, Pawlewski P. A fuzzy weighted average approach for selecting portfolio of new product development projects[J]. Neurocomputing, 2016, 231:19-27.

[31] Ghapanchi A H, Tavana M, Khakbaz M H, et al. A methodology for selecting portfolios of projects with interactions and under uncertainty[J]. International Journal of Project Management, 2012, 30:791-803.

[32] Bhattacharyya R, Kumar P, Kar S. Fuzzy R&D portfolio selection of interdependent projects[J]. Computers & Mathematics with Applications, 2011, 62:3857-3870.

[33] Alvarez-García B, Fernández-Castro A S. A comprehensive approach for the selection of a portfolio of interdependent projects. An application to subsidized projects in Spain[J]. Computers & Industrial Engineering, 2018, 153-159.

[34] Liu Y, Liu Y K. Distributionally robust fuzzy project portfolio optimization problem with interactive returns[J]. Applied Soft Computing, 2016, 56:655-668.

[35] Jafarzadeh H, Akbari P, Abedin B. A methodology for project portfolio selection under criteria prioritisation, uncertainty and projects interdependency – combination of fuzzy QFD and DEA[J]. Expert Systems with Applications, 2018, 110:237-249.

[36] Yu L, Wen F, Lai K K. Genetic algorithm-based multi-criteria project portfolio selection[J]. Annals of Operations Research, 2012, 197:71-86.

[37] Oh J, Yang J, Lee S. Managing uncertainty to improve decision-making in NPD portfolio management with a fuzzy expert system[J]. Expert Systems with Applications, 2012, 39:9868-9885.

[38] Hassanzadeh F, Nemati H, Sun M. Robust optimization for interactive multiobjective programming with imprecise information applied to R&D project portfolio selection[J]. European Journal of Operational Research, 2014, 238:41-53.

[39] Wu Y, Li J, Wang J, et al. Project portfolio management applied to building energy projects management system[J]. Renewable & Sustainable Energy Reviews, 2012, 16:718-724.

[40] Golabi K, Kirkwood C W, Sicherman A. Selecting a Portfolio of Solar Energy Projects Using Multiattribute Preference Theory[J]. Management Science, 1981, 27:174-189.

[41] Mavromatidis G, Orehounig K, Carmeliet J. Comparison of alternative decision-making criteria in a two-stage stochastic program for the design of distributed energy systems under uncertainty[J]. Energy, 2018, 56:709-724.

[42] Ren H, Gao W, Zhou W, et al. Multi-criteria evaluation for the optimal adoption of distributed residential energy systems in Japan[J]. Energy Policy, 2009, 37:5484-5493.

[43] Jing R, Zhu X, Zhu Z, et al. A multi-objective optimization and multi-criteria evaluation integrated framework for distributed energy system optimal planning[J]. Energy Conversion and Management, 2018, 166:445-562.

[44] Väisänen S, Mikkilä M, Havukainen J, et al. Using a multi-method approach for decision-making about a sustainable local distributed energy system: A case study from Finland[J]. Journal of Cleaner Production, 2016, 137:1330-1338.

[45] Hajibandeh N, Shafie-khaha M, Osório G J, te al. A heuristic multi-objective multi-criteria demand response planning in a system with high penetration of wind power generators[J]. Applied Energy, 2018, 212:721-732.

[46] Hassan Z, Garni A. Solar PV power plant site selection using a GIS-AHP based approach with application in Saudi Arabia[J]. Applied Energy, 2017, 206: 1225-1240.

[47] Wang J, Du P, Niu T, et al. A novel hybrid system based on a new proposed algorithm-Multi-Objective Whale Optimization Algorithm for wind speed forecasting[J]. Applied Energy, 1970, 208:344-360.

[48] Voss M, Kock A. Impact of relationship value on project portfolio success — Investigating the moderating effects of portfolio characteristics and external turbulence[J]. International Journal of Project Management, 2013, 31:847-861.

[49] Kaiser M G, Arbi F E, Ahlemann F. Successful project portfolio management beyond project selection techniques: Understanding the role of structural alignment[J]. International Journal of Project Management, 2015, 33:126-139.

[50] Hernandez-Perdomo E A, Mun J, Claudio M R S. Active management in state-owned energy companies: Integrating a real options approach into multicriteria analysis to make companies sustainable[J]. Applied Energy, 2017, 195:487-502.

[51] Srivannaboon S, Milosevic D Z. A two-way influence between business strategy and project management[J]. International Journal of Project Management, 2006, 24:493-505.

[52] Turner R. The Handbook of Project Based Management: Improving the Process for Achieving Your Strategic Objectives[M]. New York:McGraw-Hill Professional, 2002.

[53] Lin C, Hsieh P J. A fuzzy decision support system for strategic portfolio management[J]. Decision Support Systems, 2004, 38:383-398.

[54] Relich M, Pawlewski P. A fuzzy weighted average approach for selecting portfolio of new product development projects[J]. Neurocomputing, 2017, 231:19-27.

[55] Zadeh L A. Fuzzy sets [J]. Information & Control, 1965, 8:338-353.

[56] Huang C C, Chu P Y, Chiang Y H. A fuzzy AHP application in government-sponsored R&D project

selection [J]. Omega, 2008, 36:1038-1052.

[57] Chen C T, Cheng H L. A comprehensive model for selecting information system project under fuzzy environment[J]. International Journal of Project Management, 2009, 27:389-399.

[58] Zeng Z, Nasri E, Chini A, et al. A multiple objective decision making model for energy generation portfolio under fuzzy uncertainty: Case study of large scale investor-owned utilities in Florida[J]. Renewable Energy, 2015, 75:224-242.

[59] Baker N, Freeland J. Recent Advances in R&D Benefit Measurement and Project Selection Methods[J]. Management Science, 1975, 21:1164-1175.

[60] Mcfarlan F W. Portfolio Approach to Information Systems[J]. Harvard Business Review, 1981, 59.

[61] Keil M, Marchewka J T. Portfolio Theory Approach For Selecting and Managing IT Projects[J]. Information Resources Management Journal, 1995, 8:5-16.

[62] Alvarez-García B, Fernández-Castro A S. A comprehensive approach for the selection of a portfolio of interdependent projects. An application to subsidized projects in Spain[J]. Computers & Industrial Engineering, 2018, 153-159.

[63] Banihashemi S, Hosseini M R, Golizadeh H, et al. Critical success factors (CSFs) for integration of sustainability into construction project management practices in developing countries[J]. International Journal of Project Management, 2017, 35:1103-1119.

[64] Chen T Y. A linear assignment method for multiple-criteria decision analysis with interval type-2 fuzzy sets[J]. Applied Soft Computing Journal, 2013, 13:2735-2748.

[65] Saaty T L. The analytic hierarchy process: Planning, priority setting, resource Allocation[M]. McGraw-Hill, NY, USA, 1980.

[66] Buckley J J. Fuzzy hierarchical analysis[J]. Fuzzy sets and systems, 1985, 17:233-247.

[67] Kahraman C. Fuzzy analytic hierarchy process with interval type-2 fuzzy sets. [J]. Knowledge-Based Systems, 2014, 59:48-57.

[68] Kahraman C, Öztayşi B, Sarı İU, et al. Fuzzy analytic hierarchy process with interval type-2 fuzzy sets[J]. Knowledge-Based Systems, 2014, 59:48-57.

[69] Gong M, Jiao L, Du H, et al. Multiobjective Immune Algorithm with Nondominated Neighbor-Based Selection[J]. Evolutionary Computation, 2008, 16:225-255.

[70] Deb K, Pratap A, Agarwal S, et al. A fast and elitist multiobjective genetic algorithm: NSGA-II[J]. IEEE Transactions on Evolutionary Computation, 2002, 6:182-197.

[71] Qin J, Liu X, Pedrycz W. An extended TODIM multi-criteria group decision making method for green supplier selection in interval type-2 fuzzy environment[J]. European Journal of Operational Research, 2017, 258:626-638.

[72] Kahraman C, Kaya İ, Cebi S. A comparative analysis for multiattribute selection among renewable energy alternatives using fuzzy axiomatic design and fuzzy analytic hierarchy process[J]. Energy, 2009, 34:1603-1616.

[73] Büyüközkan G, Güleryüz S. Evaluation of Renewable Energy Resources in Turkey using an integrated MCDM approach with linguistic interval fuzzy preference relations[J]. Energy, 2017, 123:149-163.

[74] Haddad B, Liazid A, Ferreira P. A multi-criteria approach to rank renewables for the Algerian electricity system[J]. Renewable Energy, 2017, 107:462-472.

[75] Wu Y, Xu C, Zhang T. Evaluation of renewable power sources using a fuzzy MCDM based on

cumulative prospect theory: A case in China[J]. Energy, 2018, 147:1227-1239.
[76] Amer M, Daim T U. Selection of renewable energy technologies for a developing county: A case of Pakistan[J]. Energy for Sustainable Development, 2011, 15:420-435.
[77] Kaya T, Kahraman C. Multicriteria renewable energy planning using an integrated fuzzy VIKOR & AHP methodology: The case of Istanbul[J]. Energy, 2010, 35:2517-2527.
[78] Streimikiene D, Balezentis T, Krisciukaitienė I, et al. Prioritizing sustainable electricity production technologies: MCDM approach[J]. Renewable & Sustainable Energy Reviews, 2012, 16:3302-3311.
[79] Şengül Ü, Eren M, Shiraz S E, et al. Fuzzy TOPSIS method for ranking renewable energy supply systems in Turkey[J]. Renewable Energy, 2015, 75:617-625.
[80] Tasri A, Susilawati A. Selection among renewable energy alternatives based on a fuzzy analytic hierarchy process in Indonesia[J]. Sustainable Energy Technologies & Assessments, 2014, 156:34-44.

Chapter 8

A DEMATEL-TODIM based decision framework for PV power generation project in expressway service area under an intuitionistic fuzzy environment

Yunna Wu [a, b], Chenghao Wu [a, b*], Jianli Zhou [a, b], Buyuan Zhang [a, b], Chuanbo Xu [a, b], Yudong Yan [a, b], Fangtong Liu [a, b]

a. School of Economics and Management, North China Electric Power University, Beijing, China

b. Beijing Key Laboratory of New Energy and Low-Carbon Development (North China Electric Power University), Changping Beijing 102206, China

Abstract: The expressway service area photovoltaic (ESAPV) projects have been greatly promoted due to the increasing passenger volume and the current development of electric vehicle industry. Site selection based on sustainability perspective is critical to the future construction of ESAPV. This paper puts forward a decision-making framework to ensure the validity of the ESAPV site selection. First, the index system meeting the characteristics of the ESAPV project is established. Second, in order to take into account the influence of subjective preference and objective justice on the results, this study chooses the Decision Making Trial and Evaluation Laboratory (DEMATEL) method to determine the weights of first-level indicators that lack objective data support and employs an integrated weighting method to determine the weights of second-level indicators. Third, the TODIM (an acronym in Portuguese of interactive and multi-criteria decision making) method which considers decision makers' risk aversion psychology is extended to triangular intuitionistic fuzzy environment combined with group decision-making theory. Finally, a case study in Hebei of China is carried out to verify the practicability of the systematic framework. The results indicate that the optimal project is located in Shijiazhuang.

Keywords: Expressway Service Area Photovoltaic (ESAPV); Site Selection; DEMATEL; Maximum Cross-Entropy; Extended TODIM; Triangular Intuitionistic Fuzzy Environment

1. Introduction

With the rapid development of the economy and enormous progress of the society, people's demand for energy is growing, and conventional energy is increasingly in short supply, which results in the crisis of energy shortage. As a category of clean energy, solar energy is not limited by the region, and it is inexhaustible (Hao et al., 2018). In recent years, it has been widely exploited and utilized under the active promotion of Chinese government. Data from the National Energy Administration (NEA) of China show that there are 174.45 million kilowatts installed capacity of photovoltaic (PV) power generation in the country by the end of 2018, with an increase of 44.26 million kilowatts over the previous year. However, China's PV industry is still facing a high rate of solar curtailment for various reasons (NEA, 2018). In order to advance the utilization of solar energy and settle the excess capacity issues, it is necessary to think about the furtherance of distributed photovoltaic (DPV) (Zhao et al., 2015). DPV power generation has the advantages of adapting measures to local conditions, cleanliness and higher efficiency, and it can prevent the happening of power loss during transportation. On basis of the above advantages, the DPV of China is increasing rapidly with a year-on-year growth rate of 71% (NEA, 2018).

Nomenclature list abbreviation			
ESA	expressway service area	S_{co_2}	carbon dioxide emissions
ESAPV	expressway service area photovoltaic	$\tilde{\alpha}$	A TIFN
DPV	distributed photovoltaic	$d(\tilde{\alpha}_1,\tilde{\alpha}_2)$	distance between two TIFNs
DEMATEL	Decision Making Trial and Evaluation Laboratory	$\mu_{\tilde{\alpha}}$	maximum membership degree
MCDM	Multi-criteria Decision-Making	$v_{\tilde{\alpha}}$	minimum non-membership degree
LINGO	Linear Interactive and General Optimizer	X	standardized direct influence matrix
RNs	real numbers	T	comprehensive influence matrix
TFNs	triangular fuzzy numbers	r_i	influence degree of each criterion
TIFNs	triangular intuitionistic fuzzy numbers	q_j	being influenced degree of each criterion
		ζ_p	global dominance of each project
Symbol		w_{sj}	weight of first-grade criteria
C_i	initial investment cost	w_{jr}	relative weight of each criterion C_j to the reference criterion C_r

Continued

Nomenclature list abbreviation			
C_m	annual operation and maintenance cost	$\delta_j(A_p, A_q)$	dominance degree of the project A_p compared to the project A_q under criterion C_j
PP	investment payoff period	$\delta(A_p, A_q)$	dominance degree of the project A_p compared to the project A_q under all criteria

For the purpose of further boost the development of DPV, the NEA of China encourages the usage of PV power generation in public facilities. The expressway service area (ESA) is indispensable to the national logistics and passenger transportation. In recent years, the increasing passenger volume, coupled with the current development of electric vehicle industry, has put forward higher requirements for the power consumption of ESA. However, ESAs are usually located in remote areas far from the city, mostly relying on the rural power grid, which leads to unstable power supply and large power loss. Consequently, the construction of expressway service area photovoltaic (ESAPV) projects can not only realize the purpose of intensive utilization of land resources in service area, but also effectively alleviate regional power load pressure and improve the security of power supply in ESA. Moreover, compared with toll-free roads, the hardware facilities and staff of ESA will save plenty of unnecessary costs. In the future, an increasing number of ESAs will be equipped with PV power generation equipment, which is emerging as an extraordinary opportunity for PV enterprises.

The significance of this paper lies in two aspects. First, in terms of actual situation, the construction of PV power stations in the ESAs has enormous economic value with the increasing demand for power in the areas. Second, in terms of theoretical aspects, this paper also has tremendous reference implication. At present, the researches on DPV power generation mainly focus on the following aspects: efficiency improvement (Kai et al., 2011), grid-connected intelligent peaking strategy (Martin et al., 2015), economic factor (Sommerfeldt and Madani, 2017) and policy influence (Yuan et al., 2014). However, few studies exist on the indispensable topic of site selection. It is one of the crucial steps to ensure the electricity generating capacity and comprehensive benefits in the future and it needs to take multiple factors into consideration (Fang et al., 2018; Yunna and Geng, 2014). Garni and Awasthi (2017) evaluated and chose an optimal DPV project based on the target of maximal production capacity. Wu et al. (2018a) established a multi-criteria decision-making (MCDM) framework for the selection of rooftop DPV projects. In addition, Haghdadi et al. (2017) studied the orientation and location of small-scale DPV systems. The above literature has a certain referential significance for this study, but in terms of the location of ESAPV, some theoretical problems still exist in the current decision-making framework:

Firstly, the index system for the location of DPV is not rigorous and comprehensive enough, and no specific index exists for the ESAPV.

Secondly, hesitation and uncertainty in the site selection of ESAPV cannot be neglected.

Thirdly, previous methods to determine the weights of indicators are not scientific enough to satisfy the actual circumstances.

Fourthly, previous studies rarely consider the impact of investors' risk aversion psychology on decision-making.

In order to solve the existing problems in the current research, this study will improve the decision-making process from the following four aspects:

This paper will analyze the existing literature about the location of the DPV, and select representative indicators according to the frequency of each index. Moreover, this study will also put forward some targeted indicators based on the characteristics of ESAs, and then establish a rigorous index system.

For the sake of solving the second problem mentioned above, triangular intuitionistic fuzzy numbers (TIFNs) will be utilized in this paper. In recent years, TIFNs have been introduced into location decision-making due to their better flexibility and applicability in dealing with hesitation and uncertainty(Wu et al., 2018b; Xin and Liu, 2010).

As for the problems involved in the process of weight determination, this paper will adhere to the principle that the subjective method is applied to determine the weights of first-level indicators lacking objective data support, and the integrated weighting method is presented to determine the weights of second-level indicators that include both qualitative criteria and quantitative criteria.

In order to solve the fourth problem mentioned above, this paper will make use of the TODIM method. This method can reflect the influence of investor psychology in risky situations functionally (Wu et al., 2018c).

Compared with previous studies, the innovation of this paper lies in the following aspects. Firstly, a scientific criteria system for the location of ESAPV has been established innovatively considering the characteristics of ESAs. Secondly, this paper introduces triangular intuitionistic fuzzy environment to express the uncertainty of decision information. Thirdly, utilize the Decision-Making Trial and Evaluation Laboratory (DEMATEL) method to determine the weights of first-level criteria subjectively and adopt the integrated weighting method to determine the weights of sub-criteria. Fourthly, this paper employs the TODIM method which considers the influence of investors' risk aversion psychology to rank the alternatives. This decision-making model has a complete theoretical basis and immense practical significance.

2. Literature review

The site selection of ESAPV belongs to the MCDM problem. And the problem can be separated into three modules: description of the data, determination of the index weight and selection of the ranking method. This section will focus on these three modules.

2.1 Description of the data

At present, data are mainly represented by real numbers (RNs), probability interval numbers, triangular fuzzy numbers (TFNs), trapezoidal fuzzy numbers and TIFNs. Compared with previous methods of describing the data, the TIFNs consider three aspects of membership degree, non-membership degree and hesitation degree, possessing more flexibility and practicability in dealing with ambiguity and uncertainty. Therefore, it has wider application in decision-making field. Xin and Liu (2010) defined weighted arithmetic mean operators and weighted geometric average operators for TIFNs and used them in MCDM problems. Yi and Li (2018) developed triangular norm (T-Norm) based cuts of TIFNs, introduced a ranking method of TIFNs and used it to make multi-criteria decision. Wu et al. (2018b) used TIFNs to describe uncertain information and established a decision framework for the location of large commercial rooftop PV system projects. Wu, Y. et al. (2019) made use of TIFNs during the risk assessment in PV poverty alleviation projects of China. In summary, TIFNs are widely utilized to express uncertainty in MCDM problems. And it is necessary to introduce TIFNs to better express the decision makers' opinion in the location of ESAPV project.

2.2 Method to determine the weights of criteria

The methods to determine index weight include subjective methods and objective methods. For example, Wu and Zhou (2019) utilized Intuitionistic Fuzzy-Decision Making Trial and Evaluation Laboratory (IF-DEMATEL) to get the weights of criteria during the risk assessment of urban rooftop DPV in Energy Performance Contracting (EPC) projects. Aragonés-Beltrán et al. (2010) proposed an (Analytic Network Process) ANP-based approach for the selection of PV power plant investment project. The methods involved in the above documents represent subjective methods, and the objective methods are illustrated as follows. As we know, the concept of entropy is derived from thermodynamics, and cross-entropy can determine the weights of information sources according to the degree of mutual support, Wu et al. (2017) used maximum cross-entropy method to determine the weights of criteria when making site selection of electric vehicle charging station. Tang et al. (2016) applied entropy method to the weight determination of short-term PV power generation project.

But in reality, a scientific method to determine weights should not only contain the subjective judgment of experts, but also reflect the information of the data itself. Consequently, a large number of scholars have applied integrated methods to determine the weights of indicators. For example, Xu et al. (2016) applied Analytic Hierarchy Process (AHP) and entropy method to the construction of water supply in remote areas of China. Wu et al. (2018c) used ANP and the entropy method to get the comprehensive weights of indicators when choosing the optimal DPV project. However, their mode is to use subjective method and objective method to calculate the weights separately, and then assign the weights calculated by the two methods to different coefficients to integrate the weights. This method is too rough to meet the actual situation. A more scientific approach is to use a subjective method to determine the weights of first-level criteria that lack objective data support, and use an integrated weighting method to determine the weights of second-level criteria including both qualitative indicators and quantitative indicators.

2.3 Method to rank the alternatives

The last stage of MCDM is to use an appropriate method to rank the alternatives. Muhsen et al. (2018) considered photovoltaic water pumping system (PVPS) would be extremely important for the utilization of solar energy in remote areas, and they used Technique for Order Preference by Similarity to Ideal Solution (TOPSIS) and AHP to optimally size PVPS according to the economic and technological factors. Wu et al. (2018b) utilized Vlsekriterijumska Optimizacija IKompromisno Resenje (VIKOR) to rank the alternative commercial rooftop PV projects. Stamatakis et al. (2016) applied the Preference Ranking Organization Methods for Enrichment Evaluations (PROMETHEE) method to the multi-criteria analysis for PV integrated in shading devices for Mediterranean region. Cavallaro (2010) adopted the ELECTRE III method which belongs to the ELECTRE family to evaluate the thin-film PV production processes. Wu et al. (2018c) employed TODIM method to rank the alternative DPV projects. Through literature review, it can be seen that the above ranking methods have been widely applied to MCDM problems in the energy field. Table 8.1 gives a brief description and analysis of the above methods.

Table 8.1 Description and analysis of the ranking methods.

Method	Brief description	Advantages and disadvantages
TOPSIS	This method weighs the overall benefits of the evaluation object according to the relative proximity. The greater the relative proximity, the better the overall benefit of the evaluation object.	It is easy to understand and the results are intuitive. It does not take the relative importance of the distances into account.
VIKOR	It is an improved version of the TOPSIS method and it considers the maximum benefit of the group and the minimum regret of the individual in order to obtain a compromise solution (Wu, Z. et al., 2019).	Compared with TOPSIS method, the results obtained are more reasonable (Wu et al., 2018b). It cannot specifically show the reason why some alternatives don't satisfy a certain condition.
ELECTRE	It is a sequential decision-making method that uses hierarchical priority relation to solve MCDM problems of limited schemes.	This method is simple to calculate and can be programmed. The information provided by decision matrix is not fully utilized (Sevkli, 2010).

Continued

Method	Brief description	Advantages and disadvantages
PROMETHEE	This method judges the superiority of the schemes according to the difference between attribute values of each scheme.	This method does not require standardization of the data and can avoid information loss in the data procession (Brans and Mareschal, 2005). It does not take the risk aversion psychology of decision makers into account.
TODIM	This method assumes that the decision maker is bounded rational and ranks the projects by calculating the global dominance of each project.	It fully considers the influence of decision makers' risk aversion psychology. It is a relatively new MCDM method, which needs to be expanded and deepened (Fan et al., 2013).

Thus, we can find that the TODIM method has attracted a great deal of attention because of considering the risk aversion psychology of decision makers. In reality, due to the limited knowledge of decision makers and the complexity of the decision-making problem itself, decision makers are often bounded rational. TODIM is a behavioral decision-making method based on prospect theory and it can better describe the bounded rational behavior of decision makers. However, the classical TODIM method is only applicable to the MCDM problem of a single decision maker in an accurate number environment, and it can't do anything about the group decision problem in the fuzzy environment (Krohling et al., 2013). Therefore, in order to make the behavioral decision-making method more suitable for reality, this paper fully considers the uncertainty of decision information and extends the TODIM method to the triangular intuitionistic fuzzy environment (Zhang and Xu, 2014). At the same time, due to the increase of realistic complexity, it is difficult for a single decision maker to take all the relevant factors into account, so this study introduces three experts to expand behavioral decision-making to group decision-making. The three experts are a scholar proficient in PV system, an engineer with long-term experience in the field and an economic expert with professional financial knowledge. Hence, according to the principles above, this study will improve the TODIM method and use the extended one to rank the ESAPV projects.

Based on the above analysis, this paper intends to use TIFNs to express the evaluation information of decision makers in order to cope with the hesitation and uncertainty generated in the evaluation process. In the process of weight determination, since the first-level indicators involved in the site selection of ESAPV have much relevance, this study will choose the DEMATEL method to determine the weights of first-level indicators. In addition, compared with entropy weight method, the maximum cross-entropy method can pre-set the range of weight and then use the software of Linear Interactive and General Optimizer (LINGO) to derive the results, which is more scientific, efficient and more in line with the needs of site selection of ESAPV. Therefore, this paper will choose the DEMATEL and maximum cross-entropy method to determine the weights of second-level indicators. Finally, in terms of project sequencing, due to the fact that the location of ESAPV is affected by massive complex factors, decision makers usually have the psychology of risk aversion in the process of site selection. Therefore, this paper applies the TODIM method which considers the psychological factors of decision makers to the ranking of alternatives.

3. Evaluation criteria system of ESAPV

The location of DPV power station involves numerous factors. On basis of this, site selection of ESAPV contains some novel connotations and requirements. After inquiring a large number of documents on location decision-making and consulting experts, the evaluation index system for the location of ESAPV is summarized as follows.

3.1 Resource criteria (C1)

Annual sunshine hours (C11) (Islam et al., 2011; Wu et al., 2018b; Yunna and Geng, 2014): It represents the local level of solar energy resources. The more electricity will be generated with an increasing number of sunshine hours.

Annual solar radiation (C12) (Tavana et al., 2017; Wu et al., 2018b; Yunna and Geng, 2014): Annual solar radiation directly determines the capacity of DPV plants, which has a vital impact on the construction of ESAPV projects.

Average temperature (C13) (Chumpolrat et al., 2014; Radziemska, 2014; Sánchez-Lozano et al., 2016; Sagani et al., 2017): Temperature will have an essential impact on PV modules and even the entire PV power station. It is generally believed that it is more beneficial for PV power generation in the hotter weather. However, the reality case will be distinct. The researches indicate that excessive temperature will influence the work performance of PV modules (Ghazvini and Olamaei, 2019; Kaabeche and Bakelli, 2019).

Relative humidity (C14) (Sagani et al., 2017; Wu et al., 2018c): The increase of relative humidity means the increase of water vapor content in the air and the decrease of solar radiation, which leads to the decrease of electricity generation of PV equipment.

3.2 Economy criteria (C2)

Initial investment cost (C21) (Azoumah et al., 2010; Tavana et al., 2015): The initial investment cost is made up of the hardware investment and software investment, calculated by Eq. (8-1).

$$C_i = C_h + C_s \tag{8-1}$$

where C_i is the initial investment cost, C_h is the hardware investment and C_s is the software investment.

Annual operation and maintenance cost (C22) (Dong et al., 2014; Wu et al., 2013): Operation and maintenance costs include wages of workers and managers, cleaning and maintaining equipment costs, equipment overhaul costs, and aging line replacement costs. It can be calculated as:

$$C_m = C_i \cdot R_i \tag{8-2}$$

where C_m is the annual operation and maintenance cost, and R_i is the rate of maintenance (Liu et al., 2017; Wu et al., 2018a).

Annual project income (C23) (Liu et al., 2017; Shakouri et al., 2017; Wu et al., 2018c): This indicator reflects the profitability of the project. Based on the EPC mode that meets the goal of China's 13th Five-Year Plan, this paper derives the calculation formula of ESAPV project income, as shown in Table 8.2.

Table 8.2 Annual project income of ESAPV under Energy Performance Contracting (EPC) model.

Formula	Remark
$W = W_1 + W_2 + W_3 + W_4$ $W_1 = GK$ $W_2 = G_1P$ $W_3 = G_2P_0C$ $W_4 = (G_2P_o - G_2P_oC)r$	W : General income W_1 : Subsidy income W_2 : On-grid income W_3 : Income from electricity consumption of expressway service area W_4 : Energy-saving benefits G : Power generation K : kWh subsidy G_1 : Power generation amount to network P : Benchmark price of desulfurized coal G_2 : Electricity consumption of expressway service area P_o : Spot price C : Pre-agreed discount r : Contractual earnings ratio

Investment payoff period (C24) (Dong et al., 2014; Guo and Zhao, 2015; Wu et al., 2017): The ESAPV project requires a great deal of capital investment, and the investment recovery period will be an enduring time, which indicates the project investment risk in a certain sense, so it has attracted much attention. The value of investment payoff period can be calculated as:

$$PP = C_i / W \tag{8-3}$$

where PP is the investment payoff period, and W is the annual project income which could be calculated according to Table 8.2.

3.3 Construction criteria (C3)

Infrastructure conditions (C31) (Amer and Daim, 2011; Kurt, 2014; Wu et al., 2014b): The infrastructure conditions discussed in this paper mainly include the quality of the roof in ESAs, the degree to which the roof is easy to install PV equipment, and the space on the ground for crane to use.

Available area (C32) (Wu et al., 2018a; Wu et al., 2018b): The construction of ESAPV needs to make full use of its own building roof, carport and other unused areas so as to better absorb solar radiation, reduce the impact on the surrounding environment, and help to reduce costs.

Possibility of capacity expansion in the future (C33) (Guo and Zhao, 2015; Wu et al., 2013; Yao et al., 2014): When making investment decisions on ESAPV projects, we should fully consider the available land area near ESAs and evaluate the possibility of capacity expansion in the future.

3.4 Social & Environmental criteria (C4)

Public support (C41) (Carlisle et al., 2016; Mir-Artigues et al., 2015): A high degree of public support will be conducive to the promotion and popularization of PV projects in the whole city. It will not only contribute to the construction of a green city, but also promote the maximization of investors' income.

Carbon emission reduction (C42) (Bo et al., 2014; Matulaitis et al., 2016): Both the public and experts need to know how much carbon emissions can be reduced by an ESAPV project. And the value of carbon emission reduction can be calculated as:

$$S_{\mathrm{co}_2} = G \cdot g \cdot m \tag{8-4}$$

where S_{co_2} is the carbon dioxide emissions, g is the average amount of standard coal consumed by per kilowatt hour, and m is the amount of carbon dioxide produced by burning a ton of standard coal.

Ecological harmony (C43) (Wu et al., 2014b; Yunna and Geng, 2014): In addition to occupying the roof of ESA, the project also needs to develop part of the land around the service area, which may affect local vegetation and soil. So, we need to assess the ecological harmony degree of different projects.

3.5 Risk Criteria (C5)

Extreme weather damage risk (C51) (Guerin, 2017; Wu et al., 2018b): Extreme low temperature and extreme high temperature will both affect the PV equipment. Other extreme weather conditions, such as strong winds, thunderstorms and heavy snow, can damage PV modules to a certain extent.

Policy risk (C52) (Angelopoulos et al., 2017; Frisari and Stadelmann, 2015): The ESAPV projects are greatly influenced by policies. At the national level, PV subsidies are unstable and may face the risk of cancellation in recent years. At the provincial and municipal level, the support of local governments for ESAPV projects may also change.

Grid-connected risk (C53) (Azoumah et al., 2010; Gorsevski et al., 2013; Mir-Artigues et al., 2015; Wu et al., 2014a; Wu et al., 2018c): There are wave crests and troughs in PV power generation. And it is necessary to incorporate the surplus electricity generated during the wave crests into the local power grid so as to utilize the solar energy resources to full advantage. But it will probably lead to grid-connected risk at the same time.

As shown in Fig. 8.1, there is the evaluation criteria system of ESAPV.

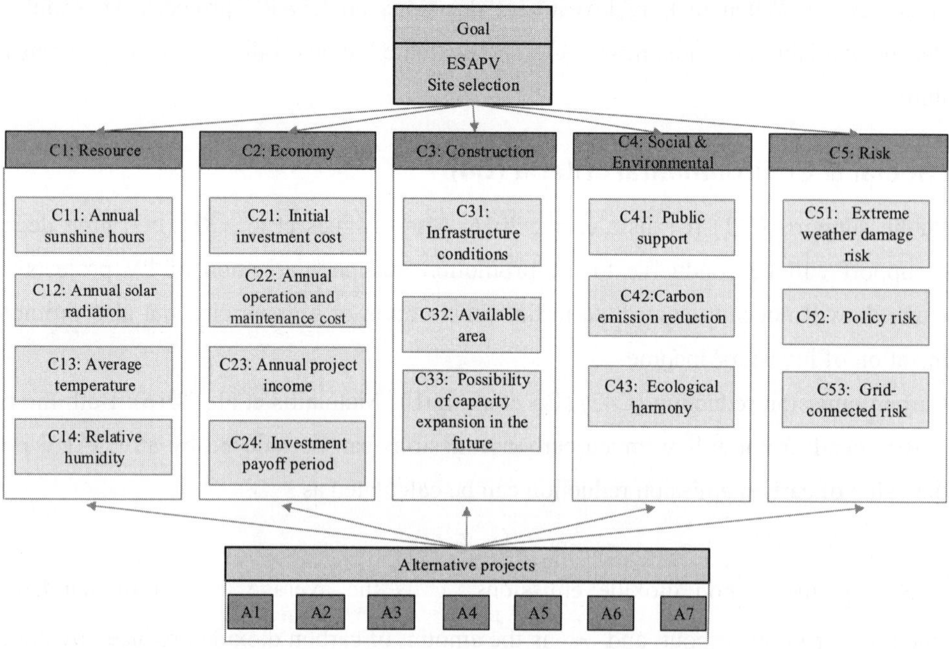

Fig. 8.1 Criteria system for the location of ESAPV.

4. Decision framework of ESAPV projects

This section will elaborate on the triangular intuitionistic fuzzy environment, the decision-making steps and the theoretical methods involved in each step.

4.1 Triangular intuitionistic fuzzy environment in MCDM problem

Definition 1. (Li, 2010) Let $\tilde{\alpha}=((\underline{\alpha},\alpha,\overline{\alpha});\mu_{\tilde{\alpha}},\nu_{\tilde{\alpha}})$ be a TIFN on the real number set, and its membership function and non-membership function are respectively defined as follows:

$$\mu_{\tilde{\alpha}}(x)=\begin{cases}\dfrac{\mu_{\tilde{\alpha}}(x-\underline{\alpha})}{\alpha-\underline{\alpha}} & \text{if } (\underline{\alpha}\leqslant x<\alpha)\\ \mu_{\tilde{\alpha}} & \text{if } x=\alpha\\ \dfrac{\mu_{\tilde{\alpha}}(\overline{\alpha}-x)}{\overline{\alpha}-\alpha} & \text{if } (\alpha<x\leqslant\overline{\alpha})\\ 0 & \text{if } (x<\underline{\alpha},x>\overline{\alpha})\end{cases}\qquad 0\leqslant\mu_{\tilde{\alpha}}\leqslant 1 \tag{8-5}$$

$$\nu_{\tilde{\alpha}}(x)=\begin{cases}\dfrac{\alpha-x+\nu_{\tilde{\alpha}}(x-\underline{\alpha})}{\alpha-\underline{\alpha}} & \text{if } (\underline{\alpha}\leqslant x<\alpha)\\ \nu_{\tilde{\alpha}} & \text{if } x=\alpha\\ \dfrac{x-\alpha+\nu_{\tilde{\alpha}}(\overline{\alpha}-x)}{\overline{\alpha}-\alpha} & \text{if } (\alpha<x\leqslant\overline{\alpha})\\ 1 & \text{if } (x<\underline{\alpha},x>\overline{\alpha})\end{cases}\quad 0\leqslant\nu_{\tilde{\alpha}}\leqslant 1 \tag{8-6}$$

The values $\mu_{\tilde{\alpha}}$ represent the maximum membership degree and $\nu_{\tilde{\alpha}}$ represent the minimum non-membership degree and they satisfy the condition: $0\leqslant \mu_{\tilde{\alpha}}+\nu_{\tilde{\alpha}}\leqslant 1$, as shown in Fig. 8.2.

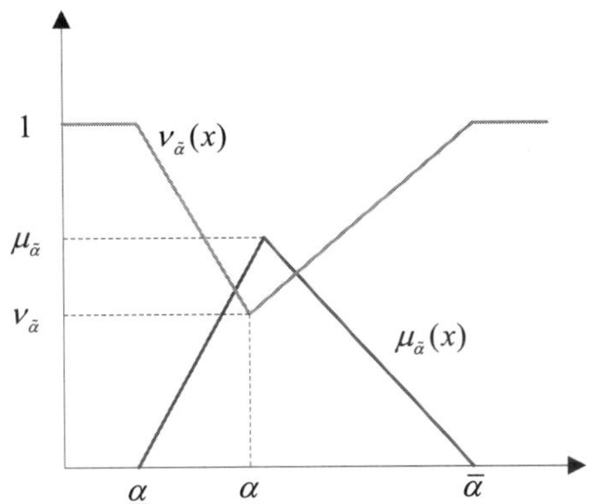

Fig. 8.2 A TIFN $\tilde{\alpha}=((\underline{\alpha},\alpha,\overline{\alpha});\mu_{\tilde{\alpha}},\nu_{\tilde{\alpha}})$.

Definition 2. (Li, 2010) Let $\tilde{\alpha}_1=((\underline{\alpha}_1,\alpha_1,\overline{\alpha}_1);\mu_{\tilde{\alpha}_1},\nu_{\tilde{\alpha}_1})$ and $\tilde{\alpha}_2=((\underline{\alpha}_2,\alpha_2,\overline{\alpha}_2);\mu_{\tilde{\alpha}_2},\nu_{\tilde{\alpha}_2})$ be two TIFNs and λ⩾0. Then the operations for TIFNs are defined as follows:

$$\tilde{\alpha}_1+\tilde{\alpha}_2=((\underline{\alpha}_1+\underline{\alpha}_2,\alpha_1+\alpha_2,\overline{\alpha}_1+\overline{\alpha}_2);\mu_{\tilde{\alpha}_1}\wedge\mu_{\tilde{\alpha}_2}\nu_{\tilde{\alpha}_1}\vee\nu_{\tilde{\alpha}_2}) \tag{8-7}$$

$$\lambda\tilde{\alpha}_1=((\lambda\underline{\alpha}_1,\lambda\alpha_1,\lambda\overline{\alpha}_1);\mu_{\tilde{\alpha}_1},\nu_{\tilde{\alpha}_1}) \tag{8-8}$$

where the symbols "$\wedge$" and "$\vee$" mean min and max operators respectively.

Definition 3. (Wan et al., 2016) Let $\tilde{\alpha}_1=((\underline{\alpha}_1,\alpha_1,\overline{\alpha}_1);\mu_{\tilde{\alpha}_1},\nu_{\tilde{\alpha}_1})$ and $\tilde{\alpha}_2=((\underline{\alpha}_2,\alpha_2,\overline{\alpha}_2);\mu_{\tilde{\alpha}_2},\nu_{\tilde{\alpha}_2})$ be two TIFNs. The Hamming distance between them is defined as follows:

$$\begin{aligned}d(\tilde{\alpha}_1,\tilde{\alpha}_2)=\frac{1}{6}[&\left|(1+\mu_{\tilde{\alpha}_1}-\nu_{\tilde{\alpha}_1})\underline{\alpha}_1-(1+\mu_{\tilde{\alpha}_2}-\nu_{\tilde{\alpha}_2})\underline{\alpha}_2\right|\\&+\left|(1+\mu_{\tilde{\alpha}_1}-\nu_{\tilde{\alpha}_1})\alpha_1-(1+\mu_{\tilde{\alpha}_2}-\nu_{\tilde{\alpha}_2})\alpha_2\right|\\&+\left|(1+\mu_{\tilde{\alpha}_1}-\nu_{\tilde{\alpha}_1})\overline{\alpha}_1-(1+\mu_{\tilde{\alpha}_2}-\nu_{\tilde{\alpha}_2})\overline{\alpha}_2\right|]\end{aligned} \tag{8-9}$$

Definition 4. (Li, 2010) A ratio ranking formula developed for ranking the TIFNs $\tilde{\alpha}_i$ (i=1, 2, …, *n*), is summarized as follows:

$$R(\tilde{\alpha}_i,\lambda)=\frac{(\underline{\alpha}_i+4\alpha_i+\overline{\alpha}_i)+(\lambda\mu_{\tilde{\alpha}_i}^2+(1-\lambda)(1-\nu_{\tilde{\alpha}_i})^2)}{6+(\overline{\alpha}_i-\underline{\alpha}_i)(\lambda\mu_{\tilde{\alpha}_i}^2+(1-\lambda)(1-\nu_{\tilde{\alpha}_i})^2)} \tag{8-10}$$

where, $\lambda\in(0,1)$ reflects the attitude toward uncertainties' degree of decision makers, and we make λ be 1/2 in this study.

In this paper, a four-stage decision-making framework for the location of ESAPV is established under triangular intuitionistic fuzzy environment. And in order to illustrate the theory and logic of this framework more vividly and concretely, the corresponding decision-making flow chart is provided, as shown in Fig. 8.3.

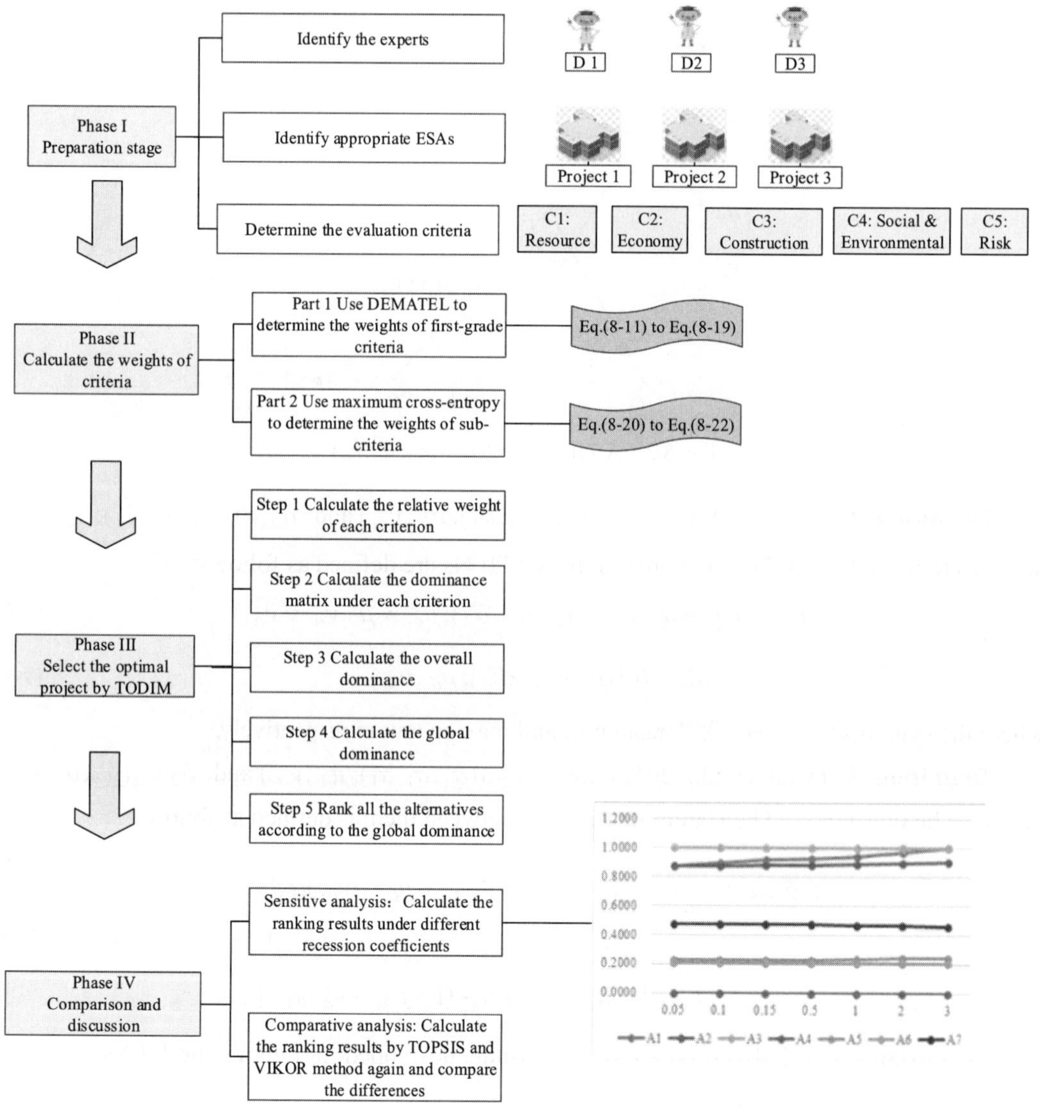

Fig. 8.3 The decision framework for the location of ESAPV.

4.2 Phase I-Preparation process

The preparation process consists of three steps:

Step 1. Identify the experts. A scientific and rigorous decision-making process requires the participation of multiple experts and needs to fully adopt their opinions. The location of ESAPV projects requires scholars, engineers, as well as economic experts. Only in this way can we ensure the validity of decision-making.

Step 2. Identify appropriate ESAs. First, ESAs with large available area are identified by Google Map. Second, communicate with the managers of the service areas to find out whether they have the willingness to cooperate. And then carry out field investigation to collect information such as roof quality, building conditions and so on. Finally, the experts choose several ESAs for later decision-making.

Step 3. Determine the evaluation criteria. Determine the evaluation criteria of ESAPV by literature review and suggestions from experts. And the complete evaluation index system has been shown in Section 3 of this paper.

4.3 Phase II-Calculate the weights of criteria

This study adopts DEMATEL and maximum cross-entropy method to determine the weights of the indicators.

Part 1. It should be noted that the thoughts of this IF-DEMATEL are based on the works developed by Seyed-Hosseini et al. (2006) and Chen and Li (2009). There are the steps of IF-DEMATEL method, and it will be applied to the weight determination process of both first-level indicators and second-level indicators.

Step 1. Construct the direct influence matrix. The influence of criterion C_i on criterion C_j is represented by $\tilde{\alpha}_{ijk}$ which is selected by expert "k" from Table 8.3, and all assessment results form matrix A.

Table 8.3 Degree of influence and corresponding TIFNs for expert assessment.

Degree of influence	TIFNS
No (N)	((0, 0, 0); μ, ν)
Low (L)	((0, 1/2, 1); μ, ν)
Medium (M)	((1/2, 1, 3/2); μ, ν)
High (H)	((3/2, 2, 5/2); μ, ν)
Very high (VH)	((5/2, 3, 7/2); μ, ν)

$$\tilde{A}_k = \begin{bmatrix} & C_1 & C_2 & \cdots & C_n \\ C_1 & 0 & \tilde{\alpha}_{12k} & \cdots & \tilde{\alpha}_{1nk} \\ C_2 & \tilde{\alpha}_{21k} & 0 & \cdots & \tilde{\alpha}_{2nk} \\ . & . & . & & . \\ . & . & . & \tilde{\alpha}_{ijk} & . \\ . & . & . & & . \\ C_n & \tilde{\alpha}_{n1k} & \tilde{\alpha}_{n2k} & \cdots & 0 \end{bmatrix}, i=1,2,\ldots,n; j=1,2,\ldots,n$$

Step 2. Determine the total direct influence matrix based on Eq. (8-11).

$$\tilde{\alpha}_{ij} = \sum_{k=1}^{K} \sigma_k \tilde{\alpha}_{ijk} = ((\underline{\alpha}_{ij}, \alpha_{ij}, \overline{\alpha}_{ij}); \mu_{\tilde{\alpha}_{ij}}, \nu_{\tilde{\alpha}_{ij}}) \tag{8-11}$$

where σ_k represents the weight of expert "k", satisfying the condition that $\sum_{k=1}^{K} \sigma_k = 1$ and $\sigma_k > 0$ for $k = 1,2,3,\ldots,K$.

The total direct influence matrix can be expressed as:

$$\tilde{A} = \begin{bmatrix} & C_1 & C_2 & \cdots & C_n \\ C_1 & 0 & \tilde{\alpha}_{12} & \cdots & \tilde{\alpha}_{1n} \\ C_2 & \tilde{\alpha}_{21} & 0 & \cdots & \tilde{\alpha}_{2n} \\ . & . & . & & . \\ . & . & . & \tilde{\alpha}_{ij} & . \\ . & . & . & & . \\ C_n & \tilde{\alpha}_{n1} & \tilde{\alpha}_{n2} & \cdots & 0 \end{bmatrix}, i=1,2,\ldots,n; j=1,2,\ldots,n$$

Step 3. Calculate the defuzzified direct influence matrix B (element β_{ij}) based on Eq. (8-12).

$$\beta_{ij} = \frac{(\underline{\alpha}_{ij} + 4\alpha_{ij} + \overline{\alpha}_{ij}) + (0.5\mu_{\tilde{\alpha}_{ij}}^2 + 0.5(1-\nu_{\tilde{\alpha}_{ij}})^2)}{6 + (\overline{\alpha}_{ij} - \underline{\alpha}_{ij})(0.5\mu_{\tilde{\alpha}_{ij}}^2 + 0.5(1-\nu_{\tilde{\alpha}_{ij}})^2)} \tag{8-12}$$

Step 4. Calculate the standardized direct influence matrix as follows:

$$X = \left[x_{ij}\right]_{n\times n} = \frac{1}{s} \cdot B \tag{8-13}$$

$$s = \max_{i=1}^{n} \left\{ \sum_{j=1}^{n} \beta_{ij} \right\} \tag{8-14}$$

Step 5. Determine the comprehensive influence matrix based on Eq. (8-15).

$$T = \left[t_{ij}\right]_{n\times n} = X(I-X)^{-1} \tag{8-15}$$

where, t_{ij} represents the comprehensive influence of criterion i on criterion j, and I is the identity matrix.

Step 6. Calculate the influence degree and being influenced degree of each criterion as follows:

$$r_i = \sum_{j=1}^{n} t_{ij} \tag{8-16}$$

$$q_j = \sum_{i=1}^{n} t_{ij} \tag{8-17}$$

Step 7. Determine the weights of criteria as follows:

$$w_{sj}' = \left[(r_j + q_j)^2 + (r_j - q_j)^2 \right]^{1/2} \tag{8-18}$$

$$w_{sj} = \frac{w_{sj}'}{\sum_{j=1}^{n} w_{sj}'} \tag{8-19}$$

Part 2. There are the steps of maximum cross-entropy method, and it will be used to the weight determination process of sub-criteria.

Step 1. Construct the decision matrix.

As shown in Fig. 8.1, there are 17 sub-criteria, which can be segmented into two categories: quantitative criteria and qualitative criteria. For the first type of criteria, they can be measured or calculated accurately; for the second type of qualitative criteria, they will be evaluated by experts using TIFNs. It is worthy emphasizing that for the second type of qualitative indicators, in order to avoid the problem of one-sidedness and inaccuracy caused by only one expert decision, we still need to integrate the opinions of many experts. Assuming that this decision involves i (i=1, 2, …, m) alternatives, j (j=1, 2…, n) qualitative sub-criteria, and it is evaluated by K experts. Let $\tilde{a}_{ijk} = ((\underline{a}_{ijk}, a_{ijk}, \overline{a}_{ijk}); \mu_{\tilde{a}_{ijk}}, \nu_{\tilde{a}_{ijk}})$ be the score of the ith project on the jth sub-criteria chosen by expert "k" from Table 8.4.

Table 8.4 Linguistic variables and their corresponding TIFNs used to evaluate the projects.

Linguistic variable	TIFNS
Extremely low (EL)	((0, 1, 2); μ, ν)
Very low (VL)	((1, 2, 3); μ, ν)
Low (L)	((2, 3, 4); μ, ν)
Medium (M)	((3, 4, 5); μ, ν)
High (H)	((4, 5, 6); μ, ν)
Very high (VH)	((5, 6, 7); μ, ν)
Extremely high (EH)	((6, 7, 8); μ, ν)

The integrated opinions of experts for each qualitative sub-criterion can be calculated as follows:

$$\tilde{a}_{ij}=\sum_{k=1}^{K}\lambda_k\tilde{a}_{ijk}=((\underline{a}_{ij},a_{ij},\overline{a}_{ij});\mu_{\tilde{a}_{ij}},\nu_{\tilde{a}_{ij}}) \tag{8-20}$$

where λ_k represents the weight of expert k, satisfying the condition that $\sum_{k=1}^{K}\lambda_k=1$ and $\lambda_k>0$ for $k=1,2,3,...,K$. After collecting, sorting and calculating the values of criteria, the weighted decision matrix $[\tilde{a}_{ij}]_{m\times n}$ is established.

Step 2. Normalize the weighted decision matrix.

The sub-criteria include benefit criteria and cost criteria which are defined as F^B and F^C respectively. In addition, they belong to different physical dimensions and measurements. In order to eliminate the effects of inconsistency and different dimensions, it is necessary to normalize the decision matrix $[\tilde{a}_{ij}]_{m\times n}$ as $[\tilde{b}_{ij}]_{m\times n}$ where $\tilde{b}_{ij}=((\underline{b}_{ij},b_{ij},\overline{b}_{ij});\mu_{\tilde{b}_{ij}},\nu_{\tilde{b}_{ij}})$ with $\mu_{\tilde{b}_{ij}}=\mu_{\tilde{a}_{ij}}$, $\nu_{\tilde{b}_{ij}}=\nu_{\tilde{a}_{ij}}$ and

$$(\underline{b}_{ij},b_{ij},\overline{b}_{ij})=\begin{cases}\left(\dfrac{\underline{a}_{ij}}{\overline{a}_{\max j}},\dfrac{a_{ij}}{\overline{a}_{\max j}},\dfrac{\overline{a}_{ij}}{\overline{a}_{\max j}}\right) & \text{if} \quad a_j\in F^B\\[2ex] \left(\dfrac{\underline{a}_{\min j}}{\overline{a}_{ij}},\dfrac{\underline{a}_{\min j}}{a_{ij}},\dfrac{\underline{a}_{\min j}}{\underline{a}_{ij}}\right) & \text{if} \quad a_j\in F^C\end{cases} \tag{8-21}$$

where $\overline{a}_{\max j}=\max\{\overline{a}_{ij}\mid i=1,2,...,m\}$, $\underline{a}_{\min j}=\min\{\underline{a}_{ij}\mid i=1,2,...,m\}$.

Step 3. Determine the weights of sub-criteria.

The concept of entropy is derived from thermodynamics, cross-entropy can determine the weights of information sources according to the degree of mutual support. The weight of information source will increase with the higher degree of mutual support. Therefore, based on the principle of maximum cross-entropy, this part constructs the weight determination model when the weight information is partly known, as follows:

For the criteria C_j, the deviation between project A_i and other projects is defined as: $D_{ij}(\omega_j)=\sum_{t=1}^{m}d(\tilde{b}_{ij},\tilde{b}_{tj})\omega_j$, and the total deviation between all the projects and other projects is defined as: $D_j(\omega_j)=\sum_{i=1}^{m}D_{ij}(\omega_j)=\sum_{i=1}^{m}\sum_{t=1}^{m}d(\tilde{b}_{ij},\tilde{b}_{tj})\omega_j$. For all the criteria, the total deviation between all the projects and other projects is defined as: $D(\omega_j)=\sum_{j=1}^{n}D_j(\omega_j)=\sum_{j=1}^{n}\sum_{i=1}^{m}\sum_{t=1}^{m}d(\tilde{b}_{ij},\tilde{b}_{tj})\omega_j$.

According to the principle of maximum cross-entropy, when the weight information is partly known, a non-linear optimization model is constructed as follows:

$$D(\omega_j)=\sum_{j=1}^{n}\sum_{i=1}^{m}\sum_{t=1}^{m} d\left(\tilde{b}_{ij}, \tilde{b}_{tj}\right)\omega_j \tag{8-22}$$

$$\text{s.t.} = \begin{cases} \omega_j \in P \\ \sum_{j=1}^{n} \omega_j = 1 \\ 0 \leqslant \omega_j \leqslant 1 \end{cases}$$

where P is the weight information partly known.

4.4 Phase III-Select the optimal project

TODIM method can effectively capture the risk aversion psychology of decision makers and deal with the problem of MCDM with uncertain decision information (Gomes and Rangel, 2009). The method is similar to AHP and PROMETHEE in that it compares different alternatives for the same criterion. And the TODIM method utilized in this proposed model involves the following steps (Liu and Teng, 2016):

Step 1. Choose the criterion C_r with the largest weight as the reference criterion and then calculate the relative weight of each criterion C_j to the reference criterion C_r as follows:

$$w_{jr} = \frac{w_j}{w_r} \tag{8-23}$$

Step 2. Calculate the dominance matrix under each criterion, and the dominance degree of the project A_p compared to the project A_q under criterion C_j can be calculated as follows:

$$\delta_j(A_p, A_q) = \begin{cases} \sqrt{\dfrac{(b_{pj} - b_{qj})w_{jr}}{\sum_{j=1}^{n} w_{jr}}} & \text{if } b_{pj} - b_{qj} > 0 \\ 0 & \text{if } b_{pj} - b_{qj} = 0 \\ -\dfrac{1}{\theta}\sqrt{\dfrac{(b_{qj} - b_{pj})\sum_{j=1}^{n} w_{jr}}{w_{jr}}} & \text{if } b_{pj} - b_{qj} < 0 \end{cases} \tag{8-24}$$

where θ is the coefficient of loss recession. Different risk preferences correspond to different recession coefficients θ. The value of θ should satisfy the condition that $\theta > 0$, if $0 < \theta < 1$, then the effect of expense will rise; if $\theta > 1$, then the effect of expense will decline (Qin et al., 2017).

Step 3. Calculate the overall dominance of project A_p over project A_q under all criteria as below:

$$\delta(A_p, A_q) = \sum_{j=1}^{n} \delta_j (A_p, A_q) \tag{8-25}$$

Step 4. Calculate the global dominance of each project as follows:

$$\zeta_p = \frac{\sum_{q=1}^{n} \delta(A_p, A_q) - \min_p (\sum_{q=1}^{n} \delta(A_p, A_q))}{\max_p (\sum_{q=1}^{n} \delta(A_p, A_q)) - \min_p (\sum_{q=1}^{n} \delta(A_p, A_q))} \tag{8-26}$$

Step 5. Rank all the projects according to the global dominance. The ranking order of project A_p will rise as the ζ_p takes bigger value.

4.5 Phase IV-Comparison and discussion

In order to prove the validity of the decision framework proposed in this paper, sensitivity analysis and comparative analysis should be carried out. First, decision makers will have different attitudes when facing risks due to factors such as their cultural background and corporate strategy, different risk preferences correspond to different recession coefficients θ, and θ will be set to different values to conduct sensitivity analysis. Second, in order to verify the advancement and feasibility of the TODIM method, TOPSIS (Lai et al., 1994) and VIKOR (Opricovic and Tzeng, 2004) are used to rank the alternatives again. Moreover, the coefficient v in the VIKOR method will be set to ½ based on existing researches (Kim and Ahn, 2019; Wu et al., 2018b; Zeng et al., 2019).

5. Case study and discussion

The decision framework proposed in Section 4 will be applied to a case study in this part. Moreover, sensitivity analysis and comparative analysis will be made to verify the validity of the decision framework.

5.1 Problem statement

A PV company in Beijing intends to invest in a PV power station in the ESAs of Hebei Province. Seven ESAs are identified after investigation and research, which are located in Zhangjiakou, Baoding, Shijiazhuang, Xingtai, Handan, Hengshui and Cangzhou, as shown in Fig. 8.4. Each of these projects has its own advantages and disadvantages. This enterprise has to select an optimal project.

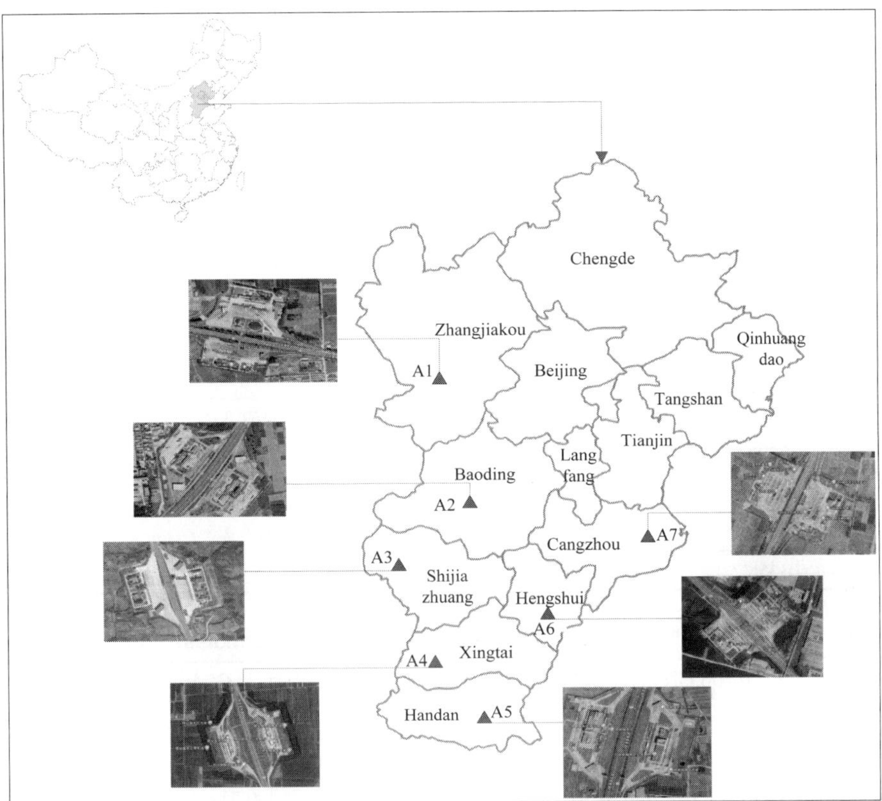

Fig. 8.4 Geographical positions of the seven ESAPV projects.

5.2 Attribute data collection

The evaluation index system of ESAPV includes 10 quantitative indicators and 7 qualitative indicators. For quantitative indicators, we can find exact data from specific data sources or calculate them through formulas, as shown in Table 8.5, Table 8.6 and Table 8.7. For qualitative indicators, linguistic variables are selected from Table 8.4 by experts to fill in Questionnaire II (Appendix A), and then transformed into corresponding TIFNs. Finally, weighted TIFNs for calculation are generated by summing up the opinions of three experts, as shown in Appendix B (we make the weights of experts be 1/3 in this article).

Table 8.5 Approaches to obtaining quantitative data.

Criteria	Unit	Approaches
C11	h	NASA (National Aeronautics and Space Administration)
C12	MJ/㎡	NASA
C13	℃	NASA
C14	%	NASA
C21	106.CNY	Calculated by Eq. (8-1)
C22	106.CNY	Calculated by Eq. (8-2)
C23	106.CNY	Calculated according to Table 8.2

Continued

Criteria	Unit	Approaches
C24	year	Calculated by Eq. (8-3)
C32	㎡	Google Map
C42	103 t	Calculated by Eq. (8-4)

Table 8.6 Quantitative data inquired from the Internet.

Project	C11(h)	C12(MJ/㎡)	C13(℃)	C14(%)	C32(㎡)
A1	3812.3	7152.3	7.3	44.9	16739.9
A2	3324.2	6347.5	10.1	56.7	10178.5
A3	3050.1	5723.4	11.4	61.3	17642.3
A4	2790.6	5517.8	12.6	62.7	11345.9
A5	2753.3	5224.2	13.7	64.3	12847.5
A6	3234.1	5526.7	11.6	63.2	16581.4
A7	3458.2	5673.9	10.9	61.8	13247.3

Table 8.7 Quantitative data calculated by formulas.

Project	C21(106.CNY)	C22(106.CNY)	C23(106.CNY)	C24(year)	C42(103 t)
A1	26.45	0.50	2.89	9.16	2.62
A2	16.08	0.29	1.66	9.67	2.23
A3	27.87	0.50	2.87	9.71	2.70
A4	17.93	0.32	1.82	9.86	2.27
A5	20.30	0.36	2.01	10.08	2.31
A6	26.20	0.48	2.74	9.54	2.58
A7	20.93	0.38	2.18	9.59	2.41

As for the PV subsidies that need to be used in Table 8.2, this paper also conducts a detailed investigation. Because the ESAPV project adopts the operation mode of “self-use, surplus electricity access to the Internet”, the current state subsidy for the project is 0.32 yuan per kilowatt hour. In addition, the government of Hebei Province provides a subsidy of 0.2 yuan per kilowatt hour. Finally, for each prefecture-level city, there are different municipal financial subsidy policies. And the details are shown in Table 8.8.

Table 8.8 Different municipal financial subsidies for DPV projects in Hebei Province.

City	Zhangjiakou	Baoding	Shijiazhuang	Xingtai	Handan	Hengshui	Cangzhou
Subsidy(yuan/kWh)	0.05	0.10	0.10	0.05	0.15	0.05	0.05

Data source: Hebei Province Development and Reform Commission.

5.3 Calculate the weights of criteria

The weight determination method proposed in Section 4.3 will be applied to this part.

Part 1. Establish the weights of first-level indicators using DEMATEL. The three experts evaluate five criteria of resource, economy, construction, social & environmental, as well as risk, and fill in Questionnaire I (Appendix A) to generate three fuzzy direct influence matrices (Appendix B). Then the weighted influence matrix is calculated according to the operation rules of TIFNs, assuming that the weights of experts are the same. Finally, import this weighted matrix into Matlab to generate the weights of each first-level indicators.

Part 2. According to the steps of DEMATEL method, the subjective weights of sub-criteria can be obtained, then construct a non-linear optimization model based on the maximum cross-entropy principle to establish the objective weights of sub-criteria. In this paper, objective weight and subjective weight account for 50% respectively (Wu et al., 2018c) .

Step 1. Standardize the quantitative data.

Step 2. Collect three experts' scoring tables on qualitative indicators which are represented by TIFNs. Calculate the weighted scoring table and make it standardized. Finally, calculate the distance between the weighted and standardized TIFNs according to Eq. (8-9).

Step 3. Based on the detailed steps of maximum cross-entropy method, calculate the total deviations between all projects and other projects for all attributes.

Step 4. Construct a non-linear optimization model based on the maximum cross-entropy principle, and then utilize the software of LINGO to get the weights of sub-criteria.

Finally, we get the weights of the indicators, as shown in Table 8.9. From the table, we can see that the criterion with the highest weight is the investment payoff period C24, followed by the annual project income C23, which reflects that the decision makers attach the most importance to the economic benefits. Similarly, in order to illustrate the weights of indicators at all levels intuitively, this paper provides the corresponding pie chart, as shown in Fig. 8.5.

Table 8.9 Summary of the criteria weights.

Indicators	Objective Weights	Subjective Weights	Comprehensive Weights
C11	0.0525	0.1199	0.0862
C12	0.0375	0.0785	0.0580
C13	0.0300	0.0375	0.0338
C14	0.0300	0.0228	0.0264
C21	0.0325	0.0610	0.0468
C22	0.0520	0.0696	0.0608
C23	0.1105	0.0967	0.1036
C24	0.0650	0.1505	0.1078
C31	0.0550	0.0255	0.0403
C32	0.0726	0.0551	0.0639
C33	0.0924	0.0389	0.0657
C41	0.0627	0.0486	0.0557
C42	0.0323	0.0644	0.0484
C43	0.0950	0.0105	0.0528

Continued

Indicators	Objective Weights	Subjective Weights	Comprehensive Weights
C51	0.0846	0.0268	0.0557
C52	0.0594	0.0669	0.0632
C53	0.0360	0.0269	0.0315

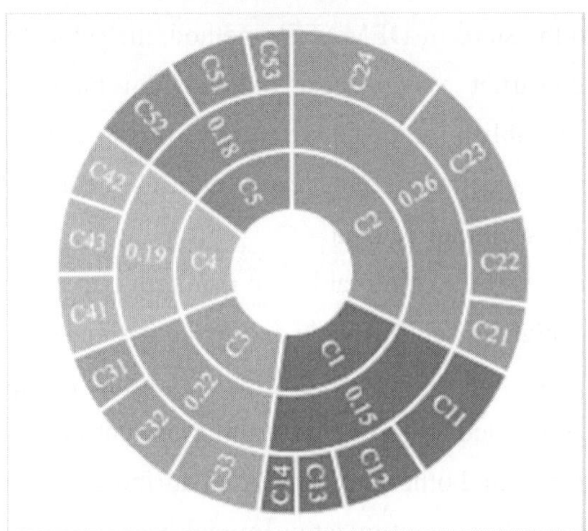

Fig. 8.5 Weights of criteria at all levels.

5.4 Select the optimal project

Since the quantitative data and weighted qualitative data which are standardized have been obtained when calculating the weights of sub-criteria, it can be used directly here.

Step 1. Calculate the relative weights of the index according to Eq. (8-23).

Step 2. Calculate the dominance relationship between the projects for attribute Cj based on Eq. (8-24), where θ is 1 (Xu et al., 2017; Zhang et al., 2017; Zhang and Xu, 2014). In consideration of the simplicity and legibility of the paper, the dominance matrix under C21 is exhibited representatively, as shown in Table 8.10.

Step 3. Add the dominances under 17 indicators according to Eq. (8-25) to get the overall dominance matrix, as shown in Table 8.11.

Step 4. Calculate the global dominance of each project based on Eq. (8-26) and rank the projects, as shown in Table 8.12.

Table 8.10 Dominance matrix under indicator C21.

C21	A1	A2	A3	A4	A5	A6	A7
A1	0.0000	-2.8940	0.0382	-2.4853	-1.9840	-0.3524	-1.8508
A2	0.1354	0.0000	0.1407	0.0694	0.0986	0.1344	0.1041
A3	-0.8152	-3.0066	0.0000	-2.6156	-2.1450	-0.8881	-2.0224
A4	0.1163	-1.4827	0.1224	0.0000	0.0701	0.1151	0.0776
A5	0.0929	-2.1069	0.1004	-1.4968	0.0000	0.0914	0.0335

Continued

C21	A1	A2	A3	A4	A5	A6	A7
A6	0.0165	-2.8725	0.0416	-2.4602	-1.9525	0.0000	-1.8169
A7	0.0866	-2.2248	0.0946	-1.6587	-0.7148	0.0850	0.0000

Table 8.11 Overall dominance matrix.

	A1	A2	A3	A4	A5	A6	A7
A1	0.0000	-11.7685	-8.9217	-6.8693	-11.3479	-4.3250	-6.0168
A2	-18.5347	0.0000	-10.5186	-3.1694	-7.1942	-5.9072	-6.3564
A3	-13.6851	-12.9995	0.0000	-3.8174	-7.2502	-2.0018	-7.0887
A4	-21.5615	-18.0476	-18.8287	0.0000	-8.9628	-10.5638	-11.5602
A5	-19.3833	-16.0169	-15.5958	-7.3591	0.0000	-9.8667	-11.4328
A6	-17.9042	-17.4779	-13.2529	-9.8514	-11.5598	0.0000	-10.7191
A7	-17.9068	-15.2998	-13.4556	-6.6620	-9.2599	-6.9999	0.0000

Table 8.12 Ranking results of projects.

	A1	A2	A3	A4	A5	A6	A7
ξ	0.9436	0.8867	1.0000	0.0000	0.2312	0.2052	0.4672
R	2	3	1	7	5	6	4

According to the global dominance obtained, the projects are ranked as follows: A3>A1>A2>A7>A5>A6>A4. Thus A3 is the optimal alternative for the enterprise to invest in when θ=1.

In addition, the ranking results under different types of data are calculated, as shown in Table 8.13. Compared with RNs, TFNs take into account the ambiguity and uncertainty of experts in evaluating alternatives, which causes a slight change in the results. While TIFNs consider three aspects of membership degree, non-membership degree and hesitation degree, possessing more flexibility and practicability, which results in the optimal project being replaced by A3.

Table 8.13 Ranking results under different types of data.

	A1	A2	A3	A4	A5	A6	A7
RNs	1	3	2	7	5	6	4
TFNs	1	3	2	7	4	6	5
TIFNs	2	3	1	7	5	6	4

5.5 Sensitivity and comparative analysis

Part 1. Sensitivity analysis.

Since the loss recession coefficient θ reflects the sensitivity of decision makers to loss, we decide to set θ to different values to test the impact of investors' risk aversion psychology on decision results. In addition, the decision makers' loss aversion degree will increase as the θ takes smaller value, so the study is more meaningful when the value of θ changes from 0 to 1. And this paper chooses the global dominance (Table 8.14) when θ is set to 0.05, 0.1, 0.15, 0.5, 1, 2 and 3 respectively to illustrate the results of sensitivity analysis.

Table 8.14 Ranking results under different recession coefficients.

θ	0.05		0.1		0.15		0.5		1		2		3	
	ξ	R	ξ	R	ξ	R	ξ	R	ξ	R	ξ	R	ξ	R
A1	0.8754	3	0.8946	2	0.9163	2	0.9279	2	0.9436	2	0.9724	2	0.9982	2
A2	0.8769	2	0.8774	3	0.8779	3	0.8816	3	0.8867	3	0.8958	3	0.9040	3
A3	1.0000	1	1.0000	1	1.0000	1	1.0000	1	1.0000	1	1.0000	1	1.0000	1
A4	0.0000	7	0.0000	7	0.0000	7	0.0000	7	0.0000	7	0.0000	7	0.0000	7
A5	0.2237	5	0.2241	5	0.2245	5	0.2274	5	0.2312	5	0.2383	5	0.2447	5
A6	0.2053	6	0.2053	6	0.2053	6	0.2053	6	0.2052	6	0.2051	6	0.2051	6
A7	0.4724	4	0.4721	4	0.4718	4	0.4699	4	0.4672	4	0.4623	4	0.4579	4

Then, by further analyzing Table 8.14 and Fig. 8.6, we can find that when $\theta<0.1$, the ranking results is A3>A2>A1>A7>A5>A6>A4, but when $0.1\leqslant\theta\leqslant3$, the ranking results is A3>A1>A2>A7>A5>A6>A4. The results above show that the ranking of the projects is stable overall and A3 is always the optimal project no matter how the value of θ changes. But with the adjustment of the parameter θ, the ranking results will also change accordingly. When the parameter value changes from 0.05 to 0.1, the order of A1 and A2 will change at the same time, which reflects the characteristic of sensitivity. Therefore, when evaluating ESAPV projects, the risk aversion psychology of decision makers is an important factor to consider.

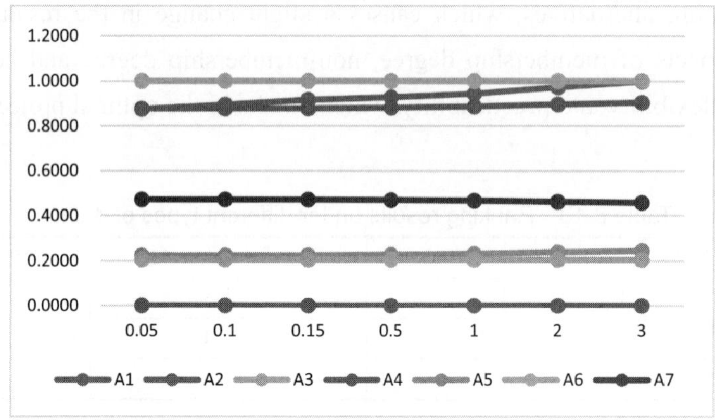

Fig. 8.6 Global dominances under different recession coefficients.

Part 2. Comparative analysis.

There are the ranking results obtained by different methods, as shown in Table 8.15.

Table 8.15 Ranking results calculated by different methods.

		A1	A2	A3	A4	A5	A6	A7
TODIM	$\theta < 0.1$	3	2	1	7	5	6	4
	$0.1 \leqslant \theta \leqslant 3$	2	3	1	7	5	6	4
VIKOR	S	0.3097	0.5255	0.4649	0.6821	0.6635	0.5329	0.5581
	R	0.0597	0.1036	0.0664	0.0906	0.1078	0.0565	0.0597
	Q	0.0312	0.7488	0.3050	0.8319	0.9751	0.2996	0.3646
	Rank	1	5	3	6	7	2	4
TOPSIS		1	5	3	7	6	2	4

As shown in Table 8.15, the ranking results obtained by these three methods are different from each other. And we can get three conclusions through observation and analysis. First, the TOPSIS method and the VIKOR method are both based on the common idea that determine the priority of projects according to the proximity of each project to the ideal project. As a result, the optimal project calculated by these two methods is the same one, A1. Second, compared with TOPSIS, the VIKOR method takes the maximum benefit of the group and the minimum regret of the individual into consideration, which causes the orders of A4 and A5 change slightly. Third, TOPSIS and VIKOR are based on the assumption that the decision makers are absolutely rational, while the TODIM method takes the decision makers' psychological factor into account, hence the optimal project changes from A1 to A3. In general, the ranking results obtained by the TODIM method are more convincing because of its paying attention to the risk aversion psychology of decision makers and this comparison analysis shows the practicability of the proposed model.

6. Conclusion

The rapid development of electric vehicle industry in recent years has put forward higher requirements for the power consumption of ESAs. Therefore, the construction of ESAPV projects becomes an important issue to be studied urgently. And the main conclusions of this article are summarized as follows:

(1) The location of ESAPV is a brand-new topic, whose criteria system has been innovatively established in this paper.

(2) This article applies triangular intuitionistic fuzzy environment to the location of ESAPV for the first time, which ensures the feasibility and validity of the evaluation results.

(3) The DEMATEL method is utilized to determine the weights of first-level indicators that lack objective data support and the integrated weighting method is applied to determine the weights of second-level indicators. This weight determination method is more in line with the actual needs, which can be referred by other researchers.

(4) The TODIM method which considers decision makers' risk aversion psychology is improved by a combination with triangular intuitionistic fuzzy environment and group decision-making theory. The sensitive analysis and comparative analysis have verified the practicability of the improved TODIM method.

As a new research object, the location decision of ESAPV projects is affected by multiple factors and faces numerous uncertainties. This study introduces triangular intuitionistic fuzzy environment to solve the problem of randomness and uncertainty. In addition, facing the current complex investment environment, investors may have different risk aversion awareness. In this paper, TODIM method considering investors' psychological factors is introduced to rank the projects, which is more in line with the actual situation. In conclusion, the decision-making framework proposed in this paper can effectively solve the location problem of ESAPV projects. The decision-making ideas and decision-making methods involved in the framework will contribute to the investment decisions of other renewable energy projects, thus contributing to the cleaner production and environmental sustainability. In the future, with the large-scale development of ESAPV projects, the combination of these projects and energy storage technology will be the directions for future work.

Acknowledgments

This paper is supported by the National Social Science Fund of China (19AGL027), the Fundamental Research Funds for the Central Universities (No. 2018ZD14) and the 2017 Special Project of Cultivation and Development of Innovation Base (No. Z171100002217024).

Appendix A

Questionnaire I

Introductions:

(1) This questionnaire is designed for academic research. Please fill it in carefully. Thank you very much!

(2) This article contains five first-level criteria, they are C1 Resource criteria, C2 Economy criteria, C3 Construction criteria, C4 Social & Environmental criteria and C5 Risk Criteria. You can employ No (N), Low (L), Medium (M), High (H) and Very high (VH) to evaluate the influence degree among all the criteria.

Table A.1 Questionnaire I.

	C1	C2	C3	C4	C5
C1					

Continued

C2					
C3					
C4					
C5					

Questionnaire II

Introductions:

(1) This questionnaire is designed for academic research. Please fill it in carefully. Thank you very much!

(2) This article contains seven qualitative sub-criteria, they are C31 Infrastructure conditions, C33 Possibility of capacity expansion in the future, C41 Public support, C43 Ecological harmony, C51 Extreme weather damage risk, C52 Policy risk, C53 Grid-connected risk. You can employ Extremely low (EL), Very low (VL), Low (L), Medium (M), High (H), Very high (VH), Extremely high (EH) to evaluate the projects.

Table A.2 Questionnaire II.

	C31	C33	C41	C43	C51	C52	C53
A1							
A2							
A3							
A4							
A5							
A6							
A7							

Appendix B

Three fuzzy direct influence matrices of first-level criteria represented by linguistic variables.

$$\tilde{A}_1 = \begin{bmatrix} & C_1 & C_2 & C_3 & C_4 & C_5 \\ C_1 & N & VH & M & M & N \\ C_2 & N & N & M & L & N \\ C_3 & N & H & N & L & M \\ C_4 & N & L & M & N & N \\ C_5 & N & H & N & H & N \end{bmatrix} \quad \tilde{A}_2 = \begin{bmatrix} & C_1 & C_2 & C_3 & C_4 & C_5 \\ C_1 & N & H & L & M & N \\ C_2 & N & N & L & M & N \\ C_3 & N & VH & N & M & H \\ C_4 & N & M & M & N & N \\ C_5 & N & VH & M & VH & N \end{bmatrix}$$

$$\tilde{A}_3 = \begin{bmatrix} & C_1 & C_2 & C_3 & C_4 & C_5 \\ C_1 & N & VH & L & H & N \\ C_2 & N & N & H & L & N \\ C_3 & N & H & N & M & M \\ C_4 & N & M & H & N & N \\ C_5 & N & VH & L & H & N \end{bmatrix}$$

Three scoring tables on qualitative sub-criteria represented by linguistic variables.

$$\begin{bmatrix} D_1 & C_{31} & C_{33} & C_{41} & C_{43} & C_{51} & C_{52} & C_{53} \\ A_1 & M & VH & M & EH & M & EL & VL \\ A_2 & H & H & H & VH & L & VL & M \\ A_3 & EH & M & VH & EH & EL & EL & M \\ A_4 & M & H & H & VH & M & VL & L \\ A_5 & EH & M & VH & EH & L & EL & M \\ A_6 & EH & H & M & H & VL & L & L \\ A_7 & M & VH & M & H & L & L & VL \end{bmatrix}$$

$$\begin{bmatrix} D_2 & C_{31} & C_{33} & C_{41} & C_{43} & C_{51} & C_{52} & C_{53} \\ A_1 & L & EH & H & VH & L & VL & L \\ A_2 & VH & VH & VH & EH & EL & EL & M \\ A_3 & H & H & EH & EH & VL & VL & L \\ A_4 & H & H & VH & VH & L & EL & M \\ A_5 & EH & H & VH & EH & VL & VL & L \\ A_6 & H & L & H & M & L & EL & L \\ A_7 & H & EH & M & H & VL & EL & L \end{bmatrix}$$

$$\begin{bmatrix} D_3 & C_{31} & C_{33} & C_{41} & C_{43} & C_{51} & C_{52} & C_{53} \\ A_1 & L & VH & H & EH & M & VL & VL \\ A_2 & EH & VH & EH & VH & EL & EL & L \\ A_3 & H & H & EH & EH & EL & EL & VL \\ A_4 & H & M & EH & VH & L & L & L \\ A_5 & H & M & H & EH & L & EL & VL \\ A_6 & H & H & VH & H & VL & L & M \\ A_7 & M & VH & VH & H & VL & L & M \end{bmatrix}$$

Table B.1 Three scoring tables on qualitative sub-criteria represented by TIFNs.

D1	C31	C33	C41	C43	C51	C52	C53
A1	((3, 4, 5); 0.8, 0.1)	((5, 6, 7); 0.6, 0.2)	((3, 4, 5); 0.8, 0.1)	((6, 7, 8); 0.8, 0.2)	((3, 4, 5); 0.7, 0.1)	((0, 1, 2); 0.7, 0.2)	((1, 2, 3); 0.6, 0.3)
A2	((4, 5, 6); 0.7, 0.1)	((4, 5, 6); .0.7, 0.3)	((4, 5, 6); .0.7, 0.3)	((5, 6, 7); 0.6, 0.3)	((2, 3, 4); 0.8, 0.1)	((1, 2, 3); 0.8, 0.1)	((3, 4, 5); 0.8, 0.1)

Continued

D1	C31	C33	C41	C43	C51	C52	C53
A3	((6, 7, 8); 0.7, 0.2)	((3, 4, 5); .0.8, 0.1)	((5, 6, 7); 0.7, 0.2)	((6, 7, 8); 0.7, 0.2)	((0, 1, 2); 0.7, 0.3)	((0, 1, 2); 0.8, 0.2)	((3, 4, 5); 0.7, 0.1)
A4	((3, 4, 5); 0.8, 0.2)	((4, 5, 6); .0.8, 0.1)	((4, 5, 6); 0.8, 0.1)	((5, 6, 7); 0.8, 0.1)	((3, 4, 5); 0.7, 0.2)	((1, 2, 3); 0.7, 0.1)	((2, 3, 4); 0.7, 0.2)
A5	((6, 7, 8); 0.8, 0.2)	((3, 4, 5); .0.7, 0.2)	((5.6.7); 0.8, 0.1)	((6, 7, 8); 0.7, 0.1)	((2, 3, 4); 0.7, 0.1)	((0, 1, 2); 0.7, 0.3)	((3, 4, 5); 0.6, 0.2)
A6	((6, 7, 8); 0.8, 0.1)	((4, 5, 6); .0.7, 0.2)	((3.4.5); 0.6, 0.1)	((4, 5, 6); 0.6, 0.2)	((1, 2, 3); 0.6, 0.3)	((2, 3, 4); 0.7, 0.2)	((2, 3, 4); 0.6, 0.3)
A7	((3, 4, 5); 0.7, 0.1)	((5, 6, 7); 0.6, 0.3)	((3, 4, 5); 0.7, 0.2)	((4, 5, 6); 0.7, 0.3)	((2, 3, 4); 0.8, 0.1)	((2, 3, 4); 0.7, 0.1)	((1, 2, 3); 0.7, 0.1)

D2	C31	C33	C41	C43	C51	C52	C53
A1	((2, 3, 4); 0.8, 0.2)	((6, 7, 8); 0.7, 0.3)	((4, 5, 6); 0.8, 0.1)	((5, 6, 7); 0.6, 0.2)	((2, 3, 4); 0.7, 0.2)	((1, 2, 3); 0.8, 0.1)	((2, 3, 4); 0.6, 0.4)
A2	((5, 6, 7); 0.7, 0.2)	((5, 6, 7); 0.8, 0.2)	((5, 6, 7); 0.7, 0.2)	((6, 7, 8); 0.5, 0.5)	((0, 1, 2); 0.8, 0.2)	((0, 1, 2); 0.8, 0.2)	((3, 4, 5); 0.7, 0.2)
A3	((4, 5, 6); 0.8, 0.1)	((4, 5, 6); 0.7, 0.1)	((6, 7, 8); 0.6, 0.3)	((6, 7, 8); 0.5, 0.3)	((1, 2, 3); 0.7, 0.1)	((1, 2, 3); 0.6, 0.3)	((2, 3, 4); 0.7, 0.3)
A4	((4, 5, 6); 0.7, 0.3)	((4, 5, 6); 0.6, 0.3)	((5, 6, 7); 0.7, 0.2)	((5, 6, 7); 0.7, 0.1)	((2, 3, 4); 0.7, 0.3)	((0, 1, 2); 0.7, 0.3)	((3, 4, 5); 0.8, 0.2)
A5	((6, 7, 8); 0.8, 0.1)	((4, 5, 6); 0.7, 0.2)	((5, 6, 7); 0.8, 0.1)	((6, 7, 8); 0.8, 0.1)	((1, 2, 3); 0.6, 0.3)	((1, 2, 3); 0.8, 0.1)	((2, 3, 4); 0.7, 0.3)
A6	((4, 5, 6); 0.7, 0.2)	((2, 3, 4); 0.7, 0.2)	((4, 5, 6); 0.8, 0.1)	((3, 4, 5); 0.7, 0.2)	((2, 3, 4); 0.7, 0.2)	((0, 1, 2); 0.8, 0.1)	((2, 3, 4); 0.6, 0.2)
A7	((4, 5, 6); 0.7, 0.2)	((6, 7, 8); 0.7, 0.2)	((3, 4, 5); 0.7, 0.1)	((4, 5, 6); 0.8, 0.1)	((1, 2, 3); 0.8, 0.1)	((0, 1, 2); 0.6, 0.3)	((2, 3, 4); 0.7, 0.2)

D3	C31	C33	C41	C43	C51	C52	C53
A1	((2, 3, 4); 0.7, 0.2)	((5, 6, 7); 0.7, 0.2)	((4, 5, 6); 0.7, 0.3)	((6, 7, 8); 0.7, 0.3)	((3, 4, 5); 0.7, 0.2)	((1, 2, 3); 0.7, 0.2)	((1, 2, 3); 0.7, 0.2)
A2	((6, 7, 8); 0.7, 0.2)	((5, 6, 7); 0.7, 0.3)	((6, 7, 8); 0.7, 0.3)	((5, 6, 7); 0.8, 0.1)	((0, 1, 2); 0.8, 0.2)	((0, 1, 2); 0.8, 0)	((2, 3, 4); 0.8, 0.1)
A3	((4, 5, 6); 0.7, 0.1)	((4, 5, 6); 0.8, 0.1)	((6, 7, 8); 0.7, 0.2)	((6, 7, 8); 0.6, 0.3)	((0, 1, 2); 0.7, 0.2)	((0, 1, 2); 0.8, 0.1)	((1, 2, 3); 0.9, 0)
A4	((4, 5, 6); 0.7, 0.3)	((3, 4, 5); 0.7, 0.2)	((6, 7, 8); 0.8, 0.2)	((5, 6, 7); 0.8, 0.2)	((2, 3, 4); 0.7, 0.1)	((2, 3, 4); 0.9, 0.1)	((2, 3, 4); 0.8, 0)
A5	((4, 5, 6); 0.8, 0.1)	((3, 4, 5); 0.7, 0.1)	((4, 5, 6); 0.9, 0.1)	((6, 7, 8); 0.9, 0.1)	((2, 3, 4); 0.7, 0.2)	((0, 1, 2); 0.9, 0)	((1, 2, 3); 0.8, 0.1)
A6	((4, 5, 6); 0.8, 0.1)	((4, 5, 6); 0.7, 0.1)	((5, 6, 7); 0.8, 0.1)	((4, 5, 6); 0.9, 0.1)	((1, 2, 3); 0.6, 0.3)	((2, 3, 4); 0.8, 0.1)	((3, 4, 5); 0.7, 0.2)
A7	((3, 4, 5); 0.7, 0.2)	((5, 6, 7); 0.7, 0.3)	((5, 6, 7); 0.7, 0.2)	((4, 5, 6); 0.8, 0.1)	((1, 2, 3); 0.8, 0.1)	((2, 3, 4); 0.7, 0.2)	((3, 4, 5); 0.8, 0.1)

Table B.2 The weighted scoring tables on qualitative sub-criteria represented by TIFNs.

	C31	C33	C41	C43	C51	C52	C53
A1	((2.33, 3.33, 4.33); 0.7, 0.2)	((5.33, 6.33, 7.33); 0.6, 0.3)	((3.67, 4.67, 5.67); 0.7, 0.3)	((5.67, 6.67, 7.67); 0.6, 0.3)	((2.67, 3.67, 4.67); 0.7, 0.2)	((0.67, 1.67, 2.67); 0.7, 0.2)	((1.33, 2.33, 3.33); 0.6, 0.4)
A2	((5.00, 6.00, 7.00); 0.7, 0.2)	((4.67, 5.67, 6.67); 0.7, 0.3)	((5.00, 6.00, 7.00); 0.7, 0.3)	((5.33, 6.33, 7.33); 0.5, 0.5)	((0.67, 1.67, 2.67); 0.8, 0.2)	((0.33, 1.33, 2.33); 0.8, 0.2)	((2.67, 3.67, 4.67); 0.7, 0.2)
A3	((4.67, 5.67, 6.67); 0.7, 0.2)	((3.67, 4.67, 5.67); 0.7, 0.1)	((5.67, 6.67, 7.67); 0.6, 0.3)	((6.00, 7.00, 8.00); 0.5, 0.3)	((0.33, 1.33, 2.33); 0.7, 0.3)	((0.33, 1.33, 2.33); 0.6, 0.3)	((2.00, 3.00, 4.00); 0.7, 0.3)
A4	((3.67, 4.67, 5.67); 0.7, 0.3)	((3.67, 4.67, 5.67); 0.6, 0.3)	((5.00, 6.00, 7.00); 0.7, 0.2)	((5.00, 6.00, 7.00); 0.7, 0.2)	((2.33, 3.33, 4.33); 0.7, 0.3)	((1.00, 2.00, 3.00); 0.7, 0.3)	((2.33, 3.33, 4.33); 0.7, 0.2)
A5	((5.33, 6.33, 7.33); 0.8, 0.2)	((3.33, 4.33, 5.33); 0.7, 0.2)	((4.67, 5.67, 6.67); 0.8, 0.1)	((6.00, 7.00, 8.00); 0.7, 0.1)	((1.67, 2.67, 3.67); 0.6, 0.3)	((0.33, 1.33, 2.33); 0.7, 0.3)	((2.00, 3.00, 4.00); 0.6, 0.3)
A6	((4.67, 5.67, 6.67); 0.7, 0.2)	((3.33, 4.33, 5.33); 0.7, 0.2)	((4.00, 5.00, 6.00); 0.6, 0.1)	((3.67, 4.67, 5.67); 0.6, 0.2)	((1.33, 2.33, 3.33); 0.6, 0.3)	((1.33, 2.33, 3.33); 0.7, 0.2)	((2.33, 3.33, 4.33); 0.6, 0.3)
A7	((3.33, 4.33, 5.33); 0.7, 0.2)	((5.33, 6.33, 7.33); 0.6, 0.3)	((3.67, 4.67, 5.67); 0.7, 0.2)	((4.00, 5.00, 6.00); 0.7, 0.3)	((1.33, 2.33, 3.33); 0.8, 0.1)	((1.33, 2.33, 3.33); 0.6, 0.3)	((2.00, 3.00, 4.00); 0.7, 0.2)

References

[1] Amer M, Daim T U. Selection of renewable energy technologies for a developing county: A case of Pakistan[J]. Energy for Sustainable Development, 2011, 15(4): 420-435.

[2] Angelopoulos D, Doukas H, Psarras J, et al. Risk-based analysis and policy implications for renewable energy investments in Greece[J]. Energy Policy, 2017, 105(105): 512-523.

[3] Aragonés-Beltrán P, Chaparro-González F, Pastor-Ferrando J, et al. An ANP-based approach for the selection of photovoltaic solar power plant investment projects[J]. Renewable and sustainable energy reviews, 2010, 14(1): 249-264.

[4] Azoumah Y, Ramdé E W, Tapsoba G, et al. Siting guidelines for concentrating solar power plants in the Sahel: Case study of Burkina Faso[J]. Solar Energy, 2010, 84(8): 1545-1553.

[5] Bo Z, Zhang X, Peng L, et al. Optimal sizing, operating strategy and operational experience of a stand-alone microgrid on Dongfushan Island[J]. Applied Energy, 2014, 113(2): 1656-1666.

[6] Brans J P, Mareschal B. Promethee Methods[J]. Multiple Criteria Decision Analysis State of the Art Surveys, 2005, 78: 163-186.

[7] Carlisle J E, Solan D, Kane S L, et al. Utility-scale solar and public attitudes toward siting: A critical examination of proximity[J]. Land Use Policy, 2016, 58: 491-501.

[8] Cavallaro F. A comparative assessment of thin-film photovoltaic production processes using the ELECTRE III method[J]. Energy Policy, 2010, 38(1): 463-474.

[9] Chen S, Li J. Assessing the architectural design services by using DEMATEL approach, 2009 International Conference on Computational Intelligence and Natural Computing. IEEE, 2009, pp. 463-466.

[10] Chumpolrat K, Sangsuwan V, Udomdachanut N, et al.Effect of Ambient Temperature on Performance of Grid-Connected Inverter Installed in Thailand[J]. International Journal of Photoenergy, 2014, 2:

1-6.

[11] Dong J, Feng T T, Yang Y S, et al. Macro-site selection of wind/solar hybrid power station based on ELECTRE - II[J]. Renewable & Sustainable Energy Reviews, 2014, 35: 194-204.

[12] Fan Z P, Zhang X, Chen F D, et al. Extended TODIM method for hybrid multiple attribute decision making problems[J]. Knowledge-Based Systems, 2013, 42(2): 40-48.

[13] Fang H, Li J, Song, W. Sustainable site selection for photovoltaic power plant: An integrated approach based on prospect theory[J]. Energy Conversion and Management, 2018, 174:755-768.

[14] Frisari G, Stadelmann, M. De-risking concentrated solar power in emerging markets: The role of policies and international finance institutions[J]. Energy Policy, 2015, 82: 12-22.

[15] Garni H Z A, Awasthi A. Solar PV power plant site selection using a GIS-AHP based approach with application in Saudi Arabia[J]. Applied Energy, 2017, 206: 1225-1240.

[16] Ghazvini A M, Olamaei J. Optimal sizing of autonomous hybrid PV system with considerations for V2G parking lot as controllable load based on a heuristic optimization algorithm[J]. Solar Energy, 2019, 184: 30-39.

[17] Gomes L F A M, Rangel L S A D. An application of the TODIM method to the multicriteria rental evaluation of residential properties. European Journal of Operational Research, 2009, 193(1): 204-211.

[18] Gorsevski P V, Cathcart S C, Mirzaei G, et al. A group-based spatial decision support system for wind farm site selection in Northwest Ohio[J]. Energy Policy, 2013, 55(249): 374-385.

[19] Guerin T F, Evaluating expected and comparing with observed risks on a large-scale solar photovoltaic construction project: A case for reducing the regulatory burden[J]. Renewable & Sustainable Energy Reviews, 2017, 74: 333-348.

[20] Guo S, Zhao H. Optimal site selection of electric vehicle charging station by using fuzzy TOPSIS based on sustainability perspective[J]. Applied Energy, 2015, 158: 390-402.

[21] Haghdadi N, Copper J, Bruce A, et al. A method to estimate the location and orientation of distributed photovoltaic systems from their generation output data[J]. Renewable Energy, 2017, 108: 390-400.

[22] Hao J, Cheng X, Zhu J, et al. Mathematical and Experimental Analysis on Solar Thermal Energy Harvesting Performance of the Textile-based Solar Thermal Energy Collector[J]. Renewable Energy, 2018, 129: 553-560.

[23] Islam M K, Ahammad T, Pathan E H, et al. Analysis of Maximum Possible Utilization of Solar Radiation on a Solar Photovoltaic Cell with a Proposed Model[J]. International Journal of Modeling & Optimization, 2011, 1(1): 66-69.

[24] Kaabeche A, Bakelli Y. Renewable hybrid system size optimization considering various electrochemical energy storage technologies[J]. Energy Conversion and Management, 2019, 193: 162-175.

[25] Kai S, Li Z, Yan X, et al. A Distributed Control Strategy Based on DC Bus Signaling for Modular Photovoltaic Generation Systems With Battery Energy Storage[J]. IEEE Transactions on Power Electronics, 2011, 26(10): 3032-3045.

[26] Kim J H, Ahn B S. Extended VIKOR method using incomplete criteria weights[J]. Expert Systems with Applications, 2019, 126: 124-132.

[27] Krohling R A, Pacheco A G C, Siviero A L T. IF-TODIM: An intuitionistic fuzzy TODIM to multi-criteria decision making[J]. Knowledge-Based Systems, 2013, 53(9): 142-146.

[28] Kurt Ü. The fuzzy TOPSIS and generalized Choquet fuzzy integral algorithm for nuclear power plant site selection – a case study from Turkey[J]. Journal of Nuclear Science\s&\stechnology, 2014, 51(10): 1241-1255.

[29] Lai Y-J, Liu T-Y, Hwang C-L. Topsis for MODM[J]. European journal of operational research, 1994, 76(3): 486-500.

[30] Li D F. A ratio ranking method of triangular intuitionistic fuzzy numbers and its application to MADM problems[J]. Computers & Mathematics with Applications, 2010, 60(6): 1557-1570.

[31] Liu J, Xu F, Lin S. Site selection of photovoltaic power plants in a value chain based on grey cumulative prospect theory for sustainability: A case study in Northwest China[J]. Journal of Cleaner Production, 2017, 148: 386-397.

[32] Liu P, Teng F. An extended TODIM method for multiple attribute group decision-making based on 2-dimension uncertain linguistic Variable[J]. Complexity, 2016, 21(5): 20-30.

[33] Martin A D, Cano J M, Silva J F A, et al. Backstepping Control of Smart Grid-Connected Distributed Photovoltaic Power Supplies for Telecom Equipment[J]. IEEE Transactions on Energy Conversion, 2015, 30(4): 1496-1504.

[34] Matulaitis V, Straukaitė G, Azzopardi B, et al. Multi-criteria decision making for PV deployment on a multinational level[J]. Solar Energy Materials & Solar Cells, 2016, 156: 122-127.

[35] Mir-Artigues P, Cerdá E, Río P D. Analyzing the impact of cost-containment mechanisms on the profitability of solar PV plants in Spain[J]. Renewable & Sustainable Energy Reviews, 2015, 46: 166-177.

[36] Muhsen D H, Khatib T, Abdulabbas T.E. Sizing of a standalone photovoltaic water pumping system using hybrid multi-criteria decision making methods[J]. Solar Energy, 2018, 159: 1003-1015.

[37] NEA. Operational status of photovoltaic construction in the year of 2018. http://www.nea.gov.cn/2018-11/19/c_137617256.htm.

[38] Opricovic S, Tzeng G-H. Compromise solution by MCDM methods: A comparative analysis of VIKOR and TOPSIS[J]. European journal of operational research, 2004, 156(2): 445-455.

[39] Qin J, Liu X, Pedrycz, W. An extended TODIM multi-criteria group decision making method for green supplier selection in interval type-2 fuzzy environment[J]. European Journal of Operational Research, 2017, 258(2): 626-638.

[40] Radziemska, E. The effect of temperature on the power drop in crystalline silicon solar cells[J]. Renewable Energy, 2014, 28(1): 1-12.

[41] Sánchez-Lozano J M, García-Cascales M S, Lamata M T. Comparative TOPSIS-ELECTRE TRI methods for optimal sites for photovoltaic solar farms[J]. Case study in Spain. Journal of Cleaner Production, 2016, 127:387-398.

[42] Sagani A, Mihelis J, Dedoussis V. Techno-economic analysis and life-cycle environmental impacts of small-scale building-integrated PV systems in Greece[J]. Energy & Buildings, 2017, 139: 277-290.

[43] Sevkli M. An application of the fuzzy ELECTRE method for supplier selection[J]. International Journal of Production Research, 2010, 48(12): 3393-3405.

[44] Seyed-Hosseini S M, Safaei N, Asgharpour M J. Reprioritization of failures in a system failure mode and effects analysis by decision making trial and evaluation laboratory technique[J]. Reliability Engineering & System Safety, 2006, 91(8): 872-881.

[45] Shakouri M, Lee H W, Kim Y W. A probabilistic portfolio-based model for financial valuation of

community solar[J]. Applied Energy, 2017, 191: 709-726.

[46] Sommerfeldt N, Madani H. Revisiting the techno-economic analysis process for building-mounted, grid-connected solar photovoltaic systems: Part one – Review[J]. Renewable & Sustainable Energy Reviews, 2011, 74: 1379-1393.

[47] Stamatakis A, Mandalaki M, Tsoutsos, T. Multi-criteria analysis for PV integrated in shading devices for Mediterranean region[J]. Energy and Buildings, 2016, 117: 128-137.

[48] Tang P, Chen D, Hou Y. Entropy method combined with extreme learning machine method for the short-term photovoltaic power generation forecasting[J]. Chaos, Solitons & Fractals, 2016, 89: 243-248.

[49] Tavana M, Arteaga F J S, Mohammadi S, et al. A Fuzzy Multi-Criteria Spatial Decision Support System for Solar Farm Location Planning[J]. Energy Strategy Reviews, 2017, 18: 93-105.

[50] Tavana M, Keramatpour M, Santosarteaga F J, et al. A fuzzy hybrid project portfolio selection method using Data Envelopment Analysis, TOPSIS and Integer Programming[J]. Expert Systems With Applications, 2015, 42(22): 8432-8444.

[51] Wan SP, Wang F, Lin L L, et al. Some new generalized aggregation operators for triangular intuitionistic fuzzy numbers and application to multi-attribute group decision making[J]. Computers & Industrial Engineering, 2016, 93(C): 286-301.

[52] Wu Y, Geng S, Xu H, et al. Study of decision framework of wind farm project plan selection under intuitionistic fuzzy set and fuzzy measure environment[J]. Energy Conversion & Management, 2014, 87: 274-284.

[53] Wu Y, Geng S, Zhang H, et al. Decision framework of solar thermal power plant site selection based on linguistic Choquet operator[J]. Applied Energy, 2014, 136(C): 303-311.

[54] Wu Y, Ke Y, Wang J, et al. Risk assessment in photovoltaic poverty alleviation projects in China under intuitionistic fuzzy environment[J]. Journal of Cleaner Production, 2019, 219: 587-600.

[55] Wu Y, Xie C, Xu C, et al. A Decision Framework for Electric Vehicle Charging Station Site Selection for Residential Communities under an Intuitionistic Fuzzy Environment: A Case of Beijing[J]. Energies, 2017, 10(9): 1270.

[56] Wu Y, Xua C, Ke Y, et al. An intuitionistic fuzzy multi-criteria framework for large-scale rooftop PV project portfolio selection: case study in Zhejiang, China[J]. Energy, 2018, 143: 295-309.

[57] Wu Y, Zhang B, Xu C, et al. Site selection decision framework using fuzzy ANP-VIKOR for large commercial rooftop PV system based on sustainability perspective[J]. Sustainable Cities & Society, 2018, 40: 454-470.

[58] Wu Y, Zhou J. Risk assessment of urban rooftop distributed PV in energy performance contracting (EPC) projects: An extended HFLTS-DEMATEL fuzzy synthetic evaluation analysis[J]. Sustainable Cities and Society, 2019, 47: 101524.

[59] Wu Y, Zhou J, Hu Y, et al. A TODIM-Based Investment Decision Framework for Commercial Distributed PV Projects under the Energy Performance Contracting (EPC) Business Model: A Case in East-Central China[J]. Energies, 2018, 11: 1210.

[60] Wu Y N, Yang Y S, Feng T T, et al. Macro-site selection of wind/solar hybrid power station based on Ideal Matter-Element Model[J]. International Journal of Electrical Power & Energy Systems, 2013, 50(1): 76-84.

[61] Wu Z, Xu J, Jiang X, et al. Two MAGDM models based on hesitant fuzzy linguistic term sets with

possibility distributions: VIKOR and TOPSIS[J]. Information Sciences, 2019, 473: 101-120.

[62] Xin Z, Liu P. Method for aggregating triangular fuzzy intuitionistic fuzzy information and its application to decision making[J]. Ukio Technologinis Ir Ekonominis Vystymas, 2010,16(2): 280-290.

[63] Xu C, Bai P, Xin T, et al. A novel solar energy integrated low-rank coal fired power generation using coal pre-drying and an absorption heat pump[J]. Applied energy, 2017, 200: 170-179.

[64] Xu J, Feng P, Yang P. Research of development strategy on China's rural drinking water supply based on SWOT–TOPSIS method combined with AHP-Entropy: a case in Hebei Province[J]. Environmental Earth Sciences, 2016, 75(1): 58.

[65] Yao W, Zhao J, Wen F, et al. A Multi-Objective Collaborative Planning Strategy for Integrated Power Distribution and Electric Vehicle Charging Systems[J]. IEEE Transactions on Power Systems, 2014, 29(4): 1811-1821.

[66] Yi Z H, Li H Q. Triangular norm-based cuts and possibility characteristics of triangular intuitionistic fuzzy numbers for decision making[J]. International Journal of Intelligent Systems, 2018, 33(1): 1165-1179.

[67] Yuan J, Sun S, Zhang W, et al. The economy of distributed PV in China[J]. Energy, 2014, 78: 939-949.

[68] Yunna W U, Geng S. Multi-criteria decision making on selection of solar-wind hybrid power station location: A case of China[J]. Energy Conversion & Management, 2014, 81(81): 527-533.

[69] Zeng S, Chen S-M, Kuo L-W. Multiattribute decision making based on novel score function of intuitionistic fuzzy values and modified VIKOR method[J]. Information Sciences, 2019, 488: 76-92.

[70] Zhang W, Ju, Y, Gomes L F A M. The SMAA-TODIM approach: Modeling of preferences and a robustness analysis framework[J]. Computers & Industrial Engineering, 2017, 114:130-141.

[71] Zhang X, Xu Z. The TODIM analysis approach based on novel measured functions under hesitant fuzzy environment[J]. Knowledge-Based Systems, 2014, 61: 48-58.

[72] Zhao X, Zeng Y, Di Z. Distributed solar photovoltaics in China: Policies and economic performance[J]. Energy, 2015, 88: 572-583.

Chapter 9

Evaluation of renewable power sources using a fuzzy MCDM based on cumulative prospect theory: a case in China

Yunna Wu [a, b], Chuanbo Xu [a, b*], Ting Zhang [a, b]
a. School of Economics and Management, North China Electric Power University, PCR, Beijing, China
b. Beijing Key Laboratory of New Energy and Low-Carbon Development (North China Electric Power University), Changping, Beijing, 102206, China

Abstract: Under the global implementation of low-carbon economy, the development of renewable energy becomes an important way of energy saving and emission reduction. Multi-criteria decision-making (MCDM) techniques are gaining popularity in renewable power sources (RPS) evaluation since this process involves many conflicting criteria. Classical MCDM techniques assume that decisions are conducted in a deterministic environment and decision-makers (DMs) are completely rational while facing with investment risks. However, these hypotheses are not supported in the RPS selection. Fortunately, fuzzy set theory enables to cope with vagueness of evaluations in decision-making process, and cumulative prospect theory can reflect the risk preference of DMs and describe the actual behavior of them. Therefore, in this paper, a fuzzy MCDM technique based on cumulative prospect theory is proposed for selecting the most appropriate RPS in China. A case study in China is carried out to illustrate the rationality and feasibility of the proposed method. The results show that the solar PV is determined to be the best one in China, but the optimal alternative is sensitive to the prospect parameters. This research provides insightful information for the public investors with different risk preferences to evaluate the RPS and select the most appropriate one under uncertain environment.

Keywords: renewable power sources; multi-criteria decision-making; fuzzy set theory; cumulative prospect theory

1. Introduction

Renewable energy is energy that is collected from renewable resources such as sunlight, wind, rain, tides, waves, and geothermal heat. In the background of global low-carbon economy, the development of renewable energy becomes an important way of energy saving and emission reduction. Over the past decade, renewable energy has been attached to great importance and rapid development in the world. The cumulative installed capacity of various renewable power sources (RPS) in top-6 countries in 2016 is shown in Fig.9.1. It can be seen that China is the world's leading country in cumulative installed capacity of RPS, with over double the generation of the second-ranking country, the America. Even so, renewable energy in China accounted for just 11.4% of its energy consumption structure in 2016, with most of the remainder provided by traditional coal power facilities. According to the China's energy development strategy action plan, the proportion of renewable energy in the primary energy consumption is expected to rise to 15% by 2020. There is no doubt that large amounts of investments are required to accomplish such an arduous task. The selection of the most appropriate RPS plays an important role for energy investments. A rational selection of RPS can maximize economic benefits, local employment and technology transfer, while at the same time minimizing to environmental burden and resource use. These effects are conducive to long-term investment. Nevertheless, a poorly decision-making of RPS selection can lead to stakeholder reaction, ecologic damage and poor financial returns, beside others [1]. However, researches on the selection of the most appropriate RPS in China have not attracted much attention from researchers. Public investors (including the Top 5 power generation groups and their subsidiaries, other central enterprises, provincial and municipal state-owned enterprises) are the main investment bodies of renewable energy [2]. So, this paper aims to evaluate the renewable energy sources and select the most appropriate one from the perspective of public investors.

Five RPS, namely hydropower, solar PV, solar thermal power, wind power and biomass power, are being considered as alternatives in this paper since other RPS such as ocean power and geothermal power are almost uncompetitive at the present stage of China. For public investors, the selection of the best RPS is a complicate problem which cannot be simplified to economic feasibility only, requiring investors to consider environmental, social, and technical aspect as well [1]. Traditional single-criterion decision-making methods such as cost to benefit analysis are unable to resolve this problem [3]. Therefore, a flexible tool is required to handle such complex situation.

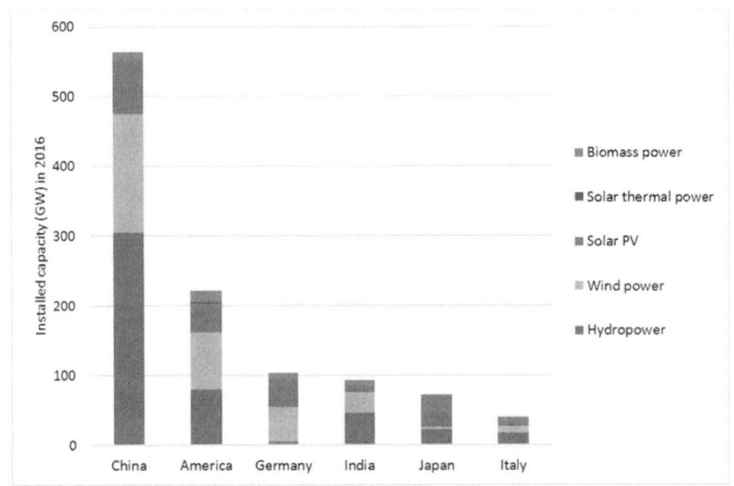

Fig. 9.1 Cumulative installed capacity of various RPS in top-6 countries in 2016.

Data source: Renewables 2017 Global Status Report.

Multi-criteria decision-making (MCDM) techniques, which provide solutions to the problems involving conflicting and multiple criteria, are the most commonly used method of decision support applied to RPS selection [4]. Haddad and Liazid [5] presented an analytic hierarchy process (AHP) model combined with experts' feedback to the evaluation of different renewable energy options for the Algerian electricity system. The performances of different RPS options were evaluated against thirteen sub-criteria reflecting economic, environmental, social and technical concerns, and solar power was selected as the particularly well-suited RPS for Algeria. Similarly, Amer and Daim [6] prioritized RPS for electricity generation in Pakistan by using AHP method. Wind power, solar PV, solar thermal and biomass power options were used as the alternatives in the decision model. It indicated that biomass power and wind power emerged as the preferred alternatives. Streimikiene [7] employed multi-objective optimization on the basis of ratio analysis (MULTIMOORA) and Technique for Order Preference by Similarity to an Ideal Solution (TOPSIS) to prioritize sustainable electricity production technologies, hydropower and solar power systems were identified as the most sustainable. Cristóbal [3] applied the VlseKriterijumska Optimizacija I Kompromisno Resenje in serbian (VIKOR) combined with AHP method in the selection of a RPS corresponding to the Renewable Energy Plan launched by the Spanish Government. The results showed that the biomass plant option is the best choice, followed by the wind power and solar thermo-electric alternatives. Büyüközkan and Güleryüz [8] applied the Decision-Making Trial and Evaluation Laboratory Model (DEMATEL) technique integrated with Analytic Network Process (ANP) for selecting the most appropriate RPS in Turkey from an investor-focused perspective. The results showed that the first alternative which is wind power has the largest score among all other alternatives. In addition, MCDM techniques have been also applied in other fields of renewable energy such as plant location selection [9], material supplier selection [10] and efficiency assessment [11]. A state-of-art of MCDM towards sustainable renewable energy development can be referred to [12].

The classic MCDM techniques generally assume that all criteria are expressed in crisp values. However, on the one hand, investment is a forward-looking activity, the evaluations of criteria performance in the next few years are hard to predict accurately due to the dynamics of electricity market and continuous innovation of energy technology. On the other hand, some evaluations in RPS selection are dependent on the knowledge of experts. Because of the inherent vagueness of human thinking as well as the cognitive limitation of human beings, it is relatively difficult for experts to make exact evaluations on the criteria. Thus, the problem of RPS selection is fraught with uncertainties. Fuzzy set theory, which was developed by Zadeh [13], provides easiness to deal with uncertainties in decision-making problems.

The combination of MCDM techniques and fuzzy set theory, named as fuzzy MCDM, is so admirable and has been widely accepted as suitable techniques in RPS selection field. For instance, fuzzy AHP and fuzzy axiomatic design methods were used respectively to determine the best renewable energy alternative for Turkey [14]. Research findings showed that wind energy was selected as the best renewable energy alternative in both methods. Fuzzy TOPSIS was employed to rank renewable energy supply systems in Turkey, and the interval Shannon's Entropy methodology was used to determine weight values of the criteria [15]. An integrated fuzzy VIKOR and AHP methodology were employed for determining the best renewable energy alternative in Istanbul by Kaya and Kahraman [16] and Büyüközkan and Güleryüz [17]. For these two studies, the fuzzy AHP was used to determine the weights of criteria and sub-criteria while the fuzzy VIKOR was employed to rank the alternatives. However, the former study found that wind power is the most appropriate renewable energy option, while geothermal power is chosen as the suitable one in the latter study. Fuzzy TOPSIS and fuzzy AHP were also proposed for prioritization of renewable energy alternatives in Turkey [18]. And fuzzy AHP and weight sum model were used to the selection among the renewable energy alternatives for Indonesia [19]. Therefore, it has very important significance in applying fuzzy MCDM techniques into RPS selection to handle its inherent uncertainty.

Another flaw of classic MCDM techniques is that they are usually based on the expected utility theory where investors are assumed to be completely rational. However, in real-life decision-makings, the investors are always limited rational while facing the risk, and investors have different subjective risk preferences under different risk environment. Prospect theory developed by Kahneman and Tversky [20] is a descriptive model of individual decision making under condition of risk. In Kahneman and Tversky [20], it was shown that investors' psychological behavior exhibits a risk-averse tendency for gains and a risk-seeking tendency for losses. Inspired by prospect theory, some behavioral decision-making theories have also been developed, such as regret theory, disappointment theory, cumulative prospect theory, third generation prospect theory and so on. Among these theories, cumulative prospect theory [21], which can be deemed as a combination of the original prospect theory and the rank dependent expected utility model, has been regarded as the most popular theory since it describes the decision-makers (DMs)' behavioral characteristics well and gives the calculation formulas on values and weights of potential outcomes.

Since the formulas have features of clear logic and simple computation process, cumulative prospect theory has been widely used to solve various decision-making problems considering DMs' behavior [22, 23]. Moreover, some applications of cumulative prospect theory in renewable energy decision making have been found. For example, Wilton et al. [24] adopted cumulative prospect theory to investigate DM risk propensity toward various capacity credit of wind power. Liu et al. [25] employed grey cumulative prospect theory to study the site selection of PV power plants from the perspective of sustainability. And Klein and Deissenroth [26] reported a model based on cumulative prospect theory showing that the question of when people invest in residential PV systems is found to be not only determined by profitability, but also by profitability's change compared to the status quo. However, the cumulative prospect theory is rarely used in the RPS selection. Actually, on the one hand, the risks in the process of RPS selection are significant due to the uncertain and dynamics of electricity market. On the other hand, the risk preferences of investors are different such as risk neutral, risk aversion and risk seeking, and the different risk preferences of investors will inevitably affect the final selection results. Therefore, how to incorporate the cumulative prospect theory into decision-making of RPS selection deserves more attention.

Based on the above analysis, in this study, we propose a fuzzy MCDM model based on cumulative prospect theory to help public investors in choosing the most appropriate RPS. To begin with, a comprehensive evaluation criteria system of RPS selection consisting of criteria and sub-criteria is constructed on the basis of literature analysis. Then, triangular fuzzy numbers (TFNs), as one of the most commonly used fuzzy numbers, are adopted to represent the performance of each RPS with respect to each sub-criterion. Following this, the AHP method combining with experts' knowledge and experience is applied to obtain the weights of criteria and sub-criteria. At last, the cumulative prospect theory is employed to rank the RPS alternatives by taking into account the risk preferences of investors. The originality of this paper comes from that it is the first time to apply the combination of the fuzzy set theory and cumulative prospect theory to the field of RPS selection.

The remainder of this paper is organized as follows. Section 2 establishes the evaluation criteria system of RPS selection, and introduces the basic concepts of TFN and cumulative prospect theory. Section 3 analyzes the decision framework of RPS selection. Section 4 gives a study case in China. The last section concludes this paper.

2. Research methodology

2.1 Evaluation criteria system

The establishment of criteria system plays an important role in the RPS selection decision-making. In this section, four main criteria directly related to the sustainability objective were selected for the analysis: economical, environmental, socio-political and technical aspect. Moreover, sub-criteria associated with each criterion were identified from the scientific literature. Fig. 9.2 is the evaluation criteria system of RPS selection. The explanations of the sub-criteria are as follows:

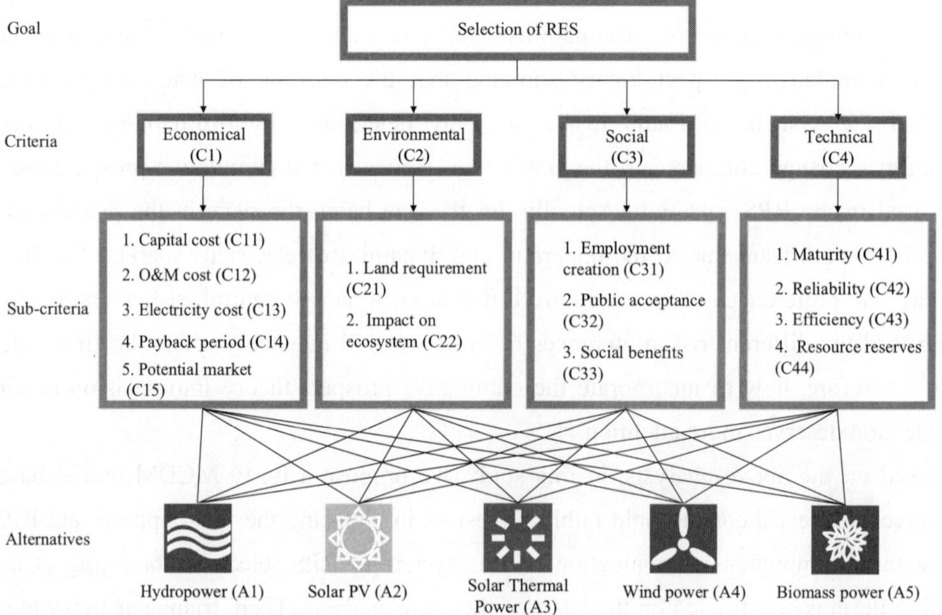

Fig. 9.2 Evaluation criteria system for RPS evaluation.

2.1.1 Economical criterion

- Capital cost (C11) [6, 16, 27, 28]. Capital cost includes total expenditure occurred in establishing a plant including the equipment, labor, installation, infrastructure and commissioning cost.
- Operations and maintenance (O&M) cost (C12) [6, 16, 27-29]. Operations and maintenance cost consist of the plant running cost including salaries of the employees, cost of the parts/spares required for scheduled maintenance purposes etc. The O&M cost of renewable energy plants are lower compared to fossil fuel-fired power plants, but are still

significant.

- Electricity cost (C13) [6, 16, 27, 30]. It is the net present value of the unit-cost of electricity over the lifetime of a generating asset.
- Payback period (C14) [5, 15, 16, 18]. The payback period of an energy project refers to the period of time required for the return on an investment to "repay" the sum of the original investment.
- Potential market (C15) [14, 27]. Potential market is one of the most critical factors for the energy profitable investment.

2.1.2 Environmental criterion

- Land requirement (C21) [6, 16, 27, 30-32]. Every power plant occupies some land, which may affect the landscape and increase the project cost especially if it is near a city.
- Impact on ecosystem (C22) [6, 31]. It is a measure of environmental friendliness and impact of the power plant on the environment.

2.1.3 Social criterion

- Employment creation (C31) [6, 7, 27, 30, 31, 33]. Energy supply systems employ many people during their life cycle, from construction and operation until decommissioning.
- Public acceptance (C32) [16, 29, 30, 32, 34, 35]. Public acceptability expresses the overview of opinions related to the energy systems by the local residents.
- Social benefits (C33) [6, 15, 16]. Social benefit represents the social progress in the local community and region by initiating a power project.

2.1.4 Technical criterion

- Maturity (C41) [6, 16, 27, 31, 32]. It indicates how technology is widespread at regional, national and international levels. This measure also indicates if the technology has already reached the theoretical efficiency limit or if there is still room for improvement.
- Reliability (C42) [6, 16, 34, 35]. Reliability is defined as the ability of a system to perform as intended/designed under stated conditions. Reliability of a power plant is very critical.
- Efficiency (C43) [6, 16, 27, 31]. Efficiency refers to how much useful energy we can obtain from an energy demand growth. It is the most used technical criteria to evaluate RPS. Efficient energy use is essential in slowing the energy. The calculation equation of efficiency varies from sources to sources. Take the case of PV modules, the efficiency is calculated as $\eta_t = \frac{P_{\max}}{G \times S_t} \times 100\%$, where η_t is the efficiency, $P_{\max}$ is the maximum power value of a module under a given test condition (unit: W), G denotes the irradiance in the test condition of $P_{\max}$ (unit: $W \cdot m^{-2}$) and S_t represents the total area of module (unit: m^{-2}).

- Resource availability (C44) [6, 17, 36]. It is the availability of RER to generate energy, which is a measure for the secure operation of a RPS, such as river flow rate, sun radiation and wind speed.

2.2 Relative method and theory

2.2.1 Triangular fuzzy number

Triangular fuzzy number (TFN) and trapezoidal fuzzy number are two restrict fuzzy sets with convexity and normalization, and have been widely applied to modeling fuzzy data. TFN is used in this study for the reasons that it has a good ability to ensure integrality of decision information, and at the same time the inside elements in it are readily available than trapezoidal fuzzy numbers.

In this section, we introduce the basic concepts of TFN, defuzzification method of TFN, and distance measure of TFNs.

Definition 1. [37] A fuzzy number $\tilde{a}$ is a triangular fuzzy number if its membership degree function is expressed mathematically as follows:

$$\mu_{\tilde{a}}(x)=\begin{cases}0 & \text{if} \quad x<\underline{a}\\(x-\underline{a})/(a-\underline{a}) & \text{if} \quad \underline{a}\leqslant x\leqslant\overline{a}\\(\overline{a}-x)/(\overline{a}-a) & \text{if} \quad a\leqslant x\leqslant\overline{a}\\0 & \text{if} \quad x>\overline{a}\end{cases} \tag{9-1}$$

where the $\underline{a}$, a and $\overline{a}$ are the lower value, modal value, and upper value, respectively. They satisfy. $\underline{a}\leqslant a\leqslant\overline{a}$ For the convenience, we denote a TFN by $\tilde{a}=(\underline{a},a,\overline{a})$.

Since it is difficult to compare two TFNs directly, the defuzzification of the TFNs is necessary. Various defuzzification strategies have been suggested in the literature. In this paper, the graded mean integration approach is used.

Definition 2. [38] Let $\tilde{a}=(\underline{a},a,\overline{a})$ be a TFN, the value of defuzzification $S(\tilde{a})$ is given as follows:

$$S(\tilde{a})=\frac{\underline{a}+4a+\overline{a}}{6} \tag{9-2}$$

Definition 3. Let $\tilde{a}=(\underline{a},a,\overline{a})$ and $\tilde{b}=(\underline{b},b,\overline{b})$ be two TFNs, then the Euclidean distance between them is shown as follows:

$$d(\tilde{a},\tilde{b})=\left[\frac{(\overline{a}-\overline{b})^2+(a-b)^2+(\underline{a}-\underline{b})^2}{3}\right]^{1/2} \tag{9-3}$$

2.2.2 Cumulative prospect theory

Cumulative prospect theory proposed by Tversky and Kahneman [21] in 1992 is an extended version of prospect theory. It is a descriptive theory for human decision behavior under risk. In cumulative prospect theory, prospect value V is obtained by the value function $v(x)$ and the weight function $w(p)$, calculated by Eq. (9-4).

$$V = \sum_{i=1}^{n} \pi(w_j) \cdot v(x_i) \tag{9-4}$$

The value function represents the risk preference are determined by Eq. (9-5).

$$v(x) = \begin{cases} x^{\alpha} & \text{if } x \geqslant 0 \\ -\lambda(-x)^{\beta} & \text{if } x < 0 \end{cases} \tag{9-5}$$

where x denotes the gains or losses; $x \geqslant 0$ represents the gains and $x < 0$ represents the losses. α and β are exponential parameters related to gains and losses, respectively, $0 \leqslant \alpha \leqslant \beta \leqslant 1$. λ is the risk aversion parameter, which represents the characteristic of steeper for losses than for gains, $\lambda > 1$. In this study, we adopt the values of these parameters as $\alpha = \beta = 0.88, \lambda = 2.25$, which are determined by Tversky and Kahneman's empirical research [21]. A graphical representation of the value function is shown in Fig. 9.3.

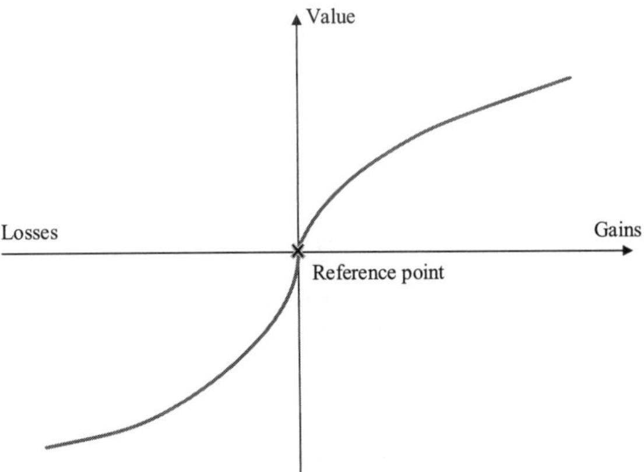

Fig. 9.3 A value function of cumulative prospect theory.

The major improvement of cumulative prospect theory on the basis of prospect theory is that the weight function used is not a linear function, but an inverse S-type curve, which indicates individual investors tend to overestimate the likelihood of small probability events, while underestimate the likelihood of high and medium probability events. Therefore, the weight function can be expressed by Eq. (9-6).

$$\pi(w_j) = \begin{cases} \dfrac{w_j{}^{\chi}}{(w_j{}^{\chi} + (1-w_j)^{\chi})^{1/\chi}} & \text{if } x \geqslant 0 \\ \dfrac{w_j{}^{\delta}}{(w_j{}^{\delta} + (1-w_j)^{\delta})^{1/\delta}} & \text{if } x < 0 \end{cases} \tag{9-6}$$

where χ and δ is attitude coefficient of risk gains and losses, respectively, $0<\chi,\delta<1$. Similarly, the values of χ and δ are also determined as 0.61 and 0.69 respective through experiments [21].

3. Decision framework of RPS selection

The decision framework integrates the TFN, AHP and cumulative prospect theory together in a very structure and systematic framework. The proposed framework composes of two main phases: a preparations stage and a decision-making stage, which can be seen in Fig. 9.4. A detailed description of each phase and their corresponding steps is presented in Sections 3.1and Sections 3.2.

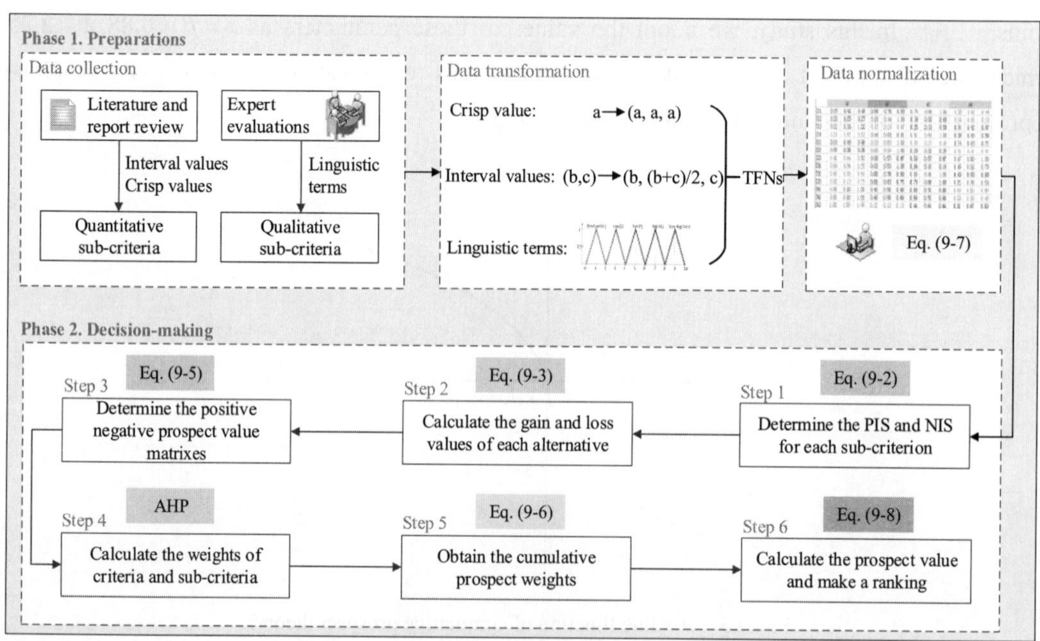

Fig. 9.4 Decision framework of RPS selection.

3.1 Preparations

3.1.1 Data collection

The quantitative criteria and qualitative criteria coexist in the established evaluation criteria system. Data for the quantitative criteria generally come from relative literature and reports. For the data collection of the qualitative criteria, a common practice is to ask several authoritative experts to express their opinions based on their knowledge and experience [39]. And linguistic terms introduced by Zadeh [40] are often employed by experts to deal with qualitative data since linguistic terms are much closer to the humans' thinking and knowledge than numerical representation. Before the evaluation, generally it is necessary to set an appropriate linguistic assessment set in advance. Let the linguistic assessment set be $S=\{s_\alpha \mid \alpha=-l,\ldots,0,\ldots,l\}$, where s_α represents a linguistic term, l is positive integer and its value is set to be 2 in this study, so the linguistic assessment set can be represented as follows:

$$S=\{s_{-2},s_{-1},s_0,s_1,s_2\}=\{\text{Very Low (VL), Low (L), Fair (F), High (H), Very High (VH)}\}.$$

3.1.2 Data transformation

The collected data are heterogeneous which may consist of different representation forms. In general, crisp values, interval values and linguistic terms are most likely to be included. The three representations can be transformed into TFNs in the following manners:

- The crisp value is actually a special form of TFN. A TFN can be degenerated into a certain crisp value in the case of the three elements of the TFN are equal. In other words, a crisp value can be extended to a TFN without losing information. For example, the crisp value 3.1 can be transformed as the TFN (3.1, 3.1, 3.1).
- In contrast to the interval value, the TFN need to determine an intermediate value. To find this value of a fuzzy number, the lower bound and upper bound of the interval value are averaged arithmetically [41]. For example, the interval value (3, 4) can be transformed as the TFN (3, 3.5, 4).
- For the transformation between linguistic terms and TFNs, it is necessary to define their mapping relations. For example, the linguistic term 'High' can be transformed as the TFN (6, 7, 8). The relations between linguistic terms and their corresponding TFNs are depicted in Fig. 9.5.

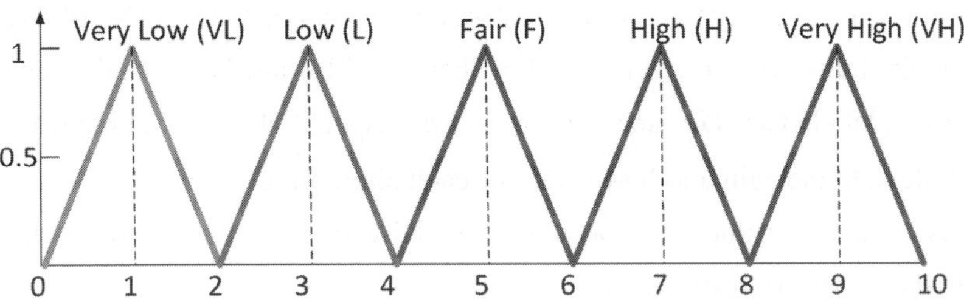

Fig. 9.5 Linguistic terms and their corresponding TFNs.

After the transformation, the decision matrix $[\bar{a}_{ij}]_{m\times n}$ made up by pure TFNs can be obtained.

3.1.3 Data normalization

To eliminate the influence of different physical dimensions and measurements on the final decision, the decision matrix $[\bar{a}_{ij}]_{m\times n}$ needs be normalized as $[\bar{r}_{ij}]_{m\times n}$ where $\tilde{r}_{ij}=(\underline{r}_{ij},r_{ij},\overline{r}_{ij})$ and

$$(\underline{r}_{ij}, r_{ij}, \overline{r}_{ij}) = \begin{cases} (\dfrac{\underline{a}_{ij}}{\overline{a}_{\max j}}, \dfrac{a_{ij}}{\overline{a}_{\max j}}, \dfrac{\overline{a}_{ij}}{\overline{a}_{\max j}}) & \text{if } x_j \in F^B \\ (\dfrac{\underline{a}_{\min j}}{\overline{a}_{ij}}, \dfrac{\underline{a}_{\min j}}{a_{ij}}, \dfrac{\underline{a}_{\min j}}{\underline{a}_{ij}}) & \text{if } x_j \in F^C \end{cases} \tag{9-7}$$

where $\overline{a}_{\max j} = \max\{\overline{a}_{ij} \mid i = 1,2,\ldots,m\}$, $\underline{a}_{\min j} = \min\{\overline{a}_{ij} \mid i = 1,2,\ldots,m\}$. F^B and F^C are the subsets of benefit criteria and cost criteria, respectively.

3.2 Decision-making

The reference point plays a vital role in decision-making when the cumulative prospect theory is employed. In generally, the reference points can be selected from the following key points: zero-point; mean value; maximum value; and minimum value. Based on the maximum value and minimum value as well as inspired by the concept of TOPSIS method, this paper considers the positive ideal solution (PIS) and the negative ideal solution (NIS) as the reference points which embody the attitudes of investors toward risks. When the reference point is the PIS, the investors tend to be risk seekers because they are confronted with losses while when the reference point is the NIS, the benefits enable the investors inclined to risk aversion. Then the formula of prospect value V can be deduced as follows:

$$V_i = \sum_{j=1}^{m} v_{ij}^{+} \pi^{+}(w_j) + \sum_{j=1}^{m} v_{ij}^{-} \pi^{-}(w_j) \tag{9-8}$$

Step 1. Determine the PIS and NIS for each sub-criterion.

Firstly, the defuzzification values of all TFNs in the normalized decision matrix are calculated by the Eq. (9-2). Then, for each sub-criterion, ranking the TFNs of the alternatives according to their defuzzification values. After that, the PIS and NIS of all alternatives under each sub-criterion, labeled as G_j and $B_j (j = 1,\ldots,m)$ respectively, can be obtained.

Step 2. Calculate the gain and loss values of each alternative.

The gains or losses values can be represented by the distance between alternative and NIS/PIS using the Eq. (9-3), respectively.

Step 3. Determine the positive and negative prospect value matrixes.

After the gain and loss values are obtained, the following positive and negative prospect value matrixes V_{ij}^{+} and V_{ij}^{-} can be determined by the Eq. (9-5).

Step 4. Calculate the weights of criteria and sub-criteria.

Reasonable weights for decision criteria may be obtained by many techniques, one of which is the AHP. It utilizes pair-wise comparisons for a set of criteria to judge the relative importance of one criteria to another. In this context, the fundamental "1-9 scale" defined by Saaty is employed for experts to evaluate the priority score. Then, the weights of sub-criteria w_j can be calculated.

Step 5. Calculate the cumulative prospect weights.

Based on the Eq. (9-6) and the obtained weights of sub-criteria, the cumulative prospect weights $\pi^{+}(w_j)$ and $\pi^{-}(w_j)$ can be calculated.

Step 6. Calculate the integrated prospect value of each alternative and make a ranking.

Since the prospect value and cumulative prospect weight are determined, the integrated prospect values of each alternative V_i can be calculated by the Eq. (9-8).

4. A study case in China

In recent years, the utilization of renewable energy has received attention in China. Chinese renewables now account for 16.7% of the global total, up from 1.2% just ten years ago. Fig. 9.6 shows the China's cumulative installed capacity of various RPS by the end of 2016 and its goals in 2020 formulated in the 13th Five-Year Plan (2015–2020). There is still a lot of room for investment in renewable energy. It is estimated that a total of 2.5 trillion RMB investments are required for renewable energy during the 13th Five-Year period. To help investors make better investment decisions, the following part will briefly introduce the development status of RPS in China.

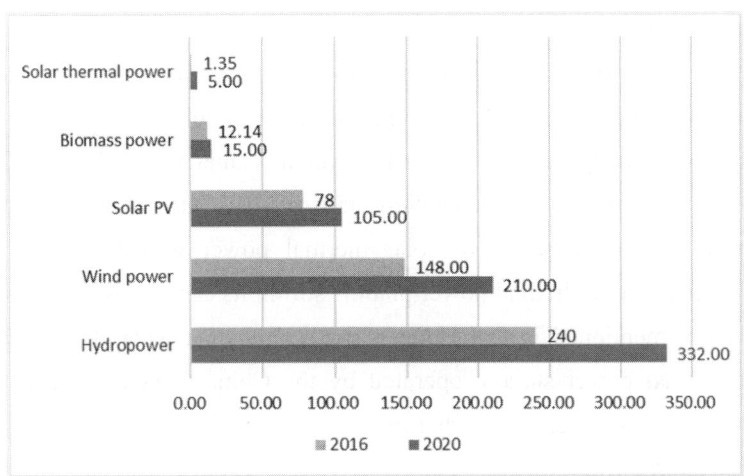

Fig. 9.6 China's cumulative installed capacity of various RPS in 2016 and corresponding goals in 2020 (GW, data source: National Energy Administration).

4.1 Review the development status of RPS in China

4.1.1 Hydropower

China has the richest hydro resources in the world with a total theoretical hydropower potential of 694 GW. Among all RPS, the hydropower is the earliest development, and it is also the most mature technique in China. At the end of 2016, the newly installed hydropower capacity is 12.74 GW, including conventional hydropower of 9.08 GW and pumped storage of 3.66 GW. The annual utilization hour of hydropower is 3621 h, which basically reached the same level of the previous year. Due to the increasing cost of hydropower development and recent hydropower curtailment, the speed of investment is slowing down. The overall development of hydropower has entered a stable and mature stage.

4.1.2 Solar PV

China lies in the northeastern part of East Asia between 4° and 53° North latitude and 73°–135° East longitude with an area of 9.6 million km^2 [42]. The abundant area of solar energy has a high proportion of more than 2/3, with its radiation of more than 5000 MJ/ m^2 yr. and more than 2200 h of sunshine. With abundant solar energy, China enjoys a fast growth of its photovoltaic industry since 2004, which increases more than 100% averagely per year [43]. China's solar PV cumulative installed capacity has reached 43.18 GW by the end of 2015, including 37.12 GW of stationary PV and 6.06 GW of distributed PV. National Energy Administration (NEA) statistics show that the newly and cumulative installed capacity of photovoltaic power generation was 34.54GW and 77.42GW respectively by the end of 2016.

4.1.3 Solar thermal power

Solar thermal power generation is another basic way of solar power generation. The provinces that meet the solar thermal power resources in China are mainly concentrated in Qinghai, Tibet, Xinjiang, Gansu, Ningxia and Inner Mongolia. At the end of 2015, the cumulative installed capacity of solar thermal power in China was only 0.13 GW. Then, the development of solar thermal power generation industry steps into the fast growth stage during 2016. The newly installed capacity of solar thermal power was 1.34 GW. However, the development of China's solar thermal power plant is still in its early construction stage currently. What is particularly mentioned is that China's first commercial solar thermal power station, Delingha solar thermal power station, operated by the China General Nuclear Power Group (CGN) in northwestern province of Qinghai made its first test run on August 31, 2017 with all equipment running normally.

4.1.4 Wind power

The wind energy potential in China is considerable, according to the 3rd national wind energy resource survey, the exploitable wind power potential is 600–1000 GW onshore and 400–500 GW offshore. And by 2012, China's accumulated installed capacity had surged to 75 GW, allowing China to surpass the U.S. as the country with the most installed wind capacity [44]. At present, the total installed capacity of wind power in China accounted for 33.6% of the world. Wind power is now the second largest renewable energy source following by hydropower in China [45]. However, the phenomenon of wind power curtailment has emerged because China's wind energy resources are concentrated in the Three North regions (northeast, north and northwest China) which are far from the load center [46].

4.1.5 Biomass power

As a large agricultural country, China is rich in biomass resources. The annual available number of agricultural residues, forest residues, manure, and municipal solid waste throughout the country is equivalent to 440 million tce, 350 million tce, 28 million tce and 12 million tce, respectively. Unlike hydropower, wind power, and solar PV, it doesn't exist the problem of power curtailment. So, it is welcomed by the power grid. China's biomass power installed capacity reached 12.14 GW by the end of 2016, accounting for 0.7% of the national total installed capacity, and 2.1% of the installed capacity of renewable energy power generation. The development of biomass in China is in its infancy. Some factors restrict the development of biomass power generation, including high raw material cost, difficult collection in raw materials, lack of core technology, and low feed-in-tariff.

4.2 RPS selection in China using the proposed method

Data for the quantitative and qualitative criteria are collected and shown in Table 9.1. Then, the crisp values, interval values and linguistic terms are all transformed into TFNs. After the transformation, the decision matrix $[\bar{a}_{ij}]_{m\times n}$ made up of pure TFNs can be obtained. Then, the decision matrix $[\bar{a}_{ij}]_{m\times n}$ can be normalized as $[\bar{r}_{ij}]_{m\times n}$ using the Eq. (9-7), and is shown in Table 9.2.

Table 9.1 The values of sub-criteria in term of the four RPS with their references.

Sub-criteria	Unit	Hydropower	Solar PV	Solar thermal power	Wind power	Biomass power	Refere-nce
Capital Cost (C11)	USD/kW	1 000-3500	1150-1400	4500-7150	950-1250	2000-2500	[41]
O&M cost (C12)	USD/kWa	45-52	12-42	65-70	17.31-31	63.8-84.7	[41]
Electricity Cost (C13)	USD/kWh	0.25	2.1-3.5	0.2-0.33	0.52	0.56-0.84	[41]
Payback period (C14)	Year	5-10	7-13	8-12	13-16	6-9.5	[15]
Market maturity (C15)	-	F	H	F	H	F	EA
Land requirement (C21)	Km^2 /GW	750	35-42	15-24	100-120	5000	[50, 51]
Impact on ecosystem (C22)	-	VH	H	L	H	F	EA
Employment creation (C31)	Jobs/MW	0.9-1.2	0.7-25	0.2-5.0	0.9-4.0	11.2-19.7	[52, 53]
Public acceptance (C32)	-	F	H	H	VH	H	EA
Social benefits (C33)	-	VL	L	H	H	VH	EA
Maturity (C41)	-	VH	F	L	H	F	EA
Reliability (C42)	-	VH	H	L	F	H	EA

Continued

Sub-criteria	Unit	Hydropower	Solar PV	Solar thermal power	Wind power	Biomass power	Refere-nce
Efficiency (C43)	%	80	9.5-12	21	35	25-50	[27]
Resource availability (C44)	kwh/m2/year	1100	2130	2200	570	200	[27]

Note: EA means expert assessment.

Table 9.2 The normalized decision matrix.

	A1	A2	A3	A4	A5
C11	(0.27, 0.42, 0.95)	(0.68, 0.75, 0.83)	(0.13, 0.16, 0.21)	(0.76, 0.86, 1.00)	(0.38, 0.42, 0.48)
C12	(0.23, 0.25, 0.27)	(0.29, 0.44, 1.00)	(0.17, 0.18, 0.18)	(0.39, 0.50, 0.69)	(0.14, 0.16, 0.19)
C13	(0.22, 0.36, 1.00)	(0.15, 0.24, 0.67)	(0.12, 0.15, 0.20)	(0.25, 0.33, 0.50)	(0.31, 0.42, 0.67)
C14	(0.50, 0.67, 1.00)	(0.38, 0.63, 0.81)	(0.42, 0.50, 0.63)	(0.31, 0.34, 0.38)	(0.53, 0.65, 0.83)
C15	(0.50, 0.63, 0.75)	(0.75, 0.88, 1.00)	(0.50, 0.63, 0.75)	(0.75, 0.88, 1.00)	(0.59, 0.63, 0.75)
C21	(0.02, 0.02, 0.02)	(0.36, 0.39, 0.43)	(0.63, 0.77, 1.00)	(0.13, 0.14, 0.15)	(0.00, 0.00, 0.00)
C22	(0.20, 0.22, 0.25)	(0.25, 0.29, 0.33)	(0.50, 0.67, 1.00)	(0.25, 0.29, 0.33)	(0.33, 0.40, 0.50)
C31	(0.04, 0.04, 0.05)	(0.03, 0.51, 1.00)	(0.01, 0.10, 0.20)	(0.04, 0.10, 0.16)	(0.45, 0.62, 0.79)
C32	(0.40, 0.50, 0.60)	(0.60, 0.70, 0.80)	(0.60, 0.70, 0.80)	(0.80, 0.90, 1.00)	(0.60, 0.70, 0.80)
C33	(0.00, 0.10, 0.20)	(0.20, 0.30, 0.40)	(0.60, 0.70, 0.80)	(0.60, 0.70, 0.80)	(0.80, 0.90, 1.00)
C41	(0.80, 0.90, 1.00)	(0.40, 0.50, 0.60)	(0.30, 0.40, 0.60)	(0.60, 0.70, 0.80)	(0.40, 0.50, 0.60)
C42	(0.80, 0.90, 1.00)	(0.60, 0.70, 0.80)	(0.20, 0.30, 0.40)	(0.40, 0.50, 0.60)	(0.60, 0.70, 0.80)
C43	(1.00, 1.00, 1.00)	(0.12, 0.13, 0.15)	(0.26, 0.26, 0.26)	(0.44, 0.44, 0.44)	(0.31, 0.47, 0.63)
C44	(0.50, 0.50, 0.50)	(0.97, 0.97, 0.97)	(1.00, 1.00, 1.00)	(0.26, 0.26, 0.26)	(0.09, 0.09, 0.09)

Based on the normalized decision matrix, the defuzzification values of all TFNs are calculated by the Eq. (9-2). Then, the PIS and NIS of all alternatives under each sub-criterion are determined as follows:

$$G=\{G_1,G_2,\ldots,G_m\}=\{\max_{1\leqslant i\leqslant n}(\tilde{r}_{i1}),\max_{1\leqslant i\leqslant n}(\tilde{r}_{i2}),\ldots,\max_{1\leqslant i\leqslant n}(\tilde{r}_{im})\}=\{(0.76,0.86,1.00),(0.29,0.44,1.00),$$
$$(0.22,0.36,1.00),(0.50,0.67,1.00),(0.75,0.88,1.00),(0.63,0.77,1.00),(0.50,0.67,1.00),$$
$$(0.45,0.62,0.79),(0.80,0.90,1.00),(0.80,0.90,1.00),(0.80,0.90,1.00),(0.80,0.90,1.00),$$
$$(1.00,1.00,1.00),\ (1.00,1.00,1.00)\};$$

$$B=\{B_1,B_2,\ldots,B_m\}=\{\min_{1\leqslant i\leqslant n}(\tilde{r}_{i1}),\min_{1\leqslant i\leqslant n}(\tilde{r}_{i2}),\ldots,\min_{1\leqslant i\leqslant n}(\tilde{r}_{im})\}=\{(0.13,0.16,0.21),(0.14,0.16,0.19),$$
$$(0.12,0.15,0.20),(0.31,0.34,0.38),(0.50,0.63,0.75),(0.00,0.00,0.00),(0.20,0.22,0.25),$$
$$(0.04,0.04,0.05),(0.40,0.50,0.60),(0.00,0.10,0.20),(0.20,0.30,0.40),(0.20,0.30,0.40),$$
$$(0.12,0.13,0.15),(0.09,0.09,0.09)\}.$$

The gains or losses values can be represented by the distance between alternative and NIS or PIS using Eq. (9-3), respectively. They are calculated and presented as follows:

$$\begin{Bmatrix} d(A_1,G) \\ d(A_2,G) \\ d(A_3,G) \\ d(A_4,G) \\ d(A_5,G) \end{Bmatrix} = \begin{Bmatrix} 0.38,0.44,0.00,0.00,0.25,0.79,0.53,0.59,0.40,0.80,0.00,0.00,0.00,0.50; \\ 0.13,0.00,0.21,0.20,0.00,0.43,0.47,0.28,0.20,0.60,0.40,0.20,0.87,0.03; \\ 0.71,0.50,0.48,0.24,0.25,0.00,0.00,0.52,0.20,0.20,0.60,0.60,0.74,0.00; \\ 0.00,0.19,0.29,0.42,0.00,0.68,0.47,0.53,0.00,0.20,0.20,0.40,0.56,0.74; \\ 0.45,0.50,0.20,0.10,0.25,0.81,0.34,0.00,0.20,0.00,0.40,0.20,0.55,0.91. \end{Bmatrix};$$

$$\begin{Bmatrix} d(A_1,B) \\ d(A_2,B) \\ d(A_3,B) \\ d(A_4,B) \\ d(A_5,B) \end{Bmatrix} = \begin{Bmatrix} 0.46,0.08,0.48,0.42,0.00,0.02,0.00,0.00,0.00,0.00,0.60,0.60,0.87,0.41; \\ 0.58,0.50,0.27,0.21,0.25,0.39,0.07,0.61,0.20,0.20,0.20,0.40,0.00,0.88; \\ 0.00,0.02,0.00,0.18,0.00,0.81,0.53,0.10,0.20,0.60,0.00,0.00,0.13,0.91; \\ 0.71,0.38,0.22,0.00,0.25,0.13,0.07,0.07,0.40,0.60,0.40,0.20,0.30,0.17; \\ 0.26,0.00,0.33,0.34,0.00,0.00,0.19,0.59,0.20,0.80,0.20,0.40,0.35,0.00. \end{Bmatrix}$$

After the gain and loss values are obtained, the following positive and negative prospect value matrixes V_{ij}^+ and V_{ij}^- are determined by the Eq. (9-5).

$$V_{ij}^+ = \begin{pmatrix} 0.50 & 0.11 & 0.53 & 0.46 & 0.00 & 0.03 & 0.00 & 0.00 & 0.00 & 0.00 & 0.64 & 0.64 & 0.88 & 0.46 \\ 0.62 & 0.55 & 0.32 & 0.26 & 0.30 & 0.44 & 0.09 & 0.65 & 0.24 & 0.24 & 0.24 & 0.45 & 0.00 & 0.89 \\ 0.00 & 0.03 & 0.00 & 0.22 & 0.00 & 0.83 & 0.57 & 0.13 & 0.24 & 0.64 & 0.00 & 0.00 & 0.16 & 0.92 \\ 0.74 & 0.42 & 0.26 & 0.00 & 0.30 & 0.17 & 0.09 & 0.10 & 0.45 & 0.64 & 0.45 & 0.24 & 0.35 & 0.21 \\ 0.30 & 0.00 & 0.38 & 0.38 & 0.00 & 0.00 & 0.24 & 0.63 & 0.24 & 0.82 & 0.24 & 0.45 & 0.40 & 0.00 \end{pmatrix}$$

$$V_{ij}^- = -\begin{pmatrix} 0.96 & 1.09 & 0.00 & 0.00 & 0.66 & 1.84 & 1.29 & 1.42 & 1.00 & 1.85 & 0.00 & 0.00 & 0.00 & 1.22 \\ 0.37 & 0.00 & 0.57 & 0.55 & 0.00 & 1.06 & 1.15 & 0.73 & 0.55 & 1.44 & 1.00 & 0.55 & 1.98 & 0.11 \\ 1.66 & 1.22 & 1.18 & 0.65 & 0.66 & 0.00 & 0.00 & 1.26 & 0.55 & 0.55 & 1.44 & 1.44 & 1.72 & 0.00 \\ 0.00 & 0.52 & 0.76 & 1.04 & 0.00 & 1.60 & 1.15 & 1.28 & 0.00 & 0.55 & 0.55 & 1.00 & 1.36 & 1.73 \\ 1.12 & 1.23 & 0.55 & 0.29 & 0.66 & 1.87 & 0.87 & 0.00 & 0.55 & 0.00 & 1.00 & 0.55 & 1.32 & 2.07 \end{pmatrix}$$

The pair-wise comparison judgment matrices are provided by the experts (see Appendix). Based on these matrices, the weights of criteria and sub-criteria are obtained, as shown in Fig. 9.7.

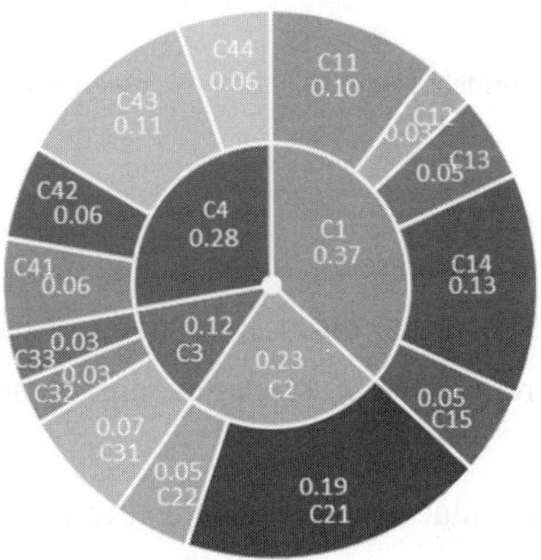

Fig.9.7 Criteria and sub-criteria weights.

Based on the Eq. (9-6) and the obtained weights of sub-criteria, the cumulative prospect weights are calculated and shown as follows:

$$\pi^{+}(w_j)=[0.19,0.10,0.13,0.21,0.13,0.25,0.13,0.15,0.09,0.10,0.14,0.14,0.20,0.14];$$

$$\pi^{-}(w_j)=[0.17,0.08,0.11,0.20,0.11,0.25,0.11,0.13,0.07,0.08,0.12,0.12,0.18,0.12].$$

Since the prospect value and cumulative prospect weight are determined, the integrated prospect values of each alternative are calculated as:

$V_1=-0.783$, $V_2=-0.636$, $V_3=-1.034$, $V_4=-1.076$, $V_5=-1.157$.

The ranking of RPS alternatives in descending order is determined as follows: $A2>A1>A3>A4>A5$. It means the solar PV is the optimal RPS, followed by the hydropower, solar thermal power, wind power, and biomass power.

In addition, further analysis reveals that none of RPS performs equally well on all four criteria considered. This behavior is described vividly in Fig. 9.8. Solar PV ranks first in economical criteria, while solar thermal power is inclined towards environmental criteria and biomass power is inclined towards social criteria. Whereas, hydropower accounts for an absolute advantage in technical criteria.

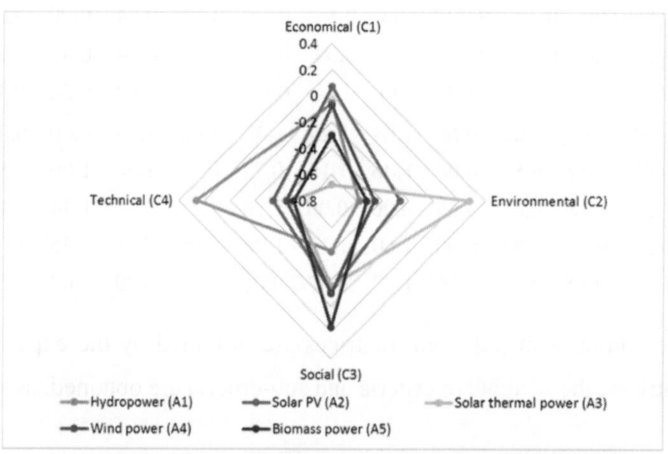

Fig. 9.8 Performance of RPS alternatives with respect to criteria.

4.3 Sensitivity analysis

Since the risk attitudes of investor are mainly reflected by the prospect parameters (λ,α,β) in prospect value function, it is necessary to discuss the effect of parameters change on alternative ranking. For this purpose, three different scenarios are created by changing the prospect parameters.

Scenario 1. By changing the value of the parameter λ from -1 to -10.

Scenario 2. By changing the value of the parameter α from 0 to 1.

Scenario 3. By changing the value of the parameter β from 0 to 1.

The ranking of RPS alternatives obtained from sensitivity analysis with respect to the three scenarios are presented in Fig. 9.9 to Fig.9.11 respectively. It can be concluded from these figures that the ranking results are sensitive to the parameters of α and β, but not sensitive to the parameter of λ. With the value of α decreases to 0.22, the ranking results are changed to $A2 > A4 > A1 > A3 > A5$. While value of α is between 0.22 and 0.75, the ranking results are changed to $A2 > A1 > A4 > A3 > A5$. Although the optimal alternative has remained unchanged, the investment planning toward RPS will change if investors want to invest multiple sources at the same time. Similarly, the ranking results will also change to when the value of β varies. And it is noteworthy that the optimal alternative turns to A1 with the value of β decreases to 0.64. It means the investors' risk preference can affect the selection decision. Actually, α represents the concavity degree of gain region in the prospect value function, β represents the convexity degree of loss region in the prospect value function. So, the greater the value of α or β, the more likely investors are to seek risk. While λ indicates the sensitivity of investors to losses. So, with the decrease of the α or β value, investors tend to be more conservative when faced with risks. From the perspective of investment security, Chinese public investors would give more attention to the hydropower (A1).

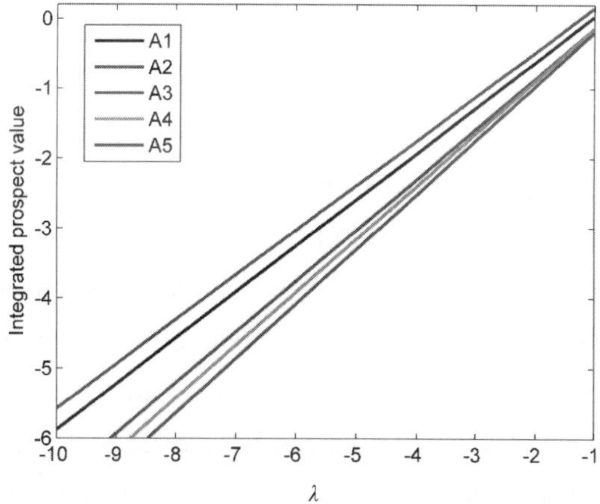

Fig. 9.9 Sensitivity analysis in the case of the parameter λ changes.

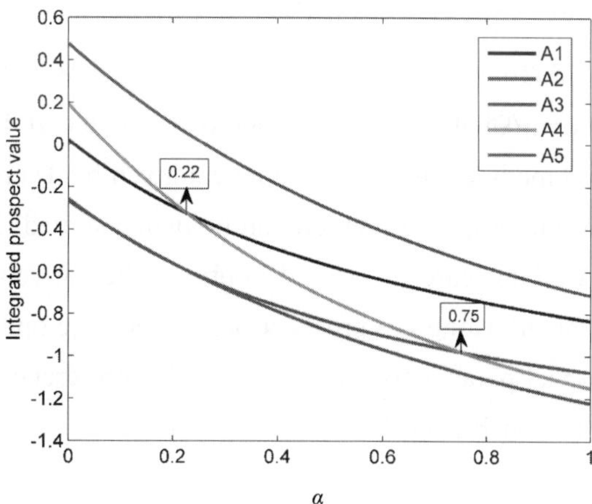

Fig. 9.10 Sensitivity analysis in the case of the parameter α changes.

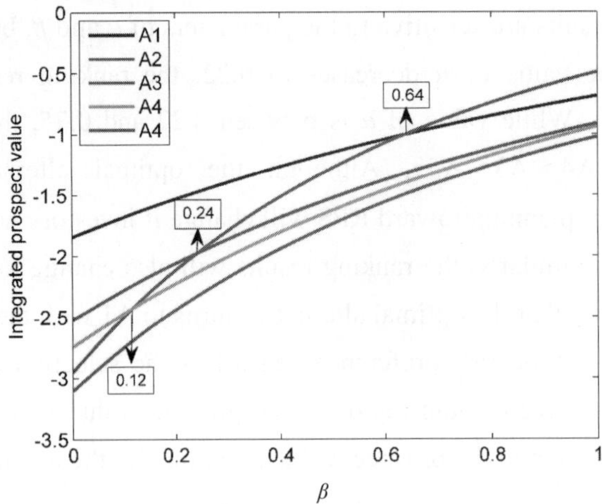

Fig. 9.11 Sensitivity analysis in the case of the parameter β changes.

4.4 Comparative analysis

In this section, a comparative analysis with two existing methods, fuzzy TOPSIS and fuzzy simple additive weighting (SAW), are presented to highlight the importance of risk preference in the RPS selection. The fuzzy TOPSIS technique was proposed by Shahbazi [47] to solve MCDM problems under fuzzy environment and to deal efficiently with uncertainty in the evaluations. Its principle is based on the fact that, the chosen alternative should have the shortest distance from the PIS and the farthest distance from the NIS. Fuzzy SAW is one of the most often used techniques for resolving fuzzy MCDM problems. A total score is obtained for each alternative by multiplying the importance weight assigned for each criterion by the fuzzy value to the alternative on each criterion and summing the products over all criteria. A detailed steps of fuzzy TOPSIS and SAW under the TFN environment can be referred to [48] and [49]. The input data for both methods are derived from Table 9.2 and Fig. 9.8. Then, the output ranking results are calculated and shown as follows:

- By the fuzzy TOPSIS: A2(0.512) > A1(0.483) > A3(0.454) > A4(0.381) > A5(0.365)
- By the fuzzy SAW: A2(0.507) > A1(0.482) > A3(0.473) > A4(0.433) > A5(0.421)

It can be seen that the optimal alternative obtained by the fuzzy TOPSIS and fuzzy SAM is same as that of the proposed method when the parameters given by Tversky and Kahneman are used. So, the correctness of the proposed method can be demonstrated. Moreover, as shown in Section 4.3, with the value of β decreases to 0.64, the optimal alternative would be changed from A2 to A1. In other words, by adjusting the prospect parameters, the optimal alternative will be changed. Acutally, the prospect parameters vary with the risk preference of investors. It makes the proposed method more reasonable for the selection of RPS.

5. Conclusions

Evaluating the RPS and selecting the most appropriate one to invest is critical for investors. MCDM techniques can be employed to identify the most suitable RPS. However, classic MCDM techniques cannot be operated in the uncertain environment, and take into account the risk preferences of investors. Therefore, a fuzzy MCDM technique based on the cumulative prospect theory is proposed to select the most appropriate RPS. Firstly, the comprehensive criteria system is established on the basis of literature review, which decomposes the complex goal hierarchically into four criteria and 14 sub-criteria that can be operated. Secondly, the TFNs are used to evaluate the criteria value collected from literature and reports as well as expert consultation to depict the uncertainty in the decision-making. Thirdly, the AHP combining with experts' knowledge and experience is applied to obtain the weights of criteria and sub-criteria. Fourthly, taking into account the risk preferences of investors, the cumulative prospect theory is employed to rank the alternatives. Subsequently, the case study in China is proposed to illustrate the rationality and feasibility of the proposed method. The weight results show that economical aspect and technical aspect are the most important criteria. And the ranking results suggest the solar PV as the best alternative, followed by the hydropower, solar thermal power, wind power, and biomass power. After that, the sensitivity analysis is carried out, and the results show that the ranking results are sensitive to the parameters of α and β. Furthermore, the comparative analysis is also given to clarify the rationality of the proposed method.

The merits of the proposed method are three-folds: ①it considers both uncertainties of evaluations and risk preference of investors in the RPS selection, which can simulate actual situation better. Note that the uncertainties here refer to the fuzziness, which are caused by dynamics of electricity market and policy, advance of energy technology, the vagueness of human thinking as well as the cognitive limitation of human beings. In uncertain environment, investors can adjust the parameters according to their own risk preferences, so as to choose the most suitable RPS to invest; ②it deals with mixed decision information including the crisp values, interval values and linguistic terms simultaneously. The merit solves the complex problem with the different kinds of evaluation information without information lossing; ③it provides not only the rankings of alternatives under the overall goal, but also the rankings of alternatives under each criterion. This merit will help the investors to analyze the advantages and disadvantages of alternative RPS clearly and easily. Therefore, based on the above improvements, the probability of decision-making mistake can be decreased.

In the future research, similar studies can be conducted under an intuitionistic fuzzy environment to deal with more complex problems. In addition, since the portfolio becomes an important means of risk diversification, renewable energy portfolio selection under fuzzy environment is a topic worthy of further study.

Appendix A

$$\begin{pmatrix} & C1 & C2 & C3 & C4 \\ C1 & 1 & 2 & 3 & 1 \\ C2 & 1/2 & 1 & 2 & 1 \\ C3 & 1/3 & 1/2 & 1 & 1/2 \\ C4 & 1 & 1 & 2 & 1 \end{pmatrix} \begin{pmatrix} & C11 & C12 & C13 & C14 & C15 \\ C11 & 1 & 3 & 2 & 1 & 2 \\ C12 & 1/3 & 1 & 1/2 & 1/4 & 1/2 \\ C13 & 1/2 & 2 & 1 & 1/3 & 1 \\ C14 & 1 & 4 & 3 & 1 & 3 \\ C15 & 1/2 & 2 & 1 & 1/3 & 1 \end{pmatrix}$$

$$\begin{pmatrix} & C21 & C22 \\ C21 & 1 & 4 \\ C22 & 1/4 & 1 \end{pmatrix} \begin{pmatrix} & C31 & C32 & C33 \\ C31 & 1 & 3 & 2 \\ C32 & 1/3 & 1 & 1 \\ C33 & 1/2 & 1 & 1 \end{pmatrix} \begin{pmatrix} & C41 & C42 & C43 & C44 \\ C41 & 1 & 1 & 1/2 & 1 \\ C42 & 1 & 1 & 1/2 & 1 \\ C43 & 2 & 2 & 1 & 2 \\ C44 & 1 & 1 & 1/2 & 1 \end{pmatrix}$$

Acknowledgments

Project supported by the 2017 Special Project of Cultivation and Development of Innovation Base (No. Z171100002217024) and the Fundamental Research Funds for the Central Universities (No. 2017XS099).

References

[1] Büyüközkan G, Karabulut Y. Energy project performance evaluation with sustainability perspective[J]. Energy, 2017, 119:549-560.

[2] Zeng M, Liu X, Li Y, et al. Review of renewable energy investment and financing in China: Status, mode, issues and countermeasures[J]. Renewable & Sustainable Energy Reviews, 2014, 31(2):23-37.

[3] Cristóbal J R S. Multi-criteria decision-making in the selection of a renewable energy project in spain: The Vikor method[J]. Renewable Energy, 2011, 36(2):498-502.

[4] Strantzali E, Aravossis K. Decision making in renewable energy investments: A review[J]. Renewable & Sustainable Energy Reviews, 2016, 55:885-898.

[5] Haddad B, Liazid A, Ferreira P. A multi-criteria approach to rank renewables for the Algerian electricity system[J]. Renewable Energy, 2017, 107:462-472.

[6] Amer M, Daim T U. Selection of renewable energy technologies for a developing county: A case of Pakistan[J]. Energy for Sustainable Development, 2011, 15(4):420-35.

[7] Streimikiene D, Balezentis T, Krisciukaitienė I, et al. Prioritizing sustainable electricity production technologies: MCDM approach[J]. Renewable & Sustainable Energy Reviews, 2012, 16(5):3302-3311.

[8] Büyüközkan G, Güleryüz S. An integrated DEMATEL-ANP approach for renewable energy resources selection in Turkey[J]. International Journal of Production Economics, 2016, 182:435-448.

[9] Wu Y, Geng S, Zhang H, Gao M. Decision framework of solar thermal power plant site selection

based on linguistic Choquet operator[J]. Applied Energy, 2014, 136(C):303-311.

[10] Wu Y, Zeng B, Zhang H, et al. Cloud decision framework in pure 2-tuple linguistic setting and its application for low-speed wind farm site selection[J]. Journal of Cleaner Production, 2017, 142:2154-2165.

[11] Wu Y, Hu Y, Xiao X, et al. Efficiency assessment of wind farms in China using two-stage data envelopment analysis[J]. Energy Conversion & Management. 2016, 123:46-55.

[12] Kumar A, Sah B, Singh A R, et al. A review of multi criteria decision making (MCDM) towards sustainable renewable energy development[J]. Renewable & Sustainable Energy Reviews, 2017, 69:596-609.

[13] Zadeh L A. Fuzzy sets [J]. Information & Control, 1965, 8(3):338-353.

[14] Kahraman C, Kaya İ, Cebi S. A comparative analysis for multiattribute selection among renewable energy alternatives using fuzzy axiomatic design and fuzzy analytic hierarchy process[J]. Energy, 2009, 34(10):1603-161611.

[15] Şengül Ü, Eren M, Shiraz S E, et al. Fuzzy TOPSIS method for ranking renewable energy supply systems in Turkey[J]. Renewable Energy, 2015, 75(C):617-625.

[16] Kaya T, Kahraman C. Multicriteria renewable energy planning using an integrated fuzzy VIKOR & AHP methodology: The case of Istanbul[J]. Energy, 2010, 35(6):2517-2527.

[17] Büyüközkan G, Güleryüz S. Evaluation of Renewable Energy Resources in Turkey using an integrated MCDM approach with linguistic interval fuzzy preference relations[J]. Energy, 2017, 123:149-163.

[18] Çolak M, Kaya İ. Prioritization of renewable energy alternatives by using an integrated fuzzy MCDM model: A real case application for Turkey[J]. Renewable & Sustainable Energy Reviews, 2017, 80:840-853.

[19] Tasri A, Susilawati A. Selection among renewable energy alternatives based on a fuzzy analytic hierarchy process in Indonesia[J]. Sustainable Energy Technologies & Assessments, 2014, 7:34-44.

[20] Kahneman D, Tversky A. Prospect theory: An analysis of decision under risk[J]. Econometrica, 1979, 47(2):263-291.

[21] Tversky A, Kahneman D. Advances in prospect theory: Cumulative representation of uncertainty[J]. Journal of Risk & Uncertainty, 1992, 5(4):297-323.

[22] Liu Y, Fan Z P, Zhang Y. Risk decision analysis in emergency response: A method based on cumulative prospect theory[J]. Computers & Operations Research, 2014, 42(2):75-82.

[23] Wang L, Wang Y M, Martínez L. A group decision method based on prospect theory for emergency situations[J]. Information Sciences, 2017, 418-419:119-135.

[24] Wilton E, Delarue E, D'Haeseleer W, et al. Reconsidering the capacity credit of wind power: Application of cumulative prospect theory[J]. Renewable Energy, 2014, 68(3):752-760.

[25] Liu J, Xu F, Lin S. Site selection of photovoltaic power plants in a value chain based on grey cumulative prospect theory for sustainability: A case study in Northwest China[J]. Journal of Cleaner Production, 2017, 148:386-397.

[26] Klein M, Deissenroth M. When do households invest in solar photovoltaics? An application of prospect theory[J]. Energy Policy, 2017, 109:270-278.

[27] Garni H A, Kassem A, Awasthi A, et al. A multicriteria decision making approach for evaluating renewable power generation sources in Saudi Arabia[J]. Sustainable Energy Technologies &

Assessments, 2016, 16:137-150.

[28] Chatzimouratidis A I, Pilavachi P A. Technological, economic and sustainability evaluation of power plants using the Analytic Hierarchy Process[J]. Energy Policy, 2009, 37(3):788-798.

[29] Heo E, Kim J, Cho S. Selecting hydrogen production methods using fuzzy analytic hierarchy process with opportunities, costs, and risks[J]. International Journal of Hydrogen Energy, 2012, 37(23):17655-17662.

[30] Malkawi S, Al-Nimr M D, Azizi D. A multi-criteria optimization analysis for Jordan's energy mix[J]. Energy, 2017, 127:680-696.

[31] Ahmad S, Tahar R M. Selection of renewable energy sources for sustainable development of electricity generation system using analytic hierarchy process: a case of Malaysia[J]. Renewable Energy, 2014, 63(1):458-466.

[32] Troldborg M, Heslop S, Hough R L. Assessing the sustainability of renewable energy technologies using multi-criteria analysis: Suitability of approach for national-scale assessments and associated uncertainties[J]. Renewable & Sustainable Energy Reviews, 2014, 39(6):1173-1184.

[33] Brand B, Missaoui R. Multi-criteria analysis of electricity generation mix scenarios in Tunisia[J]. Renewable & Sustainable Energy Reviews, 2014, 39(6):251-261.

[34] Ren J, Lützen M. Selection of sustainable alternative energy source for shipping: Multi-criteria decision making under incomplete information[J]. Renewable & Sustainable Energy Reviews, 2017, 74:1003-1019.

[35] Heo E, Kim J, Boo K J. Analysis of the assessment factors for renewable energy dissemination program evaluation using fuzzy AHP[J]. Renewable & Sustainable Energy Reviews, 2010, 14(8):2214-2220.

[36] Ahmad S, Nadeem A, Akhanova G, et al. Multi-criteria evaluation of renewable and nuclear resources for electricity generation in Kazakhstan[J]. Energy, 2017, 141:1880-1891.

[37] Chang D Y. Applications of the extent analysis method on fuzzy AHP[J]. European Journal of Operational Research, 1996, 95(3):649-655.

[38] Yu X, Hua L. Improvement on Judgement Matrix Based on Triangle Fuzzy Number[J]. Fuzzy Systems & Mathematics, 2003, 17(2):59-64.

[39] Chen S, Liu J, Wang H, et al. A linguistic multi-criteria decision making approach based on logical reasoning[J]. Information Sciences An International Journal, 2014, 258(3):266-276.

[40] Zadeh L A. The concept of a linguistic variable and its application to approximate reasoning – II[J].Information Sciences, 1975, 8(3):199-249.

[41] IRENA. Renewable energy technologies: cost analysis series [EB/OL]. http://www.irena.org/Publications/Publications, 2012.

[42] Liu L Q, Wang Z X, Zhang H Q, et al. Solar energy development in China—A review[J]. Renewable & Sustainable Energy Reviews, 2010, 14(1):301-311.

[43] Zhang D, Wang J, Lin Y, et al. Present situation and future prospect of renewable energy in China[J]. Renewable & Sustainable Energy Reviews, 2017, 76:865-871.

[44] Long T L, Branstetter L, Azevedo I M L. China's wind industry: Leading in deployment, lagging in innovation[J]. Energy Policy, 2017, 106:588-599.

[45] Shen J, Luo C. Overall review of renewable energy subsidy policies in China – Contradictions of intentions and effects[J]. Renewable & Sustainable Energy Reviews, 2015, 41(C):1478-1488.

[46] He G, Kammen D M. Where, when and how much wind is available? A provincial-scale wind resource assessment for China[J]. Energy Policy, 2014, 74:116-122.

[47] Shahbazi F, Sarmadian F, Jafarzadeh A A, et al. Application of SAW, TOPSIS and fuzzy TOPSIS models in cultivation priority planning for maize, rapeseed and soybean crops[J]. Geoderma, 2018, 310:178-190.

[48] Ye F, Li Y. An extended TOPSIS model based on the Possibility theory under fuzzy environment[J]. Knowledge-Based Systems, 2014, 67(3):263-269.

[49] Goyal R K, Kaushal S, Sangaiah A K. The utility based non-linear fuzzy AHP optimization model for network selection in heterogeneous wireless networks[M]. Applied Soft Computing, 2017.

[50] Chatzimouratidis A I, Pilavachi P A. Multicriteria evaluation of power plants impact on the living standard using the analytic hierarchy process[J]. Energy Policy, 2008, 36(3):1074-1089.

[51] Reddy V S, Kaushik S C, Tyagi S K. Exergetic analysis and performance evaluation of parabolic trough concentrating solar thermal power plant (PTCSTPP) [J]. Energy, 2012, 39(1):258-273.

[52] Dvořák P, Martinát S, Dan V D H, et al. Renewable energy investment and job creation; a cross-sectoral assessment for the Czech Republic with reference to EU benchmarks[J]. Renewable & Sustainable Energy Reviews, 2017, 69:360-368.

[53] Rodríguez-Huerta E, Rosas-Casals M, Sorman A H. A societal metabolism approach to job creation and renewable energy transitions in Catalonia[J]. Energy Policy, 2017, 108:551-564.

Chapter 10

Sustainability performance assessment of wind power coupling hydrogen storage projects using a hybrid evaluation technique based on interval type-2 fuzzy set

Yunna Wu [a, b], Chuanbo Xu [a, b*], Buyuan Zhang [a], Yao Tao [a], Xinying Li [a], Han Chu [a], Fangtong Liu [a]

a. School of Economics and Management, North China Electric Power University, Beijing, PCR

b. Beijing Key Laboratory of New Energy and Low-Carbon Development (North China Electric Power University), Changping Beijing, 102206

Abstract: The purpose of this study is to assess the performance of wind power coupling hydrogen storage projects from the perspective of sustainability. Firstly, an evaluation criteria system for sustainability performance assessment is established, which includes economic, environmental and social aspects. Then, the criteria performances of each alternative are determined by expert groups in the fields of energy economy, energy environment and society sciences. Later, considering the uncertainty in the decision-making, the interval type-2 fuzzy Analytic Hierarchy Process and the interval type-2 fuzzy Technique for Order Preference by Similarity to an Ideal Solution technique are employed to weight the criteria and sort the alternatives, respectively. Finally, a case study in Tibet autonomous, China is given to illustrate the effective of the proposed evaluation criteria and technique. The result shows the alternatives A4 gets the highest score. Moreover, the results of sensitivity analysis reveal that the alternative A4 always secures its top ranking when its weight is floating within a certain range. Meanwhile, the weight results show that the criteria of levelized cost of energy and poverty alleviation promotion should gain more attention. This research can offer references for investors to make investment decisions and for the government to make corresponding policies.

Keywords: wind power coupling hydrogen storage project; sustainability; performance evaluation; interval type-2 fuzzy Analytic Hierarchy Process; interval type-2 fuzzy Technique for Order Preference by Similarity to an Ideal Solution

Nomenclature

$\tilde{\tilde{A}}_i$	An IT2FS	$\tilde{\tilde{w}}_i$	Fuzzy weight of criteria
$H_j(\tilde{A}_i^U)$	Membership value of the element in the upper trapezoidal membership function	$\tilde{\tilde{r}}_i$	Geometric mean of each row of matrix
$H_j(\tilde{A}_i^L)$	Membership value of the element in the lower trapezoidal membership function	D^k	Decision-making matrix of kth decision-maker
$\text{Def}(\tilde{\tilde{a}}_i)$	Defuzzified value of an IT2FS	$\overline{Y}$	Weighted normalized fuzzy decision matrix
CI	Consistency index of a judgement matrix	x^+	Positive ideal solution
$\lambda_{\max}$	Largest principal eigenvalue of a matrix	x^-	Negative ideal solution
m	Matrix order	F_1	Set of benefit criteria
w	Main eigenvector which corresponds to maximum eigenvalue $\lambda_{\max}$.	F_2	Set of cost criteria
CR	Random consistency ratio of a judgement matrix	$d^+(x_i)$	Distance of each alternative from positive ideal solution
RI	Average random consistency index of a judgement matrix	$d^-(x_i)$	Distance of each alternative from negative ideal solution
$C(x_j)$	Closeness coefficient of each alternative		

1. Introduction

Coal is the most significant primary energy in China at this stage, accounting for 70% of the total primary energy consumption. This figure is 40 percentage points higher than the world average [1]. However, the uncontrolled usage of coal resources has brought enormous environmental challenges to China for a long time, including serious haze status, greenhouse gases emissions, ecological disruption and so on [2]. In addition, the excessive reliance on non-renewable coal resources will lead to the crisis of national energy security. Predictably, China's energy structure will undergo tremendous changes in the near future. Clean and renewable energy sources will gradually replace non-renewable fossil fuels and become the main source of energy supply.

Wind power with the clean and renewable advantages increasingly valued by many countries, and China is no exception. China has abundant wind power resources. It is estimated that the total exploitable wind power is 1400 GW onshore and 600 GW offshore, respectively [3]. Under this circumstance, China's wind power installed capacity has increased exponentially over the past decade, as shown in Fig. 10.1. Since 2012, the new installed capacity of wind power in China has been ranked first in the world for 4 consecutive years. At the same time, China's accumulative wind power installed capacity has exceeded 1.78 billion kW by the end of 2017, ranking the first place in the world [4].

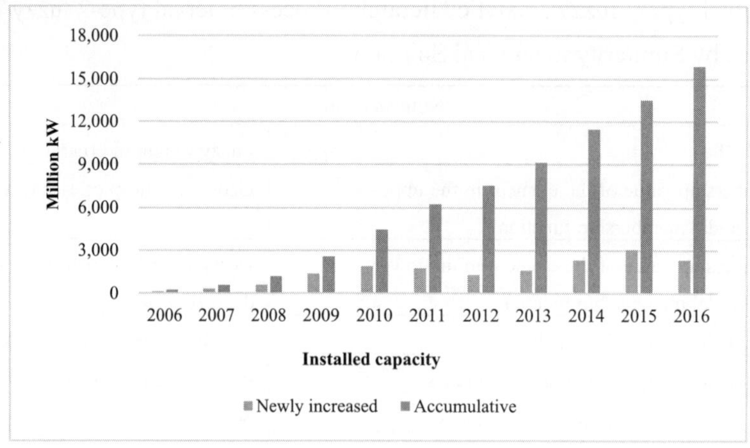

Fig. 10.1 China's wind power installed capacity in the past decade [5].

However, due to its random and intermittent characteristics, wind power has a great impact on the security and stability of the power grid [6]. The problem of wind power grid-connected is becoming increasingly prominent in China. The National Energy Administration (NEA) data showed that the amount of abandoned wind power reached 49.7 billion kWh in 2016 [7]. The phenomenon of wind power abandonment in 2017 is still grim, though it has improved compared with last year [8].

Storing the abandoned wind power is undoubtedly a good choice to solve this problem. In recent years, energy storage technologies have attracted wide attentions [9]. Because of its large-scale and long-term storage as well as high conversion efficiency, hydrogen energy storage technology is considered as an important support for the development of wind power generation, and is becoming the focus of wind power technology innovation in many countries [10]. The development of wind power coupling hydrogen storage (WPCHS) project is still in its early stages in China. The performance of proposed WPCHS project is the most concerned problem for local government as well as potential investors. Being clear about the performance of WPCHS project can help the investors select the most promising project, and at the same time facilitate the government to take measures to improve the project performance so as to encourage more private capitals to enter in. As the preliminary work of WPCHS project, the performance assessment is essential in the whole life cycle.

The term "sustainability" is defined through the following interconnected dimensions: environment, economy and society. This concept has been emphasized in the development of renewable energy project [11]. As a matter of fact, WPCHS project has remarkable environmental benefits such as carbon emission reduction and social benefits such as employment creation. Moreover, as awareness of sustainable development enhances, more and more power companies starting to pay attention to the harmonious development of environment, society and economy. Therefore, this research aims to evaluate the performance of WPCHS projects from the sustainability perspective. Considering that the WPCHS project performance evaluation includes multiple dimensions, a hybrid multi-criteria decision-making (MCDM) technique, namely interval type-2 fuzzy AHP (Analytic Hierarchy Process)-TOPSIS (Technique for Order Preference by Similarity to an Ideal Solution), is used to select the optimal WPCHS project from all alternatives in this paper.

2. Literature review

Nowadays, the researches on performance evaluation of WPCHS project or system are quite fruitful. Schuster and Walther [12] measured the profitability of a WPCHS project in Germany using the Decision Tree Approach. It was concluded that the mode of re-electrification is unprofitable but the wholesale of hydrogen can generate revenue, depending on the underlying parameters, regardless of the location of the power plant. Loisel et al. [13] assessed the economic performance of a hybrid power plant which consists of an offshore wind power farm and a hydrogen production-storage system. The results showed that the wind power abandonment can be about one-third lower than the total excess in some simulations due to the limited capacity to store the hydrogen. Siyal et al. [14] carried out an economic performance analysis of standalone wind powered hydrogen refueling stations at three selected sites. The results indicated that the levelized cost of hydrogen achieved by refueling stations having V112 wind turbine ranged from 5.18 to 7.25 US$/kg$H_2$, whereas it ranged from 6.52 to 9.62 US$/kg$H_2$ for stations having V82 wind turbines. Besides, Ghandehariun and Kumar [15] performed a life cycle assessment (LCA) to determine the greenhouse gas (GHG) emissions per unit mass of produced hydrogen by considering the emissions starting from the extraction of wind energy to the production of hydrogen. Ji-Yong et al. [16] assessed the environmental and economic performances of the wind-hydrogen system using LCA and life cycle costing (LCC) methodologies.

Moreover, some scholars also studied the benefits of wind-PV power coupling hydrogen storage (WPVPCHS) system which combines photovoltaic (PV) system on the basis of WPCHS system. Gökçek and Kale [17] performed a techno-economic performance assessment of hydrogen refuelling station powered by wind-PV complementary power system in İzmir-Çeşme, Turkey. The levelized cost of the hybrid system was found to be US$7.526–7.866/kg in different system configurations, which proved that it is economically appropriate. Qolipour et al. [18] carried out a techno-economic performance assessment for a wind-PV power plant construction for electric and hydrogen production. The findings showed that the area under study annually produces 3, 153, 762 kWh of electricity for a wind-PV power hybrid system, and 31, 680 kg of hydrogen for constructing a hybrid system. Al-Sharafi et al. [19] investigated the potentials of power generation and hydrogen production via solar and wind energy resources at different locations in the Kingdom of Saudi Arabia. The results showed that integration of 2 kW PV array, 3 wind turbines, 2 kW converter and 7 batteries storage bank is the best configuration that leads to the minimum levelized cost of energy (COE) of 0.609 $/kWh at Yanbu area.

From these literature reviews, it is concluded that the existing studies on WPCHS project performance evaluation mainly focus on two aspects: ①economic aspect by calculating the internal rate of return, net present value, cost of energy levelized cost of energy; ②environment aspect by using the LCA methodology. However, the research on sustainability performance evaluation of WPCHS project is quite scarce. Hacatoglu et al. [20] developed a novel sustainability assessment methodology for energy systems using life-cycle emission factors and sustainability indicators. Subsequently, Hacatoglu et al. [21] also applied an existing method to evaluate the sustainability performance of a wind-hydrogen system. It suggested that superficial assessments of sustainability should be avoided and that multi-criteria analysis is essential. However, only quantitative criteria are considered in their two researches. Actually, some environmental and social impacts of WPCHS projects are qualitative and cannot be treated quantitatively.

MCDM techniques are the most commonly used approaches to deal with the problem of sustainability performance assessment. MCDM includes numerous techniques such as AHP, analytic network process (ANP), decision making trial and evaluation laboratory (DEMATEL), TOPSIS, VIse Kriterijumska Optimizacija kompromisno Resenje (VIKOR), Preference Ranking Organization Methods for Enrichment Evaluation (PROMETHEE), Elimination Et Choix Tradulsant la REaltite (ELECTRE) and so on. Among them, AHP is one of the most classical MCDM techniques. It is easy to use because of its hierarchical structure and pairwise comparison that allow decision-makers to give different weight for each criterion [22]. TOPSIS is a compensatory aggregation MCDM technique with the advantages of high computational efficiency and superior ability to acquire objective results [23]. The ANP and DEMATEL are applied to situations where there is a correlation between indicators. The VIKOR takes into account the individual regrets of decision-making. Moreover, the PROMETHEE and ELECTRE focus on compensation issue between alternatives. Compared with other MCDM techniques, the AHP and TOPSIS are more suitable for solving the problem of WPCHS sustainability performance assessment because it does not involve the criteria correlation issue, individual regrets issue, and alternative compensation issue. Besides, the algorithms of AHP and TOPSIS are easier to understand and operator. Because of their outstanding advantages, the combination of AHP and TOPSIS has been widely researched. For instance, Azimifard et al. [24] selected sustainable supplier countries for Iran's steel industry using the AHP-TOPSIS technique. Sindhu et al. [25] investigated the deployment of solar farms using the AHP-TOPSIS technique.

Moreover, the AHP-TOPSIS technique is also applied in the study of [26] to determine the optimal load shedding scheme for large pulp mill electrical system.

However, some criteria are difficult to be measured by crisp numbers in the process of WPCHS project performance evaluation. The reasons are elaborated in two-fold: on the one hand, the performance evaluation of WPCHS project is a beforehand decision-making process. The impact of some uncertain factors such as policy changes and technological innovation on criteria values are difficult to predict accurately. On the other hand, some criteria (e.g. ecological impact, residential satisfaction) are qualitative and their values depend on the experience and knowledge of decision-makers. It is unrealistic to require decision-makers to express their preferences in the form of crisp numbers due to the ambiguity of human-thinking [27].

Fortunately, the fuzzy set theory put forward by Zadeh [28] can effectively solve this problem. Some studies on AHP-TOPSIS technique under the fuzzy environment were carried out. Taylan et al. [29] selected construction projects and made risk assessment by fuzzy AHP-TOPSIS under the environment of triangular fuzzy numbers. Amiri et al. [30] evaluated the competence of the firms using AHP-TOPSIS technique while the criteria values were expressed as trapezoidal fuzzy numbers. To depict more uncertainty and obtain more robust results, Celik and Akyuz [31] proposed an AHP-TOPSIS technique under interval type-2 fuzzy number environment for decision-making problems in maritime transportation engineering.

The interval type-2 fuzzy number is used in this paper because it could deal with imprecise and incomplete information in practical application better than ordinary fuzzy sets. Compared with type-1 fuzzy numbers like interval fuzzy numbers, triangular fuzzy numbers or trapezoidal fuzzy number, such number has a better processing ability for dealing with high-order uncertainty [32]. And many high-order uncertainties exist in the problem of WPCHS project performance evaluation as mentioned earlier. Thus, for handling with the highly complex issue of WPCHS project performance evaluation, the interval type-2 fuzzy number is more suitable.

The contributions of this paper are highlighted as follows:

(1) It can be found that the current criteria systems for the performance of WPCHS project contain only a few economic criteria or some quantitative criteria. This is the first study to establish a comprehensive evaluation criteria system, which includes quantitative and qualitative criteria, for WPCHS project performance evaluation from the three aspects of economy, society and environment.

(2) The interval type-2 fuzzy AHP-TOPSIS technique has been successfully employed in some performance evaluation problems, indicating that the technology has good property. However, to the best of our knowledge, this technique has not been introduced into the energy field. This study extends the application field of interval type-2 fuzzy AHP-TOPSIS technique.

(3) Through analyzing a case study in China, some generally managerial implications are

conducted. These can help potential investors to clearly analyze the pros and cons of WPCHS projects and at the same time provide ideas for local governments to formulate corresponding policies.

3. Introduction of wind power coupling hydrogen storage technology

This part mainly introduces the system composition and basic principle of wind power coupling hydrogen storage technology.

3.1 System composition

The WPCHS system includes the following five sub-systems:

(1) Control system: power electronic control module (include AC rectifier), safety control facilities.

(2) Electrolytic hydrogen manufacturing system: medium pressure alkaline electrolyzer, hydrogen-oxygen demister separator, hydrogen-oxygen balance valve.

(3) Storage system: medium pressure buffer hydrogen storage tank, high pressure hydrogen storage tank.

(4) Compression system: compressor.

(5) Auxiliary system: separator, scrubber, cooler, lye pump water, supply equipment, water temperature control equipment, suction pump, ventilation system, heating supply equipment, power supply equipment.

3.2 Basic principle

Hydrogen production from electrolyzed water is a process powered by electricity to break down water into hydrogen and oxygen through a chemical reaction. Electrolytic hydrogen production systems can be divided into alkaline electrolysis cell, polymer membrane electrolysis cell, and solid oxide electrolysis cell, depending on the type of electrolyte [33]. Among them, the alkaline electrolyzer is the oldest electrolysis way, which has the advantages of mature technology, good economy and easy operation. Therefore, this electrolysis way is the research object of this work.

The basic principle of WPCHS is to electrolyze water powered by wind energy to produce hydrogen and oxygen. The framework of a WPCHS system is shown in Fig. 10.2. The wind farm's discarded power is first turned into a direct current (DC) through the power electronic control module. Then, the DC enters the medium pressure alkaline electrolyzer to electrolyze water into hydrogen. The produced hydrogen is separated, washed and purified and then enters the medium pressure buffer hydrogen storage tank. The hydrogen is long-term stored in the high-pressure hydrogen storage tank after passing through the compressor. When electricity is needed, the stored hydrogen is transformed to electricity through different ways such as fuel cell [34]. In addition to converting to electrical, the produced hydrogen can be also used to meet industrial needs.

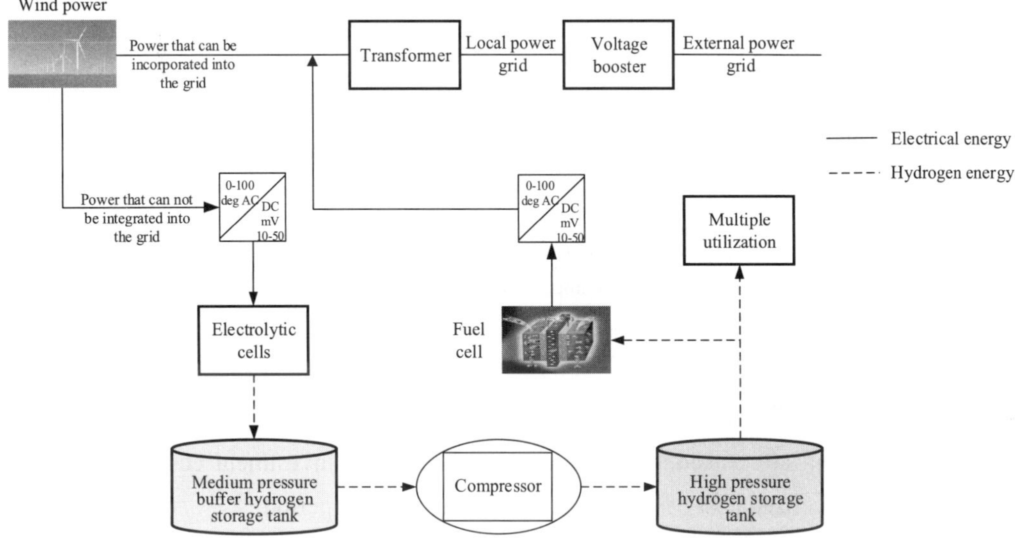

Fig. 10.2 Framework of wind power coupling hydrogen storage system [35].

4. Sustainable criteria for wind power coupling hydrogen storage project performance evaluation

A reasonable evaluation criteria system is critical to the performance evaluation of WPCHS projects. In this paper, the evaluation criteria system for WPCHS project performance evaluation is established from the perspective of sustainability. The evaluation criteria system includes economic, environmental and social dimensions. After that, the criteria associated with the three dimensions are identified via the next steps: first of all, an initial evaluation criteria list is collected through studying the relative academic literatures; secondly, experts whose background are energy environment, energy economy and energy society are invited to screen the list and then determine the importance of each criterion on the basis of their knowledge and experience; in the last, the unimportant criteria are removed from the list according to the experts' feedback, and the evaluation criteria system for WPCHS project performance evaluation is finally built, as shown in Table 10.1. The explanations of these criteria are elaborated as follows.

Table 10.1 Sustainable criteria for WPCHS project performance evaluation.

Aspect	Criteria	Type
Economic aspect (C1)	Investment cost (C11)	Cost
	Operation and maintenance cost (C12)	Cost
	Levelized cost of energy (C13)	Cost
	Payback period (C14)	Cost
Environmental aspect (C2)	Carbon dioxide emission reduction (C21)	Benefit
	PM 2.5 emission reduction (C22)	Benefit
	Ecological impact (C23)	Cost
	Land occupation (C24)	Cost
Social aspect (C3)	Poverty alleviation promotion (C31)	Benefit
	Technology innovative promotion (C32)	Benefit
	Power quality improvement (C33)	Benefit
	Residential satisfaction (C34)	Benefit

4.1 Economic aspect (C1)

Four key criteria are considered in the economic aspect: investment cost, operation and maintenance cost, levelized cost of energy (LCOE), and payback period.

(1) Investment cost. It includes land cost, equipment (e.g. wind turbine and hydrogen storage tanks) acquisition cost, construction cost and labor cost.

(2) Operation and maintenance cost. It consists of the system running cost including salaries of the employees, cost of the parts/spares required for scheduled maintenance purposes etc.

(3) LCOE. It measures the net present value of the unit-cost of electricity over the lifetime of a WPCHS project. It is an important criterion for the energy industry to evaluate the economic benefits of WPCHS projects from the perspective of the life cycle [36].

(4) Payback period. It refers to the time required to make the cumulative economic benefit equal to the initial investment cost. Investors often care about what time they can recover costs and thus to reduce risks.

4.2 Environmental criteria (C2)

The environmental impacts of the development of WPCHS projects are twofold. On the one hand, neither wind energy nor hydrogen energy is pollution-free, which protects the environment to a certain extent. On the other hand, however, the construction of a WPCHS is a major engineering which will inevitably cause damage to land, vegetation and water.

(1) Carbon dioxide emission reduction. Compared to traditional thermal power station, WPCHS projects will emit much less carbon dioxide (such as CO2 and CH4).

(2) PM2.5 emission reduction (C4). It measures the emission reduction of PM2.5 induced by using WPCHS projects rather than a traditional thermal power station.

(3) Ecological impact. It mainly estimates the vegetation degradation, water loss and soil erosion as well as birds decrease due to the construction of WPCHS projects.

(4) Land occupation. WPCHS projects occupy a great deal of land resources, which may affect the landscape and increase the project cost especially if it is near a city [37].

4.3 Social criteria (C3)

A WPCHS project can bring great social benefits, including poverty alleviation promotion, technology innovative promotion and power quality improvement.

(1) Poverty alleviation promotion (C31). The establishment of a WPCHS project will not only increase local employment, but boost local economic development. All these play an important role in helping the poor. Nowadays, the government is more and more concerned about people's well-being. On November 3, 2013, Chinese President Xi put forward the concept of "precise poverty alleviation" for the first time. Therefore, it is necessary to response the government order in the energy industry.

(2) Technology innovative promotion (C32). The technologies of hydrogen production by wind power, hydrogen storage and transportation are not yet fully mature. The development of a new WPCHS project could promote the innovative of relative technologies.

(3) Power quality improvement (C33). The inherent uncertainty of wind resources makes the output power of wind turbines fluctuate, which may affect the power quality of power grid, such as voltage deviation, voltage fluctuation and flicker, harmonics and so on. Hydrogen storage can improve the power quality in the local power network.

(4) Residential satisfaction (C34). Residential satisfaction expresses the views of local residents' opinions on WPCHS projects. It is very essential to consider residential satisfaction because many power plants fail due to public opposition.

5. Interval type-2 fuzzy hybrid evaluation technique for project performance evaluation

The Interval type-2 fuzzy sets (IT2FSs), interval type-2 fuzzy AHP as well as interval type-2 fuzzy TOPSIS are introduced in this section.

5.1 Interval type-2 fuzzy sets

The problem of WPCHS project performance evaluation is a complex issue and its results are affected by many complicated factors. Type-1 fuzzy sets cannot fully represent such uncertainties. IT2FSs, proposed by Zadeh [38], can represent more uncertainty and can produce more robust results because the upper and lower membership functions of an IT2FS are type-1 membership functions. Since put forward, the IT2FSs have been successfully applied to various kinds of evaluation problems, such as air quality evaluation [39], R&D project evaluation [40], supplier evaluation [41] and so on. In this section, basic conceptions and operations of IT2FSs are introduced.

Definition [42]. Let $\tilde{\tilde{A}}_i$ be an IT2FS $\tilde{\tilde{A}}_i=[\tilde{A}_i^U,\tilde{A}_i^L]=\left[\left(a_{i1}^U,a_{i2}^U,a_{i3}^U,a_{i4}^U;H_1(\tilde{A}_i^U),H_2(\tilde{A}_i^U)\right),\left(a_{i1}^L,a_{i2}^L,a_{i3}^L,a_{i4}^L;H_1(\tilde{A}_i^L),H_2(\tilde{A}_i^L)\right)\right]$, where $\tilde{A}_i^U$ and $\tilde{A}_i^L$ are type-1 fuzzy sets, $a_{i1}^U,a_{i2}^U,a_{i3}^U,a_{i4}^U,a_{i1}^U,a_{i2}^U,a_{i3}^U,a_{i4}^U$ are the characteristic points of the $\tilde{\tilde{A}}_i$. $H_j(\tilde{A}_i^U)$ denotes the membership value of the element $a^U{}_{i(j+1)}$ in the upper trapezoidal membership function $\tilde{A}_i^U$, $1\leqslant j\leqslant 2$, $H_j(\tilde{A}_i^L)$ denotes the membership value of the element $a^L{}_{i(j+1)}$ in the lower trapezoidal membership function. A classical trapezoidal IT2FS is depicted in Fig.10.3.

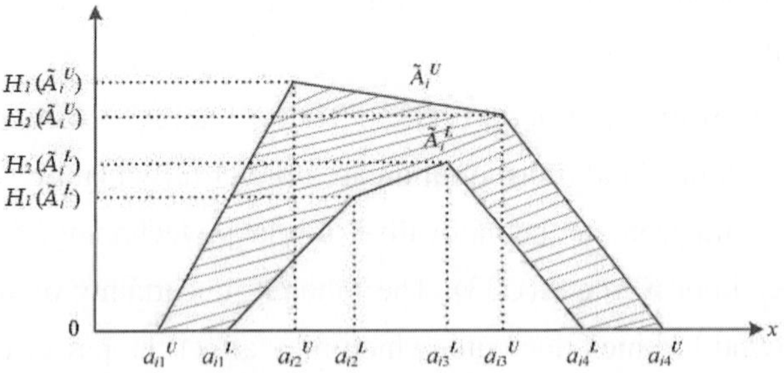

Fig. 10.3 A trapezoidal interval type-2 fuzzy number [43].

Moreover, the basic operations of IT2FSs are as follows:

$$\tilde{\tilde{A}}_1\oplus\tilde{\tilde{A}}_2=(\tilde{A}_1^U,\tilde{A}_1^L)\oplus(\tilde{A}_2^U,\tilde{A}_2^L)=$$
$$\begin{pmatrix} a_{11}{}^U+a_{21}{}^U,a_{12}{}^U+a_{22}{}^U,a_{13}{}^U+a_{23}{}^U,a_{14}{}^U+a_{24}{}^U;\min\left(H_1(\tilde{A}_1^U),H_1(\tilde{A}_2^U)\right),\min\left(H_2(\tilde{A}_1^U),H_2(\tilde{A}_2^U)\right),\\ a_{11}{}^L+a_{21}{}^L,a_{12}{}^L+a_{22}{}^L,a_{13}{}^L+a_{23}{}^L,a_{14}{}^L+a_{24}{}^L;\min\left(H_1(\tilde{A}_1^L),H_1(\tilde{A}_2^L)\right),\min\left(H_2(\tilde{A}_1^L),H_2(\tilde{A}_2^L)\right)\end{pmatrix} \tag{10-1}$$

$$\tilde{\tilde{A}}_1\otimes\tilde{\tilde{A}}_2=(\tilde{A}_1^U,\tilde{A}_1^L)\otimes(\tilde{A}_2^U,\tilde{A}_2^L)=$$
$$\begin{pmatrix} a_{11}{}^U\times a_{21}{}^U,a_{12}{}^U\times a_{22}{}^U,a_{13}{}^U\times a_{23}{}^U,a_{14}{}^U\times a_{24}{}^U;\min\left(H_1(\tilde{A}_1^U),H_1(\tilde{A}_2^U)\right),\min\left(H_2(\tilde{A}_1^U),H_2(\tilde{A}_2^U)\right),\\ a_{11}{}^L\times a_{21}{}^L,a_{12}{}^L\times a_{22}{}^L,a_{13}{}^L\times a_{23}{}^L,a_{14}{}^L\times a_{24}{}^L;\min\left(H_1(\tilde{A}_1^L),H_1(\tilde{A}_2^L)\right),\min\left(H_2(\tilde{A}_1^L),H_2(\tilde{A}_2^L)\right)\end{pmatrix} \tag{10-2}$$

$$k\otimes\tilde{\tilde{A}}_1=\begin{pmatrix}\left(ka_{11}{}^U,ka_{12}{}^U,ka_{13}{}^U,ka_{14}{}^U;H_1(\tilde{A}_1^U),H_2(\tilde{A}_1^U)\right),\\ \left(ka_{11}{}^L,ka_{12}{}^L,ka_{13}{}^L,ka_{14}{}^L;H_1(\tilde{A}_1^L),H_2(\tilde{A}_1^L)\right)\end{pmatrix} \tag{10-3}$$

5.2 Interval type-2 fuzzy Analytic Hierarchy Process

AHP proposed by Saaty [44] is a popular MCDM method for its rational hierarchy structure and clear logic relations. Subsequently, Buckley [45] extended Saaty's AHP into fuzzy AHP by integrating with fuzzy sets. In this paper, AHP method under IT2FS environment, which is called interval type-2 fuzzy AHP, is employed to obtain fuzzy weights of the criteria involved in WPCHS project performance evaluation. The steps of the interval type-2 fuzzy AHP technique are given as follows:

Step 1. The pair wise comparison matrix under IT2FS environment is established. The linguistic terms and their corresponding IT2FSs are shown in Table 10.2.

Table 10.2 Linguistic variables for criteria weights [46].

Linguistic variables	IT2FSs	Reciprocal IT2FSs
Absolutely Strong (AS)	((7, 8, 9, 9; 1, 1),(7.2, 8.2, 8.8, 9; 0.8, 0.8))	((0.11, 0.11, 0.12, 0.14; 1, 1), (0.11, 0.11, 0.12, 0.14; 0.8, 0.8))
Very Strong (VS)	((5, 6, 8, 9; 1, 1), (5.2, 6.2, 7.8, 8.8; 0.8, 0.8))	((0.11, 0.12, 0.17, 0.2; 1, 1), (0.11, 0.13, 0.16, 0.19; 0.8, 0.8))
Fairly Strong (FS)	((3, 4, 6, 7; 1, 1), (3.2, 4.2, 5.8, 6.8; 0.8, 0.8))	((0.14, 0.17, 0.25, 0.33; 1, 1), (0.15, 0.17, 0.24, 0.31; 0.8, 0.8))
Slightly Strong (SS)	((1, 2, 4, 5; 1, 1), (1.2, 2.2, 3.8, 4.8; 0.8, 0.8))	((0.2, 0.25, 0.5, 1; 1, 1), 0.21, 0.26, 0.45, 0.83; 0.8, 0.8))
Exactly Equal (E)	((1, 1, 1, 1; 1, 1), (1, 1, 1, 1; 1, 1))	((1, 1, 1, 1; 1, 1), (1, 1, 1, 1; 1, 1))

Step 2. Test the consistency of the IT2FSs pair wise comparison. In this manner, the IT2FSs matrices are defuzzified as Eq. (10-4) [46] and checked for consistency.

$$\mathrm{Def}(\tilde{\tilde{a}}_i)=\frac{\dfrac{(a_{i4}^U-a_{i1}^U)+\left(H_1(\tilde{A}_i^U)\bullet a_{i2}^U-a_{i1}^U\right)+\left(H_2(\tilde{A}_i^U)\bullet a_{i3}^U-a_{i1}^U\right)}{4}+a_{i1}^U+\dfrac{(a_{i4}^L-a_{i1}^L)+\left(H_1(\tilde{A}_i^L)\bullet a_{i2}^L-a_{i1}^L\right)+\left(H_2(\tilde{A}_i^L)\bullet a_{i3}^L-a_{i1}^L\right)}{4}+a_{i1}^L}{2} \tag{10-4}$$

The matrix consistency index CI is calculated as follows:

$$CI=(\lambda_{\max}-m)/(m-1) \tag{10-5}$$

where $Aw=\lambda_{\max}w$, $\lambda_{\max}$ is the largest principal eigenvalue of the decision matrix; m is matrix order.

Then, the random consistency ratio CR is calculated using:

$$CR=CI/RI \tag{10-6}$$

where RI is the average random consistency index of judgement matrix.

Step 3. Aggregate the assessment of each expert by using geometric mean operator.

$$\tilde{\tilde{A}}_{ij}=\left[\tilde{\tilde{A}}^1\otimes\cdots\otimes\tilde{\tilde{A}}^n\right]^{1/n} \tag{10-7}$$

where $\sqrt[n]{\tilde{\tilde{A}}_{ij}}=\begin{pmatrix}\sqrt[n]{\tilde{\tilde{A}}_{ij1}{}^U},\sqrt[n]{\tilde{\tilde{A}}_{ij2}{}^U},\sqrt[n]{\tilde{\tilde{A}}_{ij3}{}^U},\sqrt[n]{\tilde{\tilde{A}}_{ij4}{}^U};H_1(a_{ij}{}^U),H_2(a_{ij}{}^U),\\ \sqrt[n]{\tilde{\tilde{A}}_{ij1}{}^L},\sqrt[n]{\tilde{\tilde{A}}_{ij2}{}^L},\sqrt[n]{\tilde{\tilde{A}}_{ij3}{}^L},\sqrt[n]{\tilde{\tilde{A}}_{ij4}{}^L};H_1(a_{ij}{}^L),H_2(a_{ij}{}^L)\end{pmatrix}$

Step 4. Calculate the interval type-2 fuzzy weights of each criterion as follows.

$$\tilde{\tilde{w}}_i = \tilde{\tilde{r}}_i \times (\tilde{\tilde{r}}_1 + \tilde{\tilde{r}}_2 + ... + \tilde{\tilde{r}}_m)^{-1} \tag{10-8}$$

where $\tilde{\tilde{r}}_i$ represents the geometric mean of each row of the matrix.

5.3 Interval type-2 fuzzy Technique for Order Preference by Similarity to an Ideal Solution

TOPSIS, as a one of the classical MCDM methods, was proposed by Hwang and Yoon [47]. It is a sorting method based on the approximation degree between a limited number of evaluation alternatives and the idealized alternatives, and it is a relatively good or bad evaluation in the existing alternatives [48]. For interval type-2 fuzzy TOPSIS method, the elements in the decision matrix have adopted the form of interval type-2 fuzzy numbers. The steps of interval type-2 fuzzy TOPSIS method are as below:

Assuming that there are m WPCHS projects and n evaluation criteria, a total of t decision-makers $D_1, D_2, ..., D_t$ are responsible for this evaluation.

Step 1. Transform the linguistic variables into IT2FSs

As can be seen from the established evaluation criteria system, qualitative and quantitative criteria exist simultaneously. Because of the different dimensions, it is necessary to normalize them. Linguistic variables are usually employed by decision-makers and then the linguistic variables are transformed into IT2FSs using mapping relationships shown in Table 10.3.

Table 10.3 Linguistic variables and their corresponding IT2FSs [49].

Linguistic variables	Trapezoidal IT2FSs
Very Low (VL)	((0, 0, 0, 0.1; 1, 1), (0, 0, 0, 0.05; 0.9, 0.9))
Low (L)	((0, 0.1, 0.1, 0.3; 1, 1), (0.05, 0.1, 0.1, 0.2; 0.9, 0.9))
Medium Low (ML)	((0.1, 0.3, 0.3, 0.5; 1, 1), (0.2, 0.3, 0.3, 0.4; 0.9, 0.9))
Medium (M)	((0.3, 0.5, 0.5, 0.7; 1, 1), (0.4, 0.5, 0.5, 0.6; 0.9, 0.9))
Medium high (MH)	((0.5, 0.7, 0.7, 0.9; 1, 1), (0.6, 0.7, 0.7, 0.8; 0.9, 0.9))
High (H)	((0.7, 0.9, 0.9, 1; 1, 1), (0.8, 0.9, 0.9, 0.95; 0.9, 0.9))
Very High (VH)	((0.9, 1, 1, 1; 1, 1), (0.95, 1, 1, 1; 0.9, 0.9))

Then, the interval type-2 fuzzy decision-making matrix of kth decision-maker can be constructed, as shown in Eq. (10-9).

$$D^k = (\tilde{\tilde{d}}_{ij}{}^k) = \begin{pmatrix} \tilde{\tilde{d}}_{11}{}^k & \tilde{\tilde{d}}_{12}{}^k & \tilde{\tilde{d}}_{13}{}^k & \tilde{\tilde{d}}_{14}{}^k \\ \tilde{\tilde{d}}_{21}{}^k & \tilde{\tilde{d}}_{22}{}^k & \tilde{\tilde{d}}_{23}{}^k & \tilde{\tilde{d}}_{24}{}^k \\ \vdots & \vdots & \vdots & \vdots \\ \tilde{\tilde{d}}_{m1}{}^k & \tilde{\tilde{d}}_{m2}{}^k & \cdots & \tilde{\tilde{d}}_{mn}{}^k \end{pmatrix} \tag{10-9}$$

Step 2. Aggregate the interval type-2 fuzzy decision matrix of the decision-makers.

After inputting the criteria data of each WPCHS project, the aggregated interval type-2 fuzzy decision matrix can be constructed, as expressed in Eq. (10-10).

$$\bar{D} = (\tilde{\tilde{d}}_{ij})_{m\times n} = \begin{pmatrix} \tilde{\tilde{d}}_{11} & \tilde{\tilde{d}}_{12} & \tilde{\tilde{d}}_{13} & \tilde{\tilde{d}}_{14} \\ \tilde{\tilde{d}}_{21} & \tilde{\tilde{d}}_{22} & \tilde{\tilde{d}}_{23} & \tilde{\tilde{d}}_{24} \\ \vdots & \vdots & \vdots & \vdots \\ \tilde{\tilde{d}}_{m1} & \tilde{\tilde{d}}_{m2} & \tilde{\tilde{d}}_{m3} & \tilde{\tilde{d}}_{mn} \end{pmatrix} \tag{10-10}$$

where $\tilde{\tilde{d}}_{ij} = \dfrac{\left(\tilde{\tilde{d}}_{ij}{}^{1} \oplus \tilde{\tilde{d}}_{ij}{}^{2} \oplus \cdots \oplus \tilde{\tilde{d}}_{ij}{}^{t}\right)}{t}$ is an IT2FS $1 \leqslant i \leqslant m, 1 \leqslant j \leqslant n, 1 \leqslant k \leqslant t$.

Step 3. Establish the weighted normalized fuzzy decision matrix

$$\bar{Y} = (\tilde{\tilde{v}}_{ij})_{m\times n} = \begin{bmatrix} \tilde{\tilde{v}}_{11}{}^{k} & \tilde{\tilde{v}}_{12}{}^{k} & \tilde{\tilde{v}}_{13}{}^{k} & \tilde{\tilde{v}}_{14}{}^{k} \\ \tilde{\tilde{v}}_{21}{}^{k} & \tilde{\tilde{v}}_{22}{}^{k} & \tilde{\tilde{v}}_{23}{}^{k} & \tilde{\tilde{v}}_{24}{}^{k} \\ \vdots & \vdots & \vdots & \vdots \\ \tilde{\tilde{v}}_{m1}{}^{k} & \tilde{\tilde{v}}_{m2}{}^{k} & \cdots & \tilde{\tilde{v}}_{mn}{}^{k} \end{bmatrix} \tag{10-11}$$

where $\tilde{\tilde{v}}_{ij} = \tilde{\tilde{w}}_i \otimes \tilde{\tilde{d}}_{ij}, 1 \leqslant i \leqslant m, 1 \leqslant j \leqslant n$.

Step 4. Determine the interval type-2 fuzzy positive/negative ideal solution

Determine the positive ideal solution $x^{+} = (v_1{}^{+} v_2{}^{+}, \ldots, v_m{}^{+})$ and the negative-ideal solution $x^{-} = (v_1{}^{-} v_2{}^{-}, \ldots, v_m{}^{-})$, where

$$v_i{}^{+} = \begin{cases} \max\limits_{1\leqslant j\leqslant n} (\mathrm{Def}(\tilde{\tilde{v}}_{ij})), \text{ if } f_i \in F_1 \\ \min\limits_{1\leqslant j\leqslant n} (\mathrm{Def}(\tilde{\tilde{v}}_{ij})), \text{ if } f_i \in F_2 \end{cases} \tag{10-12}$$

and

$$v_i{}^{-} = \begin{cases} \min\limits_{1\leqslant j\leqslant n} (\mathrm{Def}(\tilde{\tilde{v}}_{ij})), \text{ if } f_i \in F_1 \\ \max\limits_{1\leqslant j\leqslant n} (\mathrm{Def}(\tilde{\tilde{v}}_{ij})), \text{ if } f_i \in F_2 \end{cases} \tag{10-13}$$

where F_1 denotes the set of benefit criteria, F_2 denotes the set of cost criteria, and $1 \leqslant i \leqslant m$.

Step 5. Calculate the distance of each alternative from a fuzzy positive and negative ideal solution, shown as follows:

$$d^{+}(x_i) = \sqrt{\sum_{i=1}^{m} (\mathrm{Def}(\tilde{\tilde{v}}_{ij}) - v_i{}^{+})^2} \tag{10-14}$$

$$d^{-}(x_i) = \sqrt{\sum_{i=1}^{m} (\mathrm{Def}(\tilde{\tilde{v}}_{ij}) - v_i{}^{-})^2} \tag{10-15}$$

Step 6. Compute the closeness coefficient of each alternative and rank the alternatives.

$$C(x_j)=\frac{d^-(x_j)}{d^+(x_j)+d^-(x_j)} \tag{10-16}$$

where $1 \leqslant j \leqslant n$. The larger the value of $C(x_j)$, the better of the alternative.

The decision framework of WPCHS project performance evaluation by using interval type-2 fuzzy AHP-TOPSIS method is displayed in Fig. 10.4.

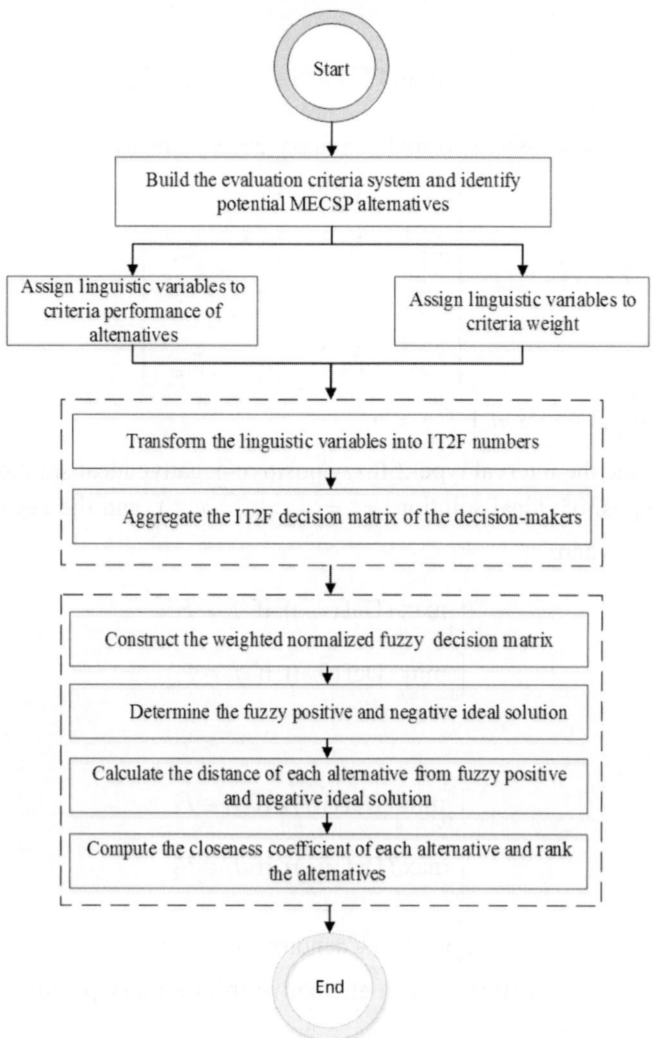

Fig. 10.4 Decision framework of WPCHS project performance evaluation.

6. A case study

A large-scale energy group is planning to invest in WPCHS project in China. The condition of wind resources is their primary concern. After a round of high-level meeting, the Tibet autonomous region, located in southwest areas, are selected as investment regions. The reasons for this selection are as follows:

(1) Tibet autonomous region is vast in territory and its land cost is very low. Actually, high land cost has become a heavy burden for energy enterprises, which accounts for more than half of the total investment cost.

(2) Tibet autonomous region is the only centralized poverty-stricken region in China. Investment in the Tibet autonomous region can actively respond to the call of the nation for precision poverty alleviation, and at the same time assume the social responsibilities of enterprises to enhance the visibility of enterprises.

(3) The phenomena of wind power abandonment in Tibet autonomous region is serious. In 2014, the rate of wind power abandonment in Tibet autonomous region reached 17.25%, ranking second in the whole country.

After that, through a series of field investigations and public opinion polls, a total of 13 WPCHS projects are identified. In order to select the optimal investment plan, a decision-making committee is set up which consists of three experts whose background are energy environment, energy economy, and society sciences. After consulting the feasibility study reports, the committee preliminarily selects four potential WPCHS projects (i=1,2,3,4).

Every expert assigns the linguistic rating judgments for the criteria performance of WPCHS each alternative, as shown in Tables 10.4.

Table 10.4 Linguistic ratings for criteria performances of four WPCHS alternatives.

		C11	C12	C13	C14	C21	C22	C23	C24	C31	C32	C33	C34
E1	A1	VL	L	L	L	VH	H	ML	ML	M	ML	M	M
	A2	L	ML	L	VL	ML	M	M	MH	H	ML	M	H
	A3	VL	L	L	ML	M	L	L	VL	L	ML	L	VL
	A4	H	VH	MH	ML	H	L	H	L	MH	ML	H	VH
E2	A1	L	ML	VL	L	ML	ML	MH	M	L	L	M	M
	A2	H	VH	L	ML	VL	ML	ML	MH	VL	VL	H	M
	A3	VH	VH	L	L	VH	M	M	H	VL	L	H	L
	A4	VH	VH	H	L	VH	VL	VH	L	ML	MH	VH	H
E3	A1	ML	M	L	ML	H	VH	VH	VL	L	H	H	VL
	A2	L	ML	ML	H	VH	VH	VL	L	H	H	VL	M
	A3	M	MH	M	L	ML	ML	H	H	ML	L	H	H
	A4	ML	M	L	H	VL	MH	MH	H	H	ML	ML	L

Note: E means expert.

Then, these linguistic variables are transformed into IT2FSs based on the mapping relationships given in Table 10.3.

Subsequently, experts individually make the importance comparison of the criteria, as shown in the following matrixes. Similarly, these linguistic variables are transformed into IT2FSs based on the mapping relationships given in Table 10.2. Consistency check is carried out using Eq. (10-4) to Eq. (10-6), and results show all the comparison matrixes pass the consistency test.

$$\begin{pmatrix} & C1 & C2 & C3 \\ C1 & [E,E,E] & [SS,SS,E] & [E,E,1/SS] \\ C2 & [1/SS,1/SS,E] & [E,E,E] & [E,1/SS,1/SS] \\ C3 & [E,E,SS] & [E,SS,SS] & [E,E,E] \end{pmatrix}$$

$$\begin{pmatrix} & C11 & C12 & C13 & C14 \\ C11 & [E,E,E] & [FS,SS,SS] & [1/SS,E,E] & [SS,E,SS] \\ C12 & [1/FS,SS,SS] & [E,E,E] & [1/SS,E,E] & [1/SS,E,1/SS] \\ C13 & [SS,E,E] & [SS,E,E] & [E,E,E] & [FS,SS,SS] \\ C14 & [1/SS,E,1/SS] & [SS,E,SS] & [1/FS,1/SS,1/SS] & [E,E,E] \end{pmatrix}$$

$$\begin{pmatrix} & C21 & C22 & C23 & C24 \\ C21 & [E,E,E] & [SS,E,E] & [SS,SS,E] & [E,1/SS,E] \\ C22 & [1/SS,E,E] & [E,E,E] & [E,E,E] & [1/SS,1/SS,E] \\ C23 & [1/SS,1/SS,E] & [E,E,E] & [E,E,E] & [1/FS,1/SS,E] \\ C24 & [E,SS,E] & [SS,SS,E] & [1/FS,1/SS,E] & [E,E,E] \end{pmatrix}$$

$$\begin{pmatrix} & C31 & C32 & C33 & C34 \\ C31 & [E,E,E] & [VS,SS,SS] & [SS,E,E] & [SS,SS,E] \\ C32 & [1/VS,1/SS,1/SS] & [E,E,E] & [1/SS,1/SS,E] & [1/SS,1/SS,E] \\ C33 & [1/SS,E,E] & [SS,SS,E] & [E,E,E] & [SS,E,E] \\ C34 & [1/SS,1/SS,E] & [SS,SS,E] & [1/SS,E,E] & [E,E,E] \end{pmatrix}$$

Following this, the fuzzy weights of these criteria are calculated using Eq. (10-7) and Eq. (10-8) and given in Table 10.5.

Table 10.5 Fuzzy weights of the criteria.

Criteria	Absolute weights
C1	((0.211, 0.375, 0.816, 1.246; 1, 1), (0.244, 0.410, 0.758, 1.131; 0.8, 0.8))
C2	((0.156, 0.219, 0.39, 0.587; 1, 1), (0.169, 0.231, 0.366, 0.531; 0.8, 0.8))
C3	((0.088, 0.113, 0.211, 0.363; 1, 1), (0.093, 0.118, 0.194, 0.315; 0.8, 0.8))
C11	((0.028, 0.082, 0.357, 0.849; 1, 1), (0.037, 0.096, 0.310, 0.692; 0.8, 0.8))
C12	((0.014, 0.039, 0.190, 0.533; 1, 1); (0.018, 0.046, 0.161, 0.415; 0.8, 0.8))
C13	((0.034, 0.103, 0.464, 1.072; 1, 1); (0.045, 0.123, 0.403, 0.882; 0.8, 0.8))
C14	((0.012, 0.034, 0.176, 0.533; 1, 1); (0.015, 0.039, 0.148, 0.407; 0.8, 0.8))
C21	((0.028, 0.057, 0.168, 0.338; 1, 1), (0.033, 0.064, 0.151, 0.285; 0.8, 0.8))
C22	((0.019, 0.034, 0.257, 0.384; 1, 1), (0.021, 0.037, 0.089, 0.184; 0.8, 0.8))
C23	((0.015, 0.028, 0.086, 0.200; 1, 1), (0.017, 0.031, 0.075, 0.161; 0.8, 0.8))
C24	((0.021, 0.048, 0.159, 0.341; 1, 1), (0.026, 0.054, 0.141, 0.284; 0.8, 0.8))
C31	((0.016, 0.034, 0.122, 0.301; 1, 1), (0.019, 0.038, 0.105, 0.240; 0.8, 0.8))
C32	((0.004, 0.007, 0.030, 0.107; 1, 1), (0.004, 0.008, 0.024, 0.077; 0.8, 0.8))
C33	((0.012, 0.024, 0.084, 0.219; 1, 1), (0.014, 0.026, 0.073, 0.172; 0.8, 0.8))
C34	((0.008, 0.016, 0.062, 0.183; 1, 1), (0.010, 0.018, 0.052, 0.139; 0.8, 0.8))

Combined the criteria performance and criteria weight, the weighted normalized fuzzy decision matrix can be obtained, as shown in Table 10.6.

Table 10.6 Weighted normalized fuzzy decision matrix.

	A1	A2	A3	A4
C11	((0,0,0,0.013; 1,1), (0,0,0,0.003; 0.8,0.8))	((0,0.001,0.003,0.076; 1,1), (0,0.001,0.003,0.026; 0.8,0.8))	((0,0,0,0.059; 1,1), (0,0,0,0.021; 0.8,0.8))	((0.002,0.022,0.097,0.424; 1,1), (0.006,0.026,0.084,0.263; 0.8,0.8))
C12	((0.002,0.012,0.057,0.267; 1,1), (0.004,0.014,0.048,0.166; 0.8,0.8))	((0.005,0.021,0.101,0.356; 1,1), (0.008,0.025,0.086,0.249; 0.8,0.8))	((0.007,0.023,0.114,0.391; 1,1), (0.01,0.028,0.097,0.277; 0.8,0.8))	((0.01,0.033,0.158,0.48; 1,1), (0.014,0.038,0.135,0.36; 0.8,0.8))
C13	((0,0,0,0.01; 1,1), (0,0,0,0.002; 0.8,0.8))	((0,0,0.001,0.048; 1,1), (0,0,0.001,0.014; 0.8,0.8))	((0,0.001,0.002,0.068; 1,1), (0,0.001,0.002,0.021; 0.8,0.8))	((0,0,0.003,0.035; 1,1), (0,0.001,0.002,0.014; 0.8,0.8))
C14	((0,0,0.001,0.024; 1,1), (0,0,0,0.007; 0.8,0.8))	((0,0,0,0.027; 1,1), (0,0,0,0.01; 0.8,0.8))	((0,0,0.001,0.024; 1,1), (0,0,0,0.007; 0.8,0.8))	((0,0,0.005,0.08; 1,1), (0,0.001,0.004,0.031; 0.8,0.8))
C21	((0.001,0.011,0.031,0.124; 1,1), (0.004,0.012,0.027,0.077; 0.8,0.8))	((0,0,0,0.012; 1,1), (0,0,0,0.004; 0.8,0.8))	((0.001,0.006,0.017,0.087; 1,1), (0.002,0.007,0.015,0.047; 0.8,0.8))	((0,0,0,0.025; 1,1), (0,0,0,0.01; 0.8,0.8))
C22	((0.001,0.006,0.018,0.083; 1,1), (0.002,0.007,0.016,0.05; 0.8,0.8))	((0,0.004,0.01,0.058; 1,1), (0.001,0.004,0.009,0.031; 0.8,0.8))	((0,0,0.001,0.017; 1,1), (0,0,0,0.006; 0.8,0.8))	((0,0,0,0.005; 1,1), (0,0,0,0.001; 0.8,0.8))
C23	((0.001,0.004,0.012,0.066; 1,1), (0.002,0.004,0.011,0.037; 0.8,0.8))	((0,0,0,0.005; 1,1), (0,0,0,0.001; 0.8,0.8))	((0,0.001,0.003,0.031; 1,1), (0,0.001,0.002,0.013; 0.8,0.8))	((0.004,0.012,0.036,0.132; 1,1), (0.006,0.013,0.032,0.087; 0.8,0.8))
C24	((0,0,0,0.009; 1,1), (0,0,0,0.002; 0.8,0.8))	((0,0.002,0.005,0.061; 1,1), (0,0.002,0.005,0.026; 0.8,0.8))	((0,0,0,0.03; 1,1), (0,0,0,0.009; 0.8,0.8))	((0,0,0.001,0.023; 1,1), (0,0,0.001,0.008; 0.8,0.8))
C31	((0,0.001,0.002,0.038; 1,1), (0.0.001,0.002,0.013; 0.8,0.8))	((0,0,0,0.061; 1,1), (0,0,0,0.024; 0.8,0.8))	((0,0,0,0.009; 1,1), (0,0,0,0.01; 0.8,0.8))	((0.002,0.02,0.62,0.274; 1,1), (0,0.001,0.056,0.16; 0.8,0.8))
C32	((0,0.001,0.002,0.033; 1,1), (0,0.001,0.002,0.013; 0.8,0.8))	((0,0,0,0.011; 1,1), (0,0,0,0.003; 0.8,0.8))	((0,0,0,0.003; 1,1), (0,0,0,0.001; 0.8,0.8))	((0,0,0.005,0.049; 1,1), (0,0.002,0.004,0.022; 0.8,0.8))
C33	((0.002,0.017,0.051,0.218; 1,1), (0.005,0.019,0.046,0.129; 0.8,0.8))	((0,0,0,0.03; 1,1), (0,0,0,0.011; 0.8,0.8))	((0,0.006,0.018,0.133; 1,1), (0.001,0.007,0.016,0.068; 0.8,0.8))	((0.002,0.02,0.061,0.222; 1,1), (0.006,0.023,0.055,0.144; 0.8,0.8))
C34	((0,0,0,0.018; 1,1), (0,0,0,0.006; 0.8,0.8))	((0.001,0.011,0.038,0.182; 1,1), (0.004,0.013,0.033,0.104; 0.8,0.8))	((0,0,0,0.011; 1,1), (0,0,0,0.003; 0.8,0.8))	((0,0.005,0.015,0.111; 1,1), (0.001,0.005,0.013,0.058; 0.8,0.8))

Then, the interval type-2 fuzzy positive/negative ideal solution can be calculated via Eq. (10-12) and Eq. (10-13):

$$v_i^+ = (0.113,0.07,0.001,0.015,0.049,0.031,0.001,0.002,0.033,0.005,0.029,0.021)$$

$$v_i^- = (0.002,0.15,0.061,0.004,0.003,0.001,0.055,0.017,0.001,0.001,0.003,0.001)$$

The distances between each WPCHS alternative from the positive/negative ideal solution can be computed according to Eq. (10-14) and Eq. (10-15):

$$d_1^+ = 0.139,\ d_2^+ = 0.120,\ d_3^+ = 0.114,\ d_4^+ = 0.106;$$

$$d_1^- = 0.122,\ d_2^- = 0.094,\ d_3^- = 0.083,\ d_4^- = 0.120.$$

In the last, the closeness coefficient $C(x_j)$ of each WPCHS alternative can be determined by Eq. (10-16):

$$C(x_1)=0.468,\ C(x_2)=0.439,\ C(x_3)=0.421,\ C(x_4)=0.523.$$

So, $C(x_4) \geqslant C(x_1) \geqslant C(x_2) \geqslant C(x_3)$. It means that the alternative A4 ranks first, followed by A1. Therefore, A4 should be selected as the optimal one.

7. Discussions

The result analysis, sensitivity analysis, and comparative analysis are provided in this section.

7.1 Result analysis

In order to reflect the criteria weights more intuitively, the fuzzy weights are defuzzified based on Eq. (10-4). The results are given in Fig. 10.5. Among all the criteria, the weight of LCOE is the largest and has the greatest influence on the results of the performance evaluation. This is because the LCOE is a vital index for the international energy industry to evaluate the economic benefits of power generation projects from the perspective of life cycle. Besides this, the criterion of poverty alleviation promotion is also important. As a key link in the national economy and people's livelihood, energy industry plays a unique and important role in "precise poverty alleviation". Therefore, the development of WPCHS projects will play an important role in speeding up poverty alleviation in poor areas.

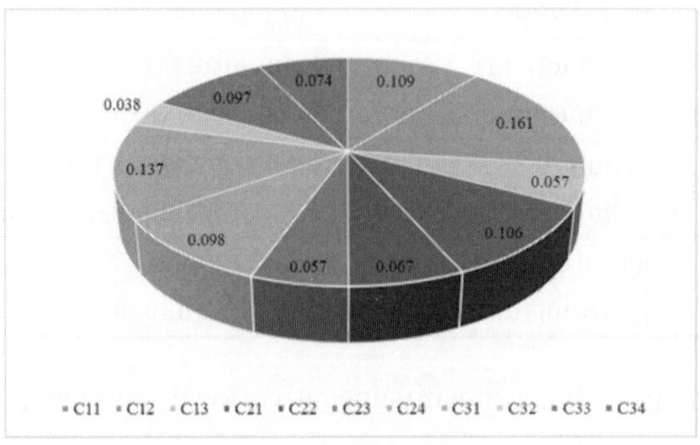

Fig. 10.5 Defuzzified weights of the criteria.

In addition, the defuzzified values of each alternative on the aspects of economy, environment, and society can be obtained, as described vividly in Fig. 10.6. As can be observed from this Figure, none of the alternatives equally well on all three aspects. The alternative A1 ranks first regarding the environmental aspect while the alternative A4 holds absolute advantage regarding the economic and social aspects. So, the performance evaluation of WPCHS projects cannot be viewed unilaterally, but need to be considered from the whole. It can be seen that the main reason why A4 ranked first is its outstanding performances on economic and social aspects. Although its environmental performance obtains the lowest values, the weights of the criteria under the environmental aspect are quite small.

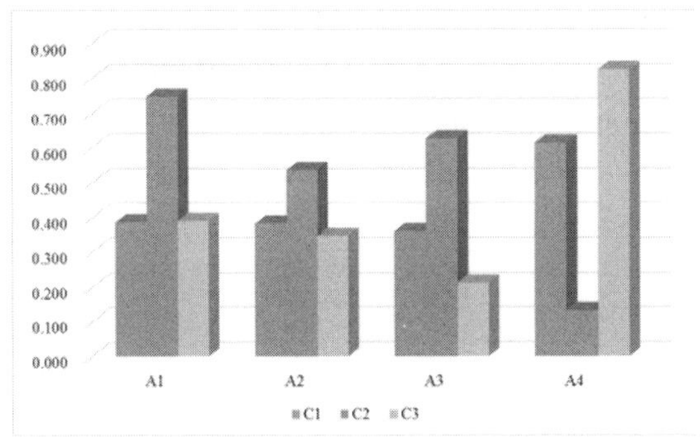

Fig. 10.6 Performance of WPCHS projects on each aspect.

7.2 Sensitivity analysis

A sensitivity analysis is carried out to examine whether the results would be different when the criteria weights change. These cases where the criteria in economic aspect have 5%, 10% and 15% lighter and 5%, 10% and 15% heavier than the base weight are shown in Fig. 10.7. It can be observed that the change trend of A4 is opposite with the other three in the case of C11 and C12 weight change. The reason for this lies that the performance of A4 on criteria C11 is far better than others. It can be also found that as the weight of criteria C11 becomes small and the weight of criteria C12 becomes big, A1 has the potential to exceed A4 and becomes the optimal one. In the case of C13 weight change, the scores of four alternatives are hardly changed.

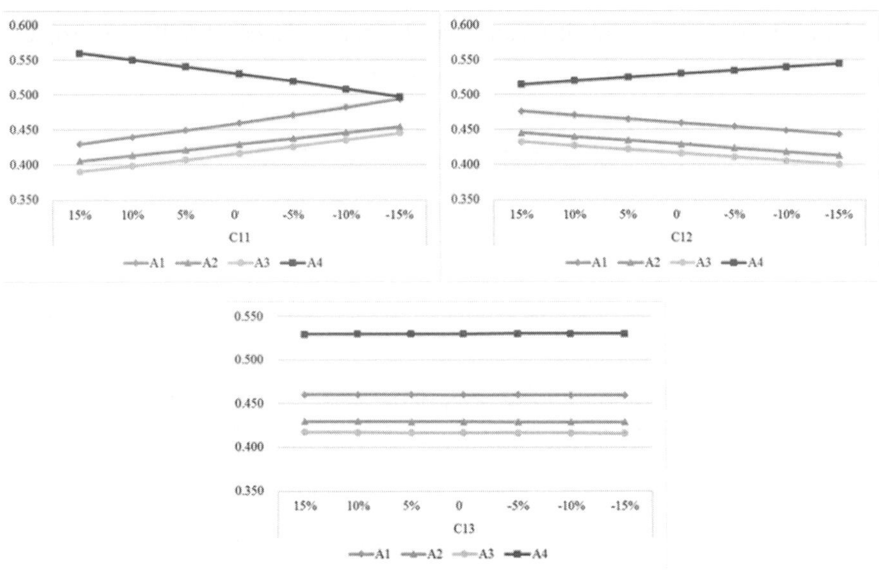

Fig. 10.7 Sensitivity analysis result of economic aspect.

Cases in which the criteria in environmental aspect have 5%, 10% and 15% less and 5%,

10% and 15% more than the base weight are shown in Fig. 10.8. It can be seen that the ranking results change from A4>A1>A2>A3 to A4>A1>A3>A2 when the weight of C12 changes more than 15%. Different from this criterion, the scores of four alternatives change little when the weights of the other three criteria fluctuate.

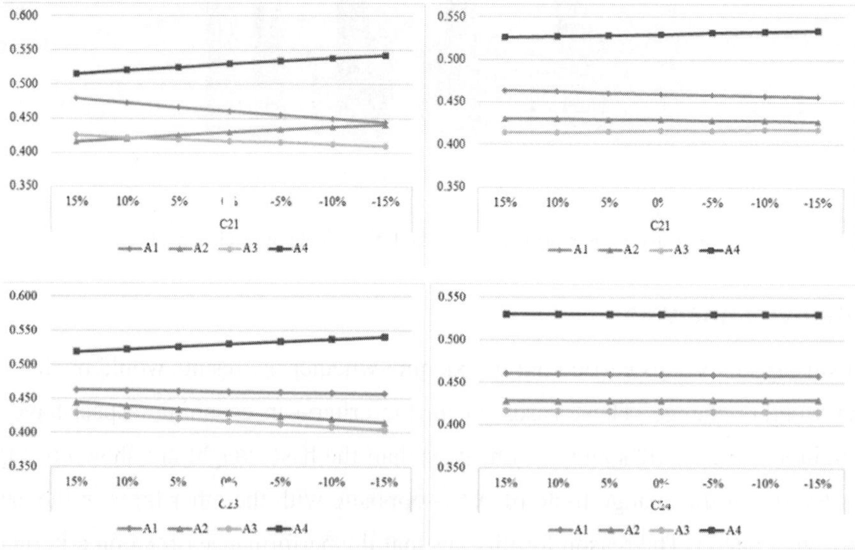

Fig. 10.8 Sensitivity analysis result of environmental aspect.

Fig. 10.9 gives those cases in which the criteria in social aspect have 5%, 10% and 15% change compared with the base weight. The scores of the WPCHS projects in these cases are nearly unchanged. In some extent, it means that the performance of WPCHS projects has less sensitive towards the changing of social criteria weight.

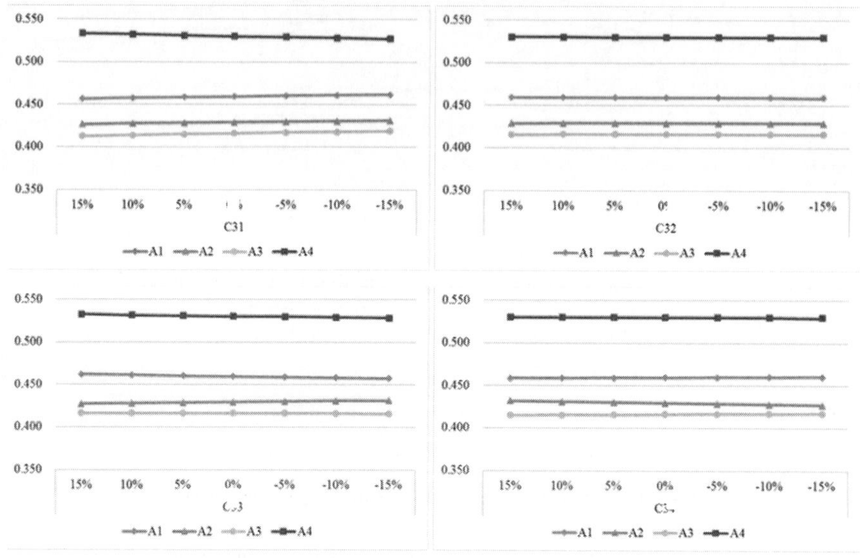

Fig. 10.9 Sensitivity analysis result of social aspect.

From the above analysis, it can be seen that the alternative A4 always secures its top ranking when its weight is floating within a certain range (−15% to 15%). It reveals that the WPCHS project performance evaluation by using the interval type-2 fuzzy AHP-TOPSIS technique is robust.

7.3 Comparative analysis

In this section, a comparative analysis with type-1 fuzzy AHP-TOPSIS is presented to validate the effectiveness of the proposed approach.

Triangular fuzzy AHP-TOPSIS has been successfully used in many studies [50]. Therefore, this approach is selected as the comparative objective to highlight the importance of high-order uncertainties. The linguistic variables for alternative performance with respect to criteria are shown in Table 10.7, and the linguistic variables for criteria weights are presented in Table 10.8.

Table 10.7 Linguistic variables for alternative performance with respect to criteria [50].

Linguistic variables	Trapezoidal fuzzy numbers (TFNs)
Very Low (VL)	(1, 1, 2)
Low (L)	(2, 3, 4)
Medium Low (ML)	(3, 4, 5)
Medium (M)	(4, 5, 6)
Medium high (MH)	(5, 6, 7)
High (H)	(6, 7, 8)
Very High (VH)	(7, 8, 9)

Table 10.8 Linguistic variables for criteria weights [50].

Linguistic variables	TFNs	Reciprocal TFNs
Absolutely Strong (AS)	(7, 9, 9)	(1/9, 1/9, 1/7)
Very Strong (VS)	(5, 7, 9)	(1/9, 1/7, 1/5)
Fairly Strong (FS)	(3, 5, 7)	(1/7, 1/5, 1/3)
Slightly Strong (SS)	(1, 3, 5)	(1/5, 1/3, 1)
Exactly Equal (E)	(1, 1, 1)	(1, 1, 1)

The positive/negative ideal solution can be calculated via Eq. (10-12) and Eq. (10-13):

$$v_i^+ = (0.104, 0.081, 0.022, 0.012, 0.005, 0.037, 0.012, 0.037, 0.003, 0.029, 0.019, 0.02)$$

$$v_i^- = (0.017, 0.004, 0.012, 0.006, 0.017, 0.013, 0.005, 0.022, 0.006, 0.018, 0.02, 0.011)$$

Then, the distances between each WPCHS alternative from the positive/negative ideal solution can be computed according to Eq. (10-14)and Eq. (10-15):

$$d_1^+ = 0.084,\ d_2^+ = 0.148,\ d_3^+ = 0.089,\ d_4^+ = 0.118;$$

$$d_1^- = 0.075,\ d_2^- = 0.124,\ d_3^- = 0.072,\ d_4^- = 0.113.$$

Finally, the closeness coefficient $C(x_j)$ of each WPCHS alternative can be determined by Eq. (10-16):

$$C(x_1) = 0.473,\ C(x_2) = 0.456,\ C(x_3) = 0.447,\ C(x_4) = 0.492.$$

Therefore, the ranking result is A4>A1>A2>A3.

It can be seen that the ranking results obtained by the type-1 triangular fuzzy AHP-TOPSIS are the same with the proposed approach. The correctness of the proposed approach can be justified. And the credibility of the results is also confirmed.

To further compare the stability of the two results, the standard deviation is introduced as follows [51, 52]:

$$s = \sqrt{(x_1 - \overline{x})^2 + (x_2 - \overline{x})^2 + \cdots + (x_n - \overline{x})^2} \tag{10-17}$$

where $\overline{x}$ is the average number.

Therefore, the standard deviation of the result obtained by type-1 triangular fuzzy AHP-TOPSIS is calculated as 0.020 while the standard deviation of the result obtained by the type-2 fuzzy AHP-TOPSIS is 0.045. It means that the proposed approach can distinguish alternative performance more clearly, which proves the effectiveness of the proposed approach.

8. Conclusions, managerial implications and future work

At present, the phenomenon of wind power curtailment is still serious in China, which affects the healthy development of wind industry. Thus, the research and development of energy storage technology attract much attention from all countries. The hydrogen storage is one of the most promising technologies since it can store energy for a long time. Under this circumstance, the construction and development of WPCHS projects is very meaningful and urgent. Performance assessment, as a key link in the early stage of the project, is essential. Therefore, this paper assesses the performance of WPCHS projects from the sustainability perspective. A comprehensive evaluation criteria system is established to decompose the sustainability perspective into eleven criteria from three dimensions of economy, environment and society. Considering the uncertainties of decision-making environment, an interval type-2 fuzzy AHP-TOPSIS technique is utilized to determine the weights of criteria and rank the alternatives, respectively. The weight results show that the economic aspect has the largest weight, as proved by many scholars. The ranking results show that the alternative A4 ranks first in all scenarios of sensitive analysis.

From the results of the WPCHS project performance assessment, some managerial implications can be carried out: ①investors should comprehensively consider the various aspects of criteria. When investors conduct in WPCHS project construction, it should not only focus on a single criterion. In order to maintain sustainable development, various kinds of criteria must be taken into account simultaneously; ②the uncertainties of criteria performance must be considered in the process of WPCHS project performance assessment due to the change of policies and technologies.

In future work, some other MCDM techniques such as VIKOR and PROMETHEE will be applied to solve the problem of WPCHS project performance assessment. In addition, considering that the risk preference will affect the decision results, integrating various kinds of investors' risk preference in the decision process is a topic worthy of further study.

Acknowledgements

Project supported by the 2017 Special Project of Cultivation and Development of Innovation Base (No. Z171100002217024), the Fundamental Research Funds for the Central Universities (No. 2017XS099) and (No. 2018ZD14) and the NCEPU "Double First-Class" Graduate Talent Cultivation Program.

References

[1] Hong H, Peng S, Zhang H, et al. Performance assessment of hybrid solar energy and coal-fired power plant based on feed-water preheating[J]. Energy, 2017, 128:830-838.

[2] Zhang X, Winchester N, Zhang X. The future of coal in China[J]. Energy Policy, 2017, 110:644-652.

[3] Da Z, Zhang X, He J, et al. Offshore wind energy development in China: Current status and future perspective[J]. Renewable & Sustainable Energy Reviews, 2011, 15(9):4673-4684.

[4] Hayashi D, Huenteler J, Lewis J I. Gone with the wind: A learning curve analysis of China's wind power industry[J]. Energy Policy, 2018, 120:38-51.

[5] NEA. China Renewable Energy Development Report 2017. http://www.nea.gov.cn/2018-05/24/c_137202940.htm. 2017.

[6] Yang Z, Noori M, Tatari O. Boosting the adoption and the reliability of renewable energy sources: Mitigating the large-scale wind power intermittency through vehicle to grid technology[J]. Energy, 2017, 120:608-618.

[7] NEA. Wind power grid-connected operation in 2016. http://www.nea.gov.cn/2017-01/26/c_136014615htm.2017.

[8] Sahu B K. Wind energy developments and policies in China: A short review[J]. Renewable & Sustainable Energy Reviews, 2018, 81:1393-1405.

[9] Zhao H, Guo S, Zhao H. Comprehensive assessment for battery energy storage systems based on fuzzy-MCDM considering risk preferences[J].Energy, 2019, 168:450-461.

[10] Chung Y, Hong S, Kim J. Which of the technologies for producing hydrogen is the most prospective in Korea? Evaluating the competitive priority of those in near-, mid-, and long-term[J]. Energy Policy, 2014, 65(4):115-125.

[11] Dombi M, Kuti I, Balogh P. Sustainability assessment of renewable power and heat generation technologies[J]. Energy Policy, 2014, 67(1):264-271.

[12] Schuster M, Walther T. Valuation of combined wind power plant and hydrogen storage: A decision tree approach[R]. 2017 14th International Conference on the European Energy Market: IEEE, 2017, 1-6.

[13] Loisel R, Baranger L, Chemouri N, et al. Economic evaluation of hybrid off-shore wind power and hydrogen storage system[J]. International Journal of Hydrogen Energy, 2015, 40(21):6727-6739.

[14] Siyal S H, Mentis D, Howells M. Economic analysis of standalone wind-powered hydrogen refueling stations for road transport atselected sites in Sweden[J]. International Journal of Hydrogen Energy, 2015, 40(32):9855-9865.

[15] Ghandehariun S, Kumar A. Life cycle assessment of wind-based hydrogen production in Western Canada[J]. International Journal of Hydrogen Energy, 2016, 41(22):9696-9704.

[16] Ji-Yong L, Sanghyuk A, Kyounghoon C, et al. Life cycle environmental and economic analyses of a hydrogen station with wind energy[J]. International Journal of Hydrogen Energy, 2010, 35:2213-2225.

[17] Gökçek M, Kale C. Techno-economical evaluation of a hydrogen refuelling station powered by Wind-PV hybrid power system: A case study for İzmir-Çeşme[J]. International Journal of Hydrogen Energy, 2018, 43(23):10615-10625.

[18] Qolipour M, Mostafaeipour A, Tousi O M. Techno-economic feasibility of a photovoltaic-wind power plant construction for electric and hydrogen production: A case study[J]. Renewable & Sustainable Energy Reviews, 2017, 78:113-123.

[19] Al-Sharafi A, Sahin A Z, Ayar T, et al. Techno-economic analysis and optimization of solar and wind energy systems for power generation and hydrogen production in Saudi Arabia[J]. Renewable & Sustainable Energy Reviews, 2017, 69:33-49.

[20] Hacatoglu K, Dincer I, Rosen M A. Sustainability assessment of a hybrid energy system with hydrogen-based storage[J]. International Journal of Hydrogen Energy, 2015, 40(3):1559-1568.

[21] Hacatoglu K, Dincer I, Rosen M A. Sustainability of a wind-hydrogen energy system: Assessment using a novel index and comparison to a conventional gas-fired system[J]. International Journal of Hydrogen Energy, 2016, 41(19):8376-8385.

[22] Wu Y, Xu C, Ke Y, et al. Portfolio selection of distributed energy generation projects considering uncertainty and project interaction under different enterprise strategic scenarios[J]. Applied Energy, 2019, 236:444-464.

[23] Geng S, Yin Y, Lin L, et al. Social capital selection framework of public-private partnership project of electrochemical storage power station under linguistic environment[J]. Journal of cleaner production, 2018, 199: 751-762.

[24] Azimifard A, Moosavirad S H, Ariafar S. Selecting sustainable supplier countries for Iran's steel industry at three levels by using AHP and TOPSIS methods[J]. Resources Policy, 2018, 57:30-44.

[25] Sindhu S, Nehra V, Luthra S. Investigation of feasibility study of solar farms deployment using hybrid AHP-TOPSIS analysis: Case study of India[J]. Renewable & Sustainable Energy Reviews, 2017, 73:496-511.

[26] Goh H H, Kok B C, Yeo H T, et al. Combination of TOPSIS and AHP in load shedding scheme for large pulp; mill electrical system[J]. International Journal of Electrical Power & Energy Systems,

2013, 47(6):198-204.

[27] Wu Y, Xu C, Ke Y, et al. An intuitionistic fuzzy multi-criteria framework for large-scale rooftop PV project portfolio selection: Case study in Zhejiang, China[J]. Energy, 2018, 143:295-309.

[28] Zadeh L A. Fuzzy sets[J]. Information & Control, 1965, 8(3):338-353.

[29] Taylan O, Bafail A O, Abdulaal R M S, et al. Construction projects selection and risk assessment by fuzzy AHP and fuzzy TOPSIS methodologies[J]. Applied Soft Computing Journal, 2014, 17(4): 105-116.

[30] Amiri M, Zandieh M, Soltani R, et al. A hybrid multi-criteria decision-making model for firms competence evaluation[J]. Expert Systems with Applications, 2009, 36(10):12314-12322.

[31] Celik E, Akyuz E. An interval type-2 fuzzy AHP and TOPSIS methods for decision-making problems in maritime transportation engineering: The case of ship loader[J]. Ocean Engineering, 2018, 155:371-381.

[32] Jin L, Huang G H, Cong D, et al. A Robust Inexact Joint-optimal α cut Interval Type-2 Fuzzy Boundary Linear Programming (RIJ-IT2FBLP) for energy systems planning under uncertainty[J]. International Journal of Electrical Power & Energy Systems, 2014, 56:19-32.

[33] Fan X C, Wang W Q, Shi R J, et al. Hybrid pluripotent coupling system with wind and photovoltaic-hydrogen energy storage and the coal chemical industry in Hami, Xinjiang[J]. Renewable & Sustainable Energy Reviews, 2017, 72:950-960.

[34] Aiche-Hamane L, Belhamel M, Benyoucef B, et al. Feasibility study of hydrogen production from wind power in the region of Ghardaia[J]. International Journal of Hydrogen Energy, 2009, 34(11):4947-4952.

[35] Shao Z, Wu J, Zhao Q. Evaluation and Simulation of Energy Interconnection[M]. Beijing: Science Press (in Chinese), 2018.

[36] Çolak M, Kaya İ. Prioritization of renewable energy alternatives by using an integrated fuzzy MCDM model: A real case application for Turkey[J]. Renewable & Sustainable Energy Reviews, 2017, 80:840-853.

[37] Wu Y, Xu C, Zhang T. Evaluation of renewable power sources using a fuzzy MCDM based on cumulative prospect theory: A case in China[J]. Energy, 2018, 147:1227-1239.

[38] Zadeh L A. The concept of a linguistic variable and its application to approximate reasoning-III[J]. Information Sciences, 1975, 9(1):43-80.

[39] Debnath J, Majumder D, Biswas A. Air quality assessment using weighted interval type-2 fuzzy inference system[J]. Ecological Informatics, 2018, 46:133-146.

[40] Mohagheghi V, Mousavi S M, Vahdani B, et al. R&D project evaluation and project portfolio selection by a new interval type-2 fuzzy optimization approach[J]. Neural Computing & Applications, 2017, 28(12):3869-3888.

[41] Ghorabaee M K, Amiri M, Zavadskas E K, et al, Antucheviciene J. A new multi-criteria model based on interval type-2 fuzzy sets and EDAS method for supplier evaluation and order allocation with environmental considerations[J]. Computers & Industrial Engineering, 2017, 112:156-174.

[42] Chen T Y. A linear assignment method for multiple-criteria decision analysis with interval type-2 fuzzy sets[J]. Applied Soft Computing Journal, 2013, 13(5):2735-2748.

[43] Lee L W, Chen S M. Fuzzy multiple attributes group decision-making based on the extension of TOPSIS method and interval type-2 fuzzy sets[J]. International Conference on Machine Learning and

Cybernetics, 2008, 6(12):3260-3265.

[44] Saaty T L. The analytic hierarchy process: Planning, priority setting, resource Allocation[M]. New York: McGraw-Hill, 1980.

[45] Buckley J J, Uppuluri V R R. Fuzzy Hierarchical Analysis[M]. Berlin:Springer, 1987.

[46] Kahraman C. Fuzzy analytic hierarchy process with interval type-2 fuzzy sets[J]. Knowledge-Based Systems, 2014, 59(2):48-57.

[47] Tzeng G H, Huang J J. Multiple attribute decision making: methods and appliations[J]. European Journal of Operational Research, 1995, 4(4):287-288.

[48] Celik E, Erdogan M, Gumus A T. An extended fuzzy TOPSIS–GRA method based on different separation measures for green logistics service provider selection[J]. International Journal of Environmental Science & Technology, 2016, 13(5):1377-1392.

[49] Qin J, Liu X, Pedrycz W. An extended TODIM multi-criteria group decision making method for green supplier selection in interval type-2 fuzzy environment[J]. European Journal of Operational Research, 2017, 258(2):626-638.

[50] Zyoud S H, Kaufmann L G, Shaheen H, et al. A framework for water loss management in developing countries under fuzzy environment: Integration of Fuzzy AHP with Fuzzy TOPSIS[J]. Expert Systems with Applications, 2016, 61(C):86-105.

[51] Guo S, Zhao H. Fuzzy best-worst multi-criteria decision-making method and its applications[J]. Knowledge-Based Systems, 2017, 121: 23-31.

[52] Geng S, Lin L. The extensible evaluation framework of urban green house gas emission reduction responsibility: A case of Shandong province in China[J]. Energy, 2018, 162: 171-184.

Chapter 11

A fuzzy analysis framework for waste incineration power plant comprehensive benefit evaluation from refuse classification perspective

Yunna Wu [a, b], Yao Tao [a, b*], Zhongqing Deng [a, b], Jianli Zhou [a, b], Chuanbo Xu [a, b], Buyuan Zhang [a, b]

a. School of Economics and Management, North China Electric Power University, Beijing, China

b. Beijing Key Laboratory of New Energy and Low-Carbon Development (North China Electric Power University), Changping, Beijing, 102206, China

Abstract: The waste-to-energy project has been concerned a lot due to its environmental friendliness. With the implementation of refuse classification, the utilization rate of resources has been improved and the comprehensive benefit of incineration power plant has been impacted as well. Thus, to assess the incineration power plant performance from refuse classification perspective, the article constructs a complete decision framework. Firstly, 13 sub-criteria are identified into 3 categories and the hesitant fuzzy linguistic term sets (HFLTS) is employed to ensure the completeness of evaluation information. Secondly, the analytic hierarchy process (AHP) method and entropy method are combined to obtain the indexes weights, avoiding the subjectivity in weight judgment. Thirdly, based on principle of fuzzy relation synthesis, fuzzy synthetic evaluation (FSE) method is used to calculate the final result. A case study is carried out to validate the applicability of the proposed framework. In addition, the article puts forward suggestions in economics, environment and society to improve the overall benefit of incineration power plant. From a new perspective, this paper provides a theoretical reference for the future development of incineration power plants and expands literature in benefit evaluation.

Keywords: Refuse classification; Incineration power plant; Comprehensive benefit evaluation; HFLTS; Combined weight; FSE method

1. Introduction

With the rapid development of population, urbanization and consumption, the increasing quantity of municipal solid waste (MSW) is deemed as an important issue that had a large negative impact on life quality. Generally speaking, the treatments to waste mainly include landfill, compost and incineration. Requiring resource-saving and environment-friendly, the incineration performs best compared with other treatments (Dong et al., 2014). At the same time, in view of the shortage of energy sources, waste to energy provides an approach to address the energy demand and obtains a great attention for its higher energy recovery rate and less land occupation (He and Lin, 2019) (Assamoi and Lawryshyn, 2012). Incineration power plant which uses incineration to convert MSW to electricity, meeting the requirement of waste reduction, recycling and harmlessness, has a great potential. It can be seen that the incineration power plant not only plays a role in solving the problem of MSW disposal but also generates energy from waste material (Cheng and Hu, 2010).

The initial MSW management was born after the industrial revolution (Perry, 1992). During the last quarter of the 19th century, human found that incinerating and recovering can handle the increasing waste volumes, then the first batch of incineration plants appeared in US and Europe (Makarichi, 2018). After decades of advancement, the technologies of incineration have developed from simple open pit burning to highly efficient incineration power plant (Wang, Y. et al., 2016). In China, the incineration technology was first introduced at end of 1980s and the first modernized incineration plant was built in Guangdong province in 1988 (Liu et al., 2006). In order to utilize the resource in waste fully, Chinese government promotes construction of waste classification system. Generally, the garbage can be divided into four categories, recyclables, kitchen waste, harmful waste and other wastes. The recyclables mainly include waste paper, plastic, glass, metal and cloth, which can be reused after recycling and processing. For the kitchen waste, it also named wet waste due to the high moisture content, has a negative impact on calorific value of fuel. Harmful waste contains heavy metals, toxic substances and waste do harm to human health or the environment. Except these three categories, the other wastes mainly refers to bricks, ceramics, paper towels and others that hard to recycle. Unclassified waste holds inhomogeneous mixtures and would produce large amount of aromatic hydrocarbons after combustion, however, the classification could make waste more homogeneous and stable which improves the calorific value of material and reduces the emission of pollutants (Li et al., 2019).

Totally, the main goal of waste classification is to classify the waste as available resource, and the more detailed classification of waste is beneficial to the utilization of back-end resources (Nie et al., 2018). Under the classification of waste management, the waste incineration industry gains huge business opportunities but also faces several challenges. For example, waste classification brings a high calories value but fewer number of combustion materials, so that whether the calorific value hedging would reduce the generation benefits or not. Besides, the problems such as how to balance the relationship among the business related to the incineration industry, how to guide the residents participate in waste classification automatically (Meng et al., 2018) and how to determine the contribution of incineration power plant after waste classification are also noteworthy. However, the former researches on incineration power plant focused on technologies a lot but the overall benefit of power plant a few (Hui et al., 2012) (Feng et al., 2018) (Khalil et al., 2019) (Caneghem et al., 2012). Distinguish from the single evaluation on ecology or biology, the comprehensive benefit evaluation is more macroscopic and defined as the sum of identifiable and quantifiable total benefits. That is to say, the comprehensive benefits indicate the integrated representation of performance in all aspects. Thus, doing a comprehensive benefit evaluation of incineration power plant is conductive to realize the status of plant and meaningful to the further development.

Comprehensive benefit evaluation is a multi-criteria decision making (MCDM) problem. Suffering from the complex evaluation factors, especially under the refuse classification, the assessment of incineration power plant comprehensive benefit has much to optimize. Several shortcomings and inadequacies still exist in performance decision process. On the one hand, comprehensive benefit includes many factors such as market benefit, safety benefit or economic benefit, the traditional evaluation index system is no longer adapted to current standard in sustainable development. Meanwhile, considering the garbage classification, some fresh criteria need to be added in the evaluation system. On the other hand, uncertainty and fuzziness are inevitable problems in decision making. Description of decision information is often incomplete and the experts' views could not have a good expression. Furthermore, the calculation methods to criteria weights and alternative ratings are so various that the employee of decision methods depends on the specific circumstances.

Up to now, there are so many researches about MCDM. In the aspect of information description, fuzzy set theory is studied by scholars. Proposed by Zadeh (1965), the fuzzy set has an advantage in disposing of uncertain, incomplete and ambiguous information than traditional crisp number (Wu et al., 2018a). It improved the information adequacy and rich the expression. Nevertheless, when there are several sources of vagueness appeared simultaneously, original fuzzy set could not handle these information well (Wu et al., 2019b). For this reason, the fuzzy sets are expanded into type-2 fuzzy set (Zadeh, 1974) (Wu et al., 2019d) and interval fuzzy set (Zeng and Zhao, 2006), which could process high-order uncertainty but difficult to calculate.Moreover, facing the situation that the experts are restricted in knowledge area or thinking model, it is difficult to use only one linguistic set to express their information clearly. Thus, to manage the situation that expert hovers between the several values to assess an attribute, hesitant fuzzy sets was put forward (Torra, 2010). And considering the completeness that expression with several values is richer than a single term, hesitant fuzzy linguistic term sets (HFLTS) is proposed by Rodríguez et al. (2012). For the purpose of calculating easily, quantify the linguistic language is a necessary step. Fuzzy number, transforming the language into a connected set of possible values with a weight between 0 and 1, was developed by scholars (Dubois and Prade, 1978). Based on this, Zadeh et al. (1996) promoted it to triangular fuzzy number (TFN) which including lower bound, upper bound and most possible value. Because of the good ability to ensure integrality of decision information and availability of data, TFN is applied to modeling fuzzy data widely (Wu et al., 2018c). Sánchez-Lozano et al. (2016) transformed criteria into a fuzzy decision matrix through triangular fuzzy number in a site selection of wind farm and pointed out that the criteria in decision-making not only include the crisp numbers but also the qualitative values which could be showed by fuzzy membership. Sheen (2005) emphasized that the TFN represented a rational basis to quantify the vagueness in decision-making problems and did a financial evaluation with a fuzzy profitability model. Gan et al. (2017) proposed a model with TFN to study the economic feasibility analysis of renewable energy projects in the whole life. Zhao et al. (2014) deepened the application of TFN into hesitant triangular fuzzy information aggregation in MCDM problems. Wu et al. (2019b) introduced TFN to risk assessment on offshore PV power generation projects, the result showed that TFN could handle vague information well in MCDM problems. It can be seen that TFN could protect the integrity of information, therefore, utilizing the TFN in the comprehensive benefit evaluation of incineration power plant has theoretical reliability and practical significance.

At the same time, the ranking method is also a very significant step in MCDM. In view of the difference between alternatives, the ranking method is mainly used to quantify this distance and compare their size. Some methods like Technique for Order Preference by Similarity to Ideal Solution (TOPSIS), Analytic Hierarchy Process (AHP), Vlsekriterijumska Optimizacija IKompromisno Resenje (VIKOR) are commonly used in alternative ranking (Kumar et al., 2017). Vavrek and Chovancová (2019) proposed the CV-TOPSIS technique to assess the energy sustainability development in EU and quantified the performance of economy and environment. Long and Geng (2015) utilized the Entropy method to ensure the objectivity of criteria weight and proposed a decision framework with TOPSIS of photovoltaic module selection under fuzzy environment. Nixon et al. (2013) expanded the application of AHP and provided a framework for selection of waste management in India. Khoshand et al. (2018) built a model with AHP to assess comprehensive benefits of different cases for energy recovery from waste according to the criteria including technical feasibility, economic issues and so on. Liu et al. (2014) put forward a framework with interval 2-tuple linguistic VIKOR to select the disposal site for MSW. Büyüközkan and Karabulut (2017) constructed a model with AHP and VIKOR methods to evaluate the property of renewable energy projects, and pointed out that the evaluation was deemed as not only an economic problem but also an environment and social one.

However, the above methods largely focus on difference between reality and optimum but can not assess the performance degree well. Only the membership of each degree can be determined, the decision-makers (DMs) can understand the project situation more intuitively. Thus, considering the process of decision making always exists an interaction among indexes and the complexity of decision system, employing fuzzy synthetic evaluation (FSE) based on the fuzzy relation principle could handle these problems well (Shidpour et al., 2016). Evaluating membership grade of a project from multiple attributes through the principle of fuzzy relation synthesis, FSE method gains a wide concentration on MCDM field (Mu et al., 2014). Wang et al. (2018) transformed a multi-dimensional index system into one-dimensional and assessed the energy-saving technologies with AHP-FSE method, the result shows more credible after qualitative analysis and quantitative calculation. Li et al. (2018) introduced Entropy method into FSE, improving the utilization of objective data during the decision making. Li and Yu (2017) combined Entropy and FSE to evaluate the air pollution, the result shows that Entropy method leads a more objective consequence. Wu et al. (2017a) utilized a multi-criteria fuzzy comprehensive evaluation framework to assess the risk of straw power generation project under PPP mode and identify the key risk factors. Wu and Zhou (2019) applied FSE to do a risk assessment of rooftop distributed PV under EPC mode. Wang, J. et al. (2016) utilized triangular fuzzy number to represent decision information and FSE to determine the knowledge management performance, and the group support system was introduced to improve the efficiency of evaluation. Tseng et al. (2017) employed FSE to do a benefit evaluation of industry from economic, environmental aspects. Obviously, FSE has strong practicability and operability in the problems of multi-criteria and multi-objective. Considering that the comprehensive benefit evaluation of incineration power plant related with uncertain and fuzzy factors from many aspects, thus, employ a model with FSE to do a comprehensive benefit evaluation is feasible.

Based on the description above, this paper aims to: ①determine the factors which have an influence on incineration power plant comprehensive benefit; ②propose a novel decision framework to evaluate incineration power plant performance. Taking a refuse classification perspective, the originality of paper includes the following aspects: ①build a three-dimensional evaluation index system including economic benefit, environmental benefit and social benefit; ②a performance evaluation model is built based on combined weight method and fuzzy comprehensive evaluation method. Meanwhile, with the help of HFLTS and TFN, the fuzziness of decision has been handled well and the reliability of decision information has been enhanced greatly; ③for the purpose of improving the overall performance, the measurements to improve efficiency are put forward in economy, environment and society. The contribution of current study are multifaceted: ①this paper can contribute to the theory about waste-to-energy performance from a new visual angle and expand the knowledge of benefit management; ②an evaluation index system for incineration power plant comprehensive benefit can assist managers in realizing and analyzing performance factors better; ③with awareness of final comprehensive benefit, the project manager could do a better choice whether the operation of plant is shut off or maintained or improved; ④the suggestions to improve the benefit in economy, environment and society can provide a reference for project leaders and policy makers.

The rest of article is structured as follows. Section 2 builds a novel performance evaluation index system based on the existed study. Section 3 explains the principle of decision-making methods and presents a complete decision framework. Section 4 applies the model in a case study. Section 5 gives suggestions to optimize the comprehensive benefits of incineration power plant. Section 6 concludes this study and points out its limitations.

2. Index system for incineration power plant comprehensive benefit

Evaluation index system describes the project from several aspects, playing a significant role in decision making. For the renewable energy project performance evaluation, Zhang et al. (2019) constructed a criteria system included economic, environmental, social and technical for dimensions. It is note that the emission reduction, land requirement, investment cost and job creation were employed as sub-criteria in the index system. Nie et al. (2018) suggested the economic factor should be given priority in analysis of MSW problems, and the classification of MSW depended on classification and environmental consciousness of residents heavily. Meanwhile, some sub-criteria like operating cost, recycling profits, leachate, management system were mentioned in the text. Ezeah and Roberts (2012) considered population quality, education levels, living habits and other factors were essential in the classification of MSW. Labuschagne et al. (2005) entailed social equity, economic efficiency and environmental performance into the performance evaluation of business sustainability. Wu et al. (2018a) put forward an evaluation index system for waste-to-energy plant site including impacts on air, waste discharge, public acceptability, local economy development, improvement of living standards and so on. Wu et al. (2016) established a criteria system for a refuse power plant investment decision, depending on production, environment, land, policy and others. According to referring the relative literatures and realizing the influence of refuse classification, we establish an index system for comprehensive benefit evaluation of incineration power plant including economic factors, environmental factors and social factors. The details are shown as follows:

2.1 Economic benefit (C1)

- Waste disposal fees (C11) (Mak et al., 2019) (Chu et al., 2019): Waste disposal fees mainly refer to the fees that residents should pay for domestic waste disposal services. Because of the large amount of garbage, the difficulty of measurement and the high cost of collection, the current way of garbage disposal fees is mainly to levy garbage treatment fees on public utilities such as water and electricity, and to collect garbage fees directly through property agencies. With the development of refuse classification, establishing a proper waste treatment charging system can promote the construction of an incentive and restraint mechanism in waste reduction, resource-based and harmless treatment.
- Investment cost (C12) (Badgett et al., 2019): The investment of incineration power plant is generally high, mainly containing construction cost and operation cost. The former is closely related to incineration equipment and technology, with a cost of about 300-500 thousand yuan per ton. And the latter mainly includes maintenance, depreciation and management fees, nearly costs 80-100 yuan per ton.
- Profit (C13) (Eboh et al., 2019): The profits of garbage power plants mainly come from electricity sales, government subsidies, heating and slag sales. Generally speaking, electricity sales account for about 70% of revenue. Government subsidy is mainly to encourage and support the development of the industry. Heating and slag selling are to improve the comprehensive economic value of power plants. Furthermore, the high calories of waste through refuse classification could provide a steady generation in incineration, which means the benefit in electricity sales could be improved.
- Power generation per ton garbage (C14) (Ibikunle et al., 2019): As an economic and technical index, it mainly refers to electricity generation of each ton of waste incineration. On the one hand, this criterion indicates the technological advance. On the other hand, with the refuse classification, the calories of waste is higher than before which could improve the power generation of per ton of garbage leading a better economic performance.
- Payback period (C15) (Wu et al., 2019c): The time it takes for the total income of the project to reach the total investment of the project after putting into operation. Generally, the payback period of incineration power plants is 8-12 years.

2.2 Environmental benefit (C2)

- Leachate (C21) (Moody and Townsend, 2017): The component of the landfill leachate contains heavy metals and many dissolved organic matters. Be derived from refuse burning, the leachate has a harm to land and air without a proper dealing. A garbage classification is conducive to improve the dry wet separation and reduce the moisture of waste.

- Land savings (C22) (Cheng et al., 2007): Compared with composting and landfill plant, incineration power plant has less impact on land pollution. Therefore, due to the scarcity of land, introducing land savings in environmental benefit would conduce to indicate the protection and utilization of land.
- Air pollution (C23) (Tabata, 2013) (Lim et al., 2014): Dioxins, acid gases, heavy metals and other pollutants produced by incineration power plant have a negative impact on air quality. Classifying rubbish could remove the polluted substances and reduce the production of harmful gases.
- Waste recycle (C24) (Meng et al., 2019): Municipal garbage is a resource that in a mistaken time and mistaken place. Recycling the garbage not only avoids resource waste but also improves the utilization of materials. According to the refuse classification, the valuable is identified before incineration and the residue is processed to produce cement additives, brick or paving based materials in high quality. Thus, the index is significant to the macro environment benefit.

2.3 Social benefit (C3)

- Disposal quantity of waste (C31) (Nagpure, 2019): The increasing number of garbage causes the Garbage Siege phenomenon, which has a negative influence on human activities. Considering that the one of the key roles of incineration power plant is taking care of garbage, thus introducing this criterion could reflect the impact of incineration plant on society.
- Promotion of local development (C32) (Savva et al., 2013): The operation of incineration power plant would promote development of related industries which include plastic, kitchen and other industries. Meanwhile, the incineration power generation has less pollution and improves regional environmental quality greatly which could attract foreign investment and is conductive to other tertiary industries, so as to have a contribution to local development.
- Public acceptability (C33) (Liu et al., 2019): For a long time, NIMBY (not in my back yard) is a thorny problem in waste incineration industry, impeding its development. Negative public acceptability always brings a hinder at the beginning of the project, publicizing emission targets in time and accepting public supervision are important ways to solve this problem. Thus, building a harmonious factory-citizen relationship will provide tremendous impetus for the development and survival of power plants.

- Job creation (C34) (Lim et al., 2014) The incineration power generation project has a characteristic in long time and wide range, referring project planning, mechanical equipment placement, equipment maintenance, and various fields in the operation process. These activities which all have a large demand of labors produce good social benefits in job creation.

From above, we can gain an index system which is classified into three categories and 13 sub-criteria, as shown in Fig. 11.1.

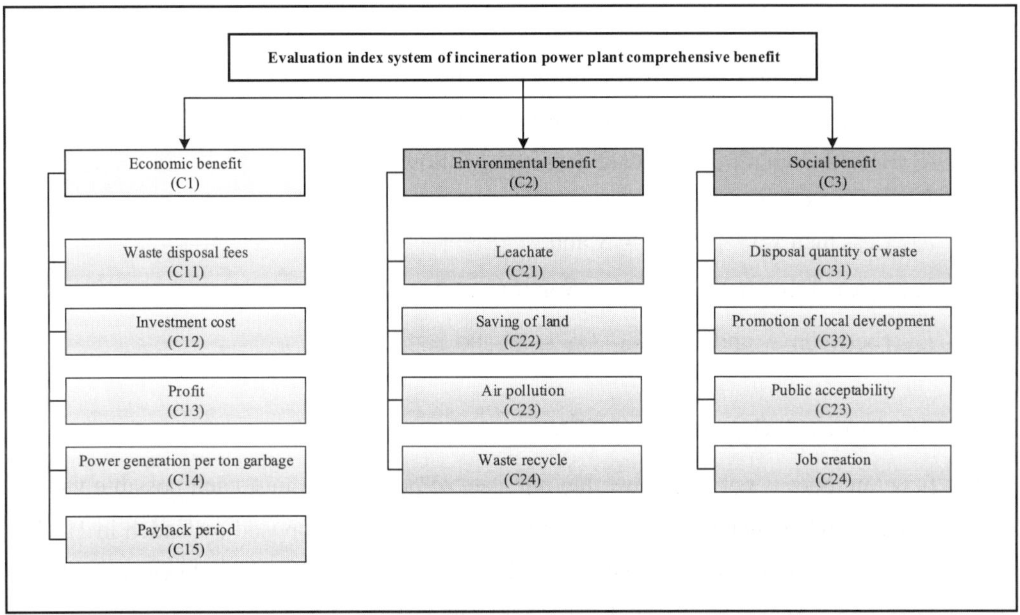

Fig. 11.1 Criteria system of comprehensive benefit on incineration power plant.

3. Materials and methods

3.1 Definitions and operations of HFLTS

The HFLTS is an expanded hesitant fuzzy sets. By means of multiple language terms, HFLTS performances well in retaining evaluation information given by DMs. As an extension, HFLTS not only reflects the evaluation value when DMs make a decision, but also takes the situation that DMs hesitate in the evaluation of program into consideration. Unlike the traditional single linguistic term, HFLTS contains multiple linguistic terminology which describe the criteria more comprehensive, reduced the loss of information and became more applicable. The basic definitions of HFTLS are shown as follows (Rodríguez et al., 2012).

Let $S=\{s_0,s_1,s_2,\ldots,s_n\}$ be a set of linguistic terms. A HFLTS, H_S is a continuous linguistic term ordered in S. Let G_H be a generation represented by HFTLS, the elements of

$G_H=(V_N,V_T,I,P)$ are defined as follows:

(1) $V_N=\begin{Bmatrix}\text{(primary term), (composite term),}\\ \text{(unary relation), (binary relation), (conjunction)}\end{Bmatrix}$;

(2) $V_T=\{\text{lower than, greater than, between, and, } s_0,\ldots,s_n\}$;

(3) $I\in V_N$.

Next, transforming the expression l produced by G_H into HFLTS through the function E_{G_H}. The function E_{G_H} is defined as follows:

$$E_{G_H}:l\rightarrow H_S \tag{11-1}$$

According to the DMs' knowledge and experience to the project, the linguistic expression about evaluation criteria would be given. Furthermore, transforming these initial language value into HFLTS form, the operation rules are defined as follows:

(1) $E_{G_H}(s_i)=\{s_i\ /\ s_i\in S\}$;

(2) $E_{G_H}(\text{less than } s_i)=\{s_j\ /\ s_j\in S \text{ and } s_j\leqslant s_i\}$;

(3) $E_{G_H}(\text{greater than } s_i)=\{s_j\ /\ s_j\in S \text{ and } s_j\geqslant s_i\}$;

(4) $E_{G_H}(\text{between } s_i \text{ and } s_j)=\{s_k\ /\ s_k\in\ S \text{ and } s_i\leqslant s_k\leqslant s_j\}$.

3.2 Definition and algorithm of TFN

The fuzzy number is not a single value but a set of possible values, each possible value has its own membership between 0 and 1. Triangular fuzzy number, proposed by Zadeh in 1965, has an advantage in description of information for the reason that it consists of lower bound, upper bound and most possible value (Jie et al., 2017), shown in Fig. 11.2.

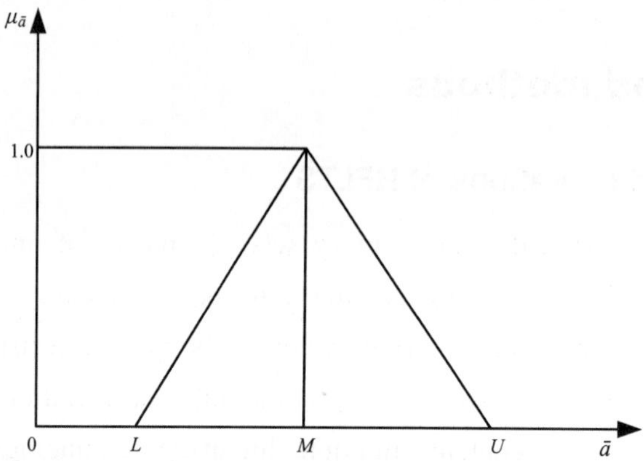

Fig. 11.2 Triangular fuzzy number.

$\bar{a}=(a^L,a^M,a^U)$ represents a triangular fuzzy number, the membership degree is expressed as follows:

$$\mu_{\bar{a}}(x)=\begin{cases}0 & x<a^L\\ (x-a^L)/(a^M-a^L) & a^L\leqslant x\leqslant a^M\\ (a^U-x)/(a^U-a^M) & a^M\leqslant x\leqslant a^U\\ 0 & x>a^U\end{cases} \tag{11-2}$$

where a^L, a^U and a^M are the lower bound, upper bound and most possible value.

If there are m triangular fuzzy numbers, the aggregated value can be gained through the follow formula:

$$h=(\tfrac{1}{m}\sum\bar{a}_i)=(\tfrac{1}{m}\sum a_i^L,\tfrac{1}{m}\sum a_i^M,\tfrac{1}{m}\sum a_i^U) \tag{11-3}$$

Fuzzy number describes evaluation information well in decision-making progress but the calculation methodology is difficult, thus de-fuzzing the fuzzy values into best non-fuzzy performance (BNP) can solve this problem. Generally speaking, the center of area (COA) method is simple and practical and do not need to consider DMs' preferences, the formula is defined as follows (Rostamzadeh et al., 2015):

$$\text{BNP: } D_{\bar{a}}=a^L+\frac{(a^U-a^L)+(a^M-a^L)}{3} \tag{11-4}$$

Moreover, determining the similarity degree between two TFNs is a meaningful step which could gain an intuitive and visual result. To sure the distance between TFNs, the formula can be defined as follows (Wu et al., 2017b):

$$Sd(\alpha,\beta)=1-\frac{\left|\alpha^L-\beta^L\right|+\left|\alpha^M-\beta^M\right|+\left|\alpha^U-\beta^U\right|}{3} \tag{11-5}$$

where $\alpha=(\alpha^L,\alpha^M,\alpha^U)$ and $\beta=(\beta^L,\beta^M,\beta^U)$ are two triangular fuzzy numbers, $Sd(\alpha,\beta)$ is a similarity degree between α and β. So, it can be seen that the value of similarity degree higher the two TFNs closer.

3.3 Entropy

Entropy method is an objective weighting method, which only depends on the data itself. Based on the entropy value of decision information, the subjectivity of expert weight method could be avoided effectively. The detail steps of calculation are defined as follows (Yuan et al., 2019):

Suppose a decision matrix $D=\begin{bmatrix}x_{11} & x_{12} & \cdots & x_{1m}\\ x_{21} & x_{22} & \cdots & x_{2m}\\ \vdots & \vdots & \ddots & \vdots\\ x_{n1} & x_{n2} & \cdots & x_{nm}\end{bmatrix}$, where x_{ij} means the value of alternative i on criterion j.

Step 1. Calculate the contribution degree p_{ij}.

$$p_{ij} = x_{ij} / \sum_{i=1}^{n} x_{ij} \tag{11-6}$$

where p_{ij} means the contribution degree of alternative i regarding the criterion j.

Step 2. Calculate the entropy value e_j for the criterion j.

$$e_j = -k\sum_{i=1}^{n} p_{ij} \cdot \ln p_{ij} \tag{11-7}$$

where e_j means the contribution degree of all alternatives to criterion j, and the constant k is generally taken $1/\ln n$.

Step 3. Calculate the otherness coefficient g_j for the criterion j.

$$g_j = 1 - e_j \tag{11-8}$$

where g_j means the deviation degree of each alternative on criterion j.

Step 4. Calculate the weight value of each criterion.

$$w_j = g_j / \sum_{i=1}^{m} g_i \tag{11-9}$$

3.4 AHP

AHP is a subjective weighting method (Saaty, 1990). Depending on the relative importance among the indexes, it makes full use of experts' knowledge and experience and measures the importance of criteria effectively. The specific process are shown as follows (Wu et al., 2019a):

Step 1. Build a judgment matrix. The expert committee determines the relative importance among indexes with a help of 1-9 scale method. Then, a judgment matrix A can be obtained.

$$A = \begin{pmatrix} a_{11} & a_{12} & \cdots & a_{1n} \\ a_{21} & a_{22} & \cdots & a_{2n} \\ \cdots & \cdots & \cdots & \cdots \\ a_{n1} & a_{n2} & \cdots & a_{nn} \end{pmatrix}$$

where a_{ij} means the relative importance that criterion i to the criterion j and $a_{ii} = 1$.

Step 2. Normalize $\overline{W} = \left[\overline{W}_1, \overline{W}_2, \ldots, \overline{W}_n\right]^T$ and gain a weight vector through following formula:

$$W_{si} = \frac{(\prod_{j=1}^{n} a_{ij})^{1/n}}{\sum_{i=1}^{n} (\prod_{j=1}^{n} a_{ij})^{1/n}} \tag{11-10}$$

Step 3. Examine the consistency. In the AHP method, a random consistency ratio CR is usually used to check the matrix consistency to avoid the deviations. If the CR is lower than 0.1, then the judgment matrix A passes the consistency check.

$$CI = \frac{\sum_{i=1}^{n} \frac{(AW_s)_i}{nW_{si}} - n}{n-1} \tag{11-11}$$

$$CR = \frac{CI}{RI} \tag{11-12}$$

where $(AW_s)_i$ means the element i in vector AW, CI means consistency test index and RI means random consistency index.

3.5 Fuzzy synthetic evaluation method

Based on the fuzzy mathematics, fuzzy synthetic evaluation is mainly applied to quantify factors with hazy situation or unclear boundaries. Transforming the qualitative evaluation into quantitative evaluation, the method has strong practicability and a great advantage to solve the problems which are difficult to quantify. The process of fuzzy synthetic evaluation is mainly divided into three steps (Wu et al., 2018b):

Step 1. Construct first-level evaluation vector B_{ci}.

$$B_{ci} = \begin{pmatrix} h_{ci1} \\ \vdots \\ h_{cij} \end{pmatrix} \tag{11-13}$$

Step 2. Calculate the second-level evaluation vector B_c.

$$h_{ci} = W_{ci} \bullet B_{ci} = \begin{pmatrix} w_{ci1} & \cdots & w_{cij} \end{pmatrix} \bullet \begin{pmatrix} h_{ci1} \\ \vdots \\ h_{cij} \end{pmatrix} \tag{11-14}$$

$$B_c = \begin{pmatrix} h_{c1} \\ \vdots \\ h_{ci} \end{pmatrix} \tag{11-15}$$

where w_{cij} means the weight of each evaluation criterion within every group.

Step 3. Calculate the overall evaluation value.

$$B = W_i \bullet B_c = \begin{pmatrix} w_{c1} & \cdots & w_{ci} \end{pmatrix} \bullet \begin{pmatrix} h_{c1} \\ \vdots \\ h_{ci} \end{pmatrix} \tag{11-16}$$

where w_{ci} means the weight of first-level criteria.

3.6 Framework

In order to visual the whole process of decision-making, this section summarizes the methodology introduced above and proposes a three-phase decision framework. Fig. 11.3

displays the brief method flow and overall research procedure of comprehensive benefits evaluation.

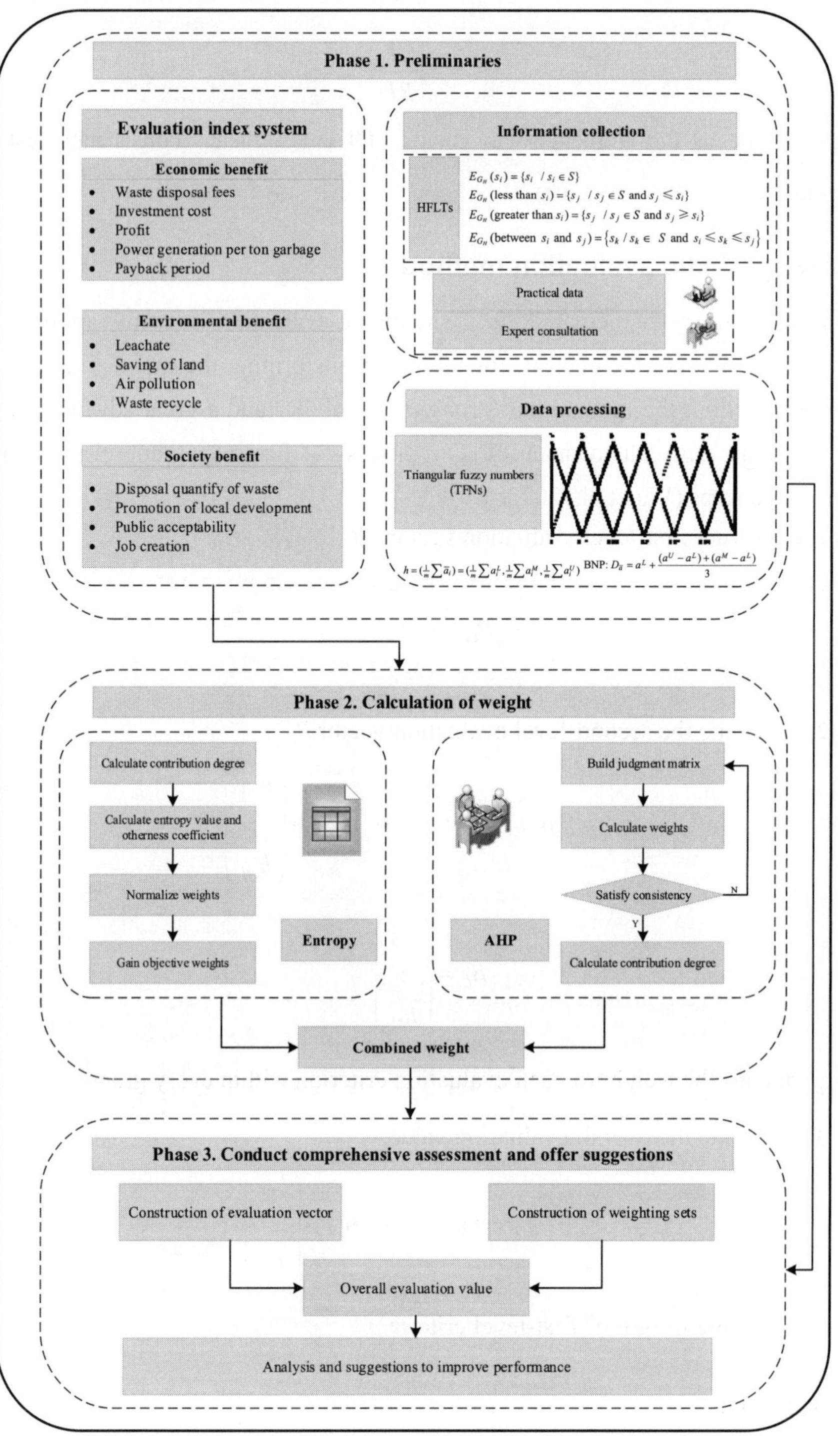

Fig. 11.3 A framework for incineration power plant comprehensive benefit evaluation.

4. Case study

In this section, the decision framework proposed in current paper would be applied in a case study to testify its validation. Now, there are three incineration power plants A, B, C. Firstly, the plant A is far away from the city center. In order to response a require of green development, plant A carries out the implementation of classified garbage which can save resources and land, cut down cost and reduce environmental pollution. Plant B, near the crowded areas, has an advanced technology and a considerable generation benefit. Meanwhile, it is in high status of the implementation of waste classification so that the local development and the satisfaction of residents are increasing. As for plant C, it still operated in the traditional ways which made it a little backward. No implementation of waste classification, its emission is more polluted than A and B, and the relevant industries are lifeless. To judge whether the comprehensive benefit of incineration power plant is good or not, the detail evaluation processions with data are acted as follows.

4.1 Weight determination

4.1.1 Objective weight

Based on the principle of difference driving, the objective weight of criteria can be calculated by comparing the differences of objective data among indicators. Considering there are both quantitative and qualitative factors in evaluation system, we decide the following methods for information collection: for the quantitative indicators, we employ the practical value directly; for the qualitative indicators, the 0-100 score method is chosen to evaluate their performance, and the higher the score is the better the indicator performs. The details are as seen in Table 11.1.

Table 11.1 Relevant data of each evaluation index.

Index	Unit	A	B	C	Qualitative/Quantitative
C11	Yuan/ton	70	84	62	Quantitative
C12	Billion yuan	9	12	7	Quantitative
C13	Billion yuan	3.1	4	2.5	Quantitative
C14	kWh/ton	390	470	350	Quantitative
C15	Year	9	12	8	Quantitative
C21	/	64	45	75	Qualitative
C22	/	70	80	72	Qualitative
C23	/	45	53	65	Qualitative
C24	/	70	90	52	Qualitative
C31	Ton	1400	2000	1200	Quantitative
C32	/	62	75	60	Qualitative
C33	/	90	80	57	Qualitative
C34	/	80	73	62	Qualitative

With the help of Eq. (11-6) to Eq. (11-9), the results of entropy method are shown in Table 11.2.

Table 11.2 Objective weights of evaluation index.

Index	e_j	g_j	w_j
C11	0.9928119	0.0071881	0.0431302
C12	0.9780668	0.0219332	0.1316049
C13	0.9832172	0.0167828	0.1007014
C14	0.9931209	0.0068791	0.0412765
C15	0.9862645	0.0137355	0.0824168
C21	0.9808235	0.0191765	0.1150638
C22	0.9984653	0.0015347	0.0092088
C23	0.9896524	0.0103476	0.0620881
C24	0.9778806	0.0221194	0.1327219
C31	0.9782534	0.0217466	0.1304852
C32	0.9954252	0.0045748	0.0274498
C33	0.9842803	0.0157197	0.0943224
C34	0.9950785	0.0049215	0.0295303

4.1.2 Subjective weight

Inviting the experts to analyze the correlations among the indexes and using a brainstorm to do a pair-wise comparison. Then determining the pair-wise comparison judgment matrices by means of 1-9 scale method, the detail data are shown in Table 11.3.

Table 11.3 The judgment matrix of each criterion.

	C11	C12	C13	C14	C15	C21	C22	C23	C24	C31	C32	C33	C34
C11	1	2	1/2	2	2	1	1	2	1	3	1/2	1	2
C12	1/2	1	1/3	1	3	1	2	1/2	2	1	1/2	1/2	1
C13	2	3	1	2	2	2	3	1	1	1/2	1	1/3	2
C14	1/2	1	1/2	1	1/2	1/2	2	1/2	1/2	1/2	1/2	1/2	1/2
C15	1/2	1/3	1/2	2	1	1/3	1/2	1/2	1/2	1	1/2	1/2	1
C21	1	1	1/2	2	3	1	2	2	1	2	1	1/2	3
C22	1	1/2	1/3	1/2	2	1/2	1	1/2	1/2	3	1/2	1/2	1
C23	1/2	2	1	2	2	1/2	2	1	1	2	2	2	1/2
C24	1	1/2	1	2	2	1	2	1	1	2	1/2	2	4
C31	1/3	1	2	2	1	1/2	1/3	1/2	1/2	1	2	1/2	1
C32	2	2	1	2	2	1	2	1/2	2	1/2	1	1	3
C33	1	2	3	2	2	2	2	1/2	1/2	2	1	1	3
C34	1/2	1	1/2	2	1	1/3	1	2	1/4	1	1/3	1/3	1

According to the principle of AHP mentioned in current paper, the weight of each criterion can be calculated through Eq. (11-10) to Eq. (11-12) and the final results are shown in Table 11.4.

Table 11.4 Subjective weights of evaluation index.

Index	w
C11	0.0908
C12	0.0665
C13	0.0998
C14	0.0436
C15	0.0423
C21	0.0917
C22	0.0552
C23	0.0929
C24	0.095
C31	0.0649
C32	0.097
C33	0.1076
C34	0.0528
CR=0.0875<0.1	

4.1.3 Combined weight

For the purpose that the final weight can represent the information not only in subjectivity but also in objectivity, a combined criterion weight W^* can be decided through the following formula (Yuan et al., 2019):

$$W^* = \lambda W_{Entropy} + (1-\lambda)W_{AHP} \tag{11-17}$$

where λ is a preference coefficient. To ensure a generality, here the value of λ is determined as 0.5.

With the help of Eq. (11-17), the final results are shown in Fig. 11.4.

With the results of subjective weights, objective weights and combined weight, a comparative analysis of evaluation index importance is carried out in Fig. 11.5.

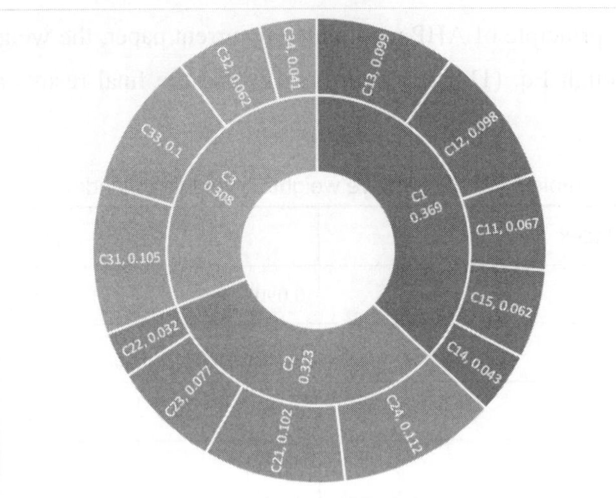

Fig. 11.4 The combined weight of each evaluation index.

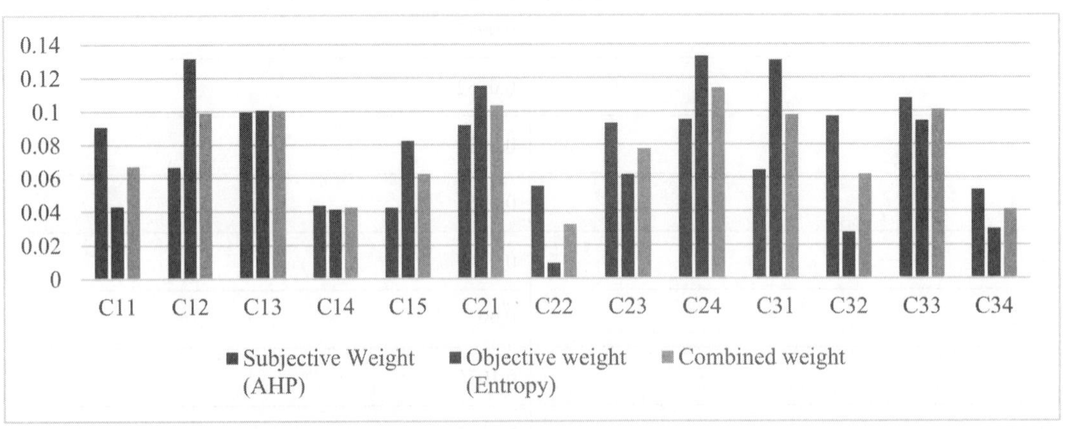

Fig. 11.5 Comparative criteria weights determined by ANP, Entropy and combined method.

The results show that a gap existed between the objective and subjective weight of criteria, which indicates the weights calculated by objective method are often deviate from DMs' psychological expectations, particularly in C12, C22 and C32. Nevertheless, the gap also reflects the necessity of using combined weight method, which avoids weight values being too objective or subjective. In addition, it can be found that economic benefit (C1) always has most weight in each method. Therefore, economic benefit is the key factor to determine the comprehensive benefit of incineration power plant. As a basis of all materials, its decline would affect the overall benefit directly. Meanwhile, the weights of environmental benefit (C2) and social benefit (C3) are similar, which indicates these two factors are both worthy of attention. For the sub-criteria, C24 has the highest weight value, which means that waste management gets a great attention in the comprehensive benefit evaluation from the refuse classification perspective. It impacted the mechanism of classification and recovery but also ensured the calorific value of raw materials and the quality of residues in the incineration. At the same time, the values of C12,

C13, C21, C31 and C33 are in the range of 0.08-0.1 states that these indexes are also vital in evaluation, the several reasons could explain this situation. Firstly, investment and profit are concerns of any projects. Secondly, paying attention to the impact of leachate can represent the effect of waste classification policy in environment and the ecological efficiency. Thirdly, the initial use of incineration power plant is waste treatment, paying attention to capacity of disposal is helpful to settlement of "Junk-Besieged-City". At the same time, due to the garbage classification is a spring implementation that a part of residents do not adapt to the new reform, so the employing public acceptability is also significant. From the above analysis, the key factors in incineration power plant are examined, certainly, the others in evaluation index system are also important.

4.2 Data transforming

In this section, the three expert groups are invited to give their judgment about the performance level towards each criterion through linguistic expressions. Considering their differences in cognition and practical experience of incineration power plant, the weights of experts in groups A, B and C are 0.3, 0.4 and 0.3 respectively. At first, the linguistic term set is determined as {s0=Very Bad (VB), s1=Bad (B), s2=Medium Bad (MB), s3=Moderate (M), s4=Medium Good (MG), s5=Good (G), s6=Very Good (VG)}. According to the meaning of HFLTS, the detail messages given by experts are expressed in Table 11.5.

Table 11.5 Linguistic expressions and HFLTS of each criterion in plant A.

	Group 1		Group 2		Group 3	
	Linguistic expression	HFLTS	Linguistic expression	HFLTS	Linguistic expression	HFLTS
C11	between M and G	{s3, s4, s5}	between M and VG	{s3, s4, s5, s6}	between MG and G	{s4, s5}
C12	between M and MG	{s3, s4}	M	{s3}	between MG and G	{s4, s5}
C13	between M and MG	{s3, s4}	between MB and G	{s2, s3, s4, s5}	MG	{s4}
C14	G	{s4}	between M and G	{s3, s4, s5}	between MG and G	{s4, s5}
C15	between M and MG	{s3, s4}	between MG and G	{s4, s5}	MG	{s4}
C21	between MB and MG	{s2, s3, s4}	M	{s3}	between M and MG	{s3, s4}
C22	M	{s3}	between MB and M	{s2, s3}	between M and MG	{s3, s4}
C23	between MG and G	{s4, s5}	greater than MG	{s4, s5, s6}	VG	{s6}
C24	between M and MG	{s3, s4}	between MB and G	{s2, s3, s4, s5}	MG	{s4}
C31	M	{s3}	between M and MG	{s3, s4}	between MG and G	{s4, s5}
C32	between MB and M	{s2, s3}	MB	{s2}	between B and MG	{s1, s2, s3, s4}
C33	greater than VG	{s5, s6}	greater than VG	{s5, s6}	greater than MG	{s4, s5, s6}
C34	between MG and G	{s4, s5}	greater than MG	{s4, s5, s6}	MG	{s4}

Owing to the limited space of paper, we only present the hesitant fuzzy linguistic terms about plant A and the rest data would be given in Appendix A. After a collection of evaluation information, we transform these linguistic terms into triangular fuzzy number. Fig. 11.6 shows the lower value, middle value and upper value of the seven terms where y-axis refers to the membership of number and the x-axis refers to the value of triangular fuzzy number.

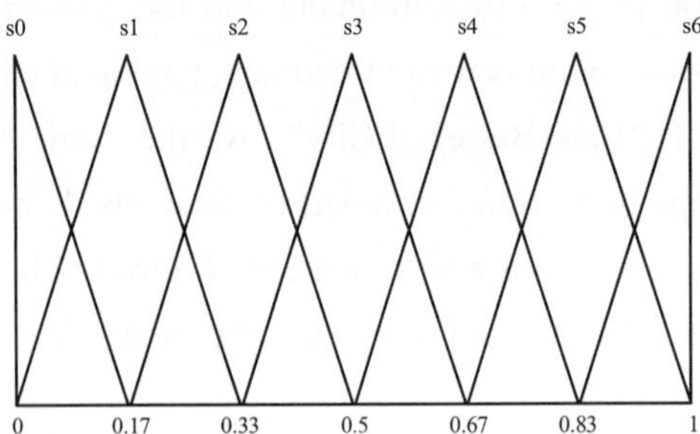

Fig. 11.6 Set of seven terms with its semantics.

To gain the overall consequence, aggregation of expert opinion is a significant step. Through the Eq. (11-3) introduced in section 3, the aggregated results of plan A can be gained, as shown in Table 11.6.

Table 11.6 Triangular fuzzy numbers of each criterion in plant A.

	Group 1	Group 2	Group 3	Aggregated results
C11	(0.5, 0.67, 0.83)	(0.58, 0.75, 0.88)	(0.59, 0.75, 0.92)	(0.559, 0.726, 0.877)
C12	(0.42, 0.58, 0.75)	(0.33, 0.5, 0.67)	(0.59, 0.5, 0.92)	(0.435, 0.599, 0.769)
C13	(0.42, 0.58, 0.75)	(0.42, 0.58, 0.75)	(0.5, 0.67, 0.83)	(0.444, 0.607, 0.774)
C14	(0.5, 0.67, 0.83)	(0.5, 0.67, 0.83)	(0.59, 0.75, 0.92)	(0.527, 0.694, 0.857)
C15	(0.42, 0.58, 0.75)	(0.59, 0.75, 0.92)	(0.5, 0.67, 0.83)	(0.512, 0.675, 0.842)
C21	(0.33, 0.5, 0.67)	(0.33, 0.5, 0.67)	(0.42, 0.58, 0.75)	(0.357, 0.524, 0.694)
C22	(0.33, 0.5, 0.67)	(0.25, 0.42, 0.59)	(0.42, 0.58, 0.75)	(0.325, 0.492, 0.662)
C23	(0.59, 0.75, 0.92)	(0.67, 0.83, 1)	(0.83, 1, 1)	(0.694, 0.857, 0.976)
C24	(0.42, 0.58, 0.75)	(0.42, 0.85, 0.75)	(0.5, 0.67, 0.83)	(0.444, 0.607, 0.774)
C31	(0.33, 0.5, 0.67)	(0.42, 0.58, 0.75)	(0.59, 0.75, 0.92)	(0.444, 0.607, 0.777)
C32	(0.25, 0.42, 0.59)	(0.17, 0.33, 0.5)	(0.25, 0.42, 0.58)	(0.218, 0.384, 0.551)
C33	(0.75, 0.92, 1)	(0.75, 0.92, 1)	(0.67, 0.83, 1)	(0.726, 0.893, 1)
C34	(0.59, 0.75, 0.92)	(0.67, 0.83, 1)	(0.5, 0.67, 0.83)	(0.595, 0.758, 0.925)

4.3 Fuzzy synthetic operation of comprehensive benefit

The final value of comprehensive benefit evaluation would be calculate based on the above data. According to the Eq. (11-13) to Eq. (11-16), the overall comprehensive benefit evaluation results of each incineration power plant are shown as follows:

$$B = W^{*} \bullet B_k = (w_{11}, w_{12}, \ldots, w_{34}) \bullet (B_a, B_b, B_c) = (B_A, B_B, B_C)$$

$$B = ((0.485, 0.65, 0.807), (0.548, 0.711, 0.858), (0.301, 0.462, 0.63))$$

where B_a, B_b and B_c mean the initial aggregated results of plant A, plant B and plant C, respectively.

From the calculation results, the comprehensive evaluation value of each incineration power plant is obtained (see in Fig. 11.7).

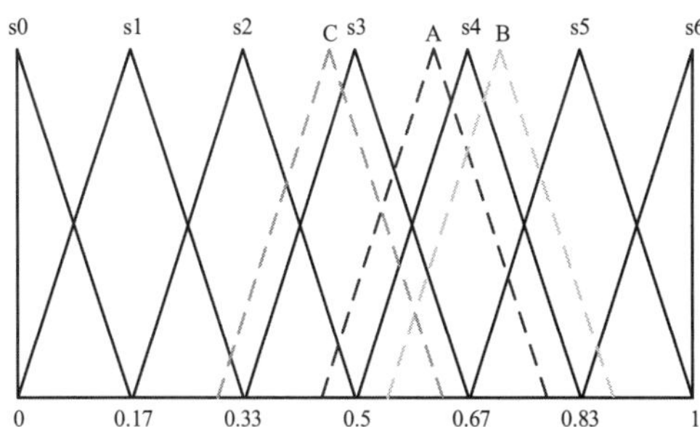

Fig. 11.7 The final comprehensive benefit result of each plant.

In order to compare these data objectively, removing the fuzziness of value becomes a necessary process. Based on the Eq. (11-4), the BNP of each plant is calculated as follows:

$$BNP_A = 0.485 + \frac{((0.807 - 0.485) + (0.65 - 0.485))}{3} = 0.648$$

$$BNP_B = 0.548 + \frac{((0.858 - 0.548) + (0.711 - 0.548))}{3} = 0.706$$

$$BNP_C = 0.301 + \frac{((0.63 - 0.301) + (0.462 - 0.301))}{3} = 0.464$$

At the same time, to determine the certain comprehensive benefit performance, the similarity degrees between the assessment result and linguistic terms could be measured through Eq. (11-5):

$$Sd(B_A, s_3) = 1 - \frac{|B_A^L - s_3^L| + |B_A^M - s_3^M| + |B_A^U - s_3^U|}{3} = 0.852$$

$$Sd(B_A, s_4) = 1 - \frac{|B_A^L - s_4^L| + |B_A^M - s_4^M| + |B_A^U - s_4^U|}{3} = 0.981$$

$$Sd(B_B, s_4) = 1 - \frac{|B_B^L - s_4^L| + |B_B^M - s_4^M| + |B_B^U - s_4^U|}{3} = 0.882$$

$$Sd(B_B, s_5) = 1 - \frac{|B_B^L - s_5^L| + |B_B^M - s_5^M| + |B_B^U - s_5^U|}{3} = 0.873$$

$$Sd(B_C, s_2) = 1 - \frac{|B_C^L - s_2^L| + |B_C^M - s_2^M| + |B_C^U - s_2^U|}{3} = 0.869$$

$$Sd(B_C, s_3) = 1 - \frac{|B_C^L - s_3^L| + |B_C^M - s_3^M| + |B_C^U - s_3^U|}{3} = 0.964$$

It can be seen that the comprehensive benefit performance of plant A is closer to s4, the plant B is closer to s4 and the plant C is closer to s3. That is to say, the detail situation of comprehensive benefit level is that the A is located in medium good, the B is located in medium good and the C is located in moderate. Furthermore, combined with the BNP of each plant, a conclusion can be found that the comprehensive benefit of plant B is best, the A is second and the C is lowest.

5. Discussion

It can be seen that the comprehensive benefit of incineration power plant under the waste classification is higher than no waste classification. Taking an effective measurement in performance management improves the overall benefit indeed. Profited from the waste separation, the incineration power plant could not only act better in the treatment efficiency of incinerator, but also improve its environment ability. However, a single policy about waste classification does not have a decisive effect on power plant comprehensive benefit. Thus, the article takes the economic, environment and society aspects into consideration to analyze the comprehensive performance, combining the characteristic of incineration power plant, and obtains a result that the comprehensive benefit of power plant under garbage classification almost performed better than moderate. Meanwhile, for the purpose of further development of incineration power plant in the future, several measurements to raise the plant's performance are given in this section.

(1) Economic aspect: Paying attention to monitoring and assessment of waste incineration power projects, planning guidance and the policy support in financial subsidies. In the meantime, inviting society capital to join in the plant construction and applying financing models like PPP or BOT into the lifecycle of plant also are pretty ways to improve economics benefit too. Furthermore, considering the requirement of refuse classification, strengthening the construction of municipal solid waste treatment facilities as well as public service capacity that improve the calorific value of garbage and reduce the cost of sorting are benefit to efficiency of power generation plant. Also, making full use of power generation, heat supply and slag sale would bring a good profit, but it is also necessary to note that balance the interests of parties in the waste power generation industry chain and build a circular economic chain. Moreover, clarifying the current demand in power market and economic circumstance, participating in power market reform, adding the auxiliary services as frequency modulation transactions, building an integrated energy service model are also the ways to enhance the efficiency in economy.

(2) Environmental aspect: Implementing the national environmental protection standards strictly, even becoming superior to them. Employing mature incineration technology and advanced equipment to eliminate the negative impact of harmful gases like dioxin and minimize the pollution emissions so that achieving a harmless and resourced-based development. Improving the management of refuse classification and waste incineration through actions in

source classification and multistage utilization. Besides, transforming the governance route of waste from single treatment to comprehensive treatment is an efficient method to speed up the settlement of waste siege. With the significant goal of resource conversion and environmental protection, we should establish thorough legislation and develop innovative technologies. Attaching importance to environmental protection can realize the friendly development among industry and environment, which is in line with the trend of green development and can lead incineration power plant achieving more environmental benefits.

(3) Social aspect: the definition of various kinds of rubbish should be clarified and some leading policies for the social benefit in waste field ought to be developed by governors. To encourage the residents to take part in refuse classification, a mechanism with excitation and punishment could be proposed. Moreover, some mandatory measures could be taken when necessary, which can not only improve the utilization of resources, but also reduce the pressure of garbage disposal in the incineration power plant. Meanwhile, disclosing the emission information of incineration plant to the public in time and accepting the supervision of public are meaningful to public acceptability. The sponsors could organize masses to visit the plant on site, which would updates their cognitions to the incineration power plant and releases the tension in NIMBY. Furthermore, building the waste incineration power plants into a green energy regeneration base, ecological protection and Science Education Park is a pretty idea, which can not only play a role of demonstration and radiation in local development, improve the quality of life of residents, but also demonstrate the concept of ecological civilization of sustainable development.

6. Conclusion

Based on the perspective of refuse classification, our research proposes a complete framework to evaluate the comprehensive benefit of incineration power plant. Existing researches centralized on benefit of the waste-to-energy are still hold several flaws. Firstly, the attention on benefit are often concentrating on economy during evaluation. Ignorance of environment and society, some incineration power plants are far from beautiful in the beginning and leading the loss of benefit is floating. Secondly, due to the considerable evaluation indexes existed in decision-making, the interaction and fuzziness among the criteria are difficult to determine with simple number. Moreover, the ranking techniques used in previous researches could not take the objectivity and subjectivity during the calculation into consideration. Lastly, after gaining the final consequence, most suggestions to improve the incineration power plant in the future operation have a great space to optimal.

Considering the shortcomings mentioned above, the current paper mainly works as follows: Firstly, a benefit evaluation index system of incineration power plant, from the refuse classification perspective, is built including 13 performance factors that divided into three categories, namely economic benefit, environmental benefit and social benefit. Secondly, the article employs HFLTs to solve the fuzziness from decision information and transforms them into TFNs that reduces the loss of message. Combining the Entropy method and AHP method, the weights of evaluation indexes are suitable to complex situation. Next, the paper applies fuzzy comprehensive evaluation method and principle of maximum similarity to calculate the overall benefit level, and the applicability of model is confirmed through a case study. Lastly, aiming at the economy, environment and society three aspects, several suggestions are put forward under the characteristic of refuse classification. For the further development of incineration power plant, our study can provide a decision support and theoretical reference.

However, due to the experience of writers, there are still some limitations in the paper. On the one hand, the evaluation index system might not be perfect. Facing the intricate impacts on incineration power plant comprehensive benefit, the index system should be adjusted properly based on the specific situation. On the other hand, some countermeasures to improve the incineration power plant comprehensive benefit are not permanent that should be updated slightly with the time going by or in the particular case. Thus, we would pay more attention to these parts in future research to gain more practical results.

Acknowledgements

This research is supported by the National Social Science Fund of China (19AGL027), the Fundamental Research Funds for the Central Universities (No. 2018ZD14), the 2017 Special Project of Cultivation and Development of Innovation Base (No. Z171100002217024).

Appendix A

Table A.1 Linguistic expressions and HFLTS of each criterion in plant B.

	Group 1		Group 2		Group 3	
	Linguistic expression	HFLTS	Linguistic expression	HFLTS	Linguistic expression	HFLTS
C11	G	{s5}	greater than VG	{s5, s6}	between MG and G	{s4, s5}
C12	less than M	{s0, s1, s2, s3}	between MB and M	{s3}	between B and M	{s1, s2, s3}
C13	between MG and G	{s4, s5}	between M and MG	{s2, s3, s4, s5}	greater than VG	{s5, s6}
C14	greater than MG	{s4, s5, s6}	G	{s3, s4, s5}	greater than VG	{s5, s6}
C15	between MB and G	{s2, s3, s4, s5}	between M and MG	{s4, s5}	between MB and M	{s2, s3}
C21	greater than VG	{s5, s6}	between M and G	{s3}	between MG and G	{s4, s5}
C22	between MG and G	{s4, s5}	between M and MG	{s2, s3}	MG	{s4}
C23	between M and G	{s3, s4, s5}	between M and MG	{s4, s5, s6}	between MB and G	{s2, s3, s4, s5}
C24	greater than VG	{s5, s6}	greater than MG	{s2, s3, s4, s5}	VG	{s6}

Continued

	Group 1		Group 2		Group 3	
	Linguistic expression	HFLTS	Linguistic expression	HFLTS	Linguistic expression	HFLTS
C31	greater than MG	{s4, s5, s6}	between MG and G	{s3, s4}	greater than VG	{s5, s6}
C32	between M and MG	{s3, s4}	MG	{s2}	between M and VG	{s3, s4, s5, s6}
C33	greater than MG	{s4, s5, s6}	between MG and G	{s5, s6}	MG	{s4}
C34	between MG and G	{s4, s5}	between M and MG	{s4, s5, s6}	between M and VG	{s3, s4, s5, s6}

Table A.2 Linguistic expressions and HFLTS of each criterion in plant C.

	Group 1		Group 2		Group 3	
	Linguistic expression	HFLTS	Linguistic expression	HFLTS	Linguistic expression	HFLTS
C11	between MB and MG	{s2, s3, s4}	G	{s5}	between MG and G	{s4, s5}
C12	between MG and G	{s4, s5}	MG	{s4}	greater than MG	{s4, s5, s6}
C13	less than M	{s0, s1, s2, s3}	between MB and M	{s2, s3}	between B and MB	{s1, s2}
C14	between MG and G	{s4, s5}	between MB and G	{s2, s3, s4, s5}	between M and MG	{s3, s4}
C15	greater than MG	{s4, s5, s6}	between M and MG	{s3, s4}	between M and G	{s3, s4, s5}
C21	between B and M	{s1, s2, s3}	MB	{s2}	less than M	{s0, s1, s2, s3}
C22	between M and G	{s3, s4, s5}	between M and MG	{s3, s4}	MG	{s4}
C23	between MB and M	{s2, s3}	between B and M	{s1, s2, s3}	between MB and MG	{s2, s3, s4}
C24	between MB and MG	{s2, s3, s4}	between B and M	{s1, s2, s3}	between MB and M	{s2, s3}
C31	between MB and M	{s2, s3}	M	{s3}	between B and MG	{s1, s2, s3, s4}
C32	between B and MB	{s1, s2}	MB	{s2}	between MB and M	{s2, s3}
C33	less than MB	{s0, s1, s2}	between B and MB	{s1, s2}	between B and MB	{s1, s2}
C34	between MB and MG	{s2, s3, s4}	between M and MG	{s3, s4}	between MB and MG	{s2, s3, s4}

Table A.3 Triangular fuzzy numbers of each criterion in plant B.

	Group 1	Group 2	Group 3	Aggregated results
C11	(0.67, 0.83, 1)	(0.75, 0.92, 1)	(0.59, 0.75, 0.92)	(0.678, 0.842, 0.976)
C12	(0.12, 0.25, 0.42)	(0.25, 0.42, 0.59)	(0.17, 0.33, 0.5)	(0.187, 0.342, 0.512)
C13	(0.59, 0.75, 0.92)	(0.42, 0.58, 0.75)	(0.75, 0.92, 1)	(0.57, 0.733, 0.876)
C14	(0.67, 0.83, 1)	(0.67, 0.83, 1)	(0.75, 0.92, 1)	(0.694, 0.857, 0.1)
C15	(0.42, 0.58, 0.75)	(0.42, 0.58, 0.75)	(0.25, 0.42, 0.59)	(0.369, 0.532, 0.702)
C21	(0.75, 0.92, 1)	(0.5, 0.67, 0.83)	(0.59, 0.75, 0.92)	(0.602, 0.769, 0.908)
C22	(0.59, 0.75, 0.92)	(0.42, 0.58, 0.75)	(0.5, 0.67, 0.83)	(0.495, 0.658, 0.825)
C23	(0.5, 0.67, 0.83)	(0.42, 0.58, 0.75)	(0.42, 0.58, 0.75)	(0.444, 0.607, 0.774)
C24	(0.75, 0.92, 1)	(0.67, 0.83, 1)	(0.83, 1, 1)	(0.742, 0.908, 0.1)
C31	(0.67, 0.83, 1)	(0.59, 0.75, 0.92)	(0.75, 0.92, 1)	(0.662, 0.825, 0.968)
C32	(0.42, 0.58, 0.75)	(0.5, 0.67, 0.83)	(0.58, 0.72, 0.88)	(0.5, 0.667, 0.821)
C33	(0.67, 0.83, 1)	(0.59, 0.75, 0.92)	(0.5, 0.67, 0.83)	(0.587, 0.75, 0.917)
C34	(0.59, 0.75, 0.92)	(0.42, 0.58, 0.75)	(0.58, 0.72, 0.88)	(0.519, 0.682, 0.84)

Table A.4 Triangular fuzzy numbers of each criterion in plant C.

	Group 1	Group 2	Group 3	Aggregated results
C11	(0.33, 0.5, 0.67)	(0.67, 0.83, 1)	(0.59, 0.75, 0.92)	(0.544, 0.707, 0.877)
C12	(0.59, 0.75, 0.92)	(0.5, 0.67, 0.83)	(0.67, 0.83, 1)	(0.578, 0.742, 0.908)
C13	(0.12, 0.25, 0.42)	(0.25, 0.42, 0.59)	(0.09, 0.25, 0.42)	(0, 163, 0.318, 0.488)
C14	(0.59, 0.75, 0.92)	(0.42, 0.58, 0.75)	(0.42, 0.58, 0.75)	(0.471, 0.631, 0.801)
C15	(0.67, 0.83, 1)	(0.42, 0.58, 0.75)	(0.5, 0.67, 0.83)	(0.519, 0.682, 0.849)
C21	(0.17, 0.33, 0.5)	(0.17, 0.33, 0.5)	(0.12, 0.25, 0.42)	(0.155, 0.306, 0.476)
C22	(0.5, 0.67, 0.83)	(0.42, 0.58, 0.75)	(0.5, 0.67, 0.83)	(0.468, 0.634, 0.798)
C23	(0.25, 0.42, 0.59)	(0.17, 0.33, 0.5)	(0.33, 0.5, 0.67)	(0.242, 0.408, 0.578)
C24	(0.33, 0.5, 0.67)	(0.17, 0.33, 0.5)	(0.25, 0.42, 0.59)	(0.242, 0.408, 0.578)
C31	(0.25, 0.42, 0.59)	(0.33, 0.5, 0.67)	(0.25, 0.42, 0.59)	(0.282, 0.452, 0.619)
C32	(0.09, 0.25, 0.42)	(0.17, 0.33, 0.5)	(0.25, 0.42, 0.59)	(0.17, 0.333, 0.503)
C33	(0.06, 0.17, 0.33)	(0.09, 0.25, 0.42)	(0.09, 0.25, 0.42)	(0.081, 0.226, 0.393)
C34	(0.33, 0.5, 0.67)	(0.42, 0.58, 0.75)	(0.33, 0.5, 0.67)	(0.366, 0.532, 0.702)

References

[1] Assamoi B, Lawryshyn Y. The environmental comparison of landfilling vs. incineration of MSW accounting for waste diversion[J]. Waste Management, 2012, 32(5):1019-1030.

[2] Badgett A, Newes E, Milbrandt A.Economic Analysis of Wet Waste-to-Energy Resources in the United States[J]. Energy, 2019.

[3] Büyüközkan G, Karabulut Y. Energy project performance evaluation with sustainability perspective[J]. Energy, 2017, 119:549-560.

[4] Caneghem J V, Brems A, Lievens P, et al. Fluidized bed waste incinerators: Design, operational and environmental issues[J]. Progress in Energy & Combustion Science, 2012, 38(4): 551-582.

[5] Cheng H, Hu Y. Municipal solid waste (MSW) as a renewable source of energy: Current and future practices in China[J]. Bioresource Technology, 2010, 101(11):3816-3824.

[6] Cheng H, Zhang Y, Meng I H, et al. Municipal Solid Waste Fueled Power Generation in China:A Case Study of Waste-to-Energy in Changchun City[J]. Environmental Science & Technology, 2007, 41(21):7509-7515.

[7] Chu Z, Wang W, Zhou A, et al. Charging for municipal solid waste disposal in Beijing[J]. Waste Management, 2019, 94: 85-94.

[8] Dong J, Yong C, Zou D, et al. Energy–environment–economy assessment of waste management systems from a life cycle perspective: Model development and case study[J]. Applied Energy, 2014, 114(2):400-408.

[9] Dubois D, Prade H. Operations on fuzzy numbers[J]. International Journal of systems science, 1978, 9(6): 613-626.

[10] Eboh F C, Andersson B-Å, Richards T. Economic evaluation of improvements in a waste-to-energy combined heat and power plant[J]. Waste Management, 2019, 100:75-83.

[11] Ezeah C, Roberts C L. Analysis of barriers and success factors affecting the adoption of sustainable

management of municipal solid waste in Nigeria[J]. Journal of environmental management, 2012, 103:9-14.

[12] Feng Z, Li X, Lu J W, et al. Emission characteristics of PCDD/Fs in stack gas from municipal solid waste incineration plants in Northern China[J]. Chemosphere, 2018, 200: 23-29.

[13] Gan L, Xu D, Hu L, et al. Economic feasibility analysis for renewable energy project using an integrated TFN–AHP–DEA approach on the basis of consumer utility[J]. Energies, 2017, 10(12):2089.

[14] He J, Lin B. Assessment of waste incineration power with considerations of subsidies and emissions in China[J]. Energy Policy, 2019.

[15] Hui L, Kong S, Liu Y, et al. Pollution Control Technologies of Dioxins in Municipal Solid Waste Incinerator[J]. Procedia Environmental Sciences, 2012, 16(4):661-668.

[16] Ibikunle R A, Titiladunayo I F, Akinnuli B O, et al. Estimation of power generation from municipal solid wastes: A case Study of Ilorin metropolis, Nigeria[J]. Energy Reports, 2019.

[17] Jie C, Hui Q, Gao Y, et al. Human Health Risk Assessment of Contaminants in Drinking Water Based on Triangular Fuzzy Numbers Approach in Yinchuan City, Northwest China[J]. Exposure & Health, 2017, (6):1-12.

[18] Khalil M, Berawi M A, Heryanto R, et al. Waste to energy technology: The potential of sustainable biogas production from animal waste in Indonesia[J]. Renewable & Sustainable Energy Reviews, 2019, 105:323-331.

[19] Khoshand A, Kamalan H, Rezaei H. Application of analytical hierarchy process (AHP) to assess options of energy recovery from municipal solid waste: a case study in Tehran, Iran[J]. Journal of Material Cycles & Waste Management, 2018, 20(3): 1689-1700.

[20] Kumar A, Sah B, Singh A R, et al.A review of multi criteria decision making (MCDM) towards sustainable renewable energy development[J]. Renewable & Sustainable Energy Reviews 69(Complete), 2017, 69:596-609.

[21] Labuschagne C, Brent A C, Erck R P G V. Assessing the sustainability performances of industries[J]. Journal of Cleaner Production, 2005, 13(4):373-385.

[22] Li R, Yu J. The early-warning system based on hybrid optimization algorithm and fuzzy synthetic evaluation model[J]. Information Sciences, 2017, 435: S002002551632254X.

[23] Li X, Cundy A B, Chen W. Fuzzy synthetic evaluation of contaminated site management policy from the perspective of stakeholders: A case study from China[J]. Journal of cleaner production, 2018, 198:1593-1601.

[24] Li X, Ma Y, Zhang M, et al. Study on the relationship between waste classification, combustion condition and dioxin emission from waste incineration[J]. Waste Disposal & Sustainable Energy, 2019, 1(2): 91-98.

[25] Lim S-Y, Lim K-M, Yoo S-H. External benefits of waste-to-energy in Korea: A choice experiment study[J]. Renewable and Sustainable Energy Reviews, 2014, 34: 588-595.

[26] Liu H C, You J X, Fan X J, et al. Site selection in waste management by the VIKOR method using linguistic assessment[J]. Applied Soft Computing, 2014, 21(5):453-461.

[27] Liu Y, Ge Y, Xia B, et al. Enhancing public acceptance towards waste-to-energy incineration projects: Lessons learned from a case study in China[J]. Sustainable Cities and Society, 2019, 48:101582.

[28] Liu Z, Liu Z, Li X. Status and prospect of the application of municipal solid waste incineration in

China[J]. Applied Thermal Engineering, 2006, 26(11):1193-1197.

[29] Long S, Geng S. Decision framework of photovoltaic module selection under interval-valued intuitionistic fuzzy environment[J]. Energy Conversion and Management, 2015, 106:1242-1250.

[30] Mak T M W, Yu I K M, Wang L, et al. Extended theory of planned behaviour for promoting construction waste recycling in Hong Kong[J]. Waste Management, 2019, 83:161-170.

[31] Makarichi L. The evolution of waste-to-energy incineration: A review[J]. Renewable and Sustainable Energy Reviews, 2018, 91: 812-821.

[32] Meng X, Tan X, Wang Y, et al. Investigation on decision-making mechanism of residents' household solid waste classification and recycling behaviors[J]. Resources, Conservation & Recycling., 2018, 140: 224-234.

[33] Meng X, Tan X, Wang Y, et al. Investigation on decision-making mechanism of residents' household solid waste classification and recycling behaviors[J]. Resources, Conservation and Recycling, 2019, 140:224-234.

[34] Moody C M, Townsend T G. A comparison of landfill leachates based on waste composition[J]. Waste Management, 2017, 63:267-274.

[35] Mu S, Hu C, Chohr M, et al. Assessing risk management capability of contractors in subway projects in mainland China[J]. International Journal of Project Management, 2014, 32(3):452-460.

[36] Nagpure A S. Assessment of quantity and composition of illegal dumped municipal solid waste (MSW) in Delhi[J]. Resources, Conservation and Recycling, 2019, 141: 54-60.

[37] Nie Y, Wu Y, Zhao J, et al. Is the finer the better for municipal solid waste (MSW) classification in view of recyclable constituents? A comprehensive social, economic and environmental analysis[J]. Waste management, 2018, 79:472-480.

[38] Nixon J D, Dey P K, Ghosh S K, et al. Evaluation of options for energy recovery from municipal solid waste in India using the hierarchical analytical network process[J]. Energy, 2013, 59(59): 215-223.

[39] Perry W E. The utilization of by-products and waste products in the production of commercial fertilizers[J]. Fertilizer Research, 1992, 32(1):111-114.

[40] Rodríguez R M, Martínez L, Herrera F. Hesitant Fuzzy Linguistic Term Sets[J]. IEEE Transactions on Fuzzy Systems, 2012, 20(1):109-119.

[41] Rostamzadeh R, Govindan K, Esmaeili A, et al. Application of fuzzy VIKOR for evaluation of green supply chain management practices[J]. Ecological Indicators, 2015, 49: 188-203.

[42] Saaty T L. How to make a decision: the analytic hierarchy process[J]. European journal of operational research, 1990, 48(1):9-26.

[43] Sánchez-Lozano J, García-Cascales M, Lamata M. GIS-based onshore wind farm site selection using Fuzzy Multi-Criteria Decision Making methods[J]. Evaluating the case of Southeastern Spain. Applied Energy, 2016, 171: 86-102.

[44] Savva P, Costa C, Charalambides A. Environmental, economical and marketing aspects of the operation of a waste-to-energy plant in the kotsiatis landfill in cyprus[J]. Waste and Biomass Valorization, 2013, 4(2):259-269.

[45] Sheen J. Fuzzy financial profitability analyses of demand side management alternatives from participant perspective[J]. Information Sciences, 2005, 169(3-4): 329-364.

[46] Shidpour H, Cunha C D, Bernard A. Group multi-criteria design concept evaluation using combined rough set theory and fuzzy set theory[J]. Expert Systems with Applications, 2016, 64: 633-644.

[47] Tabata T. Waste-to-energy incineration plants as greenhouse gas reducers: A case study of seven Japanese metropolises[J]. Waste Management & Research, 2013, 31(11): 1110-1117.

[48] Torra V. Hesitant Fuzzy Sets[J]. International Journal of Intelligent Systems, 2010, 25(6):529-539.

[49] Tseng M-L, Wu K-J, Ma L, et al. A hierarchical framework for assessing corporate sustainability performance using a hybrid fuzzy synthetic method-DEMATEL[J]. Technological Forecasting and Social Change, 2019, 144:524-533.

[50] Vavrek R, Chovancová J. Assessment of economic and environmental energy performance of EU countries using CV-TOPSIS technique[J]. Ecological Indicators, 2019, 106: 105519.

[51] Wang J, Ding D, Liu O, et al. A synthetic method for knowledge management performance evaluation based on triangular fuzzy number and group support systems[J]. Applied Soft Computing, 2016, 39(C): 11-20.

[52] Wang Q, Han R, Huang Q, et al. Research on energy conservation and emissions reduction based on AHP-fuzzy synthetic evaluation model: A case study of tobacco enterprises[J]. Journal of cleaner production, 2018, 201: 88-97.

[53] Wang Y, Lai N, Zuo J, et al. Characteristics and trends of research on waste-to-energy incineration: A bibliometric analysis, 1999–2015[J]. Renewable & Sustainable Energy Reviews, 2016, 66:95-104.

[54] Wu Y, Chen, K, Zeng B, et al. Cloud-based decision framework for waste-to-energy plant site selection – A case study from China[J]. Waste Management, 2016, 48:593-603.

[55] Wu Y, Jing W, Yong H, et al. An Extended TODIM-PROMETHEE Method for Waste-to-energy Plant Site Selection Based on Sustainability Perspective[J]. Energy, 2018, 156:1-16.

[56] Wu Y, Ke Y, Xu C, et al. An integrated decision-making model for sustainable photovoltaic module supplier selection based on combined weight and cumulative prospect theory[J]. Energy, 2019a.

[57] Wu Y, Li L, Song Z, et al. Risk assessment on offshore photovoltaic power generation projects in China based on a fuzzy analysis framework[J]. Journal of cleaner production, 2019b, 215:46-62.

[58] Wu Y, Li L, Xu R, et al. Risk assessment in straw-based power generation public-private partnership projects in China: A fuzzy synthetic evaluation analysis[J]. Journal of Cleaner Production, 2017a, 161:977-990.

[59] Wu Y, Song Z, Li L, et al. Risk management of public-private partnership charging infrastructure projects in China based on a three-dimension framework[J]. Energy, 2018b, 165:1089-1101.

[60] Wu Y, Tao Y, Zhang B, et al. A decision framework of offshore wind power station site selection using a PROMETHEE method under intuitionistic fuzzy environment: A case in China[J]. Ocean & Coastal Management, 2020, 184:105016.

[61] Wu Y, Wang Y, Chen K, et al. Social sustainability assessment of small hydropower with hesitant PROMETHEE method[J]. Sustainable cities and society, 2017b, 35: 522-537.

[62] Wu Y, Xu C, Ke Y, et al. Portfolio optimization of renewable energy projects under type-2 fuzzy environment with sustainability perspective[J]. Computers & Industrial Engineering, 2019d, 133: 69-82.

[63] Wu Y, Xu C, Zhang T. Evaluation of renewable power sources using a fuzzy MCDM based on cumulative prospect theory: A case in China[J]. Energy, 2018c, 147: 1227-1239.

[64] Wu Y, Zhou J. Risk assessment of urban rooftop distributed PV in energy performance contracting (EPC) projects: An extended HFLTS-DEMATEL fuzzy synthetic evaluation analysis[J]. Sustainable Cities and Society, 2019, 47:101524.

[65] Yuan J, Li X, Xu C, et al. Investment risk assessment of coal-fired power plants in countries along the Belt and Road initiative based on ANP-Entropy-TODIM method[J]. Energy, 2019, 176:623-640.

[66] Zadeh L A. Fuzzy sets [J]. Information & Control, 1965, 8(3):338-353.

[67] Zadeh L A. The Concept of a Linguistic Variable and its Application to Approximate Reasoning[J]. Inf Sci, 1974, 8(3):199-249.

[68] Zadeh L A, Klir G J, Yuan B. Fuzzy sets, fuzzy logic, and fuzzy systems: selected papers[J]. World Scientific, 1996.

[69] Zeng W Y, Zhao Y B. Relationship between Similarity Measure and Entropy of Interval-valued Fuzzy Sets Based on Interval-number Measurement[J]. Fuzzy Systems & Mathematics, 2006, 157(11): 1477-1484.

[70] Zhang L, Xin H, Yong H, et al. Renewable energy project performance evaluation using a hybrid multi-criteria decision-making approach: Case study in Fujian, China[J]. Journal of cleaner production, 2019, 206: 1123-1137.

[71] Zhao X, Lin R, Wei G. Hesitant triangular fuzzy information aggregation based on Einstein operations and their application to multiple attribute decision making[J]. Expert Systems with Applications, 2014, 41(4):1086-1094.

Chapter 12

Portfolio optimization of renewable energy projects under type-2 fuzzy environment with sustainability perspective

Yunna Wu [a, b], Chuanbo Xu [a, b*], Yiming Ke [a, b], Yao Tao [a, b], Xinying Li [a, b]

a. School of Economics and Management, North China Electric Power University, Beijing, China

b. Beijing Key Laboratory of New Energy and Low-Carbon Development (North China Electric Power University), Changping, Beijing, 102206, China

Abstract: In this study, a fuzzy multi-criteria decision-making (MCDM) framework is established to optimize the renewable energy project (REP) portfolio(s) in an efficient way. Firstly, from the perspective of sustainability, three objectives of economic, social and environmental impacts as well as 16 subordinated criteria are identified for REP performance evaluation via literature review. Secondly, the performance of REPs on these criteria is adopted the form of interval type-2 fuzzy (IT2F) numbers to fully describe the inherent uncertainties in the REP portfolio optimization problem. Thirdly, the fuzzy weights of these criteria are obtained using interval type-2 fuzzy analytic hierarchy process (IT2F-AHP) technique. Fourthly, based on the criteria performances and criteria weights, the interval type-2 fuzzy weighted averaging (IT2FWA) operator is used to aggregate the fuzzy values of REPs in term of the three objectives. Fifthly, a zero-one programming model is formulated and the non-dominated sorting genetic algorithm-II is employed to capture an optimal-Pareto set by considering the trade-off between the three objectives. Finally, to validate the effectiveness of the proposed framework, a case study in Southeast China is conducted. Results show that the criteria greenhouse gas emission reduction owns the highest weight, and three non-dominant solutions with uniform distribution are obtained.

Keywords: renewable energy project; portfolio optimization; sustainability perspective;

multi-criteria decision-making.

Nomenclature			
$\tilde{\tilde{A}}_i$	a trapezoidal interval type-2 fuzzy set	C	total cost constraint
$\tilde{A}_i^U$	upper value a trapezoidal IT2FS	$\tilde{\tilde{C}}_i$	fuzzy investment cost of project i
$\tilde{A}_i^L$	lower value a trapezoidal IT2FS	$\tilde{\tilde{I}}_C(x)$	cost reduction when two projects i and j are implemented
$H_j(\tilde{A}_i^U)$	upper trapezoidal membership function	MCDM	multi-criteria decision-making
$H_j(\tilde{A}_i^L)$	lower trapezoidal membership function	REP	renewable energy project
CR	consistency ratio	IT2F	interval type-2 fuzzy
CI	consistency index	IT2FS	interval type-2 fuzzy set
$\lambda_{\max}$	principal eigen value	IT2F-AHP	interval type-2 fuzzy analytic hierarchy process
m	matrix order	IT2F-WA	interval type-2 fuzzy weighted averaging
RI	random index	NSGA-II	Non-Dominated Sorting Genetic Algorithm-II
$\tilde{\tilde{r}}_i$	geometric mean of each row of matrix	DMs	decision makers
$\tilde{\tilde{S}}_i^j$	fuzzy value of project i in term of objective j		

1. Introduction

Energy is a basic natural resource for human survival, economic growth and social development, and it is an important strategic material related to the economic lifeline and safety of a country. With the deterioration of environment, the intensification of greenhouse effect and the exhaustion of conventional resource (such as coal and oil), countries around the world turn their attention to the field of renewable energy. According to the BP statistical review of world energy 2017, renewable energy ranks first in all energy growth with a 12% growth rate under the weakening trend of global primary energy consumption. Among all countries, China's renewable energy consumption has increased by 33.4% throughout the year of 2016, making China the world's largest consumer of renewable energy. However, coal is still the main energy in China, while the renewable energy only accounts for 11% of the total primary energy consumption in 2016 (Centre, 2017). To comply with the requirements of Paris Agreements requirements for a "Well Below 2°C" future, more ambitious targets for renewable energy were set recently (Fig. 12.1). And to achieve such ambitious targets, there is no doubt that more and more favorable policies and measures will be implemented to support the development of renewable energy.

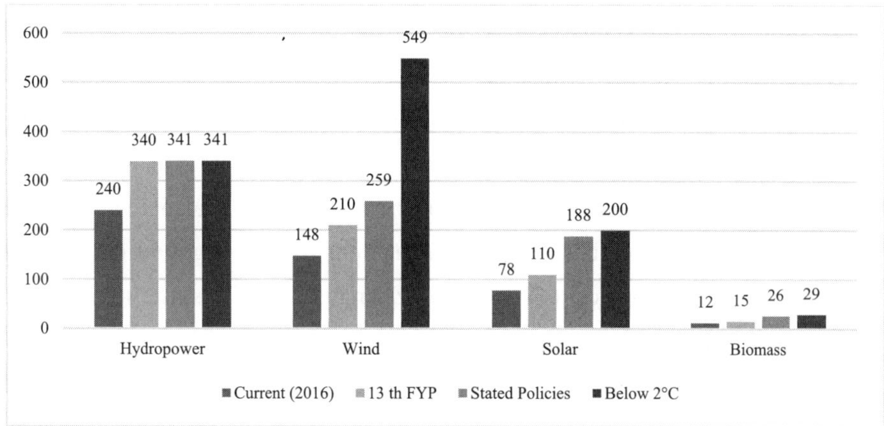

Fig. 12.1 Installed capacity of renewable energy sources in different scenarios.

With the emergence of renewable energy market, the number of optional renewable energy projects will inevitably exceed the number of executable projects under the limited resource constraints of power generation enterprises. So, an important decision for power generation enterprises is to decide effective project portfolios. Project portfolio optimization, as a vital phase of project portfolio management, is the process of selecting a portfolio of projects from available project proposals without exceeding available organizational resources or violating organizational constraints and requirements (Wu et al., 2012). Power generation enterprises have to diversify their overall risk through a variety of renewable energy sources portfolios since the diversification achieves lower overall risk compared to that for the individual renewable energy source (Cucchiella et al., 2016). For example, Cucchiella et al. (2012) applied portfolio theory in the Italian electricity market for different energy sources such as biomass, wind, hydro and photovoltaic, and demonstrated that risk can be mitigated by the diversification of investments in various renewable energies.

In the field of energy project portfolio optimization, several valuable studies have been found. Smith-Perera et al. (2010) and Garcíamelón et al. (2015) selected energy project portfolio in power generation enterprises from the perspective of strategic alignment.

Wu et al. (2017) made a selection of an optimal large-scale rooftop photovoltaic project portfolio under the objective of the total benefit maximization and the installed capacity maximization. Golabi et al. (1981) optimized a portfolio of solar energy projects with the objective of the overall technical quality. Maier et al. (2016) formulated an optimization model which maximizes the risk-averse measure value of a holding company to select renewable electricity generator investments. Moreover, Zeng et al. (2015) developed a multi-objective model of the energy generation portfolios by taking into account the trade-offs between the cost per kWh of electricity generation and the total risk for an investor-owned utility. The literature review reveals that existing literature relating to energy project portfolio optimization has little or no consideration for the sustainability issues. Sustainable development, as defined by the Brundtland Commission's Report, is to meet the needs of contemporary development without compromising the ability of future generations to meet their own needs (Nations, 1987). Sustainability means a trade-off between economic, environment and social activities. For the problem of REP investment, it is not only an economic issue, but also requires investors to consider environmental and social issues since either positive or negative environmental and social impacts of a REP are significant (Wu, Xu, & Zhang, 2018). Thus, the sustainability issues are very important for REP portfolio optimization.

As the mainstream of the portfolio optimization, the modern portfolio theory (also known as mean-variance analysis) (Markowitz, 1952) is a mathematical framework for allocating a portfolio of projects such that the expected return is maximized for a given level of risk, defined as variance. However, this theory is not applicable to the problem of REP portfolio optimization. One reason is that the modern portfolio theory focuses on the economic aspect merely, while another reason is that the modern portfolio theory is strictly quantitative, REP portfolio optimization may contain qualitative criteria that cannot be quantified. Fortunately, aiming to find the most suitable solution from a set of alternatives considering a great deal of objectives or criteria, MCDM emerges as a powerful tool to solve this problem. Recently, the MCDM has been widely applied to the project portfolio optimization problems, and more specifically, Relich and Pawlewski (2017) proposed a project portfolio selection model that uses a fuzzy weighted averaging (WA) approach for ranking new product projects and an artificial neural network approach for estimating project performance. Tavana et al. (2015) proposed a hybrid method for selecting an optimal combination of projects. Among these, data envelopment analysis (DEA) was used in the initial screening process, the TOPSIS and integer linear programming (LP) were applied for ranking the projects and for selecting the most suitable project portfolio, respectively. And Khalili-Damghani et al. (2013) employed a hybrid fuzzy rule-based multi-criteria framework consisting of DEA and Non-Dominated Sorting Genetic Algorithm-II (NSGA-II) for project portfolio optimization.

Inspired by them, this paper aims to propose a hybrid MCDM framework, which integrates the WA operator, the AHP technique and the NSGA-II algorithm, to select the optimal REP portfolio from a sustainability perspective under type-2 fuzzy environment. The main contributions and originality of this paper are three-folds: ①Current researches on REP portfolio optimization mainly focus on the consideration of enterprise strategy, investment cost, installed capacity, return and risk and so on. The paper manages to integrate the sustainability thinking into the establishment of an optimal REP portfolio which has not been tried before; and therefore, a new evaluation index system is also established; ②Although the fuzzy set such as interval number, triangular fuzzy number, and trapezoidal fuzzy numbers has been widely used in the portfolio optimization problem, the application of the type-2 fuzzy number in REP portfolio optimization problem is still novel; Compared with low-order fuzzy numbers, the fuzzification degree of IT2FNs is higher, which is more suitable for complex decision-making like REP portfolio optimization; ③Despite the combination of NSGA-II and AHP, NSGA-II and WA as well as AHP and WA have been studied by many scholars, it is the first time to combine the WA operator, the AHP technique and the NSGA- II algorithm together to solve a decision-making problem.

The rest of this paper is organized as follows: a literature review is conducted in the next Section; in section 3, an evaluation criteria system for REP sustainable performance evaluation is established; section 4 introduces the basic theory of interval type-2 fuzzy sets (IT2FSs), IT2FWA operator, IT2F-AHP technique and NGSA-II; in section 5, a decision framework for REP portfolio optimization is established; a case study in Southeast China is provided in section 6, while the section 7 draws conclusions.

2. Literature review

Many previous studies on project portfolio optimization were carried out in a deterministic environment. However, the uncertainties in the REP portfolio optimization cannot be ignored, otherwise the decision error will occur. Such uncertainties mainly stem from the following two aspects. On the one hand, REP project portfolio optimization is a beforehand event, the performance of criteria in the future are difficult to predict accurately because of the intermittent generation and the highly volatile electricity spot prices as well as the energy policy adjustment (Maier et al., 2016). On the other hand, some evaluations in renewable REP portfolio optimization are qualitative, which largely rely on the knowledge and experience of experts. It is unrealistic for experts to make evaluations in the form of the crisp number due to the ambiguity of human-thinking. Thus, the decision makers (DMs) of power generation enterprises must make decisions on REP portfolio optimization under nondeterministic conditions. Fuzzy set (FS) theory (Zadeh, 1996) is an effective tool to model such uncertain phenomena. For example, the investment capitals and the net cash flows of the projects were presented as interval-valued fuzzy numbers instead of crisp or classical fuzzy numbers (Mohagheghi et al., 2015); triangular fuzzy numbers were applied to solve the uncertainty in the data with regards to specific criteria (Tavana et al., 2015); trapezoidal fuzzy numbers were employed to present the outcome, cost, risk, fund and constraints (Bhattacharyya et al., 2011) as well as estimating future cash flows (Carlsson, 2007) in the R&D project portfolio optimization.

It is noted that the membership grade of the above type-1 fuzzy sets is a crisp number in [0, 1]. However, decision-making on REP portfolio optimization is usually confronted with the circumstances where it is difficult to determine the exact membership function for a fuzzy set since the decision is in a more complex environment. To deal with this issue, type-2 fuzzy sets (Zadeh, 1974) which are the extension of type-1 fuzzy sets have been proposed. Type-2 fuzzy sets are described by both primary and secondary membership to provide more degrees of freedom and flexibility, and they are three-dimensional. To date, IT2FS (Mendel et al., 2006) are the most widely used T2FS, and have been applied successfully for various MCDM problems, such as supplier selection (Keshavarz Ghorabaee et al., 2017), project-critical path selection (Dorfeshan et al., 2018), transportation mode selection (Kundu et al., 2015), preparedness and response ability evaluation (Celik & Gumus, 2016), car sharing station selection (Deveci et al., 2018), hydrogen underground storage site selection (Deveci, 2018) as well as R&D project portfolio optimization (V. Mohagheghi et al., 2017) and high and new technology-project portfolio optimization (Vahid Mohagheghi et al., 2017). In addition to its applications in MCDM problems, IT2FS has also been applied to fuzzy intelligent control (Castillo, Amador-Angulo, et al., 2016; Castillo, Cervantes, et al., 2016; Castillo & Melin, 2008; Cervantes & Castillo, 2015; Ontiveros-Robles et al., 2018) and information granule formation (Sanchez et al., 2015b). These valuable researches are effectively promoting the study of IT2FS.

Whereas researches for introducing IT2FS into REP portfolio optimization field are lacking, this paper tries to fill this knowledge gap. The reason of using IT2FS is that it has the advantage of more accurate modeling of high-order uncertainty in REP portfolio optimization. In addition, compared with type-1 fuzzy sets, IT2FS focus on imprecision information and give a good representation of experts' knowledge in the form of fuzzy rules (Sanchez et al., 2015a). This is suitable for solving the problems of REP portfolio optimization by depicting the imprecision of cost variables such as the levelized cost of energy and representing the recognition of experts on some qualitative variables like public acceptance.

Reasonable weights of the decision criteria can be obtained by a variety of methods, one of which is the AHP. It permits some level of inconsistency in the judgments of DMs, which is more accordant with the circumstances of real-life decisions (Garbuzova-Schlifter & Madlener, 2016). Moreover, it allows both qualitative and quantitative variables to be compared under the same framework (Ghosh et al., 2016). Following this, how to aggregate the criteria value into an objective value is also a key issue. The WA operator (also called SAW method) is a simple and most applicable MCDM method which is known as a weighted linear combination or scoring technique. The advantage of such method is that it is a proportional linear transformation of the raw data. This means that the relative order of magnitude of the standardized scores will keep equal (Afshari et al., 2010). Therefore, combining the advantages of the AHP technique and the WA operator together, the integrated method has drawn more and more attention from researchers. A summary of the related work along with the applications of AHP-WA method is given in Table 12.1. In this study, we try to apply the AHP-WA method to determine the weight of criteria and obtain the values of objectives in the REP portfolio optimization.

Table 12.1 Related work along with the applications of AHP-WA method.

Topic	Method	Literature
Site selection of landfill	AHP-WA	(Chabuk et al., 2017; Rahmat et al., 2017)
Risk assessment of supply chain	AHP-WA	(Jaberidoost et al., 2015)
Risk assessment of bridge structures	AHP-WA-DEA	(Wang et al., 2008)
Classification of inventory.	AHP-WA-DEA	(Hadi-Vencheh & Mohamadghasemi, 2011)
Cultivation priority planning for crops	AHP-WA-TOPSIS	(Seyedmohammadi et al., 2017)
Selection of cloud vendor	AHP-WA-TOPSIS	(Liu et al., 2016)
Selection of water resources strategic	AHP-WA-PROMETHEE III	(Banihabib et al., 2017)

REP portfolio optimization on the basis of sustainable thought requires optimization of multiple objectives simultaneously including economic, environmental and social impacts maximization. There are usually two approaches to solve a multi-objective optimization problem. The first class is to transform the multiple objectives problem into a single objective problem, such as the linear weighted and constraint approach. However, the difficulty lies in the determination of the weights associated with conflicting objectives (Panda & Yegireddy, 2013). The other class of approaches is to produce a set of Pareto-optimal solutions. Since there is usually no single optimal solution in multi-objective problems, the pareto-optimal solutions are reasonable. Each vector in the Pareto-optimal solution sets is non-dominated. At present, popular Pareto dominance based multi-objective evolutionary algorithms consist of the NSGA-II, the improved strength Pareto evolutionary algorithm (SPEA2), the Pareto envelope-based selection algorithm II (PESA-II) and so on. Many of recent works on multi-objective optimization problems are analyzed by comparisons of these algorithms (Afzalirad & Rezaeian, 2016; Fattahi et al., 2015; Mousavi et al., 2016). In solving most problems, the Pareto-optimal set obtained by NSGA-II algorithm has better distribution than that obtained by PAES-II and SPEA2 algorithms, and its convergence is closer to the actual Pareto-optimal level (Li et al., 2015).

In recent years, the NSGA-II algorithm has been successfully applied to project portfolio optimization problem, such as Khalili-Damghani et al. (2013) present a NSGA-II based multi-objective framework for sustainable project portfolio optimization. Gutjahr et al. (2010) made a multi-objective decision analysis for competence-oriented project portfolio optimization based on NSGA-II algorithm. Razi (2014) optimized the risk of each project using a two-objective zero-one mathematical programming model through the NSGA-II. Wu et al. (2017) applied the NSGA-II algorithm to capture an optimal-Pareto set in the process of large-scale rooftop PV project portfolio optimization. Wu et al. (2019) applied the improved NSGA-II algorithm to obtain the optimal portfolio of distributed energy generation projects under different strategic scenario. So, there is no doubt that the usage of the NSGA-II algorithm for the renewable energy project portfolio optimization is a meaningful and beneficial work.

3. Evaluation criteria system for REP sustainable performance evaluation

The construction of evaluation criteria system has a vital role in the REP portfolio optimization. In this section, three objectives related to sustainability are selected for the analysis: economic, environmental and social impacts. Economic impacts are of great significance in REP sustainable performance evaluation; environmental impacts can gain strong interests in recent years for sustainable development; and social attitudes towards REP are influential in the decision-making process. Furthermore, criteria under each objective are identified from literature review. Fig. 12.2 is the evaluation criteria system of RPS sustainable performance evaluation. The brief explanations of these criteria are as follows:

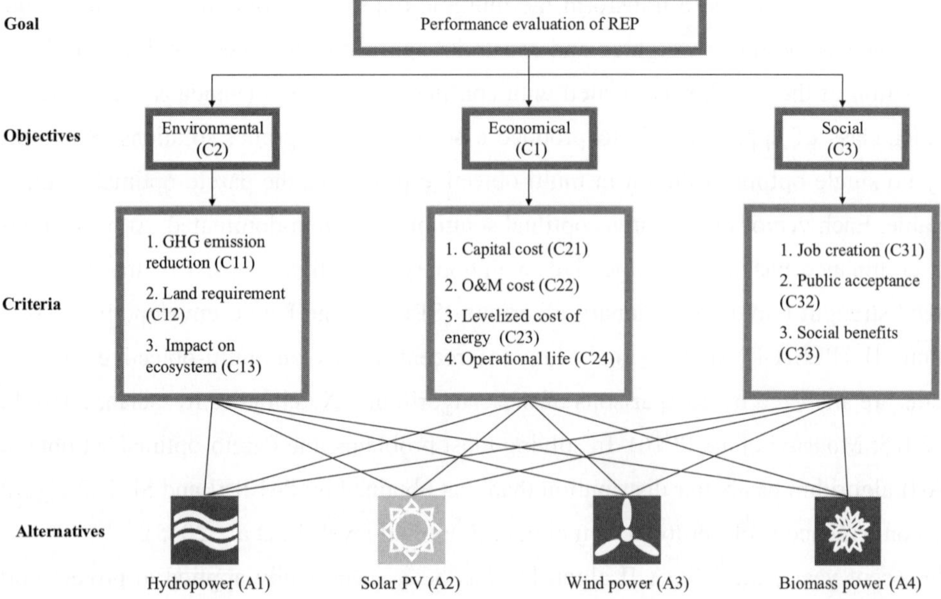

Fig. 12.2 Evaluation criteria system for REP sustainable performance evaluation.

3.1 Environmental criterion

- GHG emission reduction (C11) (Ahmad et al., 2017; Büyüközkan & Güleryüz, 2017; Çolak & Kaya, 2017; Garni et al., 2016; Haddad et al., 2017; Şengül et al., 2015; Streimikiene et al., 2012). It is calculated as the avoided emissions of each renewable energy plant. It depends not only on the performance of renewable energy technology, but on the emissions of the counterfactual technology or of the electricity system.

- Land requirement (C12) (Amer & Daim, 2011; Büyüközkan & Güleryüz, 2017; Kaya & Kahraman, 2010; Malkawi et al., 2017; Troldborg et al., 2014). Land requirement is one of the most critical factors for energy investment. Each renewable energy plant occupies some land, which may affect some farmlands or landscapes.
- Impact on ecosystem (C13) (Ahmad & Tahar, 2014; Amer & Daim, 2011; Garni et al., 2016; Haddad et al., 2017). It is a measure of environmental friendliness and the impacts of the renewable energy plant on the environment. Alternative that puts less emphasis on eco-system is considered better.

3.2 Economical criterion

- Capital cost (C21) (Amer & Daim, 2011; Büyüközkan & Güleryüz, 2017; Garni et al., 2016; Kaya & Kahraman, 2010; Şengül et al., 2015). Capital cost means the total expenditure which occurs in establishing a renewable energy plant including the equipment, labor, installation, infrastructure and commissioning costs.
- Operations and maintenance (O&M) cost (C22) (Garni et al., 2016; Haddad et al., 2017; Heo et al., 2012). Operations and maintenance cost include the plant running costs including the employees' salaries, the parts/spares costs caused by the scheduled maintenance purposes etc.
- Levelized cost of energy (C23) (Amer & Daim, 2011; Çolak & Kaya, 2017; Kaya & Kahraman, 2010; Şengül et al., 2015): This criterion includes investment, operating, fuel, maintenance and capital in the life of renewable energy source. It measures the net present values of the unit-cost of electricity over the lifetime of a generating asset.
- Operation life (C24) (Ahmad & Tahar, 2014; Çolak & Kaya, 2017; Haddad et al., 2017; Şengül et al., 2015). This criterion evaluates the service life of a renewable energy plant. It corresponds to the period during which the power plant can operate before being decommissioned.

3.3 Social criterion

- Job creation (C31) (Büyüközkan & Güleryüz, 2017; Çolak & Kaya, 2017; Streimikiene et al., 2012). Renewable energy projects generate employment opportunities especially for the local communities.
- Public acceptance (C32) (Garni et al., 2016; Haddad et al., 2017; Heo et al., 2010). Public opinions toward a type of power plant represents the public acceptance.
- Social benefits (C33) (Amer & Daim, 2011; Büyüközkan & Güleryüz, 2017; Haddad et al., 2017; Kaya & Kahraman, 2010; Şengül et al., 2015). A social benefit represents the social progress in the local community or region by initiating a power project.

4. Methodology

4.1 Basic conception of IT2FSs

Definition 1. (Chen, 2013) Let $\tilde{\tilde{A}}_i$ be a trapezoidal IT2FS. $\tilde{\tilde{A}}_i=[\tilde{A}_i^U,\tilde{A}_i^L]=\left[\left(a_{i1}^U,a_{i2}^U,a_{i3}^U,a_{i4}^U;H_1(\tilde{A}_i^U),H_2(\tilde{A}_i^U)\right),\left(a_{i1}^L,a_{i2}^L,a_{i3}^L,a_{i4}^L;H_1(\tilde{A}_i^L),H_2(\tilde{A}_i^L)\right)\right]$, where $\tilde{A}_i^U$ and $\tilde{A}_i^L$ are type-1 fuzzy sets, $a_{i1}^U,a_{i2}^U,a_{i3}^U,a_{i4}^U,a_{i1}^U,a_{i2}^U,a_{i3}^U,a_{i4}^U$ are the reference points of the $\tilde{\tilde{A}}_i$. $H_j(\tilde{A}_i^U)$ denotes the membership value of the element $a^U{}_{i(j+1)}$ in the upper trapezoidal membership function $\tilde{A}_i^U$, $1\leqslant j\leqslant 2$, $H_j(\tilde{A}_i^L)$ denotes the membership value of the element $a^L{}_{i(j+1)}$ in the lower trapezoidal membership function. A classical trapezoidal IT2FS is depicted in Fig. 12.3.

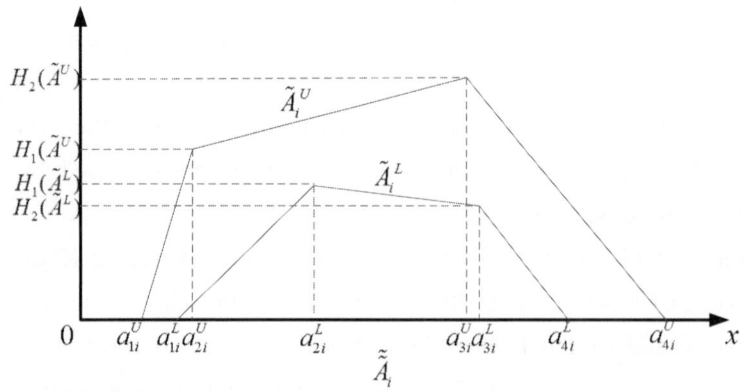

Fig. 12.3 The upper trapezoidal membership function $\tilde{A}_i^U$ and the lower trapezoidal membership function $\tilde{A}_i^L$ of the interval type-2 fuzzy set $\tilde{\tilde{A}}_i$.

4.2 IT2FWA operator

Definition 2. Let $\tilde{\tilde{A}}_i=\left[\left(a_{i1}^U,a_{i2}^U,a_{i3}^U,a_{i4}^U;H_1(\tilde{A}_i^U),H_2(\tilde{A}_i^U)\right),\left(a_{i1}^L,a_{i2}^L,a_{i3}^L,a_{i4}^L;H_1(\tilde{A}_i^L),H_2(\tilde{A}_i^L)\right)\right]$ $(i=1,2,\ldots,n)$ be a collection of trapezoidal interval type-2 fuzzy sets. The IT2FWA operator of the elements $\tilde{\tilde{A}}_1,\tilde{\tilde{A}}_2,\ldots,\tilde{\tilde{A}}_m$ shown as follows:

$$\text{TI2FWA}(\tilde{\tilde{A}}_1,\tilde{\tilde{A}}_2,\ldots,\tilde{\tilde{A}}_m)=\mathop{\oplus}_{j=1}^{m}\varpi_j\otimes\tilde{\tilde{A}}_j \tag{12-1}$$

where the ϖ_j is the corresponding weight.

The basic operation of interval type-2 fuzzy numbers are as follows:

(1) $$\tilde{\tilde{A}}_1\oplus\tilde{\tilde{A}}_2=(\tilde{A}_1^U,\tilde{A}_1^L)\oplus(\tilde{A}_2^U,\tilde{A}_2^L)=\begin{pmatrix}a_{11}{}^U+a_{21}{}^U,a_{12}{}^U+a_{22}{}^U,a_{13}{}^U+a_{23}{}^U,a_{14}{}^U+a_{24}{}^U;\min\left(H_1(\tilde{A}_1^U),H_1(\tilde{A}_2^U)\right),\min\left(H_2(\tilde{A}_1^U),H_2(\tilde{A}_2^U)\right),\\ a_{11}{}^L+a_{21}{}^L,a_{12}{}^L+a_{22}{}^L,a_{13}{}^L+a_{23}{}^L,a_{14}{}^L+a_{24}{}^L;\min\left(H_1(\tilde{A}_1^L),H_1(\tilde{A}_2^L)\right),\min\left(H_2(\tilde{A}_1^L),H_2(\tilde{A}_2^L)\right)\end{pmatrix}$$

(2) $\tilde{\tilde{A}}_1 \otimes \tilde{\tilde{A}}_2 = (\tilde{A}_1^U, \tilde{A}_1^L) \otimes (\tilde{A}_2^U, \tilde{A}_2^L) =$

$$\begin{pmatrix} a_{11}{}^U \times a_{21}{}^U, a_{12}{}^U \times a_{22}{}^U, a_{13}{}^U \times a_{23}{}^U, a_{14}{}^U \times a_{24}{}^U; \min\left(H_1(\tilde{A}_1^U), H_1(\tilde{A}_2^U)\right), \min\left(H_2(\tilde{A}_1^U), H_2(\tilde{A}_2^U)\right), \\ a_{11}{}^L \times a_{21}{}^L, a_{12}{}^L \times a_{22}{}^L, a_{13}{}^L \times a_{23}{}^L, a_{14}{}^L \times a_{24}{}^L; \min\left(H_1(\tilde{A}_1^L), H_1(\tilde{A}_2^L)\right), \min\left(H_2(\tilde{A}_1^L), H_2(\tilde{A}_2^L)\right) \end{pmatrix};$$

$$(3)\ \ k \otimes \tilde{\tilde{A}}_1 = \begin{pmatrix} \left(ka_{11}{}^U, ka_{12}{}^U, ka_{13}{}^U, ka_{14}{}^U; H_1(\tilde{A}_1^U), H_2(\tilde{A}_1^U)\right), \\ \left(ka_{11}{}^L, ka_{12}{}^L, ka_{13}{}^L, ka_{14}{}^L; H_1(\tilde{A}_1^L), H_2(\tilde{A}_1^L)\right) \end{pmatrix}.$$

4.3 IT2F-AHP technique

AHP, proposed by Saaty (1980) is a popular MCDM method for its rational hierarchy structure and clear logic relations. Subsequently, Buckley (1985) extended the Saaty's AHP into fuzzy AHP by integrating with fuzzy sets. In this paper, AHP method under Interval type-2 fuzzy set environment is employed to obtain fuzzy weights of the criteria.

The steps of IT2F-AHP technique are presented as follows:

Step 1. The pair wise comparison matrix under IT2FSs is constructed among all criteria in the hierarchical structure. The linguistic terms and their corresponding IT2Fs are shown in Table 12.2.

Table 12.2 Linguistic terms for importance weights of factors (Kahraman, 2014).

Linguistic variables	IT2F	Reciprocal IT2F
Absolutely Strong (AS)	((7, 8, 9, 9; 1, 1), (7.2, 8.2, 8.8, 9; 0.8, 0.8))	((0.11, 0.11, 0.12, 0.14; 1, 1), (0.11, 0.11, 0.12, 0.14; 0.8, 0.8))
Very Strong (VS)	((5, 6, 8, 9; 1, 1), (5.2, 6.2, 7.8, 8.8; 0.8, 0.8))	((0.11, 0.12, 0.17, 0.2; 1, 1), (0.11, 0.13, 0.16, 0.19; 0.8, 0.8))
Fairly Strong (FS)	((3, 4, 6, 7; 1, 1), (3.2, 4.2, 5.8, 6.8; 0.8, 0.8))	((0.14, 0.17, 0.25, 0.33; 1, 1), (0.15, 0.17, 0.24, 0.31; 0.8, 0.8))
Slightly Strong (SS)	((1, 2, 4, 5; 1, 1), (1.2, 2.2, 3.8, 4.8; 0.8, 0.8))	((0.2, 0.25, 0.5, 1; 1, 1), 0.21, 0.26, 0.45, 0.83; 0.8, 0.8))
Exactly Equal (E)	((1, 1, 1, 1; 1, 1), (1, 1, 1, 1; 1, 1))	((1, 1, 1, 1; 1, 1), (1, 1, 1, 1; 1, 1))

Step 2. Test the consistency of the IT2FSs pair wise comparison. In this manner, the IT2FSs matrices are defuzzified as Eq. (12-4) (Kahraman, 2014) and checked for consistency.

$$\text{Defuzzified}(\tilde{\tilde{a}}_i) = \frac{\dfrac{(a_{i4}^U - a_{i1}^U) + \left(H_1(\tilde{A}_i^U) \bullet a_{i2}^U - a_{i1}^U\right) + \left(H_2(\tilde{A}_i^U) \bullet a_{i3}^U - a_{i1}^U\right)}{4} + a_{i1}^U + \dfrac{(a_{i4}^L - a_{i1}^L) + \left(H_1(\tilde{A}_i^L) \bullet a_{i2}^L - a_{i1}^L\right) + \left(H_2(\tilde{A}_i^L) \bullet a_{i3}^L - a_{i1}^L\right)}{4} + a_{i1}^L}{2} \quad (12\text{-}2)$$

In order to identify the consistency ratio (CR) of a matrix, first the matrix consistency index CI is found as follows.

$$CI = (\lambda_{\max} - m) / (m - 1) \tag{12-3}$$

where $Aw = \lambda_{\max} w$, $\lambda_{\max}$ is the largest or principal eigen value of the A decision matrix of pairwise comparison; m is matrix order.

Then, the consistency index of a randomly generated reciprocal matrix with reciprocal forces is called the random index (RI) that depends on (m) and is calculated using the matrix order (m) and the table explained by Saaty (Saaty, 1980). It turns out that A is consistent if the value of CR less than 0.1 is considered acceptable. The matrix consistency ratio CR is calculated using:

$$CR = CI / RI \tag{12-4}$$

Step 3. Aggregate the evaluations of DMs by using geometric mean.

$$\tilde{\tilde{A}}_{ij} = \left[\tilde{\tilde{A}}^1 \otimes \cdots \otimes \tilde{\tilde{A}}^n \right]^{1/n} \tag{12-5}$$

where $\sqrt[n]{\tilde{\tilde{A}}_{ij}} = \begin{pmatrix} \sqrt[n]{\tilde{\tilde{A}}_{ij1}{}^U}, \sqrt[n]{\tilde{\tilde{A}}_{ij2}{}^U}, \sqrt[n]{\tilde{\tilde{A}}_{ij3}{}^U}, \sqrt[n]{\tilde{\tilde{A}}_{ij4}{}^U}; H_1(a_{ij}{}^U), H_2(a_{ij}{}^U), \\ \sqrt[n]{\tilde{\tilde{A}}_{ij1}{}^L}, \sqrt[n]{\tilde{\tilde{A}}_{ij2}{}^L}, \sqrt[n]{\tilde{\tilde{A}}_{ij3}{}^L}, \sqrt[n]{\tilde{\tilde{A}}_{ij4}{}^L}; H_1(a_{ij}{}^L), H_2(a_{ij}{}^L) \end{pmatrix}$

Step 4. Calculated the fuzzy weights of each criterion as follows.

$$\tilde{\tilde{w}}_i = \tilde{\tilde{r}}_i \times (\tilde{\tilde{r}}_1 + \tilde{\tilde{r}}_2 + \ldots + \tilde{\tilde{r}}_m)^{-1} \tag{12-6}$$

where $\tilde{\tilde{r}}_i$ represents the geometric mean of each row of matrix.

4.4 NSGA-II optimization algorithm

NSGA-II is a fast and elitist optimization technology. The advantage of the NSGA-II is that multiple objectives are reduced to a single fitness measure by the creation of number of fronts, sorted according to non-domination.

In order to effectively rank individuals, Deb et al. (2002) proposed two algorithms, non-dominated sorting algorithm (NDSA) and crowded distance sorting algorithm (CDSA). The former algorithm applies the concept of dominance to compare and sort individuals. It divides individuals into several fronts F_i, with rank i. The higher the fronts are, the better the individual is. In addition, the concept of crowding distance is used to rank individuals belonging to the same front. It is defined as the average distance between a specific individual and two adjacent individuals. The crowding distance can distribute the individuals in the crowded part to a lower level, thus increasing the diversity among individuals (Rajabi-Bahaabadi et al., 2015). The procedure of the NSGA-II algorithm can be expressed in Fig. 12.4.

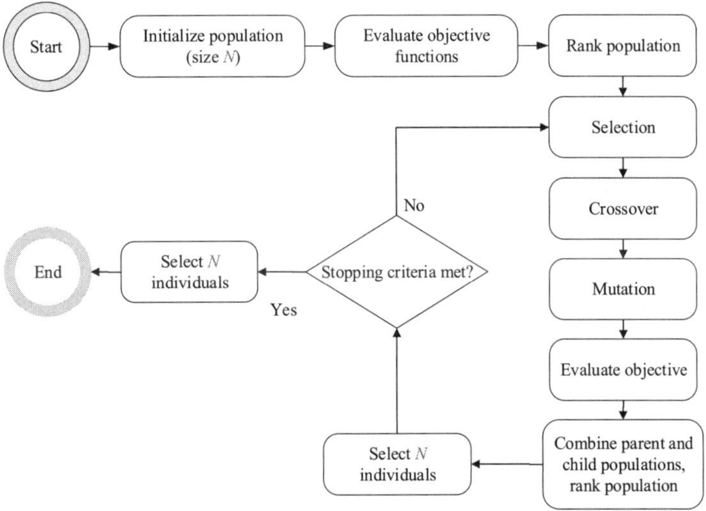

Fig. 12.4 Flowchart of the NSGA-II algorithm.

5. Decision framework for portfolio optimization of REP

Since a single MCDM method is not enough to solve the complex problem of REP portfolio optimization, a hybrid decision framework integrating the IT2F-AHP technique, the IT2FWA operator, and the NSGA-II algorithm together in a systematic framework is proposed. The proposed framework includes three stages of a preparations stage, an objective value aggregation stage and a project portfolio optimization stage. Detailed descriptions of the corresponding steps at each stage are given in subsections 5.1 to 5.3.

5.1 Preparatory stage

The preparatory stage is composed of the following two steps:

Step 1. Establish a decision-making committee.

In this step, a decision-making committee is established and includes three kinds of roles: internal senior managers, internal programmers, and an external expert group with academic background of REP management. Their duties are clarified in Table 12.3.

Table 12.3 The duties of roles.

Roles	Duties
Senior managers	Identify potential alternatives
	Determine the optimal portfolio
Expert group	Assess the relative weights of the criteria
	Assess the performance of alternatives in terms of each criterion. Assess the cost synergies between alternatives

Continued

Roles	Duties
Programmers	Aggregate the experts' opinions
	Check the consistency of the matrixes and calculate the relative weights of the criteria, and then make an aggregation
	Calculate the strategic alignment degree of each alternative
	Aggregate the experts' opinions on SIC
	Solve the multi-objective integer nonlinear programming equations and provide a Pareto-optimal set

Moreover, it is worth mentioning that the internal opinions between senior managers or experts in the expert group are inevitably disagreed. On the situation of the senior manager disagreement, the Delphi technique is used for obtaining a consensus from several senior managers through a meeting. The Delphi technique comprises of the following phases: ①a problem is posed to a panel of members; ②members expressed their own views to address the problem; ③the views gathered are analyzed and the feedback is sent towards members; ④the previous two steps are repeated for several rounds till an agreement is achieved. Nevertheless, the Delphi technique is invalid for the latter case since it's always difficult to gather all the external experts in a meeting. So, the WA operator is used here to aggregate experts' opinions.

Step 2. Form a set of alternatives.

The establishment of a complete set of alternatives is conducive to the enterprise to the discovery of valuable projects. The following three ways can be adopted to find projects as many as possible: ①employee recommendation; ②questionnaire investigation; and ③field investing-ation.

Step 3. Collect information about the alternatives and criteria.

In order to make the decision more accurate, it is necessary to provide as much information as possible for the experts on the alternative and criteria. The information is mainly obtained from reports and literatures.

5.2 Objective value aggregation stage

Step 4. Obtain and aggregate the performance of alternatives.

(1) Assess the performance of alternatives regarding each criterion.

In this step, according to the collected information and their experiences, experts in the expert group assess the performance of alternatives regarding each criterion. Linguistic variables are adopted by experts in this assessment process since linguistic variables are much closer to humans' thinking and knowledge, and can also reduce the decision-making pressure of experts (Wu, Xu, Li, et al., 2018).

(2) Convert the linguistic variables into IT2FSs.

For the transformation between linguistic terms and IT2FSs, it is necessary to define their mapping relations. The relations between linguistic terms and their corresponding IT2FSs are depicted in Table 12.4.

Table 12.4 Linguistic variables and their corresponding IT2FSs (Qin et al., 2016).

Linguistic variables	Trapezoidal IT2FSs
Very Low (VL)	(0, 0, 0, 0.1; 1, 1), (0, 0, 0, 0.05; 0.9, 0.9)
Low (L)	(0, 0.1, 0.1, 0.3; 1, 1), (0.05, 0.1, 0.1, 0.2; 0.9, 0.9)
Medium Low (ML)	(0.1, 0.3, 0.3, 0.5; 1, 1), (0.2, 0.3, 0.3, 0.4; 0.9, 0.9)
Medium (M)	(0.3, 0.5, 0.5, 0.7; 1, 1), (0.4, 0.5, 0.5, 0.6; 0.9, 0.9)
Medium high (MH)	(0.5, 0.7, 0.7, 0.9; 1, 1), (0.6, 0.7, 0.7, 0.8; 0.9, 0.9)
High (H)	(0.7, 0.9, 0.9, 1; 1, 1), (0.8, 0.9, 0.9, 0.95; 0.9, 0.9)
Very High (VL)	(0.9, 1, 1, 1; 1, 1), (0.95, 1, 1, 1; 0.9, 0.9)

(3) Aggregate the experts' preferences using IT2FWA operator.

The integrated decision-making matrix is obtained through aggregating experts' preferences using Eq. (12-1).

Step 5. Determine the weights of the criteria.

The weights of the criteria are determined using the IT2F-AHP technique as introduced in section 4.3.

Step 6. Calculate the objective values of each alternative.

The environmental, economic and social objective values of each alternative are got by using the IT2FWA operator.

5.3 Project portfolio optimization stage

Step 7. Assess the cost synergies between alternatives.

Assessing synergies between projects is particularized in the context of selecting a REP portfolio. REPs within the same enterprise often share information, technology, people and organizational properties, so there are more or less cost synergies between projects. In many project portfolio decision-making situations, synergies are evaluated in a qualitative way (Zhang, 2016). So, similarly, linguistic variables are used by experts to assess the cost synergies between alternatives. Then, the linguistic variables are converted into IT2FSs by using the mapping relations given in the Table 12.4. After that, the IT2FWA operator is employ to aggregate the IT2FSs matrices.

Step 8. Establish the multi-objective programming model.

REP portfolio optimization with the sustainability perspective requires simultaneous optimization of multiple objectives. So, a multi-objective zero-one integer programming model is formulated as follows:

$$\max\{\sum \tilde{\tilde{S}}_i(x)^j\}$$
$$\text{s.t.}\begin{cases}\sum_{i=1}^{n}\tilde{\tilde{C}}_i x_i - \tilde{\tilde{I}}_C(x) \leqslant C \\ x_j = \begin{cases}1, \text{ selected} \\ 0, \text{ not selected}\end{cases}\end{cases} \tag{12-7}$$

where the objective is to simultaneously maximize the environment, economic and social objectives of a portfolio, $\tilde{\tilde{S}}_i$ is the fuzzy value of project i in term of objective j $(j=1,2,3)$. C is the total cost constraint, and $\tilde{\tilde{C}}_i$ represents the fuzzy investment cost of project i, $\tilde{\tilde{I}}_C(x)$ is a cost reduction when two projects i and j are implemented at the same time.

Since it is difficult to deal with a multi-objective model when it involves fuzzy information (Zeng et al., 2015), an effective way is to apply a defuzzified method to transform the fuzzy variable into a deterministic one. So, the Eq. (12-2) is applied to remove the fuzziness.

Step 9. Solve the zero-one multi-objective integer nonlinear programming equations The NSGA-II is operated with the following parameters:

- Encoding style: Binary symbol sets composed of 0 and 1.
- Probability of single-point crossover operator: 0.9.
- Probability of bit-wise mutation operator: 0.01.
- Initial size: 500 individuals.
- Genetic algebra: 200 generations.

6. Case study

6.1 Background

The southeast coastal area of China is a strong economic region. However, the region's fossil resources are very poor, and electricity is often inadequate. Development of renewable energy has become a promising scheme . Under this background, a state-owned power generation enterprise located in Guangdong province plans to construct and invest some new REPs. As mentioned early, a decision-making committee is established. The invited experts' profiles are presented in Table 12.5 Since experiences and titles of the experts are at the same level, the weights of these experts are assumed to be equal.

Table 12.5 Expert profile details.

Experts	Major	Academic title	Age	Work time
E1	REP management	Doctor	46	15
E2	REP management	Doctor	45	15
E3	REP management	Doctor	42	14

After a round of employee recommendation, questionnaire investigation and field investigation, a total of 22 potential projects are initially identified. After the feasibility study, 10 projects of them are excluded and only 12 projects are economic feasibility. The economic feasibility means that the internal return rate of project is greater than the social discount rate.

The relative information of the 12 projects is presented in Fig. 12.5. Moreover, the reasonable range values of various renewable energy technology performance on the quantitative criteria are collected and given in the Appendix A.

Project	Installed capacity	Budgetary cost
P1	400	3.5
P2	250	2.5
P3	180	1.5
P4	150	1.5
P5	120	1.15
P6	100	0.97
P7	58	0.55
P8	80	0.76
P9	65	0.62
P10	60	0.6
P11	180	1.05
P12	50	0.5

Note: The unit of installed capacity is MW; the unit of budgetary cost is billion yuan

Fig. 12.5 Relative information of the 12 projects.

6.2 Decision-making process

Experts individually assess the performances of the 12 alternatives on the quantitative and qualitative criteria. Their judgments are shown in Table 12.6 to Table 12.7. After that, the difference opinions are aggregated using the IT2FWA operator. The aggregated values are given in the Appendix B.

Table 12.6 Evaluation ratings of the alternatives on the quantitative criteria.

	C11 (10•T/h)	C12 (Km^2)	C21 (10^7•USD)	C22 (10^5•USD/a)	C23 (10^3•USD/h)	C24 (Year)	C31 (Jobs)
P1	204-1000	14-4200	46-56	48-168	32-84	30-30	280-10000
	VH, VH, H	MH, H, VH	VH, VH, VH	M, MH, H	VH, VH, H	ML, M, M	VH, MH, H
P2	127.5-625	8.75-2625	28.75-35	30-10.5	20-52.5	30-30	175-6250
	H, H, MH	H, VH, H	MH, H, H	L, ML, L	MH, VH, MH	ML, M, M	H, MH, MH
P3	91.8-450	6.3-1890	20.7-25.2	21.6-75.6	14.4-37.8	30-30	126-4500
	H, H, MH	ML, M, M	M, M, L	M, MH, MH	ML, L, ML	ML, M, M	H, MH, ML
P4	76.5-375	5.25-1575	17.25-21	18-63	12-31.5	30-30	105-3750
	M, H, M	ML, M, ML	L, L, L	M, MH, M	ML, L, ML	ML, M, M	H, MH, ML
P5	15.3-75	12-14.4	11.4-15	20.77-37.2	9-44.4	40-40	108-480
	L, ML, ML	VL, L, VL	L, VL, VL	M, ML, M	ML, L, L	H, MH, H	ML, ML, L

Continued

	C11 (10•T/h)	C12 (Km^2)	C21 (10^7•USD)	C22 (10^5•USD/a)	C23 (10^3•USD/h)	C24 (Year)	C31 (Jobs)
P6	10.2-50	10-12	9.5-12.5	17.31-31	7.5-27	40-40	90-400
	L, L, ML	VL, L, VL	VL, L, VL	ML, L, ML	ML, L, L	H, MH, H	ML, L, L
P7	3.01-14.75	5.8-6.96	5.51-7.25	10.04-17.98	4.35-21.46	40-40	52.2-232
	VL, VL, VL	VL, VL, VL	VL, VL, VL	VL, VL, VL	ML, ML, L	H, MH, H	VL, L, L
P8	11.64-148.44	400-400	16-20	51.04-67.76	3.2-17.6	20-25	896-1576
	L, ML, L	M, MH, H	L, ML, L	VH, VH, H	VL, ML, ML	L, L, VL	M, MH, M
P9	9.7-123.7	325-325	13-16.25	41.47-55.06	2.6-14.3	20-25	728-1280.5
	L, ML, L	M, M, ML	L, L, L	H, H, MH	VL, L, VL	L, L, VL	M, MH, M
P0	4.66-59.38	300-300	12-15	38.28-50.82	2.4-13.2	20-25	672-1182
	L, VL, L	M, MH, MH	L, VL, L	MH, M, MH	VL, L, VL	L, L, VL	M, M, M
P11	2.91-37.11	135-135	18-63	81-93.6	4.5-19.8	40-50	162-216
	VL, VL, L	ML, ML, L	ML, M, MH	VH, VH, VH	L, L, L	H, H, MH	L, VL, L
P12	2.13-27.21	37.5-37.5	5-17.5	22.5-26	1.25-5.5	40-50	45-60
	VL, L, VL	L, VL, L	VL, VL, L	ML, L, L	VL, VL, VL	H, H, MH	VL, VL, VL

Table 12.7 Evaluation ratings of the alternatives on the qualitative sub-criteria.

	C13	C32	C33
P1	ML, L, L	L, H, H	ML, M, H
P2	ML, ML, L	ML, L, ML	L, ML, ML
P3	ML, M, M	H, MH, ML	MH, H, H
P4	M, M, MH	L, ML, M	L, ML, ML
P5	L, ML, ML	ML, L, ML	MH, H, ML
P6	L, L, L	ML, ML, ML	H, ML, ML
P7	ML, L, ML	M, M, ML	ML, H, ML
P8	H, MH, M	VL, L, L	L, L, ML
P9	H, H, H	M, M, L	ML, ML, L
P10	MH, ML, M	M, ML, M	ML, M, M
P11	H, VH, H	H, MH, M	MH, H, H
P12	VH, H, H	M, ML, MH	ML, ML, H

Subsequently, experts individually make the importance comparison of the criteria, as shown in Table 12.8 to Table 12.10. Consistency check is carried out using Eq. (12-4) to Eq. (12-4) and results show all the comparison matrixes pass the consistency test.

Table 12.8 Importance comparison of the criteria within environemental aspect.

Criteria	C11	C12	C13
C11	E, E, E	FS, SS, FS	VS, FS, FS
C12	1/FS, 1/SS, 1/FS	E, E, E	E, SS, E
C13	1/VS, 1/FS, 1/FS	1/E, 1/SS, 1/E	E, E, E

Table 12.9 Importance comparison of the criteria within economic aspect.

Criteria	C21	C22	C23	C24
C21	E, E, E	FS, SS, SS	E, SS, E	AS, VS, FS
C22	1/FS, 1/SS, 1/SS	E, E, E	1/SS, 1/SS, 1/SS	SS, FS, FS
C23	1/E, 1/SS, 1/E	SS, SS, SS	E, E, E	FS, SS, SS
C24	1/AS, 1/VS, 1/FS	1/SS, 1/FS, 1/FS	1/FS, 1/SS, 1/SS	E, E, E

Table 12.10 Importance comparison of the criteria within social aspect.

Criteria	C31	C32	C33
C31	E, E, E	SS, 1/SS, E	E, SS, SS
C32	1/SS, SS, 1/E	E, E, E	E, SS, E
C33	1/E, 1/SS, 1/SS	1/E, 1/SS, 1/E	E, E, E

Following this, the fuzzy weights of the criteria are calculated using Eq. (12-5)and Eq. (12-6)and given in Table 12.11.

Table 12.11 Fuzzy weights of the criteria.

Criteria	Fuzzy weight
C11	((0.37, 0.53, 0.93, 1.25); 1, 1, (0.4, 0.56, 0.88, 1.2); 0.8, 0.8)
C12	((0.1, 0.14, 0.23, 0.32); 1, 1, (0.11, 0.14, 0.21, 0.29); 0.8, 0.8)
C13	((0.08, 0.1, 0.16, 0.22); 1, 1, (0.09, 0.1, 0.15, 0.21); 0.8, 0.8)
C21	((0.21, 0.34, 0.73, 1.14); 1, 1, (0.16, 0.36, 0.75, 1.85); 0.8, 0.8)
C22	((0.05, 0.09, 0.26, 0.55); 1, 1, (0.03, 0.09, 0.23, 0.57); 0.8, 0.8)
C23	((0.1, 0.19, 0.47, 0.8); 1, 1, (0.07, 0.18, 0.47, 1.11); 0.8, 0.8)
C24	((0.02, 0.03, 0.07, 0.13); 1, 1, (0.01, 0.03, 0.06, 0.08); 0.8, 0.8)
C31	((0.2, 0.31, 0.54, 0.76); 1, 1, (0.22, 0.33, 0.51, 0.7); 0.8, 0.8)
C32	((0.2, 0.28, 0.46, 0.63); 1, 1, (0.22, 0.3, 0.44, 0.59); 0.8, 0.8)
C33	((0.14, 0.18, 0.29, 0.44); 1, 1, (0.15, 0.19, 0.28, 0.4); 0.8, 0.8)

Based on the performances of the projects on criteria and the weights of criteria, the performances of the alternatives on the three objectives are aggregated using the IT2FWA operator and shown in Table 12.12.

Table 12.12 Performances of the alternatives on the three objectives.

	Environmental objective	Economic objective	Social objective
P1	((0.37, 0.61, 1.06, 1.56); 1, 1, (0.44, 0.65, 1, 1.39); 0.8, 0.8)	((0.11, 0.3, 0.69, 1.59); 1, 1, (0.11, 0.31, 0.7, 2.04); 0.8, 0.8)	((0.06, 0.18, 0.31, 0.76); 1, 1, (0.1, 0.19, 0.29, 0.55); 0.8, 0.8)
P2	((0.28, 0.53, 0.91, 1.48); 1, 1, (0.36, 0.56, 0.86, 1.27); 0.8, 0.8)	((0.09, 0.26, 0.59, 1.44); 1, 1, (0.09, 0.27, 0.59, 1.78); 0.8, 0.8)	((0.12, 0.31, 0.53, 1.09); 1, 1, (0.18, 0.33, 0.5, 0.85); 0.8, 0.8)
P3	((0.3, 0.57, 0.99, 1.62); 1, 1, (0.39, 0.61, 0.94, 1.38); 0.8, 0.8)	((0.11, 0.3, 0.67, 1.58); 1, 1, (0.11, 0.31, 0.67, 1.94); 0.8, 0.8)	((0.18, 0.41, 0.68, 1.3); 1, 1, (0.26, 0.43, 0.65, 1.04); 0.8, 0.8)

Continued

	Environmental objective	Economic objective	Social objective
P4	((0.23, 0.46, 0.8, 1.41); 1, 1, (0.3, 0.49, 0.76, 1.16); 0.8, 0.8)	((0.09, 0.26, 0.59, 1.45); 1, 1, (0.09, 0.27, 0.59, 1.71); 0.8, 0.8)	((0.19, 0.43, 0.72, 1.35); 1, 1, (0.27, 0.45, 0.68, 1.08); 0.8, 0.8)
P5	((0.16, 0.33, 0.56, 1.07); 1, 1, (0.22, 0.35, 0.53, 0.85); 0.8, 0.8)	((0.04, 0.18, 0.41, 1.23); 1, 1, (0.05, 0.18, 0.39, 1.26); 0.8, 0.8)	((0.29, 0.56, 0.94, 1.62); 1, 1, (0.38, 0.59, 0.89, 1.35); 0.8, 0.8)
P6	((0.16, 0.31, 0.51, 1); 1, 1, (0.21, 0.32, 0.49, 0.8); 0.8, 0.8)	((0.09, 0.27, 0.63, 1.59); 1, 1, (0.09, 0.27, 0.62, 1.8); 0.8, 0.8)	((0.33, 0.62, 1.05, 1.75); 1, 1, (0.42, 0.66, 0.99, 1.48); 0.8, 0.8)
P7	((0.14, 0.21, 0.35, 0.66); 1, 1, (0.16, 0.22, 0.33, 0.53); 0.8, 0.8)	((0.07, 0.24, 0.56, 1.46); 1, 1, (0.07, 0.24, 0.54, 1.6); 0.8, 0.8)	((0.39, 0.67, 1.14, 1.78); 1, 1, (0.47, 0.71, 1.08, 1.56); 0.8, 0.8)
P8	((0.03, 0.14, 0.24, 0.69); 1, 1, (0.07, 0.15, 0.23, 0.47); 0.8, 0.8)	((0.04, 0.13, 0.32, 1.04); 1, 1, (0.04, 0.12, 0.29, 0.94); 0.8, 0.8)	((0.13, 0.25, 0.41, 0.82); 1, 1, (0.17, 0.26, 0.39, 0.64); 0.8, 0.8)
P9	((0.05, 0.17, 0.3, 0.77); 1, 1, (0.1, 0.18, 0.28, 0.55); 0.8, 0.8)	((0.05, 0.18, 0.43, 1.3); 1, 1, (0.05, 0.17, 0.4, 1.27); 0.8, 0.8)	((0.18, 0.34, 0.56, 1.01); 1, 1, (0.23, 0.36, 0.53, 0.82); 0.8, 0.8)
P10	((0.04, 0.13, 0.22, 0.63); 1, 1, (0.08, 0.14, 0.21, 0.44); 0.8, 0.8)	((0.05, 0.18, 0.44, 1.33); 1, 1, (0.05, 0.17, 0.41, 1.3); 0.8, 0.8)	((0.2, 0.4, 0.67, 1.17); 1, 1, (0.26, 0.42, 0.63, 0.96); 0.8, 0.8)
P11	((0.06, 0.13, 0.21, 0.56); 1, 1, (0.08, 0.13, 0.2, 0.4); 0.8, 0.8)	((0.25, 0.55, 1.3, 2.51); 1, 1, (0.21, 0.56, 1.28, 3.29); 0.8, 0.8)	((0.23, 0.4, 0.66, 1.14); 1, 1, (0.29, 0.42, 0.63, 0.95); 0.8, 0.8)
P12	((0.08, 0.15, 0.25, 0.58); 1, 1, (0.1, 0.16, 0.24, 0.43); 0.8, 0.8)	((0.26, 0.55, 1.29, 2.52); 1, 1, (0.21, 0.56, 1.27, 3.24); 0.8, 0.8)	((0.4, 0.69, 1.16, 1.79); 1, 1, (0.48, 0.73, 1.1, 1.57); 0.8, 0.8)

Cost synergies between two projects are assessed by the form of linguistic variables. The cost synergy matrix is an upper triangular matrix, as shown in the following matrix. Similarly, the linguistic variables are converted into IT2FSs using the mapping relations in the Table 12.4. Subsequently, IT2FSs are aggregating based on the IT2FWA operator.

	P1	P2	P3	P4	P5	P6	P7	P8	P9	P10	P11	P12
P1	-	L,VL,L	ML,L,L	VL,L,ML	-	-	-	-	-	-	-	-
P2		-	L,VL,M	VL,N,VL	-	-	-	N,VL,H	-	-	-	-
P3			-	VL,L,L	VL,VL,ML	-	-	-	-	-	-	-
P4				-	VL,VL,VL	VL,L,VL	-	-	-	-	VL,VL,VL	-
P5					-	VL,VL,L	N,N,VL	-	-	-	VL,N,N	-
P6						-	VL,VL,N	-	-	-	-	-
P7							-	-	-	N,N,VL	-	VL,VL,VL
P8								-	VL,VL,VL	L,VL,N	-	-
P9									-	VL,VL,N	-	-
P10										-	-	-
P11											-	VL,VL,VL
P12												-

Note: the letter N means the synergy is very small and can be ignored, the symbol "-"means no synergy exists.

Finally, inputting the defuzzied values of objectives, costs and cost synergies into the programming model established in the Eq. (12-7). And the NSGA-II is operated by MATLAB 7.1 software to solve this model.

As shown in Fig. 12.6, three homogeneously distributed solutions are obtained: (0, 0, 0, 0, 0, 1, 1, 1, 0, 1, 1, 1), (0, 0, 0, 0, 1, 0, 1, 1, 1, 0, 1, 1) and (0, 0, 1, 0, 0, 1, 1, 0, 1, 1, 0, 1). Thus, the

REP portfolios (A6, A7, A8, A10, A11, A12), (A5, A7, A8, A9, A11, A12) and (A3, A6, A7, A9, A10, A12) are selected for senior managers to make final decisions. It is easy to find that the alternatives A7 and A12 are common choices between them. In addition, none of them performs equally well on all three objectives considered. The portfolio (A6, A7, A8, A10, A11, A12) ranks first in economic objective, while the portfolio (A3, A6, A7, A9, A10, A12) is inclined towards environmental and social objective. So, the final decisions depend on the preference of the senior managers.

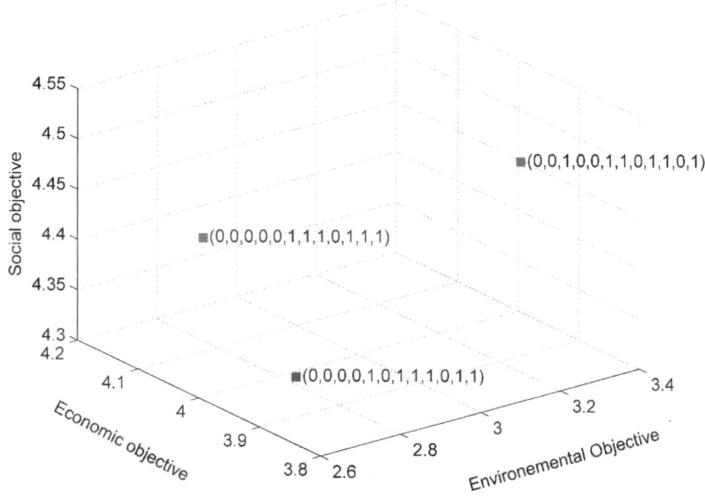

Fig. 12.6 Non-dominated solutions.

6.3 Discussion

In this section, a comparative analysis and a scenario analysis are conducted to highlight the advantages of the proposed framework.

6.3.1 Comparative analysis

The comparative analysis with type-1 fuzzy set is carried out to demonstrate the necessity of using IT2F number. A classical type-1 fuzzy set called the trapezoidal fuzzy number is employed here. Without loss of generality, the fuzzy weights of these criteria are obtained by using the triangular intuitionistic fuzzy analytic hierarchy process (TF-AHP) technique, and the aggregated fuzzy values of REPs in term of the three objectives are determined by the triangular intuitionistic fuzzy weighted averaging (TF-WA) operator. The transformation relations between linguistic variables (for alternative performance evaluation) and their corresponding trapezoidal fuzzy numbers are shown in Table 12.13. Besides, the linguistic terms for weight determination and their corresponding trapezoidal fuzzy numbers are presented in Table 12.14.

Table 12.13 Linguistic variables and their corresponding trapezoidal fuzzy numbers (Ju & Wang, 2013).

Linguistic variables	Trapezoidal fuzzy numbers
Very Low (VL)	(0, 0, 1, 2)
Low (L)	(1, 2, 2, 3)
Medium Low (ML)	(2, 3, 4, 5)
Medium (M)	(4, 5, 5, 6)
Medium high (MH)	(5, 6, 7, 8)
High (H)	(6, 7, 7, 8)
Very High (VL)	(7, 8, 9, 9)

Table 12.14 Linguistic terms for importance weights of factors (Zheng et al., 2012).

Linguistic variables	Trapezoidal fuzzy numbers	Reciprocal trapezoidal fuzzy numbers
Absolutely Strong (AS)	(8, 17/2, 9, 9)	(1/9, 1/9, 2/17, 1/8)
Very Strong (VS)	(6, 13/2, 15/2, 8)	(1/8, 2/15, 2/13, 1/6)
Fairly Strong (FS)	(4, 9/2, 11/2, 6)	(1/6, 2/11, 2/9, 1/4)
Slightly Strong (SS)	(2, 5/2, 7/2, 4)	(1/4, 2/7, 2/5, 1/2)
Exactly Equal (E)	(1, 1, 1, 1)	(1, 1, 1, 1)

The input data are derived from Table 12.6 to Table 12.10. Then, the output portfolio optimization results are calculated and shown as follows:

- $X^{(1)}$=(0, 0, 0, 0, 0, 1, 1, 1, 0, 1, 1, 1) with the environmental, economic and social objective values of (2.698, 4.112, 4.517).
- $X^{(2)}$=(0, 0, 1, 0, 0, 1, 1, 0, 1, 1, 0, 1) with the environmental, economic and social objective values of (3.124, 3.696, 4.609).

From these results, we can obviously see that the obtained portfolios under the triangular intuitionistic fuzzy environment are all included under the situation of interval type-2 fuzzy environment. However, another selected portfolio (0, 0, 0, 0, 1, 0, 1, 1, 1, 0, 1, 1) is not present under the triangular intuitionistic fuzzy environment. In addition, the objective values with higher uncertainties are smaller than the ones with lower uncertainties. This observation illustrates the advantages of considering high-ordered uncertainties of REP projects.

6.3.2 Scenario analysis

The scenario analysis is conducted to observe the portfolio optimization results under the following scenarios:

- Scenario 1. Under the environmental objective and economic objective.
- Scenario 2. Under the environmental objective and social objective.
- Scenario 3. Under the economic objectives and social objective.
- Scenario 4. Under the environmental objective.
- Scenario 5. Under the economic objective.

- Scenario 6. Under the social objective.

The selected portfolios and their objective values are shown in Table 12.15. It can be found that one selected portfolio (0, 0, 1, 0, 0, 1, 1, 0, 1, 1, 0, 1) under the sustainable scenario is contained under the scenario 3. However, the other two selected portfolios do not exist under the virtual scenarios. This observation illustrates the importance of the consideration of the three sustainable objectives at the same time in the process of REP portfolio optimization.

Table 12.15 Portfolios in different scenarios.

Scenarios	Portfolios	Objectives
Scenario 1	[0 0 0 1 0 1 1 1 0 1 0 1]	[2.977, 3.704, 0]
	[0 0 0 0 0 1 1 0 1 1 1 1]	[2.696, 4.097, 0]
	[0 0 0 0 1 0 1 0 1 1 1 1]	[2.717, 3.990, 0]
Scenario 2	[0 0 0 1 0 1 1 1 0 1 0 1]	[2.977, 0, 4.476]
	[0 0 0 0 1 1 1 1 1 0 0 1]	[2.891, 0, 4.540]
	[0 0 0 0 1 1 1 0 1 1 0 1]	[2.883, 0, 4.675]
Scenario 3	[0 0 0 0 1 1 1 1 1 0 0 1]	[0, 3.616, 4.540]
	[0 0 0 0 0 1 0 1 1 1 1 1]	[0, 3.978, 4.131]
	[0 0 1 0 0 1 1 0 1 1 0 1]	[0, 3.807, 4.535]
Scenario 4	[0 0 0 1 0 1 1 1 1 0 0 1]	[3.017, 0, 0]
Scenario 5	[0 0 0 0 0 1 1 1 1 0 1 1]	[0, 4.028, 0]
Scenario 6	[0 0 0 0 1 1 1 1 0 1 0 1]	[0, 0, 4.596]
Sustainable scenario	[0 0 0 0 0 1 1 1 0 1 1 1]	[2.663, 4.035, 4.442]
	[0 0 1 0 0 1 1 0 1 1 0 1]	[3.109, 3.807, 4.535]
	[0 0 0 0 1 0 1 1 1 0 1 1]	[2.725, 3.921, 4.330]

7. Conclusions

The portfolio optimization occupies a central role in REPs when resources are limited. However, there are few literatures on this topic, especially in China. Difficulties associated with REP portfolio optimization stem from factors including multiple conflicting objectives, uncertainties of decision-making environment and synergies between projects. Therefore, this paper constructs a hybrid fuzzy MCDM framework to select the appropriate REP portfolios. First of all, a comprehensive evaluation criteria system for REP sustainable performance evaluation is constructed from the sustainability perspective, which decomposes the sustainable goal hierarchically into three objectives and 10 criteria that can be operated. Then, the T2FNs are employed to evaluate the criteria value collected from literature, reports as well as experts' opinions to depict the uncertainties in the decision-making process. And then, the fuzzy weights of these criteria are obtained by using the IT2F-AHP technique. Results show that the weight of the criteria of GHG emission reduction is the biggest. After that, the IT2FWA operator is applied to aggregate the fuzzy values of REPs regarding the environmental, economic and social objective respectively. Subsequently, considering the cost synergies between the REPs, a fuzzy zero-one nonlinear programming model is constructed and the NSGA-II algorithm is employed to obtain an optimal-Pareto set. Last but not least, to illustrate the correctness and effectiveness of the framework, a case study in Southeast China is provided.

The merits of the proposed framework are two-folds: ①it makes clear the duties of senior managers, experts and programmers, which can largely improve the efficiency and quality of decision-making; ②it is universal that can be applied to the problem of REP portfolio optimization in other international regions.

In the future work, there are several directions that deserve further study. First, we will continue this work to select the optimal solution from the Pareto-optimal set by taking into account the different preferences of group decision-makers. In addition, with the increasing number of REPs, the decision-making information will increase exponentially. So, using in-depth learning algorithms to learn the preferences of decision-makers is an interesting topic of further study. Last but not least, the applications of the proposed hybrid fuzzy MCDM approach will be extended to other fields such as renewable energy plant site selection, renewable energy plant risk evaluation and so on.

Conflicts of interest

The authors declare no conflict of interest.

Appendix A

Table A.1 Ranges of various renewable energy technologies performance on the quantitative criteria.

Criteria	Unit	HPP	SPVP	WPP	BPP	Reference
GHG emission reduction (C11)	T/GWh	3.7-237	51-250	9.7-123.7	35-178	(Varun et al., 2009)
Land requirement (C12)	m^2 /kW	750	35-42	100-120	5000	(Chatzimouratidis & Pilavachi, 2008; Reddy et al., 2012)
Capital Cost (C21)	USD/kW	1 000-3500	1150-1400	950-1250	2000-2500	(IRENA, 2012)
O&M cost (C22)	USD/kW/a	45-52	12-42	17.31-31	63.8-84.7	(IRENA, 2012)
Levelized cost of energy (C23)	USD/kWh	0.025-0.11	0.08-0.21	0.075-0.37	0.04-0.22	(IRENA, 2018)
Operational life (C24)	Year	40-50	30	40	20-25	(Ahmad & Tahar, 2014)
Job creation (C31)	Jobs/MW	0.9-1.2	0.7-25	0.9-4.0	11.2-19.7	(Dvořák et al., 2017; Rodríguez- Huerta et al., 2017)

Note: HPP: Hydroelectric power plant; SPVP: Solar PV plant; WPP: Wind power plant; BPP: Biomass Power Plant.

Appendix B

Table B.1 Aggregated values of project performance on the criteria.

	P1	P2	P3	P4
C11	((0.83,0.97,0.97,1); 1,1, (0.9,0.97,0.97,0.98); 0.9,0.9)	((0.63,0.83,0.83,0.97); 1,1, (0.73,0.83,0.83,0.9); 0.9,0.9)	((0.63,0.83,0.83,0.97); 1,1, (0.73,0.83,0.83,0.9); 0.9,0.9)	((0.43,0.63,0.63,0.8); 1,1, (0.53,0.63,0.63,0.72); 0.9,0.9)
C12	((0.03,0.13,0.13,0.3); 1,1), (0.08,0.13,0.13,0.22); 0.9,0.9)	((0,0.07,0.07,0.23); 1,1), (0.03,0.07,0.07,0.15); 0.9,0.9)	((0.37,0.57,0.57,0.77); 1,1), (0.47,0.57,0.57,0.67); 0.9,0.9)	((0.43,0.63,0.63,0.83); 1,1), (0.53,0.63,0.63,0.73); 0.9,0.9)
C13	((0.63,0.83,0.83,0.97); 1,1), (0.73,0.83,0.83,0.9); 0.9,0.9)	((0.57,0.77,0.77,0.93); 1,1), (0.67,0.77,0.77,0.85); 0.9,0.9)	((0.37,0.57,0.57,0.77); 1,1), (0.47,0.57,0.57,0.67); 0.9,0.9)	((0.23,0.43,0.43,0.63); 1,1), (0.33,0.43,0.43,0.53); 0.9,0.9)
C21	((0,0,0,0.1); 1,1), (0,0,0,0.05); 0.9,0.9)	((0.03,0.17,0.17,0.37); 1,1), (0.1,0.17,0.17,0.27); 0.9,0.9)	((0.43,0.63,0.63,0.8); 1,1), (0.53,0.63,0.63,0.72); 0.9,0.9)	((0.7,0.9,0.9,1); 1,1), (0.8,0.9,0.9,0.95); 0.9,0.9)
C22	((0.13,0.3,0.3,0.5); 1,1), (0.22,0.3,0.3,0.4); 0.9,0.9)	((0.37,0.57,0.57,0.77); 1,1), (0.47,0.57,0.57,0.67); 0.9,0.9)	((0.17,0.37,0.37,0.57); 1,1), (0.27,0.37,0.37,0.47); 0.9,0.9)	((0.23,0.43,0.43,0.63); 1,1), (0.33,0.43,0.43,0.53); 0.9,0.9)
C23	((0,0.03,0.03,0.17); 1,1), (0.17,0.03,0.03,0.1); 0.9,0.9)	((0.07,0.2,0.2,0.37); 1,1), (0.13,0.2,0.2,0.28); 0.9,0.9)	((0.57,0.77,0.77,0.93); 1,1), (0.67,0.77,0.77,0.85); 0.9,0.9)	((0.57,0.77,0.77,0.93); 1,1), (0.67,0.77,0.77,0.85); 0.9,0.9)
C24	((0.23,0.43,0.43,0.63); 1,1), (0.33,0.43,0.43,0.53); 0.9,0.9)	((0.23,0.43,0.43,0.63); 1,1), (0.33,0.43,0.43,0.53); 0.9,0.9)	((0.23,0.43,0.43,0.63); 1,1), (0.33,0.43,0.43,0.53); 0.9,0.9)	((0.23,0.43,0.43,0.63); 1,1), (0.33,0.43,0.43,0.53); 0.9,0.9)
C31	((0.7,0.87,0.87,0.97); 1,1), (0.78,0.87,0.87,0.92); 0.9,0.9)	((0.57,0.77,0.77,0.93); 1,1), (0.67,0.77,0.77,0.85); 0.9,0.9)	((0.43,0.63,0.63,0.8); 1,1), (0.53,0.63,0.63,0.85); 0.9,0.9)	((0.43,0.63,0.63,0.8); 1,1), (0.53,0.63,0.63,0.85); 0.9,0.9)
C32	((0.47,0.63,0.63,0.77); 1,1), (0.55,0.63,0.63,0.7); 0.9,0.9)	((0.07,0.23,0.23,0.43); 1,1), (0.15,0.23,0.23,0.33); 0.9,0.9)	((0.43,0.63,0.63,0.8); 1,1), (0.53,0.63,0.63,0.72); 0.9,0.9)	((0.13,0.3,0.3,0.5); 1,1), (0.22,0.3,0.3,0.4); 0.9,0.9)
C33	((0.37,0.57,0.57,0.73); 1,1), (0.47,0.57,0.57,0.65); 0.9,0.9)	((0.03,0.17,0.17,0.37); 1,1), (0.1,0.17,0.17,0.27); 0.9,0.9)	((0.63,0.83,0.83,0.97); 1,1), (0.73,0.83,0.83,0.9); 0.9,0.9)	((0.07,0.23,0.23,0.43); 1,1), (0.15,0.23,0.23,0.33); 0.9,0.9)

	P5	P6	P7	P8
C11	((0.07,0.23,0.23,0.43); 1,1, (0.15,0.23,0.23,0.33); 0.9,0.9)	((0.03,0.17,0.17,0.37); 1,1, (0.10,0.17,0.17,0.27); 0.9,0.9)	((0,0,0,0.1); 1,1), (0,0,0,0.05); 0.9,0.9)	((0.03,0.17,0.17,0.37); 1,1), (0.1,0.17,0.17,0.27); 0.9,0.9)
C12	((0.83,0.97,0.97,1); 1,1), (0.53,0.63,0.63,0.73); 0.9,0.9)	((0.83,0.97,0.97,1); 1,1), (0.53,0.63,0.63,0.73); 0.9,0.9)	((0.9,1,1,1); 1,1), (0.95,1,1,1); 0.9,0.9)	((0.03,0.17,0.17,0.37); 1,1), (0.1,0.17,0.17,0.27); 0.9,0.9)
C13	((0.57,0.77,0.77,0.93); 1,1), (0.67,0.77,0.77,0.85); 0.9,0.9)	((0.7,0.9,0.9,1); 1,1), (0.8,0.9,0.9,0.95); 0.9,0.9)	(0.57,0.77,0.77,0.93); 1,1), (0.67,0.77,0.77,0.85); 0.9,0.9)	((0.13,0.3,0.3,0.5); 1,1), (0.22,0.3,0.3,0.4); 0.9,0.9)
C21	((0.83,0.97,0.97,1); 1,1), (0.9,0.97,0.97,0.98); 0.9,0.9)	((0.83,0.97,0.97,1); 1,1), (0.9,0.97,0.97,0.98); 0.9,0.9)	((0,0,0,0.1); 1,1), (0,0,0,0.05); 0.9,0.9)	((0.9,1,1,1); 1,1), (0.95,1,1,1); 0.9,0.9)
C22	((0.37,0.57,0.57,0.77); 1,1), (0.47,0.57,0.57,0.67); 0.9,0.9)	((0.57,0.77,0.77,0.93); 1,1), (0.67,0.77,0.77,0.85); 0.9,0.9)	((0.9,1,1,1); 1,1), (0.95,1,1,1); 0.9,0.9)	((0,0.03,0.03,0.17); 1,1), (0.02,0.03,0.03,0.1); 0.9,0.9)
C23	((0.63,0.83,0.83,0.97); 1,1), (0.73,0.83,0.83,0.9); 0.9,0.9)	((0.63,0.83,0.83,0.97); 1,1), (0.73,0.83,0.83,0.9); 0.9,0.9)	((0.57,0.77,0.77,0.93); 1,1), (0.67,0.77,0.77,0.85); 0.9,0.9)	((0.63,0.8,0.8,0.93); 1,1), (0.72,0.8,0.8,0.87); 0.9,0.9)
C24	((0.63,0.83,0.83,0.97); 1,1), (0.73,0.83,0.83,0.9); 0.9,0.9)	((0.63,0.83,0.83,0.97); 1,1), (0.73,0.83,0.83,0.9); 0.9,0.9)	((0.63,0.83,0.83,0.97); 1,1), (0.73,0.83,0.83,0.9); 0.9,0.9)	((0,0.07,0.07,0.23); 1,1), (0.03,0.07,0.07,0.15); 0.9,0.9)
C31	((0.07,0.23,0.23,0.43); 1,1), (0.15,0.23,0.23,0.33); 0.9,0.9)	((0.03,0.17,0.17,0.37); 1,1), (0.1,0.17,0.17,0.27); 0.9,0.9)	((0,0.07,0.07,0.23); 1,1), (0.03,0.07,0.07,0.15); 0.9,0.9)	((0.37,0.57,0.57,0.77); 1,1), (0.47,0.57,0.57,0.67); 0.9,0.9)

Continued

	P5	P6	P7	P8
C32	((0.07,0.23,0.23,0.43); 1,1), (0.15,0.23,0.23,0.33); 0.9,0.9)	((0.1,0.3,0.3,0.5); 1,1), (0.2,0.3,0.3,0.4); 0.9,0.9)	((0.23,0.43,0.43,0.63); 1,1), (0.33,0.43,0.43,0.53); 0.9,0.9)	((0,0.07,0.07,0.23); 1,1), (0.03,0.07,0.07,0.15); 0.9,0.9)
C33	((0.43,0.63,0.63,0.8); 1,1), (0.53,0.63,0.63,0.72); 0.9,0.9)	((0.3,0.5,0.5,0.67); 1,1), (0.4,0.5,0.5,0.58); 0.9,0.9)	((0.3,0.5,0.5,0.67); 1,1), (0.4,0.5,0.6,0.58); 0.9,0.9)	((0.03,0.17,0.17,0.37); 1,1), (0.1,0.17,0.17,0.27); 0.9,0.9)

	P9	P10	P11	P12
C11	((0.03,0.17,0.17,0.37); 1,1), (0.1,0.17,0.17,0.27); 0.9,0.9)	((0,0.07,0.07,0.23); 1,1), (0.03,0.07,0.07,0.15); 0.9,0.9)	((0,0.03,0.03,0.17); 1,1), (0.02,0.03,0.03,0.1); 0.9,0.9)	(0,0.03,0.03,0.17); 1,1), (0.02,0.03,0.03,0.1); 0.9,0.9)
C12	((0.37,0.57,0.57,0.77); 1,1), (0.47,0.57,0.57,0.67); 0.9,0.9)	((0.17,0.37,0.37,0.57); 1,1), (0.27,0.37,0.37,0.47); 0.9,0.9)	((0.57,0.77,0.77,0.93); 1,1), (0.67,0.77,0.77,0.85); 0.9,0.9)	((0.77,0.93,0.93,1); 1,1), (0.85,0.93,0.93,0.97); 0.9,0.9)
C13	(0,0.1,0.1,0.3); 1,1), (0.05,0.1,0.1,0.2); 0.9,0.9)	((0.3,0.5,0.5,0.7); 1,1), (0.4,0.5,0.5,0.6); 0.9,0.9)	((0,0.07,0.07,0.23); 1,1), (0.03,0.07,0.07,0.15); 0.9,0.9)	((0,0.07,0.07,0.23); 1,1), (0.03,0.07,0.07,0.15); 0.9,0.9)
C21	((0.63,0.83,0.83,0.97); 1,1), (0.73,0.83,0.83,0.9); 0.9,0.9)	((0.77,0.93,0.93,1); 1,1), (0.85,0.93,0.93,0.97); 0.9,0.9)	((0.3,0.5,0.5,0.7); 1,1), (0.4,0.5,0.5,0.6); 0.9,0.9)	((0.83,0.97,0.97,1); 1,1), (0.9,0.97,0.97,0.98); 0.9,0.9)
C22	((0.03,0.17,0.17,0.37); 1,1), (0.1,0.17,0.17,0.27); 0.9,0.9)	((0.17,0.37,0.37,0.57); 1,1), (0.27,0.37,0.37,0.47); 0.9,0.9)	((0,0,0,0.1); 1,1), (0,0,0,0.05); 0.9,0.9)	((0.63,0.83,0.83,0.97); 1,1), (0.73,0.83,0.83,0.9); 0.9,0.9)
C23	((0.83,0.97,0.97,1); 1,1), (0.9,0.97,0.97,0.98); 0.9,0.9)	((0.83,0.97,0.97,1); 1,1), (0.9,0.97,0.97,0.98); 0.9,0.9)	((0.7,0.9,0.9,1); 1,1), (0.8,0.9,0.9,0.95); 0.9,0.9)	((0.9,1,1,1); 1,1), (0.95,1,1,1); 0.9,0.9)
C24	((0,0.07,0.07,0.23); 1,1), (0.03,0.07,0.07,0.15); 0.9,0.9)	((0,0.07,0.07,0.23); 1,1), (0.03,0.07,0.07,0.15); 0.9,0.9)	((0.63,0.83,0.83,0.97); 1,1), (0.73,0.83,0.83,0.9); 0.9,0.9)	((0.63,0.83,0.83,0.97); 1,1), (0.73,0.83,0.83,0.9); 0.9,0.9)
C31	((0.37,0.57,0.57,0.77); 1,1), (0.47,0.57,0.57,0.67); 0.9,0.9)	((0.3,0.5,0.5,0.7); 1,1), (0.4,0.5,0.5,0.6); 0.9,0.9)	((0,0.07,0.07,0.23); 1,1), (0.03,0.07,0.07,0.15); 0.9,0.9)	((0,0,0,0.1); 1,1), (0,0,0,0.05); 0.9,0.9)
C32	((0.2,0.37,0.37,0.57); 1,1), (0.28,0.37,0.37,0.47); 0.9,0.9)	((0.23,0.43,0.43,0.63); 1,1), (0.33,0.43,0.43,0.53); 0.9,0.9)	((0.5,0.7,0.7,0.87); 1,1), (0.6,0.7,0.7,0.78); 0.9,0.9)	((0.3,0.5,0.5,0.7); 1,1), (0.4,0.5,0.5,0.6); 0.9,0.9)
C33	((0.07,0.23,0.23,0.43); 1,1), (0.15,0.23,0.23,0.33); 0.9,0.9)	((0.23,0.43,0.43,0.63); 1,1), (0.33,0.43,0.43,0.53); 0.9,0.9)	((0.63,0.83,0.83,0.97); 1,1), (0.73,0.83,0.83,0.9); 0.9,0.9)	((0.3,0.5,0.5,0.67); 1,1), (0.4,0.5,0.5,0.58); 0.9,0.9)

References

[1] Afshari A, Mojahed M, Yusuff R M. Simple Additive Weighting Approach to Personnel Selection Problem[J]. International Journal of Innovation & Technology Management, 2010, 1(5):511-515.

[2] Afzalirad M, Rezaeian J. A realistic variant of bi-objective unrelated parallel machine scheduling problem: NSGA-II and MOACO approaches[J]. Applied Soft Computing, 2016, 50:109-123.

[3] Ahmad S, Nadeem A, Akhanova G, et al. Multi-criteria evaluation of renewable and nuclear resources for electricity generation in Kazakhstan[J].Energy, 2017, 141: 1880-1891.

[4] Ahmad S, Tahar R M. Selection of renewable energy sources for sustainable development of electricity generation system using analytic hierarchy process: A case of Malaysia[J]. Renewable Energy, 2014, 63(1): 458-466.

[5] Amer M, Daim T U. Selection of renewable energy technologies for a developing county: A case of Pakistan[J]. Energy for Sustainable Development, 2011, 15(4): 420-435.

[6] Büyüközkan G, Güleryüz S. Evaluation of Renewable Energy Resources in Turkey using an

integrated MCDM approach with linguistic interval fuzzy preference relations[J]. Energy, 2017, 123: 149-163.

[7] Banihabib M E, Hashemi-Madani F S, Forghani A. Comparison of Compensatory and non-Compensatory Multi Criteria Decision Making Models in Water Resources Strategic Management[J]. Water Resources Management, 2017, 31(12): 3745-3759.

[8] Bhattacharyya R, Kumar P, Kar S. Fuzzy R&D portfolio selection of interdependent projects[J]. Computers & Mathematics with Applications, 2011, 62(10):3857-3870.

[9] Buckley J J. Fuzzy hierarchical analysis[J]. Fuzzy sets and Systems, 1985, 17(3):233-247.

[10] Carlsson C. A fuzzy approach to R&D project portfolio selection[J]. International Journal of Approximate Reasoning, 2007, 44(2):93-105.

[11] Castillo O, Amador-Angulo L, Castro J R, et al. A comparative study of type-1 fuzzy logic systems, interval type-2 fuzzy logic systems and generalized type-2 fuzzy logic systems in control problems[J]. Information Sciences, 2016, 354:257-274.

[12] Castillo O, Cervantes L, Soria J, et al. A Generalized Type-2 Fuzzy Granular Approach with Applications to Aerospace[J]. Information Sciences, 2016, 354:165-177.

[13] Castillo O, Melin P. Intelligent systems with interval type-2 fuzzy logic[J]. International Journal of Innovative Computing, Information and Control, 2008, 4(4): 771-783.

[14] Celik E, Gumus A T. An outranking approach based on interval type-2 fuzzy sets to evaluate preparedness and response ability of non-governmental humanitarian relief organizations[J]. Computers & Industrial Engineering, 2016, 101:21-34.

[15] Centre CNRE. China Renewable Energy Outlook 2017[R]. Beijing:China Wind Power 2017.

[16] Cervantes L, Castillo, O. Type-2 fuzzy logic aggregation of multiple fuzzy controllers for airplane flight control[J]. Information Sciences, 2015, 324(3): 247-256.

[17] Chabuk A J, Al-Ansari N, Hussain H M, et al. GIS-based assessment of combined AHP and SAW methods for selecting suitable sites for landfill in Al-Musayiab Qadhaa, Babylon, Iraq[J]. Environmental Earth Sciences, 2017, 76(5):209.

[18] Chatzimouratidis A I, Pilavachi P A. Multicriteria evaluation of power plants impact on the living standard using the analytic hierarchy process[J]. Energy policy, 2008, 36(3): 1074-1089.

[19] Chen T Y. A linear assignment method for multiple-criteria decision analysis with interval type-2 fuzzy sets[J]. Applied Soft Computing Journal, 2013, 13(5): 2735-2748.

[20] Çolak M, Kaya İ. Prioritization of renewable energy alternatives by using an integrated fuzzy MCDM model: A real case application for Turkey[J]. Renewable & Sustainable Energy Reviews, 2017, 80: 840-853.

[21] Cucchiella F, D'Adamo I, Gastaldi M. Modeling optimal investments with portfolio analysis in electricity markets[J]. Energy Educationence & Technology Part A Energyence & Research, 2012, 30(1): 673-692.

[22] Cucchiella F, Gastaldi M, Trosini, M. Investments and cleaner energy production: A portfolio analysis in the Italian electricity market[J]. Journal of Cleaner Production, 2016, 142: 121-132.

[23] Deb K, Pratap A, Agarwal S, et al. A fast and elitist multiobjective genetic algorithm: NSGA-II[J]. IEEE Transactions on Evolutionary Computation, 2002, 6(2), 182-197.

[24] Deveci M. Site selection for hydrogen underground storage using interval type-2 hesitant fuzzy sets[J]. International Journal of Hydrogen Energy, 2018, S0360319918309170.

[25] Deveci M, Canıtez F, Gökaşar I. WASPAS and TOPSIS based interval type-2 fuzzy MCDM method for a selection of a car sharing station[J]. Sustainable Cities & Society, 2018, 41: 777-791.

[26] Dorfeshan Y, Mousavi S M, Mohagheghi V, et al. Selecting project-critical path by a new interval type-2 fuzzy decision methodology based on MULTIMOORA, MOOSRA and TPOP methods[J]. Computers & Industrial Engineering, 2018, 120:160-178.

[27] Dvořák P, Martinát S, Dan V D H, et al. Renewable energy investment and job creation; a cross-sectoral assessment for the Czech Republic with reference to EU benchmarks[J]. Renewable & Sustainable Energy Reviews, 2017, 69:360-368.

[28] Fattahi P, Hajipour V, Nobari A. A bi-objective continuous review inventory control model[J]. Applied Soft Computing, 2015, 32(C):211-223.

[29] Garbuzova-Schlifter M, Madlener, R. AHP-based risk analysis of energy performance contracting projects in Russia[J]. Energy policy, 2016, 97:559-581.

[30] Garcíamelón M, Povedabautista R, Del V M, et al. Using the strategic relative alignment index for the selection of portfolio projects application to a public Venezuelan Power Corporation[J]. International Journal of Production Economics, 2015, 170: 54-66.

[31] Garni H A, Kassem A, Awasthi A, et al. A multicriteria decision making approach for evaluating renewable power generation sources in Saudi Arabia[J]. Sustainable Energy Technologies & Assessments, 2016, 16:137-150.

[32] Ghosh S, Chakraborty T, Saha S, et al. Development of the location suitability index for wave energy production by ANN and MCDM techniques[J]. Renewable & Sustainable Energy Reviews, 2016, 59: 1017-1028.

[33] Golabi K, Kirkwood C W, Sicherman A. Selecting a Portfolio of Solar Energy Projects Using Multiattribute Preference Theory[J]. Management Science, 1981, 27(2): 174-189.

[34] Gutjahr W J, Katzensteiner S, Reiter P, et al. Multi-objective decision analysis for competence-oriented project portfolio selection[J]. European Journal of Operational Research, 2010, 205(3):670-679.

[35] Haddad B, Liazid A, Ferreira P. A multi-criteria approach to rank renewables for the Algerian electricity system[J]. Renewable Energy, 2017, 107:462-472.

[36] Hadi-Vencheh A, Mohamadghasemi A. A fuzzy AHP-DEA approach for multiple criteria ABC inventory classification[J]. Expert Systems with Applications, 2011, 38(4): 3346-3352.

[37] Heo E, Kim J, Boo K J. Analysis of the assessment factors for renewable energy dissemination program evaluation using fuzzy AHP[J]. Renewable & Sustainable Energy Reviews, 2010, 14(8):2214-2220.

[38] Heo E, Kim J, Cho S. Selecting hydrogen production methods using fuzzy analytic hierarchy process with opportunities, costs, and risks[J]. International Journal of Hydrogen Energy, 2012, 37(23): 17655-17662.

[39] IRENA. Renewable energy technologies: cost analysis series.2012.http://www.irena.org/Publications/Publications.

[40] IRENA.Renewable Power Generation Costs in 2017. http://www.irena.org/publications/2018/Jan/Renewable -power-generation-costs-in-2017.

[41] Jaberidoost M, Olfat L, Hosseini A, et al. Pharmaceutical supply chain risk assessment in Iran using analytic hierarchy process (AHP) and simple additive weighting (SAW) methods[J]. Journal of

Pharmaceutical Policy & Practice, 2015, 8(1): 1-10.

[42] Ju Y, Wang A. Extension of VIKOR method for multi-criteria group decision making problem with linguistic information[J]. Applied Mathematical Modelling, 2013, 37(5):3112-3125.

[43] Kahraman C. Fuzzy analytic hierarchy process with interval type-2 fuzzy sets[J]. Knowledge-Based Systems, 2014, 59(2):48-57.

[44] Kaya T, Kahraman C. Multicriteria renewable energy planning using an integrated fuzzy VIKOR & AHP methodology: The case of Istanbul[J]. Energy, 2010, 35(6):2517-2527.

[45] Keshavarz Ghorabaee M, Amiri M, Zavadskas E K, et al. A new multi-criteria model based on interval type-2 fuzzy sets and EDAS method for supplier evaluation and order allocation with environmental considerations[J]. Computers & Industrial Engineering, 2017, 112: 156-174.

[46] Khalili-Damghani K, Sadi-Nezhad S, Lotfi F H, et al. A hybrid fuzzy rule-based multi-criteria framework for sustainable project portfolio selection[J]. Information Sciences, 2013, 220(1):442-462.

[47] Kundu P, Kar S. A fuzzy multi-criteria group decision making based on ranking interval type-2 fuzzy variables and an application to transportation mode selection problem[J]. Soft Computing, 2015, 1-12.

[48] Li J, Chen J, Xin B. Efficiently solving multi-objective dynamic weapon-target assignment problems by NSGA-II[C]. Control Conference, 2015, 2556-2561.

[49] Liu S, Chan F T S, Ran, W. Decision making for the selection of cloud vendor: An improved approach under group decision-making with integrated weights and objective/subjective attributes[J]. Expert Systems with Applications, 2016, 55:37-47.

[50] Maier S, Street A, Mckinnon K. Risk-averse portfolio selection of renewable electricity generator investments in Brazil: An optimised multi-market commercialisation strategy[J]. Energy, 2016, 115:1331-1343.

[51] Malkawi S, Al-Nimr M D, Azizi D. A multi-criteria optimization analysis for Jordan's energy mix[J]. Energy, 2017, 127: 680-696.

[52] Markowitz H. Portfolio selection[J]. Journal of Finance, 1952, 7(1):77-91.

[53] Mendel J M, John R I, Liu F. Interval Type-2 Fuzzy Logic Systems Made Simple[J]. IEEE transactions on fuzzy systems, 2006, 14(6): 808-821.

[54] Mohagheghi V, Mousavi S M, Vahdani B. A New Optimization Model for Project Portfolio Selection Under Interval-Valued Fuzzy Environment[J]. Arabian Journal for Science & Engineering, 2015, 40(11):3351-3361.

[55] Mohagheghi V, Mousavi S M, Vahdani B, et al. R&D project evaluation and project portfolio selection by a new interval type-2 fuzzy optimization approach[J]. Neural Computing & Applications, 2017, 28(12):1-20.

[56] Mohagheghi V, Mousavi S M, Vahdani B, et al. A mathematical modeling approach for high and new technology-project portfolio selection under uncertain environments[J]. Journal of Intelligent & Fuzzy Systems, 2017, 32(6): 4069-4079.

[57] Mousavi S M, Sadeghi J, Niaki S T A, et al. A bi-objective inventory optimization model under inflation and discount using tuned Pareto-based algorithms[J]. Applied Soft Computing, 2016, 43(C):57-72.

[58] Nations, U. Report of the World Commission on Environment and Development: Our Common Future, 1987.http://www.un-documents.net/wced-ocf.htm.

[59] Ontiveros-Robles E, Melin P, Castillo O. Comparative analysis of noise robustness of type 2 fuzzy

logic controllers[J]. Kybernetika, 2018, 54(1):175-201.

[60] Panda S, Yegireddy N K. Automatic generation control of multi-area power system using multi-objective non-dominated sorting genetic algorithm-II[J]. International Journal of Electrical Power & Energy Systems, 2013, 53(4):54-63.

[61] Qin J, Liu X, Pedrycz W. An extended TODIM multi-criteria group decision making method for green supplier selection in interval type-2 fuzzy environment[J]. European Journal of Operational Research, 2016, 258(2): 626-638.

[62] Rahmat Z G, Niri M V, Alavi N, et al. Landfill site selection using GIS and AHP: a case study: Behbahan, Iran[J]. Ksce Journal of Civil Engineering, 2017, 21(1):111-118.

[63] Rajabi-Bahaabadi M, Shariat-Mohaymany A, Babaei M, et al. Multi-objective path finding in stochastic time-dependent road networks using non-dominated sorting genetic algorithm[J]. Expert Systems with Applications An International Journal, 2015, 42(12): 5056-5064.

[64] Razi F F. A Hybrid Grey Relational Analysis and Nondominated Sorting Genetic Algorithm-II for Project Portfolio Selection[J]. Advances in Operations Research, 2014, 1-8.

[65] Reddy V S, Kaushik S C, Tyagi S K. Exergetic analysis and performance evaluation of parabolic trough concentrating solar thermal power plant (PTCSTPP)[J]. Energy, 2012, 39(1): 258-273.

[66] Relich M, Pawlewski P. A fuzzy weighted average approach for selecting portfolio of new product development projects. 2017, 231:19-27.

[67] Rodríguez-Huerta E, Rosas-Casals M, Sorman A H. A societal metabolism approach to job creation and renewable energy transitions in Catalonia[J]. Energy policy, 2017, 108: 551-564.

[68] Saaty T L.The analytic hierarchy process: Planning, priority setting, resource Allocation[M]. New York:McGraw-Hill, 1980.

[69] Sanchez M A, Castillo O, Castro J R. Generalized Type-2 Fuzzy Systems for controlling a mobile robot and a performance comparison with Interval Type-2 and Type-1 Fuzzy Systems[J]. Expert Systems with Applications, 2015a, 42(14):5904-5914.

[70] Sanchez M A, Castillo O, Castro J R. Information granule formation via the concept of uncertainty-based information with Interval Type-2 Fuzzy Sets representation and Takagi–Sugeno–Kang consequents optimized with Cuckoo search[J]. Applied Soft Computing, 2015b, 27(C):602-609.

[71] Şengül Ü, Eren M, Shiraz S E, et al. Fuzzy TOPSIS method for ranking renewable energy supply systems in Turkey[J]. Renewable Energy, 2015, 75(C): 617-625.

[72] Seyedmohammadi J, Sarmadian F, Jafarzadeh A A, et al. Application of SAW, TOPSIS and fuzzy TOPSIS models in cultivation priority planning for maize, rapeseed and soybean crops[J]. Geoderma, 2017, 310:178-190.

[73] Smith-Perera A, García-Melón M, Poveda-Bautista R, et al. A Project Strategic Index proposal for portfolio selection in electrical company based on the Analytic Network Process[J]. Renewable & Sustainable Energy Reviews, 2010, 14(6):1569-1579.

[74] Streimikiene D, Balezentis T, Krisciukaitienė I, et al. Prioritizing sustainable electricity production technologies: MCDM approach[J]. Renewable & Sustainable Energy Reviews, 2012, 16(5): 3302-3311.

[75] Tavana M, Keramatpour M, Santos-Arteaga F J, et al. A fuzzy hybrid project portfolio selection method using Data Envelopment Analysis, TOPSIS and Integer Programming[J]. Expert Systems with Applications, 2015, 42(22):8432-8444.

[76] Troldborg M, Heslop S, Hough R L. Assessing the sustainability of renewable energy technologies using multi-criteria analysis: Suitability of approach for national-scale assessments and associated uncertainties[J]. Renewable & Sustainable Energy Reviews, 2014, 39(6):1173-1184.

[77] Varun Bhat I K, Prakash R. LCA of renewable energy for electricity generation systems—A review[J]. Renewable & Sustainable Energy Reviews, 2009, 13(5): 1067-1073.

[78] Wang Y M, Liu J, Elhag T M S. An integrated AHP-DEA methodology for bridge risk assessment[J]. Computers & Industrial Engineering, 2008, 54(3):513-525.

[79] Wu Y, Li J, Wang J, et al. Project portfolio management applied to building energy projects management system[J]. Renewable & Sustainable Energy Reviews, 2012, 16(1):718-724.

[80] Wu Y, Xu C, Ke Y, et al. An intuitionistic fuzzy multi-criteria framework for large-scale rooftop PV project portfolio selection: Case study in Zhejiang, China[J]. Energy, 2017, 143:295-309.

[81] Wu Y, Xu C, Ke Y, et al. Portfolio selection of distributed energy generation projects considering uncertainty and project interaction under different enterprise strategic scenarios[J]. Applied Energy, 2019, 236: 444-464.

[82] Wu Y, Xu C, Li L, et al. A risk assessment framework of PPP waste-to-energy incineration projects in China under 2-dimension linguistic environment[J]. Journal of Cleaner Production, 2018, 183: 602-617.

[83] Wu Y, Xu C, Zhang T. Evaluation of renewable power sources using a fuzzy MCDM based on cumulative prospect theory: A case in China[J]. Energy, 2018, (147): 1227–1239.

[84] Zadeh L A. The Concept of a Linguistic Variable and its Application to Approximate Reasoning[J]. Information Sciences, 1974, 8(3):199-249.

[85] Zadeh L A. Fuzzy sets[J]. Fuzzy Sets, Fuzzy Logic, & Fuzzy Systems, 1996, 394-432.

[86] Zeng Z, Nasri E, Chini A, et al. A multiple objective decision making model for energy generation portfolio under fuzzy uncertainty: Case study of large scale investor-owned utilities in Florida[J]. Renewable Energy, 2015, 75(75):224-242.

[87] Zhang Y. Selecting risk response strategies considering project risk interdependence[J]. International Journal of Project Management, 2016, 34(5):819-830.

[88] Zheng G, Zhu N, Tian Z, et al. Application of a trapezoidal fuzzy AHP method for work safety evaluation and early warning rating of hot and humid environments[J]. Safety Science, 2012, 50(2):228-239.

第三部分　风险决策研究

第 13 章针对光伏扶贫项目，从项目全生命周期的角度入手提取风险因素，避免了风险评估分析的局限性。此外，采用三角直觉模糊数来收集专家意见，减少了信息的损失。

第 14 章首次在海上光伏发电项目的评价指标中引入公众感受，增加了视觉影响风险这一指标，同时提出了一种基于犹豫模糊语言集和三角模糊数的海上光伏发电项目风险评估模型。

第 15 章构建了模糊环境下风险评估理论框架，弥补了 EPC 模式下城市屋顶分布式光伏风险评估的研究空白，同时运用直觉模糊理论改进了传统的 DEMATEL 法，增强了其实用性。

综上所述，论文集主要包括海上光伏发电项目、城市屋顶分布式光伏项目及光伏扶贫项目的风险决策问题。论文集中新能源电力建设项目风险评估研究实现了专家信息、公众意见保留的最大化，结合传统的风险评估理论，提高了风险决策方法的实践性。

Chapter 13

Risk assessment in photovoltaic poverty alleviation projects in China under intuitionistic fuzzy environment

Yunna Wu [a, b], Yiming Ke [a, b*], Jing Wang [a, b], Lingwenying Li [a, b], Xiaoshan Lin [a, b]

a. School of Economics and Management, North China Electric Power University, Beijing, China

b. Beijing Key Laboratory of New Energy and Low-Carbon Development (North China Electric Power University), Changping Beijing 102206, China

Abstract: The photovoltaic poverty alleviation project (PPAP) supplies clean power and creates considerable income for poor families, which is highly in accord with the concept of coordinated and sustainable development. Appropriate risk assessment is essential for the aversion and the disposal of potential problems, which can minimize the loss and promote the PPAP development. In this paper, a three-phase risk assessment model is proposed: firstly, through an approach combining the project life cycle theory and the Delphi method, 18 risk factors are identified and classified into 4 groups. Next, an extend Decision-Making and Trial Evaluation Laboratory (DEMATEL) method under intuitionistic fuzzy environment is employed for weight determination of indexes. Finally, the overall risk level is assessed and the priority disposal sequence of risk factors is highlighted based on the integrated results, the decision-maker preference theory and risk scenario analysis. According to the integrated results, "financing difficulties", "no clear division of responsibilities and obligations", "lack of operational experience" and "material supply and installation defects" are the riskiest factors that urgently need to be solved. Besides, the risk analysis reveals a fact that the overall risk level of China's PPAPs is relatively high, especially in the technical aspect. Some corresponding suggestions are proposed, which may contribute to rational resource allocation and effective risk prevention.

Keywords: rural photovoltaic, poverty alleviation, intuitionistic fuzzy numbers, project life cycle, risk assessment, DEMATEL

1. Introduction

Energy shortage, environmental pollution and unbalanced regional development have become critical factors which seriously restrict the development of global economy. As the largest developing country, China also encounters some similar problems such as frequent attacks of haze weather, the rural-urban gap and low economic development in solar-resource-rich western province. To alleviate environmental pollution and achieve regional balanced development, China formally launches the PPAP which takes grid-connected centralized photovoltaic power station as the core (Administration, 2014). The PPAP refers to the project that makes use of photovoltaic power to improve the living standards of residents in poor areas, in which the rural photovoltaic is a typical mode. According to the project form and the revenue source, the PPAP can be divided into two common modes. One is that with the help of government guarantee and supporting policies, poor households get a loan from credit cooperatives and then independently complete rooftop photovoltaic system installation. In this mode, poor households can get sufficient electricity and favorable financial subsidies. The other is that power enterprises or local governments take responsibility for the village-level ground-mounted power station and help the poor with a certain electricity sale income. Since it can not only supply environment-friendly and inexhaustible power but also create considerable income for poor families, the PPAP has developed rapidly in recent years and received widespread attention from all walks of life (Xue, 2017).

The PPAP started late in China and firstly appeared in 2014. After that, a series of supportive policy measures have promoted its rapid growth. Table 13.1 shows details of some PPAPs in recent years. Restricted to the lack of experience as well as the imperfect management system, many projects were not able to be implemented successfully or even forced to stop (He and Victor, 2017). Compared with ordinary power generation projects, PPAP involve more departments and audit procedures, so the approval time is more likely to be delayed. Due to the imperfect bidding mechanism, unqualified suppliers may fail to timely supply products or unilaterally terminate the contract. What's worse, unqualified materials may result in inefficient operation and high maintenance costs. Although a series of corresponding policies and measures are carried out to improve the situation, some uncertain risk factors, such as limited design techniques, construction defects and uncontrollable natural disasters, still greatly affect the normal operation. Therefore, it is necessary to scientifically identify risk factors and offer countermeasures for PPAPs.

Table 13.1 Some photovoltaic poverty alleviation projects in China (Administration).

No.	Project Name	Installed capacity	Poverty reduction	Fund sources
1	Shangdong Guanxian PPAP	70 MW	2333 households	G: 20%; L:80%
2	Shanxi Lanxian PPAP	30 MW	1200 households	G: 10%; E: 10%; L:80%
3	Hubei Suixian PPAP	20 MW	4000 households	G: 20%; L:80%
4	Yunnan Lanping PPAP	20 MW	815 households	G: 10%; E: 10%; L:80%
5	Jiangxi Xinfeng PPAP	20 MW	800 households	G: 10%; E: 10%; L:80%
6	Anhui Dangshan PPAP	20 MW	800 households	G: 10%; E: 20%; L:70%
7	Shanxi Hunyuan PPAP	20 MW	800 households	G: 6%; E: 14%; L:80%
8	Anhui Taihu PPAP	20 MW	667 households	G: 10%; E: 10%; L:80%
9	Jilin Helong PPAP	10 MW	1200 households	G: 6%; E: 14%; L:80%
10	Hubei Changyang PPAP	6 MW	240 households	E: 20%; L:80%

Note: "G" and "E" represent the capital provided by governments and enterprises respectively, while "L" stands for loan.

Some academic studies regarding with risk assessment have been carried out, but almost no research on photovoltaic projects with poverty alleviation characteristics has been issued at present. Moreover, some limitations exist in the present research framework, which weakens the accuracy of risk assessment: on the one hand, most researches use the fuzzy set instead of numerical values to reduce information loss, but it cannot well consider the hesitation degree of the assessment; on the other hand, few studies take into account the correlation among factors in the process of weight determination.

This paper tries to thoroughly explore risk factors and accurately dissect the risk level of China's PPAPs, so as to assist project participants to rationally allocate resources and effectively handle potential risks. Possible innovations are as follows. Firstly, the triangular intuitionistic fuzzy number (TIFN) is employed for expert opinion collection so as to reduce the loss and distortion of information. Moreover, weight vectors are determined by the hesitancy degree, which is more reasonable than subjective weighting methods. Secondly, an extended DEMATEL method is adopted to evaluate the factor importance and further provides the evidence for the weight determination of the magnitude of impact (MI) and the likelihood of occurrence (LO). Thirdly, based on the MI and LO values, 25 risk scenarios covering all the actual risk situations are formed and the priority disposal sequence of risk factors is obtained according to the decision-maker preference theory. Main contributions can be concluded as three aspects: First and foremost, since few literature materials are related to PPAP risk assessment, this study can efficiently make up for the literature vacancy and enrich the material database. Then, identification and ranking of risk factors can not only help project participants get rid of massive and disorganized risk information but also assist them to form an overall and accurate understanding of PPAP risks, which contributes to risk avoidance and loss minimum in an actual process. Finally, the objective risk analysis can provide reference for reasonable investment of enterprises. Besides, the proposed response measures not only help governments adjust macro policies in accordance with current situations, but also offer some management inspiration to PPAP practitioners.

The remainder of this study is organized as follows: Section 2 briefly probes the research situation of photovoltaic project risk evaluation and some relative methods regarding with risk assessment, including factor identification, information collection and index weight determination. Section 3 interprets the basic theory of the TIFN and the research framework. Section 4 identifies and classifies the risk factors in China's PPAPs. Section 5 explores the real risk status in China's PPAPs and proposes some response measures. Finally, Section 6 draws a conclusion.

2. Literature Review

Risk assessment can predict possible risks and strive for the maximum profits with the lowest costs, which can directly help for accurate investment and scientific decision-making. Some academic studies concerning photovoltaic projects have been carried out but most of them focus on the assessment from single aspect, such as landscape impacts (Chiabrando et al., 2009), policy threats (Lüthi and Wüstenhagen, 2012), investment problems (Kayser, 2016), technical barriers (Moser et al., 2017), economic risks (Tomosk et al., 2017), energy conservation (Ayoub et al., 2015) and recycling strategies (Perez-Gallardo et al., 2018). The object to be assessed is often influenced by many factors simultaneously and decision-makers need to determine the priority item because of resource limitation, so the comprehensive risk assessment of photovoltaic projects emerges as the times require. From multiple aspects, including the approval, costs, nature impacts and community participation, Guerin conducts a comparison between the expected and observed risks on a large-scale photovoltaic project and focuses on construction risks (Guerin, 2017). Although risks of photovoltaic projects are highly valued by the society, there are still few studies related to its assessment. Moreover, almost no research on photovoltaic projects with poverty alleviation characteristics has been issued at present.

Accurate factor identification is an important prerequisite for scientific risk assessment. Through an extensive literature review, including academic journals, case study materials as well as reports by professional bodies and the governments, Zhao et al. figure out critical factors for 'Build–Operate–Transfer' electric power projects in China (Zhao et al., 2010). Xu et al. identify critical risk factors of waste-to-energy incineration projects from real-life risk events through content analysis (Xu et al., 2015). Ameyaw and Chan determine risk factors in water supply projects by literature review, content analysis and expert decision (Ameyaw and Chan, 2015). With the continuous expansion of factor identification methods, an approach combining literature review, case study and expert screening is widely accepted and well applied in determining risk factors.

As foundational work, risk information collection is often faced with the problems of information loss and distortion. Fuzzy set theory, proposed by Zadeh (Zadeh, 1996), can not only effectively present knowledge or information which may be vague, probabilistic, or imprecise in nature but also eases assessment procedures for indefinite and linguistic expressions by capturing human prejudice (Luthra et al., 2016). Combining probability with personal experience, Cheng and Lu adopt fuzzy sets to deal with the uncertain and imprecise data in risk assessment of pipe jacking construction projects, including the occurrence probability, the severity and the probability of detecting (Cheng and Lu, 2015). In order to assess the severity of construction project risks more precisely, Samantra et al. deal with the subjectivity and the corresponding uncertain characteristics of construction risk factors through trapezoidal fuzzy numbers (Samantra et al., 2017). Solving the information loss caused by uncertainty and hesitancy degree in decision making, Rodríguez et al. use intuitionistic fuzzy sets to explore the most appropriate scheme for risk management in information technology projects (Rodríguez et al., 2017). Since project risks are uncertain and vague in nature (Taylan et al., 2014), using exact numbers would lead to information loss while applications of the fuzzy concept can reserve expert linguistic information as much as possible.

As an important bridge to integrate risk indicators and decision information, the index weight determination can greatly affect the effectiveness of project assessment. The idea that project risks should be assessed from both the impact magnitude and the occurrence likelihood is common implemented in current researches (Pinto, 2014), which puts forward new requirements for the determination of index weights. The DEMATEL methodology, originated from the Geneva Research Centre of the Battelle Memorial Institute (Gabus and Fontela, 1972), is identified as an effective approach in extracting the relationships regarding interdependencies as well as the interdependence intensity among system elements (Xia et al., 2015). Chien et al. apply the DEMATEL method to identify critical construction project risks and conduct factor analysis through the casual relationship diagram (Chien et al., 2014). Later, Dedasht et al. manage to distinguish factor interrelationships and assess the overall risk in oil and gas construction projects through a combination of the DEMATEL and Analytic Network Processes methods (Dedasht et al., 2017). These studies outline the superiority and applicability of DEMATEL in dealing with complex problems, especially in the issues of uncertain factor relationships.

3. Methodology

3.1 Basic theory of the risk assessment framework

Taking the membership, non-membership and hesitancy degree into account, intuitionistic fuzzy sets are more suitable to describe the properties of fuzzy objects. In order to express the imperfect knowledge and the uncertain assessment more effectively, the TIFN is employed (Wu et al., 2016). This subsection mainly lists some basic definitions and operations of TIFNs regarding to risk assessment in PPAPs.

Definition 1. (Li, 2010) A TIFN $\tilde{a}=((\underline{a},a,\overline{a});\tilde{u}_{\tilde{a}},\tilde{v}_{\tilde{a}})$ is a special intuitionistic fuzzy set which satisfies the conditions that $\underline{a}\leqslant a\leqslant\overline{a}\in R$, $0\leqslant u_{\tilde{a}}\leqslant 1$, $0\leqslant v_{\tilde{a}}\leqslant 1$ and $0\leqslant u_{\tilde{a}}+v_{\tilde{a}}\leqslant 1$. Its membership function and non-membership function are described as follows.

$$\mu_{\tilde{a}}(x)=\begin{cases}(x-\underline{a})u_{\tilde{a}}/(a-\underline{a}) & \text{if } \underline{a}\leqslant x<a,\\ u_{\tilde{a}} & \text{if } x=a,\\ (\overline{a}-x)u_{\tilde{a}}/(\overline{a}-a) & \text{if } a<x\leqslant\overline{a},\\ 0 & \text{if } x<\underline{a} \text{ or } x>\overline{a},\end{cases} \tag{13-1}$$

and

$$v_{\tilde{a}}(x)=\begin{cases}\left[a-x+v_{\tilde{a}}(x-\underline{a})\right]/(a-\underline{a}) & \text{if } \underline{a}\leqslant x<a,\\ v_{\tilde{a}} & \text{if } x=a,\\ \left[x-a+v_{\tilde{a}}(\overline{a}-x)\right]/(\overline{a}-a) & \text{if } a<x\leqslant\overline{a},\\ 1 & \text{if } x<\underline{a} \text{ or } x>\overline{a},\end{cases} \tag{13-2}$$

where $u_{\tilde{a}}$ and $v_{\tilde{a}}$ represent the maximum degree of membership and the minimum degree of non-membership respectively. The value $\pi_{\tilde{a}}(x)=1-\mu_{\tilde{a}}(x)-v_{\tilde{a}}(x)$, an intuitionistic fuzzy index of an element x in $\tilde{a}$, represent the hesitancy degree of experts. The smaller an intuitionistic fuzzy index is, the lower the indeterminacy is.

Definition 2. (Li, 2008) Let $\tilde{a}$ and $\tilde{b}$ be two positive TIFNs an $\lambda\geqslant 0$ TIFNs' arithmetical operations are defined as follows.

$$\tilde{a}+\tilde{b}=\left(\left(\underline{a}+\underline{b},a+b,\overline{a}+\overline{b}\right);u_{\tilde{a}}\wedge u_{\tilde{b}},v_{\tilde{a}}\vee v_{\tilde{b}}\right) \tag{13-3}$$

$$\tilde{a}\tilde{b}=\left(\left(\underline{ab},ab,\overline{ab}\right);u_{\tilde{a}}\wedge u_{\tilde{b}},v_{\tilde{a}}\vee v_{\tilde{b}}\right) \tag{13-4}$$

$$\lambda\tilde{a}=\left(\left(\lambda\underline{a},\lambda a,\lambda\overline{a}\right);u_{\tilde{a}},v_{\tilde{a}}\right) \tag{13-5}$$

$$\tilde{a}^{\lambda}=\left(\left(\underline{a}^{\lambda},a^{\lambda},\overline{a}^{\lambda}\right);u_{\tilde{a}},v_{\tilde{a}}\right) \tag{13-6}$$

where the symbols "∧" and "∨" mean taking the minimum and maximum of the both respectively.

Definition 3. (Wan, 2013) Let $\tilde{a}_j$ $(j=1,2,...,n)$ be a collection of positive TIFNs and $w=\left(w_1,w_2,...,w_n\right)^T$ be the weight vector of the collection, which satisfies the condition that $0\leqslant w_j\leqslant 1$ $\left(j=1,2,...,n\right)$ and $\sum_{j=1}^{n} w_j=1$. Then the aggregation operator $TIF-WA$ is stipulated as follows.

$$TIF-WA(\tilde{a}_1,\tilde{a}_2,...,\tilde{a}_n)=\left(\left(\sum_{j=1}^{n} w_j\underline{a}_j,\sum_{j=1}^{n} w_j a_j,\sum_{j=1}^{n} w_j\overline{a}_j\right);\min_j\left\{u_{\tilde{a}_j}\right\},\max_j\left\{v_{\tilde{a}_j}\right\}\right) \tag{13-7}$$

Definition 4. (Wan et al., 2013) Let $\tilde{a}$ be a positive TIFN and r be a risk preference index in real-life situations. Its defuzzification formula is concluded as follow.

$$h\left(\tilde{a}\right)=\begin{cases}(\underline{a}+4a+\overline{a})\left(1-v_{\tilde{a}}\right)/6 & \text{if} \quad r\to 0,\\(\underline{a}+4a+\overline{a})[2(1-v_{\tilde{a}})+u_{\tilde{a}}]/18 & \text{if} \quad r=1/2,\\(\underline{a}+4a+\overline{a})(1-v_{\tilde{a}}+u_{\tilde{a}})/12 & \text{if} \quad r=1,\\(\underline{a}+4a+\overline{a})[(1-v_{\tilde{a}})+2u_{\tilde{a}}]/18 & \text{if} \quad r=2,\\(\underline{a}+4a+\overline{a})u_{\tilde{a}}/6 & \text{if} \quad r\to\infty.\end{cases} \tag{13-8}$$

And taking the median is a universal defuzzification method, especially dealing with random sample data, which means the defuzzification model with $r=1$ is most suitable for aggregation results.

Definition 5. (Wan et al., 2016) Let $\tilde{a}$ and $\tilde{b}$ be two positive TIFNs and their Hamming distance can be concluded as follows.

$$\begin{aligned}d(\tilde{a},\tilde{b})=\frac{1}{6}\Big[&\left|(1+u_{\tilde{a}}-v_{\tilde{a}})\underline{a}-(1+u_{\tilde{b}}-v_{\tilde{b}})\underline{b}\right|\\&+\left|(1+u_{\tilde{a}}-v_{\tilde{a}})a-(1+u_{\tilde{b}}-v_{\tilde{b}})b\right|\\&+\left|(1+u_{\tilde{a}}-v_{\tilde{a}})\overline{a}-(1+u_{\tilde{b}}-v_{\tilde{b}})\overline{b}\right|\Big]\end{aligned} \tag{13-9}$$

Definition 6. Let u and v be the maximum degree of membership and the minimum degree of non-membership respectively. The linguistic variables involved in this paper and the corresponding transformation rules are listed in Table 13.2, in which the TIFN $((0,0,0);1,0)$ stands for deterministic impossible events.

Table 13.2 Linguistic variables and the corresponding TIFNs.

Ratings of Alternatives	TIFNs
No influence/ frequency/ seriousness at all (N)	$((0,0,0);1,0)$
Very low influence/ frequency/ seriousness (VL)	$((0,0.1,0.3);u,v)$
Low influence/ frequency/ seriousness (L)	$((0.1,0.3,0.5);u,v)$
Moderate influence/ frequency/ seriousness (M)	$((0.3,0.5,0.7);u,v)$

Continued

Ratings of Alternatives	TIFNs
High influence/ frequency/ seriousness (H)	$((0.5,0.7,0.9);u,v)$
Very high influence/ frequency/ seriousness (VH)	$((0.7,0.9,1);u,v)$

A three-phase analysis model is proposed to conduct risk assessment in PPAPs and the concrete procedures are described in the following subsections. Fig.13.1 is a specific flow chart of the research framework.

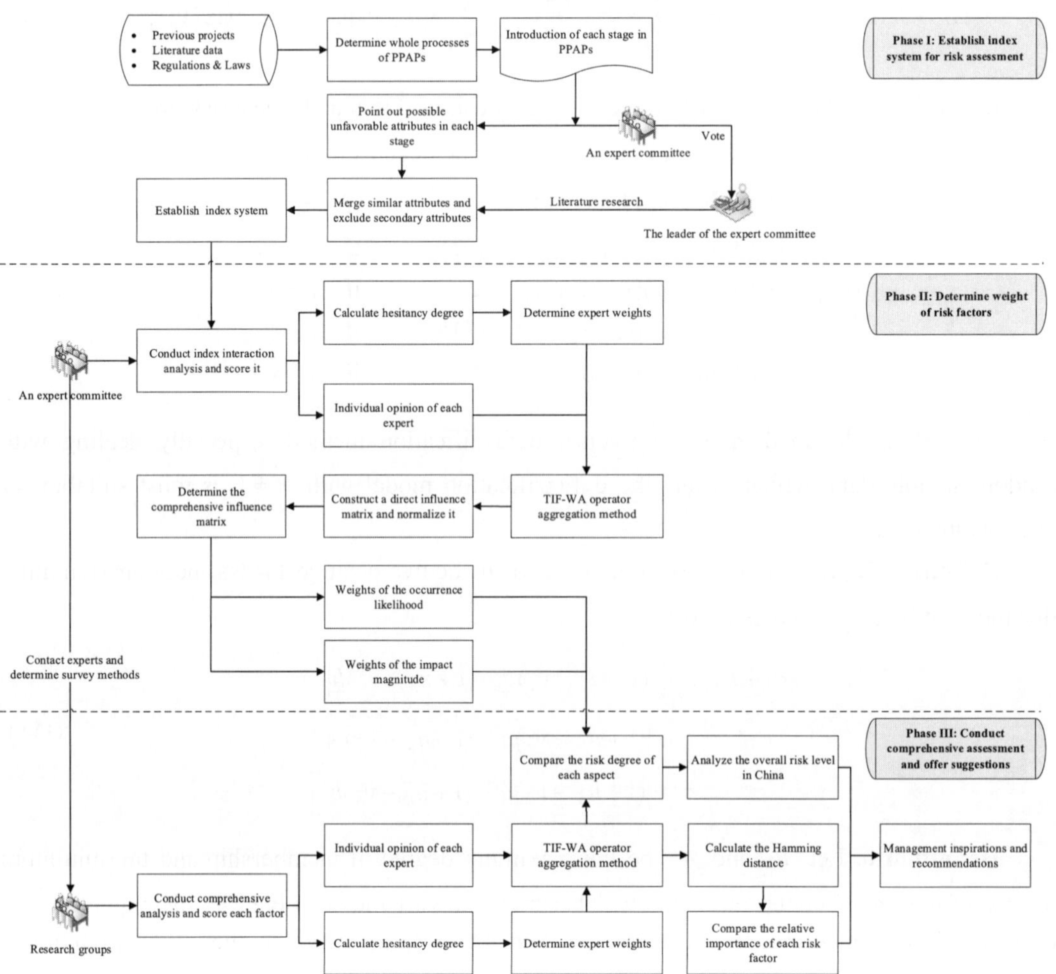

Fig. 13.1 Specific flow chart of research methodologies.

3.2 Phase I. Establish the index system for risk assessment

In this phase, a two-step approach combining project life cycle (Fourie and Brent, 2006) and the Delphi method (Linstone and Turoff, 1976) is adopted to figure out risk factors. In the Delphi process, the number of experts is determined according to the scope of knowledge required by the survey. And it is generally over 3 and not more than 20. According to the research scope and coverage of the subject, five experts whose academic backgrounds are energy, engineering, social, environmental and economical fields are selected respectively. The procedures of the Delphi method are described as follows and the corresponding flow chart is shown in Fig.13.2.

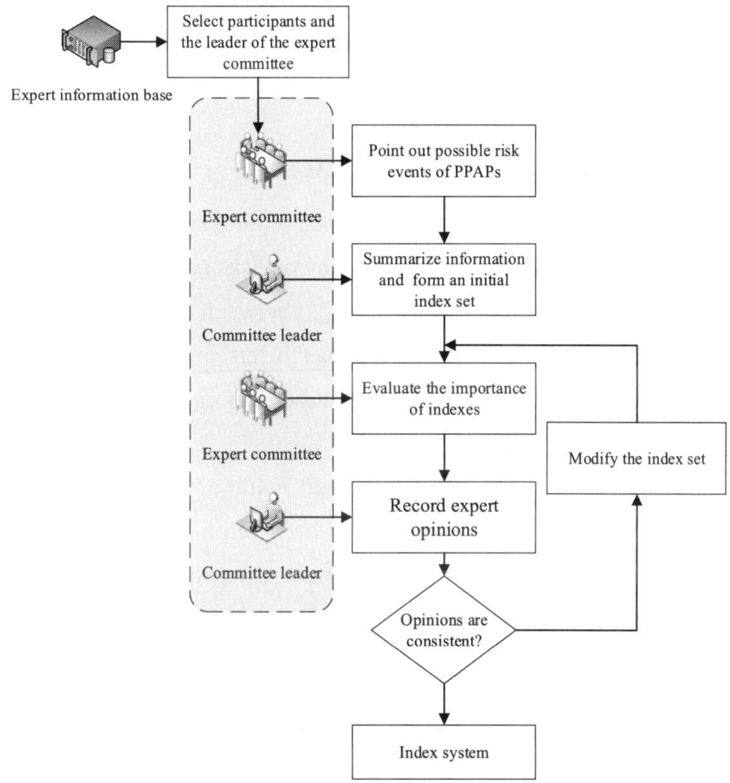

Fig. 13.2 A flow chart of the Delphi process.

Step 1. Select participants and the leader of the expert committee. According to research fields and research topics, participants are selected from the expert database and one expert with the high prestige is elected as the leader. Conducting a thorough analysis of previous projects, literature and relevant regulations, the committee concludes every stage of PPAPs' whole life cycle.

Step 2. Point out possible risk events of PPAPs. Based on the definitions of PPAPs' life cycle, Committee participants are asked to provide opinions on possible risk events of each stage. In this phase, they are not constrained by pre-defined responses and can provide as many details as possible.

Step 3. Summarize information and form an initial index set. According to the conference records and literature, the committee leader merges similar attributes and excludes secondary attributes, screening out an initial index set.

Step 4. Evaluate the importance of indexes. The obtained index set is submitted to the expert committee and experts evaluate the importance of indexes.

Step 5. Record expert opinions. The committee leader records each point of view and the corresponding evidence.

Step 6. Judge whether expert opinions towards index set are consistent. If positive, the index system is obtained. Otherwise, the index set and the corresponding feedbacks are submitted to the expert committee for further modification.

3.3 Phase II. Determine weight of risk factors

In this phase, an extend DEMATEL method (Falatoonitoosi et al., 2013) under intuitionistic fuzzy environment is adopted to improve the accuracy of risk factor weight evaluation.

Step 1. According to the direct relationships between indexes as well as degree of confidence from evaluation, each committee member offers individual linguistic variables, the maximal membership degree and the least non-membership degree on interaction situations in the acquired index system.

Step 2. Considering the theory that an expert with a large intuitionistic fuzzy index performs high uncertainty in evaluation and should be given a low confidence level, this paper follows a confidence function based on the information entropy. The calculation formula of expert weights is displayed as follows (Xu et al., 2017).

$$b_i(\pi) = -\frac{1}{(\sum_{j=1}^{n} \pi_j^i)\ln(\sum_{j=1}^{n} \pi_j^i)} \tag{13-10}$$

$$w_i = b_i(\pi) / \sum_{i=1}^{m} b_i(\pi) \tag{13-11}$$

where $w = (w_1, w_2, \ldots, w_m)$ and $\pi_i = (\pi_{i1}, \pi_{i2}, \ldots, \pi_{in})$ represent the objective weight vector of m experts and the hesitancy degree of the ith expert, respectively, while $b_i(\pi)$ is the information entropy.

Step 3. Combined with the weight vectors obtained in the previous step, expert opinions are aggregated by the $TIF-WA$ operator. The aggregation result, a collection of TIFNs, is converted to a set of real numbers called a direct influence matrix [see the Eq. (13-8)].

Step 4. Normalize the direct influence matrix. The normalized direct-relation matrix N can be obtained through the following calculation equation (Wu, 2008).

$$k = \frac{1}{\max\limits_{1 \leqslant i \leqslant n} \sum_{j=1}^{n} d_{ij}} \tag{13-12}$$

$$N = k \cdot D \tag{13-13}$$

where d_{ij} is the direct influence coefficient of the ith factor on the jth factor, and

$D = \{d_{ij}\}$ is the $n \times n$ direct influence matrix. k represents the normalized coefficient.

Step 5. The total relation matrix X is calculated through the following formula.

$$X = \lim_{\lambda \to \infty} (N + N^2 + \ldots + N^{\lambda}) = N(E - N)^{-1} \tag{13-14}$$

where λ is a real number and E represents an $n \times n$ identity matrix.

Step 6. Based on the law that factors with a higher impact coefficient tend to cause greater harm to the system and factors received more influence are more likely to get changed, the impact magnitude weights $IW = (iw_1, iw_2, \ldots, iw_m)$ and the occurrence likelihood weights $OW = (ow_1, ow_2, \ldots, ow_m)$ of risk factors can be acquired from the following equations.

$$iw_i = r_i / \sum_{j=1}^{m} r_j \tag{13-15}$$

$$ow_i = c_i / \sum_{j=1}^{m} c_j \tag{13-16}$$

where r_i illustrates both direct and indirect effects caused by the ith factor and c_j denotes all the influence that acts on the jth factor.

3.4 Phase III. Conduct comprehensive assessment and offer suggestions

In order to accurately evaluate the impact magnitude and the occurrence likelihood level of each factor, this paper adopts the questionnaire survey method to collect information. The questionnaire contains two parts: ①The main body portion set the risk factors as 18 items. For each item, experts need select the suitable linguistic values (namely very high frequency/ seriousness, high frequency/ seriousness, moderate frequency/ seriousness, low frequency/ seriousness and very low frequency/ seriousness) and provide the corresponding membership and non-membership degree; ②The auxiliary information. In order to prevent assessment error caused by the unclear boundaries of risk factors, the questionnaire provides indicator definitions.

Considering the importance of theoretical and practical experience, the criteria for expert selection are divided into three aspects: ①Having over 5-year experience in PPAP management and good understanding of risk management; ②Participating in at least one PPAP and possessing risk management knowledge; ③Writing over 3 high-level articles regarding PPAPs with in-depth knowledge of risk management. Based on the above criteria, qualified experts are selected. According to the time and the places of survey, five survey groups are set up and the details are listed in Table 13.3. Next, each committee member summarizes the survey results and offers their assessment scores of each factor. Then, the opinions of each group are aggregated as the final assessment using Eq. (13-7). Based on the combination of the factor assessment obtained in the previous step and the factor weights acquired in Phase II, the analysis of PPAPs' risks, including identification of the riskiest factor and the most important aspect as well as the overall risk level in China, is conducted and some corresponding suggestions are proposed.

Table 13.3 Some details of the survey groups.

Group	Survey methods	Survey details
Expert group 1	An expert seminar	Invite 5 experts with extensive research and practical experience in project. All of them are present in the seminar
Expert group 2	A field interview	Interview 4 managers of a photovoltaic module manufacturing company and 6 village committee secretaries
Expert group 3	A questionnaire survey	Select 18 qualified experts in the south of China and provide them with questionnaires. The response rate was 78 % and 14 questionnaires were available
Expert group 4	A questionnaire survey	Select 23 qualified experts in the east of China and provide them with questionnaires. The response rate was 87 % and 18 questionnaires were available
Expert group 5	A questionnaire survey	Select 15 qualified experts in the northwest of China and provide them with questionnaires. The response rate was 80 % and 12 questionnaires were available

4. Establishment of PPAPs' risk assessment index system

As a fundamental prerequisite, appropriate risk identification contributes a lot to risk control and final success in a project (Khameneh et al., 2016). This section includes two parts: Firstly, based on thorough analysis of previous studies and related materials on risk management in poverty alleviation projects and photovoltaic power generation, some possible risk events in each project stage are figured out and ordered by their occurrence time, which provides an effective way to understand and summarize the factors that may lead to the failure of project targets; Secondly, the preliminary list of unfavorable attributes obtained in the previous step is verified and screened. The similar attributes are integrated into a comprehensive factor and the secondary attributes are omitted. Eventually, a list containing 18 risk factors affecting PPAPs in China is obtained through the above work.

4.1 Identification of unfavorable attributes from the entire life cycle of project management

The project life cycle theory refers to the whole process of the construction project from the planning design to the construction, and then to the operation and maintenance, until the demolition (Bennett, 2007). Since the PPAP has the characteristics of high risks, quantities of units and complex factors, the division of the project life cycle stages is very important. Based on the existing risk analyses of poverty alleviation projects or photovoltaic power generation, the entire life cycle of project management consists of four phases, namely, planning, installation, operation and maintenance (O&M) as well as end-of-life: ①Planning phase, also known as the early stage of project management, mainly involves project application, site selection, feasibility studies, land requisition, project financing and so on. ②Installation phase, the core link of the PPAP, includes some risks that are related to installation quality and costs. ③Operation and maintenance phase, the power generation period, is the key to maintaining sustainable revenues. This phase mainly includes regular maintenance, power generation and grid-connection. ④End-of-life phase refers to the process of dismantling the power station and recycling the material when the project runs to the prescribed time limit. In order to achieve comprehensiveness of risk identification, this paper concludes major business processes in each phase and points out unfavorable attributes of PPAPs through a brainstorming method. The major processes of PPAPs and the corresponding unfavorable attributes are presented in Fig.13.3.

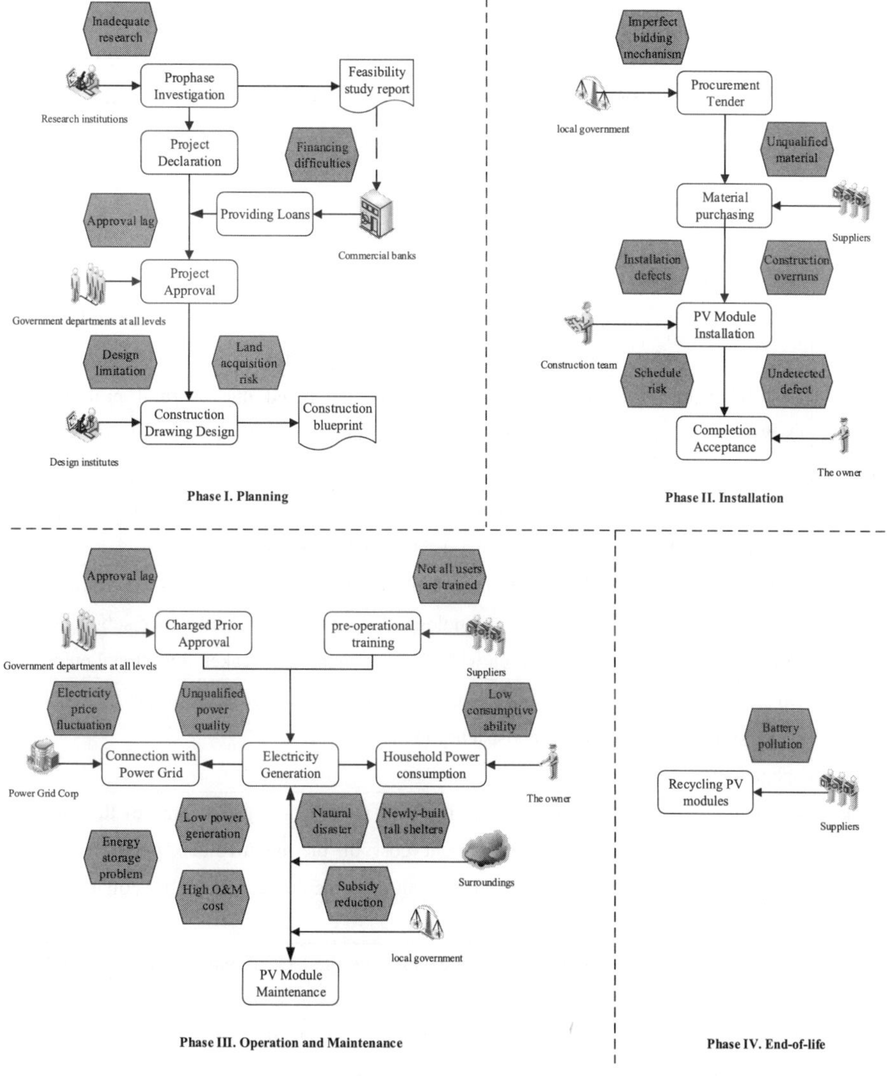

Fig. 13.3 The potential unfavorable events in PPAP life cycle.

4.2 Risk assessment index system

According to the unfavorable attributes provided above and their correlations, the risk factors are extracted and divided into 4 groups, namely political/legal risk, economic risk, technical risk and environmental risk: ①Political/legal risk (X1) is mainly caused by the unsound legal system or inadequate supervision and can only be solved through scientific legislation and strict law enforcement. It decides whether the project can be normally started and smoothly carried out. ②Economic risk (X2) mainly results from debts, costs, profits and some other factors related to revenues or expenditure. Through directly or indirectly effect on project ultimately benefits, it hinders the realization of ‘Bring sustainable incomes to the poor’. ③Technical risk (X3) consists of the threat from determined design methods, construction techniques, operation and maintenance technologies, which is greatly in line with the engineering science level. ④Environmental risk (X4) is comprised of two types of risks: the outside risks which are caused by harsh environment and the inside risks that result in environmental pollution. The concrete definitions of risk factors are explained in Table 13.4.

Table 13.4 The concrete definition of each risk factor.

Group	Risk factor	Definitions
Political/legal risk	Approval lag (X11)	This risk mainly refers to the fact that approval processes of a PPAP is too complicated, which involves many departments and application materials, posing a threat to the normal operation
	Land acquisition risk (X12)	Land acquisition may be hampered due to rural protests (Ren, 2017), environmental assessment or macro consideration of governments (Shan et al., 2017)
	Imperfect bidding mechanism (X13)	It will provide a protective umbrella for illegal bidding, which may indirectly give a rise to supplier misconduct
	Reduction of subsidy policies (X14)	With the promotion of photovoltaic projects and the maturity of PV module production technology, the governments will reduce subsidies (Zhang et al., 2016), which will affect revenues and weaken investment enthusiasm
	No clear division of responsibilities and obligations (X15)	Policies or contracts vaguely define responsibilities and obligations, and lack of consistency (Wu et al., 2017)
Economic risk	Financing difficulties (X21)	Due to low and irregular income, a large majority of the rural poor cannot afford the up-front cost of the photovoltaic power generation project (Scheutzlich et al., 2000), and neither can they offer collateral to commercial banks
	Construction overruns (X22)	Owing to design change and the lack of experience, costs in the installation phase exceed budgets
	Electricity price fluctuation (X23)	It consists of two situations: reduction of photovoltaic power generation tariffs and rise of civil electricity prices

Continued

Group	Risk factor	Definitions
Economic risk	High O&M cost (X24)	This risk originates the battery replacement overhead, external power supply expense and dust elimination cost during the operation and maintenance phase
Technical risk	Feasibility study and design limitation (X31)	In the early phase of the project, information distortion is often caused by improper information collection, which affects the overall design and planning. Moreover, data processing and modeling techniques with low precision also damage design quality
	Material supply and installation defects (X32)	Due to unreasonable production processes or outdated construction technologies (Akinyele et al., 2015), some problems such as 'not timely supply', 'unqualified photovoltaic parts' and 'construction defects' may happen
	Completion acceptance risk (X33)	During completion acceptance, inspectors cannot precisely detect all defects because of technical limitations or inadequate knowledge, which leaves hidden trouble for later operation. Besides, 'not finished on time' is a disturbing problem
	Lack of operational experience (X34)	Photovoltaic system owners who lack pre-operational training have more possibility to conduct frequent deep discharging which is assumed to have substantially contributed to battery failure (Berger, 2017). Also, lacking the experience of replacing a standby battery will increase the operational difficulties
	Consumptive and grid-connected risk (X35)	This risk refers to the fact that in poor areas, the power grid construction is relatively backward and the power consumption ability is severely low (Protopapadaki and Saelens, 2016). If the problem cannot be properly solved, photovoltaic power stations may operate at low load for a long term or even be left unused
	Energy storage problem (X36)	Since solar energy owns a feature of instability and intermittent and uncontrollable, energy storage devices become a crucial part in photovoltaic power generation system (Lai et al., 2017). Restricted by current energy storage technologies, lead-acid batteries which own problems such as poor energy storage efficiency and strong environmental corrosiveness are still the main energy storage components in PPAPs
Environmental risk	Harsh climatic conditions (X41)	Harsh climatic conditions, especially natural disaster, take great responsibility for some premature battery failures (Gustavsson and Ellegård, 2004), for example, the battery will keep low charge in a rainy season, which causes frequent cuts and wears the battery down
	Newly-built tall shelters (X42)	Since there is a common phenomenon for illegal constructions in rural areas, hot spot effect can easily occur, which reduces photovoltaic system efficiency and shortens the lifetime of photovoltaic modules (Abderrezek and Fathi, 2017)

Continued

Group	Risk factor	Definitions
Environmental risk	Battery pollution (X43)	Lead-acid batteries in photovoltaic systems consist of heavy metals such as lead, antimony, cadmium, nickel and sulfuric acid, which are highly toxic substances. If the waste batteries are not properly handled, they will have a serious impact on the human body and the ecological environment, which is contrary to the idea of environmental friendliness

5. Risk assessment in PPAPs in China based on the proposed analysis framework

5.1 Index weight calculation using an extended DEMATEL method

Thinking the proposed index system over, the committee experts are required to provide linguistic evaluation values with regard to the degree of index correlations, namely no influence, very low influence, low influence, moderate influence, high influence and very high influence. Besides, the corresponding maximal membership degree and the least non-membership degree are collected. Compared with the point scale method, it can reflect the actual choice of respondents more accurately, minimizing the loss of information and offering more persuasive base data for further analysis.

After data integration and defuzzification, the direct influence matrix is obtained and the influence with a moderate or above degree is illustrated in Fig.13.4, in which an arrow pointing represents an influence direction in the index system. The imperfect bidding mechanism presents very high impacts on material supply and installation defects with an influence coefficient of 0.7950, owing to the fact that some unqualified suppliers win the bidding and later supply equipment with quality problems or unilaterally terminate the contract. The 6 green lines in the figure indicate an important influence: Firstly, the frequent deep discharging and soot deposit problems are more likely to occur due to lack of operational experience, which adds to the burden of operation and maintenance. Secondly, unqualified parts are insecure and easily damaged, which costs a lot in the replacement and safety check of parts. Since most of constructors are paid by day, failure to supply in time will cause prolonged construction period and thereby increase the costs. Finally, feasibility studies and design materials are important basis for bank loans and government approval, so inaccurate reports tend to hinder the processes of financing and approval. Moreover, since land acquisition should conform to the government planning, the delayed approval will lead to the stagnation of expropriation processes, which further affects the normal completion.

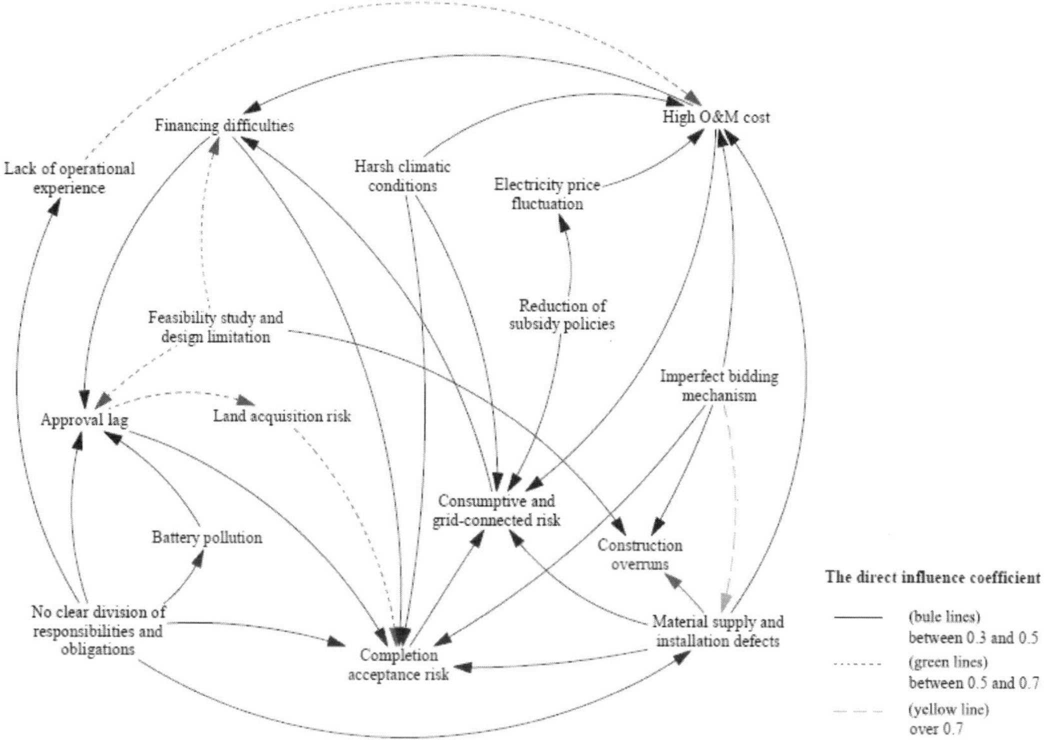

Fig. 13.4 The factor interaction with moderate or above degree.

Based on the acquired direct influence matrix and Eq. (13-12) to Eq. (13-14), the normalization is conducted and the total influence matrix is collected. Appendix A presents some information regarding to the row sums R and the column sums C of the total influence matrix. Feasibility study and design limitation (X31) and no clear division of responsibilities and obligations (X15) show their great impacts on other factors with R values of 1.45 and 1.03, relatively. Meanwhile, the consumptive and grid-connected risk (X35), ranking the top in C values, receives the highest influence from the system. Moreover, （$R+C$） values named "Prominence" stand for the factors' importance in a system: Feasibility study and design limitation (X31) is the most important factor with a score of 1.76, while newly-built tall shelters (X42) that owns only 0.32 points exhibits the least importance. Besides, （$R-C$） values called "Relation" provide division evidence of the cause and effect group: The cause group consists of factors with positive scores, namely, X13, X14, X15, X23, X31, X32, X34, X41 and X42, while other factors with negative values belong to the effect group.

Through the combination of Eq. (13-15)and Eq. (13-16) and the data in Appendix A, the impact magnitude weights and the occurrence likelihood weights of risk factors are acquired, presenting in Fig.13.5 (a) and (b), relatively. Compared with other three-aspect factors, the technical risk (X3) occupiesthe highest weights in both the impact magnitude system and the occurrence likelihood system, which indicates that the severity of the technical risk will determine the overall situation of project risks to a large extent. Imperfect bidding mechanism (X13) owns a weight of 0.101 in the impact magnitude system and a weight close to 0 in the occurrence likelihood system, laying a major influence on impact magnitude of project risks and almost no impact on the overall risk occurrence likelihood aspect.

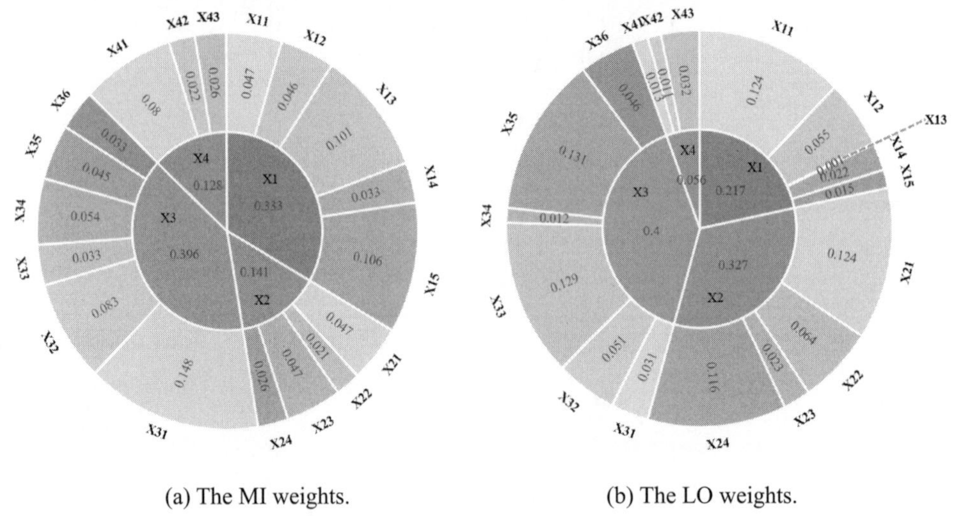

(a) The MI weights. (b) The LO weights.

Fig. 13.5 The weights of each risk group and the corresponding risk factors.

5.2 Data processing and analysis

Risk data related to current PPAPs in China is collected via conference discussions, on-the-spot interviews and questionnaires (see Appendix B). The respondents are from 27 provinces in China excluding Hainan, Qinghai, Tibet, Hongkong, Macao and Taiwan.

According to survey results, the overall hesitancy degrees of each group for risk factors are 3, 3.6, 3.2, 2.8 and 3.9, relatively. Based on the convention that “the greater hesitancy degree represents the lower confidence”, a weight vector of expert groups (0.203, 0.197, 0.202, 0.204, 0.194) is calculated by Eq. (13-10) and Eq. (13-11). Through the process that the survey data and the weight vector are substituted into Eq. (13-7), an aggregation matrix is obtained. Then, the acquired matrix is converted according to the rules in Table 13.2 and the transformed results are shown in Appendix C.

According to the basic theories and the transformation rules of TIFNs, a series of standard lines in five risk degrees, namely very low, low, moderate, high and very high, are defined as $((0,0.1,0.3);1,0)$, $((0.1,0.3,0.5);1,0)$, $((0.3,0.5,0.7);1,0)$, $((0.5,0.7,0.9);1,0)$ and $((0.7,0.9,1);1,0)$. Based on a principle of ‘similar selection’, the risk degree of a factor is judged and determined by the distance between the assessment value and the standard line. MI and LO are divided into 5 segments based on the approach degree calculation, and then 25 areas are formed after free combinations. Fig.13.6 shows 9 of the 25 areas and the position of 18 risk factors for the reason that their assessment values do not involve the "very low" and "very high"segmentations in numerical analysis. X21, X15, X34 and X32 are all located in Area 3, which represents that they all suffer from high risks in both the impact magnitude and the occurrence likelihood indicating that they are urgently needed to be solved. "Financing difficulties" (X21), the riskiest factor, is mainly caused by high initial investment costs, low incomes of the poor, limited national poverty alleviation funds, few medium-sized private enterprise investments and complicated bank loan procedures. Financing, as the economic premise and the important base, directly determines whether the project can be carried out smoothly; Due to the limited experience and the lack of local political construction, laws and regulations may be difficult to cover all aspects and PPAPs may run under the lax supervision, which further contributes to the risk "no clear division of responsibilities and obligations" (X15) and hampers the achievement of the ultimate target. For example, the replacement of a damaged inverter should belong to which groups: government procurement, supplier warranty or user payment. If the problems of responsibilities and obligations cannot be properly solved, PPAPs may be abandoned ahead of time; "Lack of operational experience" (X34) is also a common problem because of users' unavailable operational materials and the relatively low education level, which may shorten the equipment life, reduce the power quality, and further affect final benefits; In order to occupy a larger market share, some manufacturers offer abnormally lower prices, which usually ends up with contract breach or unqualified products.

Due to technical limitations, some defects in production or installation are passed, which poses a huge threat to the power generation and the equipment usage cycle. For example, as far as the installation techniques of confluence boxes are concerned, the disordered and untagged wiring is inconvenient for later troubleshooting while the untighten screw may cause long-time wire heating or even burn the line head. Besides, since most PPAP installers fail to conduct the insulation treatment for the bare parts of the wire head, it is likely to bring about great possibility to cause electric shock and short circuit events. Consumptive and grid-connected risk (X35), a very common issue with great impact in PPAPs, mainly results from two reasons: one is that the self-generated and consumed photovoltaic power will directly reduce the electricity sale profits of power grid enterprises (Luo et al., 2016); the other is that a large amount of overhead in system integration and grid reinforcement becomes a barrier of grid-connected. Newly-built tall shelters (X42), the least urgent factor lying in Area 7, which may result from the fact that the problem caused by hot spot effect is alleviated to a certain extent and it is less likely to build large buildings in poor areas.

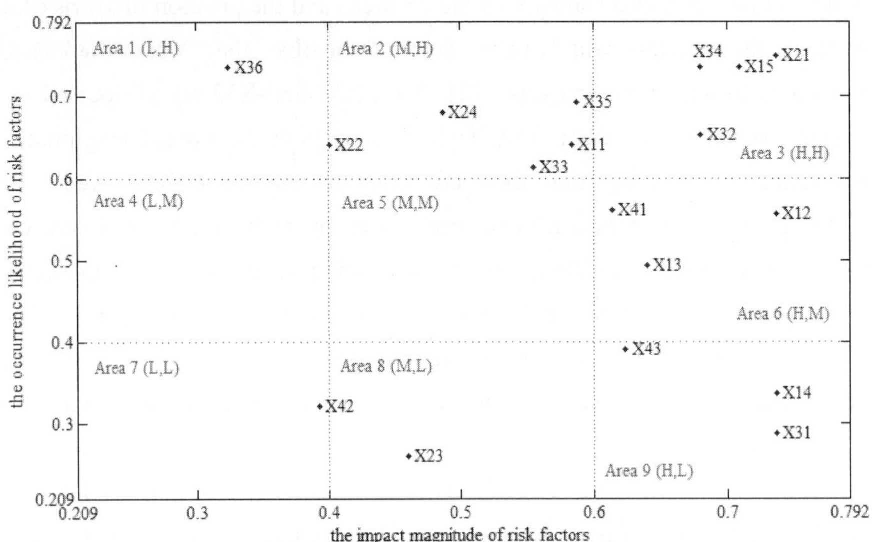

Fig. 13.6 Nine scenarios of PPAP risk factors.

Considering resource constraints and decision makers' preferences, the risks in Area 3 should be given priority and the factors in Area 7 can be moderately postponed. The priority order of each factor is not the same due to the risk preference. For example, facing a decision on ranking factors in Area 2 and Area 6, decision makers with a risk frequency preference tend to solve risks in Area 2 rather than those in Area 6, while decision makers with a risk degree preference do the opposite.

The distances between the standard line of "no seriousness/frequency at all" and the four risk aspects are (0.653, 0.583), (0.515, 0.623), (0.619, 0.624) and (0.566, 0.417), located in Area 6, Area 2, Area 3 and Area 5 respectively. The results imply that the technical risk should be firstly settled to achieve healthy and orderly development of rural photovoltaic. On the one hand, due to the restriction of production processes and component conversion efficiency, costs in photovoltaic power generation is far beyond that in other forms of energy generation, causing heavy dependence on government subsidies. On the other hand, with the backward power grid construction and the limited grid-connected technologies, such as the solution to "sub-transmission and distribution facility overload" (Zhang et al., 2012), the grid-connected approval is postponed for various reasons and a smooth consumption channel is difficult to work, which pose a threat to operational benefits. Compared with other photovoltaic power generation projects, PPAPs possess higher operation and grid connection risks due to the low knowledge level of poverty households and the backward grid construction. Moreover, unlike ordinary projects, PPAPs involve the interests of multi stakeholders, which brings about some ambiguity in the division of rights and responsibilities. Furthermore, nonstandard operations and installation defects challenge safe power generation. Considering the risk preference, decision-makers with a risk frequency preference may follow the rule X3>X2>X1>X5, while decision-makers with a risk degree preference may choose the order X3>X1>X2>X5. The overall risk level of present PPAPs in China is (0.609, 0.602), which indicates that PPAPs are suffering a situation that both the impact magnitude and the occurrence likelihood are highly risky.

5.3 Implications for practice

According to the above analysis, some corresponding suggestions and countermeasures are proposed, which may offer a valuable reference and bring a management inspiration for participants and decision-makers in PPAPs.

5.3.1 Political/legal risk

Approval lag: Firstly, to strengthen social supervision and enhance executive efficiency, governments should firstly improve the transparency of approval procedures and announce the approval status of PPAPs in real time. Secondly, it is necessary to establish a “Green” channel for PPAPs. Thirdly, optimizing administrative organizations will be an effective way to simplify, optimize and regulate approval processes. Lastly, the various departments involved in PPAPs should strengthen their information communication and achieve close cooperation.

Land acquisition risk: As the nominal owner of land, governments should offer a just, fair and open land transfer platform so as to assist developers in legally obtain the land use permit and the license of “the planning and construction land”. Besides, developers are supposed to do a good job in field investigation and project publicity, including the land requisition size, benefit distribution and compensation so as to reduce the resistance of local villagers.

Imperfect bidding mechanism: On the one hand, governments need to perfect the bidding mechanism and strengthen supervision, for example, opening complaints reporting channels for illegal rigging behaviors and setting up a particular department for supervision. On the other hand, bidders should cultivate and uphold the conception of “fair competition and integrity bidding”. Punishments such as bidding ban or fines shall be imposed on illegal bidders according to the seriousness of the circumstances.

Reduction of subsidy policies: Since it is inevitable for the subsidy reduction, the upstream photovoltaic manufacturing industry needs to apply innovation abilities to the improvement of production efficiency and product quality so as to reduce costs and seek enough profits.

No clear division of responsibilities and obligations: The responsibilities and obligations of every party involved in a PPAP should be clearly defined in a contract or relative law. Moreover, the regulations must be strictly implemented. Local governments should send staffs to project sites and provide some essential consulting services like contract consultation and dispute mediation for poor households.

5.3.2 Economic risk

Financing difficulties: The introduction of the "Public-Private-Partnership" mode into PPAPs not only reduces the financial burden of governments, but also attracts social capital, which may successfully change the situation of "single financing channel and difficult financing". Moreover, collaboration with charitable organizations would be also a good way to solve financing problems.

Construction overruns: In response to control this risk, design institutes should accurately estimate engineering quantities and finalize design details so as to reduce the possibility of demand change. Besides, a well experienced construction team and a scientific cost management system can successfully control project costs. Strengthen the management of material purchasing and select economic qualified materials can contribute to cost saving.

Electricity price fluctuation: Considering implement situations of PPAPs, governments should adopt macro-control policies to prevent abnormal fluctuations of electricity prices. Meanwhile, the National Power Grid Corp shall establish an independent system of transmission and distribution tariff under the assistance of governments.

High O&M cost: PPAPs should make use of advanced generation equipment to ensure the power generation efficiency and reduce the component failure rate. Governments should help standardize the operation and daily maintenance of rural residents by all kinds of activities, such as issuing operation manuals, pasting relative posters, and conducting advisory services regularly so that the goal of prolonging equipment service life and reducing operating costs can be realized.

5.3.3 Technical risk

Feasibility study and design limitation: Design institutes should improve the utilization rate of "building information modeling" (Ghaffarianhoseini et al., 2016) in the design and planning stage of PPAPs in order to accurately acquire the early architectural information and discover design defects in advance. Responsibility of PPAPs should be refined and the accountability system needs to be perfected so that the examination and approval departments can conscientiously perform duties and strictly audit design plans.

Material supply and installation defects: Governments need to increase the publicity and the punishment of unqualified supplier behaviors, such as cancelling their bidding right within three years and further prolonging the ban in the case of unsatisfactory rectification. Moreover, governments should also take the lead to collect information of installation defects in previous projects, including positions, causes and corresponding treatment techniques, and further form the defect database so that construction teams can obtain experience and reduce the possibility of installation defects.

Completion acceptance risk: Construction units should formulate a reasonable schedule under the consideration of installation details and sudden situations. Then project managers should carry on scientific adjustment when difference of progresses appears. Besides, project beneficiaries can ensure the completion level and after-sale service of contractors through quality assurance contracts.

Lack of operational experience: Personnel training should be included as the obligation of contractors in a contract and governments shall work as a supervisor to ensure the implementation of contracts. In addition, one or two members of each village can be selected as technical contacts for routine operation and maintenance.

Consumptive and grid-connected risk: Governments should guide rural residents to suit economic construction to local conditions, which can help improve the ability of local electric power consumption. Since the grid is the main power consumption mode in poor areas, the National Power Grid Corp should overhaul, optimize and streamline the local power grid with supporting policies or funds. Furthermore, the corporation should reduce the impacts caused by the "short-circuit current" or "unqualified power quality" through technological innovations.

Energy storage problem: Because PPAPs are located in remote areas where the power grid is weak or even no electricity is supplied, the grid-connected approval is usually postponed or canceled. In order to benefit the poverty household as soon as possible, the energy storage system is generally equipped. Since the key of energy storage technology progress is the breakthrough of material and chemistry technologies, such as hybrid potassium-ion capacitor (Comte et al., 2017), governments should not only set up special funds for battery researches, but also encourage universities and research institutions to develop related subjects and train professional talents.

5.3.4 Environmental risk

Harsh climatic conditions: Insurance institutions should offer PPAPs' comprehensive operation insurance, which can efficiently reduce economic losses caused by natural factors, such as surface cracks, ground subsidence, collapse, sudden landslides, mudslides, lightning, rain, storms, tornadoes, floods and so on. Moreover, materials need to be scientifically evaluated before the selection of photovoltaic modules. For example, in snowstorm areas, photovoltaic modules should pass the relevant tests required by IEC61215, which means their abilities to withstand extreme weather such as hail and gale are qualified.

Newly-built tall shelters: Governments should encourage anonymous complaints of "illegal construction" and strengthen the supervision and management. It is necessary to inform rural residents of unsafe construction areas. When installing photovoltaic system, system designers should refer to local planning and design the best tilt angle of photovoltaic modules on the premise of guaranteeing power generation.

Battery pollution: Some poor households pile up and throw waste batteries everywhere, causing the pollution of soil, grassland and groundwater in some areas. To cope with this issue, in a contract or agreement, the responsibility for recycling photovoltaic modules should be clearly defined and the treatment should be in a harmless manner. Moreover, it is suggested that photovoltaic suppliers can adopt the strategy of "replacing old batteries with new ones". It not only alleviates economic pressures of poor households to buy new batteries, but also effectively prevents environmental pollution of waste batteries.

6. Conclusion

Accurate risk assessment of China's PPAPs provides critical decision support for project participants to prevent potential risks, which further ensures the normal operation and the final success. However, few researches are related to risk assessment of PPAPs, and some limitations still exist in current risk assessment framework: Firstly, most studies focus on risks in a certain project phase like the construction stage, which cannot offer a thorough understanding of overall project risks; Secondly, rare researches simultaneously consider both hesitancy degree and fuzziness in project risk assessment, leading to information loss to some extent; Thirdly, the index weight vector is usually determined by factor attributes rather than index interactions in a system, which is likely to cause biased evaluations. The target of risk assessment cannot be achieved unless the limitations are successfully settled.

Therefore, a risk assessment index system for China's PPAPs is established by integrating the life cycle theory and the Delphi method. Further, a risk analysis model combing TIFNs, extended DEMATEL method and the *TIF-WA* operator is developed, which provides references for project participants to assess, avoid and dispose risks. Compared with the existing studies on risk assessment, the proposed analysis model has the following advantages: ①Risk factors are thoroughly extracted not just from a particular phase but the project life cycle, which can provide materials for risk aversion in the whole process; ②Expert decision information is collected by the way of TIFNs, including linguistic values, the maximum membership degree and the minimum non-membership degree, which can accurately describe the randomness and fuzziness of information and veritably reflect the risk level; ③Factor weight vectors are determined by the casual relationship diagram, which effectively increases objectivity in the overall risk assessment; ④The *TIF-WA* operator not only can integrate TFINs at the cost of minimal information loss, but also has advantage of simple usage. Risk groups and the corresponding factors are calculated through the proposed analysis model. The result reveals that "financing difficulties", "no clear division of responsibilities and obligations", "lack of operational experience" and "material supply and installation defects" are the riskiest factors that are urgent to be solved, while "newly-built tall shelters" expresses the minimum risk in the assessment index system. Moreover, it is pointed out that the disposal of the technical risk should be given priority and the overall risk level of China's PPAPs are relatively high. Then, by integrating factor analysis and the decision-maker preference theory, the priority disposal sequences of risk factors in each scenario are listed. Finally, some suggestions and countermeasures regarding with 18 risk factors are proposed. Since the research object is the China's PPAPs, academics who have good understanding of China's policies and economic situations are selected and the survey is conducted in China. And research results can also contribute to international PPAP risk assessment. Firstly, the risk assessment index system is extracted from the life cycle of PPAPs, which can be directly applied to risk assessment of international PPAPs. Moreover, the proposed risk assessment model can overcome limitations that exist in current risk assessment framework like information loss and biased evaluations, which can be adopted in risk assessment of other projects.

Acknowledgements

This research is supported by the 2017 Special Project of Cultivation and Development of Innovation Base (No. Z171100002217024).

Appendix A

Table A.1 The coefficient of the influencing degree, influenced degree, prominence and relation.

	R	*C*	*R*+*C*	*R*–*C*		*R*	*C*	*R*+*C*	*R*–*C*
X11	0.47	1.22	1.68	-0.75	X31	1.45	0.31	1.76	1.15
X12	0.45	0.54	1	-0.09	X32	0.81	0.5	1.31	0.32
X13	0.99	0.01	1	0.98	X33	0.33	1.27	1.59	-0.94
X14	0.33	0.22	0.55	0.11	X34	0.53	0.12	0.65	0.41
X15	1.03	0.15	1.18	0.89	X35	0.44	1.28	1.73	-0.84
X21	0.46	1.21	1.67	-0.75	X36	0.33	0.45	0.78	-0.12
X22	0.21	0.63	0.83	-0.42	X41	0.78	0.13	0.91	0.65
X23	0.46	0.22	0.68	0.24	X42	0.22	0.1	0.32	0.11
X24	0.25	1.13	1.38	-0.88	X43	0.25	0.31	0.56	-0.06

Appendix B

Table B.1 The decision information of five expert groups under intuitionistic fuzzy environment.

	Expert group 1		Expert group 2		Expert group 3		Expert group 4		Expert group 5	
	MI1	LO1	MI2	LO2	MI3	LO3	MI4	LO4	MI5	LO5
X11	(VH;0.8,0.2)	(VH;0.9,0.1)	(H;0.9,0)	(VH;0.8,0.2)	(VH;0.8,0)	(H;0.9,0.1)	(H;0.8,0.1)	(VH;0.9,0)	(M;0.8,0.1)	(H;0.9,0)

Continued

	Expert group 1		Expert group 2		Expert group 3		Expert group 4		Expert group 5	
	MI1	LO1	MI2	LO2	MI3	LO3	MI4	LO4	MI5	LO5
X12	(VH;0.8,0.1)	(M;0.8,0)	(VH;0.9,0.1)	(H;0.8,0.1)	(VH;0.9,0.1)	(H;0.9,0)	(VH;0.9,0)	(VH;0.9,0.1)	(VH;0.8,0.1)	(M;0.8,0)
X13	(VH;0.9,0)	(M;0.8,0.1)	(VH;0.8,0.2)	(H;0.8,0)	(H;0.9,0)	(M;0.8,0.1)	(H;0.8,0.1)	(H;0.8,0.1)	(VH;0.9,0)	(M;0.8,0.1)
X14	(VH;0.8,0.1)	(M;0.9,0)	(VH;0.9,0)	(L;0.8,0.1)	(VH;0.8,0.1)	(M;0.8,0.2)	(VH;0.9,0)	(M;0.9,0.1)	(VH;0.8,0)	(L;0.9,0)
X15	(VH;0.8,0.1)	(VH;1,0)	(VH;0.9,0.1)	(VH;0.9,0)	(VH;0.9,0.1)	(VH;0.9,0.1)	(VH;1,0)	(VH;1,0)	(H;0.8,0)	(VH;0.8,0.1)
X21	(VH;0.9,0)	(VH;1,0)	(VH;0.8,0.1)	(VH;0.8,0)	(VH;0.9,0)	(H;0.8,0)	(VH;1,0)	(VH;1,0)	(VH;0.9,0.1)	(VH;1,0)
X22	(M;0.9,0)	(VH;0.8,0.2)	(L;0.8,0.1)	(VH;0.9,0.1)	(M;0.8,0.2)	(H;0.8,0)	(H;0.9,0)	(VH;0.8,0.1)	(M;0.8,0.1)	(H;0.8,0.1)
X23	(H;0.8,0)	(VL;0.9,0)	(M;0.9,0)	(L;0.8,0)	(L;0.9,0)	(M;0.8,0.1)	(H;0.8,0.1)	(L;0.9,0)	(M;0.8,0.1)	(L;0.9,0)
X24	(M;0.8,0)	(VH;0.8,0.1)	(M;0.8,0)	(H;0.9,0.1)	(M;0.8,0)	(VH;0.9,0)	(H;0.8,0)	(VH;0.8,0.1)	(M;0.9,0)	(H;0.9,0)
X31	(VH;0.8,0.1)	(L;0.8,0.1)	(VH;0.9,0.1)	(M;0.8,0)	(VH;0.9,0.1)	(L;0.8,0.1)	(VH;1,0)	(L;0.8,0)	(VH;1,0)	(L;0.8,0.1)
X32	(VH;1,0)	(VH;0.9,0)	(H;0.8,0)	(H;0.8,0)	(H;0.8,0.1)	(H;0.9,0)	(VH;0.9,0.1)	(VH;0.8,0)	(VH;0.8,0.1)	(H;0.9,0.1)
X33	(H;0.8,0)	(VH;0.8,0.1)	(H;0.8,0.1)	(VH;0.8,0)	(H;0.9,0)	(H;0.8,0.2)	(M;0.8,0.2)	(H;0.8,0.1)	(H;0.8,0)	(H;0.8,0.1)
X34	(H;0.9,0.1)	(VH;0.9,0)	(H;0.9,0)	(VH;0.8,0.1)	(VH;0.8,0.1)	(VH;1,0)	(VH;0.8,0)	(VH;0.8,0)	(VH;0.9,0)	(VH;0.9,0.1)
X35	(VH;0.8,0.2)	(VH;1,0)	(H;0.9,0.1)	(VH;0.9,0)	(H;0.8,0.1)	(VH;0.9,0.1)	(H;0.8,0.2)	(VH;0.9,0.1)	(H;0.9,0.1)	(VH;0.8,0)
X36	(M;0.8,0)	(VH;0.9,0.1)	(L;0.9,0)	(VH;0.8,0.1)	(L;0.9,0)	(VH;0.8,0.1)	(M;0.9,0.1)	(VH;0.8,0.1)	(L;0.8,0)	(VH;0.8,0)
X41	(H;0.8,0.2)	(M;0.9,0.1)	(VH;0.8,0.1)	(H;0.8,0)	(H;0.8,0.1)	(H;0.8,0.1)	(VH;0.9,0.1)	(H;0.8,0)	(H;0.8,0)	(H;0.8,0.1)
X42	(H;0.8,0.1)	(L;0.9,0)	(L;0.9,0.1)	(M;0.8,0.1)	(M;0.8,0.1)	(L;0.8,0)	(M;0.9,0.1)	(L;0.8,0.1)	(L;0.9,0)	(L;0.8,0)
X43	(H;0.8,0)	(M;0.8,0.1)	(VH;0.8,0.1)	(M;0.9,0)	(H;0.9,0)	(M;0.8,0)	(H;0.8,0.1)	(L;0.9,0)	(H;0.8,0)	(M;0.9,0)

Appendix C

Table C.1 The aggregation result based on the TIF-WA operator.

Group	Risk factors	MI value	Group value	LO	Group value
X1	X11	((0.54,0.74,0.9);0.8,0.2)	((0.64,0.84,0.97);0.8,0.2)	((0.62,0.82,0.96);0.8,0.2)	((0.54,0.74,0.90);0.8,0.2)
	X12	((0.7,0.9,1);0.8,0.1)		((0.46,0.66,0.84);0.8,0.1)	
	X13	((0.62,0.82,0.96);0.8,0.2)		((0.38,0.58,0.78);0.8,0.1)	
	X14	((0.7,0.9,1);0.8,0.1)		((0.22,0.42,0.62);0.8,0.2)	
	X15	((0,66,0.86,0.98);0.8,0.1)		((0.7,0.9,0.1);0.8,0.1)	
X2	X21	((0.7,0.9,1);0.8,0.1)	((0.46,0.66,0.82);0.8,0.2)	((0.66,0.86,0.98);0.8,0)	((0.60,0.80,0.94);0.8,0.2)
	X22	((0.3,0.5,0.7);0.8,0.2)		((0.62,0.82,0.96);0.8,0.2)	
	X23	((0.34,0.54,0.74);0.8,0.1)		((0.12,0.3,0.5);0.8,0.1)	
	X24	((0.34,0.54,0.74);0.8,0)		((0.62,0.82,0.96);0.8,0.1)	
X3	X31	((0.7,0.9,1);0.8,0.1)	((0.59,0.79,0.93);0.8,0.2)	((0.14,0.34,0.54);0.8,0.1)	((0.60,0.80,0.94);0.8,0.2)
	X32	((0.62,0.82,0.96);0.8,0.1)		(0.58,0.78,0.94);0.8,0.1)	
	X33	((0.5,0.7,0.88);0.8,0.2)		(0.58,0.78,0.94);0.8,0.2)	
	X34	((0.62,0.82,0.96);0.8,0.1)		((0.7,0.9,1);0.8,0.1)	
	X35	((0.54,0.74,0.92);0.8,0.2)		((0.7,0.9,1);0.8,0.2)	
	X36	(0.18,0.38,0.58);0.8,0.1)		((0.7,0.9,1);0.8,0.1)	

Continued

Group	Risk factors	MI value	Group value	LO	Group value
X4	X41	(0.58,0.78,0.94);0.8,0.2)	((0.52,0.72,0.89);0.8,0.2)	((0.46,0.66,0.86);0.8,0.1)	((0.29,0.49,0.69);0.8,0.1)
	X42	((0.26,0.46,0.66);0.8,0.1)		((0.18,0.38,0.58);0.8,0.1)	
	X43	((0.54,0.74,0.92);0.8,0.1)		(0.26,0.46,0.66);0.8,0.1)	
sum			((0.58,0.78,0.92);0.8,0.2)		(0.57,0.77,0.91);0.8,0.2)

References

[1] Abderrezek M, Fathi M. Experimental study of the dust effect on photovoltaic panels' energy yield[J]. Solar Energy, 2017, 142: 308-320.

[2] Administration N E. Notice on the First Batch of Photovoltaic Poverty Alleviation Projects. [2018-11-20].http://zfxxgk.nea.gov.cn/auto87/201610/t20161017_2310.htm?keywords=.

[3] Administration N E. 2014. Notice on the printing and implementation of the work scheme for the implementation of the photovoltaic poverty alleviation project.[2017-11-28]. http://zfxxgk.nea.gov.cn/auto87/201411/t20141105_1862.htm.

[4] Akinyele D O, Rayudu R K, Nair N K C. Development of photovoltaic power plant for remote residential applications: The socio-technical and economic perspectives[J]. Applied Energy, 2015, 155: 131-149.

[5] Ameyaw E E, Chan A P C. Evaluation and ranking of risk factors in public–private partnership water supply projects in developing countries using fuzzy synthetic evaluation approach[J]. Expert Systems with Applications, 2015, 42:5102-5116.

[6] Ayoub N, Musharavati F, Pokharel S, et al. Risk based life cycle assessment conceptual framework for energy supply systems in large buildings[J]. Journal of Cleaner Production, 2015, 107:291-309.

[7] Bennett F L.The management of construction: A project lifecycle approach[M]. New York: Routledge, 2007.

[8] Berger T. Practical constraints for photovoltaic appliances in rural areas of developing countries: Lessons learnt from monitoring of stand-alone systems in remote health posts of North Gondar Zone, Ethiopia[J]. Energy for Sustainable Development, 2017, 40:68-76.

[9] Cheng M, Lu Y. Developing a risk assessment method for complex pipe jacking construction projects[J]. Automation in Construction, 2015, 58:48-59.

[10] Chiabrando R, Fabrizio E, Garnero G. The territorial and landscape impacts of photovoltaic systems: Definition of impacts and assessment of the glare risk[J]. Renewable & Sustainable Energy Reviews, 2009, 13:2441-2451.

[11] Chien K F, Wu Z H, Huang S C. Identifying and assessing critical risk factors for BIM projects: Empirical study[J]. Automation in Construction, 2014, 45:1-15.

[12] Comte A L, Reynier Y, Vincens C, et al. First prototypes of hybrid potassium-ion capacitor (KIC): An innovative, cost-effective energy storage technology for transportation applications[J]. Journal of Power Sources, 2017, 363:34-43.

[13] Dedasht G, Zin R M, Ferwati M S, et al. DEMATEL-ANP risk assessment in oil and gas construction

projects[J]. Sustainability, 2017, 9:1420.

[14] Falatoonitoosi E, Leman Z, Sorooshian S, et al. Decision-Making Trial and Evaluation Laboratory[J]. Research Journal of Applied Sciences Engineering & Technology, 2013, 5: 3476-3480.

[15] Fourie A, Brent A C. A project-based Mine Closure Model (MCM) for sustainable asset Life Cycle Management[J]. Journal of Cleaner Production, 2006, 14:1085-1095.

[16] Gabus A, Fontela E. World problems, an invitation to further thought within the framework of DEMATEL. Battelle Geneva Research Center, Geneva, Switzerland.1972.

[17] Ghaffarianhoseini A, Tookey J, Ghaffarianhoseini A, et al. Building Information Modelling (BIM) uptake: Clear benefits, understanding its implementation, risks and challenges[J]. Renewable & Sustainable Energy Reviews, 2016, 75.

[18] Guerin T F. Evaluating expected and comparing with observed risks on a large-scale solar photovoltaic construction project: A case for reducing the regulatory burden[J]. Renewable & Sustainable Energy Reviews, 2017, 74:333-348.

[19] Gustavsson M, Ellegård A.The impact of solar home systems on rural livelihoods. Experiences from the Nyimba Energy Service Company in Zambia[J]. Renewable energy, 2004, 29:1059-1072.

[20] He G, Victor D G. Experiences and lessons from China’s success in providing electricity for all[J]. Resources Conservation & Recycling, 2017, 122:335-338.

[21] Kayser D. Solar photovoltaic projects in China: High investment risks and the need for institutional response[J]. Applied Energy, 2016, 174:144-152.

[22] Khameneh A H, Taheri A, Ershadi M. Offering a Framework for Evaluating the Performance of Project Risk Management System[J]. Procedia - Social and Behavioral Sciences, 2016, 226:82-90.

[23] Lüthi S, Wüstenhagen R. The price of policy risk — Empirical insights from choice experiments with European photovoltaic project developers[J]. Energy Economics, 2012, 34:1001-1011.

[24] Lai C S, Jia Y, Lai L L, et al. A comprehensive review on large-scale photovoltaic system with applications of electrical energy storage[J]. Renewable & Sustainable Energy Reviews, 2017, 78:439-451.

[25] Li D F. A note on “using intuitionistic fuzzy sets for fault-tree analysis on printed circuit board assembly”[J]. Microelectronics Reliability, 2008, 48: 1741.

[26] Li D F. A ratio ranking method of triangular intuitionistic fuzzy numbers and its application to MADM problems[J]. Computers & Mathematics with Applications, 2010, 60:1557-1570.

[27] Linstone H A, Turoff M. The Delphi method: Techniques and applications[J]. Journal of Marketing Research, 1976, 18:363-364.

[28] Luo G-l, Long C-f, Wei X, et al. Financing risks involved in distributed PV power generation in China and analysis of countermeasures[J]. Renewable and Sustainable Energy Reviews, 2016, 63: 93-101.

[29] Luthra S, Govindan K, Kharb R K, et al. Evaluating the enablers in solar power developments in the current scenario using fuzzy DEMATEL: An Indian perspective[J]. Renewable and Sustainable Energy Reviews, 2016, 63:379-397.

[30] Moser D, Buono M D, Jahn U, et al. Identification of technical risks in the photovoltaic value chain and quantification of the economic impact[J]. Progress in Photovoltaics Research & Applications, 2017, 25.

[31] Perez-Gallardo J, Azzaro-Pantel C, Astier S. A Multi-objective Framework for Assessment of Recycling Strategies for Photovoltaic Modules based on Life Cycle Assessment[J]. Waste and

Biomass Valorization, 2018, 9:147-159.

[32] Pinto A. QRAM a Qualitative Occupational Safety Risk Assessment Model for the construction industry that incorporate uncertainties by the use of fuzzy sets[J]. Safety Science, 2014, 63: 57-76.

[33] Protopapadaki C, Saelens D. Heat pump and PV impact on residential low-voltage distribution grids as a function of building and district properties[J]. Applied Energy 2017, 192:268-281.

[34] Ren X F. Land acquisition, rural protests, and the local state in China and India. Environment and Planning, C:Politics and Space 2017, 35(1):25-41.

[35] Rodríguez A, Ortega F, Concepción R. An intuitionistic method for the selection of a risk management approach to information technology projects[J]. Information Sciences, 2017, 375:202-218.

[36] Samantra C, Datta S, Mahapatra SS. Fuzzy based risk assessment module for metropolitan construction project: An empirical study[J]. Engineering Applications of Artificial Intelligence, 2017.

[37] Scheutzlich T, Klinghammer W, Scholand M, et al. Financing of solar home systems in developing countries: the role of financing in the dissemination process. Vol. II: Case studies. Classical Review, 2000.

[38] Shan L, Yu A T W, Wu Y. Strategies for risk management in urban–rural conflict: Two case studies of land acquisition in urbanising China[J]. Habitat International, 2017, 59: 90-100.

[39] Taylan O, Bafail A O, Abdulaal R M S, et al. Construction projects selection and risk assessment by fuzzy AHP and fuzzy TOPSIS methodologies[J]. Applied Soft Computing Journal, 2014, 17:105-116.

[40] Tomosk S, Haysom J E, Wright D. Quantifying economic risk in photovoltaic power projects[J]. Renewable Energy, 2017, 109:422-433.

[41] Wan S P. Power average operators of trapezoidal intuitionistic fuzzy numbers and application to multi-attribute group decision making[J]. Applied Mathematical Modelling, 2013, 37:4112-4126.

[42] Wan S P, Wang F, Lin L L, et al. Some new generalized aggregation operators for triangular intuitionistic fuzzy numbers and application to multi-attribute group decision making[J]. Computers & Industrial Engineering, 2016, 93:286-301.

[43] Wan S P, Wang Q Y, Dong J Y.The extended VIKOR method for multi-attribute group decision making with triangular intuitionistic fuzzy numbers[J]. Knowledge-Based Systems, 2013, 52: 65-77.

[44] Wu W W. 2008. Choosing knowledge management strategies by using a combined ANP and DEMATEL approach[J]. Expert Systems with Applications, 2013, 35:828-835.

[45] Wu Y, Li L, Xu R, et al. Risk assessment in straw-based power generation public-private partnership projects in China: A Fuzzy Synthetic Evaluation analysis[J]. Journal of Cleaner Production, 2017.

[46] Wu Y, Zhang J, Yuan J, et al.Study of decision framework of offshore wind power station site selection based on ELECTRE-III under intuitionistic fuzzy environment: A case of China[J]. Energy Conversion & Management, 2016. 113: 66-81.

[47] Xia X, Govindan K, Zhu Q. Analyzing internal barriers for automotive parts remanufacturers in China using grey-DEMATEL approach[J]. Journal of Cleaner Production, 2015, 87:811-825.

[48] Xu F, Liu J, Lin S, et al. A VIKOR-based approach for assessing the service performance of electric vehicle sharing programs: A case study in Beijing[J]. Journal of Cleaner Production, 2017, 148: 254-267.

[49] Xu Y, Chan A P C, Xia B, et al. Critical risk factors affecting the implementation of PPP waste-to-energy projects in China[J]. Applied Energy, 2015, 158:403-411.

[50] Xue J. Photovoltaic agriculture - New opportunity for photovoltaic applications in China[J]. Renewable & Sustainable Energy Reviews, 2017, 73:1-9.

[51] Zadeh L A. Fuzzy sets, Fuzzy Sets, Fuzzy Logic, And Fuzzy Systems: Selected Papers by Lotfi A Zadeh[J]. World Scientific, 1996, 394-432.

[52] Zhang M M, Zhou D Q, Zhou P, et al. Optimal design of subsidy to stimulate renewable energy investments: The case of China[J]. Renewable & Sustainable Energy Reviews, 2016, 71:873-883.

[53] Zhang Y, Zhu S, Sparks R, et al. Impacts of solar PV generators on power system stability and voltage performance[A]. Power and Energy Society General Meeting, 2012.

[54] Zhao Z Y, Zuo J, Zillante G, et al.Critical success factors for BOT electric power projects in China: Thermal power versus wind power[J]. Renewable Energy, 2010, 35:1283-1291.

Chapter 14

Risk assessment on offshore photovoltaic power generation projects in China based on a fuzzy analysis framework

Yunna Wu[a, b], Lingwenying Li[a, b*], Zixin Song[a, b], Xiaoshan Lin[a, b]

a. School of Economics and Management, North China Electric Power University, Beijing, China

b. Beijing Key Laboratory of New Energy and Low-Carbon Development (North China Electric Power University), Changping, Beijing, 102206, China

Abstract: China has begun to promote offshore photovoltaic in coastal areas taking its advantages of saving land resources and proximity to load centers. However, the projects are bound to face a series of risk factors as the industry is in its infancy. This paper conducts a risk assessment on offshore photovoltaic power generation projects in China based on a fuzzy framework. Firstly, 16 risk factors affecting offshore photovoltaic power generation projects in China are identified and classified into 4 groups. Secondly, a risk assessment model is constructed involving Hesitant Fuzzy Linguistic Term Sets, Triangular Fuzzy Number and Fuzzy Synthetic Evaluation. Thirdly, this paper conduct an empirical study of China, and the result shows that the risk level of offshore photovoltaic power generation projects in China is medium high. Finally, some response measures are proposed. The risk index system and corresponding countermeasures can provide a reference for project managers to allocate resources to prevent risk events. Besides, the risk assessment model can help project investors to avoid too risky projects. In addition, the risk assessment on offshore photovoltaic power generation projects in China has not been discussed by scholars yet. Thus, this paper contributes to the literature and expand the knowledge.

Key words: Risk assessment, Offshore PV, Hesitant fuzzy linguistic term sets, Triangular fuzzy number, Fuzzy synthetic evaluation

Nomenclature			
$S=\{s_0,\ldots,s_g\}$	linguistic term set	H_S	HFLTS
s_i	i-th linguistic term	$G_H=(V_N,V_T,I,P)$	context-free grammar
V_N	element set	V_T	relation rule
I	element in V_N	P	generated function
ll	linguistic expression	E_{G_H}	transformation function
$\tilde{a}=(a^L,a^M,a^U)$	triangle fuzzy number	a^L	lower bound of a triangle fuzzy number
a^U	upper bound of a triangle fuzzy number	a^M	middle value of a triangular fuzzy number
m	number of linguistic terms in a H_S	h_{cij}	aggregated value of a criterion in terms of H_S by an expert
c_i	i-th criterion	u_i	order induced vector
R_c	second-level evaluation vector	$\tilde{g}_j$	second vector of the largest element in u_i
R_{ci}	first-level evaluation vector	w_{ci}	weight of the i-th risk group
w_{cij}	weight of the j-th criterion in a risk group	Sd	similarity degree between two triangle fuzzy numbers

1. Introduction

As the third renewable energy source in terms of global capacity, solar energy now is a highly appealing source of electricity by means of photovoltaic (PV) systems that cover the conversion of light into electricity using semiconducting materials that exhibit the PV effect [1]. Solar PV power generation, without pollution and greenhouse gas emissions once installed, is growing rapidly and has become a leading player in energy industry in China [2]. Wherein, the most typical form is the large-scale centralized ground-based PV power plant, mainly located in the northwest region including Xinjiang, Qinghai, Gansu, etc. However, more and more problems have emerged in ground PV. For example, installation of PV panels on the ground leads to large land occupancy, thereby bringing some pressure on agricultural production [3]. At the same time, severe solar curtailment occurs because of weak power consumption capacity in regions with adequate solar resources [4]. In contrast, the development of offshore PV power generation (an example is shown in Fig. 14.1) in China has great advantages in overcoming such problems. On one hand, China has nearly 18, 000 kilometers of continental coastline [5], and the installation of large-scale centralized offshore PV generation facilities along the sea can greatly conserve increasingly precious onshore land resources. On the other hand, China's eastern coastal regions are economically developed with a high population density, and the development of offshore PV power generation provides an ideal solution for the growing power demand of these load centers, without the need for long-distance power transmission from northwestern regions. In addition, installation of PV panels at sea can reduce the temperature of PV modules, reduce the dust adhesion of components, and increase the energy conversion efficiency, resulting in more power output than land PV [6]. Moreover, seawater contains Magnesium Chloride, which could replace the highly toxic and pricy Cadmium Chloride that is one of the key components in PV panels [7].

Fig. 14.1 An example of offshore PV power generation (Source: Solar Tribune: https://solartribune.com/offshore-solar-new-energy-opportunity-coastal-communities/).

At present, only several offshore PV power generation projects have been completed and put into operation in the southeast coastal areas of China, and some other projects are at the preparatory or construction stage. Table 1 shows part of their information. It can be said that China's offshore PV power generation is still in its infancy. Corresponding core technologies are relatively immature such as the central inverter featuring the integration of the inverter, the transformer and the switchgear. Also, the market environment is not standardized enough, and very little reference information is available for new projects. On account of these challenges, investors and owners are bound to face a series of risks in the process of project construction and operation. Thus, reasonable risk assessment and well-founded responses become especially important in project life cycle including the feasibility study, construction, operation and maintenance phase. Nevertheless, this issue has not drawn a widely attention by researchers. When studying offshore PV power generation, almost all of them are concerned about the technical aspect. Trapani et al. [8] put forward an alternative based on flexible thin film PV that floats and then concentrate on the techno-economic appraisal of offshore PV systems directly on the waterline. Trapani and Millar [9] assess the feasibility of offshore PV that is integrated with the existing fossil plant of the Maltese islands. Although Sahu et al. [10] mention some disadvantages and challenges of offshore PV when reviewing the floating photovoltaic power plant, the corresponding analysis is very limited and not deep enough.

Table 14.1 Some offshore PV power generation projects in China
(Source: Chinese National Energy Administration: http://www.nea.gov.cn/).

No.	Project Name	Capacity	Stage
1	Fujian Zhangpu Zhuyu Offshore Photovoltaic Power Generation Project	1×5MW	Formal operation
2	Zhejiang Shepantu Mariculture Photovoltaic Power Generation Project	1×99MW	Formal operation
3	Anhui Huainan Offshore Photovoltaic Power Generation Project	1×40MW	Formal operation
4	Fujian Yunxiao Dongsha Offshore Photovoltaic Power Generation Project	1×12MW	Trial operation
5	Jiangsu Donghai Quyang Offshore Photovoltaic Power Generation Project	1×15MW+1×20MW	Construction
6	Jiangsu Nantong Rudong Mariculture Photovoltaic Power Generation Project	1×10MW	Preparation
7	Jiangsu Huaian Xiangshui Mariculture Photovoltaic Power Generation Project	1×10MW+1×40MW	Preparation

As for risk assessment on general PV power generation projects, this issue has been widely discussed by many scholars from different aspects, including the financial, environmental, technical and management risk. For example, Luo et al. [11] conduct an analysis of financing risks involved in distributed PV power generation in China and put forward effective countermeasures. Manzini et al. [12] focus on the safety risk in the process of photovoltaic installations and carry out an assessment on PV systems fire events. Prusty and Jena [13] accomplished risk assessment of a PV integrated power system by means of computing the over-limit probabilities and the severities of events from a technical point of view. Liu et al. [14] put forward an improved framework to conduct uncertainty assessment on grid-connected PV system with taking weather variability and component availability into consideration. Mateo et al. [15] attach an importance to the influence of policy towards PV industry and then perform a quantitative assessment on this kind of risks. It can be seen that these researches are mainly conducted from a certain perspective and thus lack a comprehensive insight into risk assessment of PV projects. In addition to this, most of them only assess individual risks and rank them simply, without discussing the overall risk level of a project. At the same time, offshore PV power generation projects have their own unique characteristics, so it is essential to establish a risk assessment framework with pertinence. That is to say, the situation that there is a lack of literature about overall risk assessment on offshore PV power generation projects as well as a targeted comprehensive index system provides an valuable opportunity for the research of this paper.

This paper aims to: ①identify and analyze the risk factors that have an impact on offshore PV power projects in China and ②Assesse the overall risk level of offshore PV power generation projects in China. The originality of this paper comes from the following three aspects: ①an index system, for risk assessment on offshore PV projects in China, is established through a deep analysis of previous studies, actual projects and expert opinions; ②a risk assessment model is proposed for offshore PV power generation projects based on Hesitant Fuzzy Linguistic Term Sets (HFLTS) and Triangular Fuzzy Number (TFN), which could well handle the fuzziness and enhance the reliability; ③risk response measures incorporating management ideas are put forward for each risk factor aiming at improving management efficiency and quality. The contribution of this study are multifaceted: ①through the above work, this paper can contribute to the literature of renewable energy generation and expand the knowledge of risk management; ②the established index system for offshore PV power generation projects can help risk managers understand each risk factor better and thus ensure smooth implement of projects; ③with awareness of the overall risk level, project decision makers is able to make appropriate decisions and avoid too risky projects; ④the countermeasures for each risk factor can provide a reference and management inspiration for policy makers and corresponding practitioners.

The remainder of this study is structured as follows. Section 2 reviews the research status of HFLTS, TFN and ANP in existing literatures. Section 3 analyzes the risk factors that have an impact on offshore PV power generation projects in China and constructs a corresponding criteria system. Section 4 establishes a risk assessment model for offshore PV power generation projects. Section 5 conducts an empirical study of China. Section 6 gives coping strategies for each risk. Finally, Section 7 concludes this paper and proposes limitations.

2. Literature review

Multiple-criteria decision-making (MCDM) problem, as a sub-discipline of operations research, concerns structuring and solving decision and planning problems involving multiple criteria. The issue of risk assessment have been identified as a typical MCDM problem with uncertainty by many scholars [16-18]. There are two main reasons for the uncertainty of decision-making information. Firstly, risk assessment of a project is usually conducted in the planning and feasibility study stage, which can only be based primarily on pre-estimation of future circumstances. Therefore, uncertainty emerges in the process of risk assessment. Secondly, the judgement of some decision-making information in risk assessment relies on experience and knowledge of experts, with ambiguity existing in such a thinking mode. Hence, the MCDM methods to handle imperfect, vague and imprecise information play a key role in the rationality and accuracy of risk assessment. Several tools, such as fuzzy logic [19] and fuzzy sets theory [20] have been successfully applied to address this issue. Nevertheless, there is great defect in these methods when two or more sources of vagueness appear simultaneously. For this reason, some other generalizations and extensions of fuzzy sets have been introduced including type-2 fuzzy sets, intuitionistic fuzzy sets and interval fuzzy sets [21-24]. However, the experts who are involved in the MCDM problem defined under uncertainty cannot easily provide a single term as an expression of their opinions sometimes because they may think of several terms at the same time. As a result, the theory of hesitant fuzzy is introduced. Hesitant fuzzy sets (HFS) was first put forward by Torra [25] to manage situations where experts hesitate between several values to assess an indicator, alternative or variable, providing a very interesting extension of fuzzy sets. Nevertheless, similar situations may occur in qualitative settings so that experts think of several possible linguistic values or richer expressions than a single term. To solve this weakness, Rodriguez et.al [26] put forward the HFLTS method to provide a linguistic and computational basis to increase the richness of linguistic elicitation and the use of context-free grammars by using comparative terms. To illustrate the advantaged and superiority of the HFLTS method, a comparison has been made among basic fuzzy set theories, extended fuzzy set theories, the HFS and the HFLTS, as shown in Table 14.2. The HFLTS method has been studied and applied by many scholars. Chen et al. [27] propose proportional HFLTSs and a probability theory-based outranking method for MCDM problem. Liao et al. [28] research correlation coefficients of HFLTSs in the process of qualitative decision making and illustrate it applicability and validation. Wang et al. [29] employ linguistic scale functions to conduct the transformation between qualitative information and quantitative data when the HFLTS is used in multi-criteria decision-making. Proved to be an effective tool for complex and vague MCDM environment, the HFLTS method is employed in this paper to assign evaluation information by experts to each risk factor that has an impact on offshore PV power generation projects, thereby meeting the linguistic expression flexibility requirement of experts.

Table 14.2 Comparison between different fuzzy methods.

Method	Description
basic fuzzy sets (fuzzy logic, fuzzy sets)	Accords with the human cognitive habits Depict the fuzziness
extended fuzzy sets (type-2 fuzzy sets, intuitionistic fuzzy sets, interval fuzzy sets)	Accords with the human cognitive habits Depict the fuzziness Handle several vagueness resource simultaneously
hesitant fuzzy sets	Accords with the human cognitive habits Depict the fuzziness Handle hesitant fuzzy information
hesitant fuzzy linguistic term sets	Accords with the human cognitive habits Depict the fuzziness Handle several vagueness resource simultaneously Handle hesitant fuzzy term Handle multi-hesitant fuzzy terms

After assigning evaluation information to indexes, how to transfer the linguistic assessment terms into the computational form becomes a question. Fortunately, fuzzy numbers provide a solution. The fuzzy number, a generalization of a regular and real number, does not refer to one single value but rather to a connected set of possible values, and each possible value has its own weight between 0 and 1, called the membership function. After years of development, there have been many different branches of fuzzy numbers. The TFN, firstly proposed by Zadeh [30] in 1965, is one of them. The TFN consists of lower bound, upper bound and most possible value, with the advantage of containing more information in situation expression than the traditional fuzzy number. In recent years, the TFN has been applied to MCDM problems by many researchers on the purpose of making decisions more in line with real-life situations. Samantra et al. [31] employ the TFN to conduct risk assessment on metropolitan construction projects associated with uncertain characteristics. In order to evaluate the benefits of investing in safety measures for pipelines, Urbina and Aoyama [32] use the TFN as a tool to deal with uncertainty. Gul et al. propose a new Fine-Kinney-based risk assessment framework using the TFN, enabling group decision-making to be well solved under uncertain environment. When studying groundwater resources management, Ren et al. [33] develop an inexact interval-valued triangular fuzzy based multi-attribute preference model, which takes vagueness in parameter values into consideration. Zhao et al. [34] develop some hesitant triangular fuzzy aggregation operators and investigate their application to MCDM problems, with an illustrative example to show the validity of these operators. It can be seen that the TFN is able to handle the MCDM problem with vague information well. Therefore, introducing the TFN to risk assessment on offshore PV power generation projects has theoretical reliability and practical significance.

The weight reflects the relative importance of an indicator in the evaluation process. Selecting an appropriate method to determine the weight is important for obtaining a reasonable result in risk assessment. Analytic hierarchy process (AHP) is a commonly used method of weight calculation, with each element in the hierarchy considered to be independent of all the others. However, in real-world cases, there is interdependence among the items and the alternatives. Therefore, it is almost impossible for indicators to be completely independent, and correlations between indicators must be taken into consideration when determining their weight value. The analytic network process (ANP) method, put forward by Saaty [35], has provided an effective approach to addressing this issue. It is able to well handle interdependence between indicators by obtaining the composite weights through the development of super matrix. The ANP method has been widely applied to solving the MCDM problems by many scholars, especially the risk management problem [36-39]. Thus, the ANP method is utilized to calculate the weights of indicators in this paper.

Based on the review above, the applicability and superiority of the risk assessment model proposed in this paper can be explicitly stated. The established framework, including HFLTS and TFN considering correlations between the risk factors under the fuzzy environment, possesses the following advantages: ①HFLTS can allow experts to evaluate a risk factor more flexibly when they are hesitant between several linguistic terms; ②TFN is a powerful tool to express various kinds of uncertainties involved in the offshore PV projects due to their complicated and changeable environment; ③the ANP method can take into account the non-negligible fact that indicators associated with risk assessment have correlations. At present, there is no literature that makes such a combination of HFLTS, TFN and ANP in the risk assessment field. Thus, the introduction of these three methods simultaneously plus the idea of group decision making can significantly broaden and deepen the research on the fuzzy theory and the MCDM theory.

3. Criteria system of risk assessment on offshore PV projects in China

Identification of risk factors is an essential prerequisite to implement risk management and achieve project success[40]. Aiming at identifying the risks that have an impact on offshore PV projects, a three-step method is adopted in this paper. In the first step, a thorough analysis of previous studies is conducted, and the literature search is carried out according to the following boundaries. First, the Web of Science, Elsevier-Science Direct, Taylor & Francis and CNKI are chosen as the academic databases to be used for literature search and selection because they included articles in a broad scope. Then, considering the fact that almost no research on offshore PV power generation has been carried out, 'PV/offshore wind power generation' is determined as the search keywords to expand the searching scope. Following this, we select journal papers published over the period between January, 2005 and June, 2018 when PV/offshore wind power generation went through a boom. Finally, 38 qualified papers are identified. In the second step, this paper conduct an analysis of some offshore PV projects that are completed or still under construction, to identify and understand possible risk factors. All chosen projects are conducted in China because the aim of this paper is to assess the risk level of China's offshore PV power generation projects. In the third step, two professors from the field of PV power generation and project management respectively are invited to give opinions on the risk factor list obtained by the first two steps as well as the factor grouping. They point that the meanings of "high equipment purchase cost" and "interest rate increase risk" are both included in risk "high initial investment" so it would be better to delete the two risk factors. At the same time, they hold the viewpoint that feelings of the public should be taken into consideration dew to the concept of human-centered. As a result, the risk "Visual effect risk (C34)" is added. After the three steps, the criteria system of risk assessment on offshore PV projects in China is finally established and classified into four categories, as shown in Fig. 14.2.

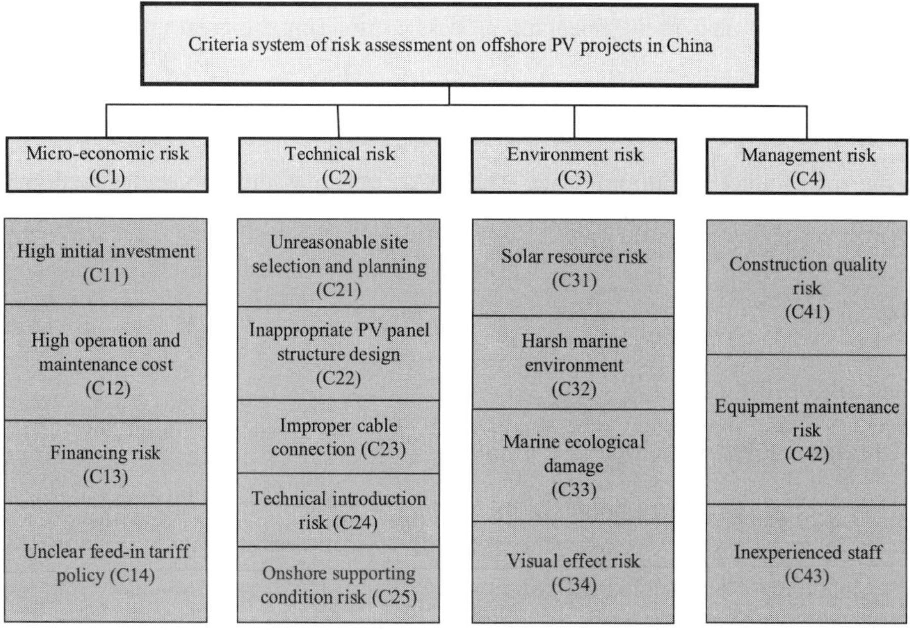

Fig. 14.2 Index system of risk assessment on offshore PV projects in China.

3.1 Micro-economic risk (C1)

3.1.1 High initial investment (C11)

Considering the complexity of the design and manufacturing process due to higher performance requirements, the offshore PV power generation project would be faced with higher costs of solar panels compared with the ground one. Moreover, underwater cables have high requirements on construction technology and professional equipment, increasing the capital pressure of initial investment of the project as a result [41].

3.1.2 High operation and maintenance cost (C12)

The operation cost of offshore PV power generation is approximately ten times more than that of other conventional fossil-fuel-based power generation projects during the first ten years of its operational phase [10]. As time goes on, the equipment tends to suffer from deformation, metal corrosion and material aging deterioration easily for various reasons in the marine environment, which virtually leads to maintenance cost increase.

3.1.3 Financing risk (C13)

As mentioned above, the offshore PV power generation requires a relative large scale of funding. Therefore, the financing process is particularly essential for the smooth development of the project. The financing risk refers to the uncertainties arising from financing activities such as financing guarantees, financing structure design and financing channel selection [42]. As the offshore PV power generation technology in China is still in the infant stage, there could exist great obstructions and risks in the financing process considering the great uncertainties in future benefits.

3.1.4 Unclear feed-in tariff policy (C14)

As the most direct manifestation of whether a project is profitable, the feed-in tariff is directly related to the income of offshore PV power generation projects. However, there is no specific tariff policy for offshore PV power generation in China at present, which would lays uncertainty in the revenue of the project.

3.2 Technical risk (C2)

3.2.1 Unreasonable site selection and planning (C21)

Site selection and planning is a critical step toward the successful development of offshore PV systems. However, the selection process involves many aspects such as solar resources, distance to load center and geological conditions [43], and thus it becomes risky. The improper offshore PV plant site may not only be unable to meet electricity demand and have a negative impact on project benefits but also give rise to failure to start construction as scheduled.

3.2.2 Inappropriate PV panel structure design (C22)

The content of PV panel structure design contains distance between the PV panels, dimensions and tilt angle of PV panels, the number of units to be installed and so on [44]. Inappropriate PV panel structure design will lead to inadequate utilization of solar radiation and sunshine duration. That is to say, if there is no scientific PV panel layout design for offshore PV systems, the maximum production efficiency cannot be guaranteed consequently.

3.2.3 Improper cable connection (C23)

Under the gravitational effect of celestial bodies, there is a periodic fluctuation in the seawater in coastal areas, which is called ocean tide [45]. This phenomenon brings the offshore PV projects another risk, that is, when the seawater falls back, the pulling force of its downward movement makes the cable to move with it. If the cable connection between the shore inverter and PV panels as well as the connection mode of the nodes are designed in an improper manner, the influence of tides on the cable lines cannot be coped with well.

3.2.4 Technical introduction risk (C24)

At present, the development of offshore PV power generation projects in China is not mature enough. The research on core technology is insufficient and relies heavily on imports. When the foreign technology does not match China’s actual situation due to different geographic conditions and staff capability, the introduction of technology will become one of the risks for the offshore PV project.

3.2.5 Onshore supporting condition risk (C25)

Onshore supporting conditions refers to the favorable factors conducive to the construction, operation and maintenance of the projects including the traffic condition, electrical transmission and distribution system. Thus, the traffic condition should be considered because of its influence on the large equipment transportation along the coast. Moreover, there is also a need to analyze whether the onshore power grid or its future planning can meet supporting requirements.

3.3 Environment risk (C3)

3.3.1 Solar resource risk (C31)

When conducting the planning and design for an offshore PV power generation project, the amount of generated power is usually estimated based on the local daily radiation and monthly radiation. However, in actual operation, the radiation in the area cannot meet the requirements of the power generation voltage if there are adverse weather conditions such as continuous rain or cloud. At the same time, haze, dust and other obstructions in the atmosphere also diminish the power output [46]. Besides, climate change may pose a risk to the prediction of the solar resource in the long-term. Thus, the power system maybe cannot achieve expected generation volume, thereby affecting project profits.

3.3.2 Harsh marine environment (C32)

Since the coastal areas of China are often attacked by typhoons in summer, the farm construction may be very difficult, and components may suffer serious damage in the operation. In addition, the coastal area of southeast China features a subtropical monsoon climate. The salt brought by prevailing land-sea breeze will cause serious salt spray corrosion and affect the durability of PV modules. Moreover, stress and vibration usually occurs in offshore PV plants owing to wind, waves and other external forces, which will cause micro-cracks in PV modules. It is worth noting that the shifting of climate change may result in aggravation of extreme ocean weather such as the increasing frequency of typhoons in China caused by the La Nina phenomenon [47], bringing a great challenge to the offshore PV projects.

3.3.3 Marine ecological damage (C33)

Owing to the large scale of offshore PV farms, the development and construction process will inevitably have a certain impact on the marine ecological environment. For example, the laying of submarine transmission cables will make seabed sediments float and thus influence the reproduction of plankton. Additionally, the projects will directly occupy the coastal habitat of birds and affect their nesting and breeding. These damages to the marine ecosystem may incur opposition from environmental protection agencies or environmentalists.

3.3.4 Visual effect risk (C34)

Although the light transmittance of tempered glass for PV modules is high, the reflection phenomenon still cannot be completely avoided, which may cause a visual impact on coastal residents. In Japan, a PV power station was sued for compensation by nearby residents because of its light reflection, resulting in considerable economic losses. Besides, large-scale PV power farms also generate visual impacts on the coastal landscape.

3.4 Management risk (C4)

3.4.1 Construction quality risk (C41)

PV cell modules will reach a very high direct-current voltage through series connection, which is much higher than the safe voltage [48]. Due to the large number of lines, open-circuit and short-circuit may occur during construction. Therefore, quality problems may be caused in the construction stage if there is a lack of good management.

3.4.2 Equipment maintenance risk (C42)

As equipment used for PV power generation projects including solar panels, inverters and transformers are all large high-tech equipment, mistakes often occur in daily maintenance, resulting in equipment failure and economic loss. Besides, the special marine environment will also bring difficulties and risks to maintenance.

3.4.3 Inexperienced staff (C43)

Most of the employees involved in the offshore PV projects are from the ground mounted PV industry. As the work environment changes from onshore to offshore, they ordinarily have the limited professional knowledge and work experience towards the marine environment, which would be risky to some extent.

4. A risk assessment model for offshore PV power generation projects

Step 1. Determining the correlation and weight of criteria.

Obviously, there are differences in the importance of each criterion in risk assessment. Thus, the relative criticality of criteria needs to be reflected by the weight. At the same time, some correlations exist between the criteria. For example, harsh marine environment i.e. risk C32 would cause corrosion of PV panels and thus increase maintenance costs i.e. risk C12. Taking such situation into consideration, the ANP method is adopted to determine the weight of criteria in this paper. Firstly, the internal dependency relationship is analyzed and determined. Then, the pairwise criticality comparison is performed among criteria with the 1-9 scale method, and the judgement matrix can be obtained. Finally, the Super Decision software is employed as the tool to achieve the weight calculation.

Step 2. Defining the linguistic term set and obtaining the HFLTS.

The risk assessment on offshore PV power generation projects is so complicated an issue involving quite a lot factors that experts cannot easily provide a single evaluation term as expression of their knowledge and may hesitant between several ones towards a criterion. Fortunately, as mentioned above, the HFLTS method is capable of handling this situation. Thus, the HFLTS method is employed in this paper to give criterion evaluation information so as to reduce information loss and improve decision-making accuracy. The basic definitions and operations of HFLTS are shown as follows [26].

Let $S=\{s_0,\dots,s_g\}$ be a linguistic term set. Then, an HFLTS, H_S, is an ordered finite subset of the continuous linguistic terms of *S*. Let G_H be a context-free grammar that generates linguistic expressions represented by HFLTS. The elements of $G_H=(V_N,V_T,I,P)$ are defined as follows:

$$\begin{aligned} &V_N=\left\{\begin{matrix}\langle\text{primary term}\rangle,\langle\text{composite term}\rangle,\\ \langle\text{unary relation}\rangle,\langle\text{binary relation}\rangle,\langle\text{conjunction}\rangle\end{matrix}\right\}\\ &V_T=\{\text{lower than, greater than, between, and, } s_0,\dots s_g\}\\ &I\in V_N\end{aligned} \tag{14-1}$$

Then, the linguistic expressions ll produced by G_H are transformed into HFLTS by means of the transformation function E_{G_H}. Let E_{G_H} be a function that transforms linguistic expressions ll obtained by G_H into HFLTS H_S, where S is the linguistic term set used by G_H:

$$E_{G_H}:ll\longrightarrow H_S$$

The linguistic expressions that are generated by using the production rules will be transformed into HFLTS in different ways according to their meaning:

$$E_{G_H}(s_i)=\{s_i/s_i\in S\} \tag{14-2}$$

$$E_{G_H}(\text{less than } s_j)=\{s_j/s_j\in S \text{ and } s_j\leqslant s_i\} \tag{14-3}$$

$$E_{G_H}(\text{greater than } s_i)=\{s_j/s_j\in S \text{ and } s_j\geqslant s_i\} \tag{14-4}$$

$$E_{G_H}(\text{between } s_i \text{ and } s_j)=\{s_k/s_k\in S \text{ and } s_i\leqslant s_k\leqslant s_j\} \tag{14-5}$$

Step 3. Transforming the HFLTS into triangular fuzzy numbers.

In order to expressing expert imperfect knowledge in decision-making utilization more effectively, the triangular fuzzy number is applied in this risk assessment model.

$\tilde{a}=(a^L,a^M,a^U)$ represents a triangle fuzzy number if its membership degree function is expressed mathematically as follows [49]:

$$\mu_{\tilde{a}}(x)=\begin{cases}0 & x<a^L\\(x-a^L)/(a^M-a^L) & a^L\leqslant x\leqslant a^M\\(a^U-x)/(a^U-a^M) & a^M\leqslant x\leqslant a^U\\0 & x>a^U\end{cases} \tag{14-6}$$

where $a^L\leqslant a^M\leqslant a^U$. a^L and a^U are the lower bound and upper bound, respectively.

Let H_S be a HFLTS provided by an expert group towards a risk factor. Suppose that there are m linguistic terms within it. Then, the HFLTS can be transformed into triangular fuzzy numbers as:

$$h_{cij}=\left(\frac{1}{m}\sum si\right)=\left(\frac{1}{m}\sum a^L,\frac{1}{m}\sum a^M,\frac{1}{m}\sum a^U\right) \tag{14-7}$$

where h_{cij} represents the aggregated value of a criterion in terms of HFLTS by an expert.

Then, the HFLTS can be aggregated as:

$$h_{cij}=\left(\sum ci\cdot si\right)=\left(\sum ci\cdot a^L,\sum ci\cdot a^M,\sum ci\cdot a^U\right) \tag{14-8}$$

where h_{cij} represents the aggregated value of a criterion in terms of HFLTS by an expert.

Step 4. Aggregating triangular fuzzy numbers of experts based on FIOWHA operator.

The risk assessment on offshore PV power generation projects studied in this paper is a group decision making problem in which a group of experts provide their evaluation terms for a risk factor. To achieve the aggregation of experts' opinion, this paper adopts the fuzzy induced ordered weighted harmonic averaging (FIOWHA) operator based on triangular fuzzy number. The following contents give the basic concepts and steps.

Let $\tilde{a}_1,\tilde{a}_2,\ldots,\tilde{a}_n$ be a set of triangular fuzzy numbers that need to be aggregated. Then the FIOWHA operator is defined as [50]:

$$\text{FIOWHA}_w\left(\left\langle u_1,\tilde{r}_1\right\rangle,\left\langle u_2,\tilde{r}_2\right\rangle,\ldots,\left\langle u_n,\tilde{r}_n\right\rangle\right)=\frac{1}{\sum_{j=1}^{n}\frac{w_j}{\tilde{g}_j}} \tag{14-9}$$

where $\tilde{r}_j=\left[r_j^L,r_j^M,r_j^U\right]$, and $w=\left(w_1,w_2,\ldots,w_n\right)^T$ is a weight vector associated with the FIOWHA operator that satisfies $w_j\in\left[0,1\right]$ and $\sum_{j=1}^{n}w_j=1$. $\tilde{g}_j$ is the second vector $\tilde{r}_i$ in $\left\langle u_i,\tilde{r}_i\right\rangle$ of the ith largest element in $u_i\left(i=1,2,\ldots,n\right)$ that ranks from the largest to the smallest. The first vector u_i in $\left\langle u_i,\tilde{r}_i\right\rangle$ is called the order induced vector.

Step 5. Aggregating triangular fuzzy numbers of criteria based on FSE method.

In order to handle the risk assessment on offshore PV power generation projects, a multi-criteria uncertainty ambiguity problem that involves subjective judgment of experts, the fuzzy synthetic evaluation (FSE) mothed is adopted in this paper to aggregate triangular fuzzy numbers of each criterion to obtain the overall risk level of the project. The fuzzy synthetic evaluation process is divided into three phases. Firstly, the first-level evaluation vector R_{ci} consisting of triangular fuzzy numbers of criteria within each group is established as:

$$R_{ci} = \begin{pmatrix} h_{ci1} \\ \vdots \\ h_{cij} \end{pmatrix} \tag{14-10}$$

Secondly, the second-level evaluation vector R_c including triangular fuzzy numbers of every group is obtained by fuzzy synthesis operation, as shown below:

$$h_{ci} = W_{ci} \bullet R_{ci} = \begin{pmatrix} w_{ci1} & \dots & w_{cij} \end{pmatrix} \bullet \begin{pmatrix} h_{ci1} \\ \vdots \\ h_{cij} \end{pmatrix} \tag{14-11}$$

$$R_c = \begin{pmatrix} h_{c1} \\ \vdots \\ h_{ci} \end{pmatrix} \tag{14-12}$$

where w_{cij} is the weight of each risk factor within every group.

Thirdly, the overall risk level of the project represented by TNFs is calculated as:

$$R = W_i \bullet R_c = \begin{pmatrix} w_{c1} & \dots & w_{ci} \end{pmatrix} \bullet \begin{pmatrix} h_{c1} \\ \vdots \\ h_{ci} \end{pmatrix} = \left(r^L, r^M, r^U \right) \tag{14-13}$$

where w_{ci} denotes the weight of each risk factor group.

Step 6. Defuzzification of the triangular fuzzy number.

Through the above steps, the risk level of offshore PV power generation projects is expressed in the form of triangular fuzzy number. In order to get a more intuitive and easy-to-understand result, the similarity degree is introduced for defuzzification treatment in this paper. The similarity degree between two triangular fuzzy numbers can be calculated as [51]:

$$Sd(\alpha, \beta) = 1 - \frac{\left|\alpha^L - \beta^L\right| + \left|\alpha^M - \beta^M\right| + \left|\alpha^U - \beta^U\right|}{3} \tag{14-14}$$

where $\alpha = \left(\alpha^L, \alpha^M, \alpha^U\right)$ and $\beta = \left(\beta^L, \beta^M, \beta^U\right)$ are two triangular fuzzy numbers, and $Sd(\alpha, \beta)$ represents the similarity degree between α and β. Thus, which risk level the evaluation result is closer to can be determined by the principle of maximum similarity.

5. Empirical study

In this section, the risk assessment on offshore PV power generation projects in China is carried out through the model proposed in Section 4. First of all, a questionnaire survey is performed to obtain the required basic data for achieving the objectives of this study. The questionnaire consisted of three parts. In the first part, the definition of each risk factor is given as a reference in case that experts cannot understand the meaning of a certain risk well. In the second and third parts, experts are requested to give weights and evaluation terms respectively towards each risk factor, which will be described in detail later. Risk assessment on offshore PV power generation projects in China requires first-hand information, extensive project experience and rich knowledge of corresponding fields. Thus, the standard for selection of target respondents included two aspects: ①Having in-depth knowledge in PV power projects as well as a good understanding about risk management of this field; ②Having been involved in at least one offshore power generation project with rich experience of risk management in such projects. According to above standards, 18 qualified experts are invited, and their general information is summarized in Table 14.3.

Table 14.3 General information of the experts.

Organization of experts				
	Power generation company	Power construction company		Academic sector
Percentage	44.4%	33.3%		22.2%
Number of PV power projects that experts have participated in				
	1-2	3-4		5 or above
Percentage	38.9%	44.4%		16.7%
Number of offshore power projects that experts have participated in				
	1-2	3-4		5 or above
Percentage	50.0%	38.9%		11.1%
Project risk management experience of experts				
	5 years or below	6-10 years	11-15 years	16 years or above
Percentage	16.7%	38.9%	27.8%	5.6%

5.1 Weight determination

As mentioned above, the second part of the questionnaire is to invite experts to determine weights of criteria. Brainstorming is firstly held within the invited experts to analyze correlations and conduct pair-wise comparisons between risk factors and risk factor groups. The risky degree of each criterion is determined by the 1-9 scale method in the light of experts' experience and judgment. After pairwise comparison matrixes are obtained, the weight of each criterion can finally be obtained by the Super Decision software when meeting the consistency requirement. The correlations between criteria and weights of criteria are shown in Table 14.4 and Table 14.5 respectively.

It can be seen from Table 14.4 that each risk factor group has a correlation with the others.

Among them, C3 has the most influence on other risk groups, followed by the C2, C4 and the C1. Accordingly, the risk factors within the C1 are affected mostly by other risk factors, which means that it is dominant in the risk assessment process. This has been fully reflected in the weight values shown in Table 14.5, i.e. C1 take up the largest weight. To be more specific, high operation and maintenance cost is attached the most importance to within C1, with the weight as 0.3484. As for C2, C3 and C4, the risk that accounts for the largest proportion is onshore supporting condition risk, solar resource risk and equipment maintenance risk, respectively. Their common feature is that they will directly affect project profits.

Table 14.4 The correlations between criterion.

		Micro-economic risk (C1)				Technical risk (C2)					Environment risk (C3)				Management risk (C4)		
		C11	C12	C13	C14	C21	C22	C23	C24	C25	C31	C32	C33	C34	C41	C42	C43
C1	C11		√		√	√	√	√	√	√		√	√		√		√
	C12			√						√		√	√				√
	C13					√	√	√	√	√					√	√	√
	C14																
C2	C21	√	√	√	√					√	√	√		√	√		
	C22	√	√	√				√	√		√	√			√	√	
	C23	√	√	√								√	√		√	√	
	C24	√	√	√	√	√	√	√			√	√		√		√	√
	C25	√	√		√		√									√	
C3	C31	√	√	√	√	√	√							√	√	√	
	C32		√	√	√				√	√	√		√		√	√	√
	C33		√	√												√	√
	C34		√	√												√	
C4	C41	√	√			√	√	√	√		√		√			√	
	C42		√	√	√						√		√				
	C43					√	√	√	√			√		√	√	√	

Table 14.5 Weights of criterion.

C1 (0.404)	C11	0.09367
	C12	0.34084
	C13	0.25382
	C14	0.31167
C2 (0.165)	C21	0.20808
	C22	0.23436
	C23	0.07628
	C24	0.17972
	C25	0.30155

Continued

C3 (0.154)	C31	0.49852
	C32	0.28521
	C33	0.0648
	C34	0.15147
C4 (0.278)	C41	0.26367
	C42	0.51473
	C43	0.2216

5.2 Data collection

The third part of questionnaire survey aims at collecting evaluation information to be used in subsequent calculations. The 18 experts are divided into three groups, and every expert group are requested to give their judgement about the risky level towards each factor by way of linguistic expressions. Firstly, the linguistic term set that is used by the context-free grammar G_H is set as {s0 = Very Low (VL), s1 = Low (L), s2 = Medium Low (ML), s3 = Moderate (M), s4 = Medium High (MH), s5 = High (H), s6 = Very High (VH)} in this paper. Then, corresponding HFLTSs are generated from the linguistic term set according to E_{G_H} described in Section 4. Table 14.6 shows the linguistic expressions and corresponding HFLTSs by the three expert groups.

Table 14.6 Linguistic expression and HFLTS towards each criterion.

	Group 1		Group 2		Group 3	
	Linguistic expression	HFLTS	Linguistic expression	HFLTS	Linguistic expression	HFLTS
C11	between MH and H	{ s4, s5 }	between M and H	{ s3, s4, s5 }	between M and MH	{ s3, s4 }
C12	greater than H	{ s5, s6 }	greater than MH	{ s4, s5, s6 }	between ML and M	{ s2, s3 }
C13	between ML and M	{ s2, s3 }	between M and MH	{ s3, s4 }	between L and ML	{ s1, s2 }
C14	greater than MH	{ s4, s5, s6 }	between ML and MH	{ s2, s3, s4 }	between MH and H	{ s4, s5 }
C21	greater than H	{ s5, s6 }	between L and M	{ s1, s2, s3 }	between L and ML	{ s1, s2 }
C22	between M and MH	{ s3, s4 }	between ML and M	{ s2, s3 }	between L and ML	{ s1, s2 }
C23	between L and ML	{ s1, s2 }	between M and H	{ s3, s4, s5 }	between L and M	{ s1, s2, s3 }
C24	between MH and H	{ s4, s5 }	between ML and M	{ s2, s3 }	greater than H	{ s5, s6 }
C25	between ML and MH	{ s2, s3, s4 }	greater than MH	{ s4, s5, s6 }	greater than H	{ s5, s6 }
C31	greater than MH	{ s4, s5, s6 }	less than ML	{ s0, s1, s2 }	between L and ML	{ s1, s2 }
C32	greater than H	{ s5, s6 }	between MH and VH	{ s4, s5, s6 }	less than L	{ s0, s1 }
C33	less than ML	{ s0, s1, s2 }	between ML and M	{ s2, s3 }	greater than MH	{ s4, s5, s6 }
C34	between L and M	{ s1, s2, s3 }	greater than H	{ s5, s6 }	between ML and M	{ s2, s3 }
C41	between L and ML	{ s1, s2 }	between M and H	{ s3, s4, s5 }	between M and MH	{ s3, s4 }
C42	greater than H	{ s5, s6 }	between MH and H	{ s4, s5 }	between M and H	{ s3, s4, s5 }
C43	between ML and M	{ s2, s3 }	between M and H	{ s3, s4, s5 }	greater than MH	{ s4, s5, s6 }

5.3 Transformation of HFLTS into triangular fuzzy number

Here the triangular fuzzy number is adopted according to seven linguistic terms with their semantics. Fig. 14.3 shows the lower value, middle value and upper value of the seven terms [52]. Wherein, the y-axis represents the membership degree of each triangular fuzzy number, and the x-axis represents the value of a set of triangular fuzzy numbers in accordance with semantics of the seven linguistic terms.

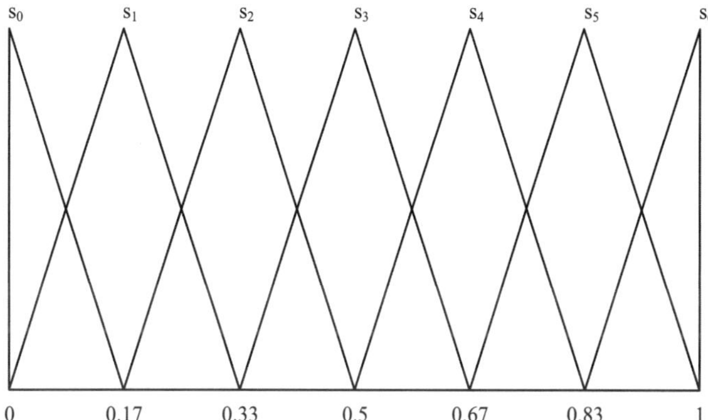

Fig. 14.3 Set of seven terms with its semantics.

Thus, the terms can be converted as follows:

$$S=\begin{Bmatrix} s_0:(0,0,0.17), s_1:(0,0.17,0.33), \\ s_2:(0.17,0.33,0.5), s_3:(0.33,0.5,0.67), \\ s_4:(0.5,0.67,0.83), s_5:(0.67,0.83,1), s_6:(0.83,1,1) \end{Bmatrix}$$

Based on Eq. (14-7), the transformation of HFLTS into triangular fuzzy number is conducted. Here we take the HFLTS of C14 by Group 1 as the example. Its corresponding triangular fuzzy number is calculated as:

$$h_{c14}=\begin{pmatrix} \frac{1}{3}(0.5+0.67+0.83), \\ \frac{1}{3}(0.67+0.83+1), \\ \frac{1}{3}(0.83+1+1) \end{pmatrix}=(0.67,0.83,0.94)$$

Similarly, the triangular fuzzy number of other criteria by each expert group can also be calculated. The results are shown in Table 14.7.

Table 14.7 Triangular numbers of each criterion.

	Group 1	Group 2	Group 3	Aggregated results
C11	(0.585, 0.75, 0.915)	(0.5, 0.667, 0.833)	(0.415, 0.585, 0.75)	(0.5, 0.667, 0.833)
C12	(0.75, 0.915, 1)	(0.667, 0.833, 0.943)	(0.25, 0.415, 0.585)	(0.583, 0.749, 0.868)
C13	(0.25, 0.415, 0.585)	(0.415, 0.585, 0.75)	(0.085, 0.25, 0.415)	(0.250, 0.416, 0.584)
C14	(0.667, 0.833, 0.943)	(0.333, 0.5, 0.667)	(0.585, 0.75, 0.922)	(0.543, 0.708, 0.86)
C21	(0.75, 0.915, 1)	(0.167, 0.333, 0.5)	(0.085, 0.25, 0.415)	(0.292, 0.458, 0.604)
C22	(0.415, 0.585, 0.75)	(0.25, 0.415, 0.585)	(0.085, 0.25, 0.415)	(0.25, 0.416, 0.584)
C23	(0.085, 0.25, 0.415)	(0.5, 0.667, 0.833)	(0.167, 0.333, 0.5)	(0.209, 0.375, 0.541)
C24	(0.585, 0.75, 0.922)	(0.25, 0.415, 0.585)	(0.75, 0.915, 1)	(0.543, 0.708, 0.854)
C25	(0.333, 0.5, 0.667)	(0.667, 0.833, 0.943)	(0.75, 0.915, 1)	(0.604, 0.77, 0.888)
C31	(0.667, 0.833, 0.943)	(0.057, 0.167, 0.333)	(0.085, 0.25, 0.415)	(0.223, 0.375, 0.527)
C32	(0.75, 0.915, 1)	(0.667, 0.833, 0.943)	(0, 0.085, 0.25)	(0.521, 0.667, 0.784)
C33	(0.057, 0.167, 0.333)	(0.25, 0.415, 0.596)	(0.667, 0.833, 0.943)	(0.306, 0.458, 0.612)
C34	(0.167, 0.333, 0.5)	(0.75, 0.915, 1)	(0.25, 0.415, 0.585)	(0.354, 0.52, 0.668)
C41	(0.085, 0.25, 0.415)	(0.5, 0.667, 0.833)	(0.415, 0.585, 0.75)	(0.354, 0.522, 0.687)
C42	(0.75, 0.915, 1)	(0.585, 0.75, 0.922)	(0.5, 0.667, 0.833)	(0.605, 0.77, 0.916)
C43	(0.25, 0.415, 0.585)	(0.5, 0.667, 0.833)	(0.667, 0.833, 0.943)	(0.479, 0.645, 0.799)

5.4 Aggregation of expert opinions

Before conducting the aggregation of expert groups' opinion, the weighting vector associated with the FIOWHA operator is determined as (0.25, 0.5, 0.25) firstly. Then, according to the calculation method described in Section 4, the aggregated results can be obtained, as show in Table 14.7.

5.5 Fuzzy synthetic operation of risk assessment

In this step, triangular fuzzy numbers of each criterion is aggregated based on the FSE method. Here the risk group "Micro-economic risk" is taken as the example. Its risk fuzzy composition operation is performed by Eq. (14-11):

$$h_{c1} = W_{c1} \bullet R_{c1} = (0.094, 0.341, 0.254, 0.312) \bullet \begin{pmatrix} (0.5, 0.667, 0.833) \\ (0.583, 0.749, 0.868) \\ (0.25, 0.416, 0.584) \\ (0.543, 0.708, 0.86) \end{pmatrix} = (0.478, 0.644, 0.79)$$

Evaluation vector of other risk groups can also be calculated and the results are:

$$h_{c2} = (0.415, 0.581, 0.725),\ h_{c3} = (0.333, 0.485, 0.627),\ h_{c4} = (0.511, 0.677, 0.830)$$

Then, the overall risk evaluation result of offshore PV power generation projects in China can be calculated according to Eq. (14-13):

$$R = W_i \bullet R_c = (0.404, 0.165, 0.154, 0.278) \bullet \begin{pmatrix} (0.478, 0.644, 0.79) \\ (0.415, 0.581, 0.725) \\ (0.333, 0.485, 0.627) \\ (0.511, 0.677, 0.830) \end{pmatrix} = (0.455, 0.619, 0.765)$$

5.6 Defuzzification process

Through the comparison between the overall risk evaluation result and the evaluation term as shown in Fig. 14.4, it can be seen that the result is between "Moderate" and "Medium high". To determine the certain overall risk level, the similarity degrees between the evaluation result and the two terms can be calculated through Eq. (14-14):

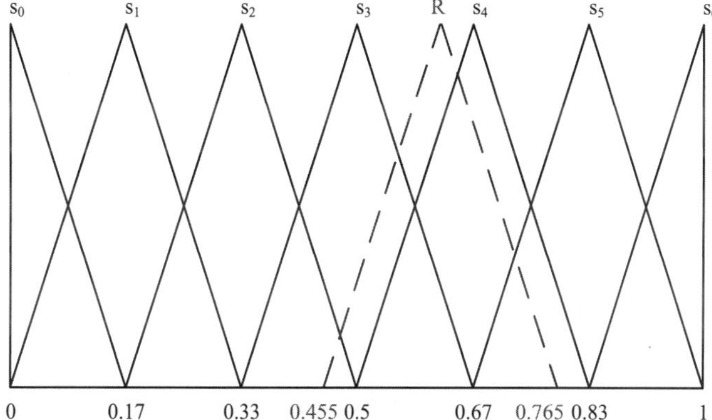

Fig. 14.4 The overall risk evaluation term.

$$Sd(R, s_3) = 1 - \frac{|R^L - s_3{}^L| + |R^M - s_3{}^M| + |R^U - s_3{}^U|}{3}$$

$$= 1 - \frac{|0.455 - 0.33| + |0.619 - 0.5| + |0.765 - 0.67|}{3}$$

$$= 0.887$$

$$Sd(R, s_4) = 1 - \frac{|R^L - s_4{}^L| + |R^M - s_4{}^M| + |R^U - s_4{}^U|}{3}$$

$$= 1 - \frac{|0.455 - 0.5| + |0.619 - 0.67| + |0.765 - 0.83|}{3}$$

$$= 0.946$$

The similarity degree between R and s_3 is 0.887, lower than that between R and s_4. Thus, the overall risk level is closer to s_4 according to the principle of maximum similarity. That is to say, the risk level of offshore PV power generation projects in China is medium high.

5.7 Discussion

According to the risk assessment result in Section 5.6, the risk level of offshore PV power generation projects in China is medium high, with the degree of membership standing between 0.455 and 0.765. Specifically, the management risk appears to own the highest risk level compared with the other three risk groups., which is consistent with the view of Gatzert and Kosub that management must be taken seriously in the project implement process for those industries that are at the infant stage because relevant experience is usually insufficient in such situations [53]. The micro-economical risk group ranked second, indicating that the capital and profits of targeted projects are faced with great threats and challenges. As for the technical and environmental risk groups, their risk level are also standing between medium and medium high, with a requirement of enough attention and relevant control. In the next section, this paper will give corresponding response strategies towards single risk factor based on the assessment results.

6. Management inspiration

As it can be seen from the result that the risk level of offshore PV power generation projects in China is medium high, it is necessary to take effective risk management measures to ensure the smooth implementation and reasonable profits of the risky project. Although risk response measures have already been discussed widely, offshore PV power generation projects have their own uniqueness and general measures are not entirely applicable. Therefore, this paper puts forward the response strategy toward each risk factor based on the review of literature that focus on general risk management plus the analysis of the characteristics of offshore PV projects, thereby achieving pertinence through such combination. The targeted countermeasures and suggestions for risk factors are given below, which could provide a reference and management inspiration for policy makers and corresponding practitioners.

6.1 Micro-economic risk

(1) High initial investment: Using a combination of economic sense and technical knowledge to locate and eliminate unnecessary project costs, value engineering (VE) can effectively reduce costs. It is estimated that the application of VE can cut back the initial investment of a construction project by 5% to 10% [54]. Thus, taking advantage of VE provides an idea for coping with this risk.

(2) High operation and maintenance cost: Firstly, predictive technology can be applied to improve the performance of PV modules [55]. Then, electronic components can be upgraded to improve the reliability of PV parts. Additionally, application-based support system can simplify the maintenance process. All the three methods are able to effectively reduce the cost of operation and maintenance.

(3) Financing risk: Reasonable financing structure design is a key step to reduce the

financing risk [56]. Another core link of the project financing risk management is the corresponding relationship between the project financing risk and the parties involved in the project, so that a risk constraint system can be formed to ensure the overall stability of project financing.

(4) Unclear feed-in tariff policy: From the perspective of government, management departments and policy makers need to formulate the long-term price policy as a guideline of price regulation so as to promote the development of the offshore PV industry. From the perspective of project owners, they should pay close attention to policy trends and refer to tariffs in similar industries.

6.2 Technical risk

(1) Unreasonable site selection and planning: As mentioned above, offshore PV farm site selection is a multiple attribute decision problem involving resource factor, economic factor, environment factor and some others. The combination of GIS technology and MCDM methods, proved to be an effective tool to improve site selection and planning reliability [57, 58], can be utilized in offshore PV projects to avoid this risk.

(2) Inappropriate PV panel structure design: PV panel structure planning is a basic but important work in the design stage, experienced professionals should be invited to take part in this process. Before production, the simulation algorithm can be adopted to find design defects and thus improvement can be made correspondingly. Moreover, panel structure design of land-based PV projects is also worth referring.

(3) Improper cable connection: Since even small cracks caused by improper connection can destroy the cable after many years, project developers should pay attention to the design of the cable connection. Taking the ocean tide effect into consideration, cables should be connected in a stronger and more endurable form compared with land-based PV power generation projects.

(4) Technical introduction risk: On one hand, the collection of intelligence information should be strengthened for better introduction screening. On the other hand, it is better for the project owner to import technologies that are in the development or growth stage of their life cycle. Such technologies can be more capable of adapting to different environments. If possible, the root technology is the best choice.

(5) Onshore supporting condition risk: In the site selection process, terrain and transportation conditions should be studied in case that unfavorable supporting conditions impede the implementation of the project. When necessary, accommodation roads must be built for large equipment. Also, the project developer should actively communicate with grid companies to ensure the supporting of onshore power grid.

6.3 Environment risk

(1) Solar resource risk: There is a saying in the industry that PV projects live at the mercy of the weather, which means that solar energy conditions directly determine project benefits. As a result, preliminary research on radiation data is particularly important. Through climate speculation, the change within a year and the long-term trend of solar energy resources can be calculated [59]. Besides, field observation is also indispensable for the sake of conducting a comparison with calculated data and ensuring a solid resource analysis.

(2) Harsh marine environment: To deal with the corrosion caused by the marine environment, the protection of surface materials should be strengthened, such as the formation of a protective film by electroplating, and the use of stainless steel anti-corrosion materials. From the macro perspective, it is necessary for Chinese government to detect and record the weather in the southeastern sea area and establish its own database in preparation for large-scale development of offshore PV power projects.

(3) Marine ecological damage: First of all, the planning and site selection of offshore PV farms should be as far away as possible from the habitats, breeding grounds, and migratory routes of marine life and birds. During the construction period, marine environmental protection warning mechanism should be established to ensure that problems can be solved in the bud. After the project is completed, the responsible party must apply for the environmental quality inspection and acceptance to the environmental protection department. The above measures can reduce the resistance from environmental protection agencies or environmentalists.

(4) Visual effect risk: In response to this risk factor, site selection would better try to avoid the marine wetland ecology area so as not to affect the natural beauty. At the same time, light reflections should be tested in advance in order to make possible adjustments.

6.4 Management risk

(1) Construction quality risk: A quality management plan should be formulated firstly with clear accountability according to the characteristics of offshore PV. During the construction stage, each step should be in strict accordance with the scientific construction process so that the construction quality can be strictly controlled. The quality inspection after project completion cannot be ignored, either.

(2) Equipment maintenance risk: The smart energy management platform is a new concept that relies on the internet of things, artificial intelligence and big data analytics to achieve digital operations. PV offshore power generation projects can utilize this concept to realize intelligent operation and maintenance and thus avoid equipment maintenance risk to some extent. In addition, the knowledge of maintenance management under special marine environment should also be studied.

(3) Inexperienced staff: Multiple measures should be taken to cultivate a skilled team. Firstly, it is necessary to conduct employee training courses with respect to theoretical knowledge of offshore PV power by means of physical explanation and practical operation. Secondly, the personnel who have participated in offshore wind projects can be absorbed into the team. Finally, in the long run, cooperation between companies and academics ought to be strengthened to cultivate excellent engineers and project managers.

7. Conclusions

This paper carries out a risk assessment on offshore PV power generation projects in China, and the main conclusions are as follows: ①An evaluation index system is constructed in the foundation of previous studies, actual projects and expert opinions. 16 risk factors influencing offshore PV power generation projects in China are included, and they are divided into four categories, namely the micro-economic risk, the technical risk, the environment risk and the management risk. ②The risk assessment model is established. In this model: the ANP method is employed to determine index weights considering the interrelationship; the HFLTS method is introduced to assign assessment information to risk factors; the TNF method is utilized to transform the linguistic terms into a computable form; the FIOWHA operator is adopted to aggregate the TNFs of each expert towards a risk factor; the FSE method and the principle of maximum similarity are used to calculate the overall risk level. ③The established model is applied to the empirical study, namely to calculate the risk level of offshore PV power generation projects in China, which is medium high as the result shows. The empirical study illustrates the applicability of the model. ④Countermeasures and suggestions for each risk factor are put forward to guarantee the smooth implementation and reasonable profits of the risky projects.

However, there are still some limitations and shortcomings in this paper. For one thing, the identification of risk factors cannot be perfect, and inevitably, there will be some omissions because of limited available information. We will continue to collect more information for the improvement of the indicator system. For another thing, different decision makers hold different attitudes towards risks, and this difference may lead to absolute opposite decision results sometimes. Therefore, we will take the risk preference of decision makers into consideration in future research.

Acknowledgements

Project supported by the 2017 Special Project of Cultivation and Development of Innovation Base (No. Z17110 0002217024) and the Fundamental Research Funds for the Central

Universities (No.2018ZD14). The authors are also thankful to all experts involved for their valuable outputs and help.

Appendix A

The calculation process of the weight of each indicator through the Super Decision software can be summarized as follows:

(1) According to the constraint relations among indicators in Table 14.4, the ANP model diagram of risk assessment of offshore PV power generation projects can be established.

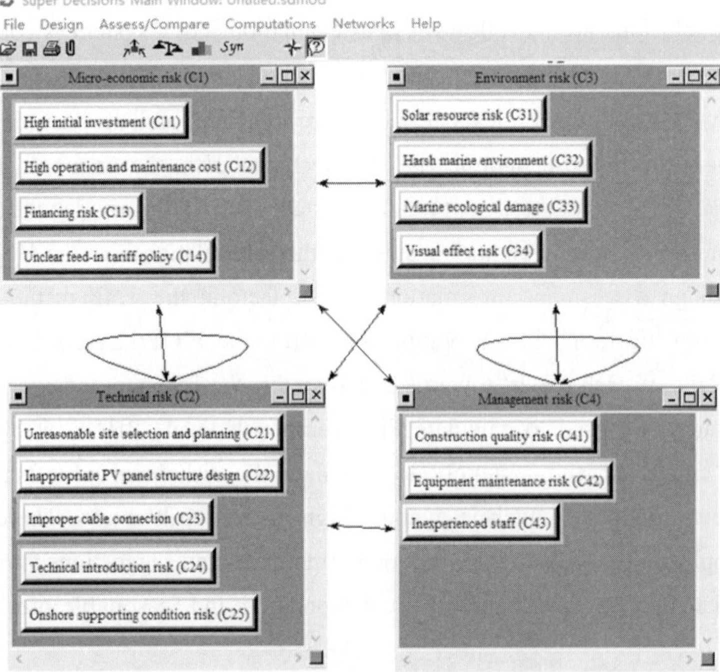

(2) The pair-wise comparison is conducted based on expert opinions, and the first-level indicators are taken as the example.

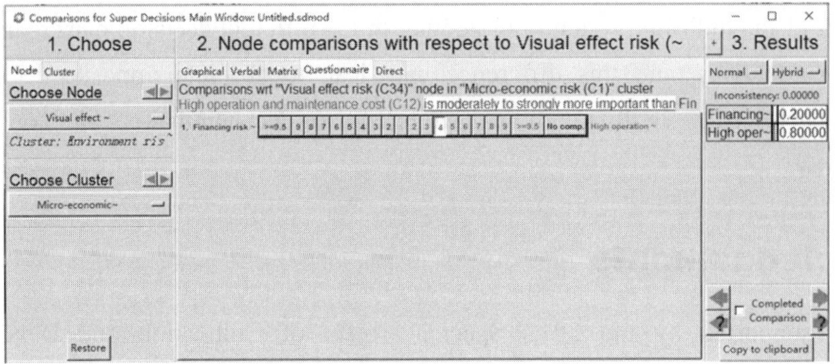

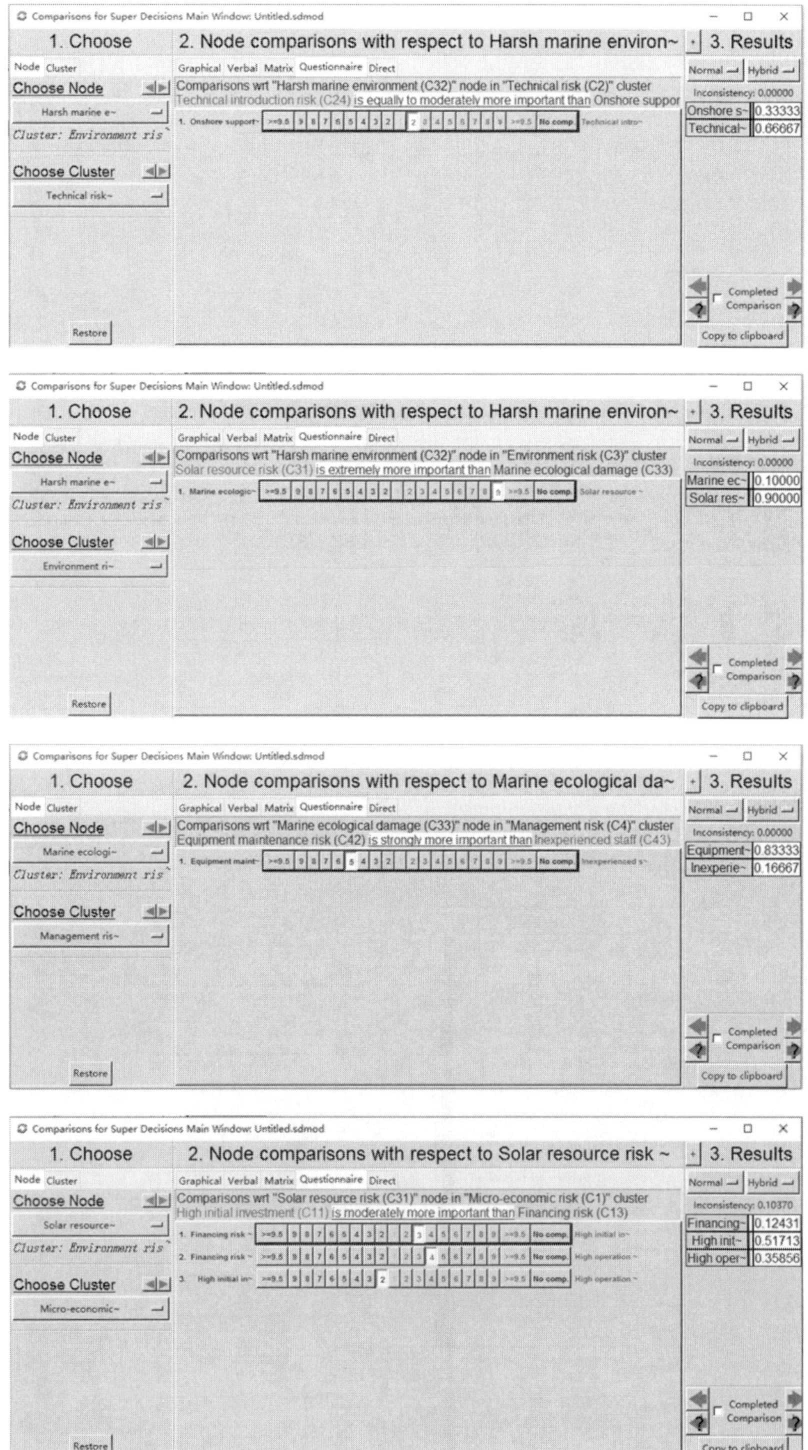
Comparisons for Super Decisions Main Window: Untitled.sdmod
1. Choose
2. Node comparisons with respect to Harsh marine environ~
3. Results
Node Cluster
Choose Node
Harsh marine e~
Cluster: Environment ris
Choose Cluster
Technical risk~
Restore
Graphical Verbal Matrix Questionnaire Direct
Comparisons wrt "Harsh marine environment (C32)" node in "Technical risk (C2)" cluster
Technical introduction risk (C24) is equally to moderately more important than Onshore suppor
Normal Hybrid
Inconsistency: 0.00000
Onshore s~ 0.33333
Technical~ 0.66667
Completed Comparison
Copy to clipboard
Comparisons for Super Decisions Main Window: Untitled.sdmod
1. Choose
2. Node comparisons with respect to Harsh marine environ~
3. Results
Choose Node
Harsh marine e~
Cluster: Environment ris
Choose Cluster
Environment ri~
Restore
Comparisons wrt "Harsh marine environment (C32)" node in "Environment risk (C3)" cluster
Solar resource risk (C31) is extremely more important than Marine ecological damage (C33)
Inconsistency: 0.00000
Marine ec~ 0.10000
Solar res~ 0.90000
Completed Comparison
Copy to clipboard
Comparisons for Super Decisions Main Window: Untitled.sdmod
1. Choose
2. Node comparisons with respect to Marine ecological da~
3. Results
Choose Node
Marine ecologi~
Cluster: Environment ris
Choose Cluster
Management ris~
Restore
Comparisons wrt "Marine ecological damage (C33)" node in "Management risk (C4)" cluster
Equipment maintenance risk (C42) is strongly more important than Inexperienced staff (C43)
Inconsistency: 0.00000
Equipment~ 0.83333
Inexperie~ 0.16667
Completed Comparison
Copy to clipboard
Comparisons for Super Decisions Main Window: Untitled.sdmod
1. Choose
2. Node comparisons with respect to Solar resource risk ~
3. Results
Choose Node
Solar resource~
Cluster: Environment ris
Choose Cluster
Micro-economic~
Restore
Comparisons wrt "Solar resource risk (C31)" node in "Micro-economic risk (C1)" cluster
High initial investment (C11) is moderately more important than Financing risk (C13)
Inconsistency: 0.10370
Financing~ 0.12431
High init~ 0.51713
High oper~ 0.35856
Completed Comparison
Copy to clipboard

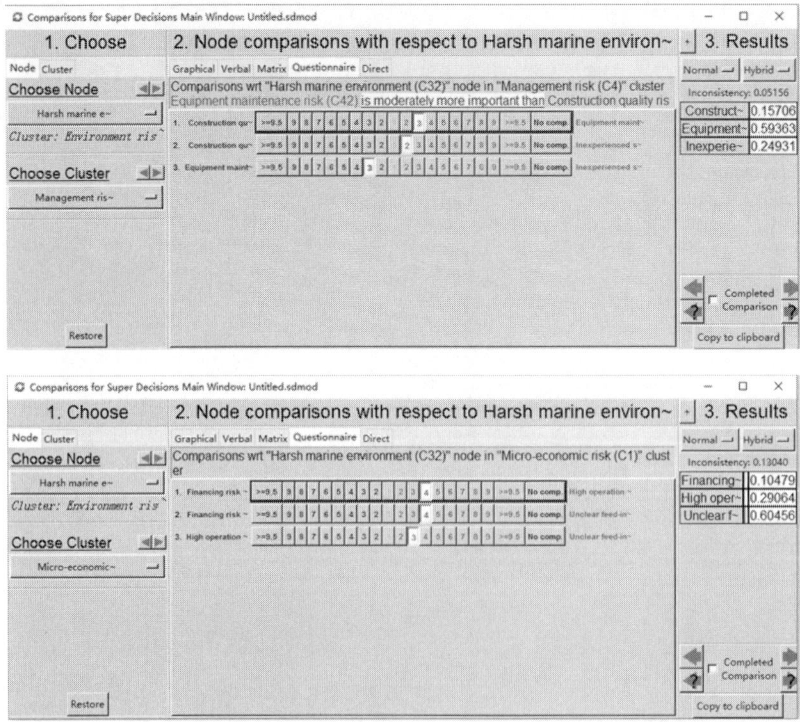

(3) The weight of each indicator could be calculated by the software, and the result is shown as follows.

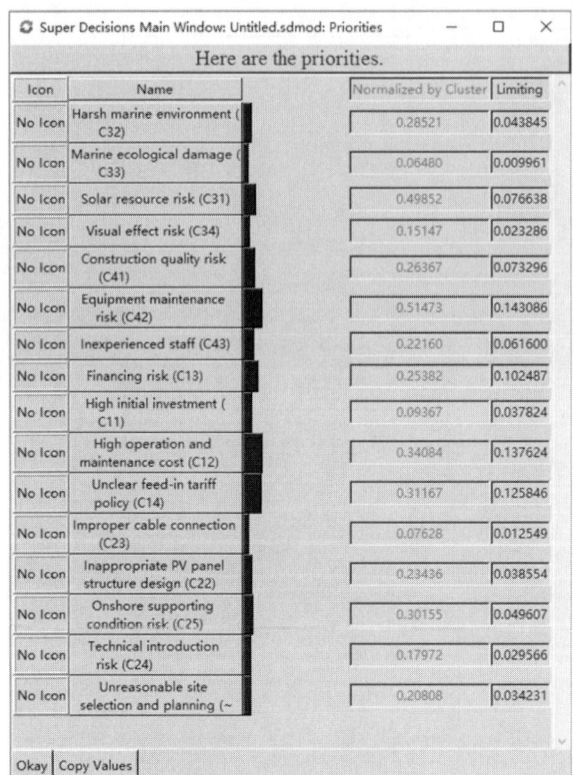

Super Decisions Main Window: Untitled.sdmod: Priorities

Here are the priorities.

Icon	Name	Normalized by Cluster	Limiting
No Icon	Harsh marine environment (C32)	0.28521	0.043845
No Icon	Marine ecological damage (C33)	0.06480	0.009961
No Icon	Solar resource risk (C31)	0.49852	0.076638
No Icon	Visual effect risk (C34)	0.15147	0.023286
No Icon	Construction quality risk (C41)	0.26367	0.073296
No Icon	Equipment maintenance risk (C42)	0.51473	0.143086
No Icon	Inexperienced staff (C43)	0.22160	0.061600
No Icon	Financing risk (C13)	0.25382	0.102487
No Icon	High initial investment (C11)	0.09367	0.037824
No Icon	High operation and maintenance cost (C12)	0.34084	0.137624
No Icon	Unclear feed-in tariff policy (C14)	0.31167	0.125846
No Icon	Improper cable connection (C23)	0.07628	0.012549
No Icon	Inappropriate PV panel structure design (C22)	0.23436	0.038554
No Icon	Onshore supporting condition risk (C25)	0.30155	0.049607
No Icon	Technical introduction risk (C24)	0.17972	0.029566
No Icon	Unreasonable site selection and planning (~	0.20808	0.034231

Okay Copy Values

References

[1] Parida B, Iniyan S, Goic R. A review of solar photovoltaic technologies[J]. Renewable & Sustainable Energy Reviews, 2011, 15(3): 1625-1636.

[2] Tan Z, Tan Q, Rong M. Analysis on the financing status of PV industry in China and the ways of improvement[J]. Renewable and Sustainable Energy Reviews, 2018, 93: 409-420.

[3] Zou H Y, Du H B, Ren J Z, et al. Market dynamics, innovation, and transition in China's solar photovoltaic (PV) industry: A critical review[J]. Renewable & Sustainable Energy Reviews, 2017, 69: 197-206.

[4] Ruhang X. Characteristics and prospective of China's PV development route: Based on data of world PV industry 2000–2010[J]. Renewable and Sustainable Energy Reviews, 2016, 56: 1032-1043.

[5] China M.o.N.R.o.P.s.R.o..Statistical bulletin of China's land, mineral and marine resources in 2017[R]. 2018.

[6] Silvério N M, et al. Use of floating PV plants for coordinated operation with hydropower plants: Case study of the hydroelectric plants of the São Francisco River basin[J]. Energy Conversion and Management, 2018, 171:339-349.

[7] Kroiß A, Präbst S, Hamberger M, et al. Development of a Seawater-proof Hybrid Photovoltaic/thermal (PV/T) Solar Collector[J] . Energy Procedia, 2014, 52(2014):93-103.

[8] Trapani K, Millar D L, Smith H C M. Novel offshore application of photovoltaics in comparison to conventional marine renewable energy technologies[J]. Renewable Energy, 2013, 50:879-888.

[9] Trapani K, Millar D L. Proposing offshore photovoltaic (PV) technology to the energy mix of the Maltese islands[J]. Energy Conversion & Management, 2013, 67(2): 18-26.

[10] Sahu A, Yadav N. Sudhakar K. Floating photovoltaic power plant: A review[J]. Renewable and Sustainable Energy Reviews, 2016, 66: 815-824.

[11] Luo G L, Long C F, Tang W J. Financing risks involved in distributed PV power generation in China and analysis of countermeasures[J]. Renewable and Sustainable Energy Reviews, 2016, 63: 93-101.

[12] Manzini G, Gramazio P, Guastella S, et al. The Fire Risk in Photovoltaic Installations – Checking the PV Modules Safety in Case of Fire[J]. Energy Procedia, 2015, 81:665-672.

[13] Prusty B R, Jena D. An over-limit risk assessment of PV integrated power system using probabilistic load flow based on multi-time instant uncertainty modeling[J]. Renewable Energy, 2018, 116: 367-383.

[14] Liu L Y, Chang D L, Xie J Y, et al. Prediction of short-term PV power output and uncertainty analysis[J]. Applied Energy, 2018, 228: 700-711.

[15] Mateo C, Cossent R, Gómez T, et al. Impact of solar PV self-consumption policies on distribution networks and regulatory implications[J]. Solar Energy, 2018, 176: 62-72.

[16] Papapostolou A, Karakosta C, Nikas A, et al. Exploring opportunities and risks for RES-E deployment under Cooperation Mechanisms between EU and Western Balkans: A multi-criteria assessment[J]. Renewable and Sustainable Energy Reviews, 2017, 80: 519-530.

[17] Okoro U, Kolios A, Cui L. Multi-criteria risk assessment approach for components risk ranking – The case study of an offshore wave energy converter[J]. International Journal of Marine Energy, 2017, 17: 21-39.

[18] Amirshenava S, Osanloo M. Mine closure risk management: An integration of 3D risk model and

MCDM techniques[J]. Journal of Cleaner Production, 2018, 184: 389-401.

[19] Emjedi M R, et al. Reliability evaluation of distribution networks using fuzzy logic[R]. Power and Energy Society General Meeting, 2010.

[20] Karasan A, Ilbahar E, Cebi S, et al. A new risk assessment approach: Safety and Critical Effect Analysis (SCEA) and its extension with Pythagorean fuzzy sets[J]. Safety Science, 2018, 108:173-187.

[21] Torres-Blanc C, Cubillo S, Hernández P. Aggregation operators on type-2 fuzzy sets[J]. Fuzzy Sets and Systems, 2017.

[22] Wang C-Y, Chen S-M. Multiple attribute decision making based on interval-valued intuitionistic fuzzy sets, linear programming methodology, and the extended TOPSIS method[J]. Information Sciences, 2017, 397-398: 155-167.

[23] Ngan S-C. An activation detection based similarity measure for intuitionistic fuzzy sets[J]. Expert Systems with Applications, 2016, 60: 62-80.

[24] Garmendia L, González D C R, Recasens J. Partial orderings for hesitant fuzzy sets[J]. International Journal of Approximate Reasoning, 2017, 84: 159-167.

[25] Torra, V. Hesitant fuzzy sets[J]. International Journal of Intelligent Systems, 2010, 25(6): 10.

[26] Rodriguez R M, Martinez L, Herrera F. Hesitant Fuzzy Linguistic Term Sets for Decision Making[J]. IEEE Transactions on Fuzzy Systems, 2012, 20(1): 109-119.

[27] Chen Z S, Chin K S, Li Y L, et al. Proportional hesitant fuzzy linguistic term set for multiple criteria group decision making[J]. Information Sciences, 2016, 357: 61-87.

[28] Liao H C, Xu Z S, Zeng X J, et al. Qualitative decision making with correlation coefficients of hesitant fuzzy linguistic term sets[J]. Knowledge-Based Systems, 2015, 76: 127-138.

[29] Wang J, Wang J Q, Zhang H Y, et al. Multi-criteria decision-making based on hesitant fuzzy linguistic term sets: An outranking approach[J]. Knowledge-Based Systems, 2015, 86: 224-236.

[30] Zadeh L A. Fuzzy sets[J]. Information & Control, 1965, 8(3): 338-353.

[31] Samantra C, Datta S, Mahapatra S S. Fuzzy based risk assessment module for metropolitan construction project: An empirical study[J]. Engineering Applications of Artificial Intelligence, 2017, 65.

[32] Urbina A G, Aoyama A. Measuring the benefit of investing in pipeline safety using fuzzy risk assessment[J]. Journal of Loss Prevention in the Process Industries, 2017, 45: 116-132.

[33] Ren L, Lu H, Xia J. An interval-valued triangular fuzzy modified multi-attribute preference model for prioritization of groundwater resources management[J]. Journal of Hydrology, 2018.

[34] Zhao X, Lin R, Wei G. Hesitant triangular fuzzy information aggregation based on Einstein operations and their application to multiple attribute decision making[J]. Expert Systems with Applications, 2014, 41(4): 1086-1094.

[35] Saaty T. Decision Making with Dependence and Feedback: The Analytic Network Process[J]. International, 1996, 95(2): 129-157.

[36] Chemweno P, Pintelon L, Horenbeek A V, et al. Development of a risk assessment selection methodology for asset maintenance decision making: An analytic network process (ANP) approach[J]. International Journal of Production Economics, 2015, 170: 663-676.

[37] Ou Yang Y P, Shieh H M, Tzeng G H. A VIKOR technique based on DEMATEL and ANP for information security risk control assessment[J]. Information Sciences, 2013, 232: 482-500.

[38] Jiang X, Fan H, Ying Z, et al. Using interpretive structural modeling and fuzzy analytic network process to identify and allocate risks in Arctic shipping strategic alliance[J]. Polar Science, 2018, 17: 83-93.

[39] Wang L E, Liu H C, Quan M Y. Evaluating the risk of failure modes with a hybrid MCDM model under interval-valued intuitionistic fuzzy environments[J]. Computers & Industrial Engineering, 2016, 102: 175-185.

[40] Lin S S, Li C B, Xu F Q, et al. Risk identification and analysis for new energy power system in China based on D numbers and decision-making trial and evaluation laboratory (DEMATEL)[J]. Journal of Cleaner Production, 2018, 180: 81-96.

[41] Sajadi A, Strezoski L, Clark K, et al. Transmission system protection screening for integration of offshore wind power plants[J]. Renewable Energy, 2018, 125.

[42] Steffen B. The importance of project finance for renewable energy projects[J]. Energy Economics, 2018, 69.

[43] Merrouni A A, Elalaoui E F, Mezrhab A, et al. Large scale PV sites selection by combining GIS and Analytical Hierarchy Process. Case study: Eastern Morocco[J]. Renewable Energy, 2018, 119.

[44] Gad H H, Haikal A Y, Ali H A. New design of the PV panel control system using FPGA-based MPSoC[J]. Solar Energy, 2017, 146: 243-256.

[45] Yin X. A novel hydro-kite like energy converter for harnessing both ocean wave and current energy[J]. Energy, 2018.

[46] Monaca S L, Ryan L. Solar PV where the sun doesn't shine: Estimating the economic impacts of support schemes for residential PV with detailed net demand profiling[J]. Working Papers, 2016, 108: 731-741.

[47] Li W, Zhai P, Cai J. Research on the Relationship of ENSO and the Frequency of Extreme Precipitation Events in China[J]. Advances in Climate Change Research, 2011, 2(2): 101-107.

[48] Jordehi A R. Enhanced leader particle swarm optimisation (ELPSO): An efficient algorithm for parameter estimation of photovoltaic (PV) cells and modules[J]. Solar Energy, 2018, 159: 78-87.

[49] Wu Y N, Wang J, Hu Y, et al. An extended TODIM-PROMETHEE method for waste-to-energy plant site selection based on sustainability perspective[J]. Energy, 2018, 156: 1-16.

[50] Rui A N, Chuancai LI. Evaluation of Grassroots Organization Construction of Grid Enterprises Based on FIOWHA Operator[J]. Water Resources & Power, 2012.

[51] Wu Y, Wang Y, Chen K F, et al. Social sustainability assessment of small hydropower with hesitant PROMETHEE method[J]. Sustainable Cities & Society, 2017, 35: 522-537.

[52] Liao H, Xu Z, Zeng X J. Distance and similarity measures for hesitant fuzzy linguistic term sets and their application in multi-criteria decision making[J]. Information Sciences, 2014, 271: 125-142.

[53] Gatzert N, Kosub T. Risks and risk management of renewable energy projects: The case of onshore and offshore wind parks[J]. Renewable and Sustainable Energy Reviews, 2016, 60: 982-998.

[54] Chen W T, Chang P Y, Huang Y H. Assessing the overall performance of value engineering workshops for construction projects[J]. International Journal of Project Management, 2010, 28(5): 514-527.

[55] Wittenberg I, Matthies E. How Do PV Households Use Their PV System and How is This Related to Their Energy Use?[J] Renewable Energy, 2018, 122:291-300.

[56] Mazzucato M, Semieniuk G. Financing renewable energy: Who is financing what and why it matters

[J]. Technological Forecasting & Social Change, 2017.

[57] Bagdanavičiūtė I, Umgiesser G, Vaičiūté D, et al. GIS-based multi-criteria site selection for zebra mussel cultivation: Addressing end-of-pipe remediation of a eutrophic coastal lagoon ecosystem[J]. Science of the Total Environment, 2018, 634.

[58] Garni H Z A, Awasthi A. Solar PV power plant site selection using a GIS-AHP based approach with application in Saudi Arabia[J]. Applied Energy, 2017, 206.

[59] Abreu E F M, Canhoto P, Prior V, et al. Solar resource assessment through long-term statistical analysis and typical data generation with different time resolutions using GHI measurements[J]. Renewable Energy, 2018, 127:398-411.

Chapter 15

Risk assessment of urban rooftop distributed PV in energy performance contracting (EPC) projects: an extended HFLTS-DEMATEL fuzzy synthetic evaluation analysis

Yunna Wu [a, b], Jianli Zhou [a, b*]

a. School of Economics and Management, North China Electric Power University, Beijing, China

b. Beijing Key Laboratory of New Energy and Low-Carbon Development (North China Electric Power University), Changping, Beijing, 102206, China

Abstract: Promoted by the policy, urban rooftop distributed photovoltaic (URDPV) has developed rapidly in China. Besides, the government is gradually applying energy performance contracting (EPC) mode to this field making use of urban rooftop resources and energy service companies' (ECOs') technological advantages, but there are still obstacles to further development. One of the main reasons that restrict the further development of EPC-URDPV projects in China is the lack of effective risk assessment method. This paper aims to identify the critical risk factors (CRFs) for such projects, and propose a comprehensive risk assessment framework. Firstly, 11 CRFs are identified based on the literature review and 4-dimensional risk analysis to composed the risk assessment index system. Secondly, the weights of CRFs are determined by the intuitionistic fuzzy-decision making trial and evaluation laboratory (IF-DEMATEL) method. It is worth noting that this paper uses the hesitant fuzzy linguistic term sets (HFLTS) to obtain evaluation information to ensure the completeness and fuzziness of experts' viewpoints. Then, an extended HFLTS-DEMATEL fuzzy synthetic evaluation method is used to conduct risk assessment. The evaluation results show that the risk levels of EPC-URDPV projects in most study areas are at "Medium" and "Relatively Low" state. The risk level of projects in Shanghai and Fujian is "Relatively High". Sensitivity analysis results show the stability and reliability of the model. After considering the causes of risk and relevant stakeholders, a risk response is proposed. This study can enrich the methods in the field of risk assessment and provide insightful references to PV investors, decision makers.

Keywords: Urban-rooftop distributed PV; Risk assessment; Energy performance contracting (EPC); Fuzzy synthetic evaluation; Hesitant fuzzy linguistic term sets (HFLTS); DEMATEL

1. Introduction

1.1 Background

At present, China is in a critical period of economic restructuring and the transformation of economic growth mode, but at the same time it has to face increasingly serious environmental challenges such as air pollution (IEA, 2017). The deterioration of the environment and the excessive consumption of resources are becoming more and more serious. Traditional fossil fuel energy is no longer able to meet the needs of the current social development. Developing low-carbon economy which can effectively resolve above huge problems has become the main development mode, new energies such as distributed photovoltaic (DPV) projects are confronted with the golden period of development (Mekhilef, Saidur, & Safari, 2011; Nugent & Sovacool, 2014). According to the scenario simulation of the International Energy Agency (IEA), in the process of domestic demand and service-led economic transformation, clean energy will play a more crucial role in the energy system, and this transformation will also create greater opportunities for the development of distributed energy in China (IEA, 2016). Besides, the development goals of China DPV are clearly put forward in relevant national documents. The 13th Five-Year Plan for Energy Development clearly points out that the installed capacity of PV power generation should reach the target of more than 110 million kilowatts in 2020, of which 60 million kilowatts are DPV (NDRC, 2016a). According to the 13th Five-Year Plan for Solar Energy Development, 100 demonstration zones for DPV applications will be built by 2020. 80% of new buildings and 50% of existing buildings will be installed with PV power generation on their roofs (NDRC, 2016b). Therefore, the policy environment is conducive to the development of URDPV projects in China.

However, the unbalanced development of the domestic PV market leads to excess capacity: there is serious solar curtailment phenomenon in Gansu and Xinjiang provinces (Xingang Zhao, Zeng, & Zhao, 2015). It is an urgent problem to excavate the factors affecting the development quality of PV projects. China's solar energy resources are unevenly distributed, and there are significant differences in both east-west distribution and north-south distribution (Zou et al., 2017). The first-class and second-class regions of solar energy resources are distributed in the western and northern regions of China. These regions mainly construct centralized PV power plants. However, these regions are relatively underdeveloped compared to the east-central and southern regions, with less electricity demand and severe solar curtailment, making them unsuitable for the development of URDPV. The east-central and southern regions are economically developed, with large populations and high electricity demand. Environmental and air pollution problems have made these areas pay more attention to the use and development of clean energy. The east-central and southern regions are China's third-class area of solar energy resources. They are not suitable for the development of centralized PV power plants due to the limitation of solar energy resources, but are fitted for large-scale development of DPV (Hou, Wang, & Liu, 2018). The growth of China's DPV mainly depends on the eastern and central South regions, and the growth rate in the eastern region is as high as 69% (IEA, 2017). The northern, northwest and northeast regions accounted for only 16% of the increase. In summary, the research area of this paper is the third-class area of solar energy resource in China, which represent the current development status and trend of URDPV in China.

Currently, the government is gradually applying energy performance contracting (EPC) mode to this field. EPC is the commercial operating mode of a URDPV project discussed in this paper. It is a management mode of energy-saving investment service which sprang up in the United States and gradually developed into a way of effectively utilizing market mechanism to promote efficient energy utilization. At present, China's energy-saving service market is mainly based on industrial enterprises, and the energy-saving potential is very large. The market prospects of EPC projects that can be implemented and have investment benefits are huge. Under this mode, the main contracting parties usually involve energy-consuming units (ECUs) and energy service companies (ECOs). ECOs provide energy-saving services to reduce energy consumption, and then gain profits by sharing ECUs' energy-saving benefits. Obviously, in EPC energy-saving scheme, ECOs and customers' interests are highly consistent (S. Zhang, 2016). The more energy-saving, the more profits both sides will get, and achieve win-win situation between ECOs and customers. At present, the main profit model of PV enterprises in China is to participate in the government-sponsored bidding for PV projects and the construction and operation of PV power plants. However, PV equipment is a product with obvious homogeneity. In the bidding process, PV enterprises often obtain bids through price war, so that most PV enterprises in China are still in a loss state. It can be said that PV has entered the "Red Sea" state in the public utilities market. In order to accelerate the development of the domestic market and solve the problem of overcapacity, it is necessary to develop DPV projects in the central and eastern regions of China (Xingang Zhao et al., 2015). The EPC-URDPV project studied in this paper can provide a new development idea for PV enterprises which are now in a revenue dilemma, and also open up a new market for PV products. Besides, it can be predicted that this mode will be frequently used in the construction of China's distributed energy projects.

1.2 EPC-URDPV projects in China

The application of EPC mode to manage URDPV projects generally involves four main bodies: Firstly, the government is the leader and promoter of relevant policies and markets, and the income and operation mode of EPC projects will be different under different policy environments; The second is the energy unit, which is not only the customer of EPC project, but also the main body of the project; Another important part is ECOs that can build, operate and maintain URDPV projects. The fourth party, power grid company should not only provide ECUs with reserve and make up for the electricity gap, but also provide power recovery services when residual power appears in URDPV. Under this scheme, the PV power supply on the roof of each building is used as the unit to enter the low-voltage user distribution box in the building, and the low-voltage entrance of the distribution box in each building is used as the grid-connected point. Then, the low-voltage line is used to access the public power grid in the nearby area. The grid connection point and the property right demarcation point are not at the same point and the wiring diagram is shown in Fig. 15.1. In this mode, PV power generation is sent directly to the user after contravariant to the low-voltage grid, and investors receive government subsidies for full power. The PV power is purchased by the power supply company according to the local desulfurization coal benchmark price. The power supply company charges the user the electricity fee according to the local sales catalogue price. This mode really realizes the nearby absorption and the surplus access to grid of PV power generation.

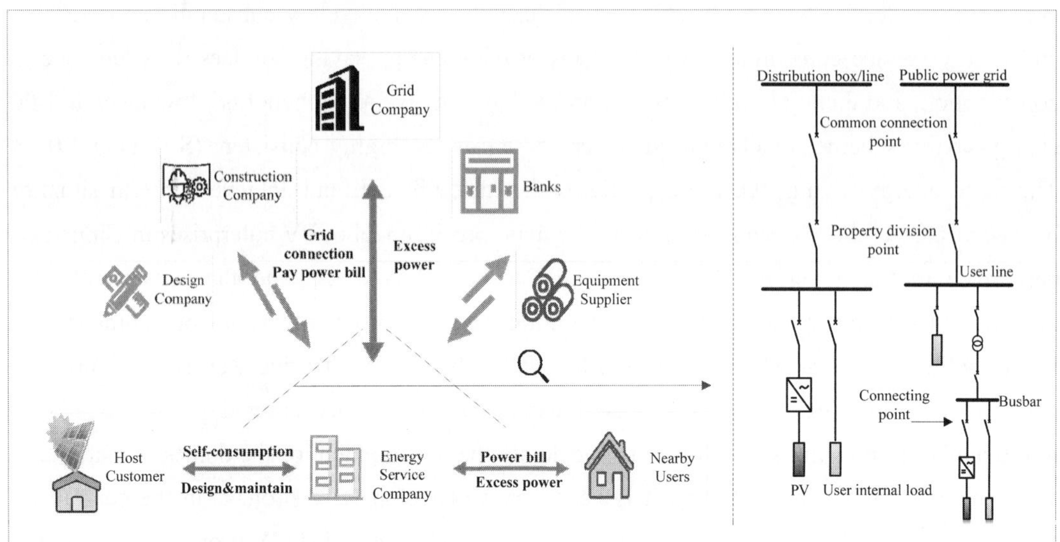

Fig. 15.1 Operating mechanism and grid-connected scheme of EPC-URDPV project.

For ECOs, the use of URDPV to provide energy-saving services for ECUs has the characteristics of easy measurement of energy-saving amount, and clear revenue situation of all parties, which reduces the uncertainty of EPC projects and makes it easier for projects to obtain financing. Since DPV can be used by multiple users, EPC-URDPV projects have obvious advantages in financing compared to energy-saving retrofit EPC projects. Table 15.1 shows part of EPC-URDPV projects in China, in the cases of successful operation, URDPV projects managed by EPC have more potential for energy saving and emission reduction, and can supply electricity, reduce the peak-valley difference of power, and ensure the safety of energy supply. It can be seen that such projects are basically utilizing rooftop resources in urban areas to place PV equipment for power generation. It is very suitable for some customers who have energy saving needs and require high reliability of power supply. The research objects of this paper are such DPV projects which make full use of urban rooftop resource.

Table 15.1 Some EPC-URDPV projects in China.

No.	Project Name	Location	Capacity	Stage
1	Tianjin Steel Tube Manufacturing Co., Ltd.—DPV power generation project on roof	Tianjin, North China	12 MW	Operation
2	Ningbo Kaiyao Electrical Appliance Manufacturing Co., Ltd.—DPV project	Zhejiang, Southeast China	0.68 MW	Operation
3	Beilun District, Ningbo, Zhejiang—DPV power generation project on Factory roof	Zhejiang, Southeast China	10 MW	Operation
4	Yuhang District, one Pavilion, three centers, DPV power generation projects	Zhejiang, Southeast China	0.256 MW	Operation
5	Hangzhou City Civic Center podium roof DPV project	Zhejiang, Southeast China	—	Preparation
6	Henan energy chemical industry group-DPV power generation project	Henan, Mid-Eastern China	15 MW	Preparation
7	Inner Mongolia Baogang Steel Pipe Company—DPV power generation project	Inner Mongolia, North China	20 MW	Preparation
8	Shanghai Fengxian District Conference Center DPV Power Generation Project	Shanghai, East China	0.36MW	Operation
9	Tianyi printing DPV power generation project	Shandong, East China	1.6 MW	Operation
10	Guangqi Honda·Hanergy 17MW Distributed Photovoltaic Power Generation Project	Guangdong, South China	17 MW	Operation

At present, most of the research on EPC focuses on energy-saving retrofit projects. For example, Lee et al. Pan Lee, Lam, Yik, and Chan (2013) used Monte Carlo simulation and sensitivity analysis to evaluate the probabilistic risk of the energy-saving gap of EPC project. The evaluation results show that the energy-saving amount is of statistical significance. It shows that EPC project has potential for development. But, their research object is energy-saving retrofit EPC project, and there is no risk study on rooftop DPV project in EPC. EPC-URDPV project is obviously different from energy-saving retrofit EPC project in many aspects, and project revenue is affected by many complex factors, such as technical maturity, construction quality, price changes, operation and maintenance in the later stage of the project. This study is to explore the risk of URDPV projects under EPC mode in China, identify the critical risk factors and give the evaluation results and corresponding measures.

1.3 Rationale and structure of the paper

Risk assessment plays an important role in URDPV projects under the EPC model as risks are accompanied with the life-cycle of the projects. However, four critical issues have not been solved well by existing study:

(1) Traditional risk assessment analysis often uses real numbers to express evaluation information, which results in serious information loss. When measuring risks, it is often impossible to describe them by specific numerical values.

(2) Risk evaluation index system is often not representative and targeted, and has not been obtained by rigorous identification methods. This kind of study usually lists the relevant risk factors directly and lacks the important risk analysis process. This problem often leads to the distortion of evaluation results.

(3) Existing risk analysis studies describe the importance of a risk factor from various dimensions, but lack of scientific and representative perspective.

(4) The method of subjective weight determination is often used to determine the weight of risk indicators. When describing the interaction between each indicator, the traditional method uses numerical scaling to describe. For example, the ANP method is implemented by using Super Decisions software. This description method is unscientific, and the interaction between indicators should also be described by fuzzy sets.

In order to solve the above issues, this paper makes the following improvements:

(1) Considering that reliable expert evaluation information is essential for risk assessment of EPC-URDPV, it is necessary to find an information description tool that can not only ensure the information is not missing, but also fully convey the opinions of the evaluator. Scholars have proposed some descriptive tools, such as the fuzzy set (Zadeh, 1965), the intuitionistic fuzzy set (Atanassov, 1986), the intuitionistic multiplicative set (Xia, Xu, & Liao, 2013), and the hesitant fuzzy set (Torra, 2010). However, these information description tools are only suitable for the description of quantitative information (H. C. Liao, Yang, & Xu, 2018), not for the description of risk assessment information (qualitative information). There are 2-tuple linguistic (Francisco Herrera & Martínez, 2000) and 2-dimension linguistic (P. Liu, 2012) tools for describing qualitative information. However, when decision-making experts are limited by factors such as their knowledge or time, they often hesitate between the values of several evaluation terms. At this time, traditional fuzzy linguistic theory cannot be used for decision-making modeling

(Rodriguez, Martinez, & Herrera, 2012). HFLTS used in this paper is suitable for describing qualitative evaluation information and can solve the above problems well.

(2) In response to the second problem, this paper first obtains the risk factors affecting the project through a large number of literature reviews, and then proposes a four-dimensional risk analysis method to identify critical risk factors (CRFs) to composed the index system.

(3) After sorting out and analyzing the existing research, this paper proposes to carry out risk analysis from four dimensions of possibility, severity, uncontrollability and urgency.

(4) This paper uses linguistic variables to express the degree of influence between factors, and then convert linguistic variables into intuitionistic fuzzy numbers (IFNs), so as to solve the problem of insufficient consideration of fuzziness in traditional Decision-Making Trial and Evaluation Laboratory (DEMATEL) method to a certain extent.

The originality of this paper can be summarized as follows: ①Through a lot of literature research, the risk factors of EPC-URDPV project are sorted out. Based on the four-dimensional risk analysis, the critical risk factors (CRFs) of EPC-URDPV project are identified and the risk evaluation index system is constructed according to the results; ②The fuzzy synthetic evaluation is developed by the HFTLS and DEMATEL to assess the risk level of EPC-URDPV project; ③A set of perfect risk assessment framework of EPC project is constructed to carry out risk management; ④The risk assessment of 15 provinces which mainly develop URDPV in China is carried out, and the risk assessment results of EPC-URDPV projects in China under three scenarios are given.

To this end, the rest of the paper is organized as follows: Literature reviews are offered in Section 2. Section 3 establishes a comprehensive risk assessment index system for EPC-URDPV projects based on the four-dimensional risk analysis. Section 4 introduces the theory and method used in this paper. Section 5, after determining the scope of the study (15 provinces), a risk assessment is conducted on China's EPC-URDPV projects. In section 6, sensitivity analysis is used to test the stability of evaluation results. In addition, scenario analysis is performed by setting three scenarios that may be faced in the future and corresponding risk response measures are given. The last section provides conclusions and outlooks.

2. Literature reviews

2.1 Risks faced by EPC-BRDPV projects in China

Despite of the booming development of URDPV, many certain and uncertain risk factors due to policy changes, technical maturity and long payback period in the whole life-cycle of an EPC-URDPV project could affect its quality development and hinder its further development. For ordinary URDPV projects, risks have been identified generally includes: ①policy risks

(Jannuzzi & Melo, 2013; Luo, Long, Wei, & Tang, 2016; Mitscher & Rüther, 2012; Wu, Zhou, Hu, Li, & Sun, 2018b; F. Zhang, Deng, Margolis, & Su, 2015); ②economic and financing risks (Chi, Lei-Jiao, Sheng-Wei, & Gao, 2017; Fetanat & Khorasaninejad, 2015; Holdermann, Kissel, & Beigel, 2014; P. Lee, Lam, & Lee, 2015; Luo et al., 2016; Wu, Zhou, et al., 2018b; Yang & Zhao, 2018); ③construction risks (Berghorn & Syal, 2016; Chi et al., 2017; Fetanat & Khorasaninejad, 2015; P. Lee et al., 2015; Wu, Zhou, et al., 2018b; Yang & Zhao, 2018); ④technical risks (Berghorn & Syal, 2016; Chi et al., 2017; Fetanat & Khorasaninejad, 2015; P. Lee et al., 2015; Ningbo, 2017; Wu, Zhou, et al., 2018b) . EPC business mode is the focus of this paper, which has been widely adopted in the United States, Japan and Germany (Strupeit & Palm, 2016). EPC mode is advocated by the new round of power system reform that China is currently vigorously promoting. Since there are special risks of EPC-URDPV project itself, risks of URDPV projects with the EPC mode will not be limited to the above, which include those brought by the EPC mode. For instance, contractual risk (24); difficulties in defining rooftop property rights (Luo et al., 2016); efficiency risk (Yang & Zhao, 2018); impact on the building (Ningbo, 2017); power generation subsidy (Chi et al., 2017; Ningbo, 2017; Wu, Zhou, et al., 2018b); operation and maintenance risk (Berghorn & Syal, 2016; Chi et al., 2017; P. Lee et al., 2015; Wu, Zhou, et al., 2018b), etc. Section 3.1. systematically collates various risk factors that EPC-URDPV project may face. Inadequate or inappropriate risk management may lead to failure of EPC-URDPV Project. Some EPC projects have failed because of poor risk assessment at an appropriate method and weak risk management (Pan Lee et al., 2013). Thus, a comprehensive risk assessment is the key to the success of EPC-URDPV projects. However, there is a lack of study about risk assessment in EPC-URDPV project, as well as a comprehensive index system for it, which provides an opportunity for the research of this paper.

2.2 Risk analysis for EPC-URDPV projects in China

Some EPC projects have failed because of poor risk assessment at an appropriate method and weak risk management (Pan Lee et al., 2013) . Similar problems exist in EPC-URDPV projects, so it is very important to carry out risk assessment and management well. There are some researches about risk analysis of DPV and energy-saving retrofit project in EPC at home and abroad. Rocchetta, Li, and Zio (2015) carried out the risk assessment of DPV under extreme weather conditions. They obtained both normal and severe weather by using Monte Carlo non-sequential algorithm. Luo et al. (2016) believed that because of the unclear definition of roof property rights, there are complex financing risks in DPV power generation projects. In addition, there are policy risks, grid access risks and uncertainties in profitability of DPV power generation projects. P. Lee et al. (2015) studied the energy retrofit projects in Hong Kong, identified the key risk factors of the EPC project through user surveys, and proposed corresponding solutions. Berghorn and Syal (2016) analyzed the risk of EPC building retrofit projects by using the Delphi method, and provide additional analysis related to risk causes and control measures as well as relative risk importance. Garbuzova-Schlifter and Madlener (2016) systematically analyzed the risk factors and causes of risk associated with EPC projects executed in three Russian sectors: industrial, housing and communal services and public. They made a qualitative risk assessment through the analytic hierarchy process (AHP) method. It can be seen that the research on EPC projects are focused on energy retrofit projects. However, for ESCOs, the use of distributed energy to provide energy-saving services for energy-using units have the characteristics of easy measurement of energy-saving amount and clear revenue situation of all parties. Therefore, after applying EPC model to URDPV projects, it is very necessary to carry out risk analysis.

In addition, for the dimensions of risk analysis, scholars have portrayed risk factors from multiple perspectives. Ebrahimnejad, Mousavi, and Mojtahedi (2008) described the risk factors from five dimensions: the probability of risk occurrence, impact, quickness of reaction, event measure quantity and event ability. AbdolrezaYazdani-Chamzini, Siamak Haji Yakhchali, and Mahmood Mahmoodian (2013); (A. P. Chan et al., 2014) portrayed risks from probability, uncertainty, ability to respond four dimensions respectively. Sarkar and Panchal (2015) proposed the exposure of risk. L. Wang, Zhang, Wang, and Li (2018) proposed two new dimensions that are unpredictability and risk urgency. Firstly, the uncertainty and unpredictability of risk occurrence are similar to the possibility to some extent. In addition, the impact of risk should be a comprehensive attribute, not suitable for a single dimension. Quickness of reaction and event measure quantity are not the characteristics that need to be focused on. After carefully considering the above research status, the four-dimensional risk analysis presented in this paper to conduct risk analysis of EPC-URDPV. The existing research results and the proposed are shown in the following Table15.2.

Table 15.2 The risk analysis dimensions of existing research and the proposed dimensions.

References	1= (Ebrahimnejad et al., 2008)	2= (AbdolrezaYazdani-Chamzini et al., 2013)	3= (A. P. Chan et al., 2014)	4= (Sarkar & Panchal, 2015)	5= (L. Wang et al., 2018)	The proposed dimension
Dimension	probability	uncertainty	probability	probability	probability	probability
	impact	impact		severity	risk impact	severity
	quickness of reaction	likelihood or probability	severity		unpredictability	uncontrollability
	event measure quantity	ability to respond		exposure	risk urgency	urgency
	event ability					

2.3 Fuzzy synthetic evaluation method

Fuzzy synthetic evaluation (FSE) is based on fuzzy mathematics and applies the principle of fuzzy relation synthesis to quantify some factors with unclear boundaries and difficult to quantify (Shidpour, Da Cunha, & Bernard, 2016). It is a method of comprehensive evaluation of the subordinate status of things from multiple attributes. The advantage of FSE method is that it can deal with complex multi-attribute evaluation problems (Mu, Cheng, Chohr, & Peng, 2014). FSE has been widely used in risk assessment research. The FSE was used to evaluate the risk of green projects in Singapore (Xianbo Zhao, Hwang, & Gao, 2016). Rai, Sharma, and Lohani (2014) used the FSE technology to evaluate the risk of International Transboundary rivers. J. Liu, Li, and Wang (2013) made a risk assessment of ultra-deep drilling project based on the method of FSE. Xianbo Zhao et al. (2016) constructed an evaluation model based on FSE method to evaluate the risks of public-private partnership (PPP) in China. This model can evaluate the risks of general PPP projects. Mu et al. (2014) used this method to evaluate the risk management capability of the contractors of metro projects in China. It is noteworthy that the method of FSE can be used not only in the field of risk assessment, but also in other fields. Haider et al. (2018) constructed the evaluation framework of community sustainable development in small-sized urban neighborhoods based on the method of FSE. Ruparathna, Hewage, and Sadiq (2017) used a FSE-based method to assess the level of service of buildings. J. Wang, Ding, Liu, and Li (2016) put forward the FSE method based on triangular fuzzy number, and carried out an empirical study, which proved that the method has strong practicability and operability. It can be seen from the above research that the FSE method can deal with multi-criteria and multi-objective problems well, especially the risk assessment problem. The risk assessment of China's EPC-URDPV project is a multi-criteria uncertainty fuzzy problem that requires expert subjective judgment. It is feasible to use FSE method to establish a risk assessment model to solve this problem.

In addition, due to the complexity and fuzziness of risk assessment, the use of qualitative linguistic set is inevitable (S. Q. Wang, Dulaimi, & Aguria, 2004), and experts often have subjectivity and uncertainty in the evaluation of each risk factor (Shan, Chan, Le, Xia, & Hu, 2015). It is important to ensure the completeness and fuzziness of evaluation information in risk assessment. The introduction of fuzzy theory is an effective solution (Xianbo Zhao, Hwang, & Low, 2013). Therefore, this paper uses HFLTS to describe the evaluation information, and uses IF-DEMATEL method to obtain the weight of index set in the process of FSE, so as to further use the method of FSE to carry out risk evaluation research.

Above all, valid research on risk management of EPC-URDPV projects is insufficient. However, the project owners generally have problems such as low technical level, limited professional quality, and poor ability to resist risks. Once the risk of such projects is not effectively controlled, it will not only lead to various problems in the process of construction and management coordination, but also extend the problems to the periphery of the project, which will lead to unnecessary civil disputes, and even affect the image of power grid and even the government. Therefore, it is a subject worthy of in-depth study to conduct risk assessment on EPC-URDPV projects, so as to reasonably and effectively avoid project risks and promote the healthy development of DPV.

3. Risk assessment index system for EPC-URDPV projects in China

Risk assessment and control are critical to the successful implementation of a project. The establishment of risk assessment index system is the basis of risk assessment and control. A reasonable indicator system can help to obtain scientific risk assessment results, and also provide a basis for measurement of investment risk analysis. Therefore, in the process of establishment, we should take all the risk into account from multiple perspectives as much as possible. EPC projects involve a large number of uncertain risks, and CRFs identification is a vital phase in the project risk management process (Hwang, Zhao, & Gay, 2013). The risk factors of EPC-URDPV projects in China are identified through literature review. It is worth noting that this study proposes four-dimensional risk analysis to select the CRFs to constitute the risk assessment index system. Given that there is little study on the risk management of EPC-URDPV projects in China, a three-phase procedure is adopted to establish the evaluation index system.

3.1 Identifying risk factors of various EPC and URDPV projects

EPC projects involve a large number of uncertain risks. Comprehensive risk identification is an important prerequisite for controlling project risks and achieving project success. To achieve this goal, this study conducted an analysis of previous literatures on risk management in EPC projects and URDPV projects to identify possible risk factors, which offers an effective way to pick up and understand the factors that may lead to the failure of the projects. These papers have studied EPC projects and URDPV projects at home and abroad. The research objects involve energy retrofits, PV power generation projects, energy-saving building projects and so on. These projects are carried out in EPC mode. It is noteworthy that EPC projects have some similar risks that need to be identified and analyzed. Finally, a list containing 38 risk factors affecting EPC-URDPV projects in China is obtained through the above work. References and distribution of the risk factors are respectively shown in Table 15.3.

Table 15.3 Risk factors associated with EPC and URDPV projects.

No.	Risk factors	Reference											
		1	2	3	4	5	6	7	8	9	10	11	12
1	Annual rate of return						√				√		√
2	Client risk	√		√	√								
3	Commissioning			√									
4	Construction-specific concerns			√			√						
5	Contractual risk				√								
6	Credit rating given by the bank	√	√		√		√						
7	Difficulties in defining rooftop property rights								√				
8	Difficulties in tariff collection								√				
9	Economic risk		√								√	√	
10	ECM selection and installation			√									
11	Efficiency risk					√							√
12	Equipment pass rate						√						
13	Financial risk	√	√		√						√		
14	Extra cost risk					√							√
15	Government service quality							√		√	√		
16	Government support						√			√		√	
17	Grid connection risk								√	√	√		√
18	Harmonic risk					√							
19	Human and behavioral risk				√								
20	Impact on the building							√					
21	Impact on the grid					√		√		√			
22	Light risk					√							
23	Management risk	√						√					
24	Market absorptive risk	√			√						√		
25	Measurement and verification risk		√	√									
26	Operation and maintenance risk		√	√		√	√	√			√		
27	Perception of performance contracting industry			√									
28	Political and legal risk	√			√	√			√			√	
29	Power generation subsidy						√	√			√		√
30	Power supply reliability risk					√					√		
31	Project design risk		√										
32	Project management over project life cycle	√	√	√	√								
33	Relay protection risk					√							
34	Service index						√			√	√		
35	Technology risk		√		√								
36	Solar energy resources							√			√	√	
37	Temperature risk					√					√		
38	volatility of energy prices			√							√		√

References:1= (Hu & Zhou, 2011); 2= (P. Lee et al., 2015); 3= (Berghorn & Syal, 2016); 4= (Garbuzova-Schlifter & Madlener, 2016); 5= (Y. Liu, Zhang, & An, 2010); 6= (Chi et al., 2017); 7= (Ningbo, 2017); 8= (Luo et al., 2016); 9= (Wu & Geng, 2014); 10= (Wu, Zhou, et al., 2018a); 11= (Fang, Li, & Song, 2018); 12=(Yang & Zhao, 2018).

3.2 Selecting CRFs by four-dimension risk analysis

After conducting the comprehensive literature review analysis, a total of 38 risk factors are gathered. This study uses the uncontrollability of risk to describe the project subject's response to risk, and proposes to analyze the risk factors from four dimensions (Fig. 15.2): possibility, severity, uncontrollability and urgency, so as to identify the CRFs.

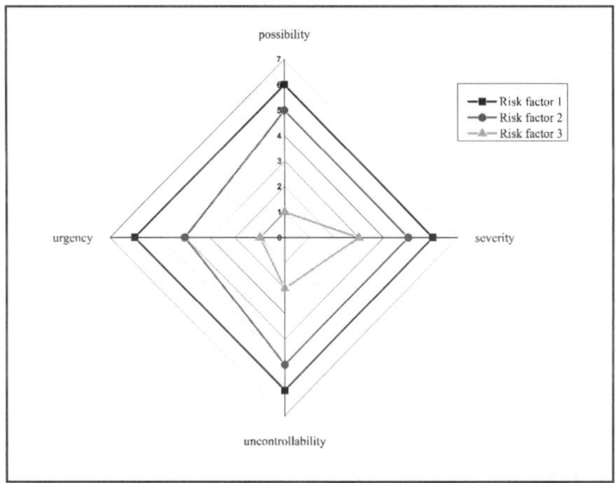

Fig. 15.2 The mechanism of Four-dimensional risk analysis.

Questionnaire survey has become a mature and effective method for risk analysis. The 38 identified risk factors in the previous step were integrated into questionnaire for a survey. The aim of the questionnaire is to require respondents to estimate the possibility, severity, uncontrollability and urgency of each risk factor. In order to obtain accurate evaluation information, the questionnaire uses a 7-point system (D. W. M. Chan & Kumaraswamy, 1996; Wu, Li, et al., 2017) to evaluate each factor's four dimension (1 = very low, 2 = low, 3 =relatively low, 4 =medium, 5 = relatively high, 6 = high, 7 = very high). Compared with the 5-point scale, 7-point system can provide more options for responders and thereby more accurate base data for subsequent processing and analysis. On the other hand, target respondents should meet the following requirements: ① Respondents engaged in research and work on DPV; ② Respondents involved in scientific research institutions, PV investment enterprises, relevant government departments and so on; ③ Scholars who have published at least four paper in international journals related to the EPC or PV projects risk management; ④ Project managers who have managed at least two DPV project in China.

In order to ensure the accuracy and validity of the risk assessment results of EPC-URDPV, it is necessary to incorporate the opinions and experiences of the related parties. When studying the risk of EPC-URDPV, this paper considers that experts from the university, energy research institutions, power planning departments, PV investment enterprises and government departments have their own understanding and views on the EPC-URDPV risk from different perspectives. Therefore, in order to carry out a comprehensive risk assessment this study decided to select experts from these five departments to build the expert group. Before collecting expert opinions, the research team was able to find 43 potential expert group members from these five departments. However, these experts differ in their experience and level of knowledge. Some experts from universities have not only made achievements in distributed PV research, but also participated in many related research topics of pre-feasibility evaluation and post-operation evaluation of distributed PV projects. Considering that these experiences are highly relevant to this study, the proportion of such experts in the expert group has been appropriately increased. In addition, as the main body of the URDPV project, the experts' opinions from PV investment enterprises are important, so the proportion of such experts in the expert group is also increased. Finally, according to above standards, we screened 15 qualified professionals (5 professors from the colleges or universities; 2 researchers from energy research institution; 2 researchers from electric power planning and engineering institution; 4 professorate senior engineer from PV investment development company; 2 researchers from government related departments) to evaluate the risk factors.

The questionnaire was distributed to professionals on September 5, 2018, with a deadline of October 8. Finally, 12 professionals responded to the questionnaire, yielding a response rate of 80%. Among them, two experts from universities did not provide feedback. Another expert, who did not give feedback on the questionnaire, came from the PV investment company. The three experts did not give us feedback before the deadline. General information about the 12 respondents is summarized in Table 15.4.

Table 15.4 neral information of the respondents.

Organization of respondents	Universities			Energy research institution		EP planning & engineering institution		PV investment company			Government related departments	
Percentage	(3) 25.00%			(2) 16.67%		(2) 16.67%		(3) 25.00%			(2) 16.67%	
Number	1	1	1	1	1	1	1	1	1	1	1	1
Number of related SCI papers	8	6	5	2	2	3	1	1	2	1	2	3
Number of participating projects	5	2	5	5	5	6	8	5	6	9	4	2
DPV experience of respondents	7 years	4 years	4 years	5 years	4 years	3 years	6 years	6 years	7 years	4 years	3 years	5 years

Based on the risk factor ranking method adopted by (A. P. Chan et al., 2014), this study extended it to four-dimensional risk analysis to obtain the comprehensive impact of each risk factor. The "Impact" of a risk factor can be calculated by Eq. (15-1).

$$\text{Impact} = \sqrt[4]{\text{possibility} \times \text{severity} \times \text{uncontrollability} \times \text{urgency}} \tag{15-1}$$

The risk factors can be ranked based on their "Impact" values. The "Impact" values and ranking results are shown in Table 15.5. The risk factors with normalized impact values $\geqslant 0.5$ are deemed as "CRF" (Wu, Xu, et al., 2018).

Table 15.5 sk factor with normalized impact values ⩾ 0.5.

No.	Risk factors	Proba-bility	Severity	Uncontro-llability	Urgency	Normalized impact	References
1	Power generation subsidy	7	6	7	6	1.00	6, 7, 10, 12
2	Political and legal risk	6	6	6	6	0.86	1, 4, 5, 8, 12
3	volatility of prices	5	6	6	6	0.78	3, 10, 12
4	Grid connection risk	6	6	5	5	0.70	8, 9, 10, 12
5	Power supply reliability risk	5	5	6	6	0.70	5, 10
6	Difficulties in defining rooftop property rights	4	6	6	6	0.68	8
7	Solar energy resources	4	6	6	6	0.68	7, 10, 11
8	Government support	4	6	6	5	0.61	6, 9, 11
9	Operation and maintenance risk	5	6	4	6	0.61	2, 3, 5, 6, 7, 10
10	Annual rate of return	3	6	6	6	0.57	6, 10, 12
11	Market absorptive risk	3	6	6	6	0.57	1, 4, 10

References:1= (Hu & Zhou, 2011); 2= (P. Lee et al., 2015); 3= (Berghorn & Syal, 2016); 4= (Garbuzova-Schlifter & Madlener, 2016); 5= (Y. Liu et al., 2010); 6= (Chi et al., 2017); 7= (Ningbo, 2017); 8= (Luo et al., 2016); 9= (Wu & Geng, 2014); 10= (Wu, Zhou, et al., 2018a); 11= (Fang et al., 2018); 12= (Yang & Zhao, 2018);

Normalized value = (impact value-minimum impact value) / (maximum impact value-minimum impact value).

3.3 Onstructing the evaluation index system

38 risk factors affecting the EPC-URDPV project were identified in the first step, and the CRFs were selected by expert scoring based on the four-dimensional risk analysis method. The 11 CRFs are classified into four categories: policy risk, economic risk, technical risk and construction environmental risk and the 4 critical risk groups are called CRGs. Thus, the risk evaluation index system of EPC-URDPV project is constructed and shown in Fig. 15.3.

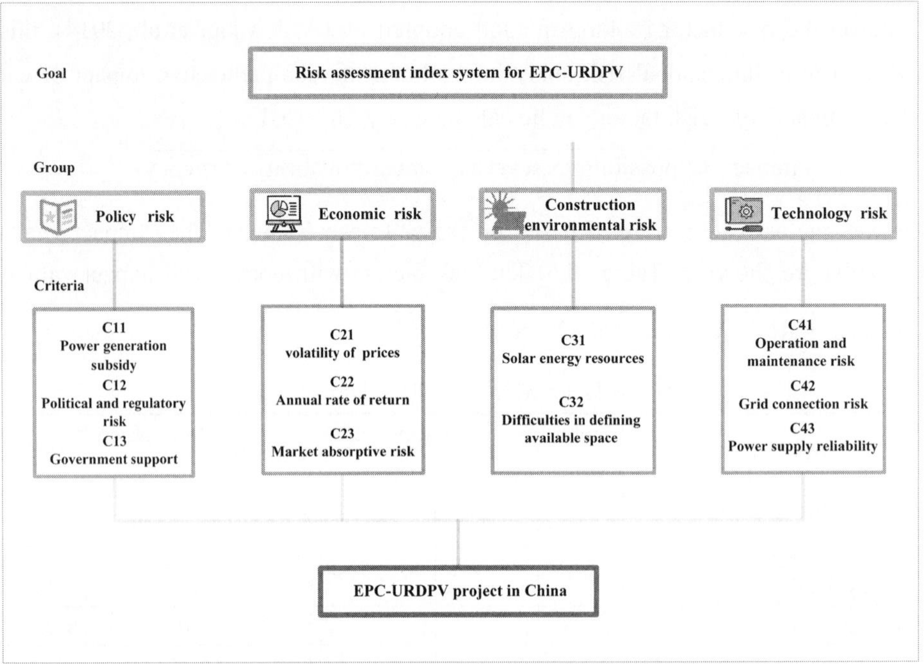

Fig. 15.3 valuation index system for risk assessment of EPC-URDPV project in China.

4. Methodology

4.1 Esitant fuzzy linguistic term sets (HFLTS) and aggregation method

With the continuous development of decision-making problems, when decision makers or experts evaluate something, the linguistic terms in the language terminology set do not match the linguistic evaluation information that the decision makers or experts want to give, but are between two linguistic terms or even between several linguistic terms. Therefore, HFLTS came into being. The HFLTS is further extended on the basis of hesitant fuzzy sets. Its function is to solve the problem that the evaluation information to be expressed by the decision maker or expert may be between multiple language terms. HFLTS can better retain the evaluation information of experts in the decision-making process, and has been widely used to solve decision-making problems in multiple management fields. It is a useful extension of the existing measurement system, which not only reflects the habits of decision makers expressing their opinions in linguistic preference, but also considers the situation in which decision makers (evaluator) hesitate in the evaluation of the program. In the risk assessment research of DPV project, the criteria evaluation information needs to be given by expert committee members in combination with their own professional knowledge and relevant experience, generally in the form of linguistic terms. In the evaluation process, it is always difficult for the expert committee to evaluate a risk assessment indicator in a single linguistic term. Thus, when experts hesitate to give linguistic evaluation information, HFLTS is a good solution to describe evaluation information. This description method can contain multiple linguistic terminology, and the description of criteria is more comprehensive. At the same time, it can effectively reduce the loss of information, make information retention more complete, and the result of aggregation is more effective. The relevant definitions of the HFLTS are as follows:

Definition 1. The set of linguistic terms considered in this paper is a finite ordered set with an odd number of linguistic terms. The intermediate linguistic terms indicate that the evaluation value is "close to 0.5" and other linguistic terms are symmetrically distributed (F. Herrera, Herrera-Viedma, & Verdegay, 1995; Yager, 1995). In these cases, the linguistic term set usually needs to meet the following conditions:

(1) Order: $s_i \geqslant s_j \Leftrightarrow i \geqslant j$;

(2) Maximum operator: if $s_i \geqslant s_j$, then $\max(s_i, s_j) = s_i$;

(3) Minimum operator: if $s_i \geqslant s_j$, then $\min(s_i, s_j) = s_j$.

Definition 2. (Rodriguez et al., 2012) Let $S = \{s_0, s_1, s_2, ..., s_n\}$ be a set of linguistic terms. If H_S is a set of sequential language terms ordered in S, then S is a set of hesitant fuzzy language terms on H_S. The mathematical form is:

$$H_S = \{< x, h(x) > | x \in X\} \tag{15-2}$$

where, function $h(x)$ represents the possible degree of membership of mapping $x \in X$ to set H_S.

Definition 3. (Rodriguez et al., 2012) Let $S = \{s_0, s_1, s_2, ..., s_n\}$ be a set of linguistic terms. H_S, H_S^1, H_S^2, and H_S^3 are the four hesitant fuzzy linguistic terms set on S, and the following operations can be defined:

(1) Upper bound H_S^+: $H_S^+ = \max(s_i) = s_k$, $s_i \in H_S$ and $s_i \leqslant s_k, \forall i$;

(2) Lower bound H_S^-: $H_S^- = \min(s_i) = s_k$, $s_i \in H_S$ and $s_i \geqslant s_k, \forall i$.

Definition 4. (Rodriguez et al., 2012) After the expert gives the initial evaluation linguistic value of the corresponding risk assessment criteria, according to the context-free semantic function E_{G_H}, the initial evaluation language value can be converted into a credibility-based HFLTS form. The operation rules are as follows:

$$E_{G_H}(s_i) = \{s_i / s_i \in S\} = \{s_i\} \tag{15-3}$$

$$E_{G_H}(\text{between } s_i \text{ and } s_j) = \{s_k / s_k \in S, s_i \leqslant s_k \leqslant s_j\} = \{s_i, s_{i+1}, ..., s_j\} \tag{15-4}$$

$$E_{G_H}(\text{below } s_i) = \{s_k / s_k \in S, s_k \leqslant s_i\} = \{s_o, s_1 ..., s_i\} \tag{15-5}$$

$$E_{G_H}(\text{above } s_i) = \{s_k / s_k \in S, s_k \geqslant s_i\} = \{s_i, s_{i+1}, ..., s_g\} \tag{15-6}$$

Considering the uncertainty of risk, the risk identification and assessment of DPV projects need to be based on certain experience or statistical data. In the process of converting the initial assessment linguistic value into HFLTS, experts often have a special preference for a certain linguistic term based on their own experience or corresponding statistical data, and give a higher degree of credibility in the process of conversion (Wu, Wang, Chen, Xu, & Li, 2017). Based on this, the credibility-based HFLTS of all investment risk assessment indicators can be obtained.

Example 1. The expert's evaluation result for the risk of government support is between small and general. Through the operation rules of context-free semantic function, the HFLTS form of this risk criteria based on credibility can be obtained as follows:

$$H_S(C_{ij}) = \left\{\frac{0.2}{S}, \frac{0.5}{RS}, \frac{0.3}{M}\right\}$$

The reliability of the linguistic value for risk assessment of government support is 0.2, 0.5 and 0.3, which corresponds to the small, the relatively small and the general respectively.

Due to the ambiguity and complexity of the actual decision-making environment, risk assessment data is often difficult to express with accurate values. The evaluation of risk indicators by the expert committee can be obtained in accordance with the linguistic terms that people are accustomed to use. However, qualitative linguistic terms cannot be mathematically operated, and it is difficult to obtain a more intuitive investment risk assessment result. Therefore, it is necessary to convert the language assessment information given by experts into a form that can be used for mathematical calculation. Triangular fuzzy number (TFN), as one of the simple and commonly used fuzzy numbers, can deal with the fuzzy information which cannot be operated well and get the result of risk assessment conveniently. In this paper, the HFLTS is transformed into TFN, and the risk assessment of the project is realized by the operation of TFN.

Definition 5. The HFLTS used in this paper contains seven language elements, and the specific features are as follows:

$$\begin{aligned} S = \{&S_{-3}\text{: Very Low (VL)}, s_{-2}\text{: Low (L)}, s_{-1}\text{: Relatively Low (RL)}, s_0\text{ : Medium(M)}, \\ &s_1\text{ : Relatively High (RH)}, s_2\text{ : High (H)}, s_3\text{ : Very High (VH)}\} \end{aligned} \tag{15-7}$$

Definition 6. (H. Liao, Xu, & Zeng, 2014) Let $S = \{s_t | t = -\tau, \cdots, -1, 0, 1, \cdots, \tau\}$ be a subscript symmetric linguistic terminology set in which the intermediate scale S_0 denotes the linguistic value as "Medium" and the other scales are evenly distributed on both sides. $S_{-\tau}$ and S_τ are the lower and upper bounds of the linguistic term set, and τ is a positive integer. A meets the following conditions:

(1) If $\alpha > \beta$, then $s_\alpha > s_\beta$,

(2) Inverse operation: $\text{neg}(s_\alpha) = s_{-\alpha}$.

The linguistic terminology set S is generally a set of discrete linguistic terms, which is not conducive to calculation and analysis. In the actual calculation process, the discrete linguistic terminology set will be expanded, and the extended linguistic terms only appear in the calculation process. Each linguistic terminology can correspond to the real number in the 0-1 interval by the corresponding membership function. Triangular membership functions (as shown in Fig. 15.4) and Gauss functions are relatively common functions (H. Liao et al., 2014). In this paper, the former is used to achieve conversion.

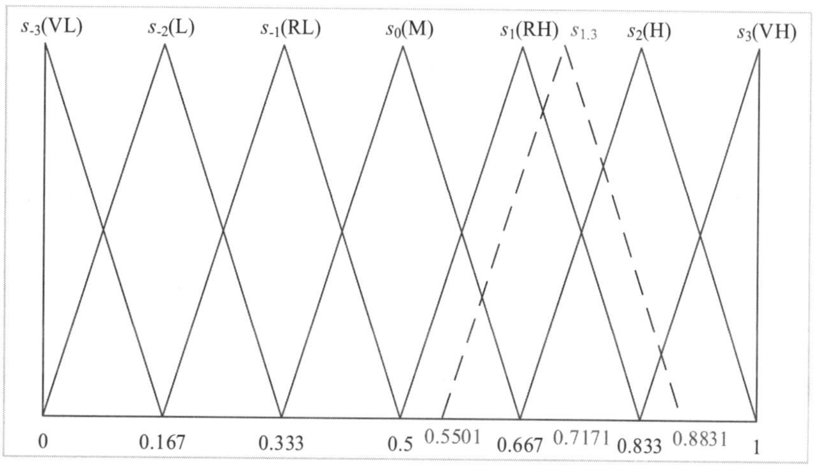

Fig. 15.4 Correspondence between linguistic terms and triangular fuzzy numbers.

Example 2. Taking $s_{1.3}$ as an example:

$$s_{1.3}:(0.5501,0.7171,0.8831)=(0.5+(1.3\text{-}1)\times 0.167,\ 0.667+(1.3-1)\times 0.167,\ 0.833+(1.3-1)\times 0.167)$$

Different types of linguistic terminology do not affect the derivation process, but differ only in the semantics they represent. The correspondence between HFLTSs (used in this paper) and TFNs can be derived from the operation relations of the subscript symmetric linguistic terminology sets. The results are as follows:

$$S=\left\{\begin{array}{l} s_{-3}:(0,0,0.167), s_{-2}:(0,0.167,0.333), \\ s_{-1}:(0.167,0.333,0.5), s_0:(0.333,0.5,0.667), \\ s_1:(0.5,0.667,0.833), s_2:(0.667,0.833,1), s_3:(0.833,1,1) \end{array}\right\}$$

Definition 7. HFLTSs can be aggregated according to the operation rules of TFNs by transforming them into TFNs (X. Wang, Jia, & Wang, 2015).

Taking the result of HFLTS based on the reliability of index C_{ij} as an example to illustrate the aggregation operation, the operation steps can be expressed as follows:

$$\begin{aligned} H_S(C_{ij}) &= \left\{\frac{0.2}{S},\frac{0.5}{RS},\frac{0.3}{M}\right\} \\ &= (0.2s_{-2},0.5s_{-1},0.3s_0) \\ &= (0.2\times(0,0.167,0.333),0.5\times(0.167,0.333,0.5),0.3\times(0.333,0.5,0.667)) \\ &= (0.183,0.35,0.517) \end{aligned}$$

4.2 Intuitionistic Fuzzy-Decision Making Trial and Evaluation Laboratory (IF-DEMATEL)

DEMATEL is an effective method for factor analysis and recognition by using graph theory and matrix tools. Digraphs are more useful than directionless graphs because digraphs can demonstrate the directed relationships of sub-systems. DEMATEL is based on digraphs, which can classify involved factors into cause group and effect Group (Chen & Li, 2009). Through the logical relationship and direct influence matrix among the factors in the system, the influence degree of each factor on other factors and the degree of each factor being influenced by other factors are calculated, and then the degree of centrality and degree of cause are calculated. In the traditional DEMATEL method, decision makers use real numbers to make judgments, but real numbers can not reflect the fuzziness and uncertainty of human decision-making. Therefore, this paper uses intuitionistic fuzzy theory to improve this method. Decision makers use linguistic variables to express the degree of influence between factors, and then convert linguistic variables into intuitionistic fuzzy numbers (IFNs), so as to solve the problem of insufficient consideration of fuzziness in traditional DEMATEL method to a certain extent.

Definition 8. (Atanassov, 1986) Let X be a non-empty set, and intuitionistic fuzzy sets on A can be defined as follows:

$$A=\left\{(x,u_A(x),v_A(x))\middle|x\in X\right\} \tag{15-8}$$

$u_A(x):X\to[0,1]$, $v_A(x):X\to[0,1]$ respectively denote that the element x belongs to the membership degree and non-membership degree of the set A, and satisfies. $0\leqslant u_A(x)+v_A(x)\leqslant 1,\forall x\in X$

For the intuitionistic fuzzy set A on X, parameter $\pi_A(x)=1-u_A(x)-v_A(x)$ is defined as the intuitionistic index, which can reflect the hesitation that element x belongs to set A. $\pi_A(x)$ satisfies. $0\leqslant\pi_A(x)\leqslant 1,\forall x\in X$ In particular, $\tilde{a}=(u_a,v_a,\pi_a)$ is called intuitionistic fuzzy number (IFN).

It should be noted that the thoughts of this IF-DEMATEL are based on the works developed by Seyed-Hosseini, Safaei, and Asgharpour (2006), Chen and Li (2009) and Lin and Tzeng (2009), and its fundamental steps are briefly described as follows.

Step 1. Establishing the linguistic measurement scale.

In this paper, a five-level linguistic scale is utilized with the following scale items: no influence, low influence, medium influence, high influence, and very high influence. The experts' evaluations are expressed by the linguistic scale. These linguistic terms and corresponding numbers are shown in Table 15.6.

Table 15.6 Linguistic variables and corresponding IFNs for expert assessment.

Traditional scale	linguistic variable	Corresponding IFNs
4	very high influence (VH)	(0.90, 0.10, 0.00)
3	high influence (H)	(0.75, 0.20, 0.05)
2	medium influence (M)	(0.50, 0.45, 0.05)
1	low influence (L)	(0.35, 0.60, 0.05)
0	no influence (N)	(0.00, 1.00, 0.00)

Step 2. Determining the direct influence matrix of each expert.

Experts use linguistic variables to represent the evaluation results, and then use Table 15.2 to convert linguistic variables into corresponding IFNs. Each expert will get a direct influence matrix $\tilde{X}^k$, which can be expressed as:

$$\tilde{X}^k = \begin{bmatrix} 0 & \tilde{x}_{12}^k & \cdots & \tilde{x}_{1n}^k \\ \tilde{x}_{21}^k & 0 & \cdots & \tilde{x}_{2n}^k \\ \vdots & \vdots & \ddots & \vdots \\ \tilde{x}_{n1}^k & \tilde{x}_{n2}^k & \cdots & 0 \end{bmatrix}$$

Step 3. Determining the total direct influence matrix.

In order to get the comprehensive evaluation result of the whole evaluation committee. In this paper, we choose the convenient intuitionistic fuzzy weighted geometric averaging (IFWGA) operator to achieve information aggregation (He, Chen, Zhou, Liu, & Tao, 2014). Let $r_{ij}^k = (u_{ij}^k, v_{ij}^k, \pi_{ij}^k)$ denote the intuitionistic fuzzy evaluation value of decision maker k on index C_j for alternative A_i, then the aggregation formula is as follows:

$$f_{ij} = \left(r_{ij}^1\right)^{\lambda_1} \otimes \left(r_{ij}^2\right)^{\lambda_2} \otimes \cdots \otimes \left(r_{ij}^k\right)^{\lambda_k} \otimes \cdots \otimes \left(r_{ij}^L\right)^{\lambda_L} = \left(\prod_{k=1}^{L}\left(u_{ij}^k\right)^{\lambda_k}, 1-\prod_{k=1}^{L}\left(1-v_{ij}^k\right)^{\lambda_k}, \prod_{k=1}^{L}\left(1-v_{ij}^k\right)^{\lambda_k} - \prod_{k=1}^{L}\left(u_{ij}^k\right)^{\lambda_k}\right) \quad (15\text{-}9)$$

where, λ_k is the weight of experts. f_{ij} represents the evaluated value after aggregation, which is an IFN. Then, the general direct influence matrix $\tilde{X}$ can be expressed as:

$$\tilde{X} = \begin{bmatrix} 0 & \tilde{x}_{12} & \cdots & \tilde{x}_{1n} \\ \tilde{x}_{21} & 0 & \cdots & \tilde{x}_{2n} \\ \vdots & \vdots & \ddots & \vdots \\ \tilde{x}_{n1} & \tilde{x}_{n2} & \cdots & 0 \end{bmatrix}$$

Step 4. The defuzzification and standardization of the direct influence matrix.

In order to facilitate the later calculation, element $\tilde{x}_{ij}$ in $\tilde{X}$ needs to be de-fuzzified to get the real number type direct influence matrix X (element x_{ij}). The transformation method is as follows (Xu & Xia, 2012):

$$x_{ij} = \frac{1}{2}\left(u_{ij} + 1 - v_{ij}\right) \quad (15\text{-}10)$$

Then, the elements in matrix X are standardized. The processing method is as follows:

$$Y = \left[y_{ij} \right]_{n \times n} = \frac{1}{s} \cdot X \tag{15-11}$$

$$s = \operatorname*{Max}_{i=1}^{n} \left\{ \sum_{j=1}^{n} x_{ij} \right\} \tag{15-12}$$

Step 5. Determining the comprehensive influence matrix.

On the basis of the direct influence matrix after standardization, the comprehensive influence matrix T is calculated by the following formula.

$$T = \left[t_{ij} \right]_{n \times n} = Y(I - Y)^{-1} \tag{15-13}$$

where, t_{ij} represents the comprehensive influence of criteria i on criteria j, including direct and indirect effects, and I is the identity matrix.

Step 6. Calculating the overall prominence and net effect of each criteria.

The sum of rows and columns in the comprehensive influence matrix T is calculated respectively to obtain the influence degree and being influenced degree of each criteria.

$$R_i = \sum_{j=1}^{n} t_{ij} \tag{15-14}$$

$$C_j = \sum_{i=1}^{n} t_{ij} \tag{15-15}$$

where, vector R_i and vector C_j respectively denote the sum of rows and the sum of columns from the comprehensive influence matrix T.

Then, we have vector ($R_i + C_j$) named "Prominence" is made by adding R_i to C_j, which reveals how much importance the criterion has. Similarly, the ($R_i - C_j$) named "net Effect" is made by subtracting R_i from C_j, which may divide criteria into a cause group and an effect group. Generally, when ($R_i - C_j$) is positive, the criterion belongs to the cause group. Otherwise, if the ($R_i - C_j$) is negative, the criterion belongs to the effect group.

Step 7. Obtaining the weight of each criteria.

According to the "Prominence" and "net Effect", the relative weight of each criteria is calculated and normalized. The calculation method is as follows:

$$w_{sj}^{'} = \left[(r_j + c_j)^2 + (r_j - c_j)^2 \right]^{1/2} \tag{15-16}$$

$$w_{sj} = \frac{w_{sj}^{'}}{\sum_{j=1}^{n} w_{sj}^{'}} \tag{15-17}$$

4.3 An extended HFLTS-Fuzzy synthetic evaluation

Risk assessment research involves the uncertainty and fuzziness of evaluation information, which are inevitable. For such problems, it is more convenient and feasible to use qualitative language such as very low, low, general and high to evaluate risk factors. The values of these languages are not specific numbers, but words. They are called linguistic variables in a vague environment. Fuzzy synthetic evaluation provides a method to express or define these variables by using mathematical logic (Zadeh, 1965). Fuzzy synthetic evaluation method can be well applied to the modeling and quantification of investment risk assessment of EPC-URDPV projects with fuzziness and uncertainty.

Its fundamental steps are briefly described as follows.

Step 1. Set up the risk evaluation criteria system for EPC-URDPV projects in China. (Factors set)

The risk evaluation criteria system for EPC-URDPV project in China has been established in chapter 3 and the 11 CRFs and the 4 CRGs can be seen in Fig.15.3.

Step 2. The definition of the risk evaluation set. (Judging set)

This paper sets the risk level evaluation set and HFLTS as the same judgment set (S).

$$\begin{aligned} S = \{ & s_{-3}\text{: Very Low (VL)}, s_{-2}\text{: Low (L)}, s_{-1}\text{: Relatively Low (RL)}, s_0 \text{ : Medium(M)}, \\ & s_1 \text{ : Relatively High (RH)}, s_2 \text{ : High (H)}, s_3 \text{ : Very High (VH)}\} \end{aligned}$$

Step 3. Determine appropriate weights for the risk criteria. (Weight set)

Section 4.3 describes in detail how to use IF-DEMATEL method to determine the relationship between risk factors and their weights. The weights obtained would be used for the next step.

Step 4. Implementation of fuzzy comprehensive evaluation.

Definition 9. The extended fuzzy synthetic evaluation model based on HFLTS is that the weight set W and the HFLTS set H_S are comprehensively evaluated through the fuzzy transformation:

$$E = \left(e^L, e^M, e^U\right) = W \cdot H_S = \left(w_1, w_2, \ldots, w_n\right) \cdot \begin{pmatrix} \left(h_1^L, h_1^M, h_1^U\right) \\ \left(h_2^L, h_2^M, h_2^U\right) \\ \cdots \\ \left(h_n^L, h_n^M, h_n^U\right) \end{pmatrix} \tag{15-18}$$

E in the formula is the result of risk assessment of EPC-URDPV project in China, which takes all risk indicators into consideration. The result is expressed in the form of TFNs. e^L, e^M and e^U represent the lower bound, the principal value and the upper bound respectively. w_n represents the weight of the nth index, and $\left(h_n^L, h_n^M, h_n^U\right)$ represents the HFLTS aggregation value of the nth index based on credibility.

Step 5. Determine the grade of evaluation object according to the principle of maximum membership.

The comprehensive evaluation results expressed in the form of TFNs cannot intuitively obtain the risk grade of EPC-URDPV project. At this time, it is necessary to judge the risk grade close to which evaluation results according to the principle of maximum membership. The greater the similarity between the two TFNs, the closer the two TFNs are.

Definition 10. The formula for calculating the similarity of the two TFNs is as follows:

$$Sd(\alpha,\beta)=1-\frac{\left|\alpha^{L}-\beta^{L}\right|+\left|\alpha^{M}-\beta^{M}\right|+\left|\alpha^{R}-\beta^{R}\right|}{3} \tag{15-19}$$

$\alpha=\left(\alpha^{L},\alpha^{M},\alpha^{U}\right)$ and $\beta=\left(\beta^{L},\beta^{M},\beta^{U}\right)$ are arbitrary two TFNs, and $Sd(\alpha,\beta)$ represents the similarity of α and β.

According to the above formulas, the similarity between the results of risk assessment and the linguistic values in the judgment set can be calculated, and then the risk level can be determined according to the principle of maximum membership.

4.4 A risk assessment framework for EPC-URDPV projects in China

At present, there are few risk studies on EPC-URDPV in China, so it is very important to construct a reasonable evaluation framework for risk assessment. This section summarizes the theoretical methods and key steps of the previous chapters to establish a five-stage risk assessment framework for EPC-URDPV in China. The specific details of each phase are described below, which will greatly improve the quality and efficiency of risk management.

Stage 1. Establish an evaluation index system based on four-dimension risk analysis.

The third part details the construction process of the risk assessment indicator system, which contains 11 important risk factors. The following work is based on this set of evaluation criteria.

Stage 2. Data processing based on HFLTS.

After establishing the risk assessment indicator system, it is necessary to collect the attribute values of the indicators corresponding to the evaluation objects and process them. The traditional numerical scoring method cannot reflect the opinions and evaluation results of the interviewed experts, and it is often impossible to give a more accurate description of the risk of the evaluation object. Risk assessment itself has great ambiguity and uncertainty. Therefore, this paper uses HFLTS to collect the scores of the interviewed experts, which fully reflects the ambiguity and hesitation of risk assessment, and makes the risk assessment process more realistic. In addition, the HFLTS is transformed into a TFN by the mapping relationship expressed in Fig. 15.4, and the attribute values of each evaluation object under each risk indicator are obtained. The specific use and transformation of HFLTS is elaborated in Section 4.1.

Stage 3. Calculate weights of evaluation indexes by IF-DEMATEL.

In the risk evaluation system of EPC-URDPV project, the relationship between the elements is uncertain. In this case, DEMATEL is suitable to determine the weight of indicators. DEMATEL is an effective method for factor analysis and identification. By sorting out the logical relationship between factors and analyzing the direct impact matrix, the "Prominence" and "net Effect" of each factor can be obtained. According to the "Prominence" and "net Effect", the relative weight of each criteria is calculated.

Stage 4. Implement risk assessment by extended Fuzzy synthetic evaluation.

Fuzzy synthetic evaluation is a common and mature risk evaluation method. In this paper, HFLTS is used to represent the evaluation information, which is different from the evaluation information used in the traditional Fuzzy synthetic evaluation method. Therefore, this paper proposes a extend for performing fuzzy comprehensive evaluation using HFLTS evaluation information, and finally determines the risk level of the evaluation object based on the closeness calculation.

Stage 5. Discussion and risk response.

Scenario analysis is an important part of risk management. The existence of risk factors makes the future development of the project multiple possibilities, and the predicted results are also multiple. Scenario analysis organically combines the objectivity of project risk evolution with human subjective initiative, so as to depict the future situation of the project more truly. As time goes by, the risk factors affecting the project will change to a large extent. Scenario analysis can be used to conduct risk analysis and risk prediction, which has great significance for project risk management. In addition, in order to prove and test the stability and robustness of the model, sensitivity analysis must be carried out accordingly.

Effective risk feedback is essential for the healthy development of EPC-URDPV projects. Based on the results of risk assessment, risk related parties are analyzed, and corresponding measures and suggestions are put forward to deal with key risk factors. This could provide a reference for the ECOs, ECUs and policy-makers in practice and give them some risk management inspiration.

5. Application of the proposed framework

The framework developed in the previous section is used to evaluate risk level of EPC-URDPV in China. The assessment object of this paper is the third-class areas of solar energy resource in China, which represent the current development status and trend of URDPV in China. The risk assessment objects of this paper, including 15 provinces, such as Shanghai, Jiangsu, Zhejiang, Anhui, Fujian, Jiangxi, Shandong, Henan, Hubei, Hunan, Guangdong,

Guangxi, Hainan, Chongqing and Guizhou.

5.1 Data collection and processing

Expert committee needs to be formed before conducting the risk assessment of EPC-URDPV in China. The risk evaluation committee includes eight experts (2 professors from the colleges or universities; 2 researchers from energy research institution; 2 professorate senior engineer from PV investment development company; 2 researchers from government related departments) whose research backgrounds are DPV and risk management. In this paper, the risk level evaluation set and the hesitant vague linguistic terms set are combined into a same judgment set. As shown in definition 5.

According to their professional background and relevant experience, the experts give the corresponding language values for the risk indicators of the evaluation objects based on the judgment set. Then, the aggregated risk assessment language information is redistributed to the members of the expert committee so that they can revise their assessment results. Repeat the above steps, the expert committee gives the evaluation language value of each risk assessment indicator of the final EPC project in a certain region. According to the method given in definition 7, HFLTS can be transformed into TFNs. Finally, the evaluation information tables corresponding to 15 evaluation provinces can be obtained. Take Shanghai for example, the linguistic values of risk indicators of EPC projects in Shanghai are shown in Table 15.7.

Table 15.7 Evaluation results of each risk indicator for EPC-URDPV in Shanghai.

Evaluation object	Criteria	Evaluation linguistic values	HS				Aggregate results
EPC-URDPV in Shanghai	C11	between M and H	0.1	0.3	0.6		(0.584, 0.750, 0.917)
			M	RH	H		
	C12	between M and H	0.3	0.3	0.4		(0.517, 0.683, 0.850)
			M	RH	H		
	C13	above RH	0.6	0.3	0.1		(0.583, 0.750, 0.900)
			RH	H	VH		
	C21	between RH and H	0.5	0.5			(0.584, 0.750, 0.900)
			RH	H			
	C22	above M	0.5	0.2	0.2	0.1	(0.483, 0.650, 0.800)
			M	RH	H	VH	
	C23	between RS and M	0.5	0.5			(0.333, 0.500, 0.667)
			RS	M			
	C31	above RH	0.7	0.1	0.2		(0.583, 0.750, 0.883)
			RH	H	VH		
	C32	between G and VH	0.7	0.3			(0.717, 0.883, 1.000)
			H	VH			

Continued

Evaluation object	Criteria	Evaluation linguistic values	HS				Aggregate results
EPC-URDPV in Shanghai	C41	between M and H	0.3	0.5	0.2		(0.483, 0.650, 0.817)
			M	RH	H		
	C42	between M and H	0.1	0.3	0.6		(0.584, 0.750, 0.917)
			M	RH	H		
	C43	between M and H	0.1	0.6	0.2		(0.467, 0.617, 0.767)
			M	RH	H		

5.2 Weight calculation of risk assessment index

Each expert uses a five-level linguistic variable to evaluate the interaction between the indicators to form the direct impact matrix. The linguistic variables in the direct influence matrix are transformed into corresponding intuitionistic fuzzy numbers, and then the IFWGA operator is used to assemble the direct influence matrix of each expert into an overall direct influence matrix as shown in Table 15.8. Based on this matrix, the centrality and causality of each indicator is calculated by IF-DEMATEL method (Section 4.2). Finally, the subjective weight of each index is calculated by Eq. (15-12) and Eq. (15-13). The calculation results are shown in Table 15.9.

Table 15.8 Overall direct influence matrix after de-fuzzification.

	C11	C12	C21	C42	C43	C32	C31	C13	C41	C22	C23
C11	0	0.4435	0.9	0	0	0	0	0.525	0.525	0.9	0.8355
C12	0.9	0	0.9	0.6375	0.4435	0.525	0	0.9	0.6375	0.775	0.775
C21	0.6375	0.375	0	0.375	0.375	0.4435	0	0.525	0.6375	0.9	0.9
C42	0.4435	0.525	0.4435	0	0.8355	0.375	0	0.6375	0.525	0.525	0.775
C43	0.4435	0.4435	0.375	0.775	0	0.375	0	0.525	0.775	0.775	0.775
C32	0	0.4435	0	0.4435	0.4435	0	0	0.4435	0.4435	0.375	0.375
C31	0.4435	0.375	0.525	0.525	0.375	0	0	0.525	0.375	0.9	0.525
C13	0.775	0.775	0.6375	0.525	0.525	0.375	0	0	0.525	0.525	0.775
C41	0	0.375	0.525	0.775	0.775	0.375	0	0.4435	0	0.525	0.775
C22	0.6375	0.775	0.525	0.375	0.375	0	0	0.525	0.4435	0	0.4435
C23	0.525	0.525	0.525	0.6375	0.525	0.375	0	0.6375	0.525	0.9	0

Table 15.9 Summary of the weight of each risk indicator.

Indicator	R_i	C_j	R_i+C_j	R_i-C_j	W_{ij}'	W_{ij}	Order
C11	2.3599	2.8632	5.2230	-0.5033	5.2472	0.0858	8
C12	3.6433	3.0048	6.6481	0.6385	6.6787	0.1092	2
C21	2.8548	2.3665	5.2213	0.4884	5.2441	0.0858	9
C42	2.8660	2.9057	5.7717	-0.0396	5.7718	0.0944	5
C43	2.9344	2.7344	5.6687	0.2000	5.6722	0.0928	7

Continued

Indicator	R_i	C_j	$R_i + C_j$	$R_i - C_j$	W'_{ij}	W_{ij}	Order
C32	1.7161	1.7633	3.4795	-0.0472	3.4798	0.0569	11
C31	2.5998	0.0000	2.5998	2.5998	3.6767	0.0601	10
C13	3.0201	3.2560	6.2761	-0.2359	6.2805	0.1027	4
C41	2.6147	3.1212	5.7359	-0.5065	5.7582	0.0942	6
C22	2.3555	3.9000	6.2555	-1.5446	6.4434	0.1054	3
C23	2.8788	3.9284	6.8072	-1.0496	6.8876	0.1127	1

According to the results in the above table, the weights of market absorptive risk and political and regulatory risk are the biggest. To some extent, the most important factor affecting EPC-URDPV project risk is policy and market absorption. Investors can focus on these two aspects when evaluating EPC-URDPV project risk. Government support and annual project income are also important risk factors, with weighted results exceeding 10%. The risk factor of difficulties in defining rooftop property rights has the lowest weight, mainly because the risk will not bring risks to the project once it is properly solved before the project starts, but the risk should be given enough attention before the project is launched.

5.3 Implement risk assessment

After determining the weight, according to Eq. (15-14), the risk of EPC projects in 15 provinces can be evaluated by fuzzy comprehensive evaluation to determine the risk level. Since the obtained evaluation result is a TFN, the closeness of the TFN corresponding to each risk level is calculated by Eq. (15-14), and finally the risk level of the evaluation object is divided according to the size of the closeness. Take the EPC-URDPV in Shanghai for example and as shown in Table 15.10.

Table 15.10 Evaluation results for EPC-URDPV in Shanghai.

Indicator	Weight	Evaluation value of each indicator
C11	0.086	(0.584, 0.750, 0.917)
C12	0.109	(0.517, 0.683, 0.850)
C13	0.103	(0.583, 0.750, 0.900)
C21	0.086	(0.584, 0.750, 0.917)
C22	0.105	(0.483, 0.650, 0.800)
C23	0.113	(0.333, 0.500, 0.667)
C31	0.060	(0.583, 0.750, 0.883)
C32	0.057	(0.717, 0.883, 1.000)
C41	0.094	(0.483, 0.650, 0.817)
C42	0.094	(0.584, 0.750, 0.917)
C43	0.093	(0.467, 0.617, 0.767)
Risk evaluation results		(0.5247, 0.6898, 0.8466)

Continued

Indicator	Weight	Evaluation value of each indicator
Risk level	M	(0.333, 0.5, 0.667)
	RH	(0.5, 0.667, 0.833)

Based on the Table 15.10 and Fig. 15.4, it can be seen that the evaluation results are between "Medium" and "Relatively High". Therefore, the closeness between the evaluation result and the two risk levels need to be calculated separately by Eq. (15-15), and then the risk level is determined.

$$Sd(s_i,s_0)=1-\frac{\left|s_i^L-s_0^L\right|+\left|s_i^M-s_0^M\right|+\left|s_i^R-s_0^R\right|}{3}$$

$$=1-\frac{|0.525-0.333|+|0.690-0.5|+|0.847-0.667|}{3}=0.813$$

$$Sd(s_i,s_1)=1-\frac{\left|s_i^L-s_1^L\right|+\left|s_i^M-s_1^M\right|+\left|s_i^R-s_1^R\right|}{3}$$

$$=1-\frac{|0.525-0.5|+|0.690-0.667|+|0.847-0.833|}{3}=0.98$$

According to the calculation results (0.98 > 0.813), the risk level is " Relatively High ". The risk level results of the respective evaluation objects are shown in Table 15.11.

Table 15.11 Risk assessment result for EPC-URDPV in each province.

Order	Province	Evaluation result	Risk level
A1	Shanghai	(0.5247, 0.6898, 0.8466)	RH
A2	Fujian	(0.4831, 0.6469, 0.8000)	RH
A3	Hainan	(0.4736, 0.6387, 0.7960)	RH
A4	Chongqing	(0.4523, 0.6174, 0.7764)	RH
A5	Guangdong	(0.4418, 0.6049, 0.7678)	RH
A6	Shandong	(0.4294, 0.5946, 0.7553)	RH
A7	Henan	(0.4274, 0.5909, 0.7454)	RH
A8	Guizhou	(0.3827, 0.5479, 0.7042)	M
A9	Zhejiang	(0.3590, 0.5210, 0.63789)	M
A10	Hubei	(0.3470, 0.5121, 0.6772)	M
A11	Guangxi	(0.3456, 0.5106, 0.6729)	M
A12	Hunan	(0.3318, 0.4983, 0.6622)	M
A13	Jiangxi	(0.2956, 0.4621, 0.6290)	M
A14	Jiangsu	(0.2390, 0.4054, 0.5724)	RS
A15	Anhui	(0.2181, 0.3845, 0.5514)	RS

The risk assessment results are mainly divided into three categories: "Relatively High", "Medium" and "Relatively Low". Among them, the EPC-URDPV projects in Anhui and Jiangsu have the best risk assessment results, which are "Relatively Low" (light green). The results show that the investment environment of EPC-URDPV projects in these two provinces is relatively good, which is suitable for PV development enterprises to invest in such projects. The evaluation results of the seven provinces of Shanghai, Fujian, Hainan, Chongqing, Guangdong, Shandong and Henan are "Relatively High", and PV development enterprises need to actively carry out risk management when investing in projects in such areas; The risk assessment results of other provinces are "Medium". Overall, the risk level of EPC-URDPV projects in China is at a relatively good level, and more than half of the evaluation areas are at investable risk level. These areas are located in the central and eastern parts of China. These areas are economically developed and have large electricity demand. It is worth pointing out that the awareness of developing clean energy is relatively mature, and the basic conditions for developing DPV projects are also basically available.

6. Discussion

6.1 Sensitivity analysis

The risk analysis model (an extended HFLTS-DEMATEL fuzzy synthetic evaluation analysis) used in this paper is a weight-based evaluation method. In order to prove and test the stability and robustness of the model, sensitivity analysis must be carried out accordingly. In this part, sensitivity analysis of weights of 11 CRFs are presented. The number of tests is as high as 66. This process aims to see whether the results would qualitatively change if the CRFs weights fluctuate. 11 CRFs are classified as 4 analysis groups, namely policy risk group, economic risk group, construction environmental risk group and technology risk group. All CRFs have 10%, 20% and 30% less weight than the base weight and 10%, 20% and 30% more weight than the base weight (Wu, Wang, Hu, Ke, & Li, 2018). Based on the sensitivity analysis results, the fluctuation curve can be drawn and the changes in net flow can be seen intuitively.

Fig. 15.5 shows that the model is sensitive to risk indicators C11 and C13 to some degree. With the increase of the weight of risk index C11, only the curve corresponding to A9 shows a downward trend, indicating that the EPC-URDPV projects in this area is less affected by the risk of generation subsidies. After the weight of risk index C13 increases gradually, the risk levels of A2, A4, A5 and A7 also increase slightly, which indicates that the influence of government support on distributed photovoltaic projects in these areas is more obvious.

Fig. 15.6 shows that the model is basically insensitive to economic risk group. It is worth noting that with the increasing weight of risk indicator C23, the risk level of EPC-URDPV projects in all regions shows a downward trend, indicating that market absorption is no longer an important obstacle to the development of EPC-URDPV projects.

Generally speaking in Fig. 15.7, the model is insensitive to the change of weight of construction environmental risk group. However, with the increase of the weight of risk index C32, compared with other regions, the trend of risk increase of distributed projects in A9 region is more obvious. It shows that difficulties in defining rooftop property rights (C32) is the main obstacle to the development of distributed photovoltaic projects in this area. The overall smoothness of the curve in Fig. 15.8 shows that the model is insensitive to technology risk group.

Based on the Fig. 15.5 to Fig.15.8, it can be summarized that the curves are relatively smooth and there is no obvious fluctuation. Among all the tests, A14 and A15 are still the best investment areas, and the risk level of EPC-URDPV projects is at a relatively low level. A1 is still the region with the highest risk level, so it is necessary to focus on the project risks when investing in such projects. Above all, the risk analysis model (an extended HFLTS-DEMATEL fuzzy synthetic evaluation analysis) adopted in this paper has good adaptability and the robustness & stability of this method is verified.

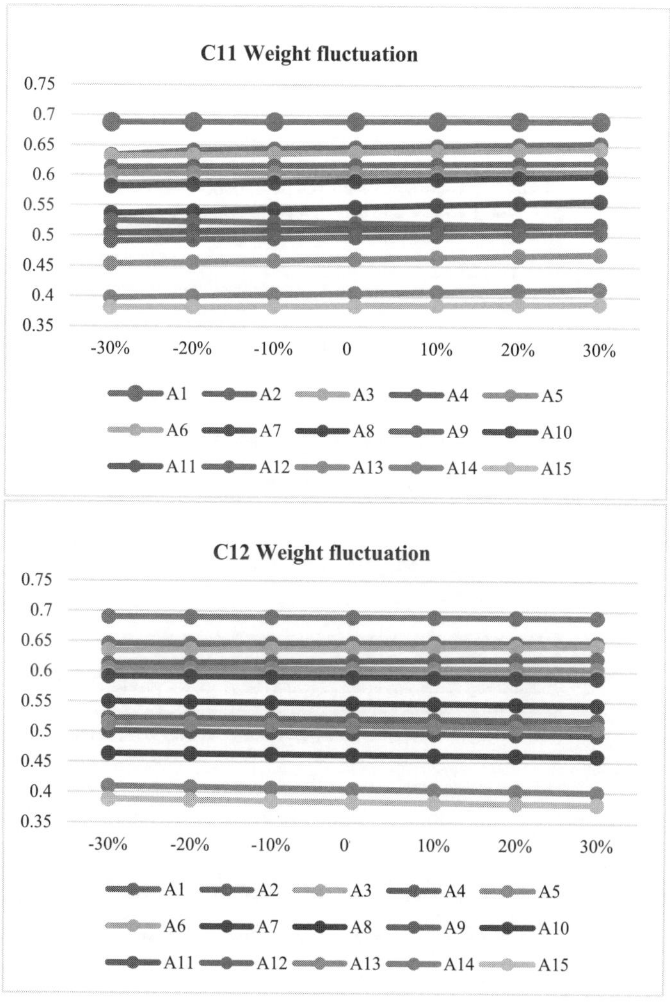

Fig. 15.5 Sensitivity analysis results of the CRFs in policy risk group.

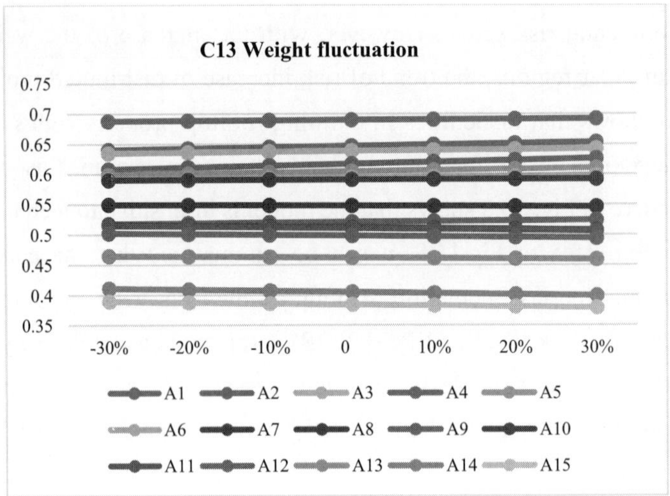

Fig. 15.5 Sensitivity analysis results of the CRFs in policy risk group.(Continued)

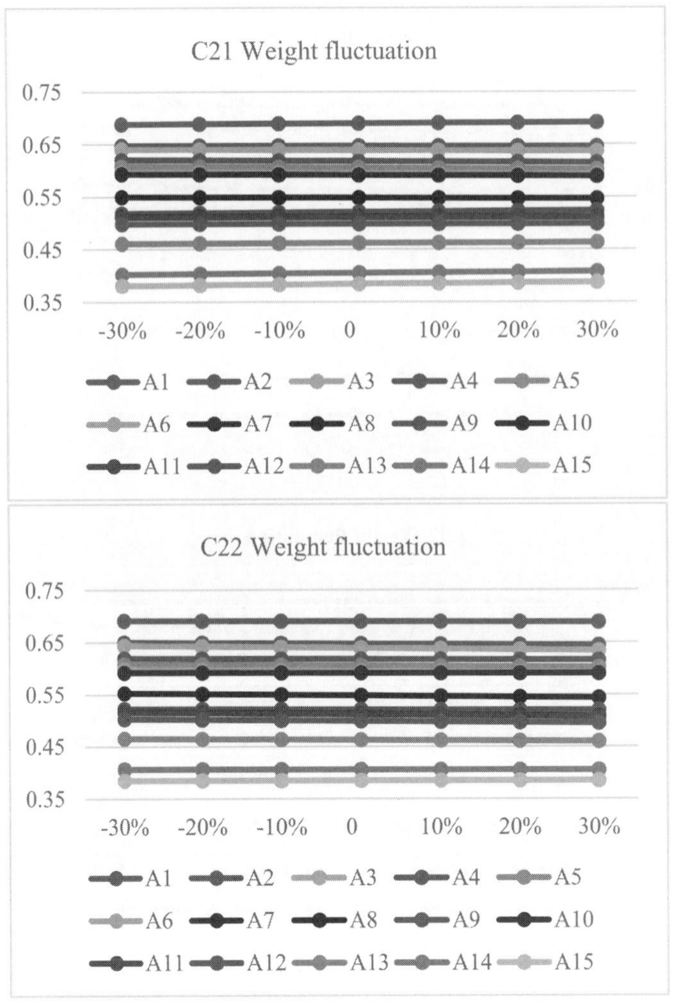

Fig. 15.6 Sensitivity analysis results of the CRFs in economic risk group.

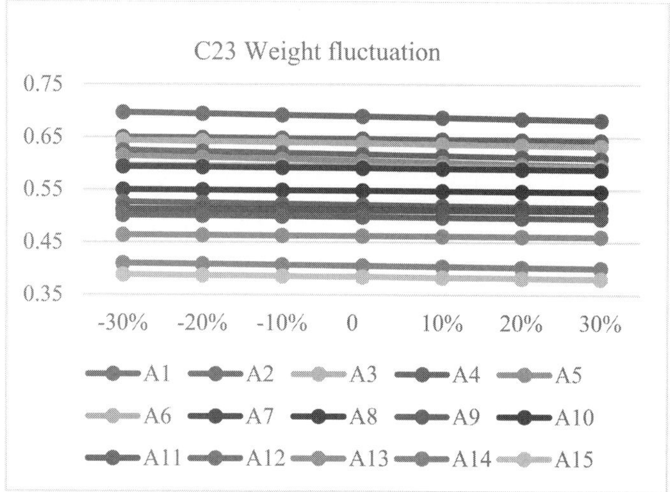

Fig. 15.6 Sensitivity analysis results of the CRFs in economic risk group. (Continued)

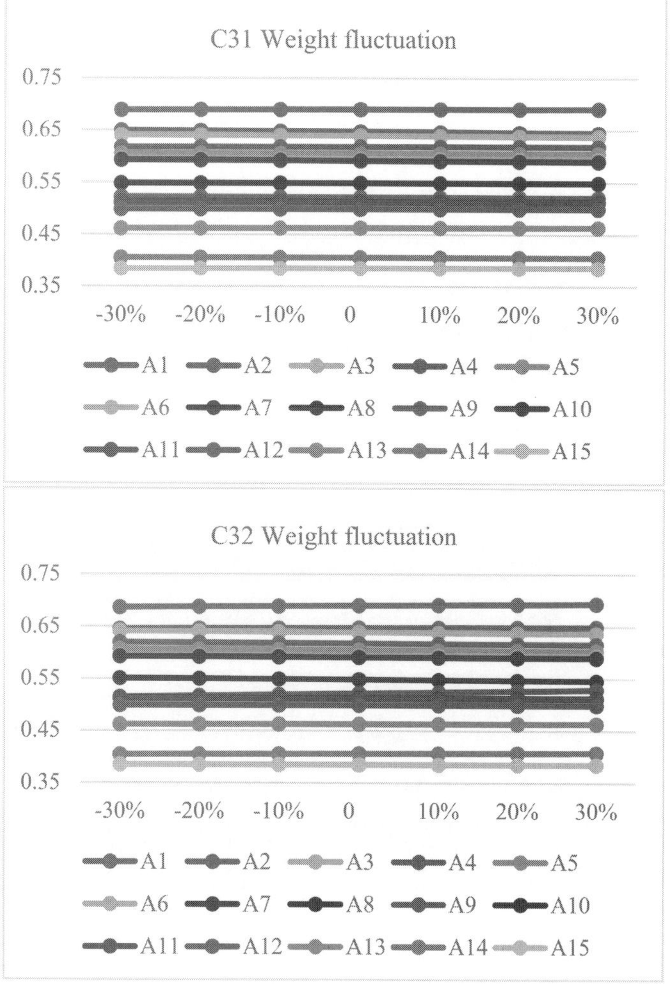

Fig. 15.7 Sensitivity analysis results of the CRFs in construction environmental risk group.

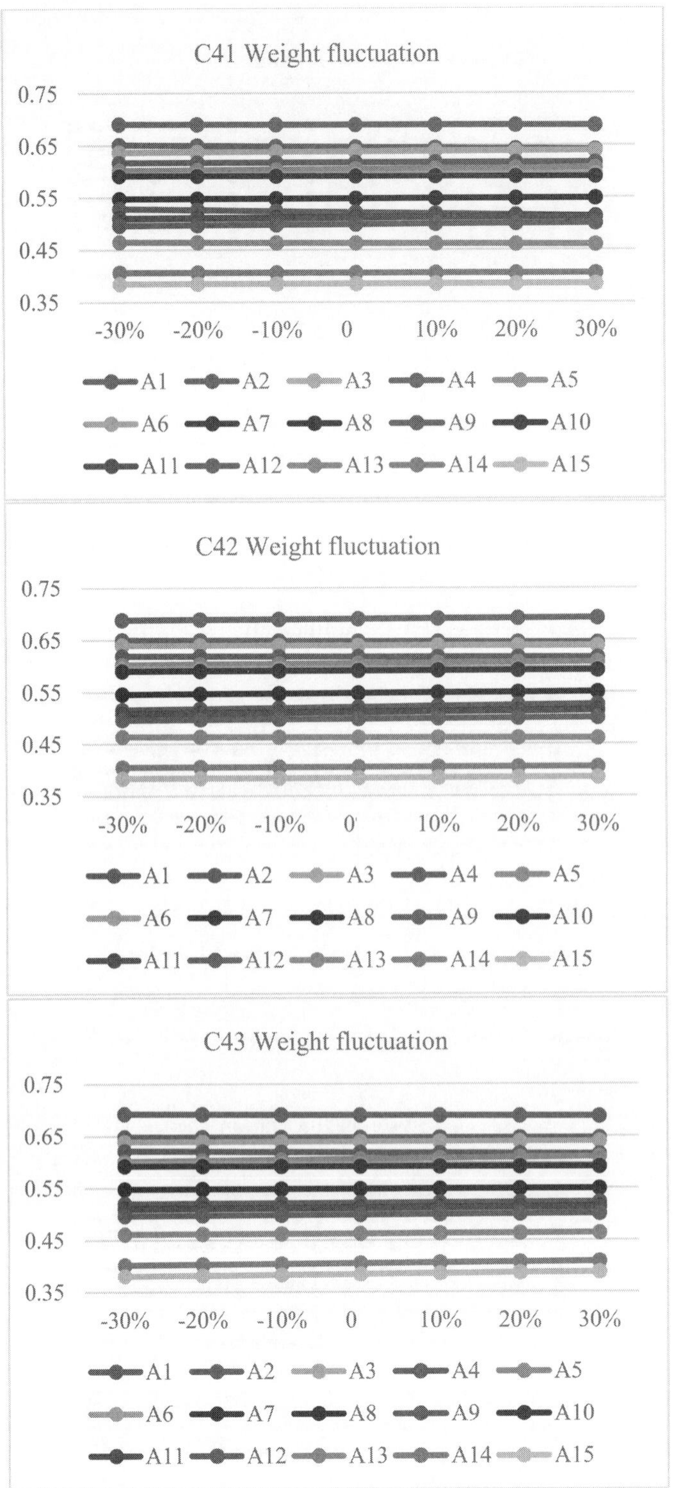

Fig. 15.8 Sensitivity analysis results of the CRFs in technology risk group.

6.2 Scenario analysis

Scenario I: Cancellation of power generation subsidies

The adjustment of the DPV policy in the past two years indicates that China is gradually reducing subsidies for PV power generation, and there is a tendency to gradually eliminate subsidies. The main reason is to force the PV industry to improve quality and increase development efficiency. The initial subsidies played a very good incentive, driving the rapid development of the PV industry, but also brought some negative effects. Some enterprises value subsidies, and their photovoltaic scale is huge but the quality is worrying. Others lack technological innovation and defraud subsidies. However, in the era of "subsidy end", PV companies must rely on technological advancement to reduce costs, improve efficiency, and enhance core competitiveness. China PV industry is slowly breaking away from policy-driven, and really developing into a high-growth industry. So, in this section, the scenario of canceling the subsidies of distributed photovoltaic generation is set to analyze the changes of risk assessment results.

Scenario II: Improvement of operation and maintenance level

In the future, continuous competition and mature development will enable PV equipment manufacturers to provide high quality and innovative equipment for EPC-URDPV projects. In addition, ECOs have accumulated rich experience in operating and maintaining EPC-URDPV projects. These good changes and developments make the overall operation and maintenance level of DPV project improved. It is necessary to set this scenario to analyze risk. Under this scenario, the importance of operational maintenance level (C9) as a risk factor in the whole risk assessment system will be reduced. This scenario is achieved by setting the weight of operational maintenance risk (C9) to 20% of the original.

Scenario III: Cancellation of power generation subsidies & Improvement of operation and maintenance level

The above two scenarios are likely to occur at the same time in the future, so the third scenario set in this paper is to cancel the power generation subsidy while the operational and maintenance level has been significantly improved. The risk assessment results in the three scenarios are shown in Table 15.12.

Table 15.12 Risk assessment result of three scenarios for EPC-URDPV in each province.

EPC-URDPV in each Province	Original scenario		Scenario I		Scenario II		Scenario III	
	Evaluation result	Risk level	Evaluation result	Risk level	Evaluation result	Risk level	Evaluation result	Risk level
Shanghai	(0.5247,0.6898,0.8466)	RH	(0.5204,0.6853,0.8409)	RH	(0.4883,0.6408,0.7851)	RH	(0.4792,0.6298,0.7712)	RH
Fujian	(0.4883,0.6469,0.8000)	RH	(0.4635,0.6214,0.7825)	RH	(0.4632,0.6092,0.7499)	RH	(0.4351,0.5787,0.7256)	M
Hainan	(0.4736,0.6387,0.7960)	RH	(0.4513,0.6162,0.7773)	RH	(0.4347,0.5873,0.7320)	RH	(0.4072,0.5579,0.7048)	M

Continued

EPC-URDPV in each Province	Original scenario		Scenario I		Scenario II		Scenario III	
	Evaluation result	Risk level	Evaluation result	Risk level	Evaluation result	Risk level	Evaluation result	Risk level
Chongqing	(0.4523,0.6174,0.7764)	RH	(0.4374,0.6023,0.7606)	RH	(0.4172,0.5709,0.7186)	M	(0.3976,0.5497,0.6952)	M
Guangdong	(0.4418,0.6049,0.7678)	RH	(0.4369,0.5999,0.7625)	RH	(0.4028,0.5534,0.7037)	M	(0.3928,0.5416,0.6899)	M
Shandong	(0.4294,0.5946,0.7553)	RH	(0.4028,0.5678,0.7325)	M	(0.3942,0.5481,0.6975)	M	(0.3629,0.5151,0.6671)	M
Henan	(0.4274,0.5909,0.7454)	RH	(0.3975,0.5607,0.7234)	M	(0.3972,0.5482,0.6902)	M	(0.3634,0.5123,0.6608)	M
Guizhou	(0.3827,0.5479,0.7042)	M	(0.3481,0.5130,0.6778)	M	(0.3526,0.5052,0.6490)	M	(0.3140.0.4647.0.6151)	M
Zhejiang	(0.3590,0.5210,0.6789)	M	(0.3746,0.5365,0.6931)	M	(0.3502,0.4996,0.6450)	M	(0.3647,0.5123,0.6546)	M
Hubei	(0.3470,0.5121,0.6772)	M	(0.3259,0.4907,0.6556)	M	(0.3169,0.4694,0.6220)	M	(0.2917,0.4423,0.5930)	M
Guangxi	(0.3456,0.5106,0.6729)	M	(0.32590.4907,0.6556)	M	(0.3154,0.4679,0.6177)	M	(0.2917,0.4423,0.5930)	M
Hunan	(0.3318,0.4983,0.6622)	M	(0.3106,0.4772,0.6439)	M	(0.3016,0.4557,0.6070)	M	(0.2764,0.4288,0.5813)	M
Jiangxi	(0.2956,0.4621,0.6290)	M	(0.2675,0.4341,0.6010)	M	(0.2793,0.4332,0.5876)	M	(0.2490,0.4014,0.5540)	RS
Jiangsu	(0.2390,0.4054,0.5724)	RS	(0.2148,0.3813,0.5481)	RS	(0.2227,0.3766,0.5309)	RS	(0.1963,0.3486,0.5012)	RS
Anhui	(0.2181,0.3845,0.5514)	RS	(0.2069,0.3733,0.5402)	RS	(0.2018,0.3557,0.5099)	RS	(0.1884,0.3406,0.4932)	RS

According to the results of the Table 15.9, it can be clearly seen that the risk assessment results under the three scenarios have changed, and the risks of the 15 provinces have shown an overall downward trend, especially scenario II and scenario III; In scenario I, the decline of risk assessment results is not obvious, indicating that the entire industry will develop in a mature and stable direction after the elimination of power generation subsidies in the DPV industry. However, there are other risks and potential risks, so the risk status of each evaluation object does not change much under the same evaluation system; When the level of operation and maintenance is greatly improved, the overall risk of EPC-URDPV project is significantly reduced, so improving the level of operation and maintenance is an important breakthrough point for managing EPC projects; The Scenario III fully reflects the development trend of China's EPC-URDPV projects in the future, the overall risk is reduced, most of them are at the medium risk level, and the whole industry tends to mature and stabilize. It is worth noting that the risk level of Anhui and Jiangsu provinces is relatively low under various scenarios, so enterprises can take them as priority areas when selecting project investments. On the contrary, the risk levels of Shanghai, Fujian and other provinces are relatively high under various scenarios. ECOs should pay more attention to project risk management when investing in such regional projects.

The risk level evaluation results are defuzzied to obtain the risk distribution of each evaluation object in three scenarios. It can be seen intuitively from Fig. 15.9 that risk trend mutations occurred in three scenarios compared with the original scenario. The risk reduction of EPC-URDPV projects in Zhejiang province is not obvious after the elimination of power generation subsidies, which leads to a sudden change in trend line, indicating that the sensitivity of EPC-URDPV projects in Zhejiang Province to power generation subsidies is low. After the improvement of operation and maintenance level, the overall risk level decreases, but the risk reduction of EPC-URDPV projects in Guangxi region is not significant, leading to a sudden change in trend line. Scenario III comprehensively reflects the trends of the first two scenarios. The risk trend mutations occurred in Zhejiang and Guangxi. According to the evaluation information, it can be seen that the main reason for the relatively high risk of EPC-URDPV projects in Zhejiang Province is the Difficulties in defining rooftop property rights. The risk assessment results of southern provinces such as Fujian, Hainan, Chongqing, and Guangdong are higher than those of the central and eastern provinces, indicating that the ideal investment areas for EPC-URDPV projects are mainly distributed in central and eastern China.

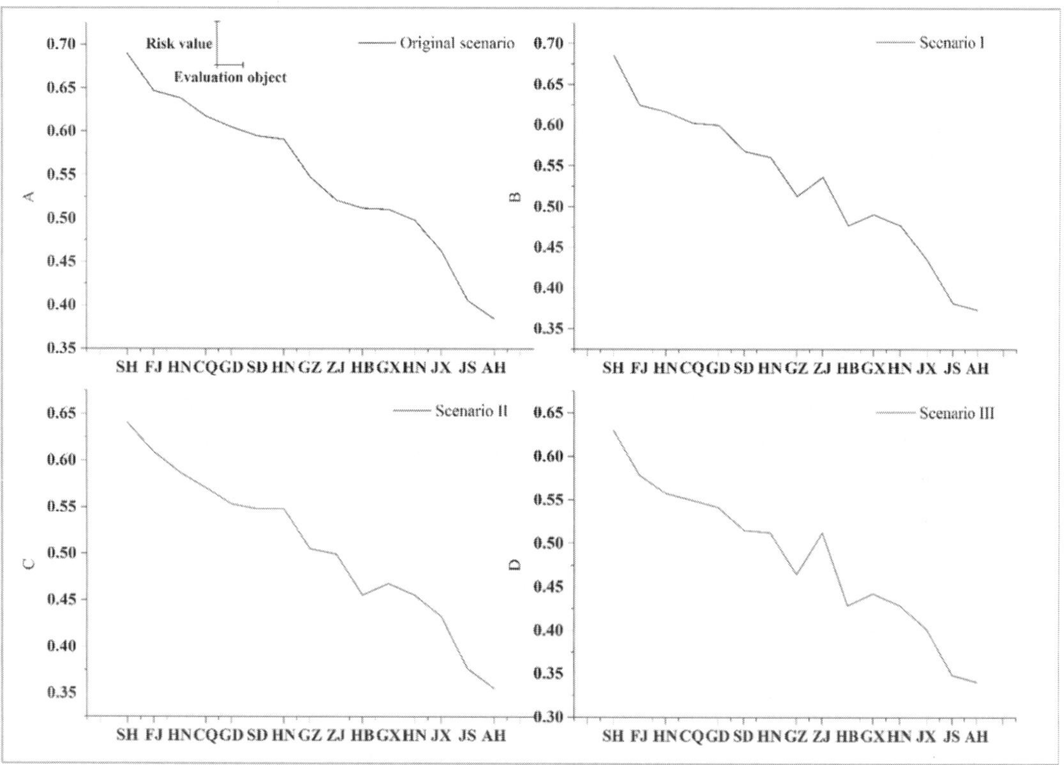

Fig. 15.9 Risk distribution in three scenarios.

6.3 Risk response

Based on the above weight results and risk assessment results, corresponding countermeasures and suggestions are put forward for CRFs to provide reference and inspiration of risk management for ECOs, policy makers and decision makers in practice. Before putting forward countermeasures to response the risks, only by analyzing the causes of risk and the parties involved (Table 15.13) can we give scientific and effective reference information. The table below summarizes the major stakeholders of the CRFs.

Table 15.13 The main parties involved in the risk factor.

No.	CRFs	ECOS	ECUs	Government	Grid company	Equipment supplier
1	Power generation subsidy	√		√		
2	Political and regulatory risk			√	√	
3	Government support			√	√	
4	volatility of prices	√	√	√	√	√
5	Annual rate of return	√	√	√		√
6	Market absorptive risk		√	√	√	
7	Solar energy resources	√	√			
8	Difficulties in defining rooftop property rights	√	√	√		
9	Operation and maintenance risk	√			√	√
10	Grid connection risk	√			√	√
11	Power supply reliability risk	√	√		√	√

6.3.1 Policy risk

Power generation subsidy(C11). Before the implementation of the EPC-URDPV project, ECOS should fully grasp and understand the power generation subsidy policy to avoid such risks due to unclear policies. The government should issue subsidies on time in accordance with the contract period, and there should be no deduction of subsidies or arrears of subsidies.

Political and regulatory risk (C12). Policy instability and non-sustainability often bring such risks. The government should actively promulgate and implement policies for the development of DPV and other new energy sources to steadily promote the development of PV industry. A great policy and regulatory environment are prerequisites for the smooth development of EPC-URDPV projects. The government and relevant departments should actively participate in the entire construction and operation of the project as participants and promoters.

Government support (C13). Government support is the key to project success. The government can properly provide preferential policies to support EPC-URDPV projects. For example, to give appropriate tax reduction policies, simplify the project approval process, etc. Grid companies should timely introduce relevant management measures for distributed energy access to the grid to provide necessary supporting facilities and services for EPC-URDPV projects.

6.3.2 Economic risk

Volatility of prices (C21). Electricity price fluctuations are mainly affected by three aspects: power generation costs, contract electricity prices, and electricity subsidies. Replacing PV modules during operation and maintenance will cause cost increase, so the quality of PV modules must be strictly controlled during the equipment selection stage of the project; Contract price involves the agreed price among ECOs, users and power grid. The determination of contract price needs to be scientifically and reasonably estimated and rigorously written into EPC contract. The implementation and sustainability of power subsidy need to be communicated and determined in advance between the government and ECOs.

Annual rate of return (C22). The sustainability of power generation subsidy directly affects annual income, and the rise of labor, material and management costs will indirectly affect annual income. The uncertainty of annual income is the result of other CRFs. The control of this risk mainly depends on the risk management of other CRFs.

Market absorptive risk (C23. The consumption of power generation is the most important indicator of the project, which not only affects the economics of the project, but also reflects the necessity of the project to some extent. "Nearby using, the surplus to grid" is currently strongly promoted model. The higher the self-use ratio of power generation, the better the economics of the project. On the premise of ensuring the stability of power generation, ECOs should properly distribute the amount of electricity required by users and the amount to the grid. Make full user load assessment in advance, and determine the docking mode and checkout cycle with the power grid in time.

6.3.3 Construction environmental risk

Solar energy resources (C31). Solar energy resource is an unchangeable risk factor. When choosing a DPV project, investors should select the appropriate solar energy resource area to carry out the project based on the expected revenue target. Solar energy resources and meteorological conditions in the areas where the alternative projects are located should be taken as important indicators for investment decisions.

Difficulties in defining rooftop property rights (C32). DPV projects need enough space to place PV modules, which are usually placed on the roof of residential buildings or factories. When looking for a suitable venue, investors often encounter issues such as property rights disputes. When choosing a project, investors should pay attention to the ownership of the property rights of the project site and specify the rights and obligations of each stakeholder in the contract. In some cases, an attempt may be made to invite the government to assist in the search for a suitable project site with a clear ownership.

6.3.4 Technology risk

Operation and maintenance risk (C41). Operational maintenance phase accounts for a large part of the life cycle of EPC-URDPV projects. Operational and maintenance risks are mainly caused by the following three aspects: ①unreasonable equipment selection; ②extreme weather effects; ③Lack of professional technicians. Therefore, it is necessary to improve the design requirements and equipment acceptance standards. Technological innovation needs to improve the efficiency of project monitoring and diagnosis. Professional technical training should be conducted regularly for operation and maintenance personnel.

Grid connection risk (C42). Project builders and grid companies are the main bodies to reduce grid-connected risks. The construction of the project must strictly comply with the requirements of the "Technical Regulations for Distributed Generation Access to Power Grid". Power grid companies should carefully check the key indicators before grid-connected and actively improve the relevant standards, norms and systems of each link of distributed generation grid-connected, so as to provide detailed basis for grass-roots units to carry out work.

Power supply reliability risk (C43). The grid-connected DPV project brings great challenges and security risks to the power supply network. PV power generation equipment must pass the joint acceptance of relevant departments. For the problems existing in acceptance, it must be completely rectified and re-acceptance completed. Only after qualified, can it be incorporated into the distribution network system for power generation. In addition, the grid-connected relay protection device must be designed and equipped at one time to improve the level of automatic operation of equipment, mainly the fault isolation ability.

7. Conclusions

The aim of this paper is to identify the critical risk factors of EPC-URDPV projects in China, at the same time a comprehensive risk assessment is carried out in 15 provinces where DPV are mainly developed in China, and corresponding risk levels are obtained. To sum up, this paper carries out risk identification, risk assessment and risk response for EPC-URDPV projects in China. Firstly, through a large number of literature studies, 38 risk factors affecting EPC-URDPV projects are identified. Then, through four-dimensional risk analysis, 11 CRFs are selected as the index system of risk assessment. The weights of 11 CRFs are calculated by using IF-DEMATEL method. The weight results show that policy and regulation risk, market absorption risk and government support are the three indicators with the largest weight. It can be explained that the development of EPC-URDPV in China is guided by two factors: policy and market. Investors need to focus on these two aspects of risk in project risk management. In order to preserve the completeness and fuzziness of the evaluation information, this paper uses HFLTs to describe the evaluation information, and finally uses fuzzy synthetic evaluation method to evaluate the projects risk in 15 provinces. The results show that the risk level of Jiangsu and Anhui provinces is the lowest, and the risk grade evaluation results are "Relatively Low"; The evaluation results of seven provinces, such as Shanghai, Fujian and Hainan, show that the risk is "Relatively High". PV development enterprises need to pay more attention to risk management when investing in projects in these areas. The results of risk assessment in other provinces are

"Medium". Overall, the risk level of China's EPC-URDPV projects is at a relatively ideal level, and more than half of the evaluation areas obtain the "Medium" risk level. The analysis results in the three scenarios indicate that the risk level of China's EPC-URDPV projects will be reduced in the future, and the scope suitable for developing DPV projects will continue to expand. The last part of the risk assessment framework is risk feedback. Through the above analysis and conclusions, this paper gives corresponding risk response strategies for 11 CRFs by analyzing the causes of risk and risk related parties.

In addition, the academic contributions of this paper are summarized as follows.

(1) Through a large number of literature studies, it can be found that the current risk factors are mainly analyzed from the perspective of possibility and severity. However, the uncontrollability and urgency of risk are also two very important perspectives. Therefore, 4D risk analysis is proposed for the first time in this paper, which identifies critical risks from four perspectives of possibility, severity, uncontrollability and urgency.

(2) By 4D risk analysis, 11 critical risk attributes of the EPC-URDPV were screened out. These risk attributes are divided into policy risk, economic risk, construction environmental risk and technical risk to build a comprehensive risk assessment index system for EPC-URDPV.

(3) At present, the risk assessment system and a complete operational framework of the EPC-URDPV are lacking. Corresponding, this paper constructs a theoretical framework for implementing risk assessment in a fuzzy environment.

(4) The classic fuzzy synthetic evaluation method is extended by the HFLTS. Fuzzy synthetic evaluation is a classic risk assessment method widely used. However, how to make this method more in line with the actual evaluation environment is worthy of further study. In this paper, HFLTS is used to describe the evaluation information in risk assessment, which expands the application environment of the method and makes it more in line with the linguistic preferences of the interviewees.

Acknowledgements

This research is supported by the Fundamental Research Funds for the Central Universities (No. 2018ZD14), the 2017 Special Project of Cultivation and Development of Innovation Base (No. Z171100002217024).

Appendix A

Table A.1 Explanation of abbreviations.

Abbreviations	
EPC	energy performance contracting

Continued

Abbreviations	
PV	photovoltaic
URDPV	Urban rooftop distributed photovoltaic
FSE	Fuzzy synthetic evaluation
HFLTS	hesitant fuzzy linguistic term sets
AHP	analytic hierarchy process
TFN	triangular fuzzy number
IF	intuitionistic fuzzy
IFN	intuitionistic fuzzy number
IFWGA	intuitionistic fuzzy weighted geometric averaging
NPV	net present value
IRR	internal rate of return
CRFs	critical risk factors
CRGs	critical risk groups
ECUs	energy-consuming units
ECOs	energy service companies
IEA	international energy agency
NDRC	National Development and Reform Commission

References

[1] Sun B, Yu Y, Qin C. Should China focus on the distributed development of wind and solar photovoltaic power generation? A comparative study[J]. Applied Energy, 2017, 185:421-439.

[2] Lu Z, Li H, Qiao Y. Probabilistic Flexibility Evaluation for Power System Planning Considering its Association with Renewable Power Curtailment[J]. IEEE Transactions on Power Systems, 2018, 33:3285-3295.

[3] Fan X C, Wang W Q, Shi R J, et al. Analysis and countermeasures of wind power curtailment in China[J]. Renewable & Sustainable Energy Reviews, 2015, 52:1429-1436.

[4] Wu Y, Xu C, Ke Y, et al. An intuitionistic fuzzy multi-criteria framework for large-scale rooftop PV project portfolio selection: case study in Zhejiang, China[J]. Energy, 2018, 143:295-309.

[5] Wang Z, Luo D, Liu L. Natural gas utilization in China: Development trends and prospects[J]. Energy Reports, 2018, 4:351-356.

[6] NDRC. Guidelines for Developing Natural Gas Distributed Energy Sources. http://www.ndrc.gov.cn/zcfb/zcfbtz/201110/t20111013_438374.html. 2011.

[7] NDRC, NEA. 13th Five-Year Plan for Energy Development. http://www.ndrc.gov.cn/zcfb/zcfbtz/201701/t20170117_835278.html. 2016.

[8] NEA. Interim Measures for the Development and Construction of Decentralized Wind Power Projects. http://zfxxgk.nea.gov.cn/auto87/201804/t20180416_3150.htm. 2018.

[9] Sefair J A, Méndez C Y, Babat O, et al. Linear solution schemes for mean-semivariance project portfolio selection problems: An application in the oil and gas industry[J]. Omega, 2016, 68:39-48.

[10] Unger B N, Kock A, Gemünden H G, et al. Enforcing strategic fit of project portfolios by project termination: An empirical study on senior management involvement[J]. International Journal of Project Management, 2012, 30:675-685.

[11] Liu P, Tan Z. How to develop distributed generation in China: In the context of the reformation of electric power system[J]. Renewable & Sustainable Energy Reviews, 2016, 66:10-26.

[12] Anadón L D, Baker E, Bosetti V. Integrating uncertainty into public energy research and development decisions[J]. Nature Energy, 2017, 2:17071.

[13] Debnath D, Whistance J, Thompson W, et al. Complement or substitute: Ethanol's uncertain relationship with gasoline under alternative petroleum price and policy scenarios[J]. Applied Energy, 2017, 191:385-397.

[14] Wu Y, Geng S. Multi-criteria decision making on selection of solar–wind hybrid power station location: A case of China[J]. Energy Conversion & Management, 2014, 81:527-533.

[15] Smith-Perera A, García-Melón M, Poveda-Bautista R, et al. A Project Strategic Index proposal for portfolio selection in electrical company based on the Analytic Network Process[J]. Renewable & Sustainable Energy Reviews, 2010, 14:1569-1579.

[16] Garcíamelón M, Povedabautista R, Del V M, et al. Using the strategic relative alignment index for the selection of portfolio projects application to a public Venezuelan Power Corporation[J]. International Journal of Production Economics, 2015, 170:54-66.

[17] Jeng J F, Huang K H. Strategic project portfolio selection for national research institutes[J]. Journal of Business Research, 2015, 68:2305-2311.

[18] Mohagheghi V, Mousavi S M, Vahdani B. A New Optimization Model for Project Portfolio Selection Under Interval-Valued Fuzzy Environment[J]. Arabian Journal for Science & Engineering, 2015, 40:3351-3361.

[19] Tavana M, Keramatpour M, Santos-Arteaga F J, et al. A fuzzy hybrid project portfolio selection method using Data Envelopment Analysis, TOPSIS and Integer Programming[J]. Expert Systems with Applications, 2015, 42:8432-8444.

[20] Khalili-Damghani K, Sadi-Nezhad S, Lotfi F H, et al. A hybrid fuzzy rule-based multi-criteria framework for sustainable project portfolio selection[J]. Information Sciences, 2013, 220:442-462.

[21] Mohagheghi V, Mousavi S M, Vahdani B, et al. R&D project evaluation and project portfolio selection by a new interval type-2 fuzzy optimization approach[J]. Neural Computing & Applications, 2017, 28:3869-3888.

[22] Pendharkar P C, Rodger J A. Information technology capital budgeting using a knapsack problem[J]. International Transactions in Operational Research, 2010, 13:333-351.

[23] Killen C P. Evaluation of project interdependency visualizations through decision scenario experimentation[J]. International Journal of Project Management, 2013, 31:804-816.

[24] Lopes Y G, Almeida A T D. Assessment of synergies for selecting a project portfolio in the petroleum industry based on a multi-attribute utility function[J]. Journal of Petroleum Science & Engineering, 2015, 126:131-140.

[25] Eilat H, Golany B, Shtub A. Constructing and evaluating balanced portfolios of R&D projects with interactions: A DEA based methodology[J]. European Journal of Operational Research, 2006, 172:1018-1039.

[26] Jiang Z, Zhang H, Sutherland J W. Development of multi-criteria decision making model for

remanufacturing technology portfolio selection[J]. Journal of Cleaner Production, 2011, 19:1939-1945.

[27] Pendharkar P C. A decision-making framework for justifying a portfolio of IT projects[J]. International Journal of Project Management, 2014, 32:625-639.

[28] Neumeier A, Radszuwill S, Garizy T Z. Modeling project criticality in IT project portfolios[J]. International Journal of Project Management, 2018, 36:833-844.

[29] Lin C, Hsieh P J. A fuzzy decision support system for strategic portfolio management[J]. Decision Support Systems, 2005, 38:383-398.

[30] Relich M, Pawlewski P. A fuzzy weighted average approach for selecting portfolio of new product development projects[J]. Neurocomputing, 2016, 231:19-27.

[31] Ghapanchi A H, Tavana M, Khakbaz M H, et al. A methodology for selecting portfolios of projects with interactions and under uncertainty[J]. International Journal of Project Management, 2012, 30:791-803.

[32] Bhattacharyya R, Kumar P, Kar S. Fuzzy R&D portfolio selection of interdependent projects[J]. Computers & Mathematics with Applications, 2011, 62:3857-3870.

[33] Alvarez-García B, Fernández-Castro A S. A comprehensive approach for the selection of a portfolio of interdependent projects. An application to subsidized projects in Spain[J]. Computers & Industrial Engineering, 2018, 153-159.

[34] Liu Y, Liu Y K. Distributionally robust fuzzy project portfolio optimization problem with interactive returns[J]. Applied Soft Computing, 2016, 56:655-668.

[35] Jafarzadeh H, Akbari P, Abedin B. A methodology for project portfolio selection under criteria prioritisation, uncertainty and projects interdependency – combination of fuzzy QFD and DEA[J]. Expert Systems with Applications, 2018, 110:237-249.

[36] Yu L, Wen F, Lai K K. Genetic algorithm-based multi-criteria project portfolio selection[J]. Annals of Operations Research. 2012; 197:71-86.

[37] Oh J, Yang J, Lee S. Managing uncertainty to improve decision-making in NPD portfolio management with a fuzzy expert system[J]. Expert Systems with Applications, 2012, 39:9868-9885.

[38] assanzadeh F, Nemati H, Sun M. Robust optimization for interactive multiobjective programming with imprecise information applied to R&D project portfolio selection[J]. European Journal of Operational Research, 2014, 238:41-53.

[39] Wu Y, Li J, Wang J, Huang Y. Project portfolio management applied to building energy projects management system[J]. Renewable & Sustainable Energy Reviews, 2012, 16:718-724.

[40] Golabi K, Kirkwood C W, Sicherman A. Selecting a Portfolio of Solar Energy Projects Using Multiattribute Preference Theory[J]. Management Science, 1981, 27:174-189.

[41] Mavromatidis G, Orehounig K, Carmeliet J. Comparison of alternative decision-making criteria in a two-stage stochastic program for the design of distributed energy systems under uncertainty[J]. Energy, 2018, 56:709-724.

[42] Ren H, Gao W, Zhou W, et al. Multi-criteria evaluation for the optimal adoption of distributed residential energy systems in Japan[J]. Energy Policy, 2009, 37:5484-5493.

[43] Jing R, Zhu X, Zhu Z, et al. A multi-objective optimization and multi-criteria evaluation integrated framework for distributed energy system optimal planning[J]. Energy Conversion and Management, 2018, 166:445-562.

[44] Väisänen S, Mikkilä M, Havukainen J, et al. Using a multi-method approach for decision-making about a sustainable local distributed energy system: A case study from Finland[J]. Journal of Cleaner Production, 2016, 137:1330-1338.
[45] Hajibandeh N, Shafie-khaha M, Osório G J, et al. A heuristic multi-objective multi-criteria demand response planning in a system with high penetration of wind power generators[J]. Applied Energy, 2018, 212:721-732.
[46] Hassan Z, Garni A. Solar PV power plant site selection using a GIS-AHP based approach with application in Saudi Arabia[J]. Applied Energy, 2017, 206: 1225-1240.
[47] Wang J, Du P, Niu T, et al. A novel hybrid system based on a new proposed algorithm-Multi-Objective Whale Optimization Algorithm for wind speed forecasting[J]. Applied Energy, 1970, 208:344-360.
[48] Voss M, Kock A. Impact of relationship value on project portfolio success — Investigating the moderating effects of portfolio characteristics and external turbulence[J]. International Journal of Project Management, 2013, 31:847-861.
[49] Kaiser M G, Arbi F E, Ahlemann F. Successful project portfolio management beyond project selection techniques: Understanding the role of structural alignment[J]. International Journal of Project Management, 2015, 33:126-139.
[50] Hernandez-Perdomo E A, Mun J, Claudio M R S. Active management in state-owned energy companies: Integrating a real options approach into multicriteria analysis to make companies sustainable[J]. Applied Energy, 2017, 195:487-502.
[51] Srivannaboon S, Milosevic D Z. A two-way influence between business strategy and project management[J]. International Journal of Project Management, 2006, 24:493-505.
[52] Turner R. The Handbook of Project Based Management: Improving the Process for Achieving Your Strategic Objectives[M]. New York: McGraw-hill, 2002.
[53] Lin C, Hsieh P J. A fuzzy decision support system for strategic portfolio management[J]. Decision Support Systems, 2004, 38:383-398.
[54] Relich M, Pawlewski P. A fuzzy weighted average approach for selecting portfolio of new product development projects[J]. Neurocomputing, 2017, 231:19-27.
[55] Zadeh L A. Fuzzy sets [J]. Information & Control, 1965, 8:338-353.
[56] Huang C C, Chu P Y, Chiang Y H. A fuzzy AHP application in government-sponsored R&D project selection [J]. Omega, 2008, 36:1038-1052.
[57] Chen C T, Cheng H L. A comprehensive model for selecting information system project under fuzzy environment[J]. International Journal of Project Management, 2009, 27:389-399.
[58] Zeng Z, Nasri E, Chini A, et al. A multiple objective decision making model for energy generation portfolio under fuzzy uncertainty: Case study of large scale investor-owned utilities in Florida[J]. Renewable Energy, 2015, 75:224-242.
[59] Baker N, Freeland J. Recent Advances in R&D Benefit Measurement and Project Selection Methods[J]. Management Science, 1975, 21:1164-1175.
[60] Mcfarlan F W. Portfolio Approach to Information Systems[J]. Harvard Business Review, 1981, 59.
[61] Keil M, Marchewka J T. Portfolio Theory Approach For Selecting and Managing IT Projects[J]. Information Resources Management Journal, 1995, 8:5-16.
[62] Alvarez-García B, Fernández-Castro A S. A comprehensive approach for the selection of a portfolio

of interdependent projects. An application to subsidized projects in Spain[J]. Computers & Industrial Engineering, 2018, 153-159.

[63] Banihashemi S, Hosseini M R, Golizadeh H, et al. Critical success factors (CSFs) for integration of sustainability into construction project management practices in developing countries[J]. International Journal of Project Management, 2017, 35:1103-1119.

[64] Chen T Y. A linear assignment method for multiple-criteria decision analysis with interval type-2 fuzzy sets[J]. Applied Soft Computing Journal, 2013, 13:2735-2748.

[65] Saaty T L. The analytic hierarchy process: Planning, priority setting, resource Allocation[M]. New York : McGraw-Hill, 1980.

[66] Buckley J J. Fuzzy hierarchical analysis[J]. Fuzzy sets and systems, 1985, 17:233-247.

[67] Kahraman C. Fuzzy analytic hierarchy process with interval type-2 fuzzy sets[J]. Knowledge-Based Systems, 2014, 59:48-57.

[68] Kahraman C, Öztayşi B, Sarı İ U, et al. Fuzzy analytic hierarchy process with interval type-2 fuzzy sets[J]. Knowledge-Based Systems, 2014, 59:48-57.

[69] Gong M, Jiao L, Du H, et al. Multiobjective Immune Algorithm with Nondominated Neighbor-Based Selection. Evolutionary Computation, 2008, 16:225-255.

[70] Deb K, Pratap A, Agarwal S, et al. A fast and elitist multiobjective genetic algorithm: NSGA-II[J]. IEEE Transactions on Evolutionary Computation, 2002, 6:182-197.

[71] Qin J, Liu X, Pedrycz W. An extended TODIM multi-criteria group decision making method for green supplier selection in interval type-2 fuzzy environment[J]. European Journal of Operational Research, 2017, 258:626-638.

[72] Kahraman C, Kaya İ, Cebi S. A comparative analysis for multiattribute selection among renewable energy alternatives using fuzzy axiomatic design and fuzzy analytic hierarchy process[J]. Energy, 2009, 34:1603-1616.

[73] Büyüközkan G, Güleryüz S. Evaluation of Renewable Energy Resources in Turkey using an integrated MCDM approach with linguistic interval fuzzy preference relations[J]. Energy, 2017, 123:149-163.

[74] Haddad B, Liazid A, Ferreira P. A multi-criteria approach to rank renewables for the Algerian electricity system[J]. Renewable Energy, 2017, 107:462-472.

[75] Wu Y, Xu C, Zhang T. Evaluation of renewable power sources using a fuzzy MCDM based on cumulative prospect theory: A case in China[J]. Energy, 2018, 147:1227-1239.

[76] Amer M, Daim T U. Selection of renewable energy technologies for a developing county: A case of Pakistan[J]. Energy for Sustainable Development, 2011, 15:420-435.

[77] Kaya T, Kahraman C. Multicriteria renewable energy planning using an integrated fuzzy VIKOR & AHP methodology: The case of Istanbul[J]. Energy, 2010, 35:2517-2527.

[78] Streimikiene D, Balezentis T, Krisciukaitienė I, et al. Prioritizing sustainable electricity production technologies: MCDM approach[J]. Renewable & Sustainable Energy Reviews, 2012, 16:3302-3311.

[79] Şengül Ü, Eren M, Shiraz S E, et al. Fuzzy TOPSIS method for ranking renewable energy supply systems in Turkey[J]. Renewable Energy, 2015, 75:617-625.

[80] Tasri A, Susilawati A. Selection among renewable energy alternatives based on a fuzzy analytic hierarchy process in Indonesia[J]. Sustainable Energy Technologies & Assessments, 2014, 156:34-44.